FROM DARKNESS TO LIGHT

HARPER & BROTHERS

Publishers : New York

FROM DARKNESS
TO LIGHT

a Confession of Faith
in the form of
an anthology

BY VICTOR GOLLANCZ

FOR RUTH

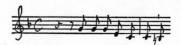

An empty book is like an Infant's Soul, in
which anything may be written. It is capable
of all things, but containeth nothing. I have
a mind to fill this with profitable wonders.
And since Love made you put it into my hands
I will fill it with those truths you love . . .

TRAHERNE

I am
As one that knows a tune but cannot sing.

COVENTRY PATMORE

That which is beneath is like that which is above: and that which is above is like that which is beneath, to work the miracles of one thing.

ROGER BACON

Si nostre vie est moins qu'une journée
En l'éternel, si l'an qui faict le tour
Chasse noz jours sans espoir de retour,
Si perissable est toute chose née,
Que songes-tu mon ame emprisonnée?
Pourquoy te plaist l'obscur de nostre jour,
Si pour voler en un plus cler sejour,
Tu as au dos l'aile bien empennée?
Là est le bien que tout esprit desire,
Là, le repos où tout le monde aspire,
Là est l'amour, là, le plaisir encore.
Là, ô mon ame, au plus hault ciel guidée,
Tu y pourras recongnoistre l'Idée
De la beauté qu'en ce monde j'adore.

JOACHIM DU BELLAY

Look down, Great Master of the feast; O shine,
And turn once more our water into wine!

HENRY VAUGHAN

FOREWORD

THE subtitle of this book—"a confession of faith in the form of an anthology"—sufficiently explains its purpose.

I would repeat, with some urgency, what I wrote in the foreword to *A Year of Grace,* namely: "The book is intended and designed to be read from beginning to end as a consecutive whole: as if, that is to say, it were a continuous piece of writing by one hand, all now appearing for the first time. I should of course be pleased if it might subsequently be found useful for the bedside." Unless the thing is read in this way it must be robbed of all its meaning as a book, and become nothing but a series of snippets: not only is each section designed to follow the previous section, but each extract is designed to follow the previous extract. I am encouraged to hope that my request will be granted by the letters I have received from so many readers of *A Year of Grace,* who have been good enough to tell me that only when they read it as a whole did they grasp what I was getting at.

The personal—and indeed semi-autobiographical—nature of this anthology explains why I have thought it in order occasionally to quote from writings of my own; and why (for instance) the places picked out for "praise" in a little coda are those particular ones rather than others doubtless equally delightful—they are places I happen specially to love.

Apart perhaps from an odd sentence or so, only three of the passages that I used for *A Year of Grace* reappear in the present anthology. Two of them—a poem by Alice Meynell and an extract from William James' *The Will to Believe*—are embedded in other passages. The third is the one from Plato's *Phaedrus,* without which the section entitled "The Soul's Memory" would have been an absurdity.

The author of each passage (with the exception mentioned below) is given at the foot of it; but the source is given in the body of the text only when, I thought, this might be useful—otherwise it is given in "Sources and Acknowledgments" at the end of the book. When there are omissions inside a passage, these are indicated by dots (which may, however, be the author's) except when, in the case of old writers, I thought it unnecessary to indicate the omissions, or when the passage is stated, in "Sources and Acknowledgments", to have been abbreviated. In the case of extracts from poems, the fact that they are extracts is not indicated by dots at the beginning and/or end of the extract, except when it seemed desirable to do so; but the poem from which the extract is taken is always given in "Sources and Acknowledgments".

The prayers at the end of the volume are printed without authors' names: which, appearing at that point, would have been irrelevant and distracting. All particulars will, however, be found in "Sources and Acknowledgments".

I have usually, but not invariably, retained old spelling and punctuation—making, however, such occasional alterations as I thought might be to the convenience of the reader. I have, for instance, always changed the old "then" to "than".

Where, under a passage, I use the words "From a Housman play", the reference is to Laurence Housman's "Little Plays of St. Francis".

An occasional word that may be unfamiliar to some readers, such as "Tao" and "Zen", is briefly explained in "Notes on Writers and Books".

The sources of the musical quotations are given on page 661. The Hebrew on page 63 is explained on page 662.

V. G.

BRIMPTON,
September 25th, 1955.

CONTENTS

Foreword   *page* 9

INTRODUCTORY: Origins   13

FIRST PART   I. From Darkness to Light   25
                II. Hope and Trust   65
                III. Serenity   79
                IV. Joy and Praise: a Prelude and Chorale,
                    with two Codas   97
                    Prelude   99
                    Chorale   105
                    Coda in praise of Places   145
                    Coda in praise of Married Love   155

SECOND PART   I. The Unity   169
                    Coda on Beasts, Plants and Earth in the
                    Unity   195
                II. ". . . of Goodness in Things Evil"   205
                    A Note on Perversity   223
                III. Divine and Human   227
                IV. The Divine Benevolence and Compassion   253
                    Coda on Suffering   267
                V. "So Panteth my Soul after Thee, O God"   277
                VI. "The Glorious Liberty of the Children of
                    God"   299

THIRD PART   I. Truth, Reason and beyond Reason   325
                II. The Soul's Memory   343
                III. Vision and Sacrament   359
                IV. Time and Eternity   413

FOURTH PART   I. Religion and Religion   425
                II. Crime and Punishment   443
                III. War and Peace   491
                    Coda to Fourth Part: on Justice   519

FIFTH PART   I. The Just Life for Man—the one thing
needful   *page* 527

II. The Just Life for Man—desirable things 559

AFTER THE BOOK. Prayer · and Prayers   609

L'ENVOI I   626

L'ENVOI II   627

Notes on Writers and Books   631

Sources and Acknowledgments   642

Index of Authors   663

Index of Subjects   669

INTRODUCTORY
ORIGINS

ISRAEL

I am a Jew because, for Israel, the world is not yet completed: men are completing it.

I am a Jew because, for Israel, Man is not created: men are creating him.

I am a Jew because, above the nations and Israel, Israel places Man and his Unity.

I am a Jew because, above Man, image of the divine Unity, Israel places the divine Unity, and its divinity.

*   *   *

Sometimes, my child, when I wander through a museum, and stand before all the pictures and statues and furniture and armour, the faïence, the crystals, the mosaics, the garments and the finery, the coins and the jewels, gathered there, from every place and every age, to hang on the walls, to stand on the plinths, to line up behind the balustrades, to be classified, numbered and ticketed in the glass cases, I think that one or other of my ancestors may have seen, touched, handled or admired one or other of these things, in the very place where it was made, and at the very time when it was made, for the use, the labour, the pain or the joy of men.

This door with the grey nails, between two poplars, in a gilded frame, this is the Geneva synagogue where my father went in to pray. And see this bridge of boats on the Rhine: my grandfather crossed the Rhine, at Hüningen. And his grandfather, where did he live? Perhaps as he dreamily calculated the mystical numbers of the Cabbala he saw, through his quiet window, this sledge glide over the snow of Germany or Poland? And the grandfather of his grandfather's grandfather? Perhaps he was this money-changer, in this Amsterdam ghetto, painted by Rembrandt.

One of my ancestors may have drunk from this wine goblet, on returning home from the lesson of his master Rashi, at the school of Troyes in Champagne; one of my ancestors may have sat on this jade-incrusted armchair as he felt a sultan's pulse; one of my ancestors may have been led to the auto-da-fé by a hooded monk who carried this cross of Castille; one of my ancestors may have seen his children trampled down by the horse of the Crusader who bore this armour.

These feather head-dresses, did another get them from an American savage? These African ivories, these Chinese silks, did another buy them by the banks of the Congo or the Amur, to sell

15

them again on the shores of the Ganges or on the Venetian lagoons?

One of them drove this plough, tempered in the fire, through the plain of Sharon; one of them went up to the Temple to offer, in these plaited baskets, his tithe of figs.

When this marble Titus was in the flesh, one of my ancestors was dragged bleeding at his chariot wheels in a Roman triumph; beneath the feet of this bearded mage with the fringed robe, flanked by two winged bulls of human profile, one of my ancestors smelt the dust of Babylon; at the breath of this porphyry Pharaoh, with the two flat hands on the two flat thighs, one of my ancestors bowed himself down, before girding on his girdle and taking up his staff to follow Moses across the Red Sea; and this Sumerian idol, with spherical eyes and angular jaws, is perhaps the very one that Abraham broke when he left his Chaldean home to follow the call of his invisible God.

And I say to myself: from this remote father right up to my own father, all these fathers have handed on to me a truth which flowed in their blood, which flows in mine; and shall I not hand it on, with my blood, to those of my blood?

Will you take it from me, my child? Will you hand it on? Perhaps you will wish to abandon it. If so, let it be for a greater truth, if there is one. I shall not blame you. It will be my fault; I shall have failed to hand it on as I received it.

But, whether you abandon it or whether you follow it, Israel will journey on to the end of days.

EDMOND FLEG (from *Why I am a Jew*)

CHRIST

And now I must return to the Person of Christ. I find myself at once in the greatest difficulty; for after sitting a long day before my library fire and brooding over the past, I am no nearer disentangling what I felt at Oxford—about the Incarnation: it is of this that I must speak—from what I felt subsequently and what I feel today. All I can do, I think, is to tell you what I have gradually come to feel about it; and I ought to wait a bit, perhaps a week or so, before making the attempt, because although my emotion is very precise I do not at the moment see how I can formulate it.

*　　　*　　　*

A way to do so came to me on Monday night, about twenty-four

16

hours after I had written the preceding paragraph, as I stood for a few minutes by the open window at Ladbroke Grove just before going to bed. I had switched off the light, and as I put my head out over the Square and smelled the leaves and the earth and the soft warm rain that was falling, I was moved once again, moved it may be for the millionth time, by an ineffable emotion of worship and gratitude. And as I lay in bed afterwards this is what I thought:

(1) I have always felt a vast, single, living bliss *behind* everything. I have always been certain it is *there*.

(2) I have always felt a life and a bliss *in* everything—I mean in every particular, in stones and chairs and mantelpieces and paper as well as in what is ordinarily called life: and it is through my meeting with these particulars, living and what are usually thought of as other than living, that I establish communion, feel myself mingled, with the bliss beyond.

(3) There is in me an imperative need, not only to establish communion, not only to merge myself, but also to worship. Or perhaps I should not speak of an imperative need, but should simply say that I *have* always worshipped—my life has been filled with a sense of worship, my being has been worshipful about the sum of things. I have worshipped the vast, single, living bliss beyond— that has been the central fact of my life; and I have worshipped it at once in and through the whole body of particulars, and in and through such single particulars—every single such single particular —as good deeds on the one hand and stocks and stones on the other.

(4) In religious language, I come to God through the world: in Platonic language I come to the Idea through the particulars. I don't mean that I deduce the Idea from the particulars: I mean that it is in the particulars that I feel and love the Idea. And Christ (whether the historic Christ or the Christ in our hearts—I shall soon deal with that) is the Supreme Particular.

(5) I worship the beyond in and through the particulars, but do not worship the particulars themselves. Not the "ordinary" particulars. I *do* worship the Supreme Particular, as I worship the beyond. I worship Him as very close, very friendly, very accessible: I worship Him in the way Blake tells of, the way common, I suppose, to all Christians:

17

"Then I see the Saviour over me,
Spreading his beams of love, and dictating the words of this mild
    song . . .
I am not a God afar off, I am a brother and a friend;
Within your bosoms I reside, and you reside in me;
Lo! we are One; forgiving all Evil; Not seeking recompense . . ."

(6) Christ, the Supreme Particular, is, for me, a concrete individual, one Person, with a man's nature: but typical of men as no
other man is typical. His nature is essentially ours—ours, not merely
a model for ours (though it is that as well): which is another way of
saying that our nature is essentially His—that this is what we really
are, the rest being error and misunderstanding. To the extent to
which we realise this—to the extent to which we "believe in" Him,
we are in Him. He is each one of us—every man—all but completely
released from bondage to error and unreality; to the error and unreality of self-centredness as opposed to communion, of what Blake
calls "selfhood":

"O Saviour, pour upon me thy Spirit of meekness and love,
    Annihilate the Selfhood in me, be thou all my life,
    Guide thou my hand which trembles exceedingly upon the rock of
        ages."

"Be thou all my life"—that is the crux.

Most men, in this sense, do die in Adam, and those of them who
"believe in" Christ do live again in Him.

And all this being so, worship by a man of Christ as the Supreme
Particular is worship both of God and of humanity.

*   *   *

This treatment of the Incarnation is of course completely subjective, and will be criticised accordingly. You must decide for
yourself whether the criticism is valid. What I have been saying,
you may think, amounts to no more than this: that I have need of a
Supreme Particular, and that when I call Christ that Particular all I
mean is that Particular for *me*. Very well; I shall not demur. And
if you go on to ask "But why Christ? Why not Krishna, or some
other Avatar?", the answer is simple: on the boy born in Elgin
Avenue to his own special heritage, and developing as he has slowly
developed through a variety of specific experiences, Christ's teaching has made an impact as of the *utterly* true, Christ's personality
has made an impact as of the *utterly* adorable, Christ's living and
dying has made an impact as of the *utterly* good. I tremble as I add,

18

but in honesty I must, that when I say utterly good I mean utterly good within human possibilities. (This is not such bad theology, either.) I do not regard Him as finally flawless. And even as I tremble I know that Christ will forgive me, for He would wish me to be divinely critical even about, perhaps specially about, Himself. But then again, I wonder: is it perhaps my own imperfection, my human imperfection, that allows me to see imperfection where nothing but perfection exists?

So my Christ, my Supreme Particular, could be no other, if I was to have one, than Christ. If I had been an Indian, Sri Krishna might have made the same impact on me. For I think that there are several Christs, but only one for each person. There are Christs, perhaps, not our Christ and yet our Christ, on earths and in dimensions of which we know nothing:

"With this ambiguous earth
His dealings have been told us. These abide:
The signal to a maid, the human birth,
The lesson, and the young Man crucified.

"But not a star of all
The innumerable host of stars has heard
How He administered this terrestrial ball.
Our race have kept their Lord's entrusted Word.

"Of His earth-visiting feet
None knows the secret, cherished, perilous,
The terrible, shamefast, frightened, whispered, sweet,
Heart-shattering secret of His way with us.

"No planet knows that this
Our wayside planet, carrying land and wave,
Love and life multiplied, and pain and bliss,
Bears, as chief treasure, one forsaken grave.

"Nor, in our little day,
May His devices with the heavens be guessed,
His pilgrimage to thread the Milky Way,
Or His bestowals there be manifest.

"But, in the eternities,
Doubtless we shall compare together, hear
A million alien Gospels, in what guise
He trod the Pleiades, the Lyre, the Bear.

19

"O be prepared, my soul!
To read the inconceivable, to scan
The million forms of God those stars unroll
When, in our turn, we show to them a Man."
ALICE MEYNELL
What a God it is who has given us, not only the "ordinary" particulars, but a Supreme Particular! And what a universe it is that can boast, not of one Supreme Particular, but of many!

*   *   *

Being the sort of person I am, if Christ had not existed I might almost have been tempted to invent Him. It may even be (though I don't believe it, Toynbee's great excursus notwithstanding) that, in one sense, men *have* invented Him: it may be, I mean, that the Gospel story is a mere amalgam of various happenings that have occurred, or have been imagined to occur, in many different places at many different times. Well, what of it? Then God, we should have to say, has put a Person, a Life and a Death into human consciousness, as a paradigm of the Way. On the one reading (to express it in its orthodox form) God was born, by God's grace, very man in a manger: on the other, God is born, by God's grace, very man in men's hearts: and I cannot for the life of me see why the one Christ should be any less "real", any less to be worshipped, than the other.

Or we should have to say, looking at it now from a slightly different angle, that out of the depths of its consciousness—out of the love and understanding in its heart—humanity has bodied forth a myth that incarnates the ultimate truth. Christ would then exist—would always have existed, would forever exist ("Before Abraham was, I am") as essential, as Divine, Humanity. Is that non-existence?

Beethoven "invented" the Quartet in C Sharp Minor, opus 131: that is to say, God put it into Beethoven's consciousness, with Beethoven's co-operation. Doesn't it then exist? Isn't it "real"? Listen to it, my dear Timothy, next time you have the chance (for you are certain to love music) and answer me.

I was delighted, the other day, to come across this passage in a book by Sri Aurobindo, the Hindu philosopher and saint who recently died:

"Such controversies as the one that has raged in Europe over the historicity of Christ would seem to a spiritually-minded Indian largely a waste of time; he would concede to it a considerable historical, but hardly any religious, importance; for what does it matter in the end whether a Jesus son of the carpenter Joseph was actually born in Nazareth or Bethlehem, lived and taught and was done to death on a real or trumped-up charge of sedition, so long as we can know by spiritual experience the inner Christ, live uplifted in the light of His teaching and escape from the yoke of the natural Law by that atonement of man with God of which the crucifixion is the symbol? If the Christ, God made man, lives within our spiritual being, it would seem to matter little whether or not a son of Mary physically lived and suffered and died in Judaea."

No, it would matter a great deal, because we are flesh and blood, and to part with a Christ of our own flesh and blood would be grievous. And yet in another sense I would go even a little further than Aurobindo. Whether or not the Incarnation—unique or otherwise—is, in the popular sense, a fact, scepticism about it would appear to be more reasonable if Christ is "historical", as you know I believe Him to be, than if He is not. If He is "historical", there is nothing far-fetched in the idea that people have drawn false deductions from a remarkable life and death. But if the Gospel narrative is a myth, it is difficult to understand how it can have come into being except by way of explaining what would then be, so to speak, a fact in its own right: the incarnation of God—his incarnation, unique or otherwise, as Christ—in innumerable men's hearts. Roughly by the same token, various parallelisms—and in particular the recurrent "dying God" beliefs—would appear to confirm Christianity, at least in one interpretation of it, rather than the reverse.

*   *   *

Such, then, is what I feel about the Incarnation: a matter partly of knowledge—of immediate experience—and partly of mood, and not at all one of "faith" or dogmatic precision. And it's no good people telling me that it's all very vague, and that I *ought* to have dogmas. I am merely describing. It is not a question of what ought to be, but of what is. The reality, for me, is that I adore Christ. Whatever may be the truth about the Gospel story, whatever may be the metaphysics of the matter, He lives and reigns for me eternally; and whether or not I should hesitate to call Him Lord, I can assuredly call Him Master.

V. G. (from My Dear Timothy)

GREECE

The conception of beauty as a joy in itself and as a guide in life
was first and most vividly expressed in Greece, and the very laws by
which things are beautiful or ugly were to a great extent discovered
there and laid down. The conception of Freedom and Justice, freedom in body, in speech and in mind, justice between the strong and
the weak, the rich and the poor, penetrates the whole of Greek
political thought, and was, amid obvious flaws, actually realized to a
remarkable degree in the best Greek communities. The conception
of Truth as an end to pursue for its own sake, a thing to discover
and puzzle out by experiment and imagination and especially by
Reason, a conception essentially allied with that of Freedom and
opposed both to anarchy and to blind obedience, has perhaps never
in the world been more clearly grasped than by the early Greek
writers on science and philosophy. One stands amazed sometimes
at the perfect freedom of their thought. Another conception came
rather later, when the small City States with exclusive rights of
citizenship had been merged in a larger whole: the conception of the
universal fellowship between man and man. Greece realized soon
after the Persian war that she had a mission to the world, that
Hellenism stood for the higher life of man as against barbarism, for
Aretē, or Excellence, as against the mere effortless average. First
came the crude patriotism which regarded every Greek as superior
to every barbarian; then came reflection, showing that not all
Greeks were true bearers of the light, nor all barbarians its enemies;
that Hellenism was a thing of the spirit and not dependent on the
race to which a man belonged or the place where he was born:
then came the new word and conception ἀνθρωπότης, *humanitas*,
which to the Stoics made the world as one brotherhood. No people
known to history clearly formulated these ideals before the Greeks,
and those who have spoken the words afterwards seem for the most
part to be merely echoing the thoughts of old Greek men.

GILBERT MURRAY

CHRIST AND GREECE

Faith in honest seeking is at the heart of the Greek view of life.
'Those who would rightly judge of truth', says Aristotle, 'must be
arbitrators, not litigants.' 'Happy is he who has learnt the value of
research', says Euripides in a fragment. Curiosity, as the Greeks
knew and the Middle Ages knew not, is a virtue, not a vice. Nature,

22

for Plato, is God's vicegerent and revealer, the Soul of the universe. Human nature is the same nature as the divine; no one has proclaimed this more strongly. Nature is for us; chaos and 'necessity' are the enemy. The divorce between religion and humanism began, it must be admitted, under Plato's successors, who unhappily were indifferent to natural science, and did not even follow the best light that was to be had in physical knowledge. In the Dark Ages, when the link with Greece was broken, the separation became absolute. . . .

It is the belief of the present writer that the unflinching eye and the open mind will bring us again to the feet of Christ, to whom Greece, with her long tradition of free and fearless inquiry, became a speedy and willing captive, bringing her manifold treasures to Him, in the well-grounded confidence that He was not come to destroy but to fulfil.

W. R. INGE

ENGLAND

We must be free or·die, who speak the tongue
That Shakspeare spake; the faith and morals hold
Which Milton held.

WORDSWORTH

O England: Modell to thy inward Greatnesse,
Like little Body with a mightie Heart . . .

SHAKESPEARE

Earth has not anything to show more fair . . .

WORDSWORTH

I. FROM DARKNESS TO LIGHT

For BETSEY BARTON

A grief without a pang, void, dark, and drear,
   A stifled, drowsy, unimpassioned grief,
   Which finds no natural outlet, no relief,
      In word, or sigh, or tear—
O Lady! in this wan and heartless mood,
To other thoughts by yonder throstle wooed,
   All this long eve, so balmy and serene,
Have I been gazing on the western sky,
   And its peculiar tint of yellow green:
And still I gaze—and with how blank an eye!
And those thin clouds above, in flakes and bars,
That give away their motion to the stars;
Those stars, that glide behind them or between,
Now sparkling, now bedimmed, but always seen:
Yon crescent Moon, as fixed as if it grew
In its own cloudless, starless lake of blue,
I see them all so excellently fair,
I see, not feel, how beautiful they are!

S. T. COLERIDGE

Why, lovely swallow, weary me with thy sweet chattering?
What dost thou hope to find in my heart? The warmth of the
    Spring?
In the great azure are flaming the almond bough and the almandine
    flower of the clear rose,
And my heart sheds its fire.

For once it was Spring. But now there is neither honey nor bee for
    me—
Neither the sting nor the sweetness.
Not mine the warm heart of Aprils and apricots, apricus,
Sunny, all gold within like the heart of the honeycomb,
Neither the honey-winged swarms of the gold thoughts of summer
Shall be mine again!

EDITH SITWELL

    The sun rises when morning comes, the mist rises from the
meadow, the dew rises from the clover; but oh, when will my heart
arise?

WELSH (TRADITIONAL)

For truly [in her dark night] the soul feels the shadow of death and the groans and tortures of Hell, as if she saw them bodily before her, for Hell to her consists in feeling herself forsaken of God, and chastised and flung aside, and that He is outraged and wrathful. All this she suffers now; and, furthermore, she is overcome by a direful terror that it is for ever. And she is haunted by this same sense of being forsaken and despised of all created people and things, particularly of her friends. She feels within herself a profound void and utter dearth of the three kinds of wealth which are ordered for her enjoyment, which are: temporal, physical, and spiritual; and she sees herself plunged into the contrary evils, to wit: miserable trifles of imperfections, aridnesses and emptinesses of the perceptions of the faculties, and desolation of the spirit in darkness. To this is added that she cannot, owing to the solitude and desolation this night produces in her, find comfort or support in any teaching or in any spiritual master. For as she is so immersed and absorbed in this passionate sorrow for her own evil doings wherein she so clearly sees her vileness, she thinks that, as others do not see what she sees and feels, they speak from lack of apprehension; and instead of comfort rather doth she receive fresh grief, thinking that this is no remedy for her hurt; and truly she is right. For the soul can do little in this condition of terror until in this purgation the spirit is softened, humbled, and purified, and becomes so refined, simple, and rarified, as to be enabled to become one with the spirit of God, according to the degree of union of love His mercy vouchsafes to concede.

ST. JOHN OF THE CROSS

And thy life shall hang in doubt before thee; and thou shalt fear day and night . . . In the morning thou shalt say, Would God it were even! And at even thou shalt say, Would God it were morning!

DEUTERONOMY

But tho' there was no prospect, no gleam of Light before, an indefinite indescribable Terror as with a scourge of ever restless, ever coiling and uncoiling serpents, drove me on from behind.

S. T. COLERIDGE

[In the dark night] glowing summer turns to autumn, all its riches are transformed into a great poverty. And the man begins to complain because of his wretchedness: for where now are the

28

ardours of love, the intimacy, the gratitude, the joyful praise: and the interior consolation, the secret joy, the sensible sweetness? How have all these things failed him? And the burning violence of his love, and all the gifts which he felt before. How has all this died in him?

RUYSBROEK

The day has foundered, and dead midnight's here:
As dark this spirit now with doubt and fear.
Doused is the candle of celestial fire,
    Lighting my secretest desire.

Put up the board! This house of life's to let.
Cold-chimneyed, void, its mouldering parapet
Surveys lost forests and a tongueless sea;
Gone joy, light, love, fire, hospitality.

Moons may perpetually wax and wane,
And morning's sun shine out again;
But when the heart at core is cold and black,
No cock, all earth for ear, will ever crow
    Its witching wildfire back.

WALTER DE LA MARE

He wandered aimlessly. The sun was setting. A special form of misery had begun to oppress him of late. There was nothing poignant, nothing acute about it; but there was a feeling of permanence, of eternity about it; it brought a foretaste of hopeless years of this cold leaden misery, a foretaste of an eternity "on a square yard of space" . . .

DOSTOEVSKY (from Crime and Punishment)

Yesterday I saw the swallows flying in the clouds. I write at the close of a beautiful day, very brilliant and very warm; but this glorious sun has passed over me like an extinct star. It has left me as it found me, cold, icy, insensible to all external impressions. My internal life withers away moment by moment; I sink into a nameless abyss, and it must be that I have already reached a great depth, for the light scarcely comes to me, and I feel the cold gaining upon me.

MAURICE DE GUÉRIN

THE SHRUBBERY

WRITTEN IN A TIME OF AFFLICTION

Oh, happy shades—to me unblest!
   Friendly to peace, but not to me!
How ill the scene that offers rest,
   And heart that cannot rest, agree!

This glassy stream, that spreading pine,
   Those alders quiv'ring to the breeze,
Might sooth a soul less hurt than mine,
   And please, if any thing could please.

But fix'd unalterable care
   Foregoes not what she feels within,
Shows the same sadness ev'ry where,
   And slights the season and the scene.

For all that pleas'd in wood or lawn,
   While peace possess'd these silent bow'rs,
Her animating smile withdrawn,
   Has lost its beauties and its pow'rs.

The saint or moralist should tread
   This moss-grown alley, musing, slow;
They seek, like me, the secret shade,
   But not, like me, to nourish woe!

Me fruitful scenes and prospects waste
   Alike admonish not to roam;
These tell me of enjoyments past,
   And those of sorrows yet to come.

WILLIAM COWPER

HATRED AND VENGEANCE

Hatred and vengeance, my eternal portion,
Scarce can endure delay of execution,
Wait, with impatient readiness, to seize my
              Soul in a moment.

Damn'd below Judas: more abhorr'd than he was,
Who for a few pence sold his holy Master.
Twice betrayed Jesus me, the last delinquent,
              Deems the profanest.

Man disavows, and Deity disowns me:
Hell might afford my miseries a shelter;
Therefore hell keeps her ever hungry mouths all
                Bolted against me.

Hard lot! encompass'd with a thousand dangers;
Weary, faint, trembling with a thousand terrors;
I'm called, if vanquish'd, to receive a sentence
                Worse than Abiram's.

Him the vindictive rod of angry justice
Sent quick and howling to the centre headlong;
I, fed with judgment, in a fleshly tomb, am
                Buried above ground.

WILLIAM COWPER

JOHN CLARE

I feel I am, I only know I am,
And plod upon the earth as dull and void;
Earth's prison chilled my body with its dram
Of dullness, and my soaring thoughts destroyed.
I fled to solitude from passion's dream,
But strife pursued: I only know I am.
I was a being created in the race
Of men, disdaining bounds of place and time;
A spirit that could travel o'er the space
Of earth and heaven like a thought sublime;
Tracing creation, like my Maker free,
A soul unshackled like eternity:
Spurning earth's vain and soul-debasing thrall—
But now I only know I am, that's all.

JOHN CLARE

INVOCATION OF DEATH

    Death, I repent
    Of these hands and feet
    That for forty years
    Have been my own
    And I repent
    Of flesh and bone,

Of heart and liver,
Of hair and skin—
Rid me, death,
Of face and form,
Of all that I am.

And I repent
Of the forms of thought,
The habit of mind
And heart crippled
By long-spent pain,
The memory-traces
Faded and worn
Of vanished places
And human faces
Not rightly seen
Or understood.
Rid me, death,
Of the words I have used.

Not this or that
But all is amiss,
That I have done,
And I have seen
Sin and sorrow
Befoul the world—
Release me, death,
Forgive, remove
From place and time
The trace of all
That I have been.

KATHLEEN RAINE

EXILE

Then, I had no doubt
That snowdrops, violets, all creatures, I myself
Were lovely, were loved, were love.
Look, they said,
And I had only to look deep into the heart,
Dark, deep into the violet, and there read,
Before I knew of any word for flower or love,
The flower, the love, the word.

32

They never wearied of telling their being; and I
Asked of the rose only more rose, the violet
More violet; untouched by time
No flower withered or flame died,
But poised in its own eternity, until the looker moved
On to another flower, opening its entity.

I see them now across a void
Wider and deeper than time and space.
All that I have come to be
Lies between my heart and the rose,
The flame, the bird, the blade of grass.
The flowers are veiled;
And in a shadow-world, appearances
Pass across a great *toile vide*
Where the image flickers, vanishes,
Where nothing is, but only seems.
But still the mind, curious to pursue,
Long followed them, as they withdrew
Deep within their inner distances,
Pulled the petals from flowers, the wings from flies,
Hunted the heart with a dissecting-knife
And scattered under a lens the dust of life;
But the remoter, stranger
Scales iridescent, cells, spindles, chromosomes,
Still merely are:
With hail, snow-crystals, mountains, stars,
Fox in the dusk, lightning, gnats in the evening air
They share the natural mystery,
Proclaim I AM, and remain nameless.

Sometimes from far away
They sign to me;
A violet smiles from the dim verge of darkness,
A raindrop hangs beckoning on the eaves,
And once, in long wet grass,
A young bird looked at me.
Their being is lovely, is love;
And if my love could cross the desert self
That lies between all that I am and all that is,
They would forgive and bless.

KATHLEEN RAINE

Again that awful sensation he had known of late passed with deadly chill over his soul. Again it became suddenly plain and perceptible to him that . . . he would never now be able to speak freely of everything—that he would never again be able to *speak* of anything to anyone. The anguish of this thought was such that for a moment he almost forgot himself. He got up from his seat, and not looking at anyone walked towards the door . . .

DOSTOEVSKY (from *Crime and Punishment*)

The essence of my hell was outlawry. By the sin which, as I felt, I had committed, I had broken the links that united me with universal living: I was separate, alone, without lot or part in the everything. I had deprived myself, treacherously, of it; I had deprived it, quite as treacherously, of me. The smell of the grass was still there, but was now all the more alien for its sweetness; the sun still shone, but not for me. If only I could no longer care! If only my senses had died! But the terrible thing was that the opposite had happened. The sweetness was sweeter than before, the sun still more radiant; happier they were, more lovable than ever I had known them since first I had awakened to their blessing. The lull of the summer streets, which had always had sadness in its magic, was now like all sadness incarnate: like an intimation of Paradise lost, of a Paradise that could never be regained. Most anguishing of all was my relation to music. I had betrayed it. And perhaps because I loved music best, my concern in this instance was almost entirely for the thing betrayed and hardly at all for myself the betrayer. The shame I should feel in its presence was something I should be unable to bear. So I kept away.

v . g . (of 1908)

For an hour past I have been the prey of a vague anxiety; I recognise my old enemy . . . It is a sense of void and anguish; a sense of something lacking: what? Love, peace—God perhaps. The feeling is one of pure want unmixed with hope, and there is anguish in it because I can clearly distinguish neither the evil nor its remedy.

Of all the hours of the day, in fine weather, the afternoon, about three o'clock, is the time which to me is most difficult to bear. I never feel more strongly than I do then *'le vide effrayant de la vie'*, the stress of mental anxiety, or the painful thirst for happiness. This torture born of the sunlight is a strange phenomenon. Is it

34

that the sun, just as it brings out the stain upon a garment, the wrinkles in a face, or the discoloration of the hair, so also it illumines with inexorable distinctness the scars and rents of the heart? Does it rouse in us a sort of shame of existence? In any case the bright hours of the day are capable of flooding the whole soul with melancholy, of kindling in us the passion for death, or suicide, or annihilation, or of driving us to that which is next akin to death, the deadening of the senses by the pursuit of pleasure. They rouse in the lonely man a horror of himself; they make him long to escape from his own misery and solitude . . .

People talk of the temptations to crime connected with darkness, but the dumb sense of desolation which is often the product of the most brilliant moment of daylight must not be forgotten either. From the one, as from the other, God is absent; but in the first case a man follows his senses and the cry of his passion; in the second, he feels himself lost and bewildered, a creature forsaken by all the world.

AMIEL

For the rest, I was utterly derelict. I felt myself banished from life and from God. And I was quite hopeless: not approximately, not in the sense people often intend when they play with this terrible word, but in the sense that to have had the very tiniest of hopes, for the very briefest of instants, would have been wholly inconceivable. The doom that I lived with in eternity was the doom that I must live in eternity with a self I detested, and must live with it alone.

V. G. (of 1943)

§ 2

One forenoon, when my terror and despair seemed to be at their height (if degrees can be spoken of in such a context, as they truly cannot), I set out for a walk with my wife. We went very slowly, my arm resting on hers: for my body was weak after a total insomnia that had lasted for twenty-two days, and every muscle and nerve in it ached. . . . About half an hour later we turned, sharply left, into a dark and narrow path that descended: and soon came out into a great open space—a sort of water-meadow, with herds grazing, and a high inland cliff just in front of us. There was dappled sunlight everywhere, and a slight breeze. I felt suddenly very still: and then I heard the inland cliff, and the grass and water and sky, say very distinctly to me "A humble and a contrite heart He will not despise". When I say I heard them say it I mean, quite literally, that I *heard* them say it: a voice came from them: but they were also themselves the voice, and the voice was also within me. . . . I said to my wife "The trouble is over": and that night I slept a little. The trouble, in one sense, was not over, for a year or two were to pass before it was more or less completely behind me: I was nevertheless right, because thenceforth, even at the worst moments, there was always a glimmer of light, however minute, at the end of the tunnel. . . . And now it is only by the greatest effort of will, if even so, that I can realise in recollection that terror and that despair, which have long appeared nothing to me; and when I live again in those days, as I often do, I live in the love that faithfully cared for me and saw me through to safety.

v. g. (of 1943)

It was like a drought—a moral drought—as if I had been absent for many years from the sources of life and hope. The inner nature was faint, all was dry and tasteless. Some instinctive feeling, uncontrollable, drove me to the sea; I was so under its influence that I could not arrange the journey so as to get the longest day. I merely started, and of course had to wait and endure much inconvenience. To get to the sea at some quiet spot was my one thought; to do so I had to travel farther, and from want of prearrangement it was between two and three in the afternoon before I reached the end of my journey. Even then, being too much preoccupied to inquire the way, I missed the road and had to walk a long distance before coming to the shore. But I found the sea at last; I walked beside it in a trance away from the houses out into the wheat. The ripe corn stood up to the beach, the waves on one side of the shingle, and the yellow wheat on the other.

There, alone, I went down to the sea. I stood where the foam came to my feet, and looked out over the sunlit waters. The great earth bearing the richness of the harvest, and its hills golden with corn, was at my back; its strength and firmness under me. The great sun shone above, the wide sea was before me, the wind came sweet and strong from the waves. The life of the earth and the sea, the glow of the sun filled me; I touched the surge with my hand, I lifted my face to the sun, I opened my lips to the wind. I prayed aloud in the roar of the waves. . . .

Then I rested, sitting by the wheat; the bank of beach was between me and the sea, but the waves beat against it; the sea was there, the sea was present and at hand. By the dry wheat I rested, I did not think, I was inhaling the richness of the sea, all the strength and depth of meaning of the sea and earth came to me again. I rubbed out some of the wheat in my hands, I took up a piece of clod and crumbled it in my fingers—it was a joy to touch it—I held my hand so that I could see the sunlight gleam on the slightly moist surface of the skin. The earth and sun were to me like my flesh and blood, and the air of the sea life.

RICHARD JEFFERIES

Towards morning I got into bed, but not to sleep; and when the dull daylight of Monday came, all support had vanished, and I seemed to be sinking into a bottomless abyss. I became gradually worse week by week, and my melancholy took a fixed form. I got a notion into my head that my brain was failing, and this was my first acquaintance with that most awful malady hypochondria. I did not know then what I know now, although I only half believe it practically, that this fixity of form is a frequent symptom of the disease, and that the general weakness manifests itself in a determinate horror, which gradually fades with returning health. For months—many months, this dreadful conviction of coming idiocy or insanity lay upon me like some poisonous reptile with its fangs driven into my very marrow, so that I could not shake it off. It went with me wherever I went, it got up with me in the morning, walked about with me all day, and lay down with me at night. I managed somehow or other to do my work, but I prayed incessantly for death; and to such a state was I reduced that I could not even make the commonest appointment for a day beforehand. The mere knowledge that something had to be done agitated me and prevented my doing it. In June next year my holiday came, and I went away home to my father's house. Father and mother were going for the first time in their lives to spend a few days by the seaside together, and I went with them to Ilfracombe. I had been there about a week, when on one memorable morning, on the top of one of those Devonshire hills, I became aware of a kind of flush in the brain and a momentary relief such as I had not known since that November night. I seemed, far away on the horizon, to see just a rim of olive light low down under the edge of the leaden cloud that hung over my head, a prophecy of the restoration of the sun, or at least a witness that somewhere it shone. It was not permanent, and perhaps the gloom was never more profound, nor the agony more intense, than it was for long after my Ilfracombe visit. But the light broadened, and gradually the darkness was mitigated. I have never been thoroughly restored. Often, with no warning, I am plunged in the Valley of the Shadow, and no outlet seems possible; but I contrive to traverse it, or to wait in calmness for access of strength.

MARK RUTHERFORD

One who was suffering tumult in his soul
Yet failed to seek the sure relief of prayer,
Went forth—his course surrendering to the care
Of the fierce wind, while mid-day lightnings prowl
Insidiously, untimely thunders growl;
While trees, dim-seen, in frenzied numbers, tear
The lingering remnant of their yellow hair,
And shivering wolves, surprised with darkness, howl
As if the sun were not. He raised his eye
Soul-smitten; for, that instant did appear
Large space ('mid dreadful clouds) of purest sky,
An azure disc—shield of Tranquillity;
Invisible, unlooked-for, minister
Of providential goodness ever nigh!

WORDSWORTH

And then all her former fear falls away, and she knows clearly that she is free, and sings with joy to see herself in such serene and tranquil peace.

ST. JOHN OF THE CROSS

38

> . . . Into my heart's night
> Along a narrow way
> I groped; and lo! the light,
> An infinite land of day.
>
> RUMI

> And first an hour of mournful musing,
> And then a gush of bitter tears,
> And then a dreary calm diffusing
> Its deadly mist o'er joys and cares;
> And then a throb, and then a lightening,
> And then a breathing from above,
> And then a star in heaven brightening—
> The star, the glorious star of love.
>
> EMILY BRONTË

I have indeed fought thro' a Hell of terrors and horrors (which none could know but myself) in a divided existence; now no longer divided nor at war with myself, I shall travel on in the strength of the Lord God, as Poor Pilgrim says.

BLAKE

For now! O Glory! and O Delight! I have entirely reduced that spectrous fiend to his station, whose annoyance has been the ruin of my labours for the last passed twenty years of my life. . . . I was a slave bound in a mill among beasts and devils; these beasts and these devils are now, together with myself, become children of light and liberty, and my feet and my wife's feet are free from fetters. . . . Suddenly, on the day after visiting the Truchsessian Gallery of pictures, I was again enlightened with the light I enjoyed in my youth, and which has for exactly twenty years been closed from me as by a door and by window-shutters. . . .

BLAKE

§ 3

PETER ABELARD

He dropped the chisel on the grass and stood up. He must not let himself think.

Yet what was a man to do in this wilderness but think? He gazed around him, and in spite of himself the tiny dwelling-places that he and Thibault had made looked at him reproachfully. They were like the little houses that he and Guillaume and Raoul used to build in the valley where the hazel-trees grew. He twitched his mind away. Was there any one channel down which it could run, now that half his life was shut off from him, and half the chambers of his brain bolted and shuttered and dark, only that his thoughts at night fluttered in them like bats? Gilles said she was prioress now. Some day perhaps, when she was an old woman, they might see one another again. But now, at the mere sight of her handwriting his heart turned over. Last year they had brought the mortuary roll of St. Vitalis to St. Denis, for the brethren to inscribe their sympathy with the bereaved house. The roll had come to St. Denis from Argenteuil: someone at Argenteuil had written half a dozen lines on death. It was not signed, but it was in her script. It had been several nights before he had quiet sleep. Some day she would cease to haunt him. Some day he would be able to think of her as God's bride, who had been his wild love in just such woods as these. But what was the desire of the flesh beside the desire of the mind?

He looked about him in despair. Under the beeches the brown hens walked and scuffled, flicking the yellow and russet leaves this way and that, absorbed and happy: from the pool below came the flat, contented voices of the ducks. He took his staff, and flung into the woods.

As he walked, the tumult in his brain died, leaving the dull, familiar ache. It was almost easier, after all, he thought, to bear the sudden resurrection of remembrance, than this grief without a ripple, without ebb or flow, a kind of dark water that lay sullen at his heart root. For a while in St. Médard he had almost gone mad. He had been so utterly confident, so sure of God: and God had forsaken him, had gone over to the side of Alberic and Ralph and Palestrina; of jealousy and stupidity and hypocrisy. They had tricked and cheated and lied, and they had won. They had destroyed his book that had been his burnt-offering to God, the symbol that he was now and for ever Christ's philosopher. They had destroyed his book and Alberic was Abel, and God had had respect to his offering, and he was the branded Cain.

Walking heedlessly but rapidly, he had covered more ground than he knew; it was with a shock of surprise that he found himself where the trees thinned on the hill above the valley where Coincy lay. Like a wild duck's nest, he thought, looking down at it, and his heart softened at the patches of the fields, the tiny roofs. He could have sat there long enough, blessing them, as he had sat watching the antics of Thibault's yellow ducklings, so small, so eager to live, so pitifully easy to crush. But even as he stood watching, brooding over them in a grim thwarted tenderness, a small sound came to his ears, high and thin almost as a gnat's voice. The tiny bell on the church had begun to ring, summoning these tiny souls, hedgers and ditchers and shambling old men and women with child, to sit down with Apostles and Martyrs, St. Ambrose and St. Augustine and the unnumbered *manes* of the unnamed holy dead. And listening, a great longing took him to go in and sit among them: to feel no more the outcast, the man whom God had rejected and would have no longer to serve Him. It might be that the miracle would happen, that he might receive the Host without such a spring of bitterness in his heart as turned the sacrament to poison.

The village seemed empty as he passed through it: every soul must be in church. He reached the graveyard and passed up the uneven stones to the low door. But there a queer reluctance seized him: he sat down on the stone ledge of the porch to take breathing-space, and courage to go in. The Alleluia was just ending: there was a pause, and Herluin's hoarse relaxed voice began the Gospel, reading aloud the Beatitudes that are for broken men, for men that are poor in spirit, for men that mourn, for men that hunger and thirst after righteousness, for men that are reviled and all manner of evil spoken against them falsely. *Rejoice and be exceeding glad, for great is your reward in heaven.* Well, he was broken enough, he had mourned, he had hungered and thirsted after righteousness, at any rate after truth, there had been evil enough said of him. But he was not blessed. There were some that God rejected, and He had rejected him.

Then fell a silence, then Thibault's young voice, the boys' voices following it. *"The souls of the just are in the hand of God, and the torment of malice shall not touch them: in the sight of the unwise they seemed to die, but they are in peace."*

He rose and went quietly out of the porch and past the quiet graves. The torment of malice had touched him: the hand of God was not for him. The whole gentleness of the November day, the day that seemed to him more than any other to have Good Friday's peace, dreamt above the world, but not on him. He had no anger now, no bitterness even. He had blasphemed God once, but he blasphemed no more. *"Though He slay me, yet will I trust in Him"*

41

—why did they never finish that sentence as Job finished it?—*"but I will maintain my ways before Him. . . . My righteousness I hold fast, and I will not let it go."*

He halted suddenly, for in this queer silence of the earth, with all the saints intent upon the prayers of the faithful, and all the world droning with devotion like a hive of bees, now if ever it seemed to him that he might speak and God would hear, with only they two left face to face. He stood quiet and grim, his face turned to the quiet sky. All the traditions of his faith, all the memories of his life were forcing him upon his knees, but he would not. His mother's silent abnegation, the humility of his father's walk with God, the whole divine consolation of psalmist and prophet pleaded with him in vain. *"As far as east is distant from the west, so far hath He removed our transgressions from us."* Let him first be shown wherein he had transgressed. *"Like as a father pitieth his children, so the Lord pitieth them that fear Him."* He asked for no pity, he asked for justice, the justice that a man would give his fellow, aye, that a lord would give his serf.

And standing there, braced against heaven, the wind that had blown upon him once and been forgotten, breathed upon him again. It came without observation, for the kingdom of God is within: a frail wisp of memory, voiceless as the drift of thistledown, inevitable as sunrise. *"Neither do I condemn thee: go, and sin no more."*

He saw no heavens opened: he saw no Son of Man. For a moment it seemed to him that all the vital forces in his body were withdrawing themselves, that the sight had left his eyes and the blood was ebbing from his heart: he felt the grey breath of dissolution, the falling asunder of body and soul. For a moment: then his spirit leapt toward heaven in naked adoration. Stripped of all human emotion, with no warmth of contrition, with no passion of devotion, but with every power of his mind, with every pulse of his body, he worshipped God.

Hours later, he found himself on the edge of the forest where the road came up from the ford and passed over the hill to Rigny-la-Vanneuse. Instinctively he had left the river for the hills, and had walked mile after mile, skirting the woods, keeping the valley below him. Yet it was no blind ecstasy that had driven him so far: his brain had never worked with so steady a rhythm. It was not so much that the first glory had passed as that it had transmuted itself into a grave clarity: and halting now at the boundary stone, he turned and looked back along the valley, its small, green meadows by the river and the patches of ploughed earth, torn open to be softened by frost and rain. The mist had cleared, and though the sky was still veiled, the veil was translucent.

"*'And now men see not the brightness in the clouds,'*" said Abelard to himself, " *'but the wind passeth and cleanseth them.'* "

It had been so with him. In the long hours of his ceaseless walking, ceaseless thinking, he had been aware of no conscious examining of himself. But as in that definition Gilles had quoted to him of infinity, the years of his intellectual majority had seemed present to him in a single moment of time, with all their implications, the shadows that they cast before and after, above all the years since he had turned his back on the world and, as he had thought, sought the Kingdom of God. Every sentence he had written stood out before him, that glorious array of embattled spears, his strong chivalry of all the powers of the soul, of all the strength of the mind, pagan and Christian; Plato and Aristotle fighting side by side with Augustine and Jerome and Origen, for the conquest of the spirit's Palestine, for the worship of the Father in spirit and in truth. But for whom was the glory of that warfare? He had fought against ignorance, against hypocrisy, against spiritual sloth, against an easy faith that was the faith of gulls and not of men: he had written for his young men, challenging them to doubt, arming them against the deadlier sin of dullness: but did dullness keep a man more insensitive to God than pride?

"If a man desire to understand God, let him prepare himself for that understanding by good life and let him take the way of humility, for by that road alone may a man come nigh that height of intellectual vision." It sounded reverent enough, but how his heart had swelled as he had written it, in a kind of pomp of abnegation: the pride of that humility was the ceremonial pride of the Roman salute. He had strutted like a beadle in a cathedral procession, forgetting that behind him came the Host.

"*I have heard of thee by the hearing of the ear, but now mine eye seeth thee; wherefore I do abhor myself.*" This very day he had challenged Heaven to show him wherein he had sinned: and Heaven's answer had been to show him itself. His righteousness he had held fast and would not let it go: it lay about him now, like farmyard trampled snow.

And now? He stood looking down at the river as it flowed through the quiet land. And something in the still, shining surface of it brought back to him a thing that he had forgotten for more than thirty years. Once when he was a youngster he had gone with his father on pilgrimage to St. Gildas de Rhuis. It was a quiet, shining day with no wind and standing on those terrible cliffs above the point and looking westward, he had seen a strange silver pathway that swept round the headland and out to sea, with no ripple upon it, counter to all the restless fleeing and pursuing of the blue gay-crested waves. His father had stood beside him, so withdrawn into himself that for a long time he had not liked to question him: and when he did, Berengar had answered heavily, with his eyes still upon it, "It is the will of God." At supper in the guest-house, the old brother who waited on them spoke of the strong current that swept round the coast and was the terror of all craft that made for home: and yet it had suffered St. Gildas to float upon it without oar or sail, and landed him unbroken in his coracle in the cove where his image stood. He saw it now, looking down into the valley, as though the river had transformed itself into that swift current, radiant, implacable and strong, and the green fields into the jabble of the tumbling waves. Well, it had brought his father to a quiet haven: it was to take himself to sea.

A shudder of premonition passed over him. To what end would it carry him, St. Brendan's Happy Isles, or the sea, shouting on an iron coast? Through what sore discipline of body and soul, through what crucifixion of his pride must he still go, before he saw the Kingdom of God? For a moment his flesh and his heart failed. Then he raised his head and began walking steadily towards home. He was chanting as he walked, the words that had held for him the torment of all longing and now were for ever his. "The souls of the just are in the hand of God, and the torment of malice shall not touch them; in the sight of the unwise they seemed to die, but they are in peace." He had turned to the stronghold of the prisoners of hope.

HELEN WADDELL (from *Peter Abelard*)

FATHER SURIN

A few months later the road had become so hard that Surin was physically and mentally incapable of describing it. From 1639 to 1657 there is a great gap in his correspondence, a total blank. During all this time he suffered from a kind of pathological illiteracy, and was incapable either of writing or reading. At moments it was difficult for him even to speak. He was in solitary confinement, cut off from all communication with the outside world. Exile from humanity was bad enough; but it was as nothing to that exile from God to which he was now condemned. Not long after his return from Annecy, Surin came to be convinced (and the conviction endured for many years) that he was already damned. Nothing now remained for him but to wait, in utter despair, for a death which was predestined to be the passage from hell on earth to an infinitely more terrible hell in hell.

His confessor and his superiors assured him that God's mercy is boundless and that, so long as there is life, there can be no certainty of damnation. . . . It was all in vain. Surin *knew* that he was lost and that the devils, over whom he had so recently triumphed, were gleefully preparing a place for him among the everlasting fires. Men might talk as they liked; but facts and his own deeds spoke louder than any words. Everything that happened, everything he felt and was inspired to do, confirmed him in his conviction. If he sat near the fire, a burning ember (the symbol of eternal damnation) was sure to jump out at him. If he entered a church, it was always at the moment when some phrase about God's justice, some denunciation of the wicked, was read or sung—for *him*. If he listened to a sermon, he would invariably hear the preacher affirm that there was a lost soul in the congregation—it was *his*. . . .

To these external and inferential proofs of his damnation were added the inward assurances inspired in his mind by some alien and evidently supernatural power. "He who speaks of God," he wrote, "speaks of a sea of rigours and (if I dare say it) of severities, passing all measure." In those long hours of helplessness, while he lay pinned to his bed by a paralysis of the will, an alternate collapse and cramping of the muscles, he received "impressions of God's fury so great that there is no pain in the world to compare with it." Year followed year, and one kind of suffering was succeeded by another; but the sense of God's enmity never wavered within him. He knew it intellectually; he felt it as an enormous weight, pressing upon him—the weight of divine judgment. *Et pondus ejus ferre non potui.* He could not bear it, and yet there it always was. . . .

On 27th October 1660 one of his relatives called to see him and, when the time came for him to go, Surin painfully dragged himself to the door to say goodbye. Standing there, after the visitor's departure, he looked out into the garden "and began to study, with a certain distinctness, the objects that were in it, a thing which, on account of an extreme debility of the nerves, I had not been able to do for fifteen years." Feeling, instead of the familiar pains, "a certain suavity", he went down the five or six steps into the garden and looked about him for a little while longer. Looked at the black mould and the shiny green of the box hedges, looked at the lawns and the Michaelmas daisies and the alley of pleached hornbeams. Looked at the low hills in the distance with their autumnal woods, fox-brown under the pale sky, in the almost silvery sunlight. There was no wind, and the silence was like an enormous crystal, and everywhere was a living mystery of colours merging, of forms distinct and separate, of the innumerable and the one, of passing time and the presence of eternity.

Next day Surin ventured out again into the universe he had almost forgotten; and, the day after that, his voyage of rediscovery took him as far as the well—and it did not invite him to suicide. He even left the garden and walked, ankle-deep in the dead leaves, through the little wood that lay beyond the walls. He was cured. . . .

In its opening phase, Surin's cure was not a passage from darkness into that "sober certainty of waking bliss", which comes when mind permits Mind to know itself, through a finite consciousness, for what it really is; it was rather the exchange of a profoundly abnormal condition for another condition of opposite sign, in which "extraordinary graces" became as ordinary as extraordinary desolations had been before. . . . [By 1663, however,] the regular and easy succession of extraordinary graces was a thing of the past. But he had something else, something better. . . . Now that the extraordinary graces were over, now that he was free to be aware of the proximity of total Awareness, he had achieved the possibility of enlightenment. For now at last he was living "in faith", precisely as Bastide had urged him to do. Now at last he was standing in intellectual and imaginative nakedness before the given facts of the world and his own life—empty that he might be filled, poor that he might be made supremely rich. "I am told," he writes two years before his death, "that there are pearl fishers, who have a pipe that goes from the sea floor to the surface, where it is buoyed up with corks, and that through this pipe they breathe—and are yet at the bottom of the sea. I do not know if this be true; but in any case it expresses very well what I have to say; for the soul has a pipe that goes to heaven, a channel, says St. Catherine of Genoa, that leads to the very heart of God. Through it she breathes wisdom and love, and is sustained. While the soul is here, fishing for pearls at the bottom of the earth, she speaks with other souls, she preaches, she does God's business; and all the time there is a pipe that goes to heaven to draw down eternal life and consolation. . . . In this state the soul is at once happy and wretched. And yet I think she is really happy. . . . For without vision or ecstasies or suspensions of the senses, in the midst of the ordinary miseries of earthly life, in weakness and many-sided impotency, our Lord gives something that passes all understanding and all measure. . . . This something is a certain wound of love which, without any visible outward effect, pierces the soul and keeps it incessantly longing for God."

And so, fishing for pearls at the bottom of the earth, his pipe between his teeth, his lungs dilated by the air from another world, the old man advanced towards his consummation. A few months before he died, Surin finished the last of his devotional writings, *Questions sur l'Amour de Dieu*. Reading certain passages of this book, we divine that the last barrier had now gone down and that, for one more soul, the Kingdom had come on earth. Through that channel to the very heart of God had flowed "a peace that is not merely a calm, like the lull of the sea, or the tranquil flow of mighty rivers; but it enters into us, this divine peace and repose, like a flooding torrent; and the soul, after so many tempests, feels, as it were, an inundation of peace; and the relish of divine repose not only enters the soul, not only takes her captive, but comes upon her, like the onrush of a multitude of waters.

"We find that, in the Apocalypse, the Spirit of God makes mention of a music of harps and lutes that is like thunder. Such are the marvellous ways of God—to make a thunder like well-tuned lutes and a symphony of lutes like thunder. Likewise, who will ever believe or imagine that there can be torrents of peace, which sweep away the dykes, which breach the levees and shatter the sea walls? And yet this is what actually happens, and it is the nature of God to make assaults of peace and silences of love. . . . God's peace is like a river, whose course was in one country and has been diverted into another by the breaking of a dyke. This invading peace does things which do not seem proper to the nature of peace; for it comes with a rush, it comes with impetuosity; and this belongs only to the peace of God. Only the peace of God can march in such equipage, like the noise of the rising tide as it comes, not to ravage the land, but to fill the bed prepared for it by God. It comes as though fiercely, it comes with a roaring, even though the sea be calm. This roaring is caused only by the abundance of the waters, and not by their fury; for the moving of the waters is not by a

47

tempest, but by the waters themselves, in all their native calm, when there is not a breath of wind. The sea in its fullness comes to visit the earth and to kiss the shores assigned for its limits. It comes in majesty and in magnificence. Even so it is in the soul when, after long suffering, the immensity of peace comes to visit her—and not a breath of wind to make a ripple on its surface. This is a divine peace, which brings with it the treasures of God and all the wealth of His Kingdom. It has its harbingers, the halcyons and heralding birds that announce its approach; these are the visits of angels which precede it. It comes like an element of the other life, with a sound of celestial harmony and with such swiftness that the soul is utterly overthrown, not because she has made any resistance to the blessing, but because of its very abundance. This abundance does no violence except to the obstacles in the way of its benediction; and all the animals that are not peaceable take flight before the onset of this peace. And with peace come all the treasures promised to Jerusalem—cassia and amber and the other rarities upon her shores. Even so comes this divine peace—comes with abundance, comes with a wealth of blessings, comes with all the precious treasures of grace."

More than thirty years before, at Marennes, Surin had often watched the calm, irresistible mounting of the Atlantic tides; and now the memory of that everyday marvel was the means by which this consummated soul was able, at last, to "disgorge herself" in a not inadequate expression of the experienced Fact. *Tel qu'en Lui-même enfin l'éternité le change*, he had come to the place where, without knowing it, he had always been; and when, in the spring of 1665, death overtook him, there was, as Jacob Boehme had said, "no necessity for him to go anywhere": he was already there.

ALDOUS HUXLEY (from *The Devils of Loudun*)

LUDWIG VAN BEETHOVEN

(a) 1798 TO 1802

It would appear that Beethoven first noticed symptoms of his deafness in 1798. His first reference to it, however, occurs in a letter to Amenda, dated June 1, 1801. The letter is most interesting as showing us Beethoven's attitude, at this time, towards the impending calamity. His first reaction, as we should expect, is rage at the *senselessness* of the hideous affliction. That he, of all men, should lose this particular sense must, indeed, have seemed the most abominable of ironies.

"Your Beethoven is most unhappy," he writes, "and at strife with nature and Creator. I have often cursed the latter for exposing his creatures to the merest accident, so that often the most beautiful buds are broken or destroyed thereby. Only think that my noblest faculty, my hearing, has greatly deteriorated."

But still he has hopes, although he fears the worst, and his self-confidence remains indomitable.

". . . I hope, indeed, that my hearing will also improve, but I am dubious, because such diseases are the most incurable. How sad is my lot! I must avoid all things that are dear to me. . . . Oh, how happy could I be if my hearing were completely restored; then would I hurry to you, but as it is I must refrain from everything and the most beautiful years of my life must pass without accomplishing the promise of my talent and powers. A sad resignation to which I must resort, although, indeed, I am resolved to rise superior to every obstacle. But how will that be possible? . . ."

In a letter to his doctor friend Wegeler, written at the end of the same month, he goes more into detail.

". . . I am living a wretched life; for two years I have avoided almost all social gatherings because it is impossible for me to say to people: 'I am deaf'. If I belonged to any other profession it would be easier, but in my profession it is an awful state, the more since my enemies, who are not few, what would they say? In order to give you an idea of this singular deafness of mine I must tell you that in the theatre I must get very close to the orchestra in order to understand the actor. If I am a little distant I do not hear the high tones of the instruments, singers, and if I be put a little farther away I do not hear at all. Frequently I can hear the tones of a low conversation, but not the words, and as soon as anybody shouts it is intolerable. It seems singular that in conversation there are people who do not notice my condition at all, attributing it to my absent-mindedness. Heaven knows what will happen to me. *Vering says that there will be an improvement if no complete cure.* I have often— cursed my existence. *Plutarch* taught me resignation. If possible I will bid defiance to my fate, although there will be moments in my life when I shall be the unhappiest of God's creatures. . . . Resignation! What a wretched refuge—and yet the only one open to me."

In November he again writes to Wegeler. His hearing has become no better, but rather worse. The slight hope of improvement that he had seems to have abandoned him, so that now he clutches eagerly at any chance. He thinks of changing his physician, accusing Vering of negligence. . . .

"Oh, if I were rid of this affliction I could embrace the world! I feel that my youth is just beginning and have I not always been ill? My physical strength has for a short time past been steadily growing more than ever and also my mental powers. Day by day I am approaching the goal which I apprehend but cannot describe. It is only in this that your Beethoven can live. Tell me nothing of rest. I know of none but sleep, and woe is me that I must give up more time to it than usual. Grant me but half freedom from my affliction and then—as a complete, ripe man I shall return to you and renew the old feelings of friendship. You must see me as happy as it is possible to be here below—not unhappy. No! I cannot endure it. I will take Fate by the throat; it shall not wholly overcome me. Oh, it is so beautiful to live—to live a thousand times! I feel that I am not made for a quiet life."

During the winter of 1801–2 Beethoven did change his physician, the new one being Dr. Schmidt, and on his advice spent the summer of 1802 at the near but quiet and secluded village of Heiligenstadt. Schmidt seems to have given Beethoven hopes that the quiet, by lessening the demands on his hearing, would effect an improvement. Up till now, as we see quite clearly from the letters, Beethoven's reaction to the impending calamity was defiance. He felt that he must assert his will in order not to be overcome. He would summon up all his strength in order to go on living and working in spite of his fate. "I will take Fate by the throat." He was, as it were, *defending* his creative power. But by the end of this summer he found that his genius, that he had felt called upon to cherish and protect, was really a mighty force using him as a channel or servant. It is probable that every genius of the first order becomes aware of this curious relation towards his own genius. Even the most fully conscious type of genius, the scientific genius, as Clerk Maxwell and Einstein, reveals this feeling of being *possessed*. A power seizes them of which they are not normally aware except by obscure premonitions. With Beethoven, so extraordinarily creative, a state of more or less unconscious tumult must have been constant. But only when the consciously defiant Beethoven had succumbed, only when his pride and strength had been so reduced that he was willing, even eager, to die and abandon the struggle, did he find that his creative power was indeed indestructible and that it was its deathless energy that made it impossible for him to die. This new and profound realization of his nature is the most significant thing in the famous Heiligenstadt Testament, written in the autumn of this year, but not discovered till after his death. It marks the complete collapse of the old morality of power, and shows the experiences that made possible the erection of a new morality of power on the ruins of the old. The document must be quoted in full.

"For my brothers Carl and — Beethoven

"O ye men who think or say that I am malevolent, stubborn or misanthropic, how greatly do ye wrong me, you do not know the secret causes of my seeming so, from childhood my heart and mind were disposed to the gentle feelings of good will, I was even ever eager to accomplish great deeds, but reflect now that for 6 years I have been in a hopeless case, aggravated by senseless physicians, cheated year after year in the hope of improvement, finally compelled to face the prospect of a *lasting malady* (whose cure will take years or, perhaps, be impossible), born with an ardent and lively temperament, even susceptible to the diversions of society, I was compelled early to isolate myself, to live in loneliness, when I at times tried to forget all this, O how harshly was I repulsed by the doubly sad experience of my bad hearing, and yet it was impossible for me to say to men speak louder, shout, for I am deaf. Ah how could I possibly admit an infirmity in the one sense which should have been more perfect in me than in others, a sense which I once possessed in highest perfection, a perfection such as few surely in my profession enjoy or ever have enjoyed—O I cannot do it, therefore forgive me when you see me draw back when I would gladly mingle with you, my misfortune is doubly painful because it must lead to my being misunderstood, for me there can be no recreation in society of my fellows, refined intercourse, mutual exchange of thought, only just as little as the greatest needs command may I mix with society. I must live like an exile, if I approach near to people a hot terror seizes upon me, a fear that I may be subjected to the danger of letting my condition be observed—thus it has been during the last year which I spent in the country, commanded by my intelligent physician to spare my hearing as much as possible, in this almost meeting my present natural disposition, although I sometimes ran counter to it yielding to my inclination for society, but what a humiliation when one stood beside me and heard a flute in the distance and *I heard nothing*, or someone heard *the shepherd singing* and again I heard nothing, such incidents brought me to the verge of despair, but little more and I would have put an end to my life—only art it was that withheld me, ah it seemed impossible to leave the world until I had produced all that I felt called upon to produce, and so I endured this wretched existence—truly wretched, an excitable body which a sudden change can throw from the best into the worst state. *Patience* it is said I must now choose for my guide, I have done so, I hope my determination will remain firm to endure until it pleases the inexorable parcae to break the thread, perhaps I shall get better, perhaps not, I am prepared. Forced already in my 28th year to become a philosopher, O it is not easy, less easy for the artist than for anyone else—Divine One thou lookest into my inmost soul, thou knowest it, thou knowest that love of man and desire to do good live therein. O men, when some day you read these words, reflect that ye did me wrong, and let the unfortunate one comfort himself if he can find one of his own kind who despite all the obstacles of nature yet did all that was in his power to be accepted among worthy artists and men. You my brothers Carl and —— as soon as I am dead if Dr. Schmid is still alive ask him in my name to describe my malady and attach this document to the history of my illness so that so far as possible at least the world may become reconciled with me after my death. At the same time I declare you two to be the heirs to my small fortune (if so it can be called), divide it fairly, bear with and help each other, what injury you have done me you know was long ago forgiven. To you brother Carl I give special thanks for the attachment you have displayed towards me of late. It is my wish that your lives may be better and freer from care than I have had, recommend virtue to your children, it alone can give happiness, not money, I speak from experience, it was virtue that upheld me in misery, to it next to my art I owe the fact that I did not end my life by suicide.—Farewell and love each other—I thank all my friends, particularly *Prince Lichnowsky* and *Professor Schmid*—I desire that the instruments from Prince L. be preserved by one of you but let no quarrel result from this, so soon as they can serve you a better purpose sell them, how glad will I be if I can still be helpful to you in my grave—with joy I hasten towards death—if it comes before I shall have had an opportunity to show all my artistic capacities it will still come too early for me despite my hard fate and I shall probably wish that it had come later—but even then I am satisfied, will it not free me from a state of endless suffering? Come when thou will I shall meet thee bravely.—Farewell and do not wholly forget me when I am dead, I deserve this of you in having often in life thought of you and how to make you happy; be so.

"Ludwig Van Beethoven

"Heiglnstadt, *October 6th, 1802*.

"For my brothers Carl and —— to be read and executed after my death.

"Heiglnstadt, October 10th, 1802, thus do I take my farewell of thee—and indeed sadly—yes that beloved hope—which I brought with me when I came here to be cured at least in a degree—I must wholly abandon, as the leaves of autumn fall and are withered so hope has been blighted, almost as I came—I go away—even the high courage—which often inspired me in the beautiful days of summer—has disappeared—O Providence—grant me at last but one day of pure joy—it is so long since real joy echoed in my heart— O when—O when, O Divine One—shall I find it again in the temple of nature and of men—Never? no—O that would be too hard."

This document marks a crisis in Beethoven's life. Never again was his attitude towards life one of defiance, where the defiance was an expression of what is called his "strength of character". He had no such need of defiance, for he no longer had any fear. He had become aware within himself of an indomitable creative energy that nothing could destroy.

(b) 1804

The first piece of music he composed that has a really profound and important spiritual content is the Eroica symphony. Indeed, the difference from the earlier music is so startling that it points to an almost catastrophic change, or extremely rapid acceleration, in his spiritual development. We have found that such a change is witnessed to by the Heiligenstadt Testament, and we shall see that the Eroica symphony is an amazingly realized and co-ordinated expression of the spiritual experiences that underlay that document. The ostensible occasion of the symphony appears to have been the career of Napoleon Bonaparte, but no amount of brooding over Napoleon's career could have given Beethoven his realization of what we may call the life-history of heroic achievement as exemplified in the Eroica. This is obviously a transcription of personal experience. He may have thought Napoleon a hero, but his conception of the heroic he had earned for himself. It has been

53

objected to the symphony that the funeral march is in the wrong place and that it should follow the scherzo. But this objection entirely misses the organic connection of the whole work. The most profound experience that Beethoven had yet passed through was when his courage and defiance of his fate had been followed by despair. He was expressing what he knew when he made the courage and heroism of the first movement succeeded by the black night of the second. And he was again speaking of what he knew when he made this to be succeeded by the indomitable uprising of creative energy in the scherzo. Beethoven was here speaking of what was perhaps the cardinal experience of his life, that when, with all his strength and courage, he had been reduced to despair, that when the conscious strong man had tasted very death, there came this turbulent, irrepressible, deathless creative energy surging up from depths he had not suspected. The whole work is a miraculously realized expression of a supremely important experience, and is justly regarded as a turning-point in Beethoven's music. The last movement is based on what we know to have been Beethoven's "Prometheus" theme. Having survived death and despair the artist turns to creation. By adopting the variation form Beethoven has been able to indicate the variety of achievement that is now open to his "Promethean" energy. The whole work is a most close-knit psychological unity. Never before in music has so important, manifold, and completely coherent an experience been communicated.

(c) 1806 TO 1813

The noble spaciousness and confidence of such works as the violin concerto and the Emperor concerto may be found in nearly all the music Beethoven composed from the Eroica symphony to the Eighth symphony. It is the work of a man full of confidence, hope, and the consciousness of indomitable power. It had appeared that he was to be shut out from life in its plenitude, that even his passion for creation might be destined to non-fulfilment. But the menace had been faced and had been found to be less terrible than it seemed. His impending deafness, which had bulked so large in Beethoven's imagination, was found to hinder neither his artistic nor, very much, his social activities. During these years it seemed to Beethoven that all things were still possible to him—at a price, it is true, but a price he had found courage enough within himself to pay. The music of this period reflects this consciousness. Again and again, in these compositions, Beethoven's last word is one of exultant confidence. . . . [But] his triumph was premature. He was to find that the fruits of victory he imagined to be within his grasp were not for him. His courage and resolution, that had taken him so far, were not enough. He had to learn submission and endurance. The key to Beethoven's spiritual development during these musically unproductive years is to be found in the statements in his journal for the years 1812 and 1813.

"Submission, absolute submission to your fate, only this can give you the sacrifice . . . to the servitude—O, hard struggle! Turn everything which remains to be done to planning the long journey—you must yourself find all that your most blessed wish can offer, you must force it to your will—keep always of the same mind.

"*Thou mayest no longer be a man*, not for thyself, only for others, *for thee there is no longer happiness except in thyself, in thy art*—O God, give me strength to conquer myself, nothing must chain me to life. . . .

"To forgo a great act which might have been and remain so—O, what a difference compared with an unstudied life which often arose in my fancy—O fearful conditions which do not suppress my feeling for domesticity, but whose execution O God, God look down upon the unhappy B., do not permit it to last thus much longer—"

These entries are concerned with Beethoven's discovery that he must forgo marriage. The "feeling for domesticity" to which he refers was very powerful at this period of Beethoven's life. The "unstudied life" he pictured must have seemed to him the natural sequel to what he had achieved. In the year 1810 Beethoven was forty years of age and, in spite of ill-health, his physical vitality was such that he appeared no more than thirty. His fame was great. He was already considered by many people to be the greatest of all composers. . . . His creative ability had steadily increased, he had found a way of life in spite of his affliction, and his position was assured. For the first time since he had come to maturity he felt that he could "let himself go" and enter upon his full heritage as a man. A wife, to a man of Beethoven's nature, was absolutely essential to this full human life. The more so, in his case, since his increasing deafness still threatened him at times with a terrible isolation. . . .

His solitariness was one of the things Beethoven found it hardest to accept. He may have known, with the profound instinctive knowledge of genius, that solitude was necessary to the highest development of his creative power. But to know is not the same thing as to accept. . . .

(d) 1818

At the time that he wrote the Hammerclavier sonata, finished in 1818, Beethoven's realization of his essential loneliness was terrible and complete. But we may suppose that even then he was becoming aware that his separation from the world was the entry into a different and more exalted region. But the Hammerclavier sonata is the expression of a man of infinite suffering, of infinite courage and will, but without God and without hope. At the time that he depicted this experience it is possible that Beethoven had already passed beyond it. The sonata is the complete expression of an important stage in Beethoven's spiritual development, but it was only after passing through this stage that the wonderful new world lay open before him, and that all his greatest work was achieved. From the Hammerclavier sonata itself nothing more could come. Its spiritual content is at the end of a process, an end that contains within itself no new beginning. The completely naked Beethoven, relying upon nothing whatever but his inner resources, has said his last word in the Hammerclavier sonata. Unless some new life is added to him, without some new organization of his experience, the undying energy of the Hammerclavier fugue can be used only to say over again what it has already said. The Hammerclavier sonata does not, in its spiritual content, belong to what is called Beethoven's third period. Neither does it belong to his second. It stands alone, a great and grim memorial to the long and painful journey between the two worlds.

The courage and resolution we find in the first movement is curiously austere. The old experience is once again to be lived through, but the spirit in which it is approached is very different. Those cold harmonies, so characteristic of Beethoven's later work, no longer convey the warm human confidence of a man who knows that victory lies at the end. There is expressed a stark, bare resolution, courageous enough, but uncoloured by any joy in conflict. And the other elements that go to make up the wealth of a Beethoven first movement have all become colder. The man who wrote this music is already a great solitary. He has abated nothing of his courage, but it has become more grim. Suffering, it would appear, has hardened him; never again, one would think, can this man melt. And there is no good humour in the scherzo. A curiously laconic savagery, with hints of the formidable passion that is expressing itself so abruptly, entirely separates this movement from the frank energy of the earlier scherzos. The slow movement is the deliberate expression, by a man who knows no reserves, of the cold and immeasurable woe in whose depths, it would seem, nothing that we could call life could endure. It seems as inimical to human existence as the icy heart of some remote mountain lake. Whether it be faithfulness to psychological experience, or whether it be the instinct of an unmatched artist, the largo that follows the slow movement is a miracle of art. To end with the slow movement would be unendurable, and any sudden shattering of the hypnotic state it produces would be equally unendurable. The gradual awakening effected by the largo from our state of dumb suspension fulfils a craving of the spirit that surely only this one artist could ever have formulated. And we awake to what? To the blind and desperate energy left in this man when there was no longer any reason to live. We are presented here with a will to live which is inexpressibly furious and inexpressibly bare. It is the expression of the final refusal of annihilation, even if no hope and no object be left in life. This sheer blind energy, this insistence on mere existence, does not contain within itself dramatic contrasts. To be expressed at all it must be expressed in a form within which its swiftness and violence can rage unchecked. No form permits so unidirectional and unhampered a flow as the fugue, and Beethoven chose the fugue. And having chosen it, he exhausts its resources to keep his mass moving with the requisite momentum. At one point the mass rises to a climax and there is an interruption. We are given a glimpse, a few bars, dolce and cantabile, of that serene, inhuman eternity that surrounds this blind, furious striving. But it is only a glimpse, a meaningless stare, and we are once more involved in this headlong rush, this most primitive, fundamental, and unconquerable of the impulses that manifest themselves in creatures that have life.

(e) 1825 TO 1827

The music of the last quartets comes from the profoundest depths of the human soul that any artist has ever sounded. . . . In the great fugue of the B flat quartet the experiences of life are seen as the conditions of creation and are accepted as such. The fugue has been called an expression of the reconciliation of freedom and necessity, or of assertion and submission, and the terms may pass since they suggest the state of consciousness that informs the fugue, a state in which the apparently opposing elements of life are seen as necessary and no longer in opposition. Beethoven had come to realize that his creative energy, which he at one time opposed to his destiny, in reality owed its very life to that destiny. It is not merely that he believed that the price was worth paying; he came to see it as necessary that a price should be paid. To be willing to suffer in order to create is one thing; to realize that one's creation necessitates one's suffering, that suffering is one of the greatest of God's gifts, is almost to reach a mystical solution of the problem of evil, a solution that it is probably for the good of the world that very few people will ever entertain. Yet, except in terms of this kind, we cannot represent to ourselves the spiritual content of the Grosse Fuge. The fugue opens with such an expression of unbridled energy and dominant will that it seems about to break the bounds of the string quartet. This vigorous, striving life is very different from the almost sub-human furious activity of the fugue of the Hammerclavier sonata, although it seems to promise an equally headlong course. But with the entry of the opposing G flat major episode it changes its character. We become aware that a truly indescribable synthesis has been effected. There is no effect conveyed to us of anything being yielded up or sacrificed. Nevertheless, there is a change, a change that makes us conscious that opposites have been reconciled, although the fugue marches to its close in indestructible might. . . .

The quartet in C sharp minor is the greatest of Beethoven's quartets, as he himself thought. It is also the most mystical of the quartets, and the one where the mystical vision is most perfectly sustained. It counts seven movements, but, regarded as an organic unity, it is the most complete of Beethoven's works. For the purposes of description, however, it is convenient to divide it into three parts. The opening fugue is the most superhuman piece of music that Beethoven has ever written. It is the completely unfaltering rendering into music of what we can only call the mystic vision. It has that serenity which, as Wagner said, speaking of these quartets, passes beyond beauty. Nowhere else in music are we made so aware, as here, of a state of consciousness surpassing our own, where our problems do not exist, and to which even our highest aspirations, those that we can formulate, provide no key. Those faint and troubling intimations we sometimes have of a vision different from and yet including our own, of a way of apprehending life, passionless, perfect and complete, that resolves all our discords, are here presented with the reality they had glimpsed. This impression of a superhuman knowledge, of a superhuman life being slowly frozen into shape, as it were, before our eyes, can be ambiguous. . . . To Beethoven himself it was the justification of, and the key to, life. In the light of this vision he surveys the world. That this vision was permanent with Beethoven is inconceivable. No men ever lived who could maintain such a state of illumination. This, we may be sure, is the last and greatest of Beethoven's spiritual discoveries, only to be grasped in the moments of his profoundest abstraction from the world. But it was sufficiently permanent to enable him to write the C sharp minor quartet in the light of it, a feat of concentration, of abstraction, of utter truthfulness, that is without equal. In the light of this experience we arrive, in the next movement, as a new-born creature in a new-born world. The virginal purity of this movement, its ethereal and crystalline quality, suggests to us a spirit not yet made flesh. After a brief introduction, which seems to usher in the act of incarnation, we find ourselves fully present in the warm, familiar human world. And yet how different it has become! The various aspects of experience that make up this human life, surveyed in the variations that follow, all have this different quality. They have the delicacy of shadows, but without their suggestion of impermanence. It is a transfigured world, where both our happiness and our prayers have become more pure and more simple. There is an indescribable lightness in this air; our bonds have become gossamer threads. And after floating through this outspread world we do, at that rapturous outbreak of trills in the last variation, rise up on wings and fly. And it is not only we, but all creation, that seems to be taking part in this exultant stirring. If ever a mystical vision of life has been presented in art it is here, in the sequence beginning with the fugue and ending with the last variation. It is this sequence, more than anything else in Beethoven's music, that convinces us that he had finally effected a synthesis of his whole experience. In these moments of illumination Beethoven had reached that state of consciousness that only the great mystics have ever reached, where there is no more discord. And in reaching it he retained the whole of his experience of life; he denied nothing. There follows an outbreak of the most exultant gaiety. There is no trace in the scherzo of anything but the purest joy. Its most human quality is its humour, but humour so carefree and radiant is scarcely human. The adagio introduction to the finale has all the quality of a sorrowful awakening. It is as if the whole of the quartet preceding this movement had been a dream. But that, we are passionately convinced, cannot be true. The note of complete authenticity in that opening fugue cannot be mistaken. But it is certain that there is a withdrawal of the vision. It signifies, perhaps, a return from those heights on which no man may permanently live to this less real but more insistent world in which we are plunged in the last movement, a world where a heroism which is also pathetic marches to its end attended by yearning and pain....

Of the three great last quartets, the one in C sharp minor is the most unearthly and serene. The first of them, in A minor, is the least mystical and the one most full of human pain. It is, as a matter of historical fact, connected with a serious illness of Beethoven's and he himself wrote over the slow movement "Heiliger Dankgesang an die Gottheit eines Genesenen, in der lydischen Tonart". ... The whole quartet may be taken as illustrating the normal aspect that life presented to the late Beethoven. Witness after witness testifies to the expression of profound sorrow that was habitual with him in the last years of his life, so that in mere contemplation of that dumb countenance the more emotional of them felt moved to tears. As we have said, we believe that in his most profound moments of insight and abstraction Beethoven was granted the solace of a more complete understanding. But such moments must have been comparatively rare, and could have occurred only in the midst of the artist's most profound isolation. We can well believe that no man ever saw the face of the transfigured Beethoven. We believe that this man had suffered so greatly that the Beethoven men saw was the normal Beethoven of those days, poor, ill, stone-deaf, wretchedly housed, utterly alone, betrayed and abandoned by the one human being whose love he so desperately and pitifully craved. And from the depths of this man rose that solemn, pure and profound song of thanksgiving to the Godhead. The yearning and the pain of the first movement (which ends, as only Beethoven would end, with what sounds like a startling and celestial trumpet call) is but little lightened in the second movement where there reigns a spiritual weariness which is quite unmistakable. But again there comes that intimation of something celestial in an *alternativo* (that some writers find "curious" and others "humorous"!) where the first violin soars high over a pedal, and then comes the first moment of joy, real joy without any *arrière-pensée*, in the whole quartet. The first part is then repeated; the dominant mood is re-established. From this matrix rises the slow movement, the most heartfelt prayer from the most manly soul that has expressed itself in music. From this pure and sincere communion with his God there comes a quickened life, a rush of celestial joy, in the passage marked "Neue Kraft fühlend". The psychological resemblance between this transition and that in the second movement is obvious. Relief from pain, in this most pessimistic of Beethoven's quartets, comes only from above. Two main experiences form the texture of this quartet, exhaustion and defeat, and the new life bestowed as an act of grace from on high. With this "new strength" the next movement steps forth, but there is a wistfulness in its bravery. This is one of those movements, that occur only in the late Beethoven, where the very quality of the heroism reveals the heartache it is intended to conceal. This forlorn and lonely little march is marching to no victory. It is a gesture, brave but pathetic. With the *Più allegro* section our forebodings are realized. Here is a shudder of realization, a resigned and hopeless cry, and we are again in the darkness of the struggle. Great waves of anguish seem to sweep over the struggling soul and at moments it seems that no resolution and faith can prevail against them. But a permanent strength, we may suppose, has come from those earlier celestial visions, from that pure and profound prayer, and the theme which before seemed to strive with difficulty against despair accelerates, until, in the final presto, it rings out victoriously, but victor in a victory so hard-won that we are left with none of that feeling of exultant triumph with which we have watched so many of Beethoven's victories, but rather with a feeling of slightly incredulous relief, of thankfulness still tinged with doubt. . . .

It so happens that Beethoven's last complete work, the quartet in F major, op. 135, makes a fitting end to his great series of explorations. It is the work of a man who is fundamentally at peace. It is the peace of a man who has known conflict, but whose conflicts are now reminiscent. This quality is most apparent in the last movement, with its motto "Muss es sein? Es muss sein!" According to Schindler this motto had its origin in a joke, but, as used here, it is a summary of the great Beethovenian problem of destiny and submission. But Beethoven had found his solution of that problem, and he treats the old question here with the lightness, even the

61

humour, of one to whom the issue is settled and familiar. There is no real conflict depicted in this last movement; the portentous question meets with a jovial, almost exultant answer, and the ending is one of perfect confidence. The question raised here is, indeed, seen in the light of the profound peace which dominates the slow movement of this quartet. If we may judge from this quartet and also from Beethoven's actual last composition, the present finale of the B flat quartet, it would appear that at the end of his life the inner Beethoven, the Beethoven who expressed himself in music, was content.

J. W. N. SULLIVAN (from *Beethoven*)

§ 4

They that sow in tears shall reap in joy.

FROM PSALM 126

> . . . But God is not like human-kind;
> Man cannot read the Almighty mind;
> Vengeance will never torture thee,
> Nor hunt thy soul eternally.
>
> Then do not in this night of grief,
> This time of overwhelming fear,
> O do not think that God can leave,
> Forget, forsake, refuse to hear!

EMILY BRONTË

He that dwelleth in the secret place of the most High shall abide under the shadow of the Almighty.

I will say of the Lord, He is my refuge and my fortress: my God; in him will I trust.

Surely he shall deliver thee from the snare of the fowler, and from the noisome pestilence.

He shall cover thee with his feathers, and under his wings shalt thou trust: his truth shall be thy shield and buckler.

Thou shalt not be afraid for the terror by night; nor for the arrow that flieth by day;

Nor for the pestilence that walketh in darkness; nor for the destruction that wasteth at noonday.

FROM PSALM 91

I waited patiently for the Lord; and he inclined unto me, and heard my cry.

He brought me up also out of an horrible pit, out of the miry clay, and set my feet upon a rock, and established my goings.

And he hath put a new song in my mouth, even praise unto our God: many shall see it, and fear, and shall trust in the Lord.

FROM PSALM 40

As Léon Bloy has well said, "Souffrir passe, avoir souffert ne passe jamais." ["Suffering disappears, but the fact of having suffered remains always with us."] . . . Victory may indeed be achieved over what has been experienced, and yet that experience is still in our possession as a permanent enhancement and extension of the reality of our spiritual life. What has once been lived through cannot possibly be effaced. That which has been continues to exist in a transfigured form. Man is by no means a completely finished product. Rather he moulds and creates himself in and through his experience of life, through spiritual conflict, and through those various trials which his destiny imposes upon him. Man is only what God is planning, a projected design.

BERDYAEV

בָּרוּךְ אַתָּה יְיָ אֱלֹהֵינוּ מֶלֶךְ הָעוֹלָם· הַגּוֹמֵל לְחַיָּבִים
טוֹבוֹת· שֶׁגְּמָלָנִי כָּל־טוֹב:

II. HOPE AND TRUST

What else is Wisdom? What of man's endeavour
Or God's high grace so lovely and so great?
To stand from fear set free, to breathe and wait . . .
EURIPIDES (tr. by Gilbert Murray)

If you do not hope, you will not find what is beyond your hopes.
CLEMENT OF ALEXANDRIA

The virtue of hope is an orientation of the soul towards a transformation after which it will be wholly and exclusively love.
SIMONE WEIL

THE DARKLING THRUSH

I leant upon a coppice gate
   When Frost was spectre-gray,
And Winter's dregs made desolate
   The weakening eye of day.
The tangled bine-stems scored the sky
   Like strings of broken lyres,
And all mankind that haunted nigh
   Had sought their household fires.

The land's sharp features seem'd to be
   The Century's corpse outleant,
His crypt the cloudy canopy,
   The wind his death-lament.
The ancient pulse of germ and birth
   Was shrunken hard and dry,
And every spirit upon earth
   Seem'd fervourless as I.

At once a voice arose among
   The bleak twigs overhead
In a full-hearted evensong
   Of joy illimited;
An aged thrush, frail, gaunt, and small,
   In blast-beruffled plume,
Had chosen thus to fling his soul
   Upon the growing gloom.

67

So little cause for carollings
   Of such ecstatic sound
Was written on terrestrial things
   Afar or nigh around,
That I could think there trembled through
   His happy good-night air
Some blessèd Hope, whereof he knew
   And I was unaware.

THOMAS HARDY

OCCLUDED

Chilled is the air with fallen rain,
   Flood-deep the river flows;
A sullen gloom daunts heart and brain,
   And no light shows.

Yet, in a mind as dark, a hint may steal
Of what lies hidden from an earth-bound eye:
Beyond the clouds the stars in splendour wheel,
The virgin huntress horns the silent sky.

WALTER DE LA MARE

THE GOOD MAN IN HELL

If a good man were ever housed in Hell
   By needful error of the qualities,
Perhaps to prove the rule or shame the devil,
   Or speak the truth only a stranger sees,

Would he, surrendering quick to obvious hate,
   Fill half eternity with cries and tears,
Or watch beside Hell's little wicket gate
   In patience for the first ten thousand years,

Feeling the curse climb slowly to his throat
   That, uttered, dooms him to rescindless ill,
Forcing his praying tongue to run by rote,
   Eternity entire before him still?

Would he at last, grown faithful in his station,
   Kindle a little hope in hopeless Hell,
And sow among the damned doubts of damnation,
   Since here someone could live and could live well?

One doubt of evil would bring down such a grace,
  Open such a gate, all Eden could enter in,
Hell be a place like any other place,
  And love and hate and life and death begin.

EDWIN MUIR

Another flower shall spring, because the soul of sweet delight
Can never pass away.

BLAKE

"ANOTHER FLOWER SHALL SPRING"

Marya Nikolaevna's predictions came true. By the evening Nikolai could no longer raise his hands, and only lay staring in front of him with a fixed concentrated gaze. Even when Kitty and his brother bent over him he took no notice of them, but continued looking in the same direction. Kitty sent for a priest to read the prayer for the dying.

During the reading Nikolai lay with his eyes closed, showing no sign of life. Levin, Kitty, and Marya Nikolaevna were standing by the bed. The prayers were not yet over when Nikolai suddenly stretched himself, sighed, and opened his eyes. Having ended his prayer, the priest put the cross against the cold brow, then wrapped it up in the scapulary. He stood still for a minute or two, then touched the huge, bloodless hand of the dying man.

"He is dead," the priest said, stepping aside, but suddenly the matted moustache of the dying man moved, and from the depths of his chest came the distinct words, that sounded so piercing in the stillness:

"Not yet . . . soon . . ."

A minute had scarcely gone by when his face lighted up and a smile appeared on his lips. He had passed away. The women hastened to dress him.

Levin's horror at the terrible enigma of death came upon him with the same intensity as on that autumn night when his brother had come to see him. Only now, in the very presence of it, he felt worse than ever. His wife's nearness saved him from falling into utter despair; for in spite of his terror he felt the need of loving and living. Love alone had saved him from the despair threatening him and he felt it growing stronger and purer.

The mystery of death had scarcely accomplished itself, when

69

another, just as insoluble, rose up and called him to life and love.

The doctor confirmed his suspicions regarding Kitty. Her indisposition was due to pregnancy.

TOLSTOY (from *Anna Karenina*)

A CONTEMPLATION UPON FLOWERS

Brave flowers, that I could gallant it like you
And be as little vaine,
You come abroad, and make a harmelesse shew,
And to your bedds of Earthe againe;
You are not proud, you know your birth
For your Embroiderd garments are from Earth:

You doe obey your moneths, and times, but I
Would have it ever springe,
My fate would know noe winter, never dye
Nor thinke of such a thing;
Oh that I could my bedd of Earth but view
And Smile, and looke as Chearefully as you:

Oh teach me to see Death, and not to feare
But rather to take truce;
How often have I seene you at a Beere,
And there look fresh and spruce;
You fragrant flowers then teach me that my breath
Like yours may sweeten and perfume my Death.

H. KINGE

SOCRATES AWAITS THE HEMLOCK

Socrates replied with a smile: O Simmias, what are you saying? I am not very likely to persuade other men that I do not regard my present situation as a misfortune, if I cannot even persuade you that I am no worse off now than at any other time in my life. Will you not allow that I have as much of the spirit of prophecy in me as the swans? For they, when they perceive that they must die, having sung all their life long, do then sing more lustily than ever, rejoicing in the thought that they are about to go away to the god whose ministers they are. But men, because they are themselves afraid of death, slanderously affirm of the swans that they sing a lament at the last, not considering that no bird sings when cold, or hungry, or in pain, not even the nightingale, nor the swallow, nor yet the hoopoe; which are said indeed to tune a lay of sorrow, although I do not believe this to be true of them any more than of the swans. But because they are sacred to Apollo, they have the gift of prophecy, and anticipate the good things of another world; wherefore they sing and rejoice in that day more than ever they did before. And I too, believing myself to be the consecrated servant of the same God, and the fellow-servant of the swans, and thinking that I have received from my master gifts of prophecy which are not inferior to theirs, would not go out of life less merrily than the swans.

PLATO

> . . . And why should mortals fear to tread
> The pathway to their future home?

EMILY BRONTË

§ 2

"THE WORLD WAS ALL BEFORE THEM"

So spake our mother Eve; and Adam heard
Well pleased, but answered not; for now too nigh
The archangel stood, and from the other hill
To their fixed station, all in bright array,
The cherubim descended, on the ground
Gliding meteorous, as evening mist
Risen from a river o'er the marish glides,
And gathers ground fast at the labourer's heel
Homeward returning. High in front advanced,
The brandished sword of God before them blazed,
Fierce as a comet; which with torrid heat,
And vapour as the Libyan air adust,
Began to parch that temperate clime; whereat
In either hand the hastening angel caught
Our lingering parents, and to the eastern gate
Led them direct, and down the cliff as fast
To the subjected plain—then disappeared.
They, looking back, all the eastern side beheld
Of Paradise, so late their happy seat,

71

Waved over by that flaming brand; the gate
With dreadful faces thronged and fiery arms.
Some natural tears they dropped, but wiped them soon;
The world was all before them, where to choose
Their place of rest, and Providence their guide.
They, hand in hand, with wandering steps and slow,
Through Eden took their solitary way.

MILTON (from *Paradise Lost*)

"THE DAY SOON TO BE BORN"

Saint Christophe has crossed the river. All night long he has
marched against the stream. Like a rock his huge-limbed body
stands above the water. On his shoulders is the Child, frail and
heavy. Saint Christophe leans on a pine-tree that he has plucked
up, and it bends. His back also bends. Those who saw him set out
vowed that he would never win through, and for a long time their
mockery and their laughter followed him. Then the night fell and
they grew weary. Now Christophe is too far away for the cries of
those standing on the water's brink to reach him. Through the roar
of the torrent he hears only the tranquil voice of the Child, clasping
a lock of hair on the giant's forehead in his little hand, and crying:
"March on."—And with bowed back, and eyes fixed straight in
front of him on the dark bank whose towering slopes are beginning
to gleam white, he marches on.

Suddenly the Angelus sounds, and the flock of bells suddenly
springs into wakefulness. It is the new dawn! Behind the sheer
black cliff rises the golden glory of the invisible sun. Almost falling,
Christophe at last reaches the bank, and he says to the Child:

"Here we are! How heavy thou wert! Child, who art thou?"
And the Child answers:
"I am the day soon to be born."

ROMAIN ROLLAND (from *Jean-Christophe*)

POET'S FULFILMENT

Lodged in a corner of his breast
Like a black hole torn by the loss
Of an ancestral treasure, like a thorn
Implanted ineradicably by his first
Sharp realisation of the world, or like a cross

72

To which his life was to be nailed, he bore
Always the ache of an anxiety, a grief
Which nothing could explain, but which some nights
Would make him cry that he could fight no more.

Time ploughed its way through him; and change
Immersed him in disorder and decay.
Only the strange
Interior ray of the bleak flame
Which charred his heart's core could illuminate
The hidden unity of his life's theme.

He knew how the extremity of night
Can sterilize the final germ of faith;
Appearance crushed him with its steady weight;
Futility discoloured with its breath
His tragic vision. All his strength was spent
In holding to some sense from day to day . . .
Slowly he fell towards dismemberment.

Yet when he lay
At last exhausted under his stilled blood's
Thick cover and eyes' earth-stained lids,
The constant burden of his breast
(Long work of yeast) arose with joy
Into its first full freedom, metamorphosised, released.

DAVID GASCOYNE

§ 3

. . . A careless trust
In the divine occasion of our dust.

GERALD GOULD

Give me my scallop shell of quiet,
My staff of faith to walk upon. . . .

SIR WALTER RALEIGH

One does not doubt the existence of air because a strong wind is
not always blowing, or of sunlight because night intervenes between
dawn and dusk.

AUROBINDO

We have, then, three schemes of value—truth, goodness, and beauty, which cannot be reduced to each other. They are the three aspects under which the life of God is known to us. . . .

These three have, each of them, the marks of the spiritual world. That is: Firstly, they claim to exist in their own right, and will not be made means or instruments to anything else, nor to each other. Secondly, they take us out of ourselves: they are not our tools, but we are rather their instruments. Thirdly, they are, each in its own manner and degree, a permanent enrichment of our life—a fund of inalienable spiritual wealth. The mark of spiritual wealth as opposed to the other goods of life is that spiritual wealth is unlimited in quantity, being manifestly free from such mechanical laws as the conservation of energy. In the spiritual world one man's gain is not another man's loss. The spiritual wealth of the world is capable of indefinite increment.

We are confronted, then, with a world of existence, and a world of values. The former, when contemplated in a barely abstract way, and stripped of all extraneous importations from the world of values, consists simply of brute facts, unclassified, unappraised, and even unrelated. The latter, when viewed in an equally abstract way, consists of the whole contents of the moral, intellectual, and artistic consciousness. What is the relation between them?

The relation of the world of values to the world of existence is a problem, perhaps we should say *the* problem, of philosophy. And what is sometimes called the Venture of Faith is the assumption that not only are the two related, but that all existence is capable of being truly stated and arranged in terms of value, and all value in terms of existence. Faith assures us that truth, goodness, and beauty, which are attributes of the eternal order, are also attributes of the world of existence, so that in living for and in these eternal ideas, so far as we can do so here, we are living in accordance with the fundamental laws of the world in which we are placed. I do not say that all Faith could be correctly described in the words of the last sentence; obviously it could not. But I think I am right in saying that all Faith consists essentially in the recognition of a world of spiritual values behind, yet not apart from, the world of natural phenomena.

If this be granted, it will be plain that there are several states of mind which are incompatible with Faith. There is the merely dull and stupid temper, which takes each day as it comes, eats, drinks, and sleeps, and never thinks about the meaning of things. There is the pessimistic temper, which sees behind phenomena only an alien and hostile power. There is the sceptical temper, which refuses to admit that any clear revelation of God has been made to us through truth, beauty, and goodness. There is the ironical, indifferent temper . . . There is the grumbling and rebellious temper . . . Lastly, there is the selfish temper, which by attending to nothing and noticing nothing but what promotes or thwarts our own private interests, becomes wholly blind to whatever of truth, beauty, or goodness God has spread before us for our delight and edification.

It is plain, then, that Faith requires certain personal qualities. If we are too stupid to ask for any meaning in our experience, too self-absorbed to be interested in anything that does not concern our petty affairs, too frivolous to care seriously for what can only be cared for seriously, too gloomy to hope, or too wilful to learn, we are labouring under fatal disqualifications for the experience of Faith. This is the meaning of the words of Christ: 'If any man is willing to do His will, he shall know of the doctrine,' and 'Blessed are the pure in heart, for they shall see God.'

What distinguishes Faith from existential knowledge is the recognition of an objective, external, and ideal standard of value—of an idea, or system of ideas, of goodness, truth, and beauty, by which things given in experience may be judged and classified. It is an essential part of Faith that this standard should be applied to given experience, and it is also requisite that experience should be appealed to in verification of the claims of Faith. This last point is important; and it leads us to recognise a peculiarity of the conditions under which Faith is exercised. The verification to which Faith appeals can never be complete while we live here. Truths of the eternal order seem to be always broken and refracted as they reach us. They manifest themselves to concrete experience in an oppositional, bipolar form, so that we continually find ourselves confronted by an obstinate negation. Truth, we may almost say, is a spark which is only generated by friction. This, it may be, is a necessary condition of the world of becoming. One reason why Faith cannot verify itself is that the world is still in the making. In the words of St. Paul, 'we see not yet all things put under' the Son of God, 'in whom (nevertheless) all things consist.' In all probability humanity (even if, with the latest authorities, we push back the beginnings of civilisation ten or fifteen thousand years) is still a child, and will scale heights yet undreamed of. It would indeed be strange and, to a thoughtful man, disquieting, if our experience were symmetrically rounded off, so that no further growth in knowledge could be expected. Faith, then, 'transcends experience'; it appears as a constructive activity. It employs the imagination to fill out what is wanting in experience. Faith endeavours to find harmony in apparent discord, and to anticipate the workings of the divine purpose. In a sense, all thought may be said to 'transcend experience', if by experience we mean sense-perception; and Faith, as we have seen, is not merely a function of thought, but a basal energy of the whole man. It includes an element of will; and the office of will is not to register experience, but to make it.

Faith, therefore, always contains an element of risk, of venture; and we are impelled to make the venture by the affinity and attraction which we feel in ourselves (through the infusion, as Christians believe, of a higher light and life from above) to those eternal principles which in the world around us appear to be only struggling for supremacy.

So far we have maintained that the primary ground of Faith is a normal and ineradicable feeling, instinct, or attraction, present in all minds which are not disqualified from having it by peculiarities which we should all agree, probably, in calling defects, a feeling or instinct that behind the world of phenomena there is a world of eternal values, attracting us towards itself. These values are manifested, and exercise their attraction, in and through phenomena, though the section of the world which we know, and from which we generalise, is an inadequate receptacle for them. Further, these values have been classified as ideas of Truth, Beauty, and Goodness, a threefold cord which is not quickly broken. This is the most general description possible of the objects and contents of Faith, and it is, I believe, all that this primary ground of Faith gives us. It contains vast implications, which can only be unravelled by the full experience of life, developing our personality along the lines of thought, will, and feeling. These three faculties have a natural connection with the ideals of the true, the good, and the beautiful respectively, though we must avoid most carefully the error of separating things which can never exist independently of each other.

W. R. INGE

That love shall in the end, as it is now in the eternal verities, be all in all, must remain for the Christian a postulate not of knowledge but of faith. And that too is well, since faith is possible for all men, and knowledge is not.

L. W. GRENSTED

Faith is a voluntary anticipation.

CLEMENT OF ALEXANDRIA

§ 4

THE SACRED HEARTH

(To George Barker)

You must have been still sleeping, your wife there
Asleep beside you. All the old oak breathed: while slow,
How slow the intimate Spring night swelled through those depths
Of soundlessness and dew-chill shadow on towards the day.
Yet I, alone awake close by, was summoned suddenly
By distant voice more indistinct though more distinctly clear,
While all inaudible, than any dream's, calling on me to rise
And stumble barefoot down the stairs to seek the air
Outdoors, so sweet and somnolent, not cold, and at that hour
Suspending in its glass undrifting milk-strata of mist,
Stilled by the placid beaming of the adolescent moon.
There, blackly outlined in their moss-green light, they stood,
The trees of the small crabbed and weed-grown orchard,
Perfect as part of one of Calvert's idylls. It was then,
Wondering what calm magnet had thus drawn me from my bed,
I wandered out across the briar-bound garden, spellbound.
    Most
Mysterious and unrecapturable moment, when I stood
There staring back at the dark white nocturnal house,
And saw gleam through the lattices a light more pure than gold
Made sanguine with crushed roses, from the firelight that all night
Stayed flickering about the sacred hearth. As long as dawn
Hung fire behind the branch-hid sky, the strong
Magic of rustic slumber held unbroken; yet a song
Sprang wordless from inertia in my heart, to see how near
A neighbour strangeness ever stands to home. George, in the wood
Of wandering among wood-hiding trees, where poets' art

77

Is how to whistle in the dark, where pockets all have holes,
All roofs for refugees have rents, we ought to know
That there can be for us no place quite alien and unknown,
No situation wholly hostile, if somewhere there burn
The faithful fire of vision still awaiting our return.

DAVID GASCOYNE

FIRST PART

III. SERENITY

For my dear Tessa

Make peace with yourself, and heaven and earth will make peace with you. Endeavour to enter your own inner cell, and you will see the heavens; because the one and the other are one and the same, and when you enter one you see the two.

ST. ISAAK OF SYRIA

Human nature is like a pool of water, my Lord. Cast a stone therein, it goes rough and broken; stir it, it becomes foul; give it peace, let it rest, and it will reflect the face of the Heavens which lie over it.

ST. FRANCIS (in a Housman play)

A PRISONER'S INNER PEACE

. . . But first a hush of peace, a soundless calm descends;
The struggle of distress and fierce impatience ends;
Mute music soothes my breast—unuttered harmony
That I could never dream till earth was lost to me.

Then dawns the Invisible, the Unseen its truth reveals;
My outward sense is gone, my inward essence feels—
Its wings are almost free, its home, its harbour found;
Measuring the gulf it stoops and dares the final bound!

EMILY BRONTË

CONSTRUCTION

From the mind's rafters
Out of the heart's rust
I built a city that shone a day
And crumbled into dust.

Then stood I on the scaffolding
Of my own despair,
Trembling lest I should lose hold
So frail my balance there.

O lovely unconstructed tree
O tree stretching to God
Would I could grow alike to thee
And draw from earth my food;

81

Earth tend for me, earth care for me
That I grow mellow, wrought
Without desire, without despair
And with no thought of thought.

MARGOT RUDDOCK

The third silence of our understanding is brought to pass in God, when the soul is wholly transformed in Him and tastes abundantly of His sweetness, in which it sleeps as in a wine-cellar, and keeps silence, because it desires nothing more. For it has found satisfaction, seeing itself so far deified and united with its pattern, and clothed in the brightness of God like another Moses who has entered into the cloud which was above the mount. This was that which more truly befel St. John when after the Last Supper he leaned upon the Lord's breast, and kept silence for a space concerning all that he felt.

In this third silence it comes to pass that the understanding is so still and so entirely closed—or rather, occupied—that it understands naught of that which is said to it, nor can judge of aught that passes near it, since it neither hears nor sees. Concerning this an old man whom I confessed, who had practised these things for more than fifty years, told me, among other mysteries, that he had often listened to sermons and things of God without understanding a word of them: so hushed and so busy was his innermost understanding that nothing which was of creatures could take shape within it. I told him that he should withdraw into retirement at such times, to which he replied that voices were to him as the sound of organs, in which the soul took delight even though it understood them not: he praised the Lord as it were in a counterpoint upon them, in a way that could be felt, although he could not convey the feeling to others.

FRANCISCO DE OSUNA

The more a man gives up his heart to God, to his vocation and to men, forgetful of himself and of that which belongs to him—the greater poise he will acquire, until he reaches peace, quiet, joy: the apanage of simple and humble souls.

FATHER YELCHANINOV

God's will must not be done in a grimly stoical spirit, but with full inclination and a sense of peace and joy. In other words, the

82

intention must be willing. To intend willingly excludes strain, worry and gloom, and makes the soul capable of receiving the Holy Spirit, of whom it is written, *In peace is his place established.*

FATHER BENET OF CANFIELD

In the Elysian Fields [of Gluck's 'Orfeo'] . . . virtue and effort are transcended: there is no need to be good or to strive upward any more: one has arrived, and all those accursed hygienics of the soul are done with and forgotten.

BERNARD SHAW

But there are those whose thoughts are sublime without being strained; who have never striven after goodness, yet are perfect. There are those who win no victories for their State, achieve no fame, and yet perfect its policies; who find quietness, though far from streams and lakes. . . . They have divested themselves of everything, yet lack nothing. They are passive, seek no goal; but all lovely things attend them. Such is the way of Heaven and Earth, the secret power of the Wise. Truly is it said, 'Quietness, stillness . . . these are the balancers of Heaven and Earth, the very substance of the Way and its Power.' Truly is it said, 'The Wise Man rests therein, and because he rests, he is at peace. Because he is at peace, he is quiet.' One who is at peace and is quiet no sorrow or harm can enter, no evil breath can invade. Therefore his inner power remains whole and his spirit intact.

Truly is it said, 'For the Wise Man life is conformity to the motions of Heaven, death is but part of the common law of Change. At rest, he shares the secret powers of Yin; at work, he shares the rocking of the waves of Yang. He neither invites prosperity nor courts disaster. . . . He casts away all knowledge and artifice, follows the pattern of Heaven. Therefore Heaven visits him with no calamity, the things of the world do not lay their trammels upon him, no living man blames him, no ghost attacks him. His life is like the drifting of a boat, his death is like a lying down to rest. He has no anxieties, lays no plans.

'He is full of light, yet none is dazzled; he is faithful, yet bound by no promise. His sleep is without dreams, his waking without grief. His spirit has remained stainless and unspoiled; his soul has not grown weary. Emptiness, nothingness, quiet—these have made him partner in the powers of Heaven.' . . .

83

Truly is it said, 'If the bodily frame of a man labours and has no rest, it wears itself out; if his spiritual essence is used without cessation, then it flags, and having flagged, runs dry.

'The nature of water is that if nothing is mixed with it, it remains clear; if nothing ruffles it, it remains smooth. But if it is obstructed so that it does not flow, then too it loses its clearness. In these ways it is a symbol of the heavenly powers that are in man.'

Truly is it said, 'A purity unspoiled by any contamination, a peace and unity not disturbed by any variation, detachment and inactivity broken only by such movement as is in accord with the motions of Heaven—such are the secrets that conserve the soul. Does not he who possesses a sword of Kan or Yüeh put it in a case and hide it away, not daring to make use of it? A greater treasure still is the soul. It can glide hither and thither where it will. There is no point in Heaven above to which it cannot climb, no hollow in the earth into which it cannot crawl. It infuses and transforms the ten thousand creatures. For it there is no symbol; its name is "One with God".

> Only the way of wholeness and integrity
> Can guard the soul.
> Guard it so that nothing is lost,
> And you will become one with the soul:
> The essence of this "one", blending,
> Will mingle with Heaven's law.'

It is of this that a rustic saying speaks, which says:

> The crowd cares for gain,
> The honest man for fame,
> The good man values success,
> But the Wise Man, his soul.

Therefore we talk of his simplicity, meaning that he keeps his soul free from all admixture; and of his wholeness, meaning that he keeps it intact and entire. He that can achieve such wholeness, such integrity we call a True Man.

CHUANG TZU (*tr. by Waley*)

A sense of rest, of deep quiet even. Silence within and without. A quietly-burning fire. A sense of comfort. . . . I am not dazed or stupid, but only happy in this peaceful morning. Whatever may be the charm of emotion, I do not know whether it equals the sweetness of those hours of silent meditation, in which we have a glimpse and foretaste of the contemplative joys of Paradise. Desire and fear, sadness and care, are done away. Existence is reduced to the simplest form, the most ethereal mode of being, that is, to pure self-consciousness. It is a state of harmony, without tension and without disturbance, the dominical state of the soul, perhaps the state which awaits it beyond the grave. It is happiness as the Orientals understand it, the happiness of the anchorite, who neither struggles nor wishes any more, but simply adores and enjoys. It is difficult to find words in which to express this moral situation, for our languages can only render the particular and localised vibrations of life; they are incapable of expressing this motionless concentration, this divine quietude, this state of the resting ocean, which reflects the sky, and is master of its own profundities. Things are then re-absorbed into their principles; memories are swallowed up in memory; the soul is only soul, and is no longer conscious of itself in its individuality and separateness. It is something which feels the universal life, a sensible atom of the Divine, of God. It no longer appropriates anything to itself, it is conscious of no void. Only the Yoghis and Soufis perhaps have known in its profundity this humble and yet voluptuous state, which combines the joys of being and of non-being, which is neither reflection nor will, which is above both the moral existence and the intellectual existence, which is the return to unity, to the pleroma, the vision of Plotinus and of Proclus—Nirvana in its most attractive form.

It is clear that the western nations . . . know very little of this state of feeling. For them life is devouring and incessant activity. They are eager for gold, for power, for dominion; their aim is to crush men and to enslave nature. They show an obstinate interest in means, and have not a thought for the end. They confound being with individual being, and the expansion of the self with happiness —that is to say, they do not live by the soul; they ignore the unchangeable and the eternal; they live at the periphery of their being, because they are unable to penetrate to its axis. They are excited, ardent, positive, because they are superficial. Why so much effort, noise, struggle, and greed?—it is all a mere stunning and deafening of the self. When death comes they recognise that it is so—why not then admit it sooner? Activity is only beautiful when it is holy—that is to say, when it is spent in the service of that which passeth not away.

AMIEL

It is the great mystery of human life that old grief passes gradually into quiet, tender joy. The mild serenity of age takes the place of the riotous blood of youth. I bless the rising sun each day, and, as before, my heart sings to meet it, but now I love even more its setting, its long slanting rays and the soft, tender, gentle memories that come with them, the dear images from the whole of my long, happy life—and over all the Divine Truth, softening, reconciling, forgiving! My life is ending, I know that well, but every day that is left me I feel how my earthly life is in touch with a new infinite, unknown, but approaching life, the nearness of which sets my soul quivering with rapture, my mind glowing and my heart weeping with joy.

DOSTOEVSKY (from *The Brothers Karamazov*)

§ 2

One ought not to desire the impossible.

LEONARDO DA VINCI

If thou regardest anything not in thine own choice as good or evil for thyself, it is inevitable that, on the incidence of such an evil or the miscarriage of such a good, thou shouldst upbraid the Gods, aye, and hate men as the actual or supposed cause of the one or the other; and in fact many are the wrong-doings we commit by setting a value on such things. But if we discriminate as good and evil only the things in our power, there is no occasion left for accusing the Gods or taking the stand of an enemy towards men.

MARCUS AURELIUS

I will do my best, replied Socrates. But you must first let me hear what Crito wants; he has long been wishing to say something to me.

Only this, Socrates, replied Crito: the attendant who is to give you the poison has been telling me, and he wants me to tell you, that you are not to talk much; talking, he says, increases heat, and this is apt to interfere with the action of the poison; persons who excite themselves are sometimes obliged to take a second or even a third dose.

Then, said Socrates, let him mind his business and be prepared to give the poison twice or even thrice if necessary; that is all.

I knew quite well what you would say, replied Crito; but I was obliged to satisfy him.

PLATO

I cannot leave it; I must stay under the old tree in the midst of the long grass, the luxury of the leaves, and the song in the very air. I seem as if I could feel all the glowing life the sunshine gives and the south wind calls to being. The endless grass, the endless leaves, the immense strength of the oak expanding, the unalloyed joy of finch and blackbird; from all of them I receive a little. Each gives me something of the pure joy they gather for themselves. . . . Does this reverie of flowers and waterfall and song form an ideal, a human ideal, in the mind? It does; much the same ideal that Phidias sculptured of man and woman filled with a godlike sense of the violet fields of Greece, beautiful beyond thought, calm as my turtle-dove before the lurid lightning of the unknown. To be beautiful and to be calm, without mental fear, is the ideal of nature. If I cannot achieve it, at least I can think it.

RICHARD JEFFERIES

The lake a beautiful image of stillness, clear as glass, reflecting all things; the wind was up, and the waters sounding. . . . The Church and buildings, how quiet they were!

DOROTHY WORDSWORTH

I have just come back from a solitary walk. I heard nightingales, saw white lilac and orchard trees in bloom. My heart is full of impressions showered upon it by the chaffinches, the golden orioles, the grasshoppers, the hawthorns, and the primroses. A dull, gray, fleecy sky brooded with a certain melancholy over the nuptial splendours of vegetation. Many painful memories stirred afresh in me; at Pré l'Evèque, at Jargonnant, at Villereuse, a score of phantoms—phantoms of youth—rose with sad eyes to greet me. The walls had changed, and roads which were once shady and dreamy I found now waste and treeless. But at the first trills of the nightingale a flood of tender feeling filled my heart. I felt myself soothed, grateful, melted; a mood of serenity and contemplation took possession of me. A certain little path, a very kingdom of green, with fountain, thickets, gentle ups and downs, and an abundance of singing-birds, delighted me, and did me inexpressible good. Its peaceful remoteness brought back the bloom of feeling. I had need of it.

AMIEL

FROM "ULTIMA THULE"

Marooned by choice upon an island where the sea
Serves as a citadel and only guarantee
Of freedom from the tyranny of maps and guides,
We thanked the saints who with their blood had blessed these
    tides,
Then searched with ardent eyes the rocks and roads to find
A further isolation for the heart and mind,
Some place so full of peace that we could cast away
The last remaining doubts and every fear allay.
And when the unfettered sun had banished rain and cloud
We saw between the hills a single field, new ploughed,
And there, a continent of calm at our command,
Discarded self, the sea, and all that heaving land;
We locked ourselves in solitude, and had no eyes
For anything that flowered on earth or in the skies,
Nor ears that would at other times have gladly heard
The wind in corn, the waves, the song of mounting bird,
But in the neutral presence of the simple light
We heard with inner ears and saw with second sight.

LEONARD CLARK

MOMENT IN TIME

I look out now upon the lawns and sombre trees
And see the shades of yesterday return,
The heavy homeward ploughing of the bees,
The rabbits scuttering in the tangled fern.

The single stars come out above the pointed firs,
The moon lifts up her silver looking-glass,
The glow-worms are night's gleaming harbingers,
And mushrooms shine like manna on the grass.

I hold the clock of dandelion in my hand
And blow away all lagging time and care,
As silently across the stubbled land
The starling squadrons ride the timeless air.

LEONARD CLARK

DEW IN AUTUMN

Sparkling upon the plants the gray dew lies,
In the cool misty stillness nothing stirs,
Only the tenuous twines of gossamers
Tremble with crystal drops, a young wind sighs,

A robin chirps, the trees like solemn clouds
Seem lost in the pale dawn, folded in leaves,
A dreaming hush through the green closes weaves
The tingling wonder of her glimmering shrouds.

Break not the silver string, the magic thread,
With which wise spiders by insidious care
Have linked together the dim slender towers

Of the rich Autumn's subtly smiling flowers:
O softly in the half-waked garden tread,
Nor brush the faint bloom from the untainted air.

WILFRED ROWLAND CHILDE

HOW STILL, HOW HAPPY!

How still, how happy! Those are words
That once would scarce agree together;
I loved the plashing of the surge,
The changing heaven, the breezy weather,

More than smooth seas and cloudless skies
And solemn, soothing, softened airs
That in the forest woke no sighs
And from the green spray shook no tears.

How still, how happy! Now I feel
Where silence dwells is sweeter far
Than laughing mirth's most joyous swell
However pure its raptures are.

Come, sit down on this sunny stone:
'Tis wintry light o'er flowerless moors—
But sit—for we are all alone
And clear expand heaven's breathless shores.

EMILY BRONTË

TWILIGHT GRAY

Now came still evening on, and twilight gray
Had in her sober livery all things clad;
Silence accompanied; for beast and bird,
They to their grassy couch, these to their nests
Were slunk, all but the wakeful nightingale.
She all night long her amorous descant sung:
Silence was pleased. Now glowed the firmament
With living sapphires; Hesperus, that led
The starry host, rode brightest, till the moon,
Rising in clouded majesty, at length
Apparent queen, unveiled her peerless light,
And o'er the dark her silver mantle threw.

MILTON

CALM EVENING

. . . As I have seen when on the breast of Thames
A heavenly bevy of sweet English dames,
In some calm evening of delightful May,
With music give a farewell to the day. . . .

WILLIAM BROWNE

DAY'S TURMOIL HUSHED

Clear nights are called the music of the heavens, because, when day's turmoil is hushed and all things rest, their wonderful concord and harmony are seen and in a manner heard, and, I know not how, sound in chorus in the depth of the heart, calming and setting it at rest.

LUIS DE LEON

FROM "THE NIGHT"

Dear night! this worlds defeat;
The stop to busie fools; cares check and curb;
The day of Spirits; my souls calm retreat
Which none disturb!
Christs progress, and his prayer time;
The hours to which high Heaven doth chime.

90

Gods silent, searching flight:
When my Lords head is fill'd with dew, and all
His locks are wet with the clear drops of night;
    His still, soft call;
His knocking time; The souls dumb watch,
When Spirits their fair kinred catch.

HENRY VAUGHAN

THE SILVER MOON

The silver moon
shines in the wood;
from every bough comes a song . . .

O well-beloved.

The deeps of the pond
reflect the dark willow-tree
where the wind sighs . . .

It is time to dream.

The vast earth is filled
under opal skies
with a tender peacefulness . . .

It is the hour of hours.

PAUL VERLAINE

PEACE, LIKE A LAMB

I lie sleepless in the half light,
Seeing through bare trees outside
The grey wolf sky of pallid stars.
I lie alone and wait,
Not for the tap of robin's beak upon the pane,
The unexpected wind that shakes
The icicles along the eaves
And ruffles up the new-dropped snow,
I wait for every earthly sound to die away;
Until from nothingness I slowly hear
Peace, like a lamb, move soft from field to field,
The crunching tread of strangers on the hills,
And unfamiliar voices in the trees,

And then, a waterfall of wings
Taking possession of the startled air.

LEONARD CLARK

How sweet the moone-light sleepes upon this banke,
Heere will we sit, and let the sounds of musicke
Creepe in our eares soft stilnes, and the night
Become the tutches of sweet harmonie:
Sit *Jessica*, looke how the floore of heaven
Is thicke inlayed with pattens of bright gold,
There's not the smallest orbe which thou beholdst
But in his motion like an Angell sings,
Still quiring to the young eyed Cherubins;
Such harmonie is in immortall soules,
But whilst this muddy vesture of decay
Doth grosly close in it, we cannot heare it:
Come hoe, and wake *Diana* with a hymne,
With sweetest tutches pearce your Mistresse eare,
And draw her home with musicke.

SHAKESPEARE

§ 4

It is vain for you to rise up early, to sit up late, to eat the bread
of sorrows: for so he giveth his beloved sleep.

FROM PSALM 127

Oh sleep! it is a gentle thing,
Beloved from pole to pole.
To Mary Queen the praise be given!
She sent the gentle sleep from Heaven,
That slid into my soul.

S. T. COLERIDGE

I sang my child to sleep
And her sweet sleep
Breathed like a flower on me
A peace so deep
That I did share her balm

92

And know her rest.
Sweet, in thy blessing sleep
I too am blessed.

MARGOT RUDDOCK

SLEEP AT NOONTIDE

And Zarathustra ran and ran, but he found no one else, and was alone and ever found himself again; he enjoyed and quaffed his solitude, and thought of good things—for hours. About the hour of noontide, however, when the sun stood exactly over Zarathustra's head, he passed an old, bent and gnarled tree, which was encircled round by the ardent love of a vine, and hidden from itself; from this there hung yellow grapes in abundance, confronting the wanderer. Then he felt inclined to quench a little thirst, and to break off for himself a cluster of grapes. When, however, he had already his arm outstretched for that purpose, he felt still more inclined for something else—namely, to lie down beside the tree at the hour of perfect noontide and sleep.

This Zarathustra did; and no sooner had he laid himself on the ground in the stillness and secrecy of the variegated grass, than he had forgotten his little thirst, and fell asleep. For as the proverb of Zarathustra saith: "One thing is more necessary than the other". Only that his eyes remained open:—for they never grew weary of viewing and admiring the tree and the love of the vine. In falling asleep, however, Zarathustra spake thus to his heart:

"Hush! Hush! Hath not the world now become perfect? What hath happened unto me?

As a delicate wind danceth invisibly upon parqueted seas, light, feather-light, so—danceth sleep upon me.

No eye doth it close to me, it leaveth my soul awake. Light is it, verily, feather-light.

It persuadeth me, I know not how, it toucheth me inwardly with a caressing hand, it constraineth me. Yea, it constraineth me, so that my soul stretcheth itself out:—

—How long and weary it becometh, my strange soul! Hath a seventh-day evening come to it precisely at noontide? Hath it already wandered too long, blissfully, among good and ripe things?

It stretcheth itself out, long—longer! it lieth still, my strange soul. Too many good things hath it already tasted; this golden sadness oppresseth it, it distorteth its mouth.

—As a ship that putteth into the calmest cove:—it now draweth up to the land, weary of long voyages and uncertain seas. Is not the land more faithful?

As such a ship huggeth the shore, tuggeth the shore:—then it sufficeth for a spider to spin its thread from the ship to the land. No stronger ropes are required there.

As such a weary ship in the calmest cove, so do I also now repose, nigh to the earth, faithful, trusting, waiting, bound to it with the lightest threads.

O happiness! O happiness! Wilt thou perhaps sing, O my soul? Thou liest in the grass. But this is the secret, solemn hour, when no shepherd playeth his pipe.

Take care! Hot noontide sleepeth on the fields. Do not sing! Hush! The world is perfect.

Do not sing, thou prairie-bird, my soul! Do not even whisper! Lo—hush! The old noontide sleepeth, it moveth its mouth: doth it not just now drink a drop of happiness—

—An old brown drop of golden happiness, golden wine? Something whisketh over it, its happiness laugheth. Thus—laugheth a God. Hush!—

—'For happiness, how little sufficeth for happiness!' Thus spake I once and thought myself wise. But it was a blasphemy: *that* have I now learned. Wise fools speak better.

The least thing precisely, the gentlest thing, the lightest thing, a lizard's rustling, a breath, a whisk, an eye-glance—*little* maketh up the *best* happiness. Hush!

—What hath befallen me: Hark! Hath time flown away? Do I not fall? Have I not fallen—hark! into the well of eternity?

—What happeneth to me? Hush! It stingeth me—alas—to the heart? To the heart! Oh, break up, break up, my heart, after such happiness, after such a sting!

—What? Hath not the world just now become perfect? Round and ripe? Oh, for the golden round ring—whither doth it fly? Let me run after it! Quick!

Hush——" (and here Zarathustra stretched himself, and felt that he was asleep.)

"Up!" said he to himself, "thou sleeper! Thou noontide sleeper! Well then, up, ye old legs! It is time and more than time; many a good stretch of road is still awaiting you—

Now have ye slept your fill; for how long a time? A half-eternity! Well then, up now, mine old heart! For how long after such a sleep mayest thou—remain awake?"

(But then did he fall asleep anew, and his soul spake against him and defended itself, and lay down again)—"Leave me alone! Hush! Hath not the world just now become perfect? Oh, for the golden round ball!"—

"Get up," said Zarathustra, "thou little thief, thou sluggard! What! Still stretching thyself, yawning, sighing, falling into deep wells?

Who art thou then, O my soul?" (and here he became frightened, for a sunbeam shot down from heaven upon his face.)

"O heaven above me," said he sighing, and sat upright, "thou gazest at me? Thou hearkenest unto my strange soul?

When wilt thou drink this drop of dew that fell down upon all earthly things,—when wilt thou drink this strange soul—

—When, thou well of eternity! thou joyous, awful, noontide abyss! when wilt thou drink my soul back into thee?"

Thus spake Zarathustra, and rose from his couch beside the tree, as if awakening from a strange drunkenness: and behold! there stood the sun still exactly above his head. One might, however, rightly infer therefrom that Zarathustra had not then slept long.

NIETZSCHE (from *Thus Spake Zarathustra*)

BLESSED IS HE WHO SLEEPS

I don't like the man who doesn't sleep, says God.
Sleep is the friend of man.
Sleep is the friend of God.
Sleep is perhaps the most beautiful thing I have created.
And I myself rested on the seventh day.
He whose heart is pure, sleeps. And he who sleeps has a pure heart.
That is the great secret of being as indefatigable as a child.
Of having that strength in the legs that a child has.
Those new legs, those new souls,
And to begin afresh every morning, ever new,
Like young hope, new hope . . .
He who doesn't sleep is unfaithful to Hope.
And it is the greatest infidelity.
Because it is infidelity to the greatest Faith.
Poor children, they conduct their business with wisdom during the day.

But when evening comes, they can't make up their minds,
They can't be resigned to trust my wisdom for the space of one
night
With the conduct and the governing of their business.
As if I wasn't capable, if you please, of looking after it a little.
Of watching over it.
Of governing and conducting, and all that kind of stuff.
I have a great deal more business to look after, poor people, I
govern creation, maybe that is more difficult.
You might perhaps, and no harm done, leave your business in my
hands, O wise men.
Maybe I am just as wise as you are.
You might perhaps leave it to me for the space of a night.
While you are asleep
At last
And the next morning you might find it not too badly damaged
perhaps . . .
Put off until tomorrow those tears which fill your eyes and your
head,
Flooding you, rolling down your cheeks, those tears which stream
down your cheeks.
Because between now and tomorrow, maybe I, God, will have
passed by your way.
Human wisdom says: Woe to the man who puts off what he has to
do until tomorrow.
And I say Blessed, blessed is the man who puts off what he has to
do until tomorrow.
Blessed is he who puts off. That is to say Blessed is he who hopes.
And who sleeps.

CHARLES PÉGUY (*tr. by Anne and Julian Green*)

IV. JOY AND PRAISE

A Prelude and Chorale with two Codas

Prelude

"THE GREAT CREATOR FROM HIS WORK RETURNED"

"Open, ye everlasting gates!" they sung;
"Open, ye Heavens, your living doors! let in
The great Creator, from his work returned
Magnificent, his six days' work, a World!
Open, and henceforth oft; for God will deign
To visit oft the dwellings of just men
Delighted, and with frequent intercourse
Thither will send his wingèd messengers
On errands of supernal grace." So sung
The glorious train ascending. He through Heaven,
That opened wide her blazing portals, led
To God's eternal house direct the way—
A broad and ample road, whose dust is gold
And pavement stars, as stars to thee appear
Seen in the Galaxy, that milky way
Which nightly as a circling zone thou seest
Powdered with stars. And now on Earth the seventh
Evening arose in Eden—for the sun
Was set, and twilight from the east came on,
Forerunning night—when at the holy mount
Of Heaven's high-seated top, the imperial throne
Of Godhead, fixed for ever firm and sure,
The Filial Power arrived, and sat him down
With his great Father; for he also went
Invisible, yet stayed (such privilege
Hath Omnipresence) and the work ordained,
Author and end of all things, and, from work
Now resting, blessed and hallowed the seventh Day,
As resting on that day from all his work;
But not in silence holy kept: the harp
Had work, and rested not; the solemn pipe
And dulcimer, all organs of sweet stop,
All sounds on fret by string or golden wire,
Tempered soft tunings, intermixed with voice
Choral or unison; of incense clouds,
Fuming from golden censers, hid the Mount.
Creation and the Six Days' acts they sung.

MILTON (from *Paradise Lost*)

"AND GOD RENEWS HIS ANCIENT RAPTURE"

I knew, I felt, (perception unexpressed,
Uncomprehended by our narrow thought,
But somehow felt and known in every shift
And change in the spirit,—nay, in every pore
Of the body, even,)—what God is, what we are,
What life is—how God tastes an infinite joy
In infinite ways—one everlasting bliss,
From whom all being emanates, all power
Proceeds; in whom is life for evermore,
Yet whom existence in its lowest form
Includes; where dwells enjoyment there is He!
With still a flying point of bliss remote,
A happiness in store afar, a sphere
Of distant glory in full view; thus climbs
Pleasure its heights for ever and for ever!
The centre-fire heaves underneath the earth,
And the earth changes like a human face;
The molten ore bursts up among the rocks,
Winds into the stone's heart, outbranches bright
In hidden mines, spots barren river-beds,
Crumbles into fine sand where sunbeams bask—
God joys therein! The wroth sea's waves are edged
With foam, white as the bitten lip of hate,
When, in the solitary waste, strange groups
Of young volcanos come up, cyclops-like,
Staring together with their eyes on flame—
God tastes a pleasure in their uncouth pride!
Then all is still; earth is a wintry clod:
But spring-wind, like a dancing psaltress, passes
Over its breast to waken it, rare verdure
Buds tenderly upon rough banks, between
The withered tree-roots and the cracks of frost,
Like a smile striving with a wrinkled face;
The grass grows bright, the boughs are swoln with blooms
Like chrysalids impatient for the air,
The shining dorrs are busy, beetles run
Along the furrows, ants make their ado;
Above, birds fly in merry flocks, the lark
Soars up and up, shivering for very joy;

Afar the ocean sleeps; white fishing-gulls
Flit where the strand is purple with its tribe
Of nested limpets; savage creatures seek
Their loves in wood and plain—and God renews
His ancient rapture!

BROWNING (from Paracelsus)

Chorale

The fetters of my tongue do Thou unbind,
That I may have the power to sing of Thee,
And sound thy praises everlastingly.

WORDSWORTH (*after Michelangelo*)

We bless Thee for our creation.

THE BOOK OF COMMON PRAYER

Serve the Lord with gladness: come before his presence with singing.

FROM PSALM 100

To breathe is a beatitude.

AMIEL

For who could live or breathe if there were not this delight of existence as the ether in which we dwell?
From Delight all these beings are born, by Delight they exist and grow, to Delight they return.

TAITTIRIYA UPANISHAD

Wherever there is a bit of colour, a note of song, a grace of form, there comes the call for our love.

TAGORE

I am a son of Earth, the soil is my mother. May we speak the beauty of thee, O Earth, that is in thy villages and forests and assemblies!

THE VEDAS

Song I call when in a plenteous soul the sweetness of eternal love with burning is taken, and thought into song is turned, and the mind into full sweet sound is changed.

RICHARD ROLLE

Is it not a great thing that you should be Heir of the World?

TRAHERNE

We need nothing but open eyes, to be ravished like the Cherubims.

TRAHERNE

Oh we crazy-pates! What joys our eyes give us.

VINCENT VAN GOGH

The soul is There all that it can be: Here it is to rejoice in what it may be.

TRAHERNE

To enjoy, to create (which is to love) and to try to understand is all that at the moment I can see of duty.

JACQUETTA HAWKES

... for me
Life's morning radiance hath not left the hills,
Her dew is on the flowers.

WORDSWORTH

What? Imitate with dull paints the Light of the World?

R. G. (*asked to paint a flower-bed in June*)

'Tis little I could care for pearls
    Who own the ample sea;
Or brooches, when the Emperor
    With rubies pelteth me;

Or gold, who am the Prince of Mines;
    Or diamonds, when I see
A diadem to fit a dome
    Continual crowning me.

EMILY DICKINSON

'And when they wanted wine, the mother of Jesus saith unto him, They have no wine' . . . Alyosha heard.

" Ah, yes, I was missing that, and I didn't want to miss it, I love that passage: it's Cana of Galilee, the first miracle. . . . Ah, that miracle! Ah, that sweet miracle! It was not men's grief but their joy Christ visited, He worked His first miracle to help men's gladness."

DOSTOEVSKY (from *The Brothers Karamazov*)

I read somewhere of a shepherd who, when asked why he made, from within fairy rings, ritual observances to the moon to protect

108

his flocks, replied: 'I'd be a damn' fool if I didn't!' These poems, with all their crudities, doubts, and confusions, are written for the love of Man and in praise of God, and I'd be a damn' fool if they weren't.

DYLAN THOMAS (note to his collected poems)

Gratitude is heaven itself.

BLAKE

§ 2

Have you noticed how the pebbles of the road are polished and pure after the rain? And the flowers? No word can describe them. One can only murmur an 'Ah!' of admiration. A Japanese writer and bonze has said that one should understand the 'Ah!' of things.

A MASTER OF ZEN BUDDHISM

The frog leaps, the cricket sings, a dew-drop glitters on the lotus leaf, a breeze passes through the pine branches, and the moonlight falls on the murmuring mountain stream.

D. T. SUZUKI

I taste a liquor never brewed,
From tankards scooped in pearl;
Not all the vats upon the Rhine
Yield such an alcohol!

Inebriate of air am I,
And debauchee of dew,
Reeling, through endless summer days,
From inns of molten blue.

When landlords turn the drunken bee
Out of the foxglove's door,
When butterflies renounce their drams,
I shall but drink the more!

Till seraphs swing their snowy hats,
And saints to windows run,
To see the little tippler
Leaning against the sun!

EMILY DICKINSON

The murmur of a bee
A witchcraft yieldeth me.
If any ask me why,
'Twere easier to die
Than tell.

The red upon the hill
Taketh away my will;
If anybody sneer,
Take care, for God is here,
That's all.

The breaking of the day
Addeth to my degree;
If any ask me how,
Artist, who drew me so,
Must tell!

EMILY DICKINSON

Lovely is the flock of birds which keeps the Tree of Life; on
every bright and goodly bird a hundred feathers, and without sin,
with pure glory, they sing a hundred tunes for every feather.

IRISH (c. 950)

... White Sirius glittering o'er the southern crags,
Orion with his belt, and those fair Seven,
Acquaintances of every little child,
And Jupiter, my own beloved star!

WORDSWORTH

Waters above! eternal Springs!
The dew, that silvers the Doves wings!
O welcom, welcom to the sad:
Give dry dust drink; drink that makes glad!
Many fair Ev'nings, many Flowr's
Sweeten'd with rich and gentle showers
Have I enjoy'd, and down have run
Many a fine and shining Sun;
But never till this happy hour
Was blest with such an Evening-shower!

HENRY VAUGHAN

It has just been raining. Nature is fresh and radiant; the earth seems to taste with rapture the water which brings it life. One would say that the throats of the birds had also been refreshed by this rain; their song is purer, more vivacious, more brilliant, and vibrates wonderfully in the air, which has become more sonorous and resounding. The nightingales, the bullfinches, the blackbirds, the thrushes, the golden orioles, the finches, the wrens—all these sing and rejoice. A goose, shrieking like a trumpet, adds by contrast to the charm. The motionless trees seem to listen to all these sounds. Innumerable apple-trees in full bloom look like balls of snow in the distance; the cherry-trees, all white as well, rise like pyramids or spread out like fans of flowers. . . .

MAURICE DE GUÉRIN

> Look children,
> Hail-stones!
> Let's rush out!

BASHO

The calm green lakes are sleeping in the mountain shadow, and on the water's canvas bright sunshine paints the picture of the day.

GWILYM COWLYD

It is Thou who givest the bright sun, together with the ice; it is Thou who createdst the rivers and the salmon in the river.

That the nut-tree should be flowering, O Christ, it is a rare craft; through Thy skill too comes the kernel, Thou fair ear of our wheat.

Though the children of Eve ill deserve the bird-flocks and the salmon, it was the Immortal One on the cross who made both salmon and birds.

It is He who makes the flower of the sloe grow through the bark of the blackthorn, and the nut-flower on the trees; beside this, what miracle is greater?

TADHG ÓG Ó HUIGINN

> Along the mountain path
> The scent of plum-blossoms—
> And on a sudden the rising sun!

BASHO

III

. . . as ruddy as a morning when
The ripe fruit blushes into joy in heaven's eternal halls . . .
BLAKE

. . . Magnificent
The morning rose, in memorable pomp,
Glorious as e'er I had beheld—in front,
The sea lay laughing at a distance; near,
The solid mountains shone, bright as the clouds,
Grain-tinctured, drenched in empyrean light;
And in the meadows and the lower grounds
Was all the sweetness of a common dawn—
Dews, vapours, and the melody of birds,
And labourers going forth to till the fields.
WORDSWORTH

DAY

Wherefore, then, up I went full soon
And gazed upon the stars and moon—
The soundless mansion of the night
Filled with a still and silent light:

And lo! night, stars and moon swept by,
And the great sun streamed up the sky,
Filling the air as with a sea
Of fiery-hued serenity.

Then turned I in, and cried, O soul,
Thank God thine eyes are clear and whole;
Thank God who hath with viewless heaven
Drenched this gross globe, the earth, and given,
In Time's small space, a heart that may
Hold in its span all night, all day!
WALTER DE LA MARE

THE RISEN SUN

I lay a while, exulting in its light,
My Druid heart drenched through with awe and praise;
Then into darkness turned a dazzled sight,
    That dared not meet its gaze.
WALTER DE LA MARE

SUNSHINE THROUGH THE WINDOW

Pleasant to me is the glittering of the sun to-day upon these margins, because it flickers so.

IRISH (*marginal note by scribe, 9th century*)

GOLDEN LIE THE MEADOWS

Golden lie the meadows: golden run the streams; red gold is on the pine-stems. The sun is coming down to earth, and walks the fields and the waters.

The sun is coming down to earth, and the fields and the waters shout to him golden shouts. He comes, and his heralds run before him, and touch the leaves of oaks and planes and beeches lucid green, and the pine-stems redder gold; leaving brightest footprints upon thickly-weeded banks, where the foxglove's last upper-bells incline, and bramble-shoots wander amid moist rich herbage. The plumes of the woodland are alight; and beyond them, over the open, 'tis a race with the long-thrown shadows; a race across the heaths and up the hills, till, at the farthest bourne of mounted eastern cloud, the heralds of the sun lay rosy fingers and rest.

GEORGE MEREDITH

THE SONG OF THE SINLESS SOUL

Rise up, O sun, most glorious minister & light of day.
Flow on, ye gentle airs, & bear the voice of my rejoicing.
Wave freshly, clear waters flowing around the tender grass;
And thou, sweet-smelling ground, put forth thy life in fruit & flowers.
Follow me, O my flocks, & hear me sing my rapturous song.
I will cause my voice to be heard on the clouds that glitter in the sun.
I will call; and who shall answer me? I will sing; who shall reply?
For from my pleasant hills behold the living, living springs,
Running among my green pastures, delighting among my trees.
I am not here alone: my flocks, you are my brethren;
And you birds that sing & adorn the sky, you are my sisters.
I sing, & you reply to my song; I rejoice, & you are glad.
Follow me, O my flocks; we will now descend into the valley.
O how delicious are the grapes, flourishing in the sun!
How clear the spring of the rock, running among the golden sand!

How cool the breezes of the valley, & the arms of the branching
  trees!
Cover us from the sun; come & let us sit in the shade . . .
Here will I build myself a house, & here I'll call on his name,
Here I'll return when I am weary & take my pleasant rest.

BLAKE

"THE ROSY FLOOD OF TWILIGHT'S SKY"

Ave Maria! blessed be the hour!
  The time, the clime, the spot, where I so oft
Have felt that moment in its fullest power
  Sink o'er the earth so beautiful and soft,
While swung the deep bell in the distant tower,
  Or the faint dying day-hymn stole aloft,
And not a breath crept through the rosy air,
And yet the forest leaves seem'd stirr'd with prayer. . . .

Sweet hour of twilight!—in the solitude
  Of the pine forest, and the silent shore
Which bounds Ravenna's immemorial wood,
  Rooted where once the Adrian wave flow'd o'er,
To where the last Caesarean fortress stood,
  Evergreen forest! which Boccaccio's lore
And Dryden's lay made haunted ground to me,
How have I loved the twilight hour and thee!

The shrill cicalas, people of the pine,
  Making their summer lives one ceaseless song,
Were the sole echoes, save my steed's and mine,
  And vesper bell's that rose the boughs along;
The spectre huntsman of Onesti's line,
  His hell-dogs, and their chase, and the fair throng
Which learn'd from this example not to fly
From a true lover,—shadow'd my mind's eye.

Oh, Hesperus! thou bringest all good things—
  Home to the weary, to the hungry cheer,
To the young bird the parent's brooding wings,
  The welcome stall to the o'erlabour'd steer;
Whate'er of peace about our hearthstone clings,
  Whate'er our household gods protect of dear,

114

Are gather'd round us by thy look of rest;
Thou bring'st the child, too, to the mother's breast.

BYRON (from *Don Juan*)

Everything that he saw from the carriage window, in the pale light of the dying day, appeared to him just as fresh, happy, and strong as he himself. The roofs of the houses shining in the setting sun, the sharp outlines of fences and corner buildings, the forms of occasional pedestrians and carriages, the motionless leaves, the green grass, the fields with their straight rows of potatoes, the slanting shadows from the houses, trees, and bushes—everything was beautiful, like an exquisite landscape fresh from the artist's hand.

TOLSTOY (from *Anna Karenina*)

§ 3

Of all things the beginning
　　Was on an April morn,
In spring the earth remembereth
　　The day that she was born.

CARMINA BURANA (*tr. by Waddell*)

Long-idling Spring may come
With such sweet suddenness
It's past the wit of man
　　His joy to express.

To see in the cold clods
Green weed 'twixt stone and stone!
The violet nod in flower
　　Its frail stalk on;

To watch the wintry sky
Shed pallor from its blue:
And beams of purest light
　　And heat pierce through!

To share, to live, to be
Merely a reflex of
Earth's old divine delight,
　　And peace, and love!

WALTER DE LA MARE

115

Leaves of the summer, lovely summer's pride,
  Sweet is the shade below your silent tree,
Whether in waving copses, where ye hide
  My roamings, or in fields that let me see
  The open sky; and whether ye may be
Around the low-stemm'd oak, robust and wide;
Or taper ash upon the mountain side;
  Or lowland elm; your shade is sweet to me.

Whether ye wave above the early flow'rs
  In lively green; or whether, rustling sere,
  Ye fly on playful winds, around my feet,
In dying autumn; lovely are your bow'rs,
  Ye early dying children of the year;
  Holy the silence of your calm retreat.

WILLIAM BARNES

In the Summer translate thy self to the Fields, where all are green with the Breath of God, or fresh with the Powers of Heaven. Sometimes thou may'st walk in Groves, which being full of Majestie will much advance the Soul. Sometimes by clear, Active Rivers, for by such (say the Mystick Poets) Apollo contemplated.

THOMAS VAUGHAN

All the sweetness of nature was buried in black winter's grave, and the wind sings a sad lament with its cold plaintive cry; but oh, the teeming summer will come, bringing life in its arms, and will strew rosy flowers on the face of hill and dale.

In lovely harmony the wood has put on its green mantle, and summer is on its throne, playing its string-music; the willow, whose harp hung silent when it was withered in winter, now gives forth its melody—Hush! Listen! The world is alive.

THOMAS TELYNOG EVANS

          Thereafter, as the shades
Of twilight deepened, going forth, I spied
A glow-worm underneath a dusky plume
Or canopy of yet unwithered fern,
Clear-shining, like a hermit's taper seen
Through a thick forest. Silence touched me here
No less than sound had done before; the child

Of Summer, lingering, shining, by herself,
The voiceless worm on the unfrequented hills,
Seemed sent on the same errand with the choir
Of Winter that had warbled at my door,
And the whole year breathed tenderness and love.

WORDSWORTH

He said the pleasantest manner of spending a hot July day was lying from morning till evening on a bank of heath in the middle of the moors, with the bees humming dreamily about among the bloom, and the larks singing high up over head, and the blue sky and bright sun shining steadily and cloudlessly. That was his most perfect idea of heaven's happiness: mine was rocking in a rustling green tree, with a west wind blowing, and bright white clouds flitting rapidly above; and not only larks, but throstles, and blackbirds, and linnets, and cuckoos pouring out music on every side, and the moors seen at a distance, broken into cool dusky dells; but close by great swells of long grass undulating in waves to the breeze; and woods and sounding water, and the whole world awake and wild with joy.

EMILY BRONTË (from Wuthering Heights)

Besides the singing and calling, there is a peculiar sound which is only heard in summer. Waiting quietly to discover what birds are about, I become aware of a sound in the very air. It is not the midsummer hum which will soon be heard over the heated hay in the valley and over the cooler hills alike. It is not enough to be called a hum, and does but just tremble at the extreme edge of hearing. If the branches wave and rustle they overbear it; the buzz of a passing bee is so much louder it overcomes all of it that is in the whole field. I cannot define it, except by calling the hours of winter to mind—they are silent; you hear a branch crack or creak as it rubs another in the wood, you hear the hoar frost crunch on the grass beneath your feet, but the air is without sound in itself. The sound of summer is everywhere—in the passing breeze, in the hedge, in the broad-branching trees, in the grass as it swings; all the myriad particles that together make the summer are in motion. The sap moves in the trees, the pollen is pushed out from grass and flower, and yet again these acres and acres of leaves and square miles of grass blades—for they would cover acres and square miles if reckoned edge to edge—are drawing their strength from the atmosphere. Exceedingly minute as these vibrations must be, their numbers perhaps may give them a volume almost reaching in the aggregate to the power of the ear. Besides the quivering leaf, the swinging grass, the fluttering bird's wing, and the thousand oval membranes which innumerable insects whirl about, a faint resonance seems to come from the very earth itself. The fervour of the sunbeams descending in a tidal flood rings on the strung harp of earth. It is this exquisite undertone, heard and yet unheard, which brings the mind into sweet accordance with the wonderful instrument of nature.

RICHARD JEFFERIES

Magnificent weather. The morning seems bathed in happy peace, and a heavenly fragrance rises from mountain and shore; it is as though a benediction were laid upon us. . . . One might believe oneself in a church—a vast temple in which every being and every natural beauty has its place. I dare not breathe for fear of putting the dream to flight—a dream traversed by angels. . . .

In these heavenly moments the cry of Pauline rises to one's lips. 'I feel! I believe! I see!' All the miseries, the cares, the vexations of life, are forgotten; the universal joy absorbs us; we enter into the divine order, and into the blessedness of the Lord. Labour and tears, sin, pain, and death have passed away. To exist is to bless; life is happiness. In this sublime pause of things all dissonances have disappeared. It is as though creation were but one vast symphony, glorifying the God of goodness with an inexhaustible wealth of praise and harmony. We question no longer whether it is so or not. We have ourselves become notes in the great concert; and the soul breaks the silence of ecstasy only to vibrate in unison with the eternal joy.

AMIEL

So I and Eucritus and the fair Amyntichus turned aside into the house of Phrasidamus, and lay down with delight in beds of sweet tamarisk and fresh cuttings from the vines, strewn on the ground. Many poplars and elm-trees were waving over our heads, and not far off the running of the sacred water from the cave of the nymphs warbled to us: in the shimmering branches the sun-burnt grasshoppers were busy with their talk, and from afar the little owl cried softly out of the tangled thorns of the blackberry; the larks were singing and the hedge-birds, and the turtle-dove moaned; the bees

flew round and round the fountains, murmuring softly; the scent
of late summer and of the fall of the year was everywhere; the pears
fell from the trees at our feet, and apples in number rolled down at
our sides, and the young plum-trees were bent to the earth with the
weight of their fruit.

THEOCRITUS (*tr. by Walter Pater*)

The double door of the house stood open to an effect of hazy
autumn sunshine, a wonderful windless waiting golden hour . . .

HENRY JAMES

A SIMPLETON

In the autumn the season of ripeness when final redness
Comes to the ore and the earth is with child by the Sun,
Like the bright gold spangles fall'n from the light of Nature
Flying over the happy fields, the Simpleton
Feeling the warm gold ripen, sat by the wayside
—His broad face having an animal nature (the beast of burden
Who has turned prophet, the beast in our earth unconscious),
A simple creature, happy as butterflies,
Or as the dancing star that has risen from Chaos.
And the world hangs like a ripe apple—the great gold planets
Lying with Evil and Good in the ripened core.
The old men Abraham-bearded like the auburn
Sun of harvest walk in the holy fields
Where the Sun forgives and remakes the shape of Evil
And, laughing, forgives lean Virtue . . . Gravity yields
The gold that was hidden deep in the earth, in the map-like
Lines of a smile made holy by Light, and the Sun
With his gold mouth kisses the skin that shines like red fire,
And shouts to the lowly, the dust that is his lover:
'See how of my love and my shining I never tire,
But rule over thunders and Chaos: the lore of the bee and the great
   lion's raging
To me are equal in grandeur, the hump of the cripple
And the mountain that hides the veins of brute gold are as one—
And to me the jarring atoms are parted lovers!'
And this is the lore the Simpleton learns from his nature—
Lifting his face in blindness and happiness up to the Sun.

EDITH SITWELL

119

GOD'S WORLD

O world, I cannot hold thee close enough!
  Thy winds, thy wide gray skies!
  Thy mists that roll and rise!
Thy woods, this autumn day, that ache and sag
And all but cry with color! That gaunt crag
To crush! To lift the lean of that black bluff!
World, world, I cannot get thee close enough!

Long have I known a glory in it all,
  But never knew I this;
  Here such a passion is
As stretcheth me apart. Lord, I do fear
Thou'st made the world too beautiful this year.
My soul is all but out of me,—let fall
No burning leaf; prithee, let no bird call.

EDNA ST. VINCENT MILLAY

THE MONTHS

September. The pear trees a bright yellow. The apple trees green still. A sweet lovely afternoon.

October. The colours of the mountains soft and rich, with orange fern; the cattle pasturing upon the hill-tops; kites sailing in the sky above our heads; sheep bleating and in lines and chains and patterns scattered over the mountains.

November. Catkins are coming out; palm trees budding; the alder, with its plum-coloured buds. We came home over the stepping-stones. The lake was foamy with white waves. I saw a solitary butter-flower in the wood.

December. O! the bonny nooks and windings and curlings of the beck, down at the bottom of the steep green mossy banks.

January. A beautiful mild morning—the sun shone, the lake was still, and all the shores reflected in it.

February. The sun shone bright and clear. A deep stillness in the thickest part of the wood, undisturbed except by the occasional dropping of the snow from the holly boughs; no other sound but that of the water, and the slender notes of a redbreast, which sang at intervals on the outskirts of the southern side of the wood. There the bright green moss was bare at the roots of the trees, and the little birds were upon it. The whole appearance of the wood was enchanting; and each tree, taken singly, was beautiful. The branches of the hollies pendent with their white burden, but still showing their bright red berries, and their glossy green leaves. The bare branches of the oaks thickened by the snow.

March. The catkins are beautiful in the hedges, the ivy is very green.

April (Good Friday). We watched the crows at a little distance from us become white as silver as they flew in the sunshine, and when they went still further they looked like shapes of water passing over the green fields.

May. It was a strange night. The hills were covered over with a slight covering of hail or snow, just so as to give them a hoary winter look with the black rocks. . . . O, thought I! what a beautiful thing God has made winter to be, by stripping the trees, and letting us see their shapes and forms.

June. We lay upon the sloping turf. Earth and sky were so lovely that they melted our very hearts. The sky to the north was of a chastened yet rich yellow, fading into pale blue, and streaked and scattered over with steady islands of purple, melting away into shades of pink. It made my heart almost feel like a vision to me.

DOROTHY WORDSWORTH (Grasmere Journal)

§ 4

THIS LIME-TREE BOWER MY PRISON

[In the June of 1797, some long-expected Friends paid a visit to the author's cottage; and on the morning of their arrival he met with an accident, which disabled him from walking during the whole time of their stay. One evening, when they had left him for a few hours, he composed the following lines in the garden-bower.]

Well, they are gone, and here must I remain,
This lime-tree bower my prison! I have lost
Beauties and feelings, such as would have been
Most sweet to my remembrance even when age
Had dimmed mine eyes to blindness! They, meanwhile,
Friends, whom I never more may meet again,
On springy heath, along the hill-top edge,
Wander in gladness, and wind down, perchance,
To that still roaring dell, of which I told;
The roaring dell, o'erwooded, narrow, deep,
And only speckled by the mid-day sun;

Where its slim trunk the ash from rock to rock
Flings arching like a bridge;—that branchless ash,
Unsunned and damp, whose few poor yellow leaves
Ne'er tremble in the gale, yet tremble still,
Fanned by the water-fall! and there my friends
Behold the dark green file of long lank weeds,
That all at once (a most fantastic sight!)
Still nod and drip beneath the dripping edge
Of the blue clay-stone.

                Now, my friends emerge
Beneath the wide wide Heaven—and view again
The many-steepled tract magnificent
Of hilly fields and meadows, and the sea,
With some fair bark, perhaps, whose sails light up
The slip of smooth clear blue betwixt two Isles
Of purple shadow! Yes! they wander on
In gladness all; but thou, methinks, most glad,
My gentle-hearted Charles! for thou hast pined
And hungered after Nature, many a year,
In the great City pent, winning thy way
With sad yet patient soul, through evil and pain
And strange calamity! Ah! slowly sink
Behind the western ridge, thou glorious sun!
Shine in the slant beams of the sinking orb,
Ye purple heath-flowers! richlier burn, ye clouds!
Live in the yellow light, ye distant groves!
And kindle, thou blue ocean! So my Friend
Struck with deep joy may stand, as I have stood,
Silent with swimming sense; yea, gazing round
On the wide landscape, gaze till all doth seem
Less gross than bodily; and of such hues
As veil the Almighty Spirit, when yet he makes
Spirits perceive his presence.

                   A delight
Comes sudden on my heart, and I am glad
As I myself were there! Nor in this bower,
This little lime-tree bower, have I not marked
Much that has soothed me. Pale beneath the blaze
Hung the transparent foliage; and I watched
Some broad and sunny leaf, and loved to see

The shadow of the leaf and stem above
Dappling its sunshine! And that walnut-tree
Was richly tinged, and a deep radiance lay
Full on the ancient ivy, which usurps
Those fronting elms, and now, with blackest mass
Makes their dark branches gleam a lighter hue
Through the late twilight: and though now the bat
Wheels silent by, and not a swallow twitters,
Yet still the solitary humble bee
Sings in the bean-flower! Henceforth I shall know
That Nature ne'er deserts the wise and pure;
No plot so narrow, be but Nature there,
No waste so vacant, but may well employ
Each faculty of sense, and keep the heart
Awake to Love and Beauty! and sometimes
'Tis well to be bereft of promised good,
That we may lift the Soul, and contemplate
With lively joy the joys we cannot share.
My gentle-hearted Charles! when the last rook
Beat its straight path along the dusky air
Homewards, I blest it! deeming, its black wing
(Now a dim speck, now vanishing in light)
Had crossed the mighty orb's dilated glory,
While thou stood'st gazing; or when all was still,
Flew creaking o'er thy head, and had a charm
For thee, my gentle-hearted Charles, to whom
No sound is dissonant which tells of Life.

S. T. COLERIDGE

THE GROVE

> ... And I know a grove
Of large extent, hard by a castle huge,
Which the great lord inhabits not; and so
This grove is wild with tangling underwood,
And the trim walks are broken up, and grass,
Thin grass and king-cups grow within the paths.
But never elsewhere in one place I knew
So many nightingales; and far and near,
In wood and thicket, over the wide grove,
They answer and provoke each other's song,

With skirmish and capricious passagings,
And murmurs musical and swift jug jug,
And one low piping sound more sweet than all—
Stirring the air with such a harmony,
That should you close your eyes, you might almost
Forget it was not day! On moon-lit bushes,
Whose dewy leaflets are but half disclosed,
You may perchance behold them on the twigs,
Their bright, bright eyes, their eyes both bright and full,
Glistening, while many a glow-worm in the shade
Lights up her love-torch.

S. T. COLERIDGE

THE WOOD

There was a wood of beech trees near my home
Whose roots were twisted round the pitted rocks,
And in the branches every spring
The thrushes sang so constantly
The glens became a single chord of sound.
The sun lay all along the faces of the leaves
And on the swinging rows of scentless flowers;
The wood stretched far into the silences,
But as you leaped from rock to rock, you heard
The tiny notes of water dripping on bright stones
And orchestras of insects underground,
You saw the ferns uncurling baby fronds
And sudden islands of forget-me-nots.
And when at last you reached the circling wire
That cut in two this trembling forest world,
You plunged into a hundred seas of bluebell light
And like a crazy traveller drugged and lost
In undiscovered continents,
You sank, defeated, drenched with flowers,
Beneath the drowning tides that wandered there.

LEONARD CLARK

Almighty One, in the woods I am blessed. Happy everyone in
the woods. Every tree speaks through thee. O God! What glory
in the woodland! On the heights is peace—peace to serve Him.

BEETHOVEN

The clouds indeed were heavy in the sky. The river ran equally
heavily with the weight of its mirk. A few boats rode on it; the
Thames traffic, at this height of its course, had not renewed itself.
Lester's attention turned to it, and the dwarf, folding her arms,
paused conformably and leaned on the parapet. The Thames was
dirty and messy. Twigs, bits of paper and wood, cords, old boxes
drifted on it. Yet to the new-eyed Lester it was not a depressing
sight. The dirtiness of the water was, at that particular point, what
it should be, and therefore pleasant enough. The evacuations of the
City had their place in the City; how else could the City be the
City? Corruption (so to call it) was tolerable, even adequate and
proper, even glorious. These things also were facts. They could
not be forgotten or lost in fantasy; all that had been, was; all that
was, was. A sodden mass of cardboard and paper drifted by, but the
soddenness was itself a joy, for this was what happened, and all that
happened, in this great material world, was good. The very
heaviness of the heavy sky was a wonder, and the unutilitarian
expectation of rain a delight. . . .

CHARLES WILLIAMS (from *All Hallows' Eve*)

§ 6

TILL EVERY MORNING YOU AWAKE IN HEAVEN

Your enjoyment of the world is never right, till every morning
you awake in Heaven; see yourself in your Father's Palace; and look
upon the skies, the earth, and the air as Celestial Joys: having such a
reverend esteem of all, as if you were among the Angels. The bride
of a monarch, in her husband's chamber, hath no such causes of
delight as you. . . .

You never enjoy the world aright, till the Sea itself floweth in
your veins, till you are clothed with the heavens, and crowned with
the stars: and perceive yourself to be the sole heir of the whole
world, and more than so, because men are in it who are every one
sole heirs as well as you. Till you can sing and rejoice and delight in
God, as misers do in gold, and Kings in sceptres, you never enjoy
the world. . . .

All things were made to be yours, and you were made to prize
them according to their value: which is your office and duty, the

end for which you were created, and the means whereby you enjoy. The end for which you were created, is that by prizing all that God hath done, you may enjoy yourself and Him in Blessedness.

TRAHERNE

A YEAR OF WONDER

How shall I find the words to describe to you, my dear Timothy, what I felt in my year of wonder 1942? I had a heightened perception of everything, and everything was perceived as beautiful and good. But it was more than a perception; it was a meeting, for which I had gone out to the other and for which the other had gone out to me: a meeting with everything's self which at the same time was my self, but was nevertheless of a difference in selfhood which alone made the meeting a possibility. But the going out and the meeting were not different things but the same thing, not successive but simultaneous; which is to say that they were not in time but in eternity. And the meeting, I say again, was with everything. With the greenness, the freshness, the slenderness, the littleness, the gentleness, the strength, the taperingness, the sun-acceptingness, the daisy-and-buttercup-enclosingness, of the benign and far-stretching grass. With the trees in their various species, and with every branch and every twig and every leaf of them. With stones and mould and air and sun and a deck-chair in the garden and a car down the lane and a spire on the downs and the wall of our house as I come in for lunch at one. And with people. I would sit, going up to London, in a crowded railway-compartment, and know myself as in every one of my fellow travellers, and know every one of them as in me.

I was in the Royal Automobile Club, of all places, on an afternoon that summer, and my eye happened to fall on a door. It was quite an ordinary door, in so far as any single thing in the universe is ordinary, with small panels and big panels and a knob; but I tell you that this door, and the look and the sound and the life of it, filled me with joy inexpressible. And I remember that on the same afternoon, in the same club, I suddenly saw something green through the doors of the winter garden, and saluted it with delighted recognition. . . .

V. G. (from My Dear Timothy)

THE GATES OF PARADISE

He leaned back at length in the deep chair. 'What a world!' he said. 'Mabel, will you play something on the piano that expresses mere joy, the genuine article, nothing feverish or like thorns under a pot, but joy that has decided in favour of the universe? It's a mood that can't last altogether, so we had better get all we can out of it.'

She went to the instrument and struck a few chords while she thought. Then she began to work with all her soul at the theme in the last movement of the Ninth Symphony which is like the sound of the opening of the gates of Paradise.

E. C. BENTLEY (from *Trent's Last Case*)

§ 7

Beasts, and all cattle; creeping things, and flying fowl. . . . praise ye the Lord.

FROM PSALM 148

THE BIRD

Hither thou com'st: the busie wind all night
Blew through thy lodging, where thy own warm wing
Thy pillow was. Many a sullen storm
(For which course man seems much the fitter born)
    Rain'd on thy bed
    And harmless head.

And now as fresh and chearful as the light
Thy little heart in early hymns doth sing
Unto that Providence, whose unseen arm
Curb'd them, and cloath'd thee well and warm.
   All things that be, praise him; and had
   Their lesson taught them, when first made.

So hills and valleys into singing break,
And though poor stones have neither speech nor tongue,
While active winds and streams both run and speak,
Yet stones are deep in admiration.
Thus Praise and Prayer here beneath the Sun
Make lesser mornings, when the great are done.

For each inclosed Spirit is a star
　　Inlightning his own little sphaere,
Whose light, though fetcht and borrowed from far,
　　Both mornings makes, and evenings there . . .

HENRY VAUGHAN

BLACK AND WHITE

On the black mountains the white lambs are straying,
Crying all night to their dams in the fold;
Falling down fissures, on crevices swaying,
The white lambs are calling with new tongues of gold.

Down in the valleys, through white mountain passes,
Running all night each one with his sire,
Playing together in frost-tangled grasses,
The black colts are neighing with new tongues of fire.

White sheep and black colts in flight on the mountains,
Singing all night where the starred snow is blown;
Raising to heaven its ice-gloried fountains,
All winter is praising the Lamb on His throne.

LEONARD CLARK

SAINT BENNO AND THE FROG

　　It was often the habit of the man of God to go about the fields
in meditation and prayer: and once as he passed by a certain marsh,
a talkative frog was croaking in its slimy waters: and lest it should
disturb his contemplation, he bade it to be a Seraphian, inasmuch
as all the frogs in Seraphus are mute. But when he had gone on a
little way, he called to mind the saying in Daniel: "O ye whales
and all that move in the waters, bless ye the Lord. O all ye beasts
and cattle, bless ye the Lord." And fearing lest the singing of the
frogs might perchance be more agreeable to God than his own
praying, he again issued his command to them, that they should
praise God in their accustomed fashion: and soon the air and the
fields were vehement with their conversation.

ACTA SANCTORUM (tr. by Waddell)

SAINT ROSE OF LIMA AND THE BIRDS

When at sunrise she passed through the garden to go to her retreat, she called upon nature to praise with her the Author of all things. Then the trees were seen to bow as she passed by, and clasp their leaves together, making a harmonious sound. The flowers swayed upon their stalks, and opened their blossoms that they might scent the air; thus according to their manner praising God. At the same time the birds began to sing, and came and perched upon the hands and shoulders of Rose. The insects greeted her with a joyous murmur, and all which had life and movement joined in the concert of praise she addressed to the Lord. . . .

Each evening at sunset a little bird with an enchanting voice came and perched upon a tree beside her window, and waited till she gave the sign to him to sing. Rose, as soon as she saw her little feathered chorister, made herself ready to sing the praises of God, and challenged the bird to this musical duel in a song which she had composed for this purpose. 'Begin, dear little bird,' she said, 'begin thy lovely song! Let thy little throat, so full of sweet melodies, pour them forth: that together we may praise the Lord. Thou dost praise thy Creator, I my sweet Saviour: thus we together bless the Deity. Open thy little beak, begin and I will follow thee: and our voices shall blend in a song of holy joy.'

· At once the little bird began to sing, running through his scale to the highest note. Then he ceased, that the saint might sing in her turn. . . . Thus did they celebrate the greatness of God, turn by turn, for a whole hour: and with such perfect order, that when the bird sang Rose said nothing, and when she sang in her turn the bird was silent, and listened to her with a marvellous attention. At last, towards the sixth hour, the saint dismissed him, saying, 'Go, my little chorister, go, fly far away. But blessed be my God who never leaves me!'

RENOUARD DE BUSSIERRE

SAINT FRANCIS AND THE BIRDS

And journeying on in that same fervour of spirit, he lifted up his eyes and beheld some trees by the wayside whereon were an infinite multitude of birds; so that he marvelled and said to his companions, "Tarry here for me by the way and I will go and preach to my little sisters the birds." And he entered into the field and began to preach to the birds that were on the ground; and anon those that were on the trees flew down to hear him, and all stood still the while St. Francis made an end of his sermon; and even then they departed not until he had given them his blessing. And according as Friar Masseo and Friar James of Massa thereafter related, St. Francis went among them, touching them with the hem of his garment, and not one stirred. And the substance of the sermon St. Francis preached was this, "My little sisters the birds, much are ye beholden to God your Creator, and alway and in every place ye ought to praise Him for that He hath given you a double and a triple vesture; He hath given you freedom to go into every place, and also did preserve the seed of you in the ark of Noe, in order that your kind might not perish from the earth. Again, ye are beholden to Him for the element of air which He hath appointed for you; moreover, ye sow not, neither do ye reap, and God feedeth you and giveth you the rivers and the fountains for your drink; He giveth you the mountains and the valleys for your refuge, and the tall trees wherein to build your nests, and forasmuch as ye can neither spin nor sew God clotheth you, you and your children: wherefore your Creator loveth you much, since He hath dealt so bounteously with you; and therefore beware, little sisters mine, of the sin of ingratitude, but ever strive to praise God." While St. Francis was uttering these words, all those birds began to open their beaks, and stretch their necks, and spread their wings, and reverently to bow their heads to the ground, showing by their gestures and songs that the holy father's words gave them greatest joy: and St. Francis was glad and rejoiced with them, and marvelled much at so great a multitude of birds and at their manifold loveliness, and at their attention and familiarity; for which things he devoutly praised the Creator in them. Finally, his sermon ended, St. Francis made the sign of holy cross over them and gave them leave to depart; and all those birds soared up into the air in one flock with wondrous songs, and then divided themselves into four parts after the form of the cross St. Francis had made over them; and one part flew towards the east; another towards the west; the third towards the south, and the fourth towards the north. And each flock sped forth singing wondrously, betokening thereby that even as St. Francis, standard-bearer of the cross of Christ, had preached to them and had made the sign of the cross over them, according to which they had divided themselves, singing, among the four quarters of the world, so the preaching of Christ's cross, renewed by St. Francis, was, through him and his friars, to be borne throughout the whole world; the

130

which friars possessing nothing of their own in this world, after the manner of birds, committed their lives wholly to the providence of God.

FROM ''THE LITTLE FLOWERS''

THE ADORATION OF THE BEASTS

I dreamed that I was lying asleep, when a light in my room wakened me. A man was standing by my bedside. He was wearing a long robe, which fell about him in motionless folds, while he stood like a column. The light that filled the room came from his hair, which rose straight up from his head, burning, like a motionless brazier. He raised his hand, and without touching me, merely by making that sign, lifted me to my feet in one movement, so that I stood before him. He turned and went out through the door, and I followed him. We were in the gallery of a cloister; the moon was shining, and the shadows of the arches made black ribs on the flagstones. We went through a street, at the end of which there was a field, and while we walked on the moonlight changed to the white light of early morning. As we passed the last houses I saw a dark, shabby man with a dagger in his hand; he was wearing rags bound round his feet, so that he walked quite soundlessly; there was a stain as of blood on one of his sleeves; I took him to be a robber or a murderer and was afraid. But as he came nearer I saw that his eyes, which were fixed immovably on the figure beside me, were filled with a profound, violent adoration such as I had never seen in human eyes before. Then, behind him, I caught sight of a confused crowd of other men and women in curious or ragged clothes, and all had their eyes fixed with the same look on the man walking beside me. I saw their faces only for a moment. Presently we came to the field, which as we drew near changed into a great plain dotted with little conical hills a little higher than a man's head. All over the plain animals were standing or sitting on their haunches on these little hills; lions, tigers, bulls, deer, elephants, were there; serpents too wreathed their lengths on the knolls; and each was separate and alone, and each slowly lifted its head upward as if in prayer. This upward-lifting motion had a strange solemnity and deliberation; I watched head after head upraised as if proclaiming some truth just realized, and yet as if moved by an irresistible power beyond them. The elephant wreathed its trunk upward, and there was something pathetic and absurd in that indirect act of adoration. But the other

131

animals raised their heads with the inevitability of the sun's rising, as if they knew, like the sun, that a new day was about to begin, and were giving the signal for its coming. Then I saw a little dog busily running about with his nose tied to the ground, as if he did not know that the animals had been redeemed. He was a friendly little dog, officiously going about his business, and it seemed to me that he too had a place in this day, and that his oblivious concern with the earth was also a sort of worship. How the dream ended I do not remember: I have now only a memory of the great animals with all their heads raised to heaven.

EDWIN MUIR

They do say that on this night
          in the warm byres
shippons, hoggots and out-barns of Britain
in the closes and the pannage-runs and on the sweet lawns of
  Britain
the breathing animals-all
             do kneel.

DAVID JONES

Standing at the masthead of my ship during a sunrise that crimsoned sky and sea, I once saw a large herd of whales in the east, all heading towards the sun, and for a moment vibrating in concert with peaked flukes.* As it seemed to me at the time, such a grand embodiment of adoration of the gods was never beheld, even in Persia, the home of the fire worshippers. As Ptolemy Philopator testified of the African elephant, I then testified of the whale, pronouncing him the most devout of all beings. For according to King John, the military elephants of antiquity often hailed the morning with their trunks uplifted in the profoundest silence.

* tails   FROM "MOBY DICK"

§ 8

(for Clarissa, Jeremy and Robert)

Little Boy,
Full of joy;
Little Girl,
Sweet and small;

132

Cock does crow,
So do you;
Merry voice,
Infant noise. . . .

BLAKE

WONDER

How like an Angel came I down!
How Bright are all Things here!
When first among his Works I did appear
,O how their Glory me did Crown!
The World resembled his Eternitie,
In which my Soul did Walk;
And evry Thing that I did see,
Did with me talk.

The Skies in their Magnificence,
The Lively, Lovely Air;
Oh how Divine, how Soft, how Sweet, how fair!
The Stars did entertain my Sence,
And all the Works of God so Bright and pure,
So Rich and Great did seem,
As if they ever must endure,
In my Esteem.

A Native Health and Innocence
Within my Bones did grow,
And while my God did all his Glories shew,
I felt a Vigour in my Sence
That was all Spirit. I within did flow
With Seas of Life, like Wine;
I nothing in the World did know,
But 'twas Divine. . . .

The Streets were pavd with Golden Stones,
The Boys and Girles were mine,
Oh how did all their Lovly faces shine!
The Sons of Men were Holy Ones.
In Joy, and Beauty, they appear'd to me,
And evry Thing which here I found,
While like an Angel I did See,
Adornd the Ground.

133

Rich Diamond and Pearl and Gold
    In evry Place was seen;
Rare Splendors, Yellow, Blew, Red, White and Green,
    Mine Eys did evry where behold.
Great Wonders clothd with Glory did appear,
    Amazement was my Bliss.
That and my Wealth was evry where:
    No Joy to this! . . .

TRAHERNL

I was standing, one of the stationary row, on an escalator at Paddington. Just behind me a little girl of six or seven was looking round us and up; and such an eagerness for life was on her face, such a glow of enchantment at the wonder of things (and of escalators in particular), that I went on my way as if from watching the dawn, or looking at crocuses in grass, or hearing a melody by Haydn.

V. G.

A LITTLE BLIND GIRL

Sometimes I rose at dawn and stole into the garden while the heavy dew lay on the grass and flowers. Few know what joy it is to feel the roses pressing softly into the hand, or the beautiful motion of the lilies as they sway in the morning breeze. Sometimes I caught an insect in the flower I was plucking, and I felt the faint noise of a pair of wings rubbed together in a sudden terror, as the little creature became aware of a pressure from without.

Another favourite haunt of mine was the orchard, where the fruit ripened early in July. The large, downy peaches would reach themselves into my hand, and as the joyous breezes flew about the trees the apples tumbled at my feet. Oh, the delight with which I gathered up the fruit in my pinafore, pressed my face against the smooth cheeks of the apples, still warm from the sun, and skipped back to the house!

HELEN KELLER

She, too, would dream: but in her own fashion. She would spend the day prowling round the garden, eating, watching, laughing, picking at the grapes on the vines like a thrush, secretly plucking a peach from the trellis, climbing a plum-tree, or giving it a little surreptitious shake as she passed to bring down a rain of the golden mirabelles which melt in the mouth like scented honey. Or she would pick the flowers, although that was forbidden: quickly she would pluck a rose that she had been coveting all day, and run away with it to the arbour at the end of the garden. Then she would bury her little nose in the delicious scented flower, and kiss it, and bite it, and suck it: and then she would conceal her booty, and hide it in her bosom between her little breasts, at the wonder of whose coming she would gaze in eager fondness. . . . And there was an exquisite forbidden joy in taking off her shoes and stockings, and walking barefoot on the cool sand of the paths, and on the dewy turf, and on the stones, cold in the shadow, burning in the sun, and in the little stream that ran along the outskirts of the wood, and kissing with her feet, and legs, and knees, water, earth, and light. Lying in the shadow of the pines, she would hold her hands up to the sun, and watch the light play through them, and she would press her lips upon the soft satin skin of her pretty rounded arms. She would make herself crowns and necklets and gowns of ivy-leaves and oak-leaves: and she would deck them with the blue thistles, and barberry and little pine-branches, with their green fruit: and then she looked like a little savage Princess. And she would dance for her own delight round and round the fountain: and, with arms outstretched, she would turn and turn until her head whirled, and she would slip down on the lawn and bury her face in the grass, and shout with laughter for minutes on end, unable to stop herself, without knowing why. . . .

ROMAIN ROLLAND (from *Jean-Christophe*)

            . . . the ever-living universe,
Turn where I might, was opening out its glories,
And the independent spirit of pure youth
Called forth, at every season, new delights
Spread round my steps like sunshine o'er green fields.

WORDSWORTH

            . . . already I began
To love the sun; a boy I loved the sun,
Not as I since have loved him, as a pledge
And surety of our earthly life, a light
Which we behold and feel we are alive;

Nor for his bounty to so many worlds—
But for this cause, that I had seen him lay
His beauty on the morning hills, had seen
The western mountain touch his setting orb,
In many a thoughtless hour, when, from excess
Of happiness, my blood appeared to flow
For its own pleasure, and I breathed with joy.

WORDSWORTH

There was another thing I loved, when a boy, with a love as big and peaceful as my love of earth, and this was rain. I was a sun-worshipper, naturally, as most children are, and my pleasure was, on fine summer days, to sit unprotected in the glare, upturning my face to the sky: a habit that continued through most of my life, until, a year or two ago, I began to prefer the shade. But my love for rain was different in kind: with more of equality in it, more of something joint. I loved the rain on my face as, going out of the breakfast-room door on an autumn night, I would stand for a time in the garden and look up to the sky and sniff the quiet air; but most of all I loved it at its point of meeting with earth, and with earth's common coverings—pavements in London, and grass and trees in gardens and parks and in what little country I knew. I loved morning dew, glistening leaves after torrents of rain, and pavements that dried, to a smell of stone, when a summer shower was over; and often I would watch as the circle of wetness—deep at the centre and thin on the edges—grew ever smaller and smaller, until suddenly, as if caught up into the air, the last little sixpenny had vanished. . . .

I loved everything young: tightly packed buds that struggled to open; and my own birthday month of April—the smell, in particular, of garden mould as evening came on after sunshine and shower. The smell, too, of privet leaves, crushed between the fingers, from roadside hedges in London gardens. And sweeping winds. And ice and snow. And autumn mists—these especially—touched with gold. And cut grass. And hay. And poppies. All seasons, all weathers.

I loved the spiritual solidity of things. I felt joy, I mean, at the existence, the life, of solid objects, joy because the objects were *there*: things like fenders and mantelpieces and walls; and my father's safe; and large thick books; and a table that stood in our nursery, with a rough deal top and "mahogany" legs. Not that I

136

didn't like small things too; I remember my feeling of happiness as I watched a scrap of paper, in a classroom, go fluttering to the floor. But that was a joy in movement; my joy in these solider things was a joy in thereness.

V. G.

. . . Those recollected hours that have the charm
Of visionary things, those lovely forms
And sweet sensations that throw back our life,
And almost make remotest infancy
A visible scene, on which the sun is shining . . .

WORDSWORTH

A walk. The atmosphere incredibly pure—a warm, caressing gentleness in the sunshine—joy in one's whole being. . . . Forgotten impressions of childhood and youth came back to me—all those indescribable effects wrought by colour, shadow, sunlight, green hedges, and songs of birds, upon the soul just opening to poetry. I became again young, wondering, and simple, as candour and ignorance are simple. I abandoned myself to life and to nature, and they cradled me with an infinite gentleness. To open one's heart in purity to this ever pure nature, to allow this immortal life of things to penetrate into one's soul, is at the same time to listen to the voice of God. Sensation may be a prayer, and self-abandonment an act of devotion.

AMIEL

§ 9

The praises of the sick and the broken excuse the silence of the healthy and whole.

RABBI MOSHE HAKOTUN

SAINT FRANCIS SPEAKS TO THE LEPERS

Dost thou not see the sun shine? Canst thou not taste the air? Do not our ears tell us that the whole world is alive? Does not the earth give forth scent after rain? Is there no fragrance in flowers and herbs? Is not that a bird singing? Man's senses are a palace wherein all these do minister. Aye, though this gate be locked, they enter to give you joy. Wheresoever the eye travels, yonder it finds

137

greeting; and where it goes there we go also. See, Brothers, there are birds; and yonder are woods and mountains; and thereunder lies Assisi. Ye have not forgotten Assisi. And that which ye have in your hearts is yours still.

IN A HOUSMAN PLAY

THE VESTURE OF THE SOUL

I pitied one whose tattered dress
Was patched, and stained with dust and rain;
He smiled on me; I could not guess
The viewless spirit's wide domain.

He said, "The royal robe I wear
Trails all along the fields of light:
Its silent blue and silver bear
For gems the starry dust of night.

"The breath of Joy unceasingly
Waves to and fro its folds starlit,
And far beyond earth's misery
I live and breathe the joy of it."

A. E.

CHARLES

He was born blind with the snow on a winter's day;
The moon blank as marble stared at him from the full,
But his mother wept to see the vacant rolling of his eyes;
His father dared not look and despairingly turned away
When hands like feelers fumbled in space to pull
Fingers and lips to upturned face to recognize.
Growing older he sat in the dark learning voices by heart,
Carried on conversations with birds singing in summer trees,
Heard brooks changing their sound at floodtime, the angled dart
Of dazzled bats diving through twilight air.
But music played by wandering band or organ at the fair
Moved him to tears and fingers to invisible keys,
So that at twenty-five he began to drown the village church
With ceaseless tides of Handel, Bach and Mendelssohn,

138

And magnified the Lord for seven-and-thirty years.
With egg-shaped head he sat upright upon his perch,
Praying on flute we might depart in peace,
Triumphant came from Egypt on the bombardon,
Made thunderstorms at will, stars race like charioteers,
Captivity to turn, the harvest to increase;
He brought sweet healing to the troubled mind,
Fearlessly opened the eyes of the blind.

LEONARD CLARK

HALT, MAIMED AND IMPOTENT

Halt, maimed and impotent, still travelling on,
O'er very Eye of Earth they made their way,
Till rimmed into the east the risen sun
Flooding its orbit with the joy of day—

That Eye of Heaven, mansion of secret light,
Whose beams of all that's lovely are the shrine,
Procreant, puissant, arbiter of Sight,
Emblem and symbol of the light divine—

So brilliant the least flaw beneath their feet
A tiny shadow cast where nought there was
Taller than locust in the rilling heat
To check the splendour of this sea of glass.

And if pure radiance could pure music be,
And quiet supreme its tabernacle were,
This orb, now blazing in its majesty,
With a sublime Hosanna rent the air.

Moved by an impulse beyond wit to scan,
His poor rags stirring in a fitful breeze,
This worn, outwearied, errant son of man
Paused, bowed his head, fell down upon his knees;

And, with a faint and lamentable cry,
Poured hoarsely forth a babble of praise and prayer,
Sun on his brows, above the boundless sky,
No living soul to hear or heed him there. . . .

WALTER DE LA MARE (from The Traveller)

She would not go to bed, certainly not, but hot drinks—yes; and a hot bath—yes; and a complete change—yes. Drinks and baths and changes were exquisite delights in themselves; part of an existence in which one beauty was always providing a reason and a place for an entirely opposite beauty. As society for solitude, and walking for sitting down, and one dress for another, and emotions for intellect, and snowstorms for hot drinks, and in general movement for repose, repose for movement, and even one movement for another, so highly complex was the admirable order of the created universe.

CHARLES WILLIAMS (from *The Greater Trumps*)

I have had to compose a symphony for the opening of the Concert Spirituel. It was performed on Corpus Christi day with great applause. . . . I was so happy that as soon as it was over I went off to the Palais Royal, where I had a large ice.

MOZART (*to his father*)

And on one occasion, in this long dissolving year, I remember that I boarded a London bus from a district I have forgotten, and where I certainly could have been up to little good, to an appointment that I did not want to keep.

It was a shooting green spring morning, nimble and crocus, with all the young women treading on naked flower-stalks, the metropolitan sward, swinging their milk-pail handbags, gentle, fickle, inviting, accessible, forgiving each robustly abandoned gesture of salutation before it was made or imagined, assenting, as they revelled demurely towards the manicure *salon* or the typewriting office, to all the ardent unspoken endearments of shaggy strangers and the winks and pipes of clovenfooted sandwichmen. The sun shrilled, the buses gambolled, policemen and daffodils bowed in the breeze that tasted of buttermilk. Delicate carousal plashed and babbled from the public-houses which were not yet open. I felt like a young god. I removed my collar-studs and opened my shirt. I tossed back my hair. There was an aviary in my heart, but without any owls or eagles. My cheeks were cherried warm, I smelt, I thought, of sea-pinks. To the sound of madrigals sung by slim sopranos in waterfalled valleys where I was the only tenor, I leapt on to a bus. The bus was full. Carefree, open-collared, my eyes alight, my veins full of the spring as a dancer's shoes should be full of champagne, I stood, in love and at ease and always young, on the packed lower deck. And a man of exactly my own age—or perhaps he was a little older—got up and offered me his seat. He said, in a respectful voice, as though to an old justice of the peace, 'Please, won't you take my seat?' and then he added—'Sir.'

DYLAN THOMAS

And we gathered together all the spades and buckets and towels, empty hampers and bottles, umbrellas and fish-frails, bats and balls and knitting, and went—oh, listen, Dad!—to the fair in the dusk on the bald seaside field.

Fairs were no good in the day; then they were shoddy and tired; the voices of hoop-la girls were crimped as elocutionists; no cannon-ball could shake the roosting coco-nuts; the gondolas mechanically repeated their sober lurch; the Wall of Death was safe as a governess cart; the wooden animals were waiting for the night.

But in the night, the hoop-la girls, like operatic crows, croaked at the coming moon; whizz, whirl, and ten for a tanner, the coco-nuts rained from their sawdust like grouse from the Highland sky; tipsy the griffin-prowed gondolas weaved on dizzy rails and the Wall of Death was a spinning rim of ruin, and the neighing wooden horses took, to a haunting hunting tune, a thousand Becher's Brooks as easily and breezily as hooved swallows. . . .

All the fun of the fair in the hot, bubbling night. The Man in the sand-yellow moon over the hurdy of gurdies. The swing-boats swimming to and fro like slices of the moon. Dragons and hippo-griffs at the prows of the gondolas breathing fire and Sousa. Mid-night roundabout riders tantivying under the fairy-lights, hunts-men on billygoats and zebras hallooing under a circle of glow-worms.

And as we climbed home, up the gas-lit hill, to the still homes over the mumbling bay, we heard the music die and the voices drift like sand. And we saw the lights of the fair fade. And, at the far end of the seaside field, they lit their lamps, one by one, in the caravans.

DYLAN THOMAS

Lend me your great sound, your great pace so smooth, your nightly glide across lighted Europe, O train de luxe! and the anguished

141

music that sounds along your corridors of gilded leather while behind the lacquered doors, with their locks of heavy brass, sleep the millionaires.

I sing through your corridors and I follow you to Vienna and to Budapest, mingling my voice with your hundred thousand voices, O Harmonika-Zug!

I felt for the first time all the joy of life in a carriage of the Nord-Express, between Wirballen and Pskow. We were gliding through meadows where, under clumps of great trees like hills, the shepherds were clad in sheepskins dirty and uncured. . . . (Eight o'clock of an autumn morning the fair diva with the violet eyes was singing in the carriage that lay next door to mine.)

And you great windows through which I saw Siberia pass and the mountains of Samnium, Castile bleak and flowerless, and, in a warm rain, the Sea of Marmora.

Lend me, O Orient-Express, Sud-Brenner-Bahn, lend me your mysterious deep noises and your vibrant tones of a violin; lend me the light and easy breathing of those engines tall and slender with their untrammelled motion; of those express engines that effortless precede four yellow coaches lettered all in gold into the Serbian mountain solitudes and beyond, through the roses of Bulgaria.

Ah! Those sounds, that movement must penetrate my poems and tell for me my inexpressible life, the life of a child who would know nothing but to hope eternally for indefinable things.

VALERY LARBAUD

§ 11

Look thy last on all things lovely,
Every hour. Let no night
Seal thy sense in deathly slumber
    Till to delight
Thou have paid thy utmost blessing;
Since that all things thou wouldst praise
Beauty took from those who loved them
    In other days.

WALTER DE LA MARE

Beauty crowds me till I die,
Beauty, mercy have on me!
But if I expire today,
Let it be in sight of thee.

EMILY DICKINSON

It may be, that we cease; we cannot tell.
Even if we cease, life is a miracle.

MASEFIELD

Coda:
in praise of places

JERUSALEM IN ENGLAND

The fields from Islington to Marybone,
To Primrose Hill and Saint John's Wood,
    Were builded over with pillars of gold,
And there Jerusalem's pillars stood.

    Her Little-ones ran on the fields,
The Lamb of God among them seen,
    And fair Jerusalem his Bride,
Among the little meadows green.

    Pancrass & Kentish-town repose
Among her golden pillars high,
    Among her golden arches which
Shine upon the starry sky.

    The Jew's-harp-house & the Green Man,
The Ponds where Boys to bathe delight,
    The fields of Cows by Willan's farm,
Shine in Jerusalem's pleasant sight.

    She walks upon our meadows green,
The Lamb of God walks by her side,
    And every English Child is seen
Children of Jesus & his Bride.

BLAKE

THE ROAD TO OXFORD

Yet another few miles, every reach, every bending,
Each hollow and hole known and dropped in our flight,
Up the steep pitch of bridge, down the swerved slope descending,
Then over the rails, to the first Oxford light.

Then slow, through the long shiny way growing brighter
The trees of St. Giles's, the lines of parked cars;
The turn for the Broad and the turn for the Mitre,
And Folly Bridge river reflecting the stars. . . .

MASEFIELD (from *The Long Drive—Edinburgh to Boar's Hill*)

OXFORD

Over, the four long years! And now there rings
One voice of freedom and regret: *Farewell!*
Now old remembrance sorrows, and now sings:
But song from sorrow, now, I cannot tell.

City of weather'd cloister and worn court;
Grey city of strong towers and clustering spires:
Where art's fresh loveliness would first resort;
Where lingering art kindled her latest fires!

Where on all hands, wondrous with ancient grace,
Grace touch'd with age, rise works of goodliest men:
Next Wykeman's art obtain their splendid place
The zeal of Inigo, the strength of Wren.

Where at each coign of every antique street,
A memory hath taken root in stone:
There, Raleigh shone; there, toil'd Franciscan feet;
There, Johnson flinch'd not, but endured alone.

There, Shelley dream'd his white Platonic dreams;
There, classic Landor throve on Roman thought;
There, Addison pursued his quiet themes;
There, smiled Erasmus, and there, Colet taught.

And there, O memory more sweet than all!
Lived he, whose eyes keep yet our passing light;
Whose crystal lips Athenian speech recall;
Who wears Rome's purple with least pride, most right.

That is the Oxford strong to charm us yet:
Eternal in her beauty and her past.
What, though her soul be vex'd? She can forget
Cares of an hour: only the great things last.

Only the gracious air, only the charm,
And ancient might of true humanities,
These nor assault of man, nor time, can harm:
Not these, nor Oxford with her memories.

Together have we walk'd with willing feet
Gardens of plenteous trees, bowering soft lawn;
Hills whither Arnold wander'd; and all sweet
June meadows, from the troubling world withdrawn;

Chapels of cedarn fragrance, and rich gloom
Pour'd from empurpled panes on either hand;
Cool pavements, carved with legends of the tomb;
Grave haunts, where we might dream, and understand.

Over, the four long years! And unknown powers
Call to us, going forth upon our way:
Ah! Turn we, and look back upon the towers
That rose above our lives, and cheer'd the day.

Proud and serene, against the sky they gleam:
Proud and secure, upon the earth they stand.
Our city hath the air of a pure dream,
And hers indeed is a Hesperian land.

Think of her so! The wonderful, the fair,
The immemorial, and the ever young:
The city sweet with our forefathers' care:
The city where the Muses all have sung.

Ill times may be; she hath no thought of time:
She reigns beside the waters yet in pride.
Rude voices cry: but in her ears the chime
Of full sad bells brings back her old springtide.

Like to a queen in pride of place, she wears
The splendour of a crown in Radcliffe's dome.
Well fare she—well! As perfect beauty fares,
And those high places that are beauty's home.

LIONEL JOHNSON

BIBURY

Kelmscott
Lechlade
August 8th [1890]

My Dear Kate

I will now write you a letter since I have not been able to see
you. Nothing very exciting has happened here since I came last
Friday. The weather has been very fine all along, Wednesday being
the hottest day. We chose that day for a solemn expedition in a
waggonette & pair . . . We went through Fairford up the valley
of the Colne, through Quennington, Coln St. Aldwyn's, Bibury,

Ablington, Winson, Colne Roger, Colne St. Denis and Fosse Bridge . . . Bibury is surely the most beautiful village in England; lying down in the winding valley beside the clear Colne . . . The whole valley is a mass of lime-stone, and looks indeed as if it had been made for people 4 ft high; but small as the scale is, it is most lovely . . .

I am now going out fishing with Ellis up to Buscott; & to say truth I would rather stroll about the garden this lovely fresh morning; but I really dare not propose a rest from the almost professional pursuit of fish which Ellis follows here: so to it I shall go. The hay is all cut now and the fields are most beautifully green, and the wide spreading meadows as lovely as anything can be . . .

Goodbye my dear Kate

Yours

William Morris

THE SOUTH BANK, LONDON

Go to the South Bank first by day; the rest of your times at night. Sit at a café table in the night of musical lights, by the radiant river, the glittering skylon above you rearing to be off, the lit pavilion, white, black, and silver in sweeps of stone and feathery steel, transplendent round you as you sip and think:

This is the first time I have ever truly seen that London whose sweet Thames runs softly; that minstrel mermaid of a town, the water-streeted eight-million-headed village in a blaze. *This* is London. . . . The arches of the bridges leap into light; the moon clocks glow; the river sings; the harmonious pavilions are happy. And this is what London should always be like, till St Paul's falls down and the sea slides over the Strand.

DYLAN THOMAS

PARIS

But after all I am in Paris. Almost the same Paris; almost the same George Moore, my senses awake as before to all enjoyment, my soul as enrapt as ever in the divine sensation of life. Once my youth moved through thy whiteness, O City, and its dreams lay down to dream in the freedom of thy fields! Years come and years go, but every year I see city and plain in the happy exaltation of spring, and departing before the cuckoo, while the blossom is still bright on the bough, it has come to me to think that Paris and May are one.

GEORGE MOORE

NEW YORK

We had a little apartment on the nineteenth floor of the Beverly Hotel, which is where 50th Street meets Lexington: and every morning, if I was not up too early and if it was fine—as it usually was, for often I might have been back in the bamboo lanes near Singapore, so blessedly tropical was the weather—I would stand at our bedroom window, which looked east, or rather a little north-east, straight down Lexington, and would watch the sun come up on my right. The Lexington lights would still be on, stretching almost endlessly to the horizon: and one suddenly saw oneself, back in the middle thirties, motoring, one might have imagined for ever, down a Roman road in France . . .

But what was to follow was more beautiful still—especially when the autumn mists were heavy. Gradually, as the sun rose, a broad and massive battlement, softened and mysterious, would appear in the sky to the right of Lexington; for the impression there was not of individual buildings—though an airy garage would always catch my eye—but of a rolling, curving mountain mass. Meanwhile, on the other side of Lexington, two or three dim pinnacles would be rising, with a beautifully strong grace, out of the sea of mist that bathed their lower parts; and then something ancient would revive in me, and for a moment I would be back—I had the same vivid fantasy morning after morning—amid the bastions, the hanging gardens and the ziggurats of a romanticised Babylon.

When the sun was up I would go into the sitting-room, and look for a moment, from the northern window, at Rockefeller Centre; and here I was back in another experience, for I might have been watching as I had been used, so long before, to watch—through Tuscan daybreaks by the Giotto Tower . . .

These were our American dawns. And the sunsets! Whenever we could, we would hurry back home before daylight had gone: and would sit for some moments facing northward, as the green lights came out in the slim skyey columns against a background of fading rose. This was fairyland; and often, at moments such as these, the heartache as for something absent was stilled. . . .

V. G.

THE WATERSHED

LINES WRITTEN BETWEEN MUNICH AND VERONA

Black mountains pricked with pointed pine
  A melancholy sky.
Out-distanced was the German vine,
  The sterile fields lay high.
From swarthy Alps I travelled forth
Aloft; it was the north, the north;
  Bound for the Noon was I.

I seemed to breast the streams that day;
  I met, opposed, withstood
The northward rivers on their way,
  My heart against the flood—
My heart that pressed to rise and reach,
And felt the love of altering speech,
  Of frontiers, in its blood.

But O the unfolding South! the burst
  Of summer! O to see
Of all the southward brooks the first!
  The travelling heart went free
With endless streams; that strife was stopped;
And down a thousand vales I dropped,
  I flowed to Italy.

ALICE MEYNELL

ROME

The history of Rome is drenched in blood and blackened with crime; yet all that seemed to be left now was the peace of memory. As we wandered about the Forum we could not summon up the blood-stained ghosts; they had quite gone, bleached by centuries into a luminous transparency, or evaporated into the bright still air. Their works were there, but these cast only the ordinary shadow which everything set up by mankind gathers at its foot. The grass in the courtyard of the Temple of the Vestals seemed to be drenched in peace down to the very root, and it was easy to imagine gods and men still in friendly talk together there.

EDWIN MUIR

152

FLORENCE

I had often been about for hours before breakfast. I would get up while it was still dark and go down to the Duomo. As the sun rose, the tower became lovelier even than Giotto had made it: all airy and transparent, it glowed like a piece of the rose-quartz that had given me so much pleasure when, as a boy of nine or ten, I had formed my little collection of minerals and rocks. The steps of the Cathedral itself had disappeared beneath the hillock of flowers, brought in by the market women, that rose against the marbled façade to the height of a man. The smell and the look of them in the morning air were as sweet to my senses as anything I had experienced before or have experienced since; not even sunrise in Venice, or flying into London on a summer night when all the lamps are lit, has seemed more beautiful.

And when I got back to our balcony, itself still grey with the earliness of the dawn, the houses on the opposite bank would be a long unbroken stretch of flaming brown.

V. G.

ASSISI

And with the dawn Assisi
Shines in thine eyes, and all her windowed towers
And peering walls that climb, roof above roof,
Up the steep hill. Then the dim darkling streets
Awake, doors open, and the market hums,—
And there's Assisi—dancing!

ST. FRANCIS (in a Housman play)

MERAN

It was the dead season at Meran, and we were alone in the gigantic hotel. But the town was most beautiful—more beautiful, I thought, than any small place I had ever been in, except perhaps Bibury or Winchelsea. The day we had intended to spend there lengthened into a week and then into a fortnight. In the early morning, before breakfast, I would walk barefoot on the hotel lawn, to feel the dew between my toes. For lunch we would sit alone at a little table on the veranda. In the afternoon we wandered in the cool shade of the pines down the long *Tapeiner-Weg*, or in the cobbled and arcaded streets; and at tea-time we paraded in the square for the town band, in the company of half Meran and (in patent-leather shoes) Sir Thomas Beecham. We would gladly have prolonged our stay there till winter, even at the cost of missing Salzburg.

V. G.

VENICE

. . . and, methinks growing young again, the opera we saw at Venice comes into my fancy, and I am ready to sing.

JOHN EVELYN

TORCELLO

But happiest of all, perhaps, was the first of many visits from Venice to Torcello. Apart from Santa Fosca and Santa Maria at the far end of it, there's really nothing "to" this little island; nothing but grass and a sort of canal and a very few uninteresting cottages. Then why did it delight me so when we chanced on it first in the twenties, and how did it happen that, as each subsequent visit to Venice loomed ahead, it was not the Piazza that I thought about most, or the tiny marble birds in the Miracoli, or Bellini's blue Madonna, or arriving by gondola at Verdi's Fenice, prettiest of opera-houses—but deserted Torcello? The reason must be, I think, that I cannot live without grass. Venice, which on a first visit, especially if the weather is grey, seems a trifle disappointing—such smells, such decay, such unseemly floating refuse in the world's fairyland!—draws you back to it more powerfully the better you know it, and ends by being irresistible. But after a few days you may see, as if with sudden rediscovery, a green plant or two on the roof of some building, or the shrubs in the courtyard of that one-storied, never-finished palazzo on the Grand Canal; and then you want grass, and you go to Torcello. We went, that first time, by vaporetto. In 1947, when we stayed for three weeks with a friend, the whole affair was more elaborate; we took a gondola with two gondoliers, and they sang their songs as the moon came up on the return journey and the lights of the Piazzetta appeared. I got to know one of these gondoliers well; he had once worked, if I understood him correctly, for Baron Corvo.

V. G.

LUCCA

Little Lucca.

MAX BEERBOHM

Another Coda:
in praise of married love

In three things I was beautified, and stood up beautiful before
the Lord and men: the concord of brethren, and friendship of
neighbours, and a woman and her husband that walk together in
agreement.

ECCLESIASTICUS

He went on with that fantasy, but at this point Kate ceased to
attend. He saw after a little that she had been following some
thought of her own, and he had been feeling the growth of something determinant even through the extravagance of much of the
pleasantry, the warm transparent irony, into which their livelier
intimacy kept plunging like a confident swimmer. Suddenly she said
to him with extraordinary beauty: "I engage myself to you for ever."
The beauty was in everything, and he could have separated
nothing—couldn't have thought of her face as distinct from the
whole joy. Yet her face had a new light. "And I pledge you—I call
God to witness!—every spark of my faith; I give you every drop of
my life." That was all, for the moment, but it was enough, and it
was almost as quiet as if it were nothing. They were in the open
air, in an alley of the Gardens; the great space, which seemed to
arch just then higher and spread wider for them, threw them back
into deep concentration. They moved by a common instinct to a
spot, within sight, that struck them as fairly sequestered, and there,
before their time together was spent, they had extorted from concentration every advance it could make them. They had exchanged
vows and tokens, sealed their rich compact, solemnised, so far as
breathed words and murmured sounds and lighted eyes and clasped
hands could do it, their agreement to belong only, and to belong
tremendously, to each other.

HENRY JAMES (from *The Wings of a Dove*)

§ 2

. . . all who joy would win
Must share it,—Happiness was born a twin.

BYRON

For Love is a celestiall harmonie,
Of likely harts composd of starres concent,
Which joyne together in sweet sympathie,
To work ech others joy and true content,

Which they have harbourd since their first descent
Out of their heavenly bowres, where they did see
And know ech other here belov'd to bee.

Then wrong it were that any other twaine
Should in loves gentle band combyned bee,
But those whom heaven did at first ordaine,
And made out of one mould the more t' agree:
For all that like the beautie which they see,
Streight do not love: for love is not so light,
As streight to burne at first beholders sight.

SPENSER

When essence meets with essence, and souls join
In mutual knots, that's the true nuptial twine.
Such, lady, is my love, and such is true:
All other love is to your sex, not you.

THOMAS RANDOLPH

[Man to Woman] Thou lovely Vision, this delightful Tree
Is given us for a Shelter from the tempests of Void and Solid,
Till once again the morn of ages shall renew upon us,
To reunite in those mild fields of happy Eternity
Where thou and I in undivided Essence walk'd about
Imbodied, thou my garden of delight and I the spirit in the garden;
Mutual there we dwelt in one another's joy, revolving
Days of Eternity . . .

BLAKE

§ 3

To be a person is to be essentially in search of a person.

M. C. D'ARCY

Thus as persons a married couple are a mutual creation, and to become persons is the double achievement of 'active love'.

M. C. D'ARCY

Mysterious is the fusion of two loving spirits: each takes the best from the other, but only to give it back again enriched with love.

ROMAIN ROLLAND

The mystery of love is the mystery of personality, which penetrates into another in a unique never-to-be-renewed identity. It is
the vision of another's image in God. Only the lover can contemplate the face of the beloved. The image of man is always
distorted and obscured for one who does not love. It is only
through love that we can see the beauty of the human face. Love
is not the confirmation of an identity, the discovery of a single
principle in myself and another—*tat twam asi*, as Indian thought
would have it. If "you" and "I" are but one then my love for you
is only the love of myself. There is no longer another being. The
loving subject and his love always imply the existence of another
and presuppose a going-out of the self towards this other person,
the mystery of the union of two beings who enjoy independent and
distinct reality.

BERDYAEV

> Why should your face so please me
> That if one little line should stray
> Bewilderment would seize me
> And drag me down the tortuous way
> Out of the noon into the night?
> But so, into this tranquil light
> You raise me. . . .

EDWIN MUIR

§ 4

To whom thus Eve, with perfect beauty adorned . . .
"Sweet is the breath of morn, her rising sweet,
With charm of earliest birds; pleasant the sun,
When first on this delightful land he spreads
His orient beams, on herb, tree, fruit, and flower,
Glistering with dew; fragrant the fertile earth
After soft showers; and sweet the coming on
Of grateful evening mild; then silent night,
With this her solemn bird, and this fair moon,
And these the gems of Heaven, her starry train:
But neither breath of morn, when she ascends
With charm of earliest birds; nor rising sun
On this delightful land; nor herb, fruit, flower,
Glistering with dew; nor fragrance after showers;

Nor grateful evening mild; nor silent night,
With this her solemn bird; nor walk by moon,
Or glittering starlight, without thee is sweet" . .
Thus talking, hand in hand alone they passed
On to their blissful bower. It was a place
Chosen by the sovereign Planter, when He framed
All things to man's delightful use. The roof
Of thickest covert was inwoven shade,
Laurel and myrtle, and what higher grew
Of firm and fragrant leaf; on either side
Acanthus, and each odorous bushy shrub,
Fenced up the verdant wall; each beauteous flower,
Iris all hues, roses, and jessamine,
Reared high their flourished heads between, and wrought
Mosaic; under foot the violet,
Crocus, and hyacinth, with rich inlay
Broidered the ground, more coloured than with stone
Of costliest emblem. Other creature here,
Beast, bird, insect, or worm, durst enter none;
Such was their awe of man . . .

        . . . Here, in close recess,
With flowers, garlands, and sweet-smelling herbs,
Espousèd Eve decked first her nuptial bed,
And heavenly choirs the hymenaean sung,
What day the genial angel to our sire
Brought her, in naked beauty more adorned,
More lovely, than Pandora, whom the gods
Endowed with all their gifts . . .

  Thus at their shady lodge arrived, both stood,
Both turned, and under open sky adored
The God that made both sky, air, earth, and heaven,
Which they beheld, the moon's resplendent globe,
And starry pole:—"Thou also madest the night,
Maker Omnipotent; and Thou the day,
Which we, in our appointed work employed,
Have finished, happy in our mutual help
And mutual love, the crown of all our bliss
Ordained by Thee; and this delicious place,
For us too large, where Thy abundance wants
Partakers, and uncropped falls to the ground.
But Thou hast promised from us two a race

To fill the earth, who shall with us extol
Thy goodness infinite, both when we wake,
And when we seek, as now, Thy gift of sleep."
　　This said unanimous, and other rites
Observing none, but adoration pure,
Which God likes best, into their inmost bower
Handed they went; and, eased the putting off
These troublesome disguises which we wear,
Straight side by side were laid; nor turned, I ween,
Adam from his fair spouse, nor Eve the rites
Mysterious of connubial love refused:
Whatever hypocrites austerely talk
Of purity, and place, and innocence,
Defaming as impure what God declares
Pure, and commands to some, leaves free to all.
Our Maker bids increase; who bids abstain
But our destroyer, foe to God and man?
Hail, wedded love, mysterious law, true source
Of human offspring, sole propriety
In Paradise of all things common else! . . .
These, lulled by nightingales, embracing slept,
And on their naked limbs the flowery roof
Showered roses, which the morn repaired. Sleep on,
Blest pair! and, O! yet happiest, if ye seek
No happier state, and know to know no more!
　　　　　　　　　MILTON (from *Paradise Lost*)

No mortal nature can endure, either in the actions of religion, or
study of wisdom, without sometime slackening the cords of intense
thought and labour, which lest we should think faulty, God Himself
conceals us not His own recreations before the world was built:
'I was,' saith the Eternal Wisdom, 'daily his delight, playing always
before him.' . . . We cannot always be contemplative, or prag-
matical abroad, but have need of some delightful intermissions
wherein the enlarged soul may leave off a while her severe schooling,
and, like a glad youth in wandering vacancy, may keep her holidays
to joy and harmless pastime; which as she cannot well do without
company, so in no company so well as where the different sex in
most resembling unlikeness, and most unlike resemblance, cannot
but please best and be pleased in the aptitude of that variety.
Whereof lest we should be too timorous, in the awe that our flat

sages would form us and dress us, wisest Solomon among his gravest proverbs countenances a kind of ravishment and erring fondness in the entertainment of wedded leisures; and in the Song of Songs, which is generally believed, even in the jolliest expressions, to figure the spousals of the Church with Christ, sings of a thousand raptures between those two lovely ones far on the hither side of carnal enjoyment.

MILTON

Conjugal delight, which is a purer and more exquisite delight of touch, surpasses all the rest on account of its use, which is the increase of the human race and thereby of the angels of heaven. These delights are in the organs of sense by reason of an influx from heaven, where every delight accompanies some use and varies according to its nature.

SWEDENBORG

Sex-love, if it is love at all, is a personal communion in which a man and a woman meet in the full integrity of their personal reality. And the law of reality in the relationship of persons is this: 'The integrity of persons is inviolable. You shall not use a person for your own ends, or indeed for any ends, individual or social. To use another person is to violate his personality by making an object of him; and in violating the integrity of another you violate your own.' In all enjoyment there is a choice between enjoying the other and enjoying yourself through the instrumentality of the other. The first is the enjoyment of love, the second is the enjoyment of lust. When people enjoy themselves through each other, that is merely mutual lust. They do not meet as persons at all; their reality is lost. They meet as ghosts of themselves and their pleasure is a ghostly pleasure that cannot begin to satisfy a human soul, and which only vitiates its capacity for reality.

JOHN MACMURRAY

And him thou lovest or her thou lovest—
If without confusion thou beholdest such one fixed like a star in heaven, and ever in thy most clinging burning passion rememberest Whom thou lovest,
Then art thou blessed beyond words, and thy love is surely eternal;
But if by confusion thou knowest not whom thou lovest—but

162

seest only the receptacle of desire which inhabits the world of change and suffering—

Then shalt thou be whirled and gulfed in a sea of torment, and shalt travel far and be many times lost upon that ocean before thou shalt know what is the true end of thy voyage.

EDWARD CARPENTER

And although copulation be considered among the ends of marriage, yet the act thereof in a right esteem can no longer be matrimonial, than it is an effect of conjugal love. When love finds itself utterly unmatched, and justly vanishes, nay, rather, cannot but vanish, the fleshly act indeed may continue, but not holy, not pure, not beseeming the sacred bond of marriage; being at best but an animal excretion, but more truly worse and more ignoble than that mute kindliness among the herds and flocks: in that proceeding as it ought from intellective principles, it participates of nothing rational, but that which the field and the fold equals. For in human actions the soul is the agent, the body in a manner passive.

MILTON

§ 5

The heart of her husband doth safely trust in her. . . .

PROVERBS

The form of marriage lies in an inseparable union of minds by which either is unalterably plighted to serve the other loyally.

ST. THOMAS AQUINAS

WIFE AND HUSBAND

There was even a minute, when her back was turned to him, during which she knew once more the strangeness of her desire to spare him, a strangeness that had already fifty times brushed her, in the depth of her trouble, as with the wild wing of some bird of the air who might blindly have swooped for an instant into the shaft of a well, darkening there by his momentary flutter the far-off round of sky. It was extraordinary, this quality in the taste of her wrong which made her completed sense of it seem rather to soften than to harden, and it was the more extraordinary the more she had to recognise it; for what it came to was that seeing herself finally sure

163

[of his having wronged her], knowing everything, having the fact, in all its abomination, so utterly before her that there was nothing else to add—what it came to was that merely by being *with* him there in silence she felt within her the sudden split between conviction and action. They had begun to cease on the spot, surprisingly, to be connected; conviction, that is, budged no inch, only planting its feet the more firmly in the soil—but action began to hover like some lighter and larger but easier form, excited by its very power to keep above ground. It would be free, it would be independent, it would go in—wouldn't it?—for some prodigious and superior adventure of its own. What would condemn it, so to speak, to the responsibility of freedom—this glimmered on Maggie even now—was the possibility, richer with every lapsing moment, that her husband would have on the whole question a new need of her, a need which was in fact being born between them in these very seconds. It struck her truly as so new that he would have felt hitherto none to compare with it at all; would indeed absolutely by this circumstance be *really* needing her for the first time in their whole connexion. No, he had used her, he had even exceedingly enjoyed her, before this; but there had been no precedent for that character of proved necessity to him which she was rapidly taking on.

HENRY JAMES (from *The Golden Bowl*)

TAMINO COMES THROUGH THE FIRE

And so screaming, they brought him, more dead than alive, to the prison, and shut him up without trial or judgment.

So there Tamino sat alone, with scanty food and drink, no sight of the sky, and no company but his own thoughts. These were confused enough. For, besides all he had felt and seen, at the war and after, he had been hurt by the mob in that last tumult, and no physician came to aid him. He grew weaker and weaker and more and more confused. His thoughts became more actual than the walls of his cell, but they had no order, nor could he impose one on them. One moment he would be fighting and killing, the next, a child among the haycocks, then drinking with his friends, till they turned into snarling curs or screaming parrots. So it went on, till at last all images fused in a dark flood, that bore him along through passages underground. On and on, for immeasurable time, uniform, colourless, it flowed, and then, at last, began to turn. He was in a whirlpool, falling faster and faster, deeper and deeper. Till suddenly, turning with him, he saw the featureless face, whence the eyes of an enemy-friend had looked out at him on the battlefield. He screamed and put out his hands to keep it off him. And something in him, not himself, and deeper than himself, cried through his lips the name "Pamina".

Ah then, if ever, after toil, there has been rest; if ever after torture, recreation; if ever after quarrel, friends have met in reconcilement; if ever lovers mingled after absence; such rest, such recreation, such reconcilement sweet dropped like a balm, blew like a breeze, and like a perfume distilled, over Tamino's worn and broken spirit. There he was, back in his cell, and there indeed, beside him, hovered in her loveliness, her tenderness, her plenitude of consoling beauty, that long lost, long loved, late forgotten lady. What she ministered to him he knew not; but that proceeded from her eyes which restored his mind and body to themselves. He gazed upon her with no desire, but with love for a lovely thing, that draws the soul because it has its principle of being in itself, and would please no more if it came into the power of another. And he stood on his feet, young again, and beautiful and strong, and Pamina put his flute into his hand and said "Play". And he played, and the flute sang what follows:

> Fade like a wraith, dissolve and pass away,
>   Unsolid wall, the image of his fear;
> And thou, bright spirit, the barrier and the way,
>   Appear! Appear!

> Thee let him see, who dost his prison make,
>   Only by acquiescence of his soul,
> Whom he escapes, when he his flesh shall take,
>   And cast it in thee whole.

> Before him passes, through the grove of fire,
>   What he must follow, though he never find,
> Or, shrinking, feed a perishing desire,
>   And sacrifice the mind.

> What drives within, deeper than all he wills,
>   What draws without, fairer than aught he knows,
> Than choice more strong, more cunning than all skills,
>   Shall keep him where he goes.

And as the flute thus sang, the wall of his cell went up in fire.

And Pamina looked at him and smiled, and saying "Follow me" passed through. And, still playing, he followed, though he was full of fear. And fearful indeed it was! For he felt the heat, though it did not consume him, and his flesh would fain have drawn back. But the soul was merciless and drove the body on. And as he passed through, to comfort him, the flute thus answered the fire:

> *Fire.* "I crackle and blaze!
>   Bear me who can!
>   Who cannot I craze—"
> *Flute.* "But I am a man."
> *Fire.* "What most you cherish
>   I burn away.
>   Be purged, or perish!"
> *Flute.* "I pass and pay."
> *Fire.* "No gain I offer
>   For all that's lost,
>   No prizes proffer—"
> *Flute.* "I know the cost."
> *Fire.* "What I take, I hold,
>   The rest resign.
>   And the tested gold—"
> *Flute.* "Ah, that is mine!"

So Tamino came through the fire.

G. LOWES DICKINSON (from *The Magic Flute*)

§ 6

TO HIS WIFE

Love, let us live as we have lived, nor lose
    The little names that were the first night's grace,
And never come the day that sees us old,
    I still your lad, and you my little lass.
Let me be older than old Nestor's years,
    And you the Sibyl, if we heed it not.
What should we know, we two, of ripe old age?
    We'll have its richness, and the years forgot.

AUSONIUS (*tr. by Waddell*)

166

SPIRITUAL LOVE

What care I tho' beauty fading
    Die ere Time can turn his glass?
What tho' locks the Graces braiding
    Perish like the summer grass?
      Tho' thy charms should all decay,
      Think not my affections may!

For thy charms—tho' bright as morning—
    Captured not my idle heart;
Love so grounded ends in scorning,
    Lacks the barb to hold the dart.
      My devotion more secure
      Woos thy spirit high and pure.

WILLIAM CALDWELL ROSCOE

THEY THAT LOVE BEYOND THE WORLD

They that love beyond the world cannot be separated by it.

Death cannot kill what never dies.

Nor can spirits ever be divided that love and live in the same Divine Principle, the root and record of their friendship.

If absence be not death, neither is theirs.

Death is but crossing the world, as friends do the seas; they live in one another still.

For they must needs be present, that love and live in that which is omnipresent.

In this Divine glass they see face to face; and their converse is free as well as pure.

This is the comfort of friends, that though they may be said to die, yet their friendship and society are in the best sense ever present, because immortal.

WILLIAM PENN

THE WORD

My friend, my bonny friend, when we are old,
    And hand in hand go tottering down the hill,
May we be rich in love's refinèd gold,
    May love's gold coin be current with us still.

May love be sweeter for the vanished days,
    And your most perfect beauty still as dear
As when your troubled singer stood at gaze
    In the dear March of a most sacred year.

May what we are be all we might have been,
    And that potential, perfect, O my friend,
And may there still be many sheafs to glean
    In our love's acre, comrade, till the end.

And may we find when ended is the page
Death but a tavern on our pilgrimage.

MASEFIELD

SECOND PART

I. THE UNITY

Then Vidagdha Sakalya asked him: 'How many gods are there, O Yajnavalkya?' He replied with this very Nivid: 'As many as are mentioned in the Nivid of the hymn of praise addressed to the Visvedevas, viz. three and three hundred, three and three thousand.'

'Yes,' he said, and asked again: 'How many gods are there really, O Yajnavalkya?'

'Thirty-three,' he said.

'Yes,' he said, and asked again: 'How many gods are there really, O Yajnavalkya?'

'Six,' he said.

'Yes,' he said, and asked again: 'How many gods are there really, O Yajnavalkya?'

'Three,' he said.

'Yes,' he said, and asked again: 'How many gods are there really, O Yajnavalkya?'

'Two,' he said.

'Yes,' he said, and asked again: 'How many gods are there really, O Yajnavalkya?'

'One and a half,' he said.

'Yes,' he said, and asked again: 'How many gods are there really, O Yajnavalkya?'

'One,' he said.

BRIHADARANYAKA UPANISHAD

To all things common and in all things known,
Yet incommunicable and alone.

ORPHIC HYMN

Indivisible, but as if divided in beings.

THE BHAGAVAD-GITA

And we must dare to affirm that the Creator, by reason of love, is drawn from his transcendent throne above all things to dwell within the heart of all things, while he yet stays within himself.

DIONYSIUS THE AREOPAGITE

What happy wonder, what blessed abashment may we reckon that to be, that taketh the souls, which come to have a sight of the heavenly beauty? what sweet flame? What sweet incense may a man believe that to be, which ariseth of the fountain of the sovereign and right beauty? Which is the original of all other beauty, which never encreaseth nor diminisheth, always beautiful, and of itself, as well on the one part as on the other, most simply, onely like itself, and partner of none other, but in such wise beautiful, that all other beautiful things be beautiful, because they be partners of the beauty of it.

CASTIGLIONE

The Spiritual Universe, the Realm of the Divine Mind—beautiful; the most beautiful of all; lying lapped in pure light and in clear radiance; the original of which this beautiful world is a shadow and an image; tranquil in the fullness of glory since in it there is nothing devoid of intellect, nothing dark or out of rule; a living thing in a life of blessedness—This must overwhelm with awe any that has seen it, and penetrated it, to become a unit of it.

But: as one that looks up to the heavens and sees the splendour of the stars thinks of the Maker and searches, so whoever has contemplated the Spiritual Universe and known it and wondered for it must search after its Maker too. What Being has raised so noble a fabric? And where? And how? Who has begotten such a child, this Realm of the Divine Mind, this lovely abundance so abundantly endowed?

The Source of all this cannot be a Mind; nor can it be an abundant power: it must have been before Mind and abundance were; these are later and things of lack; abundance had to be made abundant and Mind needed to know.

These are very near to the un-needing, to that which has no need of knowing; they have abundance and knowledge authentically, as being the first to possess. But there is That before them which neither needs nor possesses anything, since, needing or possessing anything else, it would not be what it is—The Father, The One, The Good, The Unconditioned Divine.

PLOTINUS

When therefore you seek to state or to conceive Him, put all else aside; abstracting all, keep solely to Him; see that you add nothing; be sure that your theory of God does not lessen Him. Even you are able to take contact with Something in which there is no more than That Thing itself to affirm and know, Something which lies away above all and is—it alone—veritably free, subject not even to its own law, solely and essentially That One Thing, while all else is thing and something added.

PLOTINUS

172

Before Heaven and Earth existed, from the beginning Tao was there. It is Tao that gave ghosts their holy power, that gave holy power to Dead Kings. It gave life to Heaven, gave life to Earth. It can mount above the Pole-star without becoming high; it can sink below [the Springs of Death] without becoming deep. It existed before Heaven and Earth, yet has no duration; its age is greater than that of the Longest Ago, yet it does not grow old.

Without it Heaven could not be high, Earth could not be wide, the sun and moon could not stay their course, the ten thousand things could not flourish.

CHUANG TZU (tr. by Waley)

Suddenly the cloud opened, Sinai tore out its roots from the wilderness, and, hurtling into the firmament, its broad summit came to rest beneath the flaming feet and flaming wings of the Four Beasts: the Four Beasts, with the heads of a man, of a lion, of an eagle, and of a bull, harnessed to the many-eyed wheels that revolve like Suns beneath the Chariot whose splendour bore the Throne, whose splendour bore the Splendour of the Lord. And all about, twice sixty myriads of angels, each one of whom bore a girdle of glory and a crown of glory for each one of the children of Israel, cried out unceasingly: "Holy, Holy, Holy is the Lord of Sabaoth: the whole world is full of His glory."

But of a sudden, as God was about to speak, there was silence in all the universe. Not an ox lowed in all the earth, not a bird twittered in all the skies, the waters ceased their murmur, the flames their crackling; the thunder was muted, every echo was dumb; the wings of the Cherubim ceased to beat, and the mouths of the Seraphim to sing: in order that, in the silence of all things, all things might know that outside God naught Is.

EDMOND FLEG (from a Midrash)

§ 2

We are all come from Zeus.

HOMER

Full of Zeus are all the streets and all the market-places of men.

ARATUS

173

We are enclosed in the Father, and we are enclosed in the Son, and we are enclosed in the Holy Ghost. And the Father is enclosed in us, and the Son is enclosed in us, and the Holy Ghost is enclosed in us: Almightiness, All Wisdom, All Goodness: one God, one Lord.

JULIANA OF NORWICH

We are all strings in the concert of His joy; the spirit from His mouth strikes the note and tune of our strings.

BOEHME

If thou conceivest a small minute circle, as small as a grain of mustard seed, yet the Heart of God is wholly and perfectly therein: and if thou art born in God, then there is in thyself (in the circle of thy life) the whole Heart of God undivided.

BOEHME

Is not everything Brahman when the name and the form have been removed from it?

THE VEDANTA

Every creature visible and invisible may be called a Theophany or manifestation of the Divine.

ERIGENA

'Why for fear of that,' he answered, 'you will remember that what is seen in you is present in all, and that the beauty of every other living creature is as bright as yours.'

CHARLES WILLIAMS

And this immortal and perfect soul must be the same in the highest God as well as in the humblest man, the difference between them being only in the degree in which this soul manifests itself.

VIVEKANANDA

KRISHNA

I paused beside the cabin door and saw the King of Kings at play,
Tumbled upon the grass I spied the little heavenly runaway.
The mother laughed upon the child made gay by its ecstatic morn,
And yet the sages spake of It as of the Ancient and Unborn.

I heard the passion breathed amid the honeysuckle scented glade,
And saw the King pass lightly from the beauty that he had betrayed.
I saw him pass from love to love; and yet the pure allowed His
claim
To be the purest of the pure, thrice holy, stainless, without blame.
I saw the open tavern door flash on the dusk a ruddy glare,
And saw the King of Kings outcast reel brawling through the starlit
air.
And yet He is the Prince of Peace of whom the ancient wisdom
tells,
And by their silence men adore the lovely silence where He dwells.
I saw the King of Kings again, a thing to shudder at and fear,
A form so darkened and so marred that childhood fled if it drew
near.
And yet He is the Light of Lights whose blossoming is Paradise,
That Beauty of the King which dawns upon the seers' enraptured
eyes.
I saw the King of Kings again, a miser with a heart grown cold,
And yet He is the Prodigal, the Spendthrift of the Heavenly Gold,
The largesse of whose glory crowns the blazing brows of cherubim,
And sun and moon and stars and flowers are jewels scattered forth
by Him.
I saw the King of Kings descend the narrow doorway to the dust
With all his fires of morning still, the beauty, bravery, and lust.
And yet He is the life within the Ever-living Living Ones,
The ancient with eternal youth, the cradle of the infant suns,
The fiery fountain of the stars, and He the golden urn where all
The glittering spray of planets in their myriad beauty fall.

A. E.

FROM "LAST LINES"

O God within my breast,
Almighty, ever-present Deity!
Life—that in me has rest,
As I—undying Life—have power in Thee! . . .

With wide-embracing love
Thy Spirit animates eternal years,
Pervades and broods above,
Changes, sustains, dissolves, creates, and rears.

Though earth and man were gone,
And suns and universes ceased to be,
And Thou were left alone,
Every existence would exist in Thee.

There is not room for Death,
Nor atom that his might could render void:
Thou—Thou art Being and Breath,
And what Thou art may never be destroy'd.

EMILY BRONTË

§ 3

He is all contradictions.

VIVEKANANDA

In Heaven all opposites, such as prohibition and permission, guilt and guiltlessness, are one unified whole.

RABBI HAYYIM OF MOGIELNICA

Thou art man and woman, boy and girl; old and worn thou walkest bent over a staff; thou art the blue bird and the green and the scarlet-eyed.

SWETASWATARA UPANISHAD

For Thou art there where seeing is one with being seen, and hearing with being heard, and tasting with being tasted, and touching with being touched, and speaking with hearing, and creating with speaking.

NICOLAS OF CUSA

The Lord said in a mystery: If ye make not the left hand as the right and the right as the left, and the things that are above as those that are below, and the things that are before as those that are behind, ye shall not know the kingdom of God.

LINUS (*quoting from the lost 'Martyrdom of Peter'*

FROM "THE HYMN OF JESUS"

I would be saved, and I would save. Amen.
I would be loosed, and I would loose. Amen.

176

I would be born, and I would bear. Amen.
I would hear and I would be heard. Amen.
Grace danceth. I would pipe; dance ye all. Amen.
I would flee and I would stay. Amen.
I would adorn, and I would be adorned. Amen.
I would be united, and I would unite. Amen.
A house I have not, and I have houses. Amen.
A place I have not, and I have places. Amen.
A temple I have not, and I have temples. Amen.
A lamp am I to thee that beholdest me. Amen.
A mirror am I to thee that perceivest me. Amen.
A door am I to thee that knockest at me. Amen.
A way am I to thee a wayfarer. Amen.
    Now answer thou unto my dancing.

ACTS OF JOHN

§ 4

The divine Nature, free and perfect and blissful, must be manifested in the individual in order that it may manifest in the world.

AUROBINDO

Difference gives at once a Knower and a Known, for, failing this, all is one, and silent.

PLOTINUS

That which resumes all under a unity is a Principle in which all things exist together and the single thing is All. From this Principle, which remains internally unmoved, particular things push forth as from a single root which never itself emerges. They are a branching into part, into multiplicity, each single outgrowth bearing its trace of the common source. Thus, phase by phase, there is finally the production into this world; some things close still to the root, others widely separate in the continuous progression until we have, in our metaphor, bough and crest, foliage and fruit. At the one side all is one point of unbroken rest, on the other is the ceaseless process—leaf and fruit. . . .

The things that act upon each other are branchings from a far-off beginning and so stand distinct; but they derive initially from the one source: all interaction is like that of brothers, resemblant as drawing life from the same parents.

PLOTINUS

Brahman is as the clay or substance out of which an infinite variety of articles is fashioned. As clay, they are all one; but form or manifestation differentiates them. Before every one of them was made, they all existed potentially in the clay; and, of course, they are identical substantially; but when formed, and so long as the form remains, they are separate and different; the clay-mouse can never become a clay-elephant, because, as manifestations, form alone makes them what they are, though as unformed clay they are all one.

VIVEKANANDA

Word whose breath is the world-circling atmosphere,
Word that utters the world that turns the wind,
Word that articulates the bird that speeds upon the air,

Word that blazes out the trumpet of the sun,
Whose silence is the violin-music of the stars,
Whose melody is the dawn, and harmony the night,

Word traced in water of lakes, and light on water,
Light on still water, moving water, waterfall
And water colours of cloud, of dew, of spectral rain,

Word inscribed on stone, mountain range upon range of stone,
Word that is fire of the sun and fire within
Order of atoms, crystalline symmetry,

Grammar of five-fold rose and six-fold lily,
Spiral of leaves on a bough, helix of shells,
Rotation of twining plants on axes of darkness and light,

Instinctive wisdom of fish and lion and ram,
Rhythm of generation in flagellate and fern,
Flash of fin, beat of wing, heartbeat, beat of the dance,

Hieroglyph in whose exact precision is defined
Feather and insect-wing, refraction of multiple eyes,
Eyes of the creatures, oh myriadfold vision of the world,

Statement of mystery, how shall we name
A spirit clothed in world, a world made man?

KATHLEEN RAINE

Since, for man, to participate in God is to live in perpetual contemplation of the Divine glory, and since the *substance* of all things is eternal, the beatified universe is not a vast sea in which the peculiar qualities of all things are absorbed in a never-ending monotony, but a perfectly harmonious composition in which all creatures live in unity yet without confusion of individual being.

ALICE GARDNER (*interpreting Erigena*)

Otherness in unity is without otherness because it is unity.

NICOLAS OF CUSA

§ 5

The end of creation is that all things may return to the Creator and be united with Him.

SWEDENBORG

All things, as they rise from a unity, come back to unity by a sheer need of nature; differences unfold themselves, contraries are produced, but all is drawn into one organised system by the unity at the source.

PLOTINUS

Every part of an element separated from its mass desires to return to it by the shortest way.

LEONARDO DA VINCI

Everything that exists proceeds from a single cause, the first cause: this first cause is the Good: and the Good is identical with the One. Everything that is caused both remains in its cause and proceeds from its cause and moreover turns back again to its cause.

Everything has a natural upward motion towards the Good, its begetter.

PROCLUS

Before we had our becoming Here we existed There, men other than now, some of us gods: we were pure souls, Spirit inbound with the entire of reality, members of the Spiritual, not fenced off, not cut away, integral to that All. Even now, it is true, we are not put apart; but upon that primal Man there has intruded another. . . . This other has wound himself about us, foisting himself upon the Man that each of us was at first. Then it was as if one voice sounded,

179

one word was uttered, and from every side an ear attended and received and there was an effective hearing, possessed through and through of what was present and active upon it: now we have lost that first simplicity; we are become the dual thing. . . .

To Real Being we go back, all that we have and are; to that we return as from that we came. Of what is There we have direct knowledge, not images or even impressions; and to know without image is to be; by our part in true knowledge we are those Beings; we do not need to bring them down into ourselves, for we are There among them. Since not only ourselves but all other things also are those Beings, we all are they; we are they while we are also one with all: therefore we and all things are one.

When we look outside of that on which we depend we ignore our unity; looking outward we see many faces; look inward and all is the one head. If a man could but be turned about—by his own motion or by the happy pull of Athene—he would see at once God and himself and the All. At first no doubt all will not be seen as one whole, but when we find no stop at which to declare a limit to our being we cease to rule ourselves out from the total of reality; we reach to the All as a unity—and this not by any stepping forward, but by the fact of being and abiding there where the All has its being.

PLOTINUS

Of Plotinus' last moments Eustochius has given me an account.

He himself was staying at Puteoli and was late in arriving: when he at last came, Plotinus said: "I have been a long time waiting for you; I am striving to give back the Divine in myself to the Divine in the All." As he spoke a snake crept under the bed on which he lay and slipped away into a hole in the wall: at the same moment Plotinus died.

PORPHYRY

We have seen that Plotinus conceives the universe as a living chain of being, an unbroken series of ascending or descending values and existences. The whole constitutes a 'harmony'; each inferior grade is 'in' the next above; each existence is vitally connected with all others. But those grades which are inferior in value are also imperfectly real, so long as we look at them in disconnexion. They are characterised by impermanence and inner discord, until we set them in their true relations to the whole. Then we perceive them to be integral parts of the eternal systole and diastole in which the life of the universe consists, a life in which there is nothing arbitrary or irregular, seeing that all is ordered by the necessity that eternal principles should act in accordance with their own nature. The perfect and unchangeable life of the Divine Spirit overflows in an incessant stream of creative activity, which spends itself only when it has reached the lowest confines of being, so that every possible manifestation of Divine energy, every hue of the Divine radiance, every variety in degree as well as in kind, is realised somewhere and somehow. And by the side of this outward flow of creative energy there is another current which carries all the creatures back toward the source of their being. It is this centripetal movement that directs the active life of all creatures endowed with Soul. They were created and sent into the world that they might be moulded a little nearer to the Divine image by yearning for the home which they have left. This aspiration, which slumbers even in unconscious beings, is the mainspring of the moral, intellectual, and aesthetic life of mankind.

W. R. INGE

"Everything is linked with everything else down to the lowest ring on the chain, and the true essence of God is above as well as below, in the heavens and on the earth, and nothing exists outside him. And this is what the sages mean when they say: When God gave the Torah to Israel, he opened the seven Heavens to them, and they saw that nothing was there in reality but his Glory; he opened the seven worlds to them and they saw that nothing was there but his Glory; he opened the seven abysses before their eyes, and they saw that nothing was there but his Glory. Meditate on these things and you will understand that God's essence is linked and connected with all worlds, and that all forms of existence are linked and connected with each other, but derived from his existence and essence." [So wrote Moses de Leon; and when Kabbalists of this school describe the state of the Messianic world] the emphasis is on the restoration of the original coexistence and correlation of all things. What is at present reserved to the mystic whose gaze penetrates through the outer shell to the core of the matter, will anon be the common property of mankind in the state of Redemption.

GERSHOM SCHOLEM

Poor copies out of Heaven's original,
Pale earthly pictures mouldering to decay,
What care although your beauties break and fall,
When that which gave them life endures for aye?

Oh, never vex thine heart with idle woes:
All high discourse enchanting the rapt ear,
All gilded landscapes and brave glistering shows
Fade—perish, but it is not as we fear.

Whilst far away the living fountains ply,
Each petty brook goes brimful to the main.
Since brook nor fountain can for ever die,
Thy fears how foolish, thy lament how vain!

What is this fountain, wouldst thou rightly know?
The Soul whence issue all created things.
Doubtless the rivers shall not cease to flow
Till silenced are the everlasting springs.

Farewell to sorrow, and with quiet mind
Drink long and deep: let others fondly deem
The channel empty they perchance may find,
Or fathom that unfathomable stream.

The moment thou to this low world wast given,
A ladder stood whereby thou mightst aspire;
And first thy steps, which upward still have striven,
From mineral mounted to the plant; then higher

To animal existence; next, the Man
With knowledge, reason, faith. O wondrous goal!
This body, which a crumb of dust began—
How fairly fashioned the consummate whole!

Yet stay not here thy journey: thou shalt grow
An angel bright and have thine home in Heaven.
Plod on, plunge last in the great Sea, that so
Thy little drop make oceans seven times seven . . .

RUMI

Consider this matter in the following similitude. A grain of
wheat has the air and light of this world enclosed or incorporated
in it. This is the mystery of its life, this is its power of growing,

182

by this it has a strong continual tendency of uniting again with that ocean of light and air from whence it came forth, and so it helps to kindle its own vegetable life. On the other hand, that great ocean of light and air, having its own offspring hidden in the heart of the grain, has a perpetual strong tendency to unite and communicate with it again. From this desire of union on both sides the vegetable life arises and all the virtues and powers contained in it.

WILLIAM LAW

I believe in the eternal harmony in which they say we shall one day be blended. I believe in the Word to Which the universe is striving, and Which Itself was " with God", and Which Itself is God, and so on, and so on, to infinity.

DOSTOEVSKY

All Human Forms identified, even Tree, Metal, Earth, & Stone; all Human Forms identified, living, going forth & returning wearied Into the Planetary lives of Years, Months, Days, & Hours; reposing, And then Awaking into his Bosom in the Life of Immortality.

BLAKE

§ 6

Goodness is a going out of the self into a union which realises selfhood.

V. G.

> . . . How long must I bear
> Self and identity—
> Shall I find at last
> My lost being?

KATHLEEN RAINE

> . . . How hast thou lost the golden virgin key
> To thine own immaculate Eden, to the place
> Where thine own face is the Beloved's Face
> Since He is *thou* and thine own self is He?
> For He is *thou*; ah couldst thou understand
> Thou wouldst be thee with Him, light blent with Light,
> There is one centre to the Infinite,
> It is within thee; God the Eremite
> Is thine own being's beauty, heart and hand!

WILFRED ROWLAND CHILDE

183

Where this Light is, the man's end and aim is not this or that, I or Thou, or the like, but only the One, who is neither I nor Thou, this nor that, but is above all I and Thou, this and that; and in Him all Good is loved as one Good.

THEOLOGIA GERMANICA

He was one who, having all his ideas and concepts merged with the Primal Cause, had eliminated the Illusion of Duality.

RECHUNG (of Milarepa)

Grandier was the average sensual man—only a little more so. His universe, as the record of his life sufficiently proves, was 'the world', in the sense in which that word is used so frequently in the Gospels and Epistles. "Woe unto the world because of offences!" "I pray not for the world". "Love not the world, neither the things that are in the world. If any man love the world, the love of the Father is not in him. For all that is in the world, the lust of the flesh, and the lust of the eyes, and the pride of life, is not of the Father, but of the world. And the world passeth away, and the lusts thereof; but he that doeth the will of God abideth for ever."

'The world' is man's experience as it appears to, and is moulded by, his ego. It is that less abundant life, which is lived according to the dictates of the insulated self. It is nature denatured by the distorting spectacles of our appetites and revulsions. It is the finite divorced from the Eternal. It is multiplicity in isolation from its non-dual Ground. It is time apprehended as one damned thing after another. It is a system of verbal categories taking the place of the fathomlessly beautiful and mysterious particulars which constitute reality. It is a notion labelled 'God'. It is the Universe equated with the words of our utilitarian vocabulary.

Over against 'the world' stands 'the other world', the Kingdom of God within.

ALDOUS HUXLEY (from The Devils of Loudun)

Soul-life is the immediate experience of an organic individual, from the moment when he begins to be an organic individual. This experience is conscious and self-conscious in various degrees. Its ideal perfection is such an all-embracing experience as will break down all barriers between the individual Soul and the Universal Soul. 'The Soul is potentially all things'. 'We are a spiritual world'.

W. R. INGE (interpreting Neoplatonism)

It is the heart indeed that tells us that our own self is a self only to the extent that it disappears into all other selves, non-sentient as well as sentient.

D. T. SUZUKI

Yes, now I live. And I feel my spirit growing, spreading, becoming tenuous, infinite. I am everywhere, in the ocean which is my blood, in the rocks that are my bones, in the trees, in the flowers; and my head reaches up to the heavens.

STRINDBERG

Pure I was before the world began,
I was the violence of wind and wave,
I was the bird before bird ever sang.

I was never still,
I turned upon the axis of my joy,
I was the lonely dancer on the hill,

The rain upon the mountainside,
The rising mist,
I was the sea's unrest.

I wove the web of colour
Before the rainbow,
The intricacy of the flower
Before the leaf grew.

I was the buried ore,
The fossil forest,
I knew the roots of things:
Before death's kingdom
I passed through the grave.

Times out of mind my journey
Circles the universe
And I remain
Before the first day.

KATHLEEN RAINE

Tell me, I pray you, Theotimus, if a drop of water, thrown into an ocean of some priceless essence, were alive, and could speak and declare its condition, would it not cry out with great joy: O mortals!

I live indeed, but I live not myself, but this ocean lives in me, and
my life is hidden in this abyss?

ST. FRANÇOIS DE SALES

WITHDRAWN IN GOLD

Light floods the mind!
And now the mind is pure,
Is naught-intent,
Is empty:

It is withdrawn into its solitude,
—As the moon withdraws,
When storm and rain have blacked the world away,
And only the great gold sun rides on the main—

The Shining Ones are vanished
In greater splendour,
Withdrawn, not lost, in gold,
In light not gone away:

Stars and the moon
Are lost in the light of life,
As the pure mind, withdrawn,
Is lost in the light of God.

JAMES STEPHENS

§ 7

Each is responsible for the evil anywhere in the world.
All that unites with the universal is virtue. All that separates is sin.
You are a part of the Infinite. This is your nature. Hence you
are your brother's keeper.

VIVEKANANDA

For not one sparrow can suffer & the whole Universe not suffer also
In all its Regions, & its Father & Saviour not pity & weep.

BLAKE

I am debtor to all, to all am I bounden,
Fellowman and beast, season and solstice, darkness and light,
And life and death. On the backs of the dead,

186

See, I am borne, on lost errands led,
By spent harvests nourished. Forgotten prayers
To gods forgotten bring blessings upon me.
Rusted arrow and broken bow, look, they preserve me
Here in this place. The never-won stronghold
That sank in the ground as the years into time,
Slowly with all its men steadfast and watching,
Keeps me safe now. The ancient waters
Cleanse me, revive me. Victor and vanquished
Give me their passion, their peace and the field.
The meadows of Lethe shed twilight around me.
The dead in their silences keep me in memory,
Have me in hold. To all I am bounden.

EDWIN MUIR

We are beholden to all, to the distant or dead as well as to the present and living; and we ought to remember from time to time the afflicted of past ages, and desire to assuage their agony. Do we succeed, then, in assuaging it by our desire? I am persuaded that somehow we do. We know little of time and still less of eternity, of their nature and significance: but what was and will be, surely is: and I grasp elusively, without the power to explain myself, a coincidence (in some dimension of reality outside our ken "here below") of affliction at whatever time it may have occurred, of our love at whatever time we may give it, and of the sufferer's response.

However that may be, some goodness accrues to the sum of things when we love the afflicted who are distant or dead, for the more love the more goodness: and we cannot in any case help ourselves loving them, if we have been granted imagination. But what we *can* control is our degree of attention: we can be lazy or otherwise. If we are to help deity help us, we must do our utmost, our little utmost, to heal the wounds of existence, by intention, with *Kavvanah*, as much as in deed: we must send out our love through the universe, irrespective of time or distance, and so contribute, if only as with a grain of sand, to restoration and unity.

V. G.

In some way or another we are part of an all-embracing psychic life, of a single "greatest" man.

C. G. JUNG

We see people in our space as separate. Man, however, is not in space, he is in humanity. But we see this 'humanity' abstractly or sentimentally, not understanding that it may have continuity in higher dimensions, and exist as a whole, of which each of us is a cross-section or certain minimum.

MAURICE NICOLL

When Man enters into human form there exists a particular man who, however, is still Man.

PLOTINUS

There is a soul above the soul of each,
    A mightier soul, which yet to each belongs:
There is a sound made of all human speech,
    And numerous as the concourse of all songs:
And in that soul lives each, in each that soul,
    Tho' all the ages are its life-time vast;
Each soul that dies in its most sacred whole
    Receiveth life that shall for ever last.

And thus for ever with a wider span
    Humanity o'erarches time and death;
Man can elect the universal man
    And live in life that ends not with his breath;
    And gather glory that increases still
    Till Time his glass with Death's last dust shall fill.

RICHARD WATSON DIXON

The Righteous, going to the Garden of Eden, passed before the gate of hell, and the wicked, going to hell, passed before the gate of Eden; and Adam, exiled in his penance between the two gates, cried to the Lord: "King of the World—whom my sin cast out from the world—when shall my penance have an end?" And the Holy One, blessèd be He, answered him: "In the beginning I made but one man, mingling the dust of all the places of earth. From thy sin are come men, separating their dust one from another. At the end, joining together all the spaces of the earth, mankind once again will be but one man. Then thy penance will be accomplished."

EDMOND FLEG (*from a Midrash*)

Most human beings, perhaps all human beings, are the battle-ground for a struggle between self-regarding impulses, issuing in greed, fear, strife, envy, jealousy, malice and hatred, and other-regarding impulses, issuing in unity and peace. Or this, rather, is how the matter presents itself to human consciousness, for it cannot be that there are two ultimate principles at work in reality. Somehow there is a rift in the created world, or reality, or existence, or whatever you may prefer to call it. How, when (if it is a matter of time) or why this rift occurred or occurs no mortal man can say. But an explanation can be suggested in the form of a theological myth. God was (or should we say, in the more appropriate language of eternity, is?) undifferentiated. But he perceives differentiation, concreteness, Blake's "minute particulars", as supreme value. He therefore creates (splits himself up into, produces as emanations?) these concrete particulars. But, by a law of reality, multiplicity involves relation; and at the same time a concrete particular, if it is to be a concrete particular, must have being and the potentiality for growth within itself. Each particular, therefore, being and growing, must be in relation with every other particular, also being and growing. Now the particulars, not being God (though being of or from God), cannot feel or know perfectly meanwhile—though they can and do have intimations about it—how the value of individual being and growth, and the value of relation, may be realised not as two conflicting values but as the one value which in fact they are: for individual being can be perfect only when there is perfect relation, and relation can be perfect only when there is perfection of individual being. The particulars cannot feel or know perfectly how to manage this, I said, "meanwhile": during the intermediate stage, that is—to use again the perhaps inapplicable language of temporality—between the undifferentiated God and the God become a unity of innumerable rejoicing particulars. The goal, if the word can be used when eternity is in question, is beautifully illuminated by a sentence from the Zohar: "When mankind is at one, God is One."

God, desiring this consummation (which may or may not be involved in the historical process), can help men understand how to live by the intimations he gives them; but he cannot do more than help; for if he did more he would be derogating from the value of individual being, which is the point, as it were, of the whole business.

Or to put it in another way. All men desire the peace of home—the same peace of the same home, always. Some of them know they can win it only by losing their lives—by co-operation, by altruism, by love: and they, even, commonly achieve no more than a few passing victories on the outskirts of the central battle—the battle against a way of life they know to be ruinous. Others think, but usually with a mingling of wiser thoughts, that they can win their desire by concentration on self. They do no worse than misunderstand.

v. g. (from My Dear Timothy)

§ 8

UNITY IN THE DWELLING-PLACE OF THE BEATIFIED

Heaven is so full of delight that, viewed in itself, it is nothing but blessedness and delight; for the Divine Good proceeding from the Lord's Divine Love constitutes heaven both in general and in particular with every one there; and Divine Love consists in desiring that all may be saved and made happy from their inmost being and in full perfection. So that it amounts to the same thing whether you say heaven or heavenly joy. . . .

How great the delight of heaven is, may be seen from this fact alone, that it is delightful to all in heaven to share their delights and blessings with others; and since all in heaven are of this character, it is plain how immense is the delight of heaven; for in the heavens there is a participation of all with each and of each with all. Such community of life results from the two heavenly loves which, as was said, are love to the Lord and to the neighbour, and it is the nature of these loves to communicate their delight to others. Love to the Lord is of this character because the Lord's love is the love of communicating all that He has to all mankind, for He desires the happiness of all. There is a similar love in every one who loves Him, because the Lord is in them; and so the angels share their delights with one another. That love to the neighbour is of a similar character will be seen in what follows. It is evident, therefore, that it is the nature of these loves to share their delights with others. . . .

Certain spirits had conceived the idea in the world that heavenly happiness consists in leading an idle life and in being waited on by others; but they were told that happiness never consists in mere inaction, because in that case every one would wish to sacrifice the happiness of others to his own; thus each would desire what no one could obtain. Such a life would not be active but idle, and would stultify all the powers of life, and every one ought to know that without activity there can be no happiness, and that rest is only for the sake of recreation in order that a man may return with fresh vigour to the activity of his life. They were afterwards shown by much evidence that angelic life consists in doing the good works of charity which are uses, and that the angels find all their happiness in use, from use, and according to use. Those who had the idea that heavenly joy consists in leading a life of indolence and idly inhaling eternal joy, were allowed some experience of such a life, in order to make them ashamed; and they found that it was extremely sad, and that, all joy being destroyed, they would in a short time feel nothing for it but disgust and loathing.

Some spirits who believed themselves better informed than others, declared that they had believed in the world that heavenly joy would consist solely in praising and giving glory to God, and that thus they would lead an active life; but they were told, that to praise and give glory to God is not properly an active life, and that God has no need of praise and worship; but His will is that all should perform uses and thus do the good works of charity. But they were unable to associate with such works any idea of heavenly joy, but only an idea of servitude; yet the angels testified that in the performance of such good works there is the fullest freedom, because it proceeds from inward affection and is attended by indescribable delight . . .

In no case is heaven exactly the same for one as for another, just as no man, spirit or angel, is ever exactly like another even in face. When I merely thought of two persons being exactly alike or identical, the angels were shocked and said that every whole is formed by the harmonious concurrence of various parts and derives its character from that concurrence; and that in this manner every society of heaven forms a whole and that all the societies of heaven also make a whole; and this is the work of the Lord alone by means of love.

Uses in the heavens are also various and diverse. The use performed by one angel is never exactly the same as that performed by another, and therefore the delight of one angel is not exactly the same as the delight of another. Furthermore, the delights of every use are innumerable, and those innumerable delights are also various; yet they are connected in such order that they are mutually related to each other, like the uses of every member, organ and viscus in the body, and still more like the uses of every vessel and fibre in every member, organ and viscus, where each and all are so related, that they seek their own good in that of another, and thus the good of each in all and of all in each. From this universal and individual relation they act as one whole.

I have spoken at times with spirits who had recently come from the world, about the state of eternal life, saying that it was of importance to know who was the Lord of the kingdom, and what kind and form of government it had. Just as nothing is more important to those entering another kingdom in the world, than to know who and what the king is, the nature of his government and many other particulars relating to his kingdom, so it must be far more important in that kingdom, in which they were to live to eternity. They were told, therefore, that it was the Lord who governs heaven and also the universe; for He who rules the one rules the other; thus, that the kingdom in which they now were was the Lord's and that the laws of this kingdom were eternal truths, founded on this single law, that they should love the Lord above all things and their neighbour as themselves. If, indeed, they were desirous to be like the angels, they ought to love their neighbour more than themselves. On hearing this, they could make no reply, because in the life of the body they had heard something of the kind, but had not believed it. They wondered that there should be such love in heaven, and that it could be possible for any one to love his neighbour more than himself. But they were told that every good increases immensely in the other life, and that while living in the body men could not do more than love the neighbour as themselves, because their minds were occupied with matters relating to the body; but that when these are laid aside their love becomes purer, and at length angelic, and then they love the neighbour more than themselves. For there is joy in heaven in doing good to another, and none in doing good to oneself, unless it be in order that the good may become another's, and consequently for the sake of others; this is what is meant by loving the neighbour more than oneself.

It was said, furthermore, that the possibility of such love is shown in the world by the marriage love of some who have suffered death to protect a married partner from injury; by the love of parents for their children, since a mother would rather suffer hunger than see her child in want of food; by sincere friendship, which prompts one friend to expose himself to danger for another; and even by polite and pretended friendship, which endeavours to emulate sincere friendship in giving of its best to those for whom it professes goodwill, such good-will being on the lips, but not in the heart; lastly by the very nature of love, whose delight is to serve others, not for its own sake but for theirs. But these things were incomprehensible to those who loved themselves more than others, and who, in the life of the body, had been greedy of gain; and they were still more incomprehensible to the avaricious. . . .

Heavenly joy, in its essence, cannot be described, because it is in the inmost life of the angels, and therefore in every detail of their thought and affection, and thus in every detail of their speech and action. It is as if the inner mind were fully open and free to receive the delight and blessedness which are diffused into every fibre, and thus throughout their whole being. The perception and sensation of this joy is indescribable; for commencing in the inmost parts, it flows into every particular derived from them, and diffuses itself with continual increase towards the exterior parts. When good spirits, who have not yet attained to that joy, because they are not yet raised up into heaven, perceive it in the sphere of love flowing from an angel, they are filled with such delight that they fall, as it were, into a delicious swoon. This sometimes occurs to those who desire to know what heavenly joy is. . . .

In order that I might know the nature and quality of heaven and heavenly joy, I have frequently, and for a long time together, been permitted by the Lord to perceive the delights of heavenly joy. I know them therefore from living experience, but I can never describe them; a few observations, however, may convey some idea.

Heavenly joy consists of innumerable delights and joys, which compose together a common whole, in which common whole or common affection there are harmonies of innumerable affections. These are not perceived distinctly, but only obscurely, because the perception of them is most general. Still I have perceived that it contains innumerable things in such order as cannot be described, all flowing from the order of heaven. The same order prevails in the most minute details of affection, which are presented and perceived only as a whole, according to the capacity of their recipient. In a word, each general affection contains infinite things arranged in most perfect order; and not one of them but lives and affects the rest from an inmost source, as all heavenly joys do.

I perceived, also, that the joy and delight came as from the heart, diffusing themselves very gently through all the inmost fibres, and thence into the bundles of fibres, with such an inmost sense of enjoyment, that every fibre was as it were nothing but joy and delight, and everything capable of perception and sensation seemed in like manner to be alive with happiness. Compared with these joys, bodily pleasure is as a thick and pungent fog compared with a pure and most gentle atmosphere. I have noticed that when I wished to transfer all my delight to another, a more interior and fuller delight than the former continually flowed in, in its place, and the more I desired this, the more it flowed in. This, also, I perceived to be from the Lord.

The inhabitants of heaven are continually advancing towards the spring-time of life, and the more thousands of years they live, the more delightful and happy is the spring to which they attain, and this to eternity, with an increase according to the increase and degree of their love, charity and faith. Women who have died old and worn out with age, if they have lived in faith in the Lord, in charity to the neighbour and in happy marriage love with a husband, come in process of time more and more into the flower of youth and early womanhood, and attain to a beauty which exceeds every conception of beauty ever seen on the earth. Goodness and charity mould their form, presenting in it a likeness of themselves, and causing the joy and beauty of charity to shine forth from every feature of their countenance, so that they are the very forms of charity itself. Some who have beheld them have been overwhelmed with astonishment . . . Charity itself is what portrays and is portrayed, and in such a manner that the whole angel, and especially the face, is as it were an evident and clearly perceptible personification of charity. This form is indescribably beautiful to behold, and affects with charity the inmost life of the mind. In a word, to grow old in heaven is to grow young. Those who have lived in love to the Lord and in charity to their neighbour, become, in the other life, such forms of beauty. All angels are such forms, with innumerable variety; and of these heaven is composed.

SWEDENBORG

Coda:
on beasts, plants and earth in the Unity

Each bush and oak doth know I AM.

HENRY VAUGHAN

There is a dim knowledge in plants and even in minerals.

CAMPANELLA (*paraphrased by Inge*)

Even stones have a love, a love that seeks the ground.

MEISTER ECKHART

On this calm morning it occurs to me that it is by a negation and voluntary act of no thinking that we think of earth, air, water, etc. as dead. . . . The truth is, we stop in the sense of life just when we are not forced to go on. . . .

S. T. COLERIDGE

One day an officer-disciple was late in arriving at his Master's house. He apologised and said that he had been watching a polo match. "Were the men tired?" asked the Master. "Yes, Master." "Were the horses tired?" "Yes, Master." "Is the wooden post here tired too?" The pupil failed to answer. That night he could not sleep, but at dawn hurried back to the Master. The answer had come to him. He asked the Master to repeat the question, which he did. "Yes, Master," he said, and the Master was delighted. A later Roshi pointed out that unless the post was tired there could be no tiredness anywhere.

D. T. SUZUKI (from *The Essence of Buddhism*)

The notion that the heavenly bodies have life or soul has been revived in all seriousness by Leibnitz and Fechner. If Plotinus and his modern followers have unconsciously been influenced by the idea that such bulky bodies must have a corresponding endowment of soul-life, they have undoubtedly exposed themselves to ridicule; but the doctrine itself does not seem to me ridiculous or improbable. Each of our bodies is a world, populated by millions of minute living beings. We are not conscious in them, nor are they conscious of the unitary life of the organism to which they belong. Why should not our planet have a life of its own, thinking thoughts of which we know nothing?

W. R. INGE

2

The love which speaks and sings and sighs in one part of creation is revealed in the other half in the form of flowers. All this efflorescence, with its wealth of forms and colours and perfumes, which gives splendour to the fields, is the expression of love, is love itself, which celebrates its sweet mysteries in the bosom of every flower. The blossoming branch, the bird that perches thereon to sing or build his nest, the man who gazes at the branch and at the bird, are all moved by the same principle at different degrees of perfection.

MAURICE DE GUÉRIN

You are about to enter upon spring. Abandon yourself to all there is of sweetness in this season of rebirth; make yourself a flower with the flowers.

LAMENNAIS

The birch tree is all over green in *small* leaf, more light and elegant than when it is full out. It bent to the breezes, as if for the love of its own delightful motions.

DOROTHY WORDSWORTH

VEGETATION

O never harm the dreaming world,
the world of green, the world of leaves,
but let its million palms unfold
the adoration of the trees.

It is love in darkness wrought
obedient to the unseen sun,
longer than memory, a thought
deeper than the graves of time.

The turning spindles of the cells
weave a slow forest over space,
the dance of love, creation,
out of time moves not a leaf,
and out of summer, not a shade.

KATHLEEN RAINE

A CUT FLOWER

I stand on slenderness all fresh and fair,
I feel root-firmness in the earth far down,
I catch in the wind and loose my scent for bees
That sack my throat for kisses and suck love.
What is the wind that brings thy body over?
Wind, I am beautiful and sick. I long
For rain that strikes and bites like cold and hurts.
Be angry, rain, for dew is kind to me
When I am cool from sleep and take my bath.

Who softens the sweet earth about my feet,
Touches my face so often and brings water?
Where does she go, taller than any sunflower
Over the grass like birds? Has she a root?
These are great animals that kneel to us,
Sent by the sun perhaps to help us grow.
I have seen death. The colors went away,
The petals grasped at nothing and curled tight.
Then the whole head fell off and left the sky.

She tended me and held me by my stalk.
Yesterday I was well, and then the gleam,
The thing sharper than frost cut me in half.
I fainted and was lifted high. I feel
Waist-deep in rain. My face is dry and drawn.
My beauty leaks into the glass like rain.
When first I opened to the sun I thought
My colors would be parched. Where are my bees?
Must I die now? Is this a part of life?

KARL SHAPIRO

THE LIVING HERBS

He [St. Francis] used also to say to the friar who made ready the
wood for the fire, that he should never cut down a whole tree; but
so that always some part of a tree should remain whole for the love
of Him Who did work out our salvation on the wood of the cross.
Likewise he used to say to the friar who did the garden, not to
till the whole ground for pot-herbs; but to leave some part of it to
produce green herbs, which in their time should produce flowers
for the friars, for the love of Him Who is called the "flower of the

field" and "The lily of the valley". Nay, he used to say to that brother gardener that he ought always to make a fair pleasaunce in some part of the garden; setting and planting there all sweet-smelling herbs and all herbs which bring forth fair flowers, that in their time they might call them that looked upon those herbs and flowers to the praise of God.

"THE MIRROR OF PERFECTION"

§ 3

THE FLY

Seest thou the little winged fly, smaller than a grain of sand?
It has a heart like thee, a brain open to heaven & hell,
Withinside wondrous & expansive: its gates are not clos'd:
I hope thine are not: hence it clothes itself in rich array:
Hence thou art cloth'd with human beauty, O thou mortal man.

BLAKE

THE GLOW-WORM

On a midsummer night, on a night that was eerie with stars,
  In a wood too deep for a single star to look through,
You led down a path whose turning you knew in the darkness,
  But the scent of the dew-dripping cedars was all that I knew.

I drank of the darkness, I was fed with the honey of fragrance,
  I was glad of my life, the drawing of breath was sweet;
I heard your voice, you said, "Look down, see the glow-worm!"
  It was there before me, a small star white at my feet.
We watched while it brightened as though it were breathed on and
    burning,
  This tiny creature moving over earth's floor—
" '*L'amor che move il sole e l'altre stelle*',"
  You said, and no more.

SARA TEASDALE

THE COW

In front of the white farm where, about noon, an old man some-times comes to sit in the cool doorway; where a hundred hens with scarlet combs gather in a gaudy concourse; where the sentinels of sleep, the watchdogs in their kennels, hearken to the cry of the

200

watchman of our waking—the fine, gleaming cock, all ashine with
the sun: here there had just halted a cow.

Great, stately creature, dappled brown and white, she stood there,
gentle as a hind with young, a beautiful cluster of children beneath
her—children with marble teeth and bushy hair, ruddy-faced and
smuttier than old walls, crying out noisily to others—who, still tiny,
came up in tremulous haste—and robbing without mercy an absent
milkmaid. With their laughing and maybe wounding mouths—
with their fingers, squeezing the milk from a thousand holes—they
pulled at the bounteous udder of the red-brown mother.

She, strong and good and full of her treasure, twitching sometimes at their touch, her fine flank more mottled than a leopard's,
gazed vaguely and dreamily out into space . . .

VICTOR HUGO

THE BEES

And, O Theocritus, so far have some
Prevailed among the powers of heaven and earth,
By their endowments, good or great, that they
Have had, as thou reportest, miracles
Wrought for them in old time: yea, not unmoved,
When thinking on my own beloved friend,
I hear thee tell how bees with honey fed
Divine Comates, by his impious lord
Within a chest imprisoned; how they came
Laden from blooming grove or flowery field,
And fed him there, alive, month after month,
Because the goatherd, blessed man! had lips
Wet with the Muses' nectar.

WORDSWORTH

THE TURTLE-DOVE AND THE MOUSE

Barbara is an old maid. She had two turtle-doves. One of them
died, the first year I think. The other bird continued to live alone
in its cage for 9 years, but for one whole year it had a companion
and daily visitor—a little mouse that used to come and feed with it;
and the dove would caress it, and cower over it with its wings, and
make a loving noise to it. The mouse, though it did not testify
equal delight in the dove's company, yet it was at perfect ease. The
poor mouse disappeared, and the dove was left solitary till its death.

It died of a short sickness, and was buried under a tree with funeral ceremony, by Barbara and her maidens, and one or two others.

DOROTHY WORDSWORTH

THE DOG

... as recently in Cordova, where a little ugly dog, in an advanced state of preparation for motherhood, came up to me; it was an undistinguished animal, and certainly full of very casual puppies, about which no fuss will have been made; but difficult as it was for her, she came over to me, as we were quite alone, and raised her eyes, enlarged by care and self-seclusion, and begged for my glance,—and truly in hers there was everything that transcends the individual and passes, I can't say where—into the future or into the incomprehensible; the result was that she obtained a piece of sugar from my coffee, but incidentally, oh so incidentally, we read the mass together, as it were; the transaction in itself was nothing but giving and taking, but the meaning and the earnestness and our whole mutual understanding were boundless. And yet such things can only happen on earth: when all is said and done, it is good to have made the passage here willingly, even though unsurely, even though guiltily, even though not at all heroically—at the end one will be wonderfully prepared for relationships with the divine.

RILKE

§ 4

Nothing grows in a spot where there is neither sentient, fibrous nor rational life. The feathers grow upon birds and change every year; hair grows upon animals and changes every year except a part such as the hair of the beard in lions and cats and creatures like these. The grass grows in the fields, the leaves upon the trees, and every year these are renewed in great part. So then we may say that the earth has a spirit of growth, and that its flesh is the soil; its bones are the successive strata of the rocks which form the mountains; its cartilage is the tufa stone; its blood the springs of its waters. The lake of blood that lies about the heart is the ocean. Its breathing is by the increase and decrease of the blood in its pulses, and even so in the earth is the ebb and flow of the sea. And the vital heat of the world is fire which is spread throughout the earth; and the dwelling place of its creative spirit is in the fires, which in divers parts of the earth are breathed out in baths and sulphur mines, and in volcanoes, such as Mount Etna in Sicily, and in many other places.

LEONARDO DA VINCI

The sap is mounting back from that unseenness
darkly renewing in the common deep,
back to the light, and feeding the pure greenness
hiding in rinds round which the winds still weep.

The inner side of Nature is reviving,
another *sursum corda* will resound;
invisibly, a whole year's youth is striving
to climb those trees that look so iron-bound.

Preserving still that grey and cool expression,
the ancient walnut's filling with event;
while the young brush-wood trembles with repression
under the perching bird's presentiment.

RILKE

II. "... OF GOODNESS IN THINGS EVIL"

There is some soul of goodness in things evil,
Would men observingly distil it out . . .
Thus may we gather honey from the weed,
And make a moral of the devil himself.

SHAKESPEARE

Tao is in the ant, in the broken tile, in dung, in mire.

CHUANG TZU (*tr. by Waley*)

There is nothing on Earth though never so simple so vile and
abject in the sight of man, but it beares the witnesse of God.

THOMAS VAUGHAN

God is . . . even in the depths of Hell.

BLAKE

Do not think that good and evil are two, are two separate essences,
for they are one and the same thing appearing in different degrees
and in different guises and producing differences of feeling in the
same mind.

THE VEDANTA

The stuff of which evil is made is one with the stuff of which
good is made. No tendency or desire could be pointed out in the
worst of lives or of actions which is incapable of being, with
addition or readjustment, incorporated in a good self.

BOSANQUET

Vice is still human, being mixed with something contrary to
itself.

PLOTINUS

There was never sin of thine
But within its heart did dwell
A beauty that could whisper thee
Of the high heaven from which it fell.

A. E.

Is there, as the medieval mystics taught, a 'spark' at the core of
the Soul, which never consents to evil, a Divine nucleus in the
heart of the personality, which can take no stain?

W. R. INGE

Man is a twofold being, one part capable of evil and the other capable of good; that which is capable of good is not also capable of evil, but that which is capable of evil is also capable of good.

BLAKE

Every being, to the extent that it is a being at all, must have, simply as a being, the attribute of goodness. So when we say that a flawed being is an evil being, we appear to say that what is good is evil: and that nothing can be evil save what is good, since every being has the attribute of goodness, nor could anything be evil unless the thing which was evil was some sort of being. So nothing can be evil except something good.

ST. AUGUSTINE

Every evil is based on some good, for it is present in a subject which is good as having some sort of nature. Evil cannot exist but in good; sheer evil is impossible.

ST. THOMAS AQUINAS

> Nathelesse the soule is faire and beauteous still,
> How ever fleshes fault it filthy make;
> For things immortall no corruption take.

SPENSER

The corruption of nature is another nature. . . . And yet there remains the original good of the soul, which is divine and akin to it and in the true sense natural. For that which is from God is not so much extinguished as obscured. It can be obscured, because it is not God; it cannot be extinguished, because it is from God.

TERTULLIAN

It is, in fact, not possible to form any other notion of the origin of vice than as the absence of virtue. For as when the light has been removed the darkness supervenes, but as long as it is present there is no darkness, so, as long as the good is present in the nature, vice is a thing that has no inherent existence; while the departure of the better state becomes the origin of its opposite.

ST. GREGORY OF NYSSA

The stain of sin is not something positive existent in the soul. . . . It is like a shadow which is the privation of light.

ST. THOMAS AQUINAS

The shadow belongs to the light as the evil belongs to the good, and *vice versa*.

C. G. JUNG

I inquired into the nature of Evil, and found no substance there.

ST. AUGUSTINE

God and Evil, in a word, are contraries: if the problem of evil is altogether insoluble, there is an end of Theism: if God exists, there is nothing absolutely evil.

JAMES WARD

Sin is a survival or misuse of habit and tendencies that were incidental to an earlier stage of development. . . . Their sinfulness would thus lie in their anachronism, in their resistance to the . . . Divine force that makes for moral development and righteousness.

QUOTED BY BARON VON HÜGEL

Remarkable in itself, Armelle's self-analysis is doubly interesting as being yet another piece among the many pieces of evidence all pointing to the same conclusion: namely, that the phenomenal self is underlain by a Pure Ego or Atman, which is of the same nature as the divine Ground of all being. Outside the central chamber where (until the soul has become selfless) "none but God may enter", between the divine Ground and the conscious self, lies the subliminal mind, almost impersonal at its melting fringe, but crystallizing, as the phenomenal self is approached, into the personal subconscious with its accumulations of septic rubbish, its swarms of rats and black beetles and its occasional scorpions and vipers. This personal subconscious is the haunt of our indwelling criminal lunatic, the *locus* of Original Sin. But the fact that the ego is associated with a maniac is not incompatible with the fact that it is also associated (all unconsciously) with the divine Ground. We are born with Original Sin; but we are also born with Original Virtue— with a capacity for grace, in the language of Western theology, with a "spark", a "fine point of the soul", a fragment of unfallen consciousness, surviving from the state of primal innocence and technically known as the *synteresis*. Freudian psychologists pay far more attention to Original Sin than to Original Virtue. They pore over the rats and the black beetles, but are reluctant to see the inner light. Jung and his followers have shown themselves to be some-what more realistic. Overstepping the limits of the personal sub-conscious, they have begun to explore the realm where the mind, growing more and more impersonal, merges into the psychic medium, out of which individual selves are crystallized. Jungian psychology goes beyond the immanent maniac, but stops short of the immanent God.

And yet, I repeat, there is plenty of evidence for the existence of an Original Virtue underlying Original Sin. Armelle's experience was not unique. The knowledge that there is a central chamber of the soul, blazing with the light of divine love and wisdom, has come, in the course of history, to multitudes of human beings. It came, among others, to Father Surin—and came in conjunction with a knowledge, no less immediate and no less overpowering, of the horrors at large in the psychic medium and the poisonous vermin in the personal subconscious. At one and the same instant he was aware of God and of Satan, he knew beyond all doubt that he was eternally united with the divine Ground of all being, and yet was convinced that he was already and irrevocably damned. In the end, it was the consciousness of God that prevailed. In that tormented mind, Original Sin was finally swallowed up in the infinity of a much more Original, because timeless, Virtue.

ALDOUS HUXLEY (from *The Devils of Loudun*)

§ 2

The power of the Soul for good is in proportion to the strength of its passions. Sanctity is not the negation of passion but its order. Hence great Saints have often been great sinners.

COVENTRY PATMORE

Wickedness is a miscalculating effort towards the Best.

PLOTINUS

The maundering of the drunken reveller proves the existence of the cupbearer.

RUMI

Certain people, we must keep in mind, have forgotten that to which, from the beginning onwards, their longing and effort are pointed: for all that exists desires and aspires towards the Supreme by a compulsion of nature, as if all had received the oracle that without it they cannot be.

The Good is inherently present to even those asleep: it is no occasional reminiscence but is always with them though in their drowse they are aware of it not.

PLOTINUS

Everything that we perceive around us is struggling towards freedom, from the atom to the man, from insentient, lifeless particle of matter to the highest existence on earth, the human soul. The whole universe is in fact the result of this struggle for freedom. . . .

It is under the impulse of this tendency that the saint prays and the robber robs. When the line of action is not a proper one we call it evil, and when the manifestation of it is proper and high we call it good. But the impulse is the same, the struggle towards freedom.

VIVEKANANDA

Kao Tzŭ said, "Human nature is like rushing water, which flows east or west according as an outlet is made for it. For human nature makes indifferently for good or for evil, precisely as water makes indifferently for the east or for the west."

Mencius replied, "Water will indeed flow indifferently towards the east or west; but will it flow indifferently up or down? It will not; and the tendency of human nature towards good is like the tendency of water to flow down. Every man has this bias towards good, just as all water flows naturally downwards. By splashing water, you may indeed cause it to fly over your head; and by turning its course you may keep it for use on the hillside; but you would hardly speak of such results as the nature of water. They are the results, of course, of a *force majeure*. And so it is when the nature of man is diverted towards evil."

MENCIUS

The spirit is always willing, always yearning for righteousness and love, but its purpose is deceived and betrayed by the delusions of experience. . . .

WARNER ALLEN

The wise man . . . beholds all men as things made for holy uses.

TAO TÊ CHING

We must look for a justification of all things. If you see something bad in a man, you must not overlook the fact that in this man too His Name is manifest. Praised be His Name, for no place is without Him.

THE BAAL-SHEM

When Christ wished to teach us what God is like He pointed to the God-like in men. Even in the worst sinner He could discover the hidden good and appeal to it, knowing that the good and not the evil is the essential man. He tells us that it is when a sinner "comes to himself" that he "arises and goes to his Father": the man's true self is that within him which responds to God.

G. H. C. MACGREGOR

The Holy Ghost is that which is good in everything. In every object, in every man, in every event, there is something good, not in a philosophical and not in a mystical sense, but in the simplest psychological and everyday sense. If a man does not see this good, if he condemns everything irrevocably, if he seeks and sees only the bad, if he is incapable of seeing the good in things and people—then this is the blasphemy against the Holy Ghost. There are different types of men. Some are capable of seeing the good even where there is very little of it. They are sometimes even inclined to exaggerate it to themselves. Others, on the contrary, are inclined to see everything worse than it is in reality, are incapable of seeing anything good. First of all, always and in everything, they find something bad, always begin with suspicion, with accusation, with calumny. This is the blasphemy against the Holy Ghost. This blasphemy is *not forgiven*; that means that it leaves a very deep trace on the inner nature of the man himself.

Usually in life people take slander too lightly, excuse it too easily in themselves and in others. Slander constitutes half their lives, fills half their interests. People slander without noticing themselves what they are doing and automatically they expect nothing but slander from others. They answer the slander of others with slander and strive only to forestall them. A particularly noticeable tendency to slander is called either a critical mind or wit. Men do not understand that even the usual everyday slander is the beginning of the blasphemy against the Holy Ghost. It is not for nothing that the *Devil* means *slanderer*. The passage in the Gospel, that they shall give account even of every idle word in the day of judgement, sounds so strange and incomprehensible to men because they do not understand that even a small slander is the beginning of the blasphemy against the Holy Ghost. They do not understand that even every idle word remains . . .

The parable of the unjust steward refers to the creation of the other, of the contrary, tendency, that is to say, the tendency to see the Holy Ghost or the 'good' even where there is very little of it, and in this way to increase the good in oneself and liberate oneself from sins, that is from 'evil'.

Man finds what he looks for. Who looks for the evil finds the evil; who looks for the good, finds the good.

OUSPENSKY

In setting forward this standard to be followed in our dealings with our fellow-men we are clearly claiming a sovereign faith in what George Fox called "that of God in every man", which, as it is led from within by the Spirit of God, is bound to respond to the supreme appeal which we make to love and truth. In such a faith and trust we are surely following Christ's own example, and we may do so with perfect confidence. For if anything is clear from the Gospel story it is this, that, knowing the evil that was in the world and in the heart of man, He yet retained His own unbounded faith that goodness would in the end prevail. He saw this goodness, still a flame beneath the surface, in Mary Magdalene, out of whom He cast seven evil spirits, and in the woman "who was a sinner" who came to Him in the house of Simon. He called Levi the publican to follow Him, and also Zacchaeus, though they belonged to a trade that was despised and hated by the Jews. He gained the name of being the "Friend of publicans and sinners". For He saw right through to the inner man or woman, and won them back to goodness by His own faith in them when everyone else condemned them and treated them as outcast. In this attitude towards human nature we must take the utmost care that we follow His example and count nothing 'common' or 'unclean', from whatever source it comes.

C. F. ANDREWS

If a man is loved by any human being condemnation is rash, and we ought at least to be silent.

MARK RUTHERFORD

At all times, all too many Christians have behaved as though the devil were a First Principle, on the same footing as God. They have paid more attention to evil and the problem of its eradications than to good and the methods by which individual goodness may be deepened, and the sum of goodness increased. The effects which follow too constant and intense a concentration upon evil are always disastrous. Those who crusade, not *for* God in themselves, but *against* the devil in others, never succeed in making the world better, but leave it either as it was, or sometimes even perceptibly worse than it was, before the crusade began. By thinking primarily of evil we tend, however excellent our intentions, to create occasions for evil to manifest itself.

Though frequently Manichaean in practice, Christianity was never Manichaean in its dogmas. In this respect it differs from our modern idolatries of Communism and Nationalism, which are Manichaean not only in action, but also in creed and theory. Today it is everywhere self-evident that *we* are on the side of Light, *they* on the side of Darkness. And being on the side of Darkness, *they* deserve to be punished and must be liquidated (since *our* divinity justifies everything) by the most fiendish means at our disposal. By idolatrously worshipping ourselves as Ormuzd, and by regarding the other fellow as Ahriman, the Principle of Evil, we of the twentieth century are doing our best to guarantee the triumph of diabolism in our time.

ALDOUS HUXLEY (from *The Devils of Loudun*)

Hatred of evil destroys the spiritual world of man just as much as hatred of the good, which does not mean to say that our attitude towards evil must not be ruthless, nor that there can be any question of a truce with it.

Our attitude to evil must be twofold: we must be tolerant of it as the Creator is tolerant, and we must mercilessly struggle against it.

True spirituality consists in believing in the power of good rather than that of ill, in God rather than Satan.

BERDYAEV

To call Good Evil is the great sin—the sin of the Puritan and the Philistine. To call Evil Good is comparatively venial.

COVENTRY PATMORE

Society suffers from a profound feeling of unhappiness, not so much when it is in material poverty as when its members are deprived of a large part of their humanity. This unhappiness goes on smouldering in the subconscious mind of the community till its life is reduced to ashes or a sudden combustion is produced. The repressed personality of man generates an inflammable moral gas deadly in its explosive force.

We have seen in the late war,* and also in some of the still more recent events of history, how human individuals freed from moral and spiritual bonds find a boisterous joy in a debauchery of destruction. There is generated a disinterested passion of ravage. Through such catastrophe we can realise what formidable forces of annihilation are kept in check in our communities by bonds of social ideas; nay, made into multitudinous manifestations of beauty and fruitfulness. Thus we know that evils are, like meteors, stray fragments of life, which need the attraction of some great ideal in order to be assimilated with the wholesomeness of creation. The evil forces are literally outlaws; they only need the control and cadence of spiritual laws to change them into good. The true goodness is not the negation of badness, it is in the mastery of it. Goodness is the miracle which turns the tumult of chaos into a dance of beauty.

*1914–1918   TAGORE

If to us things appear undivine, if we hasten to condemn this or that phenomenon as inconsistent with the nature of the divine being, it is because we are ignorant of the sense and purpose of the Divine in the world in its entirety. Because we see only parts and fragments, we judge of each by itself as if it were the whole . . . But at the same time our present feeling of this evil and imperfection, the revolt of our consciousness against them, is also a necessary valuation, for if we have first to face and endure them, the ultimate command on us is to reject, to overcome, to transform . . . To create out of Matter a temple of Divinity would seem to be the task imposed on the spirit born into the material universe.

AUROBINDO

In so far as Evil exists, the root of evil is in Matter; but Evil does not exist; all that exists, in a half-existence, is the last effort of The

Good, the point at which The Good ceases because, so to speak, endlessness has all but faded out to an end. . . . The existence, or half-existence, of Matter brings about the necessity of morality: the Divine perfection is above morality, is "unmoral"; the purely material is below morality; morality is for man; man—being divine at his topmost pitch and "human" at the mean, and brute below that and merely vegetative below that and merely Matter in the lowest range of his nature—man, if he is to reach his good, the desired of every being, must "what in him is dark illumine, what is low raise and support"; if he is to rise to the height of his great argument, must become what his highest is . . . His duty, or rather his happiness, his blessedness, his deepest inner choice, is to labour his entire being into identification with this, the Divine in him. . . .

STEPHEN MACKENNA (*interpreting Plotinus*)

"TO LABOUR HIS ENTIRE BEING"

There is an attitude of mind that regards all inner conflicts as undesirable, and to be done away with as completely as possible by whatever kind of "treatment"—and it is usually psychoanalytical —may prove most effective. This attitude is quite common in England among intellectuals of a certain type, or was when they had enough money for the purpose; and in America the thing is a perfect craze—in moneyed circles with a tinge of culture people talk of "my analyst" as glibly as our grandmothers used to talk of "my grocer", or as business men talk of "my chauffeur". You sometimes get an impression in the States that "my analyst" is a glorified version of the little black boy who pirouettes on with the Marschallin's chocolate in the first act of *Rosenkavalier* and pirouettes off with her handkerchief in the last.

The motive of such people, when it's something more than merely to be in the fashion, may be a frankly commercial one: once you've been psychoanalysed, they may imagine, your social life will be smoother, you'll "make friends and influence people" more easily, you'll buy better, you'll sell better, and, in a word, whether as hostess or salesman or whatever else it may be you'll "get on". The motive, on the other hand—and this alone need concern us— may be to save themselves from inner turmoil: to get rid of fears, hatreds, irrationalities, compulsions and the rest: in a word, to live at peace with themselves and their neighbours.

Now a man may be such, or may have become such, that he

216

cannot win through to any sort of fruitful living solely by his own effort and the unmediated grace of God. In that event there is need of aid from without. The helper may be, in the broadest sense, a priest: and by a priest I mean anybody, from a priest in the dictionary sense to a friend or just someone now living or long since dead, who by finding the right words, or by putting himself in the right relation, or (perhaps best of all) simply by example, becomes the mediator of God's grace. But the helper may also be an analyst: and an analyst will make the man far more of a man if he frees him for fruitful inner struggles by freeing him from the compulsion of sterile ones. But to free a man not for the right kind of conflict but from conflict as such, that is another matter; and to be freed in this way is sometimes a man's aim in seeking treatment, and sometimes, anyhow, what results from it. There are people who desire, morally as well as otherwise, too quiet a life.

For the struggle in our own hearts between the better and the worse in us, the higher and the lower: between generosity and meanness, mercy and ruthlessness, well-wishing and ill-wishing, gentleness and aggression, respect and contempt, tolerance and intolerance, humility and pride; this struggle is not something undesirable, something to be magicked away for the speedier calming of the turmoil within, but the very stuff and meaning of us as living human souls. The plain fact is that, whatever may be the explanation in terms of psychology or physiology or metaphysics or religion, we *are*, to a greater or lesser degree, mean and proud and revengeful and aggressive and egoistical; and we know quite as plainly, by a direct and immediate knowledge, that we ought not to be. So we struggle against our meanness and pride and aggressiveness and egoism because, compelled by some responsibility that seems put upon us in the nature of things, we feel we must. Somehow, we apprehend, these impulses within us are of a nature that spoils; they darken the universe; and since we alone can subdue them, if we make no effort to do so we are like a Moses who would have refused to speak for God because he stammered, or like an Isaiah who, after his mouth had been touched by the live coal, would have failed to answer "Send me". There is a passage in *The Will to Believe*, by William James, which expresses what I have been trying to say with superb clarity:

"I confess that I do not see why the very existence of an invisible world may not in part depend on the personal response which any one of us may make to the religious appeal. God himself, in short, may draw vital strength and increase of very being from our fidelity. For my own part, I do not know what the sweat and blood and tragedy of this life mean, if they mean anything short of this. If this life be not a real fight, in which something is eternally gained for the universe by success, it is no better than a game of private theatricals from which one may withdraw at will. But it *feels* like a real fight— as if there were something really wild in the universe which we, with all our idealities and faithfulnesses, are needed to redeem; and first of all to redeem our own hearts from atheisms and fears. For such a half-wild half-saved universe our nature is adapted. The deepest thing in our nature is this dumb region of the heart in which we dwell alone with our willingnesses and our unwillingnesses, our faiths and our fears. As through the cracks and crannies of caverns those waters exude from the earth's bosom which then form the fountain-heads of springs, so in these crepuscular depths of personality the sources of all our outer deeds and decisions take their rise. Here is our deepest organ of communication with the nature of things; and compared with these concrete movements of our soul all abstract statements and scientific arguments—the veto, for example, which the strict positivist pronounces upon our faith— sound to us like mere chatterings of the teeth . . .

"These then are my last words to you: Be not afraid of life. Believe that life *is* worth living, and your belief will help create the fact. The 'scientific' proof that you are right may not be clear before the day of judgment (or some stage of being which that expression may serve to symbolise) is reached. But the faithful fighters of this hour, or the beings that then and there will represent them, may turn to the faint-hearted, who here decline to go on, with words like those with which Henry IV greeted the tardy Crillon after a great battle had been gained: 'Hang yourself, brave Crillon! We fought at Arques, and you were not there!' "

"The sweat and blood and tragedy of this life". This is a reality and has meaning, just as the joy of this life is a reality and has meaning; and if we attempt to escape it, if we attempt to end the conflict within us, and the agony that this conflict involves, by being *acted upon*, we are giving up reality and becoming less than fully human. It is the tension of this struggle that gives us our glory: it makes us rich and meaningful, allies of and fellow workers with the divine. Or, to put it in another way, it is the combination of the evil within us and our struggle against it—precisely this—that produces, in every one of us save those rare souls that are born almost without sin, the very best of which we are capable: that produces a value greater than could ever have been there if neither evil nor struggle had existed. So evil, though a terrible reality for *us* and to be struggled against without respite, is, as so many have said, in ultimate reality non-existent: the evil and the conflict are instruments, both, of a final "rightness" beyond good and evil. The world, as Keats said in a famous letter, is the vale of soul-making: "Do you not see how necessary a World of Pains and troubles is to school an Intelligence and make it a Soul?"

Saul was cruel, intolerant, a persecutor: when cruel, intolerant, and a persecutor he was struggling already with the struggle that reached its climax on the road to Damascus: and Saul became Paul. Paul preached the gospel of love: and Paul would not have loved with Paul's love if Saul had not hated with Saul's hatred: and Paul and Saul were one: and when hating and persecuting, indeed by hating and persecuting, he was reaching out to the same reality and truth—to what, as creatures, we must call the same goodness—as he was reaching out to when he wrote the thirteenth chapter of the first epistle to the Corinthians. Would we have had this man *acted upon*—by anyone except the God in his heart and in the universe?

There is a sense, I must hasten to add, in which to be at peace with oneself and to be freed from the conflict is to have achieved a saving wisdom. Peace so comes when we have learned to accept, not so much with resignation as with a dutiful response to reality, the evil we confront as a part of our nature. We no longer hate ourselves for being what we are; we no longer blaspheme because we have been created just so and not otherwise; we are no longer in revolt, with an insolent egoism, against our own imperfection. We are content, in a word, to be men and not God. The struggle continues, for to accept ourselves for what we are is by no means to abandon the effort to change; the struggle, indeed, is more intense than before; but we struggle now with greater calm (and therefore with more depth), with a sort of detachment from any personal interestedness—we no longer desire to be good because of the *we*, but because of the *good*—and with a love of ourselves as well as with a love of our neighbours. And we struggle now with a greater steadiness. Before, we felt at every defeat as if we had failed in the final examination; now, the past is always irrelevant and the next attempt is all that matters.

There is nothing more precious in life than the gaining of this inner tranquillity. But it comes to very few (if, when it does come, it is really to be of the kind I have been attempting to describe) except after a long period of agony. For the agony is a preparation for the peace, which is something not to be induced, mechanically, from without, but to be won, in freedom and responsibility, from within.

v. g. (from My Dear Timothy)

THE PORTRAIT OF MOSES

The whole world was shaken and enthralled by the miracle of the Exodus. The name of Moses was on everyone's lips. Tidings of the great miracle reached also the wise king of Arabistan. The king summoned to him his best painter and bade him go to Moses, to paint his portrait and bring it back to him. When the painter returned the king gathered together all his sages, wise in the science of physiognomics, and asked them to define by the portrait the character of Moses, his qualities, inclinations, habits and the source of his miraculous power.

"King," answered the sages, "this is the portrait of a man cruel, haughty, greedy of gain, possessed by desire for power and by all the vices which exist in the world."

These words roused the king's indignation.

"How can it be possible," he exclaimed, "that a man whose marvellous deeds ring through the whole world should be of such a kind?"

A dispute began between the painter and the sages. The painter affirmed that the portrait of Moses had been painted by him quite accurately, while the sages maintained that Moses' character had been unerringly determined by them according to the portrait.

The wise king of Arabistan decided to verify which of the disputing parties was right, and he himself set off for the camp of Israel.

At the first glance the king became convinced that the face of Moses had been faultlessly portrayed by the painter. On entering the tent of the man of God he knelt down, bowed to the ground and told Moses of the dispute between the artist and the sages.

"At first, until I saw thy face," said the king, "I thought it must be that the artist had painted thy image badly, for my sages are men very much experienced in the science of physiognomics. Now I am convinced that they are quite worthless men and that their wisdom is vain and worthless."

"No," answered Moses, "it is not so; both the painter and the physiognomists are men highly skilled, and both parties are right. Be it known to thee that all the vices of which the sages spoke have indeed been assigned to me by nature and perhaps to an even higher degree than was found by them from my portrait. But I struggled with my vices by long and intense efforts of the will and gradually overcame and suppressed them in myself until all opposed to them became my second nature. And in this lies my greatest pride."

TALMUDIC LEGEND

There follows a note on perversity

I have germs of all possible crimes, or nearly all, within me. I became aware of this in the course of a journey, in circumstances which I have described to you. The crimes horrified me, but they did not surprise me; I felt the possibility of them within myself; it was actually because I felt this possibility in myself that they filled me with such horror. This natural disposition is dangerous and very painful, but, like every variety of natural disposition, it can be put to good purpose if one knows how to make the right use of it with the help of grace.

SIMONE WEIL

In these days, when I have heard others talk of what was the sin against the Holy Ghost, then would the tempter so provoke me to desire to sin that sin, that I was as if I could not, must not, neither should be quiet until I had committed that; now, no sin would serve but that; if it were to be committed by speaking of such a word, then I have been as if my mouth would have spoken that word, whether I would or no; and in so strong a measure was this temptation upon me, that often I have been ready to clap my hand under my chin, to hold my mouth from opening; and to that end also I have had thoughts at other times, to leap with my head downward, into some muck-hill hole or other, to keep my mouth from speaking.

BUNYAN (from *Grace Abounding*)

On all the levels of our being, from the muscular and sensational to the moral and the intellectual, every tendency generates its own opposite. We look at something red, and visual induction intensifies our perception of green and even, in certain circumstances, causes us to see a green halo round the red object, a green after-image when the object has been removed. We will a movement; one set of muscles is stimulated and, automatically, by spinal induction, the opposing muscles are inhibited. The same principle holds good on the higher levels of consciousness. Every yes begets a corresponding no. . . . Even the well-balanced and the self-controlled are sometimes aware of a paradoxical temptation to do the exact opposite of what they know they ought to do. It is a temptation, very often, to an evil without point or profit, to a gratuitous and, so to say, disinterested outrage against common sense and common decency. Most of these inductive temptations are successfully resisted—most, but by no means all. Every now and then sensible and fundamentally decent people will embark, all of a sudden, on courses of which they themselves are the first to disapprove. In these cases the evil-doer acts as though he were possessed by some entity different from and malignantly hostile to his ordinary self. In fact, he is the victim of a neutral mechanism, which (as not uncommonly happens with machines) has got out of hand and, from being the servant of its possessor, has become his master. . . . Every collection of spiritual letters abounds in references to those frightful temptations against the faith and against chastity, to which the seekers after perfection are peculiarly subject. Good directors point out that such temptations are a normal and almost inevitable feature of the spiritual life and must not be permitted to cause undue distress. In a letter dated 26th January 1923, Dom John Chapman writes as follows: "In the 17th–18th centuries most pious souls seem to have gone through a period in which they felt sure that God had reprobated them. . . . This doesn't seem to happen nowadays. But the corresponding trial of our contemporaries seems to be the feeling of not having any faith; not temptation against any particular article (usually), but a mere feeling that religion is not true. . . . The only remedy is to *despise* the whole thing and pay no attention to it except (of course) to assure our Lord that one is ready to suffer from it as long as He wishes, which seems an absurd paradox to say to a Person one doesn't believe in."

ALDOUS HUXLEY (from *The Devils of Loudun*)

> Yet be not sad:
> Evil into the mind of God or man
> May come and go, so unapproved, and leave
> No spot or blame behind.

MILTON (from *Paradise Lost*)

SECOND PART

III. DIVINE AND HUMAN

THE CREATION

And God stepped out on space
And he looked around and said:
I'm lonely—
I'll make me a world.

And far as the eye of God could see
Darkness covered everything,
Blacker than a hundred midnights
Down in a cypress swamp.

Then God smiled,
And the light broke,
And the darkness rolled up on one side,
And the light stood shining on the other,
And God said: That's good!

Then God reached out and took the light in his hands,
And God rolled the light around in his hands,
Until he made the sun;
And he set that sun a-blazing in the heavens.
And the light that was left from making the sun
God gathered it up in a shining ball
And flung against the darkness,
Spangling the night with the moon and stars.
Then down between
The darkness and the light
He hurled the world;
And God said: That's good!

Then God himself stepped down—
And the sun was in his right hand,
And the moon was on his left;
And stars were clustered about his head,
And the earth was under his feet.
And God walked, and where he trod
His footsteps hollowed the valleys out
And bulged the mountains up.

Then he stopped and looked and saw
That the earth was hot and barren.

So God stepped over to the edge of the world
And he spat out the seven seas—
He batted his eyes, and the lightnings flashed—
He clapped his hands, and the thunders rolled—
And the waters above the earth came down,
The cooling waters came down.

Then the green grass sprouted,
And the little red flowers blossomed,
The pine-tree pointed his finger to the sky,
And the oak spread out his arms,
The lakes cuddled down in the hollows of the ground,
And the rivers ran down to the sea;
And God smiled again,
And the rainbow appeared,
And curled itself around his shoulder.

Then God raised his arm and he waved his hand
Over the sea and over the land,
And he said: Bring forth! Bring forth!
And quicker than God could drop his hand,
Fishes and fowls
And beasts and birds
Swam the rivers and the seas,
Roamed the forests and the woods,
And split the air with their wings.
And God said: That's good!

Then God walked around
And God looked around
On all that he had made.
He looked at his sun,
And he looked at his moon,
And he looked at his little stars;
He looked on his world
With all its living things,
And God said: I'm lonely still.

Then God sat down—
On the side of a hill where he could think;
By a deep wide river he sat down;
With his head in his hands,

God thought and thought,
Till he thought: I'll make me a man!

Up from the bed of the river
God scooped the clay;
And by the bank of the river
He kneeled him down;
And there the great God Almighty,
Who lit the sun and fixed it in the sky,
Who flung the stars to the most far corner of the night,
Who rounded the earth in the middle of his hand;
This Great God,
Like a mammy bending over his baby,
Kneeled down in the dust
Toiling over a lump of clay
Till he shaped it in his own image;

Then into it he blew the breath of life,
And man became a living soul.
Amen. Amen.

JAMES WELDON JOHNSON

For He made Man (as it were) for his Play-fellow.

THOMAS VAUGHAN

PREPARATION FOR THE KING

Now all things were already arrived at their own end: "the heaven and the earth," as Moses says, "were finished," and all things that lie between them; and the particular things were adorned with their appropriate beauty, the heaven with the rays of the stars, the sea and air with the living creatures that swim and fly, and the earth with all varieties of plants and animals, to all which, empowered by the Divine will, it gave birth together; the earth was full, too, of her produce, bringing forth fruits at the same time with flowers; the meadows were full of all that grows therein, and all the mountain ridges, and summits, and every hill-side, and slope, and hollow, were crowned with young grass, and with the varied produce of the trees, just risen from the ground, yet shot up at once into their perfect beauty; and all the beasts that had come into life at God's command were rejoicing, we may suppose, and skipping about, running to and fro in the thickets in herds according to their kind,

231

while every sheltered and shady spot was ringing with the chants of the song-birds. And at sea, we may suppose, the sight to be seen was of the like kind, as it had just settled to quiet and calm in the gathering together of its depths, where havens and harbours spontaneously hollowed out on the coasts made the sea reconciled with the land; and the gentle motion of the waves vied in beauty with the meadows, rippling delicately with light and harmless breezes that skimmed the surface; and all the wealth of creation by land and sea was ready, and none was there to share it.

For not as yet had that great and precious thing, man, come into the world of being; it was not to be looked for that the ruler should appear before the subjects of his rule; but when his dominion was prepared, the next step was that the king should be manifested. When, then, the Maker of all had prepared beforehand, as it were, a royal lodging for the future king (and this was the land, and islands, and sea, and the heaven arching like a roof over them), and when all kinds of wealth had been stored in this palace (and by wealth I mean the whole creation, all that is in plants and trees, and all that has sense, and breath, and life; and if we are to account materials also as wealth—all that for their beauty are reckoned precious in the eyes of men, as gold and silver, and the substances of your jewels which men delight in—having concealed, I say, abundance of all these also in the bosom of the earth as in a royal treasure-house), he thus manifests man in the world, to be the beholder of some of the wonders therein, and the lord of others; that by his enjoyment he might have knowledge of the Giver, and by the beauty and majesty of the things he saw might trace out that power of the Maker which is beyond speech and language.

For this reason man was brought into the world last after the creation, not being rejected to the last as worthless, but as one whom it behoved to be king over his subjects at his very birth. And as a good host does not bring his guest to his house before the preparation of his feast, but, when he has made all due preparation, and decked with their proper adornments his house, his couches, his table, brings his guest home when things suitable for his refreshment are in readiness—in the same manner the rich and munificent Entertainer of our nature, when He had decked the habitation with beauties of every kind, and prepared this great and varied banquet, then introduced man, assigning to him as his task not the acquiring of what was not there, but the enjoyment of the things which were there; and for this reason He gives him as foundations the instincts of a two-fold organization, blending the Divine with the earthy, that by means of both he may be naturally and properly disposed to each enjoyment, enjoying God by means of his more divine nature, and the good things of earth by the sense that is akin to them.

ST. GREGORY OF NYSSA

The eyes of my soul were opened, and I beheld the plenitude of God, wherein I did comprehend the whole world, both here and beyond the sea, and the abyss and ocean and all things. In all these things I beheld naught save the divine power, in a manner assuredly indescribable; so that through excess of marvelling the soul cried with a loud voice, saying 'This whole world is full of God!' Wherefore I now comprehended how small a thing is the whole world, that is to say both here and beyond the seas, the abyss, the ocean, and all things; and that the power of God exceeds and fills all. Then He said unto me: 'I have shown thee something of My power', and I understood that after this I should better understand the rest. He then said 'Behold now My humility'. Then was I given an insight into the deep humility of God towards man. And comprehending that unspeakable power and beholding that deep humility, my soul marvelled greatly, and did esteem itself to be nothing at all.

ST. ANGELA OF FOLIGNO

§ 2

The Perfect Man was the cause of the Universe, being the epiphany of God's desire to be known.

IBN 'ARABI (paraphrased)

> What is all beauty in the world? The image,
> Like quivering boughs reflected in a stream,
> Of that eternal Orchard which abides
> Unwithered in the hearts of Perfect Men.

RUMI

This, O Lord, shows me to be equal to the angels, and even above them, for your substance is invisible to the angels, and your nature is inaccessible to them. Yet to me you are wholly visible, and your substance is fused with my nature.

ST. SYMEON THE NEW THEOLOGIAN

233

Man is the revelation of the Infinite, and it does not become finite in him. It remains the Infinite.

MARK RUTHERFORD

You may see the disc of Divinity quite clearly through the smoked glass of humanity, but no otherwise.

COVENTRY PATMORE

God said to Moses, 'In every place where you find a trace of the feet of man, there am I before you.'

THE MEKILTA

The man that was manifested at the first creation of the world, and he that shall be after the consummation of all, are alike: they equally bear in themselves the Divine image.

ST. GREGORY OF NYSSA

There are many wonders, but nothing more wondrous than man.

SOPHOCLES

I believe in the human being, mind and flesh; form and soul.

RICHARD JEFFERIES

Not believing in the glory of our own soul is what the Vedanta calls atheism.

VIVEKANANDA

None can question the being of a Deity but one that is ignorant of man's excellencies.

TRAHERNE

The soul, a divine thing, a fragment as it were of the Primal Beauty. . . .

PLOTINUS

What is great in man is that he is a bridge and not a goal.

NIETZSCHE

And as to our own soul we are to hold that it stands, in part, always in the presence of The Divine, while in part it is concerned with the things of this sphere and in part occupies a middle ground. It is one nature in graded powers; and sometimes the soul in its entirety is borne along by the loftiest in itself; sometimes, the less noble part is dragged down and drags the mid-soul with it, though the law is that the soul may never succumb entire.

The soul's disaster falls upon it when it ceases to dwell in the perfect Beauty, thence to pour forth into the frame of the All whatsoever the All can hold of good and beauty. The measure of its absorption in that vision is the measure of its grace and power, and what it draws from this contemplation it communicates to the lower sphere, illuminated and illuminating always.

PLOTINUS

THE POET RECALLS HIS VISION

... When everywhere a vital pulse was felt,
And all the several frames of things, like stars,
Through every magnitude distinguishable,
Shone mutually indebted, or half lost
Each in the other's blaze, a galaxy
Of life and glory. In the midst stood Man,
Outwardly, inwardly contemplated,
As, of all visible natures, crown, though born
Of dust, and kindred to the worm; a Being,
Both in perception and discernment, first
In every capability of rapture,
Through the divine effect of power and love;
As, more than anything we know, instinct
With godhead, and, by reason and by will,
Acknowledging dependency sublime.

WORDSWORTH

"A RELATION NEARER THAN ORDINARY"

Indeed, all things that are made show forth the power and wisdom of God and His goodness too to mankind; and therefore many men urge the creation to silence atheistical objections. But though all those things show a God, yet man does it above all the rest. He is the precious stone of the ring, and the most glorious jewel of the globe; to whose reasonable use, service, and satisfaction the whole seems to be made and dedicated. But God's delight (by whom man was made, we are told by the Holy Ghost) is "in the

235

habitable parts of the earth with the sons of men", and "with those that are contrite in spirit". And why is man His delight, but because man only of all His works was of His likeness? This is the intimate relation of man to God. Somewhat nearer than ordinary; for of all other beings man only had the honour of being His image; and by his resemblance to God, as I may say, came his kindred with God and knowledge of Him. So that the nearest and best way for man to know God and be acquainted with Him is to seek Him in himself, in His image; and, as he finds that, he comes to find and know God. Now man may be said to be God's image in a double respect. First, as he is of an immortal nature; and next, as that nature is endued with those excellencies in small, and proportionable to a creature's capacity, that are by nature infinitely and incomparably in his Creator. For instance, wisdom, justice, mercy, holiness, patience and the like. As man becomes holy, just, merciful, patient, etc., by the copy he will know the Original, and by the workmanship in himself he will be acquainted with the Holy Workman.

WILLIAM PENN

OUR ROYAL NATURE

For as in our own life artificers fashion a tool in the way suitable to its use, so the best Artificer made our nature as it were a formation fit for the exercise of royalty, preparing it at once by superior advantages of soul, and by the very form of the body, to be such as to be adapted for royalty: for the soul immediately shows its royal and exalted character, far removed as it is from the lowliness of private station, in that it owns no lord, and is self-governed, swayed autocratically by its own will; for to whom else does this belong than to a king? And further, besides these facts, the fact that it is the image of that Nature which rules over all means nothing else than this, that our nature was created to be royal from the first. For as, in men's ordinary use, those who make images of princes both mould the figure of their form, and represent along with this the royal rank by the vesture of purple, and even the likeness is commonly spoken of as "a king", so the human nature also, as it was made to rule the rest, was, by its likeness to the King of all, made as it were a living image, partaking with the archetype both in rank and in name, not vested in purple, nor giving indication of its rank by sceptre and diadem (for the archetype itself is not arrayed with these), but, instead of the purple robe, clothed in virtue, which is in truth the most royal of all raiment, and, in place of the sceptre, leaning on the bliss of immortality, and, instead of the royal diadem, decked with the crown of righteousness; so that it is shown to be perfectly like to the beauty of its archetype in all that belongs to the dignity of royalty.

It is true, indeed, that the Divine beauty is not adorned with any shape or endowment of form, or with any beauty of colour, but is contemplated as excellence in unspeakable bliss. As then painters transfer human forms to their pictures by the means of certain colours, laying on their copy the proper and corresponding tints, so that the beauty of the original may be accurately transferred to the likeness; so I would have you understand that our Maker also, painting the portrait to resemble His own beauty, by the addition of virtues, as it were with colours, shows in us His own sovereignty: and manifold and varied are the tints, so to say, by which His true form is portrayed: not red, or white, or the blending of these, whatever it may be called, nor a touch of black that paints the eyebrow and the eye, and shades, by some combination, the depressions in the figure, and all such arts which the hands of painters contrive, but, instead of these, purity, freedom from passion, blessedness, alienation from all evil, and all those attributes of the like kind which help to form in men the likeness of God: with such hues as these did the Maker of His own image mark our nature.

And if you were to examine the other points also by which the Divine beauty is expressed, you will find that there too the likeness in the image which we present is perfectly preserved. The Godhead is mind and word: for "in the beginning was the Word", and the followers of Paul "have the mind of Christ" which "speaks" in them: humanity too is not far removed from these: you see in yourself word and understanding, an imitation of the very Mind and Word. Again, God is love, and the fount of love: for this the great John declares, that "love is of God", and "God is love": the Fashioner of our nature has made this to be our feature too: for "hereby," He says, "shall all men know that ye are my disciples, if ye love one another": thus, if this be absent, the whole stamp of the likeness is transformed. The Deity beholds and hears all things, and searches all things out: you too have the power of apprehension of things by means of sight and hearing, and the understanding that inquires into things and searches them out.

ST. GREGORY OF NYSSA

My God, I heard this day,
That none doth build a stately habitation,
  But he that means to dwell therein.
  What house more stately hath there been,
Or can be, than is Man? to whose creation
    All things are in decay . . .

  For us the windes do blow,
The earth doth rest, heav'n move, and fountains flow.
  Nothing we see, but means our good,
  As our delight, or as our treasure:
The whole is, either our cupboard of food,
    Or cabinet of pleasure.

  The starres have us to bed;
Night draws the curtain, which the sunne withdraws;
  Musick and light attend our head.
  All things unto our flesh are kinde
In their descent and being; to our minde
    In their ascent and cause . . .

  Since then, my God, thou hast
So brave a Palace built; O dwell in it,
  That it may dwell with thee at last!
  Till then, afford us so much wit;
That, as the world serves us, we may serve thee,
    And both thy servants be.

GEORGE HERBERT

I had approached, like other youths, the shield
Of human nature from the golden side,
And would have fought, even to the death, to attest
The quality of the metal which I saw.

WORDSWORTH

For if the man who is subject to passion, and carnal, makes it
incredible that man was adorned, as it were, with Divine beauty,
surely the man of lofty virtue and pure from pollution will confirm
you in the better conception of human nature.

For instance (for it is better to make our argument clear by an
illustration), one of those noted for wickedness—some Jechoniah,
say, or some other of evil memory—has obliterated the beauty of his

nature by the pollution of wickedness; yet in Moses and in men like him the form of the image was kept pure. Now where the beauty of the form has not been obscured, there is made plain the faithfulness of the saying that man is an image of God.

ST. GREGORY OF NYSSA

§ 3

The central conception of Man in the Gospels is that he is an unfinished creation capable of reaching a higher level by a definite evolution which must begin by his own efforts.

MAURICE NICOLL

Theologians teach that our ultimate felicity will consist in the development of a single divine humanity made up of innumerable unique and sympathetic individualities or 'members', each one shining with its proper and peculiar lustre, which shall be as unlike any other lustre as that of a sapphire is from that of a ruby or an emerald; and they further teach that the end of this life is the awakening and growth of such individualities through a faithful following of the peculiar good which is each individual's 'ruling love'; since each has his ruling love, if he knew it, that is, his peculiar and partial way of discerning and desiring the absolute good, which no created being is capable of discerning and desiring in its fullness and universality. Every man who is humanly alive . . . is conscious that the bond of man with man consists, not in similarity, but in dissimilarity; the happiness of love, in which alone is happiness, residing . . . not in union but conjunction, which can only be between spiritual dissimilars. That man is created in the capacity for uniqueness of character is shown by the human face, which is never at all alike in any two persons, and of which the peculiarity is nothing but an expression of the latent inherent difference which it is the proper work of life to bring into actuality.

COVENTRY PATMORE

Thus there dawned upon me what is now my highest intuition. I saw clearly that each man is meant to represent humanity in his own way, continuing its elements uniquely so that it may reveal itself in every mode, and all that can issue from its womb be made actual in the fullness of unending space and time.

SCHLEIERMACHER

THE FATHER AND THE SON

ARJUNA:

Some worship you with steadfast love. Others worship God the unmanifest and changeless. Which kind of devotee has the greater understanding of yoga?

SRI KRISHNA:

Those whose minds are fixed on me in steadfast love, worshipping me with absolute faith. I consider them to have the greater understanding of yoga.

As for those others, the devotees of God the unmanifest, indefinable and changeless, they worship that which is omnipresent, constant, eternal, beyond thought's compass, never to be moved. They hold all the senses in check. They are tranquil-minded, and devoted to the welfare of humanity. They see the Atman in every creature. They also will certainly come to me.

But the devotees of the unmanifest have a harder task, because the unmanifest is very difficult for embodied souls to realise.

THE BHAGAVAD-GITA

He spoke well who said that the immeasurable Father is measured in the Son.

IRENAEUS

Our whole interior life is energized by the love of God. But whence shall we derive this love? All our loves are fed by sensible impressions of the beloved object (the world, our friends and loved ones). How shall our love, our faith, endure the ordeal if they are not nourished by evidences? Yet what sensible impression can we receive of God, Whom "no man hath ever seen"? We have Christ.

FATHER YELCHANINOV

Think of a white cloud as being holy, you cannot love it; but think of a holy man within the cloud, love springs up in your thoughts, for to think of holiness distinct from man is impossible to the affections.

BLAKE

*

And the Word was made flesh.

ST. JOHN

> . . . the source of life
> Descends to be a weeping babe . . .
>
> BLAKE

> Wellcome, all Wonders in one sight!
> Æternity shutt in a span.
> Sommer in Winter. Day in Night.
> Heaven in earth, and God in Man.
> Great little one! whose all-embracing birth
> Lifts earth to heaven, stoopes heav'n to earth.
>
> RICHARD CRASHAW

> Begotten Son, Divine Similitude,
> In whose conspicuous countenance, without cloud
> Made visible, the Almighty Father shines,
> Whom else no creature can behold. . . .
>
> MILTON

> The Divine Vision still was seen,
> Still was the Human Form Divine,
> Weeping in weak & mortal clay,
> O Jesus, still the Form was thine.
>
> And thine the Human Face, & thine
> The Human Hands & Feet & Breath,
> Entering thro' the Gates of Birth
> And passing thro' the Gates of Death.
>
> BLAKE

THE BIRTH OF GOD IN US

That Deity should be born in our nature, ought not reasonably to present any strangeness to the minds of those who do not take too narrow a view of things. For who, when he takes a survey of the universe, is so simple as not to believe that there is Deity in everything, penetrating it, embracing it, and seated in it? For all things depend on Him Who is, nor can there be anything which has not its being in Him Who is. If, therefore, all things are in Him, and He in all things, why are they scandalized at the plan of Revelation, when it teaches that God was born among men, that same God Who, we are convinced, is even now not outside mankind? For although this last form of God's presence amongst us is not the same as that

241

former presence, still His existence amongst us equally both then and now is evidenced; only now He Who holds together Nature in existence is transfused in *us*; while at that other time He was transfused throughout *our nature*, in order that our nature might by this transfusion of the Divine become itself divine, rescued as it was from death, and put beyond the reach of the caprice of the antagonist.

ST. GREGORY OF NYSSA

The Father is begetting his Son unceasingly, and furthermore I say he begets me his Son, his very own Son.

MEISTER ECKHART

When Christ was born of God, all creatures were, so to speak, mentally present in him.

LUIS DE LEON

We belong to the same race as Christ and through His humanity we are associated with His human freedom.

BERDYAEV

We are coheires with Christ; nor shall His own
Heire-ship be lesse, by our adoption:
The number here of heires, shall from the state
Of His great birth-right nothing derogate.

ROBERT HERRICK

THE CRUCIFIXION

What other objection is alleged by our adversaries? This: that (to take the preferable view) it was altogether needless that that transcendent Being should submit to the experience of death, but He might independently of this, through the superabundance of His power, have wrought with ease His purpose; still, if for some ineffable reason or other it was absolutely necessary that so it should be, at least He ought not to have been subjected to the contumely of such an ignominious kind of death. What death, they ask, could be more ignominious than that by crucifixion? What answer can we make to this? Why, that the death is rendered necessary by the birth, and that He Who had determined once for all to share the nature of man must pass through all the peculiar conditions of that nature. Seeing, then, that the life of man is determined between two boundaries, had He, after having passed the one, not touched the other that follows, His proposed design would have remained only half fulfilled, from His not having touched that second condition of our nature.

ST. GREGORY OF NYSSA

Jesus replied: "Fear not, Albion: unless I die thou canst not live;
But if I die I shall arise again & thou with me.
This is Friendship & Brotherhood: without it Man Is Not."
So Jesus spoke: the Covering Cherub coming on in darkness
Overshadow'd them, & Jesus said: "Thus do Men in Eternity
One for another to put off, by forgiveness, every sin."
Albion reply'd: "Cannot Man exist without Mysterious
Offering of Self for Another? is this Friendship & Brother-
   hood? . . ."
Jesus said: "Wouldest thou love one who never died
For thee, or ever die for one who had not died for thee?
And if God dieth not for Man & giveth not himself
Eternally for Man, Man could not exist; for Man is Love,
As God is Love: every kindness to another is a little Death
In the Divine Image, nor can Man exist but by Brotherhood."

BLAKE

Oh, speak through me now!

Would I suffer for him that I love? So wouldst Thou—so wilt
   Thou! . . .
He that did most, shall bear most; the strongest shall stand the
   most weak.
'Tis the weakness in strength, that I cry for! my flesh, that I seek
In the Godhead! I seek and I find it. O Saul, it shall be
A Face like my face that receives thee; a Man like to me,
Thou shalt love and be loved by, for ever: a Hand like this hand
Shall throw open the gates of new life to thee! See the Christ stand!

BROWNING

. . . but mild, the Saviour follow'd him,

Displaying the Eternal Vision, the Divine Similitude,
In loves and tears of brothers, sisters, sons, fathers and friends,
Which if Man ceases to behold, he ceases to exist,
Saying: "Albion! Our wars are wars of life, & wounds of love

243

With intellectual spears, & long winged arrows of thought.
Mutual in one another's love and wrath all renewing
We live as One Man; for contracting our infinite senses
We behold multitude, or expanding, we behold as one,
As One Man all the Universal Family: and that One Man
We call Jesus the Christ; and he in us, and we in him
Live in perfect harmony in Eden, the land of life,
Giving, receiving, and forgiving each other's trespasses.
He is the Good shepherd, he is the Lord and master,
He is the Shepherd of Albion, he is all in all,
In Eden, in the garden of God, and in heavenly Jerusalem . . ."

BLAKE

Jesus Christ, the Poor Man, who died for poor men.

CHARLES KINGSLEY

The coming of the Son of God and the Messiah in His power and glory as the King of the world and as a conqueror would have been the end of the freedom of the human spirit and the realisation of the Kingdom of God by means of necessity and compulsion.

BERDYAEV

✳

He said to Judas, when he betrayed him: "Friend, wherefore art thou come?" as if he would say: "Thou hatest me and art my enemy; so do I love thee, and am thy friend." . . . Just as though God in human nature were saying: "I am pure, single Goodness, and therefore I cannot will, or desire, or hope, or do, or give anything but goodness. If I am to reward thee for thy evil and wickedness, I must do it with goodness, for I am and have nothing else."

THEOLOGIA GERMANICA

It is impossible not to love Christ. If we saw Him now, we should not be able to take our eyes off Him, we should "listen to Him in rapture"; we should flock around Him as did the multitudes in the Gospels. All that is required of us is not to resist. We must yield to Him, to the contemplation of His image—in the Gospels, in the saints, in the Church—and He will capture our hearts.

FATHER YELCHANINOV

244

Our Lord says to every living soul, "I became man for you. If
you do not become God for me, you do me wrong."

MEISTER ECKHART

Show yourself always a partner of Christ, who makes the divine
ray shine from heaven; let Christ be to you continual and unceasing
joy.

CLEMENT OF ALEXANDRIA

Is it unnatural to do what Jesus Christ hath done?

TRAHERNE

§ 5

God suffers and bleeds when He fails to find in man an answer
to His love, when human freedom does not play its part in His
work, and when man does not place his creative forces at His
disposal.

LÉON BLOY

Without man and without human freedom God cannot and will
not establish His Kingdom, which is of necessity human as well as
divine in character.

BERDYAEV

Let us bring what is our own, God will supply the rest.

CHRYSOSTOM

Why stand we here trembling around
Calling on God for help, and not ourselves, in whom God dwells,
Stretching a hand to save the falling Man?

BLAKE

God expects from me a free creative act. My freedom and my
creative activity are my obedience to the secret will of God, Who
expects from man something much more than what is usually meant
when we speak of His will.

BERDYAEV

I dislike talk about obeying God, as if he were some Stalin or
Hitler: I cannot think that he wants me to obey him: what he wants,

245

I think, is that I should learn to co-operate, quietly and in complete freedom, with his blessed and blessing will, that will of his which I discover deep in my own heart as my own will also—as the best, essential me—and which, discovering it also deep in the heart of everything else, I find to be not only vaster, but also saner and more fruitful of life and peace and joy, than the self-regarding wilfulness that would deceive me with its appearance of leading me to my goal, but would in fact cut me off, if it had its way, from my birthright of unity with all things.

V. G.

"The Heavens are the Heavens of the Lord; but the earth hath He given to the children of men" means: "The Heavens are already heavenly, but the earth hath the Lord given unto men that they may make of it the Heavens."

RABBI HANOKH OF ALEXANDER

And God looked down on his work. And He saw that *it was not yet good.*

ROMAIN ROLLAND

"Ye are my witnesses, saith the Lord, and I am God" [Isaiah]. That is: when ye are my witnesses, I am God, and when ye are not my witnesses, I am, as it were, not God.

MIDRASH

Now you must know, God loves the soul so mightily, he who should rob God of loving the soul would rob him of his very life and being: would kill God, if one may so say; for the very love wherewith God loves the soul is what his Holy Breath is blowing in.

MEISTER ECKHART

In those limpid souls where God can see the reflection of himself, God is reposing in the soul and the soul is reposing in God. To deprive God of this, though but in thought, is to deprive him, to deny to him, his Godhood who is seeking rest in all things, for God's nature is rest.

MEISTER ECKHART

Thou lookest upon the Creator, praised be his name, and the Creator, being praised, looketh upon thee.

THE BAAL-SHEM

246

As far as the human mind ascends in love, so far the divine wisdom descends in mercy.

ST. MAXIMUS THE CONFESSOR

The wise man becometh a lyre which is all a-quiver and re-soundeth beneath the hand of God.

IAMBLICHUS (in the words of Merejkowski)

THE TRUE GLORIFICATION

I should now pass from this to another Particular; but because many are apt to misapprehend the Notion of God's glory, and flatter themselves with their pretended and imaginary aiming at the Glory of God, I think it may be of good use, a little further and more distinctly to unfold the Designe that a Religious mind drives on in directing it self and all its actions to God. We are therefore to consider, that this doth not consist in some Transient thoughts of God and his Glory as the End we propound to our selves in any Undertakings: a man does not direct all his actions to the Glory of God by forming a Conception in his Mind, or stirring up a strong Imagination upon any Action, That that must be for the Glory of God: it is. not the thinking of God's glory that is glorifying of him . . .

We rather glorifie God by entertaining the Impressions of his Glory upon us, than by communicating any kind of Glory to him. Then does a Good man become the Tabernacle of God wherein the Divine Shechinah does rest, and which the Divine glory fills, when the frame of his Mind and Life is wholy according to that Idea and Pattern which he receives from the Mount. We best glorifie him when we grow most like to him: and we then act most for his glory, when a true Spirit of Sanctity, Justice, Meekness, &c. runs through all our actions; when we so live in the World as becomes those that converse with the great Mind and Wisdom of the whole World, with that Almighty Spirit that made, supports and governs all things, with that Being from whence all good flows, and in which there is no Spot, Stain or Shadow of Evil; and so being captivated and overcome by the sense of the Divine loveliness and goodness, endeavour to be like him, and conform our selves as much as may be to him.

JOHN SMITH

THE FRIEND WHO SAID "I"

A certain man knocked at his friend's door: his friend asked, "Who is there?"

He answered, "I." "Begone," said his friend, " 'tis too soon: at my table there is no place for the raw."

How shall the raw one be cooked but in the fire of absence? What else will deliver him from hypocrisy?

He turned sadly away, and for a whole year the flames of separation consumed him;

Then he came back and again paced to and fro beside the house of his friend.

He knocked at the door with a hundred fears and reverences, lest any disrespectful word might escape from his lips.

"Who is there?" cried his friend. He answered, "Thou, O charmer of all hearts!"

"Now," said the friend, "since thou art I, come in: there is no room for two I's in this house.

The double end of thread is not for the needle: inasmuch as thou art single, enter the needle" . . .

RUMI

§ 6

Direction of the heart towards God, which the mystics of our race called *Kavvanah*, is only half the secret: waiting on God is the other half.

V. G.

Let him be content with the knowledge of Him that he has through faith, and apply his will and his love, since with love alone can he embrace Him and in it is the fruit of all meditation. There is scarcely anything which the understanding can know about God, but the will can love Him most deeply. Let a man imprison himself within himself, in the centre of his soul, where the image of God is, and there let him wait upon Him, as one listens to another speaking from some high tower, or as though he had Him within his heart, and as if in all creation there were nothing else save the soul and God. He should even forget himself and what he is doing, for, as one of the Fathers said, 'perfect prayer is that in which he who is praying is unaware that he is praying at all.'

ST. PETER OF ALCÁNTARA

I now know that there are men who . . . must seek no image of desire, but await that which lies beyond their mind—unities not of the mind, but unities of nature, unities of God . . . all whose pre-occupation is . . . to hollow their hearts till they are void and without form, to summon a creator by revealing chaos, to become the lamp for another's wick and oil . . . nor can *The Hound of Heaven* fling itself into any but an empty heart.

W. B. YEATS

As the Lord wrought effectually by His divine grace in the hearts of this people, so He thereby brought them to a divine worship and ministry; Christ's words they came to experience, viz., that God was a spirit, and that He would therefore be worshipped in the spirit and in the truth, and that such worshippers the Father would seek to worship Him. For bowing to the convictions of the spirit in themselves in their daily course of living, by which they were taught to eschew that which was made manifest to them to be evil, and to do that which was good, they in their assembling together sat down and waited for the preparation of this holy spirit, both to let them see their states and conditions before the Lord, and to worship Him acceptably; and as they were sensible of wants, or shortness, or infirmities, so in the secret of their own hearts prayer would spring to God, through Jesus Christ, to help, assist, and supply. But they did not dare to awake their beloved before His time; or approach the throne of the King of Glory till He held out His sceptre; or take thought what they should say, or after their own or other men's studied words and forms, for this were to offer strange fire; to pray, but not by the spirit; to ask, but not in the name, that is, in the power of our Lord Jesus Christ, who prayed as well as spoke like one having authority, that is, power, a divine energy and force to reach and pierce the heavens, which He gives to all that obey His light, grace, and spirit in their solemn waitings upon him. So that it is this people's principle that fire must come from heaven, life and power from God, to enable the soul to pour out itself acceptably before Him. And when a coal from His holy altar touches our lips, then can we pray and praise Him as we ought to do.

WILLIAM PENN

"WE MUST WAIT TRANQUILLY"

The eye is not wholly dependent upon an outside and alien light; there is an earlier light within itself, a more brilliant, which it sees sometimes in a momentary flash. At night in the darkness a gleam leaps from within the eye: or again we make no effort to see anything; the eyelids close; yet a light flashes before us; or we rub the eye and it sees the light it contains. This is sight without the act, but it is the truest seeing, for it sees light, whereas its other objects were the lit, not the light.

It is certainly thus that the spiritual sense . . . must have its vision—not of some other light in some other thing but of the light within itself, unmingled, pure, suddenly gleaming before it; so that we are left wondering whence it came, from within or without; and when it has gone, we say, "It was here. Yet no; it was beyond!" But we ought not to question whence; there is no whence, no coming or going in place; now it is seen and now not seen. We must not run after it, but fit ourselves for the vision and then wait tranquilly for its appearance, as the eye waits on the rising of the sun, which in its own time appears above the horizon—out of the ocean, as the poets say—and gives itself to our sight.

This Supreme Divinity, of which the sun is an image, where has it its dawning, what horizon does it surmount to appear?

It stands immediately above the contemplating spirit which has held itself at rest towards the vision, looking to nothing else than the good and beautiful, setting its entire being to that in a perfect surrender, and now tranquilly filled with power and taking a new beauty to itself, gleaming in the light of that presence.

This advent, still, is not by expectation: it is a coming without approach; the vision is not of something that must enter but of something that is present before all else . . .

PLOTINUS

THE COMING OF GRACE

Let us see what grace is: what strength it has, and how, by healing the will, it brings interior and exterior peace to man.

With these words, Marcello turned his eyes on the calm, translucent water which reflected as in a mirror the stars and beauty of the heavens, and seemed another heaven sown with lovely constellations. Pointing towards it, he continued: The water we see before us, which looks like another starry sky, partly helps us to understand what grace is. For as the image of the heavens, mirrored in the water, makes the lake look like the sky itself, so grace, when it comes to the soul and is enthroned in it, does not merely give it the semblance, but truly brings to it a likeness of God and his qualities, and transforms it into a very heaven as far as a creature can be so transformed without losing its substance. For grace is a quality, although created, that differs from any creature we see or that is created by the forces of nature, being neither air, nor smoke, nor born of any element; and the heavens themselves yield it precedence in the order of birth and sublimity of origin. . . . For grace rises above and surpasses them all, being, as it were, a portrait of God's most special attributes, imitating and recalling closely that which pertains solely to him.

Thus grace is like a deity or living image of Christ, which enters the soul and deifies it and is truly the soul of the soul.

LUIS DE LEON

IV. THE DIVINE BENEVOLENCE AND COMPASSION

with a Coda on suffering

It is quite certain that we must not lay any vileness to the charge of the All.

PLOTINUS

Let me tell you then why the creator made this world of generation. He was good, and the good can never have any jealousy of anything. And being free from jealousy, he desired that all things should be as like himself as they could be. This is in the truest sense the origin of creation and of the world, as we shall do well in believing on the testimony of wise men: God desired that all things should be good and nothing bad, so far as this was attainable.

PLATO

I saw soothfastly that our Lord was never wroth, nor ever shall be. For He is God: Good, Life, Truth, Love, Peace; His Charity and His Unity suffereth Him not to be wroth. For I saw truly that it is against the property of His might to be wroth, and against the property of His Wisdom, and against the property of His Goodness.

JULIANA OF NORWICH

One might lay down as a postulate:
All conceptions of God which are incompatible with a movement of pure charity are false.
All other conceptions of Him, in varying degree, are true.

SIMONE WEIL

The words 'Be ye perfect, even as your Father which is in heaven is perfect', coming immediately after the words 'Your Father which is in heaven, who maketh his sun to rise on the evil and on the good, and sendeth rain on the just and on the unjust' imply a whole doctrine. . . . For Christ cites as the supreme characteristic of God's justice precisely what is always brought forward (in the case, for example, of Job) with the object of accusing Him of injustice, namely, that He favours the good and the wicked indifferently.

There must have been in Christ's teaching the notion of a certain virtue attaching to indifference, similar to that which may be found in Greek stoicism and Hindu thought.

These words of Christ remind one of the supreme cry uttered by Prometheus: 'Heaven by whom for all the common light revolves' . . .

That is absolutely contrary to the current conception whereby

255

God arbitrarily sends down more grace on one man, less on another man, like some capricious sovereign; and that on the pretext that He does not owe it to any man! He owes it to his own infinite goodness to give to every creature good in all its fulness. We ought rather to believe that He showers continually on each one the fulness of his grace, but that we consent to receive it to a greater or lesser extent. In purely spiritual matters, God grants all desires. Those that have less have asked for less.

SIMONE WEIL

§ 2

Every man is born for heaven.

SWEDENBORG

Every living thing shall ripen and be saved.

MILAREPA

I know our souls are all divine;
I know that when we die,
What seems the vilest, even like thine
A part of God himself shall shine
In perfect purity.

EMILY BRONTË

Nor can we fall below the arms of God, how low soever it be we fall.

WILLIAM PENN

A naturalist attitude towards God, conceived of as a metaphysical transcendent Being, an immobile Substance, represents the latest form of idolatry in the history of the human spirit. Monotheism can indeed be a form of paganism. Man in bondage to the natural world conceives of God as a great exterior force, as a "supernatural" power in every respect comparable to "natural" power. God is merely the highest and most perfect of all forms of power, or in other words the projection of natural being. This supreme Power demands to be appeased. The transcendent God avenges Himself like the gods and men of the natural world. But Christianity appeared in the world to conquer decisively both idolatry and servitude. It affirmed the religion of the spirit and the spiritual life, the religion of the Trinity as the home of the spirit in which God reveals Himself as a Father who loves all and is near to all.

BERDYAEV

The doctrine of posthumous sanctions is only the product of a cruel and barbaric age which saw earthly justice in terms of punishment and torture. The idea of heaven and hell is a conception which reduces the spiritual life to the sphere of naturalism.

BERDYAEV

> I stood at Naples once, a night so dark
> I could have scarce conjectured there was earth
> Anywhere, sky or sea or world at all:
> But the night's black was burst through by a blaze—
> Thunder struck blow on blow, earth groaned and bore,
> Through her whole length of mountain visible:
> There lay the city thick and plain with spires,
> And, like a ghost disshrouded, white the sea.
> So may the truth be flashed out by one blow,
> And Guido see, one instant, and be saved.
> Else I avert my face, nor follow him
> Into that sad obscure sequestered state
> Where God unmakes but to remake the soul
> He else made first in vain; which must not be.

BROWNING (from The Ring and the Book)

His end is one, and one only; it is this: when the complete whole of our race shall have been perfected from the first man to the last—some having at once in this life been cleansed from evil, others having afterwards in the necessary periods been healed by the Fire, others having in their life here been unconscious equally of good and of evil—to offer to every one of us participation in the blessings which are in Him, which, the Scripture tells us, "eye hath not seen, nor ear heard", nor thought ever reached. But this is nothing else, as I at least understand it, but to be in God Himself; for the Good which is above hearing and eye and heart must be that Good which transcends the universe.

ST. GREGORY OF NYSSA

Before God created the world, he created Penitence and said to him: "I am going to create a man in the world, on condition that every time he turns to you you are ready to forgive him his sins." And, indeed, whenever man does turn to him, Penitence entreats God to forgive all his sins.

THE ZOHAR

He who has commanded us not to look back, when we have put our hands to the plough, does as He would have us do: He does not regard the past sins of a soul which seeks His Kingdom.

SAINT-CYRAN

Where is the foolish person who would think it in his power to commit more than God could forgive? and who will dare to measure, by the greatness of his crimes, the immensity of that infinite mercy which casts them all into the depths of the sea of oblivion, when we repent of them with love?

ST. FRANCOIS DE SALES

Some of us, because of our every-daily sins, hold not our promises nor keep our cleanness that our Lord setteth us in, but fall ofttimes into such wretchedness that shame it is to say it. And the beholding of this maketh us so sorry and so heavy that scarce can we see any comfort. And this dismay we take sometimes for a meekness—but it is a foul blindness and a weakness, and we cannot despise it as we do any other sin that we know which cometh through lack of true judgement. And it is against truth; for of all the properties of the Blissful Trinity it is God's will that we have especially faithfulness and comfort in love; for love maketh might and wisdom meekness to us. For just as by the courtesy of God He forgetteth our sin after the time that we ourselves repent, so willeth He that *we* forget our sin in regard to our stupid depression and our doubtful fears.

JULIANA OF NORWICH

And thus, in my folly, afore this time often I wondered why, by the great foreseeing wisdom of God, the beginning of sin was not letted; for then, methought, all should have been well. . . . But Jesus, who in this Vision informed me of all that is needful to me, answered by this word and said, *Sin is behovable [unavoidable], but all shall be well, and all shall be well, and all manner of thing shall be well.*

JULIANA OF NORWICH

He can never therefore be reconciled to your sin, because sin itself is incapable of being altered: but He may be reconciled to your person, because that may be restored: and, which is an infinite wonder, to greater beauty and splendour than before.

TRAHERNE

Then drew near unto him all the publicans and sinners for to hear him.

And the Pharisees and scribes murmured, saying, This man receiveth sinners, and eateth with them.

And he spake this parable unto them, saying,

What man of you, having an hundred sheep, if he lose one of them, doth not leave the ninety and nine in the wilderness, and go after that which is lost, until he find it?

And when he hath found it, he layeth it on his shoulders, rejoicing.

And when he cometh home, he calleth together his friends and neighbours, saying unto them, Rejoice with me; for I have found my sheep which was lost.

I say unto you, that likewise joy shall be in heaven over one sinner that repenteth, more than over ninety and nine just persons, which need no repentance.

Either what woman having ten pieces of silver, if she lose one piece, doth not light a candle, and sweep the house, and seek diligently till she find it?

And when she hath found it, she calleth her friends and her neighbours together, saying, Rejoice with me; for I have found the piece which I had lost.

Likewise, I say unto you, there is joy in the angels of God over one sinner that repenteth.

And he said, A certain man had two sons:

And the younger of them said to his father, Father, give me the portion of goods that falleth to me. And he divided unto them his living.

And not many days after the younger son gathered all together, and took his journey into a far country, and there wasted his substance with riotous living.

And when he had spent all, there arose a mighty famine in that land; and he began to be in want.

And he went and joined himself to a citizen of that country; and he sent him into his fields to feed swine

And he would fain have filled his belly with the husks that the swine did eat: and no man gave unto him.

And when he came to himself, he said, How many hired servants of my father's have bread enough and to spare, and I perish with hunger!

I will arise and go to my father, and will say unto him, Father, I have sinned against heaven, and before thee,

And am no more worthy to be called thy son: make me as one of thy hired servants.

And he arose, and came to his father. But when he was yet a great way off, his father saw him, and had compassion, and ran, and fell on his neck, and kissed him.

And the son said unto him, Father, I have sinned against heaven, and in thy sight, and am no more worthy to be called thy son.

But the father said to his servants, Bring forth the best robe, and put it on him; and put a ring on his hand, and shoes on his feet:

And bring hither the fatted calf, and kill it; and let us eat, and be merry:

For this my son was dead, and is alive again; he was lost, and is found. And they began to be merry.

Now his elder son was in the field: and as he came and drew nigh to the house, he heard musick and dancing.

And he called one of the servants, and asked what these things meant.

And he said unto him, Thy brother is come; and thy father hath killed the fatted calf, because he hath received him safe and sound.

And he was angry, and would not go in: therefore came his father out, and intreated him.

And he answering said to his father, Lo, these many years do I serve thee, neither transgressed I at any time thy commandment: and yet thou never gavest me a kid, that I might make merry with my friends:

But as soon as this thy son was come, which hath devoured thy living with harlots, thou hast killed for him the fatted calf.

And he said unto him, Son, thou art ever with me, and all that I have is thine.

It was meet that we should make merry, and be glad: for this thy brother was dead, and is alive again; and was lost, and is found.

ST. LUKE

After this, that other doubt did come with strength upon me, But how if the day of grace should be past and gone? How if you have overstood the time of mercy? Now, I remember that one day, as I was walking into the country, I was much in the thoughts of this, But how if the day of grace be past? ... Now was I in great distress, thinking in very deed that this might well be so; wherefore I went up and down bemoaning my sad condition, counting myself far worse than a thousand fools, for standing off thus long, and spending so many years in sin as I had done; still crying out, Oh, that I had turned sooner! Oh, that I had turned seven years ago! ...

But when I had been long vexed with this fear, and was scarce able to take one step more, just about the same place where I received my other encouragement, these words broke in upon my mind, "Compel them to come in, that my house may be filled"; "and yet there is room" (Luke xiv. 22, 23). These words, but especially them, "And yet there is room," were sweet words to me; for, truly, I thought that by them I saw there was place enough in heaven for me; and, moreover, that when the Lord Jesus did speak these words, he then did think of me; and that he knowing that the time would come that I should be afflicted with fear that there was no place left for me in his bosom, did before speak this word, and leave it upon record, that I might find help thereby against this vile temptation.

BUNYAN (from Grace Abounding)

A DIALOGUE BETWEEN GOD AND THE SOUL

> *Soul.* Whilst my Souls eye beheld no light
> But what stream'd from thy gracious sight;
> To me the worlds greatest King
> Seem'd but some little vulgar thing.

> *God.* Whilst thou prov'dst pure; and that in thee
> I could glass al my Deity:
> How glad did I from Heaven depart,
> To find a Lodging in thy heart!

Soul. Now Fame and Greatness bear the sway,
    ('Tis they that hold my prisons Key:)
    For whom my soul would dy, might shee
    Leave them her Immortality.

God. I, and some few pure Souls conspire,
    And burne both in a mutuall fire,
    For whom I'ld dy once more, ere they
    Should miss of Heavens eternal day.

Soul. But Lord! what if I turn againe,
    And with an adamantine chain,
    Lock me to thee? What if I chase
    The world away to give thee place?

God. Then though these souls in whom I joy
    Are Seraphins, Thou but a Toy,
    A foolish Toy, yet once more I
    Would with Thee live, and for thee die.

IGNOTO

Love bade me welcome: yet my soul drew back,
    Guiltie of dust and sinne.
But quick-ey'd Love, observing me grow slack
    From my first entrance in,
Drew nearer to me, sweetly questioning,
    If I lack'd any thing.

A guest, I answer'd, worthy to be here:
    Love said, You shall be he.
I the unkinde, ungratefull? Ah my deare,
    I cannot look on thee.
Love took my hand, and smiling did reply,
    Who made the eyes but I?

Truth Lord, but I have marr'd them: let my shame
    Go where it doth deserve.
And know you not, sayes Love, who bore the blame?
    My deare, then I will serve.
You must sit down, sayes Love, and taste my meat:
    So I did sit and eat.

GEORGE HERBERT

"Unto Me?"
"I do not know you—
Where may be your house?"

"I am Jesus—late of Judea,
Now of Paradise."

"Wagons have you to convey me?
This is far from thence?"—

"Arms of mine sufficient phaeton.
Trust Omnipotence."

"I am spotted."
    "I am Pardon."
"I am small."

    "The least
Is esteemed in Heaven
The chiefest.
Occupy my house."

EMILY DICKINSON

THE MAN WHO LOOKED BACK ON HIS WAY TO HELL

The guardian angels, who used to walk unseen before and behind
    him, have now become visible like policemen.
They drag him along, prodding him with goads and crying,
    "Begone, O dog, to thy kennel!"
He looks back towards the Holy Presence: his tears fall like autumn
    rain. A mere hope—what has he but that?
Then from God in the realm of Light comes the command—"Say
    ye to him: 'O ne'er-do-well destitute of merit,
Thou hast seen the black scroll of thy misdeeds. What dost thou
    expect? Why art thou tarrying in vain?' "
He answers: "Lord, Thou knowest I am a hundred hundred times
    worse than Thou hast declared;
But beyond my exertion and action, beyond good and evil and faith
    and infidelity,
Beyond living righteously or behaving disobediently—I had a great
    hope of Thy Loving-kindness.
I turn again to that pure Grace, I am not regarding my own works.
Thou gavest me my being as a robe of honour: I have always relied
    on that munificence."

When he confesses his sins, God saith to the Angels, "Bring him
back, for he never lost hope of Me.
Like one who recks of naught, I will deliver him and cancel all his
trespasses.
I will kindle such a fire of Grace that the least spark thereof con-
sumes all sin and necessity and free-will.
I will set fire to the tenement of Man and make its thorns a bower of
roses."

RUMI

THE FULNESS OF TIME

On a rusty iron throne,
Past the furthest star of space,
I saw Satan sit alone,
Old and haggard was his face;
For his work was done, and he
Rested in eternity.

And to him from out the sun
Came his father and his friend,
Saying,—Now the work is done
Enmity is at an end—
And He guided Satan to
Paradises that He knew.

Gabriel, without a frown;
Uriel, without a spear;
Raphael, came singing down,
Welcoming their ancient peer;
And they seated him beside
One who had been crucified.

JAMES STEPHENS

CATHERINE KINRADE

[A poor Manxwoman, mother of four base-born children, sundry
times (1713–1720) dragged through the sea for punishment by
order of Thomas Wilson, Bishop of Sodor and Man.]

None spake when Wilson stood before
The throne—

264

And He that sat thereon
Spake not; and all the presence-floor
Burnt deep with blushes, as the angels cast
Their faces downwards. Then at last,
Awe-stricken, he was 'ware
How on the emerald stair
A woman sat, divinely clothed in white,
And at her knees four cherubs bright,
That laid
Their heads within her lap. Then, trembling, he essay'd
To speak:—'Christ's mother, pity me!'
Then answered she:—
'Sir, I am Catherine Kinrade.'
Even so—the poor dull brain,
Drench'd in unhallow'd fire,
It had no vigour to restrain—
God's image trodden in the mire
Of impious wrongs—whom last he saw
Gazing with animal awe
Before his harsh tribunal, proved unchaste,
Incorrigible, woman's form defaced
To uttermost ruin by no fault of hers—
So gave her to the torturers;
And now—some vital spring adjusted,
Some faculty that rusted
Cleansed to legitimate use—
Some undeveloped action stirr'd, some juice
Of God's distilling dropt into the core
Of all her life—no more
In that dark grave entomb'd,
Her soul had bloom'd
To perfect woman—swift celestial growth
That mocks our temporal sloth—
To perfect woman—woman made to honour,
With all the glory of her youth upon her.
And from her lips and from her eyes there flow'd
A smile that lit all heaven; the angels smiled;
God smiled, if that were smile beneath the state that glow'd
Soft purple—and a voice:—'Be reconciled!'
So to his side the children crept,
And Catherine kiss'd him, and he wept.

Then said a seraph:—'Lo! he is forgiven.'
And for a space again there was no voice in Heaven.

T. E. BROWN

THE KNOWLEDGE OF MERCY

Mr. Head had never known before what mercy felt like because
he had been too good to deserve any, but he felt he knew now. . . .
He stood very still and felt the action of mercy touch him again
but this time he knew that there were no words in the world that
could name it. He understood that it grew out of agony, which is
not denied to any man and which is given in strange ways to
children. He understood it was all a man could carry into death to
give his Maker and he suddenly burned with shame that he had so
little of it to take with him. He stood appalled, judging himself with
the thoroughness of God, while the action of mercy covered his
pride like a flame and consumed it. He had never thought himself a
great sinner before but he saw now that his true depravity had been
hidden from him lest it cause him despair. He realised that he was
forgiven for sins from the beginning of time, when he had conceived in his own heart the sin of Adam, until the present, when he
had denied poor Nelson. He saw that no sin was too monstrous for
him to claim as his own, and since God loved in proportion as He
forgave, he felt ready at that instant to enter Paradise.

FLANNERY O'CONNOR

Coda :
on suffering

For already here below we receive the capacity for loving **God** and for representing him to ourselves with complete certainty **as** having the substance of real, eternal, perfect and infinite joy. Through our fleshly veils we receive from above presages of eternity which are enough to efface all doubts on the subject. . . .

There is only one time when I really know nothing of this certitude any longer. It is when I am in contact with the affliction of other people, those who are indifferent or unknown to me as much as the others, perhaps even more, including those of the most remote ages of antiquity. This contact causes me such atrocious pain and so utterly rends my soul, that as a result the love of God becomes almost impossible for me for a while. It would take very little more to make me say impossible. So much so that I am uneasy about myself. I reassure myself a little by remarking that Christ wept on foreseeing the horrors of the destruction of Jerusalem. I hope he will forgive me my compassion.

SIMONE WEIL

*

Any one that suffers is God's representative.

VIVEKANANDA

There is no remembrance more blessed, and nothing more blessed to remember, than suffering overcome in solidarity with God; this is the mystery of suffering.

KIERKEGAARD

In spite of loneliness, illness, poverty, and so many other causes of suffering, Christophe bore his lot patiently. He had never been so patient. He was surprised at himself. Illness is often a blessing. By ravaging the body it frees the soul and purifies it: during the nights and days of forced inaction thoughts arise which are fearful of the raw light of day, and are scorched by the sun of health. No man who has never been ill can have a thorough knowledge of himself.

ROMAIN ROLLAND (from *Jean-Christophe*)

No one truly knows happiness who has not suffered, and the redeemed are happier than the elect.

AMIEL

Only when grief finds its work done can God dispense us from it.

AMIEL

Learn thou to suffer, and thou shalt be able not to suffer.

ACTS OF JOHN

. . . for who would lose,
Though full of pain, this intellectual being,
Those thoughts that wander through eternity?

MILTON

Affliction is able to drown out every earthly voice . . . but the voice of eternity within a man it cannot drown. Or conversely: it is the voice of eternity within which demands to be heard, and to make a hearing for itself it makes use of the loud voice of affliction. Then when by the aid of affliction all irrelevant voices are brought to silence, it can be heard, this voice within.

KIERKEGAARD

Pain at a certain intensity is transmuted to the highest joy and all the great tragic poets of the Occident know it.

ROMAIN ROLLAND

Who knows what Golgotha Shakespeare endured as the price of Lear?

JOHN A. HUGHES

Through the tragic, something different speaks to us, something that is no longer tragic.

KARL JASPERS

To curse grief is easier than to bless it, but to do so is to fall back into the point of view of the earthly, the carnal, the natural man. By what has Christianity subdued the world if not by the apotheosis of grief, by its marvellous transmutation of suffering into triumph, of the crown of thorns into the crown of glory, and of a gibbet into a symbol of salvation? What does the apotheosis of the Cross mean, if not the death of death, the defeat of sin, the beatification of martyrdom, the raising to the skies of voluntary sacrifice, the defiance of pain?—'O Death, where is thy sting? O Grave, where is thy victory?' By long brooding over this theme—the agony of the

270

just, peace in the midst of agony, and the heavenly beauty of such peace—humanity came to understand that a new religion was born—a new mode, that is to say, of explaining life and of understanding suffering.

Suffering was a curse from which man fled; now it becomes a purification of the soul, a sacred trial sent by Eternal Love, a divine dispensation meant to sanctify and ennoble us, an acceptable aid to faith, a strange initiation into happiness. O power of belief! All remains the same, and yet all is changed. A new certitude arises to deny the apparent and the tangible; it pierces through the mystery of things, it places an invisible Father behind visible nature, it shows us joy shining through tears, and makes of pain the beginning of joy.

AMIEL

*

There are the extreme sufferings of body and soul. Do not let us play with words. I am speaking now of those deep sorrows, those agonies which overthrow our poor human nature altogether, which bring it as low as the very image of death. To me this kind of suffering seems to be wholly evil. By definition it is unbearable, and it leaves behind wounds which heal only with difficulty. What good can come of a sorrow which drives a man mad, using the word in a literal sense? When a mind totters and breaks down the weakness and collapse may be due to previous self-centredness; but it is not always so. The remorseless and mechanical play of events shatters over-sensitive souls. Innocent, they lack power to resist. There are certain blows of fate which no dialectical arguments can justify. We can only bow our heads and say that we do not understand. Sometimes the mystery is cleared up later on, and we realise that the sorrow has been of indirect value either to the sufferer himself or to those around him. But we are not always allowed to see this happen. Our knowledge of certain things is superficial and incomplete. Faith tells us that they have significance, but in this world we often have no means of finding out what it is. We need not be ashamed to admit this. The most elementary standard of intellectual honesty demands it.

In short, the suffering by which we profit is the suffering which we *can* overcome. Apart from love, suffering can only give rise to evil: the good things are courage and charity. The power of the

271

man who has suffered lies in his having stood the test, which in addition makes it easier for him to understand others. They say that sorrows pass; but the fact of having borne sorrow remains. Without the Resurrection, Good Friday would only be the triumph of evil.

MAURICE NÉDONCELLE

"I am poured out like water, my heart is as wax . . ." read Father Mellowes for Kavanagh [after Kavanagh's execution]. He did not read: "Though I should go down into the shadow of death, I shall fear no evil, because Thou, Lord, art with me." Because there *was* fear—untold fear. And he would not take any words that in the mouth of those who had died would have been false. He abhorred the very breath of complacency. Let there be the dark, profound and untampered at. The dark must have its hour and there was no good trying to stem it when it came, with complacent words. It could not be held back as the sea could not be held back. It was like the sea, the cold unfathomable sea, balancing and counteracting the dry land and the teeming, human dry-land activity.

Father Mellowes knew the dark. He knew that man could not bear very much of it. When a little of it got into him the very heart dissolved like wax and the bones melted like water. The dark. Manifold were its shapes and tides, as he had known it.

Ezra was waiting. There was this question that he wanted to ask, and which he did not know how to ask. They were sitting at the table in the sitting-room and the priest's tattered missal lay on the table. He had not opened it. He had repeated the words by heart. He had not wanted to turn to a book and open it. That too would have been a subtle evasion and falsity at this moment.

"All the destructive pain," Ezra said, "what can come of it? All the pain that cannot be borne or submitted to. What condemned men go through and children and others. Can there be any point in it or isn't it the sign of chaos?"

Ezra and the two women waited for an answer. . . . Ezra looked up. He saw Father Mellowes' smile, the smile that he would never get quite used to, resting on them, and he knew that that was the nearest to an answer that they would ever come.

FRANCIS STUART (from *Redemption*)

Why undeserved suffering? My God, why? The Church doesn't know the answer. Christ doesn't tell us the answer: what

Christ does is to face the suffering. He knew all our sorrows. He suffered undeservedly. Faced with this ghastly problem of undeserved suffering in His own experience, He identified Himself with the mystery: He brought Himself to say "My God, why?". But this cry of dereliction was not His last cry on the Cross. Just before He died, He said a very different word. Still on the Cross, still suffering, He said a very different word. He said "Father, into Thy hands I commend My spirit".

G. F. MACLEOD

Max Eyth recounts in his story *Berufs-Tragik* the building of the mighty bridge over the estuary of the Ennobucht. The most profound and thorough labour of the intellect, the most assiduous and devoted professional toil, had gone to the construction of the great edifice, making it in all its significance and purposefulness a marvel of human achievement. In spite of endless difficulties and gigantic obstacles, the bridge is at length finished, and stands defying winds and waves. Then there comes a raging cyclone, and building and builder are swept into the deep. Utter meaninglessness seems to triumph over richest significance, blind 'destiny' seems to stride on its way over prostrate virtue and merit. The narrator tells how he visits the scene of the tragedy and returns again:

"When we got to the end of the bridge, there was hardly a breath of wind; high above, the sky showed blue-green, and with an eerie brightness. Behind us, like a great open grave, lay the Ennobucht. The Lord of life and death hovered over the waters in silent majesty. We felt His presence, as one feels one's own hand. And the old man and I knelt down before the open grave and before Him."

Why did they kneel? Why did they feel constrained to do so? One does not kneel before a cyclone or the blind forces of nature, nor even before Omnipotence merely as such. But one does kneel before the wholly uncomprehended Mystery, revealed yet unrevealed, and one's soul is stilled by feeling the way of its working, and therein its justification.

RUDOLF OTTO

*

Simone Weil's cry—"There is only one time when I really know nothing of this certitude any longer"—must have been uttered by hundreds or thousands of millions since the beginning of thought:

and it is hard not to utter it as we watch a friend dying of a dreadful disease, or when we think of Belsen—or, perhaps most of all, when we hear a hurt animal shrieking in agony. Nor can we be satisfied by statements of which those by Milton, Romain Rolland, Vivekananda, Amiel, Kierkegaard, Jaspers and the author of the Acts of John are merely typical. These are suggestive, but no more. Still less can we be solaced by most of the ordinary theological explanations, whether or not they be based on the doctrine of Original Sin—for they are found, on examination, to postulate a God quite unworthy of human love.

Even the Crucifixion, considered as the crucifixion of Jesus in his human nature, proves no more than that suffering *can* be a means, like no other, to the highest good. This is not to be doubted: but while it justifies the aristocracy of suffering, it does not justify its democracy. And if it be replied that any human being can be an aristocrat of suffering, can wounded animals?

The fact is that no logical explanation of many kinds of suffering is possible. But in certain experiences, and in the contemplation of certain events, we can on occasion grasp, momentarily and elusively, a shadowy outskirt of the truth. We can grasp it in some passages of some of Beethoven's last quartets. We can grasp it as we contemplate the Crucifixion—considered as at once the voluntary and the necessary suffering of God Himself. And we can grasp it as we read certain myths, such as that of the death of the blind Oedipus, who had suffered so atrociously and so unjustly. But the reconciliation implied in that myth must be understood, not with reference to a future life, but as existing in eternal reality.

V. G.

THE DEATH OF OEDIPUS

How from this place he started, thou wilt know,
Who saw him, with no guide, no friend to show
The way, himself a leader to us all.
So came he to that threshold mystical
Of Earth, deep-rooted by the Brazen Stair
Precipitous. Many branching paths are there.
He made his choice among them, till he stayed
Close by the basoned rock where Theseus laid
The inviolate memorial of his pledge
Sworn to Pirithoüs, near the bason's edge,

Midway between that Stone of Triple Plume,
The hollow Pear-tree and the marble tomb.
There pausing he sat down and loosed withal
His sordid raiment. Then with a proud call
He charged his daughters water from the spring
To find, for cleansing and for offering
Libation. Swift to do their father's will,
The maidens sped to where Demeter's Hill,
Green with the goddess' gift, stood clear to view.
They brought the water, and with ritual due
Prepared him, and the raiment of the grave
About him wrapped; then, when his heart could crave
No more of service, and there rested naught
Undone of the lustration that he sought,
God's voice beneath us thundered. At that sound
The maidens sank to earth in tears, and wound
Their arms about his knee and beat their breast.
He heard their sudden cry of grief, and pressed
Both to his arms: "My children, from this day
You have no father. All is passed away
That once was mine or me, and all the sore
Toils of my tendance shall be yours no more;
Hard toils, I know well; yet one word there is
That maketh light your heaviest services.
Love I have given you, such as none beside
Could give. But now alone ye shall abide
And orphaned of that love through all your days."

So, clinging close and sobbing in amaze,
All wept; but when the rite of tears was o'er,
And that lamenting cry arose no more,
Deep silence fell; then on the silence brake
A great voice calling. All our hearts did shake
With fear and our hair stiffened, for all round
Like many divine voices, rose that sound:
"Ho Thou! Thou Oedipus! Why do we stay
Our goings? All too long is thy delay."
He heard, and, hearing, knew God's summons clear.
Straightway he called that Theseus be brought near,
And when he came, "O friend," he cried, "in troth
Give me thy right hand—man's most ancient oath—
Clasp it, my daughters!—never to forsake

275

These twain but act in all things for their sake
As love will prompt." And he, as a true friend,
Unshrinking, vowed in good faith to the end
To observe his promise. Once that deed was done,
The father laid his groping hands upon
His children's heads and spake: "Be strong of heart,
Daughters! From this place ye must now depart.
Seek not to see forbidden sights, or hear
Words spoken that are not for mortal ear.
Go with all haste. Theseus, alone with me,
Hath right this secret thing to hear and see."

   We all had heard his charge, and, with lament
And tears, followed the maidens as they went.
At last, we turned again to look; and there,
Long gazing, him we saw not anywhere,
But Theseus standing all alone, his hand
Across his face uplifted, to withstand
The sight of some dread vision which no eye
Of mortal might endure. To Earth and Sky,
To Mother Earth and Sky the House of God,
We saw him, in one movement where he stood,
Make prayer.

                    And what way Oedipus hath gone
From life none knoweth save Theseus alone.
For sure there came no visible death, no sweep
Of fire from God, no storm-wind of the deep;
But or some guide was sent from heaven above,
Or yawned the firmament of death, in love
And mercy, to receive him without pain.
For not in mortal anguish was he ta'en,
Nor sickness nor lament, but in a dream
Of wonder. For this tale if any deem
Me mad . . . for such, I care not what they say.

SOPHOCLES (tr. by Gilbert Murray)

V. "SO PANTETH MY SOUL AFTER THEE, O GOD"

As the hart panteth after the water brooks, so panteth my soul after thee, O God.

FROM PSALM 42

The desire and pursuit of the whole is called love.

PLATO

The whole atmosphere has a luminous serenity, a limpid clearness. The islands are like swans swimming in a golden stream. Peace, splendour, boundless space! . . . And I meanwhile look quietly on while the soft hours glide away. I long to catch the wild bird, happiness, and tame it. Above all, I long to share it with others. These delicious mornings impress me indescribably. They intoxicate me, they carry me away. I feel beguiled out of myself, dissolved in sunbeams, breezes, perfumes, sudden impulses of joy. Yet all the time I pine for I know not what intangible Eden.

Lamartine in the *Préludes* has admirably described this oppressive effect of happiness on fragile human nature. I suspect that the reason for it is that the finite creature feels itself invaded by the infinite, and the invasion produces dizziness, a kind of vertigo, a longing to fling oneself into the great gulf of being.

AMIEL

England in June has dawned upon Ruth and me as fresh as in the days of creation, for this is the first year since 1947 that we have been about our garden at a time when the poppies are in bloom, and the beds on the verge of the daisy-lawn are agleam with mingled lupins and day-lilies. Those other Junes we have been in America. I feel wonderfully happy to be here now, sitting by the library window and gazing across many-hued greens over to the Berkshire downs: happy, but sad as well, with that sadness inseparable from beauty—from the sight of a beauty which tells us that we are exiles still from our proper home. . . .

V.G. (from *My Dear Timothy*)

A LONG JOURNEY

The long insatiable yearning of the mortal creature, for absolute union—never accomplished;

Each mortal love the symbol, the promise, and the part-fulfilment of that for which all life exists.

Not this year or next, not this life or perhaps the next,
But day by day and day by day as long as thou art, pass thou nearer to that great joy.

Here too (as so often said before) it is no matter of chance:
It is not that these are lucky having found their mates, and thou art unfortunate standing alone (for they have not found their mates, and thou standest not alone);
But every day and every day (for thee as well as for them and all) the way lies on before—to be slowly accomplished—
To make thyself fit for the perfect love which awaits and which alone can satisfy thee.

Lo! that divine body which dwells within thy mortal body, slowly preparing its own deliverance—
What is all suffering before that? to surrender this is but to open the way for that—'tis but the law of Equality.
Begin to-day to walk the path which alone is gain;
In the sunshine, as the sunshine, calm contented and blessed, envying no one, railing not, repining not;
Receiving the message of the patient trees and herbs, and of the creatures of the earth, and of the stars above;
Possessing all within thyself, with showers of beauties and blessings every moment—to scatter again to others with free hand;
Neither hurrying nor slackening, but sure of thy great and glorious destiny, walk thou—
And presently all around thee shalt thou see the similitude of him whom thou seekest:
He shall send a multitude of messengers in advance to cheer thee on thy way.

EDWARD CARPENTER

THE STRAINING UPWARDS OF THE SOUL

But there are earlier and loftier beauties than material ones. In the sense-bound life we are no longer granted to know them, but the soul, taking no help from the organs, sees and proclaims them. To the vision of these we must mount.

As it is not for those to speak of the graceful forms of the material world who have never seen them or known their grace—men born blind, let us suppose—in the same way those must be silent upon the beauty of noble conduct and of learning and all that order who have never cared for such things, nor may those tell of the splendour of virtue who have never known the face of Justice and of Moral Wisdom beautiful beyond the beauty of Evening and of Dawn.

Such vision is for those only who see with the Soul's sight—and at the vision they will rejoice, and awe will fall upon them and a trouble deeper than all the rest could ever stir, for now they are moving in the realm of Truth.

This is the spirit that Beauty must ever induce, wonderment and a delicious trouble, longing and love and a trembling that is all delight. For the unseen all this may be felt as for the seen; and this the Souls feel for it, every soul in some degree, but those the more deeply that are the more truly apt to this higher love—just as all take delight in the beauty of the body but all are not stung as sharply, and those only that feel the keener wound are known as Lovers.

These Lovers, then, lovers of the beauty outside of sense, must be made to declare themselves.

What do you feel in presence of the grace you discern in actions, in manners, in sound morality, in all the works and fruits of virtue, in the beauty of souls? When you see that you yourselves are beautiful within, what do you feel? What is this Dionysiac exultation that thrills through your being, this straining upwards of all your Soul, this longing to break away from the body and live sunken within the veritable self?

These are no other than the emotions of Souls under the spell of love.

But what is it that awakens all this passion? No shape, no colour, no grandeur of mass: all is for a Soul, something whose beauty rests upon no colour, for the moral wisdom the Soul enshrines and all the other hueless splendour of the virtues. It is that you find in yourself, or admire in another, loftiness of spirit; righteousness of life; disciplined purity; courage of the majestic face; gravity; modesty that goes fearless and tranquil and passionless.

But we have not yet shown by what property in them these noble qualities have wrought the Soul to loveliness: what is this grace, this splendour as of Light, resting upon all the virtues?

Divinity and all that proceeds from Divinity are the Soul's beauty, a graciousness native to it and not foreign, for only with these is it truly Soul. And it is just to say that in the Soul's becoming a good and beautiful thing is its becoming like to God, for from the Divine comes all the Beauty and all the Good in beings.

Therefore we must ascend again towards the Good, the desired of every Soul. Anyone that has seen This, knows what I intend when I say that it is beautiful. Even the desire of it is to be desired as a good. To attain it is for those that will take the upward path, who will set all their forces towards it, who will divest themselves of all that we have put on in our descent, until each, in the solitude of himself, shall behold that from Which all things depend.

And one that shall know this vision—with what passion of love shall he not be seized, with what pang of desire, what longing to be molten into one with This, what wondering delight! If he that has never seen this Being must hunger for It as for all his welfare, he that has known must love and reverence It as the very Beauty; he will be flooded with awe and gladness, stricken by a salutary terror; he loves with a veritable love, with sharp desire; all other loves than this he must despise, and disdain all that once seemed fair.

Beholding this Being—the Choragos of all Existence, the Self-Intent that ever gives forth and never takes—resting, rapt, in the vision and possession of so lofty a loveliness, growing to Its likeness, what Beauty can the soul yet lack? For This, the Beauty supreme, the absolute, and the primal, fashions Its lovers to Beauty and makes them also worthy of love.

And for This, the sternest and the uttermost combat is set before the Souls; all our labour is for This, lest we be left without part in this noblest vision, which to attain is to be blessed in the blissful sight, which to fail of is to fail utterly.

For not he that has failed of the joy that is in colour or in visible forms, not he that has failed of power or of honours or of kingdom has failed, but only he that has failed of only This, for Whose winning he should renounce kingdoms, and command over earth and ocean and sky.

But what must we do? How lies the path? How come to vision of the inaccessible Beauty, dwelling as if in consecrated precincts, apart from the common ways where all may see, even the profane?

"Let us flee then to the beloved Fatherland": this is the soundest counsel. But what is this flight? How are we to gain the open sea? For Odysseus is surely a parable to us when he commands the flight from the sorceries of Circe or Calypso—not content to linger for all the pleasure offered to his eyes and all the delight of sense filling his days.

The Fatherland to us is There whence we have come, and There is The Father.

What then is our course, what the manner of our flight? This is not a journey for the feet; the feet bring us only from land to land; nor need you think of coach or ship to carry you away; all this order of things you must set aside and refuse to see: you must close the eyes and call instead upon another vision which is to be waked within you, a vision, the birth-right of all, which few turn to use.

And this inner vision, what is its operation?

Newly awakened it is all too feeble to bear the ultimate splendour. Therefore the Soul must be trained—to the habit of remarking, first, all noble pursuits, then the works of beauty produced not by the labour of the arts but by the virtue of men known for their goodness: lastly, you must search the souls of those that have shaped these beautiful forms.

But how are you to see into a virtuous soul and know its loveliness?

Withdraw into yourself and look. And if you do not find yourself beautiful yet, labour to make all one glow of beauty. Never did eye see the sun unless it had first become sunlike, and never can the soul have vision of the First Beauty unless itself be beautiful.

PLOTINUS

THE FLIGHT OF ALONE TO ALONE

Thus the Supreme is ever present with us—not that the Supreme reaches out to us, seeking our communion: we reach towards the Supreme, it is we that become present. We are always before It: but we do not always look: thus a choir, set in due order about the conductor, may turn away from that centre to which all should attend; let it but face aright, and it sings with beauty. We are ever before the Supreme, but we do not always attend: when we look, our Goal is attained; this is rest; this is the end of singing ill; standing straight and true before Him, we lift a choral song full of God.

In this choiring, the soul looks upon the wellspring of Life, wellspring also of Spirit, beginning of Being, fount of Good, root of Soul. It is not that these are poured out from the Supreme, lessening it as if it were a thing of mass: they spring from an eternal principle, which produces them not by its fragmentation but in virtue of its intact identity. Therefore they too hold firm; so long as the sun shines, so long there will be light.

We have not been cut away; we are not separate, what though

283

the body-nature has closed about us to press us to itself; we breathe and hold our ground because the Supreme does not give and pass but gives on for ever, so long as It remains What It Is.

Our being is the fuller for our turning Thither; this is our prosperity; to hold aloof is loneliness and lessening. Here is the soul's peace; here it has its Act, its authentic knowing; here it is immune. Here is living, here is the true; all living apart from Him is but a shadow, a mimicry. This state is its first and its final, because from God it comes, its good lies There, and, once turned to God again, it is what it was.

Any that have seen know what I have in mind: the soul takes another life as it approaches God; thus restored, it feels that the dispenser of true life is There, that now we have nothing to look for but, far otherwise, that we must put aside all else and rest in This alone, must become This alone. Thus we have all the vision that may be permitted us of Him and of ourselves; but it is of a self wrought to splendour, brimmed with the spiritual light, become that very light, pure, buoyant, unburdened, raised to Godhood—or, better, knowing its Godhood.

In our self-seeing There, the self is seen as belonging to that divine order, or rather we are merged into that self in us which has the quality of that order. It is a knowing of the self restored to its purity. No doubt we should not speak of seeing; but we cannot help talking in dualities, seen and seer, instead of, boldly, the achievement of unity. In this seeing, we neither hold an object nor trace distinction; there is no two. The man is changed, no longer himself nor self-belonging; he is merged with the Supreme, sunken into It, one with It: centre coincides with centre.

This is the purport of that rule of our Mysteries: Nothing Divulged to the Uninitiate: the Supreme is not to be made a common story, the holy things may not be uncovered to the stranger, to any that has not himself attained to see. There were not two; beholder was one with beheld; it was not a vision compassed but a unity apprehended. The man formed by this mingling with the Supreme must—if he only remember—carry its image impressed upon him: he is become the Unity, nothing within him or without inducing any diversity; no movement now, no passion, no outlooking desire, once this ascent is achieved; reasoning is in abeyance and even, to dare the word, the very self: caught away, filled with God, all the being calmed, he turns neither to this side nor to that, not even inwards to himself; utterly resting he has

284

become very rest. He belongs no longer to the order of the beautiful; he has risen beyond beauty; he has overpassed even the choir of the virtues; he is like one who, having penetrated the inner sanctuary, leaves the temple images behind him—though these become once more first objects of regard when he returns from the sanctuary; for There his converse was not with image, not with trace, but with the very Truth in the view of which all the rest is but of secondary concern.

There, indeed, it was scarcely vision, unless of a mode unknown; it was a going forth from the self, a simplifying, a renunciation, a reach towards contact and at the same time a repose, a meditation towards adjustment. This is the only seeing of what lies within the sanctuary: to look otherwise is to fail.

Things here are signs; they show therefore to the wiser teachers how God is known; the instructed priest reading the sign may enter the holy place and make real the vision of the inaccessible.

★   ★   ★

Thus may a man in his essence outgrow mere being and become identical with the Transcendent of Being. And when we have fallen back again from that union, we waken the virtue within us until we know ourselves all well ordered once more; once more we are lightened of our burden, through virtue become spiritual, and move through Spiritual Wisdom to the Supreme.

This is the life of gods and of the godlike and blessed among men, liberation from all that is alien here and from pleasure in it, a flight of Alone to Alone.

PLOTINUS

§ 2

We shall once more take a view of our own Souls, and observe how the Motions thereof lead us into the knowledge of a Deity. We alwaies find a restless appetite within our selves which craves for some Supreme and Chief good, and will not be satisfied with any thing less then Infinity it self; as if our own Penury and Indigency were commensurate to the Divine fulness. . . . We find by Experience that our Souls cannot live upon that thin and spare diet which they are entertain'd with at their own home; neither can they be satiated with those jejune and insipid morsels which this Outward world furnisheth their Table with. I cannot think the most voluptuous Epicurean could ever satisfie the cravings of his

285

Soul with Corporeal pleasure, though he might endeavour to perswade himself there was no better: nor the most Quintessential Stoicks find a Self-sufficiency and Tranquillity within their own Souls, arising out of the pregnancy of their own Mind and Reason. . . . The more we endeavour to extract an Autarchy out of our own Souls, the more we torment them, and force them to feel and sensate their own pinching poverty. Ever since our Minds became so dim-sighted as not to pierce into that Original and Primitive Blessedness which is above, our Wills are too big for our Understandings, and will believe their beloved prey is to be found where Reason dis-covers it not: they will pursue it through all the vast Wilderness of this World, and force our Understandings to follow the chase with them: nor may we think to tame this violent appetite or allay the heat of it, except we can look upward to some Eternal and Almighty goodness which is alone able to master it. . . .

The whole work of this World is nothing but a perpetuall con-tention for True Happiness, and men are scatter'd up and down the world, moving to and fro therein, to seek it. Our Souls by a Naturall Science as it were feeling their own Originall, are per-petually travailing with new designs and contrivances whereby they may purchase the scope of their high ambitions. Happiness is that Pearl of price which all adventure for, though few find it. It is not Gold or Silver that the Earthlings of this world seek after, but some satisfying good which they think is there treasur'd up. Neither is it a little empty breath that Ambition and Popularity soars after, but some kind of Happiness that it thinks to catch and suck in with it.

And thus indeed when men most of all flie from God, they still seek after him. Wicked men pursue indeed after a Deity in their worldly lusts; wherein yet they most blaspheme; for God is not a meer empty Name or Title, but that Self-sufficient good which brings along that Rest and Peace with it which they so much seek after, though they doe most prodigiously conjoyn it with something which it is not, nor can it be, and in a true and reall strain of blasphemy, attribute all that which God is to something else which is most unlike him, and, as S. Paul speaks of those infatuated Gentiles, *turn the glory of the uncorruptible God into the image of corruptible man, of birds and four-footed beasts and creeping things.* . . .

To conclude this particular, the Soul hath strong and weighty motions, and nothing else can bear it up but something permanent and immutable. Nothing can beget a constant serenity and com-posedness within, but something Supreme to its own Essence; as if having once departed from the primitive Fountain of its life, it were deprived of it self, perpetually contesting within it self and divided against it self: and all this evidently proves to our inward sense and feeling, That there is some Higher Good than our selves, something that is much more amiable and desirable, and . . . that calls forth and commands our adorations.

JOHN SMITH

Our whole being—soul, mind, sense, heart, will, life, body—must consecrate all its energies so entirely and in such a way that it shall become a fit vehicle for the Divine. . . . The difficulty of the task has led naturally to the pursuit of easy and trenchant solutions; it has generated and fixed deeply the tendency of religions and of schools of Yoga to separate the life of the world from the inner life. The powers of this world and their actual activities, it is felt, either do not belong to God at all or are for some obscure and puzzling cause, Maya or another, a dark contradiction of the divine Truth. And on their own opposite side the powers of the Truth and their ideal activities are seen to belong to quite another plane of consciousness than that, obscure, ignorant and perverse in its impulses and forces, on which the life of the earth is founded. There appears at once the antinomy of a bright and pure kingdom of God and a dark and impure kingdom of the devil; we feel the opposition of our crawling earthly birth and life to an exalted spiritual God-consciousness; we become readily convinced of the incompatibility of life's subjection to Maya with the soul's concentration in pure Brahman existence. The easiest way is to turn away from all that belongs to the one and to retreat by a naked and precipitous ascent into the other. Thus arises the attraction and, it would seem, the necessity of the principle of exclusive concentration which plays so prominent a part in the specialised schools of Yoga; for by that concentration we can arrive through an uncompromising renunciation of the world at an entire self-consecration to the One on whom we concentrate. It is no longer incumbent on us to compel all the lower activities to the difficult recognition of a new and higher spiritualised life and train them to be its agents or executive powers. It is enough to kill or quiet them and keep at most the few energies necessary, on one side, for the maintenance of the body, and, on the other, for communion with the Divine.

The very aim and conception of an integral Yoga debars us from adopting this simple and strenuous high-pitched process. The hope of an integral transformation forbids us to take a short cut, or to make ourselves light for the race by throwing away our impediments. For we have set out to conquer all ourselves and the world for God; we are determined to give him our becoming as well as our being, and not merely to bring the pure and naked spirit as a bare offering to a remote and secret Divinity in a distant heaven, or abolish all we are in a holocaust to an immobile Absolute. The Divine that we adore is not only a remote extra-cosmic Reality, but a half-veiled Manifestation present and near to us here in the universe. Life is the field of a divine manifestation not yet complete: here, in life, on earth, in the body, we have to unveil the Godhead; here we must make its transcendent greatness, light and sweetness real to our consciousness, here possess and, as far as may be, express it. Life then we must accept in our Yoga in order utterly to transmute it; we are forbidden to shrink from the difficulties that this acceptance may add to our struggle. Our compensation is that even if the path is more rugged, the effort more complex and bafflingly arduous, yet after a point we gain an immense advantage. For once our minds are reasonably fixed in the central vision and our wills are on the whole converted to the single pursuit, Life becomes our helper. Intent, vigilant, integrally conscious, we can take every detail of its forms and every incident of its movements as food for the sacrificial Fire within us. Victorious in the struggle, we can compel Earth herself to be an aid towards our perfection and can enrich our realisation with the booty torn from the powers that oppose us.

AUROBINDO

§ 3

The Curé of Ars noticed a peasant farmer frequently kneel in church for long periods without the slightest movement of the lips. "What do you say to our Lord during these long visits?" He replied: "I say nothing to Him. I look at Him and He looks at me."

A. MONNIN

It is said that once, when the Buddha was seated with his Bhikkhus on the Mount of Holy Vulture, a Brahma-Raja came to him and, offering him a golden flower, asked him to preach the

288

Dharma. The Blessed One received the flower and, holding it aloft, gazed at it in perfect silence. After a while the Venerable Mahâkaśyapa smiled.

CHRISTMAS HUMPHREYS

There lived in Kotzk a water-carrier, who, though illiterate, possessed deep religious feeling. Once, in synagogue, he heard the word "Tameh" (unclean), and it remained fixed in his memory. Unable to remember the customary prayers, he used the word "Tameh" as his prayer, repeating it with great vehemence hundreds of times. He became the butt of the townspeople's jests and was nicknamed "Tameh". The pious water-carrier ignored his mockers and continued to pour out his heart to the Creator in his own fashion.

It happened that Rabbi Menahem Mendel overheard his prayer. He appreciated the impossibility of teaching the untutored labourer the correct prayers, but wished him at least to substitute the word "Tahor" (clean) for "Tameh" (unclean). The water-carrier repeated "Tahor" many times, but soon became confused, and said "Tamor". He became aware that it was unlike either the first or the second word. He ran to the Rabbi and tearfully begged to be allowed his "own" word, inasmuch as he could not pray with the "Rabbi's word". The Rabbi complied with his request. To this day, the water-carrier may be heard, ardently praying: "Tameh, Tameh, Tameh."

HASIDIC LEGEND

A mountebank, who had become famous throughout France for his wonderful tumbling and juggling, grew very tired of his wandering life. At the end of each succeeding summer he found himself a little more oppressed by the noise and bustle of the world and a little more weary of his constant travelling from town to town. One very wet and windy day at the end of the harvest season, he came to the great convent of Clairvaux. The kindly monks were much amused by his clever tricks, and when his performance was finished did not fail to point out to him the great difference between their life and his, which, being a clever fellow, he could see very well for himself. He told them he had in his wallet a goodly fortune made by his profession, and would give it all to our Lord and His Holy Mother if he might spend the rest of his life in the convent. The Abbot, being appealed to, counted the contents of the wallet, and said it was evidently the will of God that they should welcome this worthy man.

So the tumbler was dressed as a monk, and he soon began to accommodate himself to his new life. The order and discipline of the convent gave him a pleasant feeling of security, and when he worked in the garden his heart was full of peace. But, as time went on, he began to feel sorrowful because his service was so poor. While the monks were busy chanting or praying or adding something more to their great learning, he was doing things of small importance to our Lord and His Holy Mother.

One day, being quite overcome by these troubling thoughts, he threw aside his spade, and, running down the steps into the crypt, fell on his knees before the image of the Virgin which was still standing on an old disused altar. There he poured out his pitiful tale, which simply amounted to this—that he loved the Holy Mother very dearly but had nothing worthy to give her. When he had finished this lamentation he was about to depart without feeling much relief, when he heard a Gentle Voice say "Give what you have!"

"Ah!" exclaimed the mountebank, speaking to himself (for there was no one else to be seen). "Alas! I have nothing at all, for my little fortune is no longer mine." Having thus spoken, he was turning away, when he heard the Gentle Voice saying the same words as before. He stood still in front of the old altar for a long time, thinking very hard. And suddenly he remembered that he had one thing left—his wonderful art.

He threw off his long monkish robe, and, having freed his arms and legs from all restrictive coverings, he performed in front of the image of the Virgin all those mirth-provoking turns and tumbles which had so often delighted crowds of admiring spectators.

One of the monks finding the tumbler's spade in the garden raised a great alarm that the Devil had carried him off. The Abbot and the monks began a long search, which ended in the crypt, where they found the pious mountebank still leaping and tumbling before the altar. As the Abbot was about to exclaim against this sacrilege, the poor man fell on the floor quite exhausted by the now unwonted exercise. Then a great miracle happened, for the Holy Virgin herself appeared, surrounded with a bright company of angels, and bending over the prostrate tumbler fanned his face with a little kerchief that she had.

The mountebank finished his life, as he had wished, in the con-

vent of Clairvaux, and when the end of it came it was not the Devil
who carried his soul away but the Madonna herself and her bright
company of angels.

ARTHUR STANLEY (based on an old French poem)

§ 4

THE SERAPHIC VISION

*On a plateau of rock, high and precipitous, a small cell,
roughly built of stones and timber, stands amid a group of pines
and cypress trees. Above the door is a narrow window slit; on the
gable a wooden cross. A narrow foot-bridge of primitive construction connects the plateau and the foreground, which is formed of
rough stones interspersed with juniper bushes. Below the foot-
bridge is a precipice, from which emerge the tops of pines. When
the scene opens it is dusk; the warmth of daylight has gone, and
behind the cell the moon has not yet risen.* BROTHER LEO *stands
alone by the foot-bridge, gazing toward the cell, the door of which
is shut.* BROTHER BERNARD *enters hastily.* BROTHER LEO *raises a
warning hand, without turning his eyes from the point on which
they are fixed.*

BERNARD Ha! Brother Leo?

LEO   Hush! Speak low; speak low!

BERNARD What canst thou hear?

LEO   Nothing! . . . Nothing!

BERNARD   Since when?

LEO Alas, 'tis three days, Brother.

BERNARD   Thou hast been here?

LEO Or Brother Angelo. We watch by turn:
       And all this while silence as of the grave!

BERNARD I will watch too.

LEO My message found thee. When?

BERNARD At yester-noon.

LEO   Thou hast been quick.

BERNARD   Ah, Brother,
       Do we not love him?

LEO   He is more to me
       Than life. God pardon me! When I need comfort,
       I speak *his* name.

BERNARD Three days, thou sayest? and all that time no sound?
       Truly, he is within there, think you, still?

LEO He is there, Brother.

BERNARD   And yet liveth?

LEO   Yea,
         He liveth! . . . Oh, fair Brother, pray for me!
         I may not leave him. Yet am I afraid!

BERNARD Why? For what cause?

LEO   Lest with these sinful eyes
         I may behold a mystery too great!

BERNARD God gave thee thine eyes, Brother.

LEO   Yea, and my heart
         Also; yet I do fear!

BERNARD   Hark, who comes here?

LEO 'Tis Brother Angelo; he bringeth bread
         Daily. . . . Ah, me!

         [*Enter* ANGELO: *he goes up to the door of the cell, stands
            and makes a gesture of distress. He exchanges the loaf
            he carries for the one he finds there.*

ANGELO (*returning*) Look, he hath eaten nothing!
         What? Brother Bernard?

BERNARD Aye. . . . This for three days!

LEO He hath had no food for seven.

BERNARD I will go in.

ANGELO We may not.

LEO So we watch helpless! Shall it never end?

BERNARD What surety have ye, Brothers, that he lives still?

LEO I know! I know!

BERNARD How knowest thou?

LEO   I have seen.
         When all is dark, there within wakes a light!
         And as a flame before the Sacrament
         So through the night it burns, and fades at dawn.

ANGELO I also have seen it, Brother.

BERNARD   Oh, what is here?
         'Tis marvel that thou tellest.

LEO   Why, so I think!

BERNARD What else? For surely in thy face I read
         More than thy speech reveals.

LEO   Well, thou shalt hear.
         On the fourth day, as I watched here alone,—
         Nigh spent, for Brother Angelo had not come,—
         About this hour, I looked, and lo, the door

292

Wide, and he standing by it. Then I heard
His voice, 'Who art thou, Lord?' and then again,
'Who art thou?' and therewith such tender words
Of adoration as I may not utter.
Then said he, 'What am I? O poor vile worm
That dieth, unworthy servant of my Lord!'
And as I looked I saw come down from Heaven
A torch of fire most beautiful and bright;
Over his head it rested; and from the flame
Came forth a voice; but of the words it spake
Naught could I understand.

BERNARD   And then?
LEO   What else
I saw not: for by the brightness of that flame
Mine eyes were blinded, and fear shook my heart.
When I awoke, 'twas Brother Angelo
Stood by me; and the place was dumb.

ANGELO   Here lying
I found him, Brother; and when he opened eyes
He did not know me; only afterwards
He told me this.

BERNARD   What mystery hast thou seen?
LEO   I have seen holiness; therefore am afraid.
BERNARD   Ah! be not troubled, Brother! Let us pray,
God's light be in our eyes, and in our hearts.
Had we but hearts like this, what light were ours!
          [*They kneel. Behind the cell the moon rises among the
          trees. The window of the cell lightens.*
ANGELO Oh, see! see!
LEO Oh, is not that light—wonderful?
BERNARD Now the door opens.
ANGELO Hush!
          [FRANCIS *appears in the doorway. A pause. He moves
          forward, rapt, with face raised and arms stretched wide.*
FRANCIS O Thou Lover of my soul, why dost thou call me
Whither I cannot follow thee? . . . (*A pause.*)
                                        Yea, I come!
I sleep; but my heart waketh. 'Tis the voice
Of my Beloved, saying, 'Open to me!'
O my sweet Lover!
BERNARD   Nay, Brothers, let us go!

This is too holy a mystery for our ears.
Come, come, away!

ANGELO (*softly*) Father, God give thee peace!

LEO (*softly, with a gesture of valediction*) Ah, little Father, hold me
in thy heart,
And pray for me!

BERNARD Quick! ere he speak, be hence!

[*They go out softly one by one.* FRANCIS *stands, rapt, then
speaks with pauses. His voice is low and tender.*

FRANCIS I opened to my Beloved, but He was gone. . . .
I sought Him, He could not be found. . . . I called. . . .
He gave no answer. . . . Be not Thou far off!
O Lord, my strength, haste Thee to succour me!

[*Slowly the radiance of the moon passes into cloud; the
form of* FRANCIS *becomes dim, only his face is discernible.
As he speaks, a deep vibration of music begins, barely
audible. Everything that surrounds him gradually fades
away; his body seems to stand no longer on earth but
cloud.*

I know, I know that my Redeemer liveth,
And at the last shall stand upon the earth.
Though with corruption worms destroy this body,
Yet in my very flesh shall I see God.
Him shall these eyes behold, and not another:
Yea, though He slay me, I will trust in Him.

[*A pause; very faintly in the distance thunder is heard.*

All things were made by Him. And without Him
Nothing was made that was made. In Him was Life;
And Life—the Light of men. And the Light shines
In darkness; and the darkness knoweth it not.

[*Soft sheet lightning begins to play, but the thunder is still
scarcely heard.*

That was the true Light, lighting every man
That cometh into the world. All flesh shall see it!

[*A prolonged flash of lightning. After it the light grows
brighter; and a fuller music is heard, accompanied by
thunder.*

O light of heaven, that with a million eyes
Dost visit space, a timeless traveller,
And wing-wide coverest the brief lives of men,
Say, hast thou seen the Passion of my Lord?

O freshening air, that through a million mouths
Hast given to mortals breath,—air, which He breathed
While yet on earth, and which my lips taste now,—
Say, didst thou taste the Passion of my Lord?
O dust of the ground, trodden by feet of men,
O broken bread of clay, from which was made
Man in God's image, meek substance formed for all,
How hast thou shared the Passion of my Lord?
O ye great hills, wherefor did ye mount up
High-headed into heaven to gaze on space,
If in that hour ye sought not Calvary?
Say, saw ye then the Passion of my Lord?
O ye green things of earth, ye covering leaves,
And tender herb, and shaken grass, and flower,
Ye drops of dew, ye mists, and sundering clouds,
Ye falling rains, and streams, ye downward torrents,
Ye firmamental tides which ebb and flow,
What part have ye in the Passion of my Lord?

> [*The lightning becomes more incessant; the air around him*
> *is charged with golden points of fire.*

O winds, His ministers, O wheeling fires,
And charioteers of space which, at His will,
Do burn continually on unseen wing,
Legions on legions, angels that attend,—
Where hold ye hid the Passion of my Lord?
Why doth not Earth sweat blood, if to her dust
From those dear Veins one drop did ever fall?
Why runs not ocean red, since water washed
His Wounds for burial? Why are not those thorns
Ruddier than rubies which once pierced His Brow?
Oh, why is Earth still Earth, since He, from Heaven,
Her Maker cometh giving life to all?

> [*His utterance becomes swift. In the air about him a*
> *mysterious commotion is seen, and the lights no longer*
> *burn steadfastly: they gloom and brighten again, as*
> *though unseen forms were passing before them.*

Ye, that with wing on wing
Your faces covering,
Do shroud the hidden thing
From the blindness of man's sight,
Undo, unloose again,

Holy and without stain,
His glory: let Christ reign,
And all be Light!
By birth, blessing, and bliss,
Creation did mean this,—
Form came for Love to kiss,
Making the whole world His!
To Chaos, a waste of shame,
Through night without end or aim,
Into the darkness came
His Word as a shaft of flame.
In silence of night and sleep,
Through the void under, above,
Lo, the Spirit of Love
Moved on the face of the deep;
He spake, and the Light did leap!
He saw, and it was done;
He found for its fires a way;
He parted the moon and sun,
And out of the night brought day.
He made new Heaven, new Earth,
And lo, where the Light did shine
Came living things to birth,
With music, and mouths of mirth,
And eyes to behold His worth,
And hearts to know Him divine.
Was not Creation this:—
By birth, blessing, and bliss,
Clasping His Feet, we kiss?
We are hers; she is His; . . .
He is mine!

> [*As* FRANCIS *ceases, a golden rain is seen falling about him;
> slowly the air begins to brighten with the coming of
> dawn. Music is heard and voices singing. He stands rapt
> and expectant.*

VOICES. Holy, holy, holy, Lord God of Hosts, Heaven and earth are
full of Thy glory; Glory be to Thee, O Lord most high!
FRANCIS. O Maker Christ, O Love made Flesh, make me!
Fashion me in Thine image ere I die!
That I may know Thy Passion, let me be
Partaker of Thy pains! Weak, weak I cry;

Oh, come Thou unto me!
I faint, for Thee I thirst. Now, lest I waste,
Let me be filled with thee! Sweet Saviour, haste,
Lift Thou me up. . . .
Give me Thy cup. . . .
To taste!

> [*A marvellous brightness falls upon the face of* FRANCIS;
> *the air becomes blue and radiant. He stands in a golden
> shower, gazing intently before him. Slowly he lifts and
> extends his arms in the form of the Cross. His voice
> becomes faint with joy and ravishment.*

O Day-star from on high,
Out of yon Eastern sky,
How swiftly Thou dost fly! . . .
And lo, with hands stretched wide,
Like my Lord, ere He died,
In form most glorified,
Thou comest! . . .
From what height?
O blessed, holy sight!
O Light of Light!

> [*He stands entranced in ecstasy. The dawn lies golden
> about him. From the world below comes a loud singing
> of birds. The mist fades and begins to disappear;
> behind him is seen faintly the cell with its door open.
> Earth appears again. Slowly he lets down his hands,
> which bear the marks of the Passion.*

LAURENCE HOUSMAN

VI. "THE GLORIOUS LIBERTY OF THE CHILDREN OF GOD"

The glorious liberty of the children of God.

ROMANS

What have we, Sons of God, to do with law?

MILTON

Where the Spirit of the Lord is, there is liberty.

II CORINTHIANS

> Our souls at least are free, and 'tis in vain
> We would against them make the flesh obey—
> The spirit in the end will have its way.

BYRON

That which Jesus founded, that which will remain eternally his, allowing for the imperfections which mix themselves with everything realised by humanity, is the doctrine of the liberty of the soul.

RENAN

When freedom is not an inner idea which imparts strength to our activities and breadth to our creations, when it is merely a thing of external circumstance, it is like an open space to one who is blindfolded.

TAGORE

Spirit is liberty. The nature of spirit is the opposite of passivity and necessity..

BERDYAEV

We moderns are faced with the necessity of rediscovering the life of the spirit; we must experience it anew for ourselves. It is the only way in which we can break the spell that binds us to the cycle of biological events.

C. G. JUNG

We are confronted with the necessarily determined everyday world in which processes are taking place in time and the future appears as fated. Man is fettered and weighed down. He both longs for freedom and fears it. The paradox of liberation is that in order to preserve freedom and to struggle for it, one must in a sense be already free, have freedom within oneself. Those who are slaves to the very core of their being do not know the name of freedom and cannot struggle for it. Ancient taboos surround man on all sides and fetter his moral life. In order to free himself from their power man must first be conscious of himself as inwardly free and only then can he struggle for freedom outwardly. The inner conquest of slavery is the fundamental task of moral life. Every kind of slavery is meant here—the slavery to the power of the past and of the future, the slavery to the external world and to oneself, to one's lower self. The awakening of çreative energy is inner liberation and is accompanied by a sense of freedom. Creativeness is the way of liberation.

BERDYAEV

A large liberty will be the law of a spiritual society, and the increase of freedom a sign of the growth of human society towards the possibility of true spiritualisation. To spiritualise in this sense a society of slaves, slaves of power, slaves of authority, slaves of custom, slaves of dogma, slaves of all sorts of imposed laws which they live under rather than live by, slaves internally of their own weakness, ignorance and passions from whose worst effect they seek or need to be protected by another and external slavery, can never be a successful endeavour. They must shake off their fetters first in order to be fit for a higher freedom. Not that man has not to wear many a yoke in his progress upward; but only the yoke which he accepts because it represents, the more perfectly the better, the highest inner law of his nature and its aspiration, will be entirely helpful to him. The rest buy their good results at a heavy cost, and may retard as much as, or even more than, they accelerate his progress.

AUROBINDO

Virtue consists, not in abstaining from vice, but in not desiring it.

BERNARD SHAW

It is a great liberty to be able not to sin; it is the greatest liberty to be unable to sin.

ST. AUGUSTINE

§ 2

Your laws, councils, decrees, canons, and your singular articles or opinions, are but mere deceit: the spirit of Christ in God will not be bound to any laws.

BOEHME

302

Accustomed long to application of each new experience to mine own spiritual growth, I have forgot all creeds and dogmas.

Accustomed long to keep my mind in the Uncreated State of Freedom, I have forgot conventional and artificial usages.

MILAREPA

The more people come to be taught immediately of God by the light of His word and spirit in their hearts, the less need of outward means.

WILLIAM PENN

THE LAW AS SIN

If I had personified all the various prescriptions and prohibitions of Jewish orthodoxy into a single living person and called it the Law, as possibly I came near to doing, I should have described it as a sinning person. "What shall we say then?" asks St. Paul. "Is the law sin?", and replies "God forbid". I should have replied "Yes". The Law seemed a sinning person because somehow, by compelling, it made everything dirty. There was something dark and nasty about it, which, as I might have put it at the time, messed everything up. This applied to its moral quite as much as to its ceremonial aspect, and the fact that what it prohibited might clearly be bad had nothing to do with the matter. There didn't seem much point in not doing a thing, however bad, when there was no possibility of your doing it anyhow; the not doing of it had been spoiled. Even when the Law, positive this time, compelled you to do something that ought obviously to have seemed good, it no longer seemed good, because the Law compelled you to do it: it had become at best neutral and uninteresting, if not, perversely, actually bad. Whenever the Law was there, and it was there the whole time, it brought the idea of sin with it; and the idea of sin and sin were really the same, or at any rate were equally dirty. ("Hath already committed adultery in his heart.") So the Law was sinful. I don't know how much of this I consciously thought out at the beginning of my revolt from Jewish orthodoxy, but I'm sure it's what I felt, however obscurely. I was getting, of course, at the ideas of freedom, intention and spontaneity. How I should put it now is that the Law was sinful because it interfered with the glorious liberty of the children of God, in which true blessedness consists.

V. G.

§ 3

My experience in the West, where I have realised the immense power of money and of organised propaganda—working everywhere behind screens of camouflage, creating an atmosphere of distrust, timidity and antipathy—has impressed me deeply with the truth that real freedom is of the mind and spirit; it can never come to us from outside. He only has freedom who ideally loves freedom himself and is glad to extend it to others. He who cares to have slaves must chain himself to them; he who builds walls to create exclusion for others builds walls across his own freedom; he who distrusts freedom in others loses his moral right to it. Sooner or later he is lured into the meshes of physical and moral servility.

TAGORE

This "I and mine" causes the whole misery. With the sense of possession comes selfishness, and selfishness brings on misery. Every act of selfishness or thought of selfishness makes us attached to something, and immediately we are made slaves. Each wave in the Chitta that says "I and mine" immediately puts a chain round us and makes us slaves; and the more we say "I and mine" the more slavery grows, the more misery increases. Therefore, Karma-Yoga tells us to enjoy the beauty of all the pictures in the world but not to identify ourselves with any of them.

VIVEKANANDA

Oh Poverty, high wisdom! to be subject to nothing, and by despising all to possess all created things. . . .

God will not lodge in a narrow heart; and it is as great as thy love. Poverty has so ample a bosom that Deity Itself may lodge therein. . . .

Poverty is naught to have, and nothing to desire: but all things to possess in the spirit of liberty.

JACOPONE DA TODI

People are happy who have no need of locks.

DOSTOEVSKY

I want nothing whatever. I am quite happy.

BLAKE

§ 4

Asked "What is Zen?", a Master replied "Walk on!"

CHRISTMAS HUMPHREYS

The Prophet said, "If ye knew God as He ought to be known, ye would walk on the seas, and the mountains would move at your call."

SUFI TRADITION

The bliss of the animals lies in this, that, on their lower level, they shadow the bliss of those—few at any moment on the earth—who do not 'look before and after, and pine for what is not' but live in the holy carelessness of the eternal *now*.

GEORGE MACDONALD

Contact with children teaches us sincerity, simplicity, the habit of living in the present hour, the present action.

Children are, as it were, reborn daily: hence their spontaneity, the lack of complexity in their souls, the simplicity of their judgments and actions.

Moreover, their intuitive distinctions between good and evil are unencumbered, their souls are free of the bonds of sin, they are not under the necessity of weighing and analyzing.

We possess all this as a birthright which we wantonly scatter on our way, so that we must afterwards painfully gather up the fragments of our lost fortune.

FATHER YELCHANINOV

I heard a herald's note announce the coming of a king.

He who came sounding his approach was a small boy;
The household trumpet that he flourished a tin toy.

Then from a bench beneath the boughs that lately Spring
Had hung again with green across the avenue, I rose
To render to the king who came the homage subjects owe.

And as I waited, wondered why it was that such a few
Were standing there with me to see him pass; but understood
As soon as he came into sight, this was a monarch no
Crowds of this world can recognize, to hail him as they should.

He drove past in a carriage that was drawn by a white goat:
King of the world to come where all that shall be now is new,
Calmly he gazed on our pretentious present that is not.

Of morals, classes, business, war, this child
Knew nothing. We were pardoned when he smiled.

If you hear it in the distance, do not scorn the herald's note.

DAVID GASCOYNE

How happy is the little stone
That rambles in the road alone,
And doesn't care about careers,
And exigencies never fears;
Whose coat of elemental brown
A passing universe put on;
And independent as the sun,
Associates or glows alone,
Fulfilling absolute decree
In casual simplicity.

EMILY DICKINSON

Consider and consider and always come back to what you said in
a flash and to what you knew when you saw it.

MARGOT RUDDOCK

Motives are symptoms of weakness, and supplements for the
deficient energy of the living principle, the law within us.

S. T. COLERIDGE

The more consciousness in our thoughts and words, and the less
in our impulses and general actions, the better and more healthful
the state both of head and heart. As the flowers from an orange
tree in its time of blossoming, that burgeon forth, expand, fall, and
are momently replaced, such is the sequence of hourly and
momently charities in a pure and gracious soul. The modern fiction
which depictures the son of Cytherea with a bandage round his
eyes, is not without a spiritual meaning. There is a sweet and holy
blindness in Christian love even as there is a blindness of life, yea,
and of genius too, in the moment of productive energy.

S. T. COLERIDGE

Serene will be our days and bright
And happy will our nature be,
When love is an unerring light,
And joy its own security . . .

WORDSWORTH

THE GOLDEN BIRD

If Joy, the Golden Bird, would fly,
Do not close an hand upon her!
She belongeth to the sky,
With all the winds of heaven on her:
Only when her wings are free
Bird of Lovely Life is she.

He who Joy of Life would store,
Heart of his be widely open;
Throw the key out with the door,
Throw the hope out with the hopen:
Give her—as she finds in sky—
Place to dip, and soar, and fly.

She will come again, I wist!
She of thee shall not be frighted!
She shall sing upon thy fist!
By her shall thy dark be lighted!
By her freedom thou art given
Right and room in joyous heaven!

JAMES STEPHENS

§ 5

Confucius visited Lao Tzu and began talking about goodness and duty. 'Chaff from the winnower's fan', said Lao Tzu, 'can so blear our eyes that we do not know if we are looking north, south, east, or west; at heaven or at the earth. One gnat or mosquito can be more than enough to keep us awake a whole night. All this talk of goodness and duty, these perpetual pin-pricks, unnerve and irritate the hearer; nothing, indeed, could be more destructive of his inner tranquillity. . . . The swan does not need a daily bath in order to remain white: the crow does not need a daily inking in order to remain black. . . . When the pool dries up, fish makes room for fish upon the dry land, they moisten one another with damp breath,

307

spray one another with foam from their jaws. But how much better are they off when they can forget one another, in the freedom of river or lake!'

CHUANG TZU (*tr. by Waley*)

How easy it is to interpret slavery as duty—the morbid attachment of flesh to flesh as duty! Men go out into the world and struggle and fight for money or for any other thing to which they get attached. Ask them why they do it. They say, "It is a duty". It is the absurd greed for gold and gain, and they try to cover it with a few flowers.

Duty becomes a disease with us; it drags us ever forward. It catches hold of us and makes our whole life miserable. It is the bane of human life. This duty, this idea of duty is the midday summer sun which scorches the innermost soul of mankind. Look at those poor slaves to duty! Duty leaves them no time to say prayers, no time to bathe. Duty is ever on them. They go out and work. Duty is on them! They come home and think of the work for the next day. Duty is on them! It is living a slave's life, at last dropping down in the street and dying in harness, like a horse. This is duty as it is understood. The only true duty is to be unattached and to work as free beings, to give up all work unto God.

VIVEKANANDA

Buddhism in the East is known as the Buddha-Dharma. The word Dharma has a vast variety of meanings, one of which is "duty". But duty in English has the unpleasant connotation of compulsion. It is something which ought to be done but which, generally speaking, we do not wish to do. Yet in the Buddhist sense it is that which is the next thing to be done, and the emotional labels of dislike or like are not applied. One just does it. In a memorable passage Chuang Tzu begins, "To act by means of inaction is Tao. To speak by means of inaction is exemplification of Tao". It ends, "To follow Tao is to be prepared. . . . And not to run counter to the natural bias of things is perfect". This "natural bias of things" is the rhythm of nature, the rhythm of the Universe. "It connotes acting in harmony with the swing of the Universe— whether spiritually, intellectually or in the least movement of the body—from the physical movements of the dance of happy youth to the dance of the planets about the sun and the systems about the infinite" . . .

There is a harmony called Tao which blends all events in each moment of the Universe into a perfect chord. The whole situation in and around you at this instant is a harmony with which you have to find your own union if you are to be in accord with Tao. The right life, therefore, is the natural life, and he who has found and lives in Zen lives naturally. To what extent his new found harmony affects his outward life, to bring his outward mode of living into accord with his inner awareness, is a matter of time and the individual, but just as the direct drive of an engine is sweet and without discordant tension, so the right use of action, direct action, is sweet and frictionless. Only self, the desire of self for self, intervenes and pulls the machine out of alignment. Alignment becomes the operative word. From the "power-house of the Universe", as Trine calls it, to the individual self the power is direct, and the right means used in the right way at the right time and place makes up increasingly the perfect act.

CHRISTMAS HUMPHREYS

P'u means wood in its natural condition, uncarved and unpainted. It is the Taoist symbol of man's natural state, when his inborn powers have not been tampered with by knowledge or circumscribed by morality. The Taoist cult of *p'u* is a philosophic restatement of ancient ritual ideas: 'If thou wilt make me an altar of stone thou shalt not build it of hewn stone: for if thou lift up thy tool upon it, thou hast polluted it'. The enemies of this simplicity are the sense-organs, with their separate and limited functions. 'The eye is a menace to clear sight, the ear is a menace to subtle hearing, the mind is a menace to wisdom, every organ of the senses is a menace to its own capacity. Sad is it indeed that man should look upon these seats of menace as his greatest treasure.'

What then is man's true treasure? It is his Inward Vision, a generalized perception that can come into play only when the distinction between 'inside' and 'outside', between 'self' and 'things', between 'this' and 'that' has been entirely obliterated. Chuang Tzu's symbol for this state of pure consciousness, which sees without looking, hears without listening, knows without thinking, is the god Hun-tun ('Chaos'): 'Fuss, the god of the Southern Ocean, and Fret, the god of the Northern Ocean, happened once to meet in the realm of Chaos, the god of the centre. Chaos treated them very handsomely and they discussed together what they could do to repay his kindness. They had noticed that, whereas everyone else has seven apertures, for sight, hearing, eating, breathing and so on, Chaos had none. So they decided to make the experiment of boring holes in him. Every day they bored a hole, and on the seventh day Chaos died.'

ARTHUR WALEY

§ 6

But whoso looketh into the perfect law of liberty, and continueth therein, he being not a forgetful hearer, but a doer of the work, this man shall be blessed in his deed.

THE EPISTLE OF JAMES

Action rightly renounced brings freedom:
Action rightly performed brings freedom:
Both are better
Than mere shunning of action.

THE BHAGAVAD-GITA

It is easy enough to stand still; the difficulty is to walk without touching the ground.

CHUANG TZU

The seers say truly
That he is wise
Who acts without lust or scheming
For the fruit of the act:
His act falls from him,
Its chain is broken,
Melted in the flame of my knowledge.
Turning his face from the fruit,
He needs nothing:
The Atman is enough.
He acts, and is beyond action.

Not hoping, not lusting,
Bridling body and mind,
He calls nothing his own:
He acts, and earns no evil.

What God's Will gives
He takes, and is contented.

Pain follows pleasure,
He is not troubled:
Gain follows loss,
He is indifferent:
Of whom should he be jealous?
He acts, and is not bound by his action.

When the bonds are broken
His illumined heart
Beats in Brahman:
His every action
Is worship of Brahman:
Can such acts bring evil?

THE BHAGAVAD-GITA

But all our best is of our own doing: such is our nature as long as we remain detached. The wise and good do perform acts; their right action is the expression of their own power: in the others it comes in the breathing spaces when the passions are in abeyance; but it is not that they draw this occasional wisdom from outside themselves; simply, they are for the time being unhindered.

PLOTINUS

For a free creative act there exist no fate and no predetermined future. At the moment when a free creative act takes place there is no thought of the future, of the inevitable death, of future suffering; it is an escape from time and from all determinateness.

BERDYAEV

And right action is freedom
From past and future also.

T. S. ELIOT

ACTION AND EGOISM

In the field of action desire takes many forms, but the most powerful of all is the vital self's craving or seeking after the fruit of our works. The fruit we covet may be a reward of internal pleasure; it may be the accomplishment of some preferred idea or some cherished will or the satisfaction of the egoistic emotions, or else the pride of success of our highest hopes and ambitions. Or it may be an external reward, a recompense entirely material—wealth,

311

position, honour, victory, good fortune or any other fulfilment of vital or physical desire. But all alike are lures by which egoism holds us. Always these satisfactions delude us with the sense of mastery and the idea of freedom, while really we are harnessed and guided or ridden and whipped by some gross or subtle, some noble or ignoble, figure of the blind Desire that drives the world. Therefore the first rule of action laid down by the Gita is to do the work that should be done without any desire for the fruit.

A simple rule in appearance, and yet how difficult to carry out with anything like an absolute sincerity and liberating entireness! In the greater part of our action we use the principle very little if at all, and then even mostly as a sort of counterpoise to the normal principle of desire and to mitigate the extreme action of that tyrant impulse. At best, we are satisfied if we arrive at a modified and disciplined egoism not too shocking to our moral sense, not too brutally offensive to others. And to our partial self-discipline we give various names and forms; we habituate ourselves by practice to the sense of duty, to a firm fidelity to principle, a stoical fortitude, or a religious resignation, a quiet or an ecstatic submission to God's will. But it is not these things that the Gita intends, useful though they are in their place; it aims at something absolute, unmitigated, uncompromising, a turn, an attitude that will change the whole poise of the soul. Not the mind's control of vital impulse is its rule, but the strong immobility of an immortal spirit.

The test it lays down is an absolute equality of the mind and the heart to all results, to all reactions, to all happenings. If good fortune and ill fortune, if respect and insult, if reputation and obloquy, if victory and defeat, if pleasant event and sorrowful event leave us not only unshaken but untouched, free in the emotions, free in the nervous reactions, free in the mental view, not responding with the least disturbance or vibration in any spot of the nature, then we have the absolute liberation to which the Gita points us, but not otherwise. The tiniest reaction is a proof that the discipline is imperfect and that some part of us accepts ignorance and bondage as its law and clings still to the old nature. Our self-conquest is only partially accomplished; it is still imperfect or unreal in some stretch or part or smallest spot of ground of our nature. And that little pebble of imperfection may throw down the whole achievement of the Yoga.

There are certain semblances of an equal spirit which must not be mistaken for the profound and vast spiritual equality which the Gita

312

teaches. There is an equality of disappointed resignation, an equality of pride, an equality of hardness and indifference; all these are egoistic in their nature. Inevitably they come in the course of the sadhana, but they must be rejected or transformed into the true quietude. There is too, on a higher level, the equality of the stoic, the equality of a devout resignation or a sage detachment, the equality of a soul aloof from the world and indifferent to its doings. These too are insufficient; first approaches they can be, but they are at most early soul-phases only or imperfect mental preparations for our entry into the true and absolute, self-existent, wide, equal oneness of the spirit.

For it is certain that so great a result cannot be arrived at immediately and without any previous stages. At first we have to learn to bear the shocks of the world with the central part of our being untouched and silent, even when the surface mind, heart, life are strongly shaken; unmoved there on the bedrock of our life, we must separate the soul watching behind, or immune deep within, from these outer workings of our nature. Afterwards, extending this calm and steadfastness of the detached soul to its instruments, it will become slowly possible to radiate peace from the luminous centre to the darker peripheries. In this process we may take the passing help of many minor phases; a certain stoicism, a certain calm philosophy, a certain religious exaltation may help us towards some nearness to our aim, or we may call in even less strong and exalted but still useful powers of our mental nature. In the end we must either discard or transform them and arrive instead at an entire equality, a perfect self-existent peace within, and even, if we can, a total unassailable, self-poised and spontaneous delight in all our members.

But how then shall we continue to act at all? For ordinarily the human being acts because he has a desire or feels a mental, vital or physical want or need; he is driven by the necessities of the body, by the lust of riches, honours or fame, or by a craving for the personal satisfactions of the mind or the heart or a craving for power or pleasure. Or he is seized and pushed about by a moral need or, at least, the need or the desire of making his ideas or his ideals or his will or his party or his country or his gods prevail in the world. If none of these desires nor any other must be the spring of our action, it would seem as if all incentive or motive power had been removed and action itself must necessarily cease. The Gita replies with its third great secret of the divine life. All action must be done in a more and more Godward and finally a God-possessed consciousness; our works must be a sacrifice to the Divine, and in the end a surrender of all our being, mind, will, heart, sense, life and body to the One must make God-love and God-service our only motive. This transformation of the motive force and very character of works is indeed its master idea; it is the foundation of its unique synthesis of works, love and knowledge. In the end not desire, but the consciously felt will of the Eternal, remains as the sole driver of our action and the sole originator of its initiative.

Equality, renunciation of all desire for the fruit of our works, action done as a sacrifice to the supreme Lord of our nature and of all nature—these are the three first Godward approaches in the Gita's way of Karmayoga.

AUROBINDO

THE EGOISM OF THE INSTRUMENT

Even when we become aware of all as the working of one cosmic Force and of the Divine behind it, that too need not liberate. If the egoism of the worker disappears, the egoism of the instrument may replace it or else prolong it in a disguise. The life of the world has been full of instances of egoism of this kind, and it can be more engrossing and enormous than any other; there is the same danger in Yoga. A man becomes a leader of men or eminent in a large or lesser circle and feels himself full of a power that he knows to be beyond his own ego-force; he may be aware of a Fate acting through him or a Will mysterious and unfathomable or a Light within of great brilliance. There are extraordinary results of his thoughts, his actions or his creative genius. He effects some tremendous destruction that clears the path for humanity or some great construction that becomes its momentary resting-place. He is a scourge or he is a bringer of light and healing, a creator of beauty or a messenger of knowledge. Or, if his work and its effects are on a lesser scale and have a limited field, still they are attended by the strong sense that he is an instrument and chosen for his mission or his labour. Men who have this destiny and these powers come easily to believe and declare themselves to be mere instruments in the hand of God or of Fate; but even in the declaration we can see that there can intrude or take refuge an intenser and more exaggerated egoism than ordinary men have the courage to assert or the strength to house within them. And often if men of this kind speak of God, it is to erect an image of him which is really nothing but a huge shadow of themselves or their own nature, a sustaining Deific Essence of their own type of will and thought and quality and force. This magnified image of their ego is the Master whom they serve. This happens only too often in Yoga to strong but crude vital natures or minds too easily exalted when they allow ambition, pride or the desire of greatness to enter into their spiritual seeking and vitiate its purity of motive; a magnified ego stands between them and their true being, and grasps for its own personal purpose the strength from a greater unseen Power—divine or undivine—acting through them, of which they become vaguely or intensely aware. An intellectual perception or vital sense of a Force greater than ours, and of ourselves as moved by it, is not sufficient to liberate from the ego.

AUROBINDO

§ 7

I shrink to give up my life, and thus do not plunge into the great waters of life.

TAGORE

FROM "THE DEATH OF IVÁN ILÝCH"

. . . It was morning. He knew it was morning because Gerásim [his peasant servant] had gone, and Peter the footman had come and put out the candles, drawn back one of the curtains, and begun quietly to tidy up. Whether it was morning or evening, Friday or Sunday, made no difference, it was all just the same: the gnawing, unmitigated, agonizing pain, never ceasing for an instant, the consciousness of life inexorably waning but not yet extinguished, the approach of that ever dreaded and hateful Death which was the only reality, and always the same falsity. What were days, weeks, hours, in such a case? . . .

Peter went to the door, but Iván Ilých dreaded being left alone. 'How can I keep him here? Oh yes, my medicine.' 'Peter, give me my medicine.' 'Why not? Perhaps it may still do me some good.' He took a spoonful and swallowed it. 'No, it won't help. It's all tomfoolery, all deception,' he decided as soon as he became aware of the familiar, sickly, hopeless taste. 'No, I can't believe in it any longer. But the pain, why this pain? If it would only cease just for a moment!' And he moaned. Peter turned towards him. 'It's all right. Go and fetch me some tea.'

Peter went out. Left alone Iván Ilých groaned not so much with pain, terrible though that was, as from mental anguish. Always and for ever the same, always these endless days and nights. If only it would come quicker! If only *what* would come quicker? Death, darkness? . . . No, no! Anything rather than death!

When Peter returned with the tea on a tray, Iván Ilých stared at him for a time in perplexity, not realizing who and what he was. Peter was disconcerted by that look and his embarrassment brought Iván Ilých to himself.

'Oh, tea! All right, put it down. Only help me to wash and put on a clean shirt.'

And Iván Ilých began to wash. With pauses for rest, he washed his hands and then his face, cleaned his teeth, brushed his hair, and looked in the glass. He was terrified by what he saw, especially by the limp way in which his hair clung to his pallid forehead.

While his shirt was being changed he knew that he would be still more frightened at the sight of his body, so he avoided looking at it. Finally he was ready. He drew on a dressing-gown, wrapped himself in a plaid, and sat down in the armchair to take his tea. For a moment he felt refreshed, but as soon as he began to drink the tea he was again aware of the same taste, and the pain also returned. He finished it with an effort, and then lay down stretching out his legs, and dismissed Peter.

Always the same. Now a spark of hope flashes up, then a sea of despair rages, and always pain; always pain, always despair, and always the same. When alone he had a dreadful and distressing desire to call someone, but he knew beforehand that with others present it would be still worse. 'Another dose of morphine—to lose consciousness. I will tell him, the doctor, that he must think of something else. It's impossible, impossible, to go on like this.'

An hour and another pass like that. But now there is a ring at the door bell. Perhaps it's the doctor? It is. He comes in fresh, hearty, plump, and cheerful, with that look on his face that seems to say: 'There now, you're in a panic about something, but we'll arrange it all for you directly!' The doctor knows this expression is out of place here, but he has put it on once for all and can't take it off—like a man who has put on a frock-coat in the morning to pay a round of calls. . . .

The doctor, kneeling on the sofa, is still sounding him when Praskóvya Fëdorovna's silk dress rustles at the door and she is heard scolding Peter for not having let her know of the doctor's arrival.

She comes in, kisses her husband, and at once proceeds to prove that she has been up a long time already, and only owing to a misunderstanding failed to be there when the doctor arrived.

Iván Ilých looks at her, scans her all over, sets against her the whiteness and plumpness and cleanness of her hands and neck, the gloss of her hair, and the sparkle of her vivacious eyes. He hates her with his whole soul. And the thrill of hatred he feels for her makes him suffer from her touch.

*   *   *

Till about three in the morning he was in a state of stupefied misery. It seemed to him that he and his pain were being thrust into a narrow, deep black sack, but though they were pushed further and further in they could not be pushed to the bottom. And this, terrible enough in itself, was accompanied by suffering. He was frightened yet wanted to fall through the sack, he struggled but yet co-operated. And suddenly he broke through, fell, and regained consciousness. Gerásim was sitting at the foot of the bed dozing quietly and patiently, while he himself lay with his emaciated stockinged legs resting on Gerásim's shoulders; the same shaded candle was there and the same unceasing pain.

'Go away, Gerásim,' he whispered.

'It's all right, sir. I'll stay a while.'

'No. Go away.'

He removed his legs from Gerásim's shoulders, turned sideways on to his arm, and felt sorry for himself. He only waited till Gerásim had gone into the next room and then restrained himself no longer but wept like a child. He wept on account of his helplessness, his terrible loneliness, the cruelty of man, the cruelty of God, and the absence of God.

'Why hast Thou done all this? Why hast Thou brought me here? Why, why dost Thou torment me so terribly?'

He did not expect an answer and yet wept because there was no answer and could be none. The pain again grew more acute, but he did not stir and did not call. He said to himself: 'Go on! Strike me! But what is it for? What have I done to Thee? What is it for?'

Then he grew quiet and not only ceased weeping but even held his breath and became all attention. It was as though he were listening not to an audible voice but to the voice of his soul, to the current of thoughts arising within him.

'What is it you want?' was the first clear conception, capable of expression in words, that he heard.

317

'What do you want? What do you want?' he repeated to himself. 'What do I want? To live and not to suffer,' he answered.

And again he listened with such concentrated attention that even his pain did not distract him.

'To live? How?' asked his inner voice.

'Why, to live as I used to—well and pleasantly.'

'As you lived before, well and pleasantly?' the voice repeated. And in imagination he began to recall the best moments of his pleasant life. But strange to say none of those best moments of his pleasant life now seemed at all what they had then seemed—none of them except the first recollections of childhood. There, in childhood, there had been something really pleasant with which it would be possible to live if it could return. But the child who had experienced that happiness existed no longer, it was like a reminiscence of somebody else.

As soon as the period began which had produced the present Iván Ilých, all that had then seemed joys now melted before his sight and turned into something trivial and often nasty.

And the further he departed from childhood and the nearer he came to the present the more worthless and doubtful were the joys. This began with the School of Law. A little that was really good was still found there—there was light-heartedness, friendship, and hope. But in the upper classes there had already been fewer of such good moments. Then during the first years of his official career, when he was in the service of the Governor, some pleasant moments again occurred: they were the memories of love for a woman. Then all became confused and there was still less of what was good; later on again there was still less that was good, and the further he went the less there was. His marriage, a mere accident, then the disenchantment that followed it, his wife's bad breath and the sensuality and hypocrisy: then that deadly official life and those preoccupations about money, a year of it, and two, and ten, and twenty, and always the same thing. And the longer it lasted the more deadly it became. 'It is as if I had been going downhill while I imagined I was going up. And that is really what it was. I was going up in public opinion, but to the same extent life was ebbing away from me. And now it is all done and there is only death.'

'Then what does it mean? Why? It can't be that life is so senseless and horrible. But if it really has been so horrible and senseless, why must I die and die in agony? There is something wrong!'

'Maybe I did not live as I ought to have done,' it suddenly

318

occurred to him. 'But how could that be, when I did everything properly?' he replied, and immediately dismissed from his mind this, the sole solution of all the riddles of life and death, as something quite impossible.

'Then what do you want now? To live? Live how? Live as you lived in the law courts when the usher proclaimed "The judge is coming!" The judge is coming, the judge!' he repeated to himself. 'Here he is, the judge. But I am not guilty!' he exclaimed angrily. 'What is it for?' And he ceased crying, but turning his face to the wall continued to ponder on the same question: Why, and for what purpose, is there all this horror? But however much he pondered he found no answer. And whenever the thought occurred to him, as it often did, that it all resulted from his not having lived as he ought to have done, he at once recalled the correctness of his whole life and dismissed so strange an idea.

*   *   *

Another fortnight passed. Iván Ilých now no longer left his sofa. He would not lie in bed but lay on the sofa, facing the wall nearly all the time. He suffered ever the same unceasing agonies and in his loneliness pondered always on the same insoluble question: 'What is this? Can it be that it is Death?' And the inner voice answered: 'Yes, it is Death.'

'Why these sufferings?' And the voice answered, 'For no reason —they just are so.' Beyond and besides this there was nothing.

From the very beginning of his illness, ever since he had first been to see the doctor, Iván Ilých's life had been divided between two contrary and alternating moods: now it was despair and the expectation of this uncomprehended and terrible death, and now hope and an intently interested observation of the functioning of his organs. Now before his eyes there was only a kidney or an intestine that temporarily evaded its duty, and now only that incomprehensible and dreadful death from which it was impossible to escape.

These two states of mind had alternated from the very beginning of his illness, but the further it progressed the more doubtful and fantastic became the conception of the kidney, and the more real the sense of impending death.

He had but to call to mind what he had been three months before and what he was now, to call to mind with what regularity he had been going downhill, for every possibility of hope to be shattered.

Latterly during that loneliness in which he found himself as he lay facing the back of the sofa, a loneliness in the midst of a populous

319

town and surrounded by numerous acquaintances and relations but that yet could not have been more complete anywhere—either at the bottom of the sea or under the earth—during that terrible loneliness Iván Ilých had lived only in memories of the past. Pictures of his past rose before him one after another. They always began with what was nearest in time and then went back to what was most remote—to his childhood—and rested there. If he thought of the stewed prunes that had been offered him that day, his mind went back to the raw shrivelled French plums of his childhood, their peculiar flavour and the flow of saliva when he sucked their stones, and along with the memory of that taste came a whole series of memories of those days: his nurse, his brother, and their toys. 'No, I mustn't think of that. . . . It is too painful,' Iván Ilých said to himself, and brought himself back to the present—to the button on the back of the sofa and the creases in its morocco. 'Morocco is expensive, but it does not wear well: there had been a quarrel about it. It was a different kind of quarrel and a different kind of morocco that time when we tore father's portfolio and were punished, and mamma brought us some tarts. . . .' And again his thoughts dwelt on his childhood, and again it was painful and he tried to banish them and fix his mind on something else.

Then again together with that chain of memories another series passed through his mind—of how his illness had progressed and grown worse. There also the further back he looked the more life there had been. There had been more of what was good in life and more of life itself. The two merged together. 'Just as the pain went on getting worse and worse, so my life grew worse and worse,' he thought. 'There is one bright spot there at the back, at the beginning of life, and afterwards all becomes blacker and blacker and proceeds more and more rapidly—in inverse ratio to the square of the distance from death,' thought Iván Ilých. And the example of a stone falling downwards with increasing velocity entered his mind. Life, a series of increasing sufferings, flies further and further towards its end—the most terrible suffering. 'I am flying . . .' He shuddered, shifted himself, and tried to resist, but was already aware that resistance was impossible, and again with eyes weary of gazing but unable to cease seeing what was before them, he stared at the back of the sofa and waited—awaiting that dreadful fall and shock and destruction.

'Resistance is impossible!' he said to himself. 'If I could only understand what it is all for! But that too is impossible. An explanation would be possible if it could be said that I have not lived as I ought to. But it is impossible to say that,' and he remembered all the legality, correctitude, and propriety of his life. 'That at any rate can certainly not be admitted,' he thought, and his lips smiled ironically as if someone could see that smile and be taken in by it. 'There is no explanation! Agony, death. . . . What for?'

★ ★ ★

Another two weeks went by in this way . . . Iván Ilých's physical sufferings were terrible, but worse than the physical sufferings were his mental sufferings which were his chief torture.

His mental sufferings were due to the fact that that night, as he looked at Gerásim's sleepy, good-natured face with its prominent cheek-bones, the question suddenly occurred to him: 'What if my whole life has really been wrong?'

It occurred to him that what had appeared perfectly impossible before, namely that he had not spent his life as he should have done, might after all be true. It occurred to him that his scarcely perceptible attempts to struggle against what was considered good by the most highly placed people, those scarcely noticeable impulses which he had immediately suppressed, might have been the real thing, and all the rest false. And his professional duties and the whole arrangement of his life and of his family, and all his social and official interests, might all have been false. He tried to defend all those things to himself and suddenly felt the weakness of what he was defending. There was nothing to defend.

'But if that is so,' he said to himself, 'and I am leaving this life with the consciousness that I have lost all that was given me and it is impossible to rectify it—what then?'

He lay on his back and began to pass his life in review in quite a new way. In the morning when he saw first his footman, then his wife, then his daughter, and then the doctor, their every word and movement confirmed to him the awful truth that had been revealed to him during the night. In them he saw himself—all that for which he had lived—and saw clearly that it was not real at all, but a terrible and huge deception which had hidden both life and death. This consciousness intensified his physical suffering tenfold. He groaned and tossed about, and pulled at his clothing which choked and stifled him. And he hated them on that account.

He was given a large dose of opium and became unconscious, but at noon his sufferings began again. He drove everybody away and tossed from side to side.

321

His wife came to him and said:

'Jean, my dear, do this for me. It can't do any harm and often helps. Healthy people often do it.'

He opened his eyes wide.

'What? Take communion? Why? It's unnecessary! However . . .'

She began to cry.

'Yes, do, my dear. I'll send for our priest. He is such a nice man.'

'All right. Very well,' he muttered.

When the priest came and heard his confession Iván Ilých was softened and seemed to feel a relief from his doubts and consequently from his sufferings, and for a moment there came a ray of hope. He again began to think of the vermiform appendix and the possibility of correcting it. He received the sacrament with tears in his eyes.

When they laid him down again afterwards he felt a moment's ease, and the hope that he might live awoke in him again. He began to think of the operation that had been suggested to him. 'To live! I want to live!' he said to himself.

His wife came in to congratulate him after his communion, and when uttering the usual conventional words she added:

'You feel better, don't you?'

Without looking at her he said 'Yes.'

Her dress, her figure, the expression of her face, the tone of her voice, all revealed the same thing. 'This is wrong, it is not as it should be. All you have lived for and still live for is falsehood and deception, hiding life and death from you.' And as soon as he admitted that thought, his hatred and his agonizing physical suffering again sprang up, and with that suffering a consciousness of the unavoidable, approaching end. And to this was added a new sensation of grinding shooting pain and a feeling of suffocation.

The expression of his face when he uttered that 'yes' was dreadful. Having uttered it, he looked her straight in the eyes, turned on his face with a rapidity extraordinary in his weak state and shouted:

'Go away! Go away and leave me alone!'

*   *   *

From that moment the screaming began that continued for three days, and was so terrible that one could not hear it through two closed doors without horror. At the moment he answered his wife he realized that he was lost, that there was no return, that the end had come, the very end, and his doubts were still unsolved and remained doubts.

'Oh! Oh! Oh!' he cried in various intonations. He had begun by screaming 'I won't!' and continued screaming on the letter 'o'.

For three whole days, during which time did not exist for him, he struggled in that black sack into which he was being thrust by an invisible, resistless force. He struggled as a man condemned to death struggles in the hands of the executioner, knowing that he cannot save himself. And every moment he felt that despite all his efforts he was drawing nearer and nearer to what terrified him. He felt that his agony was due to his being thrust into that black hole and still more to his not being able to get right into it. He was hindered from getting into it by his conviction that his life had been a good one. That very justification of his life held him fast and prevented his moving forward, and it caused him most torment of all.

Suddenly some force struck him in the chest and side, making it still harder to breathe, and he fell through the hole and there at the bottom was a light. What had happened to him was like the sensation one sometimes experiences in a railway carriage when one thinks one is going backwards while one is really going forwards and suddenly becomes aware of the real direction.

'Yes, it was all not the right thing,' he said to himself, 'but that's no matter. It can be done. But what *is* the right thing?' he asked himself, and suddenly grew quiet.

This occurred at the end of the third day, two hours before his death. Just then his schoolboy son had crept softly in and gone up to the bedside. The dying man was still screaming desperately and waving his arms. His hand fell on the boy's head, and the boy caught it, pressed it to his lips, and began to cry.

At that very moment Iván Ilých fell through and caught sight of the light, and it was revealed to him that though his life had not been what it should have been, this could still be rectified. He asked himself, 'What *is* the right thing?' and grew still, listening. Then he felt that someone was kissing his hand. He opened his eyes, looked at his son, and felt sorry for him. His wife came up to him and he glanced at her. She was gazing at him open-mouthed, with undried tears on her nose and cheek and a despairing look on her face. He felt sorry for her too.

'Yes, I am making them wretched,' he thought. 'They are sorry, but it will be better for them when I die.' He wished to say this but had not the strength to utter it. 'Besides, why speak? I must act,' he thought. With a look at his wife he indicated his son and said: 'Take him away . . . sorry for him . . . sorry for you too. . . .' He tried to add, 'forgive me', but said 'forego' and waved his hand, knowing that He whose understanding matters would understand.

And suddenly it grew clear to him that what had been oppressing him and would not leave him was all dropping away at once from two sides, from ten sides, and from all sides. He was sorry for them, he must act so as not to hurt them: release them and free himself from these sufferings. 'How good and how simple!' he thought. 'And the pain?' he asked himself. 'What has become of it? Where are you, pain?'

He turned his attention to it.

'Yes, here it is. Well, what of it? Let the pain be.'

'And death . . . where is it?'

He sought his former accustomed fear of death and did not find it. 'Where is it? What death?' There was no fear because there was no death.

In place of death there was light.

'So that's what it is!' he suddenly exclaimed aloud. 'What joy!'

To him all this happened in a single instant, and the meaning of that instant did not change. For those present his agony continued for another two hours. Something rattled in his throat, his emaciated body twitched, then the gasping and rattle became less and less frequent.

'It is finished!' said someone near him.

He heard these words and repeated them in his soul.

'Death is finished,' he said to himself. 'It is no more!'

He drew in a breath, stopped in the midst of a sigh, stretched out, and died.

TOLSTOY

THIRD PART

I. TRUTH, REASON AND BEYOND REASON

Everything which has any sort of beauty of its own is beautiful of itself, and looks no further than itself, not counting praise as part of itself. For indeed that which is praised is made neither better nor worse thereby. This is the case also with everything that in common parlance is called beautiful, such as material things and works of art. Does, then, the authentically beautiful need anything beyond? Nay, no more than truth. Does an emerald forfeit its excellence by not being praised? Does gold, ivory, purple, a lyre, a poniard, a floweret, a shrub?

MARCUS AURELIUS

Truth is a divine thing, a friend more excellent than any human friend.

ST. THOMAS AQUINAS

The essence of man lies in this, in his marvellous faculty for seeking truth, seeing it, loving it, and sacrificing himself to it.

GUISEPPE PREZZOLINI

Truth above all, even when it upsets and overwhelms us!

AMIEL

Though there is a regard due to education and the tradition of our fathers, truth will ever deserve as well as claim the preference.

WILLIAM PENN

There is an age in life when . . . we must make a clean sweep of all admiration and respect got at second-hand, and deny every-thing—truth and untruth—everything which we have not of our-selves known for truth. Through education, and through everything that he sees and hears about him, a child absorbs so many lies and blind follies mixed with the essential verities of life, that the first duty of the adolescent who wishes to grow into a healthy man is to sacrifice everything.

ROMAIN ROLLAND

Now I, Callicles, am persuaded of the truth of these things, and I consider how I shall present my soul whole and undefiled before the judge in that day. Renouncing the honours at which the world aims, I desire only to know the truth, and to live as well as I can, and, when I die, to die as well as I can. And, to the utmost of my power, I exhort all other men to do the same. And, in return for your exhortation of me, I exhort you also to take part in the great combat, which is the combat of life, and greater than every other earthly conflict.

PLATO

Pilate saith unto him: What is truth? Jesus saith unto him: Truth is of heaven. Pilate saith: Is there not truth upon earth? Jesus saith unto Pilate: Thou seest how that they which speak the truth are judged of them that have authority upon earth.

ACTS OF PILATE

And yet, my friend, I would rather that the whole world should be at odds with me, and oppose me, than that I myself should be at odds with myself, and contradict myself.

PLATO

The Devil is compromise.

IBSEN

Talk nonsense, but talk your own nonsense. . . . To go wrong in one's own way is better than to go right in someone else's.

DOSTOEVSKY

✷

There is small chance of truth at the goal where there is not a child-like humility at the starting-post.

S. T. COLERIDGE

He that will finde Truth, must seek it with a free judgment, and a sanctified minde: he that thus seeks, shall finde; he shall live in Truth, and that shall live in him; it shall be like a stream of living waters issuing out of his own Soule; he shall drink of the waters of his own cisterne, and be satisfied; he shall every morning finde this Heavenly Manna lying upon the top of his own Soule, and be fed with it to eternal life; he will finde satisfaction within, feeling himself in conjunction with Truth, though all the World should dispute against him.

JOHN SMITH

Inquiry is human; blind obedience, brutal. Truth never loses by the one but often suffers by the other.

WILLIAM PENN

The good must be doubted to be defended.

ERIC SIEPMANN

To *doubt* has more of faith, even to disbelieve, than that blank negation of all such thoughts and feelings which is the lot of the herd of church-and-meeting trotters.

S. T. COLERIDGE

He who replies to words of Doubt
Doth put the Light of Knowledge out.

BLAKE

A man may be a heretic in the truth; and if he believes things only because his pastor says so, or the assembly so determines, without knowing other reason, though his belief be true yet the very truth he holds becomes his heresy.

MILTON

Yet I still half refused, not my love but my intelligence. For it seemed to me certain, and I still think so today, that one can never wrestle enough with God, if one does so out of pure regard for the truth. Christ likes us to prefer truth to him because, before being Christ, he is truth. If one turns aside from him to go towards the truth, one will not go far before falling into his arms.

SIMONE WEIL

The degree of intellectual honesty which is obligatory for me . . . demands that my thought should be indifferent to all ideas without exception, including for instance materialism and atheism; it must be equally welcoming and equally reserved with regard to every one of them. . . . This indifference of thought on the level of the intelligence is in no way incompatible with the love of God, or even with a vow of love inwardly renewed each second of each day, each time eternal and each time wholly complete and new. I should be like this if I were what I ought to be.

SIMONE WEIL

We owe the definitions with which the Church has thought it right to surround the mysteries of the faith, and more particularly its condemnations (. . . *anathema sit*), a permanent and unconditional attitude of respectful attention, but not an adherence.

329

We likewise owe a respectful attention to opinions that have been condemned, to the extent—be it ever so small—to which their content, or the life of those who propounded them, contains some show of good.

Intellectual adherence is never owed to anything whatsoever. For it is never in any degree a voluntary thing. Attention alone is voluntary. And it *alone* forms the subject of an obligation.

If one tries to bring about in oneself an intellectual adherence by the exercise of the will, what actually results is not an intellectual adherence, but suggestion. That is what Pascal's method amounts to. Nothing degrades faith more. And there necessarily appears, sooner or later, a compensatory phenomenon in the shape of doubts and 'temptations against faith'.

Nothing has contributed more towards weakening faith and encouraging unbelief than the mistaken conception of an obligation on the part of the intelligence. All obligations other than the one of attention which itself is imposed on the intelligence in the exercise of its function stifle the soul—the whole soul, and not the intelligence only.

SIMONE WEIL

TRUTH AND FAITH

One of the widest of the gulfs that divide human beings is between the people who *know* about ultimate mysteries and the people who don't. Some of the people who know never cease to amaze me. Not the ones who by no fault of their own are deficient in a sense of enquiry, or incapable of examining themselves, or unable to think clearly, or careless about truth. These are quite intelligible: and so are those who have fled, consciously or otherwise, from the torturings of doubt (whereas a man should accept, even rejoice in, his doubts as he does in his certainties) into a bogus kind of certainty which enables them to give up the struggle and be at peace. But there are other large categories of people, good people, honest people, spiritually-minded people, brilliant people, sophisticated people, even specially Socratic people, or people with all these qualities combined, who, so far as I can make out, really *know* about ultimate mysteries in a way that is unintelligible to me. They call their knowledge faith. (I am not jeering.) You will no doubt remind me of a previous passage about things that are a matter of *immediate knowledge*, as contrasted with things that are a matter of no more than, though perhaps the strongest possible, opinion. And here I am suddenly up against it. For I must confess that there are moments *in* which, rather than *about* which, there is utter, final, unquestioning knowledge, without the smallest possible residue of scepticism, however distantly held in reserve. These are moments of personal meeting. We all know such moments in the meeting with another human being, called love; many know them in the meeting, experienced as a meeting between persons, with nature, or with poetry, or with music; some know them in the meeting, through any of these or through the self, with God. Afterwards, when it is no longer a question of *in* or *with* but of *about*, scepticism may enter: but the recollection of what happened *in* or *with* is relevant, and may be decisive, for the choice of how one responds to that scepticism. This is why a man can know, as I well understand, that God exists and is loving; but how can he know anything other about God than he has experienced in meeting him: how can he know, for instance, the exact relation of the Persons of the Godhead?

But "ah" you will say "you have used *immediate knowledge*, or implied that you were using it, about moments of another kind: about the moment, for instance, in the dining-room of the House of Commons, when someone was talking about the District Commissioner who went unarmed to his death rather than kill, and you *knew*—you spoke of a flash of lightning that illumined everything, you spoke of hearing, almost physically, the voice of Christ—you *knew* that he had been right, and that the other, who had preferred to shoot, had been wrong. What have you got to say to that? You can't fall back on your subsequent doubt because that is not, just now, the point. What have you got to say about your conviction in the moment itself?" I should have to reply that this was a moment of meeting with God. I should have to amend my "Some know them in the meeting with God through any of these or the self" by adding "or through the words or behaviour of others". And then, if you are a good dialectician, you will take me a stage further. "But do you not *know*," you will ask, "without a suspicion of your implied *caveat*— haven't you made it clear, times out of number—that love is good and hate is evil, that forgiving is good and revenge is evil, that evil, nevertheless, has no real existence, that nothing can be 'wrong' with the totality of things—and so on with a number of propositions, which are really variations of a single proposition? Don't you know such things as these invariably? Isn't the moment perpetual?

Aren't you *in* the moment always? Don't you rule out, therefore, the possibility of any subsequent agnosticism *about* it since no question of 'subsequent' can arise? And isn't this what lies behind your insistence on absolutes?" Ah, my dear Timothy, you are driving me very hard; I am driving myself very hard: the Hound of Heaven, I suppose, is after me: for I must give you, of course, the affirmative answer you desire, and say that, at certain points where the veil is rent or the barrier broken down, there can be a perpetual meeting, a meeting in the time that has then become eternity, with God. And the veil *could* be, not merely rent at certain points but completely rent: the barrier *could* be completely broken down. That is the meaning of the life and death of Christ, considered whether as history or as myth: Christ, the new Adam, and therefore the old Adam too; Christ, all humanity; Christ, the Son of God; Christ, who could say, with simple affirmation, "I and my Father are one"; and so Christ the Son eternally with God the Father—in an eternity of the Holy Spirit, their meeting and their love.

But I shall repeat, all the more defiantly for having been driven so far, that certainty about anything except what happens in moments of personal meeting, or in an eternal moment of personal meeting, is unintelligible to me; and, sympathising with all scepticism, I shall take the opportunity of proclaiming my profound respect for anyone who may be as sceptical about my own certainties as I am sceptical about his.

The fact is that I don't understand "faith", as meaning to take the actuality of something on trust when you haven't experienced the actuality of it yourself: the something in question being, naturally, a matter of reasonable doubt. That is why all creeds, beginning with such words as "I believe with a perfect faith", and continuing with a series of propositions some of which are obviously debatable and unlikely to be self-evident to at any rate a number of the people reciting them, seem so—mysterious to me.

v. g. (from *My Dear Timothy*)

The spiritual aim will recognise that man as he grows in his being must have as much free space as possible for all its members to grow in their own strength, to find out themselves and their potentialities. In their freedom they will err, because experience comes through many errors, but each has in itself a divine principle and they will find it out, disengage its presence, significance and law as their experience of themselves deepens and increases. Thus true spirituality will not lay a yoke upon science and philosophy or compel them to square their conclusions with any statement of dogmatic religious or even of assured spiritual truth, as some of the old religions attempted, vainly, ignorantly, with unspiritual obstinacy and arrogance. Each part of man's being has its own *dharma* which it must follow and will follow in the end, put on it what fetters you please. The *dharma* of science, thought and philosophy is to seek for truth by the intellect dispassionately, without prepossession and prejudgment, with no other first propositions than the law of thought and observation itself imposes. Science and philosophy are not bound to square their observations and conclusions with any current ideas of religious dogma or ethical rule or aesthetic prejudice. In the end, if left free in their action, they will find the unity of Truth with Good and Beauty and God, and give these a greater meaning than any dogmatic religion or any formal ethics or any narrower aesthetic idea can give us. But meanwhile they must be left free even to deny God and good and beauty if they will, if their sincere observation of things so points them. For all these rejections must come round in the end of their circling and return to a larger truth of the things they refuse. Often we find atheism both in individual and society a necessary passage to deeper religious and spiritual truth: one has sometimes to deny God in order to find him; the finding is inevitable at the end of all earnest scepticism and denial.

AUROBINDO

Scepticism and faith are no less necessary. Scepticism, riddling the faith of yesterday, prepares the way for the faith of to-morrow.

ROMAIN ROLLAND

*

The first and the highest are truth; in the middle there is falsehood, but it is taken between the truth on both sides of it and it draws its being from the truth.

BRIHADARANYAKA UPANISHAD

Not that all these errors have not each of them a truth behind their false constructions; for all errors of the human reason are false representations, a wrong building, effective misconstructions of the truth or of a side or a part of the truth.

AUROBINDO

333

Error struggling on towards the living truth is more fruitful and more blessed than dead truth.

ROMAIN ROLLAND

Every thing possible to be believ'd is an image of truth.

BLAKE

To be absolutely sure of the truth of matters concerning which there are many opinions is an attribute of God not given to man, Stranger; but I shall be very glad to tell you what I think . . .

PLATO

Truth is simply one in the divine mind, but many truths flow thence into the human mind, as one face may be mirrored with variety.

ST. THOMAS AQUINAS

Truth, whole and complete . . . is not available to us in life and time. Within time, truth is forever under way, always in motion and not final even in its most marvellous crystallizations. Never to retreat from this fundamental situation—that is the condition on which alone philosophic thought can remain truthful. . . .

Since there is no complete truth, our movement toward it is itself the only form in which truth can achieve completion in existence, here and now. In its very process the boundless acquisition of truth experiences that completion which it never reaches as a goal. The single idea that has been guiding us through the whole of philosophical logic has been the idea of the thinker unswerving on his way.

He is aware of what he knows and what he does not know. He does not fall prey to the falsehood of a truth completed and whole. He lives the meaning of truth in all the ways of being truthful. He is involved in ever deepening communication.

This is the vision of a great and noble life: to endure ambiguity in the movement of truth and to make light shine through it; to stand fast in uncertainty; to prove capable of unlimited love and hope.

KARL JASPERS

The highest thing a man is capable of is to make an eternal truth true. . . . Did Christ ever undertake to prove some truth or another, or to prove the truth? No, but He made the truth true. . . .

KIERKEGAARD

> . . . Sure, He that made us with such large discourse,
> Looking before and after, gave us not
> That capability and god-like reason
> To fust in us unused . . .

SHAKESPEARE

He saw the intellect and logical reason of man no longer as a sedate and necessary thing, but rather a narrow silver bridge passing over an immense depth, around the high guarded entrance of which thronged clouds of angry and malign presences. Often mistaking the causes and often misjudging the effects of all mortal sequences, this capacity of knowing cause and effect presented itself nevertheless to him as the last stability of man. Always approaching truth, it could never, he knew, *be* truth, for nothing can be truth till it has become one with its object, and such union it was not given to the intellect to achieve without losing its own nature. But in its divine and abstract reflection of the world, its passionless mirror of the holy law that governed the world, not in experiments or ecstasies or guesses, the supreme perfection of mortality moved. He saluted it as its child and servant, and dedicated himself again to it, for what remained to him of life, praying it to turn the light of its awful integrity upon him, and to preserve him from self-deception and greediness and infidelity and fear. 'If A is the same as B' he said, 'and B is the same as C, then A is the same as C. Other things may be true; for all I know, they may be different at the same time; but this at least is true.'

CHARLES WILLIAMS (from Shadows of Ecstasy)

He that misbelieves and lays aside clear and cautious reason, in things that fall under the discussion of reason, upon the pretence of hankering after some high principle, which, a thousand to one, proves but the infatuation of melancholy, and a superstitious hallucination, is as ridiculous as if he would not use his natural eyes about their proper object till the presence of some supernatural light, or till he had got a pair of spectacles made of the crystalline heaven, or of the *coelum empyreum*, to hang upon his nose for him to look through.

HENRY MORE

335

[Good men] are content and ready to deny themselves for God. I mean not that they should deny their own Reason, as some would have it; for that were to deny a Beam of Divine light, and so to deny God, in stead of denying our selves for him. It is better resolved by some Philosophers in this point, that *to follow Reason is to follow God.* . . . But by Self-denial I mean, the Soul's quitting all its own interest in it self, and an entire Resignation of it self to him as to all points of service and duty: and thus the Soul loves it self in God, and lives in the possession not so much of its own Being as of the Divinity.

JOHN SMITH

The word rational has been strangely abused of late times. This must not, however, disincline us to the weighty consideration, that thoughtfulness, and a desire to bottom all our convictions on grounds of right reason, are inseparable from the character of a Christian.

S. T. COLERIDGE

I am in all opinions to believe according to my own impartial reason; which I am bound to inform or improve, as far as my capacity and opportunities will permit.

It may be prudent to act sometimes by other men's reason, but I can think only by my own.

If another man's reason fully convinceth me, it becomes my own reason.

To say a man is bound to believe, is neither truth nor sense.

You may force men, by interest or punishment, to say or swear they believe, and to act as if they believed: You can go no further.

SWIFT

Of all Impotencies in the World, Credulity in Religion is the greatest. . . . Man is not at all settled or confirmed in his Religion, until his Religion is the self-same with the Reason of his Mind; that when he thinks he speaks Reason, he speaks Religion; or when he speaks religiously, he speaks reasonably; and his Religion and Reason is mingled together; they pass into one Principle; they are no more two, but one; just as the light in the Air makes one illuminated Sphere, so Reason and Religion in the Subject are one Principle.

BENJAMIN WHICHCOTE

Authority indeed proceeded from true reason, but not reason from authority. For all authority which is not approved by true reason is seen to be unsound, but true reason, fortified and unchangeably established by its own principles, needs no additional support from authority to confirm it.

ERIGENA

To the rational creature the same act is at once according to nature and according to reason.

MARCUS AURELIUS

All the different scholasticisms make me doubtful of what they profess to demonstrate, because, instead of examining, they affirm from the beginning. Their object is to throw up entrenchments around a prejudice, and not to discover the truth. They accumulate that which darkens rather than that which enlightens. . . . Their object is to trick men into assent, to furnish faith with arguments, and to suppress free inquiry. But to persuade me, a man must have no *parti pris*, and must begin with showing a temper of critical sincerity; he must explain to me how the matter lies, point out to me the questions involved in it, their origin, their difficulties, the different solutions attempted, and their degree of probability. He must respect my reason, my conscience, and my liberty. All scholasticism is an attempt to take by storm; the authority pretends to explain itself, but only pretends, and its deference is merely illusory. The dice are loaded and the premises are prejudged. The unknown is taken as known, and all the rest is deduced from it.

Philosophy means the complete liberty of the mind, and therefore independence of all social, political, or religious prejudice. It is to begin with neither Christian nor pagan, neither monarchical nor democratic, neither socialist nor individualist; it is critical and impartial; it loves one thing only—truth. If it disturbs the ready-made opinions of the Church or the State—of the historical medium —in which the philosopher happens to have been born, so much the worse, but there is no help for it.

Philosophy means, first, doubt; and afterwards the consciousness of what knowledge means, the consciousness of uncertainty and of ignorance, the consciousness of limit, shade, degree, possibility. The ordinary man doubts nothing and suspects nothing . . .

The philosopher is like a man fasting in the midst of universal intoxication. He alone perceives the illusion of which all creatures

337

are the willing playthings; he is less duped than his neighbour by his own nature. He judges more sanely, he sees things as they are. It is in this that his liberty consists—in the ability to see clearly and soberly, in the power of mental record. Philosophy has for its foundation critical lucidity. The end and climax of it would be the intuition of the universal law, of the first principle and the final aim of the universe. Not to be deceived is its first desire: to understand, its second. Emancipation from error is the condition of real knowledge. The philosopher is a sceptic seeking a plausible hypothesis, which may explain to him the whole of his experiences. When he imagines that he has found such a key to life he offers it to, but does not force it on, his fellow-men.

AMIEL

§ 3

As long as intellect is confined to its proper sphere of work, all is well, but the moment it steps out of it and invades a field which does not belong to it, the outcome is disastrous. For this stepping out means the setting up of the self as a reality, and this is sure to collide with our ethical and religious valuation of human life; it also runs contrary to our spiritual insight into the nature of things.

D. T. SUZUKI

Intellectual knowledge is partial, because our intellect is an instrument, it is only a part of us, it can give us information about things which can be divided and analysed, and whose properties can be classified, part by part. But Brahma is perfect, and knowledge which is partial can never be a knowledge of him.

But he can be known by joy, by love. For joy is knowledge in its completeness, it is knowing by our whole being. Intellect sets us apart from the things to be known, but love knows its object by fusion. Such knowledge is immediate and admits no doubt. It is the same as knowing our own selves, only more so.

Therefore, as the Upanishads say, mind can never know Brahma, words can never describe him; he can only be known by our soul, by her joy in him, by her love. Or, in other words, we can only come into relation with him by union—union of our whole being. We must be one with our Father, we must be perfect as he is.

TAGORE

338

Reason is in us what the sun is in the world. . . . As long as our mind shines brightly and pursues its appointed course, pouring its noontide beams into every part of the soul, we are within our sober selves and not possessed, but when it comes to set, it is not surprising that the ecstasy and madness of Divine possession should fall upon us. For when the Divine light shines, the human light sets, and when the former sets, the latter dawns and rises. . . . Our mind departs at the coming of the Divine spirit and returns when it departs. It is not lawful for mortal and immortal to dwell together.

PHILO

The intuition releases the power of poetry, and the greatest poetry springs from it. The imagination, the heart of poetry, is progressively freed to create new channels of life, to awaken in the mind the springs of joy and laughter which the drear propriety of reasoning would banish from the world. If the intellect measures all worth with the yardstick of its own creation, the intuition takes no measurements at all. It knows that all life is one yet separate, and that all the forms of life have an equal validity. It moves, serene with certainty, and therefore tolerant of all that lives. Unlike cold reasoning it has no fear of laughter, and having risen above the ordered world in which the by-laws of logic decree without appeal what is "sense", it is free to indulge in non-sense, for it shines upon a plane where every two are discounted as another of the endless, tiresome but no longer limiting pairs of opposites.

CHRISTMAS HUMPHREYS

And this is the manner of the Sons of Albion in their strength:
They take the Two Contraries which are call'd Qualities, with which
Every Substance is clothed: they name them Good & Evil.
From them they make an Abstract, which is a Negation
Not only of the Substance from which it is derived,
A murderer of its own Body, but also a murderer
Of every Divine Member: it is the Reasoning Power,
An Abstract objecting power, that Negatives every thing.
This is the Spectre of Man, the Holy Reasoning Power,
And in its Holiness is closed the Abomination of Desolation.

BLAKE

Art is the Tree of Life. God is Jesus. Science is the Tree of Death.

BLAKE

Then spake Jerusalem: "O Albion! my Father Albion!
Why wilt thou number every little fibre of my Soul,
Spreading them out before the Sun like stalks of flax to dry?
The Infant Joy is beautiful, but its anatomy
Horrible, ghast & deadly! nought shalt thou find in it
But dark despair & everlasting brooding melancholy!"

BLAKE

Knowledge is not by deduction, but Immediate by Perception or Sense at once. Christ adresses himself to the Man, not to his Reason.

BLAKE

God is not a Mathematical Diagram.

BLAKE

God forbid that Truth should be Confined to Mathematical Demonstration!

BLAKE

He who does not know Truth at Sight is unworthy of Her Notice.

BLAKE

All truth is a species of revelation.

S. T. COLERIDGE

REASON AND ILLUMINATION

The root of the difficulty is this: that at the very basis of all our life and existence, internal and external, there is something on which the intellect can never lay a controlling hold, the Absolute, the Infinite. Behind everything in life there is an Absolute, which that thing is seeking after in its own way; everything finite is striving to express an infinite which it feels to be its real truth. . . . It is because this is the reality of our existence that the intellectual reason and the intelligent will cannot deal with life as its sovereign, even though they may be at present our supreme instruments and may have been in our evolution supremely important and helpful. The reason can govern, but only as a minister, imperfectly, or as a general arbiter and giver of suggestions which are not really supreme commands, or as one channel of the sovereign authority, because

340

that hidden Power acts at present not directly but through many agents and messengers. . . .

[For] the intelligence of man is not composed entirely and exclusively of the rational intellect and the rational will; there enters into it a deeper, more intuitive, more splendid and powerful, but much less clear, much less developed and as yet hardly at all self-possessing light and force for which we have not even a name. But at any rate its character is to drive at a kind of illumination—not the dry light of the reason, nor the moist and suffused light of the heart, but a lightning and a solar splendour. It may indeed subordinate itself and merely help the reason and heart with its flashes; but there is another urge in it, its natural urge, which exceeds the reason. It tries to illuminate the intellectual being, to illuminate the ethical and aesthetic, to illuminate the emotional and the active, to illuminate even the senses and the sensations. It offers . . . a Truth greater and truer than the knowledge given by Reason and Science, a Right larger and more divine than the moralist's scheme of virtues, a Beauty more profound, universal and entrancing than the sensuous or imaginative beauty worshipped by the artist, a joy and divine sensibility which leaves the ordinary emotions poor and pallid, a Sense beyond the senses and sensations, the possibility of a diviner Life and action which man's ordinary conduct of life hides away from his impulses and from his vision. Very various, very fragmentary, often very confused and misleading are its effects upon all the lower members from the reason downward, but this in the end is what it is driving at in the midst of a hundred deformations. It is caught and killed or at least diminished and stifled in formal creeds and pious observances; it is unmercifully traded in and turned into poor and base coin by the vulgarity of conventional religions; but it is still the light of which the religious spirit and the spirituality of man is in pursuit, and some pale glow of it lingers even in their worst degradations.

AUROBINDO

II. THE SOUL'S MEMORY

Thus far I have been speaking of the fourth and last kind of madness, which is imputed to him who, when he sees the beauty of earth, is transported with the recollection of the true beauty; he would like to fly away, but he cannot; he is like a bird fluttering and looking upward and careless of the world below; and he is therefore thought to be mad. And I have shown this of all inspirations to be the noblest and highest and the offspring of the highest to him who has or shares in it, and that he who loves the beautiful is called a lover because he partakes of it. For, as has been already said, every soul of man has in the way of nature beheld true being; this was the condition of her passing into the form of man. But all souls do not easily recall the things of the other world; they may have seen them for a short time only, or they may have been unfortunate in their earthly lot, and, having had their hearts turned to unrighteousness through some corrupting influence, they may have lost the memory of the holy things which once they saw. Few only retain an adequate remembrance of them; and they, when they behold here any image of that other world, are rapt in amazement; but they are ignorant of what this rapture means, because they do not clearly perceive. For there is no light of justice or temperance or any of the higher ideas which are precious to souls in the earthly copies of them: they are seen through a glass dimly; and there are few who, going to the images, behold in them the realities, and these only with difficulty. There was a time when with the rest of the happy band they saw beauty shining in brightness—we philosophers following in the train of Zeus, others in company with other gods; and then we beheld the beatific vision and were initiated into a mystery which may be truly called most blessed, celebrated by us in our state of innocence, before we had any experience of evils to come, when we were admitted to the sight of apparitions innocent and simple and calm and happy, which we beheld shining in pure light, pure ourselves and not yet enshrined in that living tomb which we carry about, now that we are imprisoned in the body, like an oyster in his shell. Let me linger over the memory of scenes which have passed away.

But of beauty, I repeat again that we saw her there shining in company with the celestial forms; and coming to earth we find her here too, shining in clearness through the clearest aperture of sense. For sight is the most piercing of our bodily senses; though not by that is wisdom seen; her loveliness would have been transporting if there had been a visible image of her, and the other ideas, if they had visible counterparts, would be equally lovely. But this is the privilege of beauty, that being the loveliest she is also the most palpable to sight. Now he who is not newly initiated or who has become corrupted, does not easily rise out of this world to the sight of true beauty in the other; he looks only at her earthly namesake, and instead of being awed at the sight of her, he is given over to pleasure, and like a brutish beast he rushes on to enjoy and beget; he consorts with wantonness, and is not afraid or ashamed of pursuing pleasure in violation of nature. But he whose initiation is recent, and who has been the spectator of many glories in the other world, is amazed when he sees any one having a godlike face or form, which is the expression of divine beauty; and at first a shudder runs through him, and again the old awe steals over him; then looking upon the face of his beloved as of a god he reverences him, and if he were not afraid of being thought a downright madman, he would sacrifice to his beloved as to the image of a god.

PLATO

It is sound, I think, to find the primal source of love in a tendency of the Soul towards pure beauty, in a recognition, in a kinship, in an unreasoned consciousness of friendly relation. There are Souls who are reminded by earthly beauty of the Beauty Yonder, and these love the earthly as an image; those that have not attained to this memory do not understand what is happening within them, and take the image for the reality.

PLOTINUS

FROM "INTIMATIONS"

The Soul that rises with us, our life's Star,
    Hath had elsewhere its setting,
        And cometh from afar:
    Not in entire forgetfulness . . .

. . . Hence in a season of calm weather
        Though inland far we be,
Our Souls have sight of that immortal sea
    Which brought us hither. . . .

WORDSWORTH

346

THE RETREATE

Happy those early dayes! when I
Shin'd in my Angell-infancy.
Before I understood this place
Appointed for my second race,
Or taught my soul to fancy ought
But a white, Celestiall thought,
When yet I had not walkt above
A mile, or two, from my first love,
And looking back (at that short space,)
Could see a glimpse of his bright-face;
When on some gilded Cloud, or flowre
My gazing soul would dwell an houre,
And in those weaker glories spy
Some shadows of eternity;
Before I taught my tongue to wound
My Conscience with a sinfull sound,
Or had the black art to dispence
A sev'rall sinne to ev'ry sence,
But felt through all this fleshly dresse
Bright shootes of everlastingnesse.
    O how I long to travell back
And tread again that ancient track!
That I might once more reach that plaine,
Where first I left my glorious traine,
From whence th'Inlightned spirit sees
That shady City of Palme trees;
But (ah!) my soul with too much stay
Is drunk, and staggers in the way.
Some men a forward motion love,
But I by backward steps would move,
And when this dust falls to the urn
In that state I came return.

HENRY VAUGHAN

MESSAGE FROM HOME

Do you remember, when you were first a child,
Nothing in the world seemed strange to you?
You perceived, for the first time, shapes already familiar,
And seeing, you knew that you had always known

347

The lichen on the rock, fern-leaves, the flowers of thyme,
As if the elements newly met in your body,
Caught up into the momentary vortex of your living
Still kept the knowledge of a former state,
In you retained recollection of cloud and ocean,
The branching tree, the dancing flame.

Now when nature's darkness seems strange to you,
And you walk, an alien, in the streets of cities,
Remember earth breathed you into her with the air, with the sun's
    rays,
Laid you in her waters asleep, to dream
With the brown trout among the milfoil roots,
From substance of star and ocean fashioned you,
At the same source conceived you
As sun and foliage, fish and stream.

Of all created things the source is one,
Simple, single as love; remember
The cell and seed of life, the sphere
That is, of child, white bird, and small blue dragon-fly,
Green fern, and the gold four-petalled tormentilla
The ultimate memory.
Each latent cell puts out a future,
Unfolds its differing complexity
As a tree puts forth leaves, and spins a fate
Fern-traced, bird-feathered, or fish-scaled.
Moss spreads its green film on the moist peat,
The germ of dragon-fly pulses into animation and takes wing
As the water-lily from the mud ascends on its ropy stem
To open a sweet white calyx to the sky.
Man, with farther to travel from his simplicity,
From the archaic moss, fish, and lily parts,
And into exile travels his long way.

As you leave Eden behind you, remember your home,
For as you remember back into your own being
You will not be alone; the first to greet you
Will be those children playing by the burn,
The otters will swim up to you in the bay,
The wild deer on the moor will run beside you.
Recollect more deeply, and the birds will come,

348

Fish rise to meet you in their silver shoals,
And darker, stranger, more mysterious lives
Will throng about you at the source
Where the tree's deepest roots drink from the abyss.

Nothing in that abyss is alien to you.
Sleep at the tree's root, where the night is spun
Into the stuff of worlds, listen to the winds,
The tides, and the night's harmonies, and know
All that you knew before you began to forget,
Before you became estranged from your own being,
Before you had too long parted from those other
More simple children, who have stayed at home
In meadow and island and forest, in sea and river.
Earth sends a mother's love after her exiled son,
Entrusting her message to the light and the air,
The wind and waves that carry your ship, the rain that falls,
The birds that call to you, and all the shoals
That swim in the natal waters of her ocean.

KATHLEEN RAINE

I OFTEN WONDER

I often wonder where lie hidden the boundaries of recognition
between man and the beast whose heart knows no spoken language.

Through what primal paradise in a remote morning of creation
ran the simple path by which their hearts visited each other.

Those marks of their constant tread have not been effaced though
their kinship has been long forgotten.

Yet suddenly in some wordless music the dim memory wakes up
and the beast gazes into the man's face with a tender trust, and the
man looks down into its eyes with amused affection.

It seems that the two friends meet masked, and vaguely know
each other through the disguise.

TAGORE

THE SOLITARY BIRD

Why should a bird in that solitary hollow
    Flying from east to west
Seem in the silence of the snow-blanched sunshine
    Gilding the valley's crest
Envoy and symbol of a past within me
    Centuries now at rest?

Shallowly arched the horizon looms beyond it,
    Turquoise green and blue;
Not even a whisper irks the magic of the evening
    The narrowing valley through;
No faintest echo brings a syllable revealing
    The secret once I knew:
Down *whsts* the snow again, cloud masks the sunshine—
    Bird gone, and memory too.

WALTER DE LA MARE

THE RECOGNITION

Before time came or the great moon was made,
We walked in a young forest bright with dawn;
Immortal dews made beautiful the glade,
And blue the dim waves brake beside the lawn.

Before time came, I moved a scarlet hind,
And your white plumage shone with starry eyes:
Therefore in this dark land we are not blind,
And read each other's souls without surprise.

When we are dead, my dear, and turned to mould,
And this strange mortal rose has ceased to be,
Again, in that wild wood of virgin gold,
The white bird and the hind shall watch the sea.

WILFRED ROWLAND CHILDE

FROM "ADAMUS EXSUL"

. . . The shadow of those walls of emerald,
That were the trees of Eden, and the gleam
Of her sapphirine streams are with me yet,
For the whole shining world is interfused
With the memory of her cedar-fragrant mountains
And her gold-feathered doves. . . .

WILFRED ROWLAND CHILDE

REMEMBERED MUSIC

'Tis said, the pipe and lute that charm our ears
Derive their melody from rolling spheres;
But Faith, o'erpassing speculation's bound,

Can see what sweetens every jangled sound.

We, who are parts of Adam, heard with him
The song of angels and of seraphim.
Our memory, though dull and sad, retains
Some echo still of those unearthly strains.

Oh, music is the meat of all who love,
Music uplifts the soul to realms above.
The ashes glow, the latent fires increase:
We listen and are fed with joy and peace.

RUMI

ODE TO SALINAS

Calm grows the air around,
Arrayed in beauty and unwonted light,
Salinas, at the sound
Of music exquisite
That thy skilled hand doth cunningly indite.

And at that sound divine
My soul, that in forgetfulness hath lain,
With a new light doth shine
And unto memory plain
Of its first splendid origin attain.

For this new knowledge then
Its nobler thoughts and destiny restores:
Of gold, vain lure of men,
Which the blind crowd adores,
The perishable beauty it ignores.

Up through the fields of air
It wings, till in the highest sphere it dwells,
And a new music there
It hears, music that wells
Undying and all other kinds excels.

The great Master there it sees,
His hand upon the mighty lyre, with train
Of skilful cadences,
Create the holy strain
That this eternal temple doth sustain.

351

And since in sweet concent
Those numbers flow symphonious, reply
Concordant is soon sent,
And both together vie
In a mixed power of softest harmony.

Through sea of melody
In rapture sweet the soul doth onward glide
And sinks there finally,
Until whate'er betide
Beyond it to its senses is denied.

O heavenly ravishment!
Life-giving death, oblivion's sweet defence!
O might my life be spent
In thy calm rest, nor thence
Ever return to this vile earthly sense!

To such bliss I entreat
You, glory of Apollo's sacred choir,
O friend for whom doth beat
My heart beyond desire
Of treasures that bring tears and sorrows dire.

O evermore to hear
Thy heavenly music, Salinas, be mine!
Through whom awaking clear
To holy thoughts incline
The senses, to all else dull and supine.

LUIS DE LEON

This morning the music of a brass band which had stopped under
my windows moved me almost to tears. It exercised an indefinable,
nostalgic power over me; it set me dreaming of another world, of
infinite passion and supreme happiness. Such impressions are the
echoes of Paradise in the soul; memories of ideal spheres, whose sad
sweetness ravishes and intoxicates the heart. O Plato! O Pytha-
goras! ages ago you heard these harmonies—surprised these
moments of inward ecstasy—knew these divine transports! If
music thus carries us to heaven, it is because music is harmony,
harmony is perfection, perfection is our dream, and our dream is
heaven.

AMIEL

If music does not express feelings, how then does it affect the listener's emotions? There is no doubt that listeners, performers, and composers alike can be profoundly moved by perceiving, performing, or imagining music, and consequently music must touch on something in their emotional life that brings them into this state of excitation. But if these mental reactions were feelings, they could not change as rapidly as they do, and they would not begin and end precisely with the musical stimulus that aroused them. If we experience a real feeling of grief—that is, grief not caused or released by music—it is not possible to replace it at a moment's notice and without any plausible reason with the feeling of wild gaiety; and gaiety, in turn, cannot be replaced by complacency after a fraction of a second. Real feelings need a certain interval of time to develop, to reach a climax, and to fade out again; but reactions to music may change as fast as musical phrases do, they may spring up in full intensity at any given moment and disappear entirely when the musical pattern that provoked them ends or changes. Thus these reactions may within a few instants skip from the most profound degree of grief to utter hilarity and on to complacency without causing any discomfort to the mind experiencing them, which would be the case with a rapid succession of real feelings. In fact, if it happened with real feelings, we could be sure that it could be only in the event of slight insanity. The reactions music evokes are not feelings, but they are the images, memories of feelings [of feelings, as Plotinus might say but Hindemith does not say, "yonder"].

PAUL HINDEMITH

In looking at objects of Nature while I am thinking, as at yonder moon dim-glimmering through the dewy window-pane, I seem rather to be seeking, as it were *asking* for, a symbolical language for something within me that already and for ever exists, than observing anything new. Even when that latter is the case, yet still I have always an obscure feeling as if that new phenomenon were the dim awaking of a forgotten or hidden truth of my inner nature.

S. T. COLERIDGE

And Now Begins a New life, because another covering of Earth is shaken off. I am more famed in Heaven for my works than I could well conceive. In my Brain are studies and Chambers filled with books & pictures of old, which I wrote and painted in ages of

353

Eternity before my mortal life; & those works are the delight & Study of Archangels. Why, then, should I be anxious about the riches or fame of mortality? The Lord our father will do for us & with us according to his divine will for our Good.

You, O dear Flaxman, are a Sublime Archangel; My Friend & Companion from Eternity; in the Divine bosom is our dwelling place. I look back into the regions of Reminiscence & behold our ancient days before this Earth appear'd in its vegetated mortality to my mortal vegetated Eyes. I see our houses of Eternity, which can never be separated, tho' our Mortal vehicles should stand at the remotest corners of heaven from each other.

BLAKE

§ 2

Socrates I have heard from certain wise men and women who spoke of things divine that—

Meno What did they say?

Socrates They spoke of a glorious truth, as I conceive.

Meno What was it? and who were they?

Socrates Some of them were priests and priestesses, who had studied how they might be able to give a reason of their profession: there have been poets also, who spoke of these things by inspiration, like Pindar, and many others who were inspired. And they say— mark, now, and see whether their words are true—they say that the soul of man is immortal, and at one time has an end, which is termed dying, and at another time is born again, but is never destroyed. And the moral is, that a man ought to live always in perfect holiness. . . . The soul, then, as being immortal, and having been born again many times, and having seen all things that exist, whether in this world or in the world below, has knowledge of them all: and it is no wonder that she should be able to call to remembrance all that she ever knew about virtue, and about everything; for as all nature is akin, and the soul has learned all things, there is no difficulty in her eliciting (or as men say learning) out of a single recollection all the rest, if a man is strenuous and does not faint; for all enquiry and all learning is but recollection.

PLATO

Knowledge of Ideal Beauty is Not to be Acquired. It is Born with us. Innate Ideas are in Every Man, Born with him; they are truly Himself.

BLAKE

Some of the ancients, divining the truth yet from far away, reckoned that the soul knows things because it is composed of them.

ST. THOMAS AQUINAS

The immortal in us has memory of all its wisdom.

A. E.

'I tell you these things, not because you know them not, but because you know them.' All living instruction is nothing but corroboration of intuitive knowledge.

COVENTRY PATMORE

At this moment I left Caen, where I was then living, to take part in a geological conference arranged by the School of Mines. The incidents of the journey made me forget my mathematical work. When we arrived at Coutances we got into a brake to go for a drive, and just as I put my foot on the step, the idea came to me, though nothing in my former thought seemed to have prepared me for it, that the transformations I had used to define Fuchsian functions were identical with those of non-Euclidian geometry. I made no verification, and had no time to do so, since I took up the conversation again as soon as I had sat down in the brake, but I felt absolute certainty at once. When I got to Caen I verified the result at my leisure to satisfy my conscience.

I then began to study arithmetical questions without any great apparent result, and without suspecting that they could have the least connection with my previous researches. Disgusted at my want of success, I went away to spend a few days at the seaside, and thought of entirely different things. One day, as I was walking on the cliff, the idea came to me again with the same characteristics of conciseness, suddenness and immediate certainty, that arithmetical transformations of indefinite ternary quadratic forms are identical with those of non-Euclidian geometry.

HENRI POINCARÉ

355

A thought went up my mind to-day
That I have had before,
But did not finish,—some way back,
I could not fix the year.

Nor where it went, nor why it came
The second time to me,
Nor definitely what it was,
Have I the art to say.

But somewhere in my soul, I know
I've met the thing before;
It just reminded me—'twas all—
And came my way no more.

EMILY DICKINSON

Yes, it was the mountain Echo,
Solitary, clear, profound,
Answering to the shouting Cuckoo,
Giving to her sound for sound!

Unsolicited reply
To a babbling wanderer sent;
Like her ordinary cry,
Like—but oh, how different!

Hears not also mortal Life?
Hear not we, unthinking Creatures!
Slaves of folly, love, or strife—
Voices of two different natures?

Have not *we* too?—yes, we have
Answers, and we know not whence;
Echoes from beyond the grave,
Recognised intelligence!

Such rebounds our inward ear
Catches sometimes from afar—
Listen, ponder, hold them dear;
For of God,—of God they are.

WORDSWORTH

This discord in the pact of things,
This endless war twixt truth and truth,
That singly hold, yet give the lie
To him who seeks to yoke them both—
Do the gods know the reason why?

Or is truth one without a flaw,
And all things to each other turn,
But the soul, sunken in desire,
No longer can the links discern,
In glimmering of her smothered fire?

Then why with travail does she yearn
To find the hidden mysteries?
Knows she the thing for which she burns?
Yet who will seek what he hath got?
Yet who will seek he knows not what?

How shall he follow the unknown?
How shall he find it, and when found
How shall he know it? Did the soul
Once see the universal mind,
And know the part, and know the whole?

Now sunken in the mirk of sense,
Not wholly doth the soul forget,
Still grasps the whole, lets go the part:
And therefore whoso seeks the truth
Shall find in no wise peace of heart.

For neither doth he wholly know,
And neither doth he all forget.
But that high thing which once he saw,
And still remembers, that he holds,
And seeks to bring the truth forgot
Again to that which he hath yet.

BOETHIUS (*tr. by Waddell*)

III. VISION AND SACRAMENT

This is none other but the house of God, and this is the gate of heaven.

GENESIS

For this World belongs as well to the Body or Corpus of God the Father, as the Heaven does.

Thou must not therefore think, that the heavenly Light in this World is quite extinct: No; there is only a Duskishness or dim Obscurity upon it, so that we cannot apprehend it with our corrupted Eyes.

But if God did but once put away that Duskishness, which moves about the Light, and that thy Eyes were opened, then in that very place where thou standest, sittest, or liest, thou shouldst see the glorious Countenance or Face of God and the whole heavenly Gate.

Thou needest not first to cast thine Eyes up into Heaven, for it is written: 'The Word is near thee, viz. on thy Lips, and in thy Heart'.

BOEHME

But what is Paradise? All things that are; for all that is, is good and joyous. Therefore it is called a Paradise, and is so indeed. It is said also that Paradise is an outer court of Heaven. Even so all that is, is verily an outer court of the Eternal and of Eternity, and especially what we may recognise and know of God and Eternity, in time and in temporal things and in creatures. For the creatures are a guide and a way to God and to Eternity. Thus all this is an outer court or forecourt of Eternity; and therefore it may well be called a Paradise, and be so in truth.

THEOLOGIA GERMANICA

And thus have you a Gate, in the prospect even of this world, whereby you may see into God's Kingdom.

TRAHERNE

The simple vision of pure love, which is marvellously penetrating, does not stop at the outer husk of creation: it penetrates to the divinity which is hidden within.

MALAVAL

Lo, these are but the outskirts of His ways: and how small a whisper do we hear of Him!

JOB

> God keeps His holy mysteries
> Just on the outside of man's dream.

ELIZABETH BARRETT BROWNING

In every countenance the countenance of countenances is veiled as in a mystery.

NICOLAS OF CUSA

If ye do not recognise God, at least recognise His signs.

AL-HALLAJ

What idea could we have of God without the sky?

GEORGE MACDONALD

> . . . objects recognised
> In flashes, and with glory not their own.

WORDSWORTH

O what a world of evidences! We are lost in abysses, we now are absorpt in wonders, and swallowed up of demonstrations.

TRAHERNE

> A man that looks on glasse,
>   On it may stay his eye:
> Or if he pleaseth, through it passe,
>   And then the heav'n espie.

GEORGE HERBERT

As we see the sun but cannot look at it (for we see its light on all things but are blinded by its glare if we fix our eyes on it), so we may say of God that he is light and darkness, hidden and manifest. For we cannot see him, and if we raise our mind to behold him it is dazzled; yet we see him in all creation, which is resplendent with his light.

LUIS DE LEON

And Moses hid his face; for he was afraid to look upon God.

EXODUS

Our eyes shall see thee, which before saw dust.

GEORGE HERBERT

I but open my eyes,—and perfection, no more and no less,
In the kind I imagined, full-fronts me, and God is seen God
In the star, in the stone, in the flesh, in the soul and the clod.

BROWNING

God is nearer to me than I am to myself; He is just as near to
wood and stone, but they do not know it.

MEISTER ECKHART

God is an angel in an angel, and a stone in a stone, and a straw in
a straw.

JOHN DONNE

Brave wormes, and Earth! that thus could have
A God Enclos'd within your Cell,
Your maker pent up in a grave,
Life lockt in death, heav'n in a shell. . . .

HENRY VAUGHAN

The tree of God is the skeleton of the Universe; it grows throughout the whole of Creation and spreads its branches through all its
ramifications.

HEBREW DOCTRINE

The world is a temple, whose walls are covered with emblems,
pictures, and commandments of the Deity.

EMERSON

The highest and most divine things which it is given us to see
and to know are but the symbolic language of things subordinate to
Him who Himself transcendeth them all: through which things His
incomprehensible Presence is shown, walking on those heights of
His Holy Places which are perceived by the mind.

DIONYSIUS THE AREOPAGITE

It is surely inconceivable that any living thing could be beautiful
were there not a Life Absolute of a wonderful, an ineffable, beauty.

PLOTINUS

The entire aggregate of existence springs from the divine world, in greater beauty There because There unmingled but mingled here.

PLOTINUS

And indeed if the divine did not exist, the transcendently beautiful, in a beauty beyond all thought, what could be lovelier than the things we see? Certainly no reproach can rightly be brought against this world save only that it is not That.

PLOTINUS

If these be fair, O what is Heaven!

HENRY VAUGHAN

Kings lick the earth whereof the fair are made,
For God hath mingled in the dusty earth
A draught of Beauty from His choicest cup.
'Tis *that*, fond lover—not these lips of clay—
Thou art kissing with a hundred ecstasies,
Think, then, what must it be when undefiled!

RUMI

All streams of Beauty here below
Do from that immense Ocean flow,
And thither they should lead again.
Trace then these Streams, till thou shalt be
At length o'erwhelm'd in Beauty's boundless Sea.

JOHN NORRIS

Beauty is merely the Spiritual making itself known sensuously.

HEGEL

All that is sweet, delightful, and amiable in this world, in the serenity of the air, the fineness of seasons, the joy of light, the melody of sounds, the beauty of colours, the fragrancy of smells, the splendour of precious stones, is nothing else but Heaven breaking through the veil of this world, manifesting itself in such a degree and darting forth in such variety so much of its own nature.

WILLIAM LAW

Nature is the living visible garment of God.

GOETHE

   . . . Than Nature's self, which is the breath of God,
      Or His pure Word by miracle revealed.

WORDSWORTH

The loveliness that is in the realm of sense is an index of the nobleness of the spiritual sphere, displaying its power and its goodness alike: and all things are for ever linked; the one order spiritual in its being, the other of sense; one self-existent, the other eternally taking its being by participation in that first, and to the full of its power reproducing the spiritual nature.

PLOTINUS

We may think of the Divine as a fire whose outgoing warmth pervades the Universe.

PLOTINUS

This Fire is at the root and about the root—I mean, about the centre—of all things, both visible and invisible. It is in water, earth and air; it is in minerals, herbs and beasts; it is in men, stars and angels. But originally it is in God Himself for He is the Fountain of heat and fire, and from Him it is derived to the rest of the creatures in a certain stream or sunshine . . . It is an influence of the Almighty God, and it comes from the Land of the Living Ones.

THOMAS VAUGHAN

From out the great ring which represents the Eternal Godhead there flow forth little rings, which may be taken to signify the high nobility of natural creatures.

HENRY SUSO

Consider how far the engendered stands from its origin and yet, what a marvel!

PLOTINUS

He who seeks to find the inward in the outward, is in better case than he who only finds the inward in the inward.

HENRY SUSO

In the world as it is, the richness of the outer stirs us all to the wonder of the inner whose greatness is displayed in acts so splendid.

PLOTINUS

[St. Francis ordered a plot to be set aside for the cultivation of flowers when the convent garden was made] in order that all who saw them might remember the Eternal Sweetness.

THOMAS ÓF CELANO

... So flows experience: the vast Without;
Its microcosm, of the Soul, within;
Whereof the day-distracted eye may doubt,
But doubts no more as soon as dreams begin ...

WALTER DE LA MARE

The intimations which are but whispered, the Presences which are but half-disclosed, are those which we should intently obey.

MARK RUTHERFORD

The souls of those who have known God seek after the verdant pastures, the beautiful vistas, the fresh green gardens.

AL-JUNAID

— In your world, said the little prince, men cultivate five thousand roses in one garden ... and still they do not find what they seek ...
— That is true, I said.
— And yet what they are seeking may be found in a single rose or a drop of water.
— So it can, I answered.
And the little prince went on:
— But the eyes are blind: one must seek with the heart.

ANTOINE DE SAINT-EXUPÉRY

BEYOND

On such an evening—still; and crystalline
With light, to which the heavens their fairness owe,
What wakes some changeling in the heart to pine
For what is past the mortal to bestow?

Ev'n in the shallow, busy hours of day
Dreams their intangible enchantments weave;
And in the dead of dark the heart may crave
A sleep beyond sleep, and for its visions grieve.

366

For that strange absence nothing can atone;
And every hope is servant to desire;
The flower conceals a beauty not its own,
And echo sighs from even the silent wire.

WALTER DE LA MARE

SUNRISE

Morning awakes sublime; glad earth and sky
   Smile in the splendour of the day begun.
O'er the broad earth's illumined canopy,
   Shade of its Maker's majesty, the sun
Gleams in its living light from cloud to cloud;
   Streaks of all colours beautifully run
As if before heaven's gate there hung a shroud
   To hide its grand magnificence. O heaven,
Where entrance e'en to thought is disallowed,
   To view the glory that this scene is giving
What may blind reason not expect to see,
   When in immortal worlds the soul is living
Eternal as its maker, and as free
To taste the unknowns of eternity?

JOHN CLARE

FROM "IT AUTUMN WAS"

Those golden letters which so brightly shine
In heaven's great volume gorgeously divine;
The wonders all in sea, in earth, in air,
Be but dark pictures of that sovereign Fair;
Be tongues, which still thus cry unto your ear,
(Could ye amidst world's cataracts them hear,)
From fading things, fond wights, lift your desire,
And in our beauty, his, us made, admire:
If we seem fair, O think how fair is he
Of whose fair fairness shadows, steps, we be.
No shadow can compare it with the face,
No step with that dear foot which did it trace.

WILLIAM DRUMMOND

Not upon earth, as you suppose
tower these rocks that turn the wind,
for on their summits angels stand.

Nor from the earth these waters rise—
to quench not thirst, but ecstasy
the waterfall leaps from the sky.

Those nameless clouds that storm and swirl
about the mountain are the veil
that from these sightless eyes shall fall

when senses faint into the ground,
and time and place go down the wind.

KATHLEEN RAINE

Thou seest the Constellations in the deep & wondrous Night:
They rise in order and continue their immortal courses
Upon the mountains & in vales with harp & heavenly song,
With flute & clarion, with cups & measures fill'd with foaming
    wine.
Glitt'ring the streams reflect the Vision of beatitude,
And the calm Ocean joys beneath & smooths his awful waves . . .
Thou seest the gorgeous clothed Flies that dance & sport in summer
Upon the sunny brooks & meadows: every one the dance
Knows in its intricate mazes of delight artful to weave:
Each one to sound his instruments of music in the dance,
To touch each other & recede, to cross & change & return:
           . . . thou seest the Trees on mountains:
The wind blows heavy, loud they thunder thro' the darksom sky,
Uttering prophecies & speaking instructive words to the sons
Of men . . . . These the Visions of Eternity.
But we see only as it were the hems of their garments
When with our vegetable eyes we view these wondrous Visions.

BLAKE

Dear babe, that sleepest cradled by my side,
Whose gentle breathings, heard in this deep calm,
Fill up the interspersed vacancies
And momentary pauses of the thought!
My babe so beautiful! it thrills my heart

368

With tender gladness, thus to look at thee,
And think that thou shalt learn far other lore
And in far other scenes! For I was reared
In the great city, pent 'mid cloisters dim,
And saw nought lovely but the sky and stars.
But thou, my babe! shalt wander like a breeze
By lakes and sandy shores, beneath the crags
Of ancient mountain, and beneath the clouds,
Which image in their bulk both lakes and shores
And mountain crags; so shalt thou see and hear
The lovely shapes and sounds intelligible
Of that eternal language, which thy God
Utters, who from eternity doth teach
Himself in all, and all things in himself.
Great universal Teacher! he shall mould
Thy spirit, and by giving make it ask.

Therefore all seasons shall be sweet to thee,
Whether the summer clothe the general earth
With greenness, or the redbreast sit and sing
Betwixt the tufts of snow on the bare branch
Of mossy apple-tree, while the nigh thatch
Smokes in the sun-thaw; whether the eave-drops fall
Heard only in the trances of the blast,
Or if the secret ministry of frost
Shall hang them up in silent icicles,
Quietly shining to the quiet Moon.

S. T. COLERIDGE

The Creation of the whole Creation is nothing else but a Manifestation of the all-essential, unsearchable God; all whatever he is in his eternal unbeginning Generation and Dominion, of that is also the Creation, but not in the Omnipotence and Power, but like an Apple which grows upon the Tree, which is not the Tree itself, but grows from the Power of the Tree: Even so all Things are sprung forth out of the Divine Desire, and created into an Essence, where in the Beginning there was no such Essence present, but only that same Mystery of the Eternal Generation, in which there has been an Eternal Perfection.

For God has not brought forth the Creation, that he should be thereby perfect, but for his own Manifestation, *viz.* for the great

Joy and Glory; not that this Joy first began with the Creation, no, for it was from Eternity in the great Mystery, yet only as a spiritual Melody and Sport in itself.

The Creation is the same Sport out of himself, *viz.* a Platform or Instrument of the Eternal Spirit, with which he melodizes: and it is even as a great Harmony of manifold Instruments which are all tuned into one Harmony; for the Eternal Word, or Divine Sound or Voice, which is a Spirit, has introduced itself with the Generation of the great Mystery into Formings, *viz.* into an expressed Word or Sound: And as the joyful Melody is in itself in the Spirit of the eternal Generation, so likewise is the Instrument, *viz.* the expressed Form in itself, which the living Eternal Voice guides, and strikes with his own Eternal Will-Spirit, that it sounds and melodizes; as an Organ of divers and various Sounds or Notes is moved with one only Air, so that each Note, yea every Pipe has its peculiar Tune, and yet there is but one Manner of Air or Breath in all Notes, which sounds in each Note or Pipe according as the Instrument or Organ is made.

Thus in the Eternity there is only one Spirit in the whole Work of the Divine Manifestation, which is the Manifestator in the expressed Voice and also in the speaking Voice of God, which is the Life of the grand Mystery, and of all that is generated from thence; he is the Manifestator of all the Works of God.

BOEHME

The works of the Magician of the Beautiful are not like ours and in the least fragment His artistry is no less present than in the stars. We may enter the infinite through the minute no less than through contemplation of the vast. I thought in that early ecstasy of mine when I found how near to us was the King in His Beauty that I could learn to read that marvellous writing on the screen of Nature and teach it to others; and, as a child first learns its letters with difficulty, but after a time leaps to the understanding of their combination, and later, without care for letters or words, follows out the thought alone; so I thought the letters of the divine utterance might be taught and the spirit in man would leap by intuition to the thought of the Spirit making that utterance. For all that vast ambition I have not even a complete alphabet to show, much less one single illustration of how to read the letters of nature in their myriad intricacies of form, colour and sound in the world we live in. But I believe that vision has been attained by the seers, and we

370

shall all at some time attain it, and, as is said in the Divine Shepherd
of Hermes, it shall meet us everywhere, plain and easy, walking or
resting, waking or sleeping, "for there is nothing which is not the
image of God".

A. E.

What time this worlds great Work-maister did cast
To make al things such as we now behold,
It seemes that he before his eyes had plast
A goodly Paterne, to whose perfect mould
He fashiond them as comely as he could,
That now so faire and seemely they appeare,
As nought may be amended any wheare.

That wondrous Paterne, wheresoere it bee,
Whether in earth layd up in secret store,
Or else in heaven, that no man may it see
With sinfull eyes, for feare it to deflore,
Is perfect Beautie, which all men adore;
Whose face and feature doth so much excell
All mortall sence, that none the same may tell. . . .

SPENSER (from An Hymne in Honour of Beautie)

FROM "AN HYMNE OF HEAVENLY BEAUTIE"

Rapt with the rage of mine own ravisht thought,
Through contemplation of those goodly sights,
And glorious images in heaven wrought,
Whose wondrous beauty, breathing sweet delights
Do kindle love in high conceipted sprights;
I faine to tell the things that I behold,
But feele my wits to faile, and tongue to fold.

Vouchsafe then, O thou most Almightie Spright!
From whom all guifts of wit and knowledge flow,
To shed into my breast some sparkling light
Of thine eternall Truth, that I may show
Some litle beames to mortall eyes below
Of that immortall beautie, there with thee,
Which in my weake distraughted mynd I see;

That with the glorie of so goodly sight
The hearts of men, which fondly here admyre

Faire seeming shewes, and feed on vaine delight,
Transported with celestiall desyre
Of those faire formes, may lift themselves up hyer,
And learne to love, with zealous humble dewty,
Th' eternall fountaine of that heavenly beauty.

Beginning then below, with th' easie vew
Of this base world, subject to fleshly eye,
From thence to mount aloft, by order dew,
To contemplation of th' immortall sky;
Of the soare faulcon so I learne to fly,
That flags awhile her fluttering wings beneath,
Till she her selfe for stronger flight can breath.

Then looke, who list thy gazefull eyes to feed
With sight of that is faire, looke on the frame
Of this wyde universe, and therein reed
The endlesse kinds of creatures which by name
Thou canst not count, much lesse their natures aime;
All which are made with wondrous wise respect,
And all with admirable beautie deckt.

First, th' Earth, on adamantine pillers founded
Amid the Sea, engirt with brasen bands;
Then th' Aire still flitting, but yet firmely bounded
On everie side, with pyles of flaming brands,
Never consum'd, nor quencht with mortall hands;
And, last, that mightie shining christall wall,
Wherewith he hath encompassed this All.

By view whereof it plainly may appeare,
That still as every thing doth upward tend,
And further is from earth, so still more cleare
And faire it growes, till to his perfect end
Of purest beautie it at last ascend;
Ayre more than water, fire much more than ayre,
And heaven than fire, appeares more pure and fayre.

Looke thou no further, but affixe thine eye
On that bright shynie round still moving Masse,
The house of blessed God, which men call Skye,
All sowd with glistring stars more thicke than grasse,
Whereof each other doth in brightnesse passe,

But those two most, which, ruling night and day,
As King and Queene, the heavens Empire sway;

And tell me then, what hast thou ever seene
That to their beautie may compared bee,
Or can the sight that is most sharpe or keene
Endure their Captains flaming head to see?
How much lesse those, much higher in degree,
And so much fairer, and much more than these,
As these are fairer than the land and seas?

For farre above these heavens, which here we see,
Be others farre exceeding these in light,
Not bounded, not corrupt, as these same bee,
But infinite in largenesse and in hight,
Unmoving, uncorrupt, and spotlesse bright,
That need no Sunne t' illuminate their spheres,
But their owne native light farre passing theirs.

And as these heavens still by degrees arize,
Untill they come to their first Movers bound,
That in his mightie compasse doth comprize,
And carrie all the rest with him around;
So those likewise doe by degrees redound,
And rise more faire, till they at last arive
To the most faire, whereto they all do strive.

Faire is the heaven where happy soules have place,
In full enjoyment of felicitie,
Whence they doe still behold the glorious face
Of the Divine Eternall Majestie;
More faire is that, where those Idees on hie
Enraunged be, which Plato so admyred,
And pure Intelligences from God inspyred.

Yet fairer is that heaven, in which doe raine
The soveraine Powres and mightie Potentates,
Which in their high protections doe containe
All mortall Princes and imperiall States;
And fayrer yet, whereas the royall Seates
And heavenly Dominations are set,
For whom all earthly governance is fet.

Yet farre more faire be those bright Cherubins,
Which all with golden wings are overdight,
And those eternall burning Seraphins,
Which from their faces dart out fierie light;
Yet fairer than they both, and much more bright,
Be th' Angels and Archangels, which attend
On Gods owne person, without rest or end.

These thus in faire each other farre excelling,
As to the Highest they approch more neare,
Yet is that Highest farre beyond all telling,
Fairer than all the rest which there appeare,
Though all their beauties joynd together were;
How then can mortall tongue hope to expresse
The image of such endlesse perfectnesse?

Cease then, my tongue! and lend unto my mynd
Leave to bethinke how great that beautie is,
Whose utmost parts so beautifull I fynd;
How much more those essentiall parts of his,
His truth, his love, his wisedome, and his blis,
His grace, his doome, his mercy, and his might,
By which he lends us of himselfe a sight!

Those unto all he daily doth display,
And shew himselfe in th' image of his grace,
As in a looking-glasse, through which he may
Be seene of all his creatures vile and base,
That are unable else to see his face,
His glorious face! which glistereth else so bright,
That th' Angels selves can not endure his sight.

But we, fraile wights! whose sight cannot sustaine
The Suns bright beames when he on us doth shyne,
But that their points rebutted backe againe
Are duld, how can we see with feeble eyne
The glory of that Majestie Divine,
In sight of whom both Sun and Moone are darke,
Compared to his least resplendent sparke?

The meanes, therefore, which unto us is lent
Him to behold, is on his workes to looke,
Which he hath made in beauty excellent,

And in the same, as in a brasen booke,
To reade enregistred in every nooke
His goodnesse, which his beautie doth declare;
For all thats good is beautifull and faire.

Thence gathering plumes of perfect speculation,
To impe the wings of thy high flying mynd,
Mount up aloft through heavenly contemplation,
From this darke world, whose damps the soule do blynd,
And, like the native brood of Eagles kynd,
On that bright Sunne of Glorie fixe thine eyes,
Clear'd from grosse mists of fraile infirmities. . . .

SPENSER

§ 2

Learn to refer all Naturals to their Spirituals.

THOMAS VAUGHAN

What if earth
Be but the shadow of heaven, and things therein
Each to each other like, more than on earth is thought?

MILTON

There Exist in that Eternal World the Permanent Realities of
Every Thing which we see reflected in this Vegetable Glass of
Nature.

BLAKE

Whatever can be Created can be Annihilated: Forms cannot;
The Oak is cut down by the Ax, the Lamb falls by the Knife,
But their Forms Eternal Exist For-ever. Amen. Hallelujah!

BLAKE

And above Albion's Land was seen the Heavenly Canaan
As the Sustance is to the Shadow, and above Albion's Twelve Sons
Were seen Jerusalem's Sons and all the Twelve Tribes spreading
Over Albion.

BLAKE

He showed, too, an unconquerable reluctance to sit to a painter
or a sculptor, and when Amelius persisted in urging him to allow of

375

a portrait being made he asked him, "Is it not enough to carry about this image in which nature has enclosed us? Do you really think I must also consent to leave, as a desirable spectacle to posterity, an image of the image?"

PORPHYRY (*of Plotinus*)

In the same manner as lovers gradually advance from that beauty which is apparent in sensible forms, to that which is divine; so the ancient priests, when they considered that there was a certain alliance and sympathy in natural things to each other, and of things manifest to occult powers, and by this means discovered that all things subsist in all, they fabricated a sacred science from this mutual sympathy and similarity. Thus they recognised things supreme in such as are subordinate, and the subordinate in the supreme: in the celestial regions terrene properties subsisting in a causal and celestial manner; and in earth celestial properties, but according to a terrene condition. For how shall we account for those plants called heliotropes, that is, attendants on the sun, moving in correspondence with the revolutions of its orb; but selenitropes, or attendants on the moon, turning in exact conformity with her motion? It is because all things pray, and compose hymns to the leaders of their respective orders; but some intellectually, and others rationally; some in a natural, and others after a sensible manner. Hence the sunflower, as far as it is able, moves in a circular dance towards the sun; so that if anyone could hear the pulsation made by its circuit in the air, he would perceive something composed by a sound of this kind, in honour of its king, such as a plant is capable of framing. Hence we may behold the sun and moon in the earth, but according to a terrene quality; but in the celestial regions all plants, and stones, and animals, possessing an intellectual life according to a celestial nature. Now the ancients having contemplated this mutual sympathy of things, applied for occult purposes both celestial and terrene natures, by means of which through a certain similitude they deduced divine virtues into this inferior abode.

PROCLUS (*paraphrased by Thomas Taylor*)

Ah, Sun-flower! weary of time,
Who countest the steps of the Sun,
Seeking after that sweet golden clime
Where the traveller's journey is done:

376

Where the Youth pined away with desire,
And the pale Virgin shrouded in snow
Arise from their graves, and aspire
Where my Sun-flower wishes to go.

BLAKE

First, then, it shall be stated what correspondence is. The whole natural world corresponds to the spiritual world, not only in general but also in particular. Whatever, therefore, in the natural world derives its existence from the spiritual, is said to be its correspondent. The reason for correspondences is that the natural world with all that it contains exists and subsists from the spiritual world, and both worlds from the Divine Being. We say subsists as well as exists because every thing subsists from that which gave it existence, subsistence being perpetual existence; and because nothing can subsist from itself but only from something prior to itself, and thus originally from the First Cause; if it were separated from this, it would utterly perish or disappear.

An example of correspondence: When the union of good and truth is effected in a man, which occurs especially after temptations, he enters into a state of delight from heavenly peace. This peace may be compared to morning or dawn in spring, when, the night being past, at the rising of the sun everything on earth begins to live anew, the dew which falls from heaven causes plants to diffuse their scent, while the mild vernal temperature imparts fertility to the soil and gladdens the heart of man; and this takes place because morning or dawn, in the time of spring, corresponds to the state of peace of the angels in Heaven.

SWEDENBORG

Or, again, let us put it this way. Since we say that this universe here is modelled on the world of Spirit, every living thing must be There first; if the being of Spirit is complete it must be everything. Heaven There must be a living thing, and so not bare of stars (it is they which are really called heaven here, and the essence of heaven is starriness). There too, clearly, is earth, not barren but far fuller of life, and in it are all living beings which are called land animals here, and all plants clearly too, rooted in life. Sea too is There, and all water, in a flow and life which abides, and all the living beings in water: the nature of air is part of the universe There, and the creatures of air are There correspondingly. Must not the things in a

377

living medium be alive, in which there are living things even here? How could it be possible for any living creature not to be There? For just as each of the great parts of the universe is There, so it must be with the nature of the living beings in them. In just the same way in which heaven is There, the living beings in heaven are There; and it is impossible for them not to be, or the heaven itself would not be There. So he who inquires whence the living things come, is inquiring whence the heaven There comes; and this amounts to asking the origin of living reality There; and this is the same as asking whence comes life, and universal life and universal Soul and universal Spirit, in that world There where there is no poverty or impotence, but everything is filled full of life, boiling with life. Things There flow in a way from a single source, not like one particular breath or warmth, but as if there were a single quality containing in itself and preserving all qualities, sweet taste and smell and the quality of wine with all other flavours, visions of colours and all that touch perceives, all too that hearing hears, all tunes and every rhythm.

PLOTINUS

I heard flowers that sounded, and saw notes that shone.

SAINT-MARTIN

CORRESPONDENCES

Nature is a temple wherein living pillars sometimes
let words indistinctly fall; man walks therein
through forests of symbols which, with familiar looks,
are watching him.

Like those long drawn out echoes from afar that fuse
in the dim depths of unity, vast as the night and as
light itself, perfumes, sounds and colours correspond.

There are scents as fresh as a baby's flesh, sweet
as the oboe, green as the meadow—and others corrupt,
rich and triumphant, as expansive as infinite things,
like amber and musk, incense and benjamin, which hymn
the ecstasies of soul and sense.

BAUDELAIRE

§ 3

I was in the Spirit on the Lord's day . . .

REVELATION

Knowing demands the organ fitted to the object; eyes for one kind, ears for another: similarly some things, we must believe, are to be known by the Spiritual in us. We must not confuse spiritual insight with hearing or seeing; this would be trying to look with the ears or denying sound because it is not seen.

PLOTINUS

As the Eye, Such the Object.

BLAKE

. . . perciev'd by those senses that are clos'd from thought . . .

BLAKE

Apprehensions are God's introductions
Extended inscrutably.

EMILY DICKINSON

Hast never come to thee an hour,
A sudden gleam divine, precipitating, bursting all these bubbles, fashions, wealth?
These eager business aims—books, politics, art, amours,
To utter nothingness?

WALT WHITMAN

The Devout man does not only believe but feels there is a Deity. He has *actual sensations* of Him.

ADDISON

Those divinely possessed and inspired have at least the knowledge that they hold some greater thing within them though they cannot tell what it is; from the movements that stir them and the utterances that come from them they perceive the power, not themselves, that moves them.

PLOTINUS

379

Our hearts were drunk with a beauty
Our eyes could never see . . .

A. E.

I cannot see what flowers are at my feet,
Nor what soft incense hangs upon the boughs,
But, in embalmed darkness, guess each sweet . . .

KEATS

I know that This World is a World of Imagination & Vision.

BLAKE

This made it the more likely that he had seen a true vision; for instead of making common things look commonplace, as a false vision would have done, it had made common things disclose the wonderful that was in them.

GEORGE MACDONALD

We may know we have had the Vision when the soul has suddenly taken light. This light is from the Supreme and is the Supreme; we may believe in the Presence when, like that other God on the call of a certain man, He comes bringing light: the light is the proof of the advent. Thus, the soul unlit remains without that Vision; lit, it possesses what it sought. And this is the true end set before the soul, to take that light, to see the Supreme by the Supreme and not by the light of any other principle—to see the Supreme which is also the means to the Vision; for that which illumines the soul is that which it is to see just as it is by the sun's own light that we see the sun.
But how is this to be accomplished?
Cut away everything.

PLOTINUS

Most men in the course of their lives have known such Platonic hours of initiation, when the sense of beauty has risen from a pleasant feeling to a passion, and an element of strangeness and terror has been mingled with their joy. In those hours the world has seemed charged with a new vitality; with a splendour which does not belong to it but is poured through it, as light through a coloured window, grace through a sacrament, from that Perfect Beauty which "shines in company with the celestial forms" beyond the pale of appearance. In such moods of heightened consciousness each blade of grass seems fierce with meaning, and becomes a well of wondrous light: a "little emerald set in the City of God". The seeing self is indeed an initiate thrust suddenly into the sanctuary of the mysteries: and feels the "old awe and amazement" with which man encounters the Real.

EVELYN UNDERHILL

It is only in exceptional moods that we realise how wonderful are the commonest experiences of life. It seems to me sometimes that these experiences have an 'inner' side, as well as the outer side we normally perceive. At such moments one suddenly sees everything with new eyes; one feels on the brink of some great revelation. It is as if we caught a glimpse of some incredibly beautiful world that lies silently about us all the time. I remember vividly my first experience of the kind when, as a boy, I came suddenly upon the quiet miracle of an ivy-clad wall glistening under a London street-lamp. I wanted to weep and I wanted to pray; to weep for the Paradise from which I had been exiled, and to pray that I might yet be made worthy of it. Such moments are rare, in my experience. But their influence is permanent. They import a tinge of unreality into our normal acceptances; we suspect them for the dull and purblind things that they are. There are analogous moments when one suddenly sees the glory of people. On some unforgettable evening one's friend is suddenly seen as the unique, irreplaceable, and utterly delightful being that he is. It is as if he had been freshly created. One is no longer concerned with his relations to oneself, with his *pragmatic* value. He exists wholly in his own right; his significance is eternal, and the essential mystery of his being is as fathomless as that of God Himself.

J. W. N. SULLIVAN

The bright morning sun of summer heated the eastern parapet of London Bridge; I stayed in the recess to acknowledge it. The smooth water was a broad sheen of light, the built-up river flowed calm and silent by a thousand doors, rippling only where the stream chafed against a chain. Red pennants drooped, gilded vanes gleamed on polished masts, black-pitched hulls glistened like a black rook's feathers in sunlight; the clear air cut out the forward angles of the warehouses, the shadowed wharves were quiet in shadows that carried light; far down the ships that were hauling out moved in repose, and with the stream floated away into the summer mist. There was a faint blue colour in the air hovering between the built-up banks, against the lit walls, in the hollows of the houses. The swallows wheeled and climbed, twittered and glided downwards. Burning on, the great sun stood in the sky, heating the parapet, glowing steadfastly upon me as when I rested in the narrow valley grooved out in prehistoric times. Burning on steadfast, and ever present as my thought. Lighting the broad river, the broad walls; lighting the least speck of dust; lighting the great heaven; gleaming on my finger-nail. The fixed point of day—the sun. I was intensely conscious of it; I felt it; I felt the presence of the immense powers of the universe; I felt out into the depths of the ether. So intensely conscious of the sun, the sky, the limitless space, I felt too in the midst of eternity then, in the midst of the supernatural, among the immortal, and the greatness of the material realised the spirit. By these I saw my soul; by these I knew the supernatural to be more intensely real than the sun. I touched the supernatural, the immortal, there that moment.

RICHARD JEFFERIES

He never saw again what he saw that morning. The children on their way to school, the silvery grey pigeons that flew from the roofs to the pavement, the little loaves of bread that some invisible hand had put out, all seemed to him divine. Two little boys ran towards a pigeon and looked smilingly at Levin; the pigeon fluttered its wings and flew off, glistening in the sun, through the quivering snow-dust in the air; from a window came the odour of freshly-baked bread, as a few little rolls were laid on the sill. . . .

TOLSTOY (from *Anna Karenina*

WAITING FOR A SEAT AT THE OPERA

It was not only a sense of expectation that made the waiting in Floral Street so happy, poignant beyond description though this was for one who was still very young, and only beginning to grow familiar with the masterpieces. To have heard a piece of music once or twice, to have it veiled in your consciousness and struggling to reveal itself, and to know that very soon, at a moment that inevitably must come, you will see it face to face—that is a felicity such as few other experiences can equal, and of the same nature, perhaps, as the quiet of expectation with which a saint awaits the beatific vision. But there were other elements in our happiness. We were a little community, for the "regulars" all knew one another, and we passed the time in keen and surprisingly expert discussion about the merits or demerits of recent performances: our sense of fellowship was almost conspiratorial. Yet for me something sacramental in Floral Street itself was perhaps the greatest felicity of all. In the narrow, rather sordid street, with opera house on one side and high blackened buildings (for they seemed immensely high) on the other, there would come, in the early evenings of that June or July weather, patches of sunlight from a sun itself unseen. And then, for all the bustle and noise in the world's greatest city, and for all, or perhaps because of, the distant traffic—distant, though in fact only just beyond our deep and narrow chasm—there would happen, in the interior castle of one's spirit, a lull, a suspension, a silence and a peace in which joy and sadness, both incomparably intense and yet of an utter tranquillity, were one. The late sun in cities has always had this effect on me. I suppose something of the kind was meant by Omar Khayyam, when he talked of "the brave music of a *distant* drum"; and many people experience it, I think, when faintly, in a sunlit street, they catch the tones of a penny whistle or barrel organ, or the singing of a human voice. There are days in Aix-en-Provence, its blazing streets empty as the sun goes down and then footsteps ringing out—footsteps, they might be, of the mailed soldiery in some long-dead Caesar's legions—, when the sadness would be unbearable were it not happiness as well; and I remember standing one August, as a boy of six or seven, on the little stone balcony of my home near Maida Vale, and feeling myself caught up I knew not whither as hussars came riding down from a neighbouring barracks, and the paving stones echoed to their horses' hooves, and the street was afire with the afternoon sun, and everything was silent. . . .

I shall not attempt to explain the experience of which I have been speaking, and which, I am certain, a great many people share: I shall only say of it, as of many other experiences which are bound up with sights and sounds, that any explanation in purely physical or "materialistic" terms is ludicrously beside the mark. So I shall content myself with repeating the word "sacramental". All physical things are sacraments, and the world is so beautiful because it is a sacrament of the Supreme Beauty. To quote what Oscar Wilde himself quotes from Théophile Gautier, "I am one of those *pour qui le monde visible existe*": exists absolutely, but at the same time exists as an intimation. . . .

v. g. (from *My Dear Timothy*)

THE PENNY WHISTLE

The fog came in so thickly through the window that I rose to close it. He never closed that window, and I hoped he would not notice. For a sound of wretched street-music was coming nearer—some beggar playing dismally upon a penny whistle—and I feared it would disturb him. But in a flash he was up again.

'No, no!' he cried, raising his voice for the first time that night. 'Do not shut it. I shan't be able to hear then. Let all the air come in. Open it wider . . . wider! I love that sound!'

'The fog——'

'There is no fog. It's only sun and flowers and music. Let them in. Don't you hear it *now*?' he added. And, more to bring him peace than anything else, I bowed my head to signify agreement. For the last confusion of the mind, I saw, was upon him, and he made the outer world confirm some imagined detail of his inner dream. I drew the sash down lower, covering his body closely with the blankets. He flung them off impatiently at once. The damp and freezing night rushed in upon us like a presence. It made me shudder, but O'Malley only raised himself upon one elbow to taste it better, and—to listen.

Then, waiting patiently for the return of the quiet, trance-like state when I might cover him again, I moved towards the window and looked out. The street was empty, save for that beggar playing vilely on his penny whistle. The wretch came to a standstill immediately before the house. The lamplight fell from the room upon his tattered, broken figure. I could not see his face. He groped and felt his way.

Outside that homeless wanderer played his penny pipe in the night of cold and darkness.

Inside the Dreamer listened, dreaming of his gods and garden, his great Earth Mother, his visioned life of peace and simple things with a living Nature. . . .

And I felt somehow that player watched us. I made an angry sign to him to go. But it was the sudden touch upon my arm that made me turn round with such a sudden start that I almost cried aloud. O'Malley in his night-clothes stood close against me on the floor, slight as a spirit, eyes ashine, lips moving faintly into speech through the most wonderful smile a human face has ever shown me.

'Do not send him away,' he whispered, joy breaking from him like a light, 'but tell him that I love it. Go out and thank him. Tell him I hear and understand, and say that I am coming. Will you . . .?'

Something within me whirled. It seemed that I was lifted from my feet a moment. Some tide of power rushed from his person to my own. The room was filled with blinding light. But in my heart there rose a great emotion that combined tears and joy and laughter all at once.

'The moment you are back in bed,' I heard my voice like one speaking from a distance, 'I'll go——'

The momentary, wild confusion passed as suddenly as it came. I remember he obeyed at once. As I bent down to tuck the clothes about him, that fragrance as of flowers and open spaces rose about my bending face like incense—bewilderingly sweet.

And the next second I was standing in the street. The man who played upon the pipe, I saw, was blind. His hand and fingers were curiously large.

I was already close, ready to press all that my pockets held into his hand—ay, and far more than merely pockets held because O'Malley said he loved the music—when something made me turn my head away. I cannot say precisely what it was, for first it seemed a tapping at the window of his room behind me, and then a little noise within the room itself, and next—more curious than either—a feeling that something came out rushing past me through the air. It whirled and shouted as it went. . . .

I only remember clearly that in the very act of turning, and while my look still held that beggar's face within the field of vision, I saw the sightless eyes turn bright a moment as though he opened them and saw. He did most certainly smile; to that I swear.

But when I turned again the street immediately about me was empty. The beggar-man was gone.

And down the pavement, moving swiftly through the curtain of fog, I saw his vanishing figure. It was large and spreading. In the fringe of light the lamp-post gave, its upper edges seemed far above the ground. Someone else was with him. There were two figures.

I heard that sound of piping far away. It sounded faint and almost flute-like in the air. And in the mud at my feet the money lay—spurned utterly. I heard the last coins ring upon the pavement as they settled. But in the room, when I got back, the body of Terence O'Malley had ceased to breathe.

ALGERNON BLACKWOOD (from The Centaur)

THE POLICEMAN AND THE EMPEROR

A policeman's hand held them up. Henry gestured towards it. 'Behold the Emperor,' he said to Nancy.

'You're making fun of me, my dear,' she half protested.

'Never less,' he said seriously. 'Look at him.'

She looked, and, whether the hours she had given to brooding over the Tarots during the last few days, partly to certify her courage to herself, had imposed their forms on her memory, or whether something in the policeman's shape and cloak under the lights of the dark street suggested it, or whether indeed something common to Emperor and Khalif, cadi and magistrate, praetor and alcalde, lictor and constable, shone before her in those lights—whichever was true, it was certainly true that for a moment she saw in that heavy official barring their way the Emperor of the Trumps, helmed, in a white cloak, stretching out one sceptred arm, as if Charlemagne, or one like him, stretched out his controlling sword over the tribes of Europe pouring from the forests and bade them pause or march as he would. The great roads ran below him, to Rome, to Paris, to Aix, to Byzantium, and the nations established themselves in cities upon them. The noise of all the pausing street came to her as the roar of many peoples; the white cloak held them by a gesture; order and law were there. It moved, it fell aside, the torrent of obedient movement rolled on, and they with it. They flashed past the helmed face, and she found that she had dropped her eyes lest she should see it.

With the avoidance of that face she seemed to have plunged herself deeper into the dream, as if by avoiding it she had assented to it and had acknowledged its being and power. They were not stopped again, but yet, as the car ran smoothly on, she seemed to see that white-clothed arm again and again, now in the darkness beyond the headlights, now pointing forward just outside the window. The streets were busy with Christmas shoppers, but the car shut them out and her in, and, though they were there, it was running steadily away from them—as if down a sloping road while they were all on the high level banks on either hand. They never actually did go down that road, but—as in nightmare—they were always on the very point of plunging. Nancy held desperately to her recollection of a car and a policeman and Henry; she was really beginning to pull herself together when suddenly—somewhere on the outskirts of London—the car slowed for a moment outside the gate of a large building. Over the gate was a light, and under the light was a nurse holding a big key. A gate—a light—a nurse; yet one lobe of her brain showed her again a semblance of one of the Tarot cards—ceremonial robes; imperial headdress, cloak falling like folded wings, proud, austere face lifted towards where in the arch of the gate, so that the light just caught it, was a heraldic carving of some flying creature. Someone, somewhere—perhaps her father behind her—grunted a little, and the grunt seemed to her as if it were wrung from a being in profound pain. And then the car quickened again, and they were flying into the darkness, and away in the roads behind them was that sovereign figure and the sound of a suffering world coming up to it out of the night.

CHARLES WILLIAMS (from *The Greater Trumps*)

FROM "THE CITY"

. . . I know there lies
Open somewhere this hour a gate to Paradise,
Its blazing battlements with watchers thronged, O where?
I know not, but my flame-winged feet shall lead me there.
O, hurry, hurry, unknown shepherd of desires,
And with thy flock of bright imperishable fires
Pen me within the starry fold, ere the night falls
And I am left alone below immutable walls.
Or am I there already, and is it Paradise
To look on mortal things with an immortal's eyes?
Above the misty brilliance the streets assume
A night-dilated blue magnificence of gloom
Like many-templed Nineveh tower beyond tower;
And I am hurried on in this immortal hour.
Mine eyes beget new majesties: my spirit greets
The trams, the high-built glittering galleons of the streets
That float through twilight rivers from galaxies of light.
Nay, in the Fount of Days they rise, they take their flight,
And wend to the great deep, the Holy Sepulchre.
Those dark misshapen folk to be made lovely there

Hurry with me, not all ignoble as we seem,
Lured by some inexpressible and gorgeous dream.
The earth melts in my blood. The air that I inhale
Is like enchanted wine poured from the Holy Grail.
What was that glimmer then? Was it the flash of wings
As through the blinded mart rode on the King of Kings?
O stay, departing glory, stay with us but a day,
And burning seraphim shall leap from out our clay,
And plumed and crested hosts shall shine where men have been,
Heaven hold no lordlier court than earth at College Green.
Ah, no, the wizardry is over; the magic flame
That might have melted all in beauty fades as it came.
The stars are far and faint and strange. The night draws down.
Exiled from light, forlorn, I walk in Dublin Town.
Yet had I might to lift the veil, the will to dare,
The fiery rushing chariots of the Lord are there,
The whirlwind path, the blazing gates, the trumpets blown,
The halls of heaven, the majesty of throne by throne,
Enraptured faces, hands uplifted, welcome sung
By the thronged gods, tall, golden-coloured, joyful, young.

A. E.

He did not stop on the steps either, but went quickly down; his
soul, overflowing with rapture, yearned for freedom, space, open-
ness. The vault of heaven, full of soft, shining stars, stretched vast
and fathomless above him. The Milky Way ran in two pale streams
from the zenith to the horizon. The fresh, motionless, still night
enfolded the earth. The white towers and golden domes of the
cathedral gleamed out against the sapphire sky. The gorgeous
autumn flowers, in the beds round the house, were slumbering till
morning. The silence of earth seemed to melt into the silence of the
heavens. The mystery of earth was one with the mystery of the
stars. . . .

Alyosha stood, gazed, and suddenly threw himself down on the
earth. He did not know why he embraced it. He could not have
told why he longed so irresistibly to kiss it, to kiss it all. But he
kissed it weeping, sobbing and watering it with his tears, and
vowed passionately to love it, to love it for ever and ever. "Water
the earth with the tears of your joy and love those tears," echoed in
his soul.

What was he weeping over?

Oh! in his rapture he was weeping even over those stars, which were shining to him from the abyss of space, and "he was not ashamed of that ecstasy". There seemed to be threads from all those innumerable worlds of God, linking his soul to them, and it was trembling all over "in contact with other worlds". He longed to forgive everyone and for everything, and to beg forgiveness. Oh, not for himself, but for all men, for all and for everything. "And others are praying for me too," echoed again in his soul. But with every instant he felt clearly and, as it were, tangibly, that something firm and unshakable as that vault of heaven had entered into his soul. It was as though some idea had seized the sovereignty of his mind—and it was for all his life and for ever and ever. He had fallen on the earth a weak boy, but he rose up a resolute champion, and he knew and felt it suddenly at the very moment of his ecstasy. And never, never, all his life long, could Alyosha forget that minute.

"Someone visited my soul in that hour," he used to say afterwards, with implicit faith in his words.

Within three days he left the monastery in accordance with the words of his elder, who had bidden him "sojourn in the world".

DOSTOEVSKY (from *The Brothers Karamazov*)

I was crossing a little stream near Inchy Wood and actually in the middle of a stride from bank to bank, when an emotion never experienced before swept down upon me. I said, "That is what the devout Christian feels, that is how he surrenders his will to the will of God." I felt an extreme surprise, for my whole imagination was pre-occupied with the pagan mythology of ancient Ireland, I was marking in red ink, upon a large map, every sacred mountain. The next morning I awoke near dawn, to hear a voice saying, "The love of God is infinite for every human soul because every human soul is unique, no other can satisfy the same need in God."

W. B. YEATS

From 1914 to 1918 I was not able to get away for any holidays, but in 1919 I spent Monday to Saturday several times in a remote cottage in the Lune Valley, reading, writing, and going for long solitary walks. One afternoon I had been walking along a seemingly endless country lane, little more than a grassy cart-track between hedges. It rose steadily for some time till it reached a point where a gap in the hedges gave a view over a wide stretch of open country. I had been curiously restless and expectant, and I sat down on a heap of stones overgrown with wild geranium, feeling that something—I did not know what—was going to happen. And here I will quote from an account written and published, in the form of a story, soon after:

'Suddenly I knew.'

'What did you know?'

'Everything. All there is to be known. The nature of reality and the meaning of life, and the secret that all the philosophers have desired to know since thought began. I can't tell you, of course. I have heard "unspeakable words" which it is not lawful for a man to utter. But one thing I will say. I knew in that moment that all life is one. Not only the life of men, and animals, and insects, and plants. No, the life that runs in the sides of the hills and beats like a great heart in the ribs of the mountains.'

PETER GREEN

I went out one afternoon for a walk alone. I was in the empty unthinking state in which one saunters along country lanes, simply yielding oneself to the casual sights around which give a town-bred lad with country yearnings such intense delight. Suddenly I became conscious of the presence of someone else. I cannot describe it, but I felt that I had as direct perception of the being of God all round about me as I have of you when we are together. It was no longer a matter of inference, it was an immediate act of spiritual (or whatever adjective you like to employ) apprehension. It came unsought, absolutely unexpectedly. I remember the wonderful transfiguration of the far-off woods and hills as they seemed to blend in the infinite being with which I was thus brought into relation. This experience did not last long. But it sufficed to change all my feeling. I had not found God because I had never looked for him. But he had found me.

JOSEPH ESTLIN CARPENTER

So did I feel one warm summer day lying idly on the hillside, not then thinking of anything but the sunlight, and how sweet it was to drowse there, when, suddenly, I felt a fiery heart throb, and knew it was personal and intimate, and started with every sense dilated and intent, and turned inwards, and I heard first a music as of bells going away, away into that wondrous underland whither, as legend relates, the Danaan gods withdrew; and then the heart of the hills was opened to me, and I knew there was no hill for those who were there, and they were unconscious of the ponderous mountain piled above the palaces of light, and the winds were sparkling and diamond clear, yet full of colour as an opal, as they glittered through the valley, and I knew the Golden Age was all about me, and it was we who had been blind to it but that it had never passed away from the world.

A. E.

I was no longer young: in fact I was well over sixty. The winter had been dark and tedious. For some reason or other I had not been able to read much, and I began to think there were signs of the coming end. Suddenly, with hardly any warning, spring burst upon us. Day after day we had clear, warm sunshine which deepened every contrast of colour, and at intervals we were blessed with refreshing rains. I spent most of my time out of doors on the edge of a favourite wood. All my life I had been a lover of the country, and had believed, if this is the right word, that the same thought, spirit, life, God, which was in everything I beheld, was also in me. But my creed had been taken over from books; it was accepted as an intellectual proposition. Most of us are satisfied with this kind of belief, and even call it religion. We are more content the more definite the object becomes, no matter whether or not it is in any intimate relationship with us, and we do not see that the moment God can be named he ceases to be God.

One morning when I was in the wood something happened which was nothing less than a transformation of myself and the world, although I 'believed' nothing new. I was looking at a great, spreading, bursting oak. The first tinge from the greenish-yellow buds was just visible. It seemed to be no longer a tree away from me and apart from me. The enclosing barriers of consciousness were removed and the text came into my mind, *Thou in me and I in thee.* The distinction of self and not-self was an illusion. I could feel the rising sap; in me also sprang the fountain of life up-rushing from its roots, and the joy of its outbreak at the extremity of each twig right up to the summit was my own: that which kept me apart was nothing. I do not argue; I cannot explain; it will be easy to prove me absurd, but nothing can shake me. *Thou in me and I in thee.* Death! what is death? There is no death: *in thee* it is impossible, absurd.

MARK RUTHERFORD

He remembered that during his epileptic fits, or rather immediately preceding them, he had always experienced a moment or two when his whole heart, and mind, and body seemed to wake up to vigour and light; when he became filled with joy and hope, and all his anxieties seemed to be swept away for ever; these moments were but presentiments, as it were, of the one final second (it was never more than a second) in which the fit came upon him. That second, of course, was inexpressible. When his attack was over, and the prince reflected on his symptoms, he used to say to himself: "These moments, short as they are, when I feel such extreme consciousness of myself, and consequently more of life than at other times, are due only to the disease—to the sudden rupture of normal conditions. Therefore they are not really a higher kind of life, but a lower." This reasoning, however, seemed to end in a paradox, and lead to the further consideration:—"What matter though it be only disease, an abnormal tension of the brain, if, when I recall and analyse the moment, it seems to have been one of harmony and beauty in the highest degree—an instant of deepest sensation, overflowing with unbounded joy and rapture, ecstatic devotion, and completest life?" Vague though this sounds, it was perfectly comprehensible to Muishkin, though he knew that it was but a feeble expression of his sensations.

That there was, indeed, beauty and harmony in those abnormal moments, that they really contained the highest synthesis of life, he could not doubt, nor even admit the possibility of doubt. He felt that they were not analogous to the fantastic and unreal dreams due to intoxication by hashish, opium or wine. Of that he could judge, when the attack was over. These instants were characterized —to define it in a word—by an intense quickening of the sense of personality. Since, in the last conscious moment preceding the attack, he could say to himself, with full understanding of his words: "I would give my whole life for this one instant", then doubtless to him it really was worth a lifetime. For the rest, he thought the dialectical part of his argument of little worth; he saw only too clearly that the result of these ecstatic moments was stupefaction, mental darkness, idiocy. No argument was possible on that point. His conclusion, his estimate of the "moment", doubtless contained some error, yet the reality of the sensation troubled him. What more unanswerable than a fact? And this fact had occurred. The prince had confessed unreservedly to himself that the feeling of intense beatitude in that crowded moment made the moment worth a lifetime. "I feel then," he said one day to Rogojin in Moscow, "I feel then as if I understood those amazing words— 'There shall be no more time.' " And he added with a smile: "No doubt the epileptic Mahomet refers to that same moment when he says that he visited all the dwellings of Allah, in less time than was needed to empty his pitcher of water."

DOSTOEVSKY (from *The Idiot*)

When I went in the morning into the fields to work, the glory of God appeared in all His visible creation. I well remember we reaped oats, and how every straw and head of the oats seemed arrayed in a kind of rainbow glory, or to glow in the glory of God.

ANONYMOUS (*quoted by William James*)

On a certain spring morning I went out to walk. The fields were green, the birds sang, the dew glistened, the smoke was rising, here and there a man appeared; a light as of transfiguration lay on all things. It was only a little bit of the earth; it was only a moment of her existence; and yet as my look embraced her more and more it seemed to me not only so beautiful an idea, but so true and clear a fact, that she is an angel, an angel so rich and fresh and flower-like, and yet going her round in the skies so firmly and so at one with herself, turning her whole living face to Heaven and carrying me along with her into that Heaven, that I asked myself how the opinions of men could ever have so spun themselves away from life as to deem the earth only a dry clod, and to seek for angels above it or about it in the emptiness of the sky—only to find them nowhere.

GUSTAV THEODOR FECHNER

We wandered to the Pine Forest
  That skirts the Ocean's foam,
The lightest wind was in its nest,
  The tempest in its home.
The whispering waves were half asleep,
  The clouds were gone to play,
And on the bosom of the deep
  The smile of Heaven lay;
It seemed as if the hour were one
  Sent from beyond the skies,
Which scattered from above the sun
  A light of Paradise.

393

We paused amid the pines that stood
  The giants of the waste,
Tortured by storms to shapes as rude
  As serpents interlaced,
And soothed by every azure breath,
  That under Heaven is blown,
To harmonies and hues beneath,
  As tender as its own;
Now all the tree-tops lay asleep,
  Like green waves on the sea,
As still as in the silent deep
  The ocean woods may be.

How calm it was!—the silence there
  By such a chain was bound
That even the busy woodpecker
  Made stiller by her sound
The inviolable quietness;
  The breath of peace we drew
With its soft motion made not less
  The calm that round us grew.
There seemed from the remotest seat
  Of the white mountain waste,
To the soft flower beneath our feet,
  A magic circle traced,—
A spirit interfused around,
  A thrilling, silent life,—
To momentary peace it bound
  Our mortal nature's strife;
And still I felt the centre of
  The magic circle there
Was one fair form that filled with love
  The lifeless atmosphere.

SHELLEY

The snow hid all the grass, and all signs of vegetation, and the
rocks showed themselves boldly everywhere, and seemed more
stony than rock, or stone . . .
  We lay sidelong upon the turf, and gazed on the landscape till it
melted into more than natural loveliness . . .
  As I lay down on the grass, I observed the glittering silver line

on the ridge of the backs of the sheep, owing to their situation respecting the sun, which made them look beautiful, but with something of strangeness, like animals of another kind, as if belonging to a more splendid world.

DOROTHY WORDSWORTH

The clump of elms grew right over a deep and rugged hollow; their branches reached out across it, roofing in the cave.

Here was the spring, at the foot of a perpendicular rock, moss-grown low down, and overrun with creeping ivy higher. Green thorn bushes filled the chinks and made a wall to the well, and the long narrow hart's-tongue streaked the face of the cliff. Behind, the thick thorns hid the course of the streamlet, in front rose the solid rock, upon the right hand the sward came to the edge—it shook every now and then as the horses in the shade of the elms stamped their feet—on the left hand the ears of wheat peered over the verge. A rocky cell in concentrated silence of green things. . . . To this cell I used to come once now and then on a summer's day, tempted, perhaps, like the finches, by the sweet cool water, but drawn also by a feeling that could not be analysed. Stooping, I lifted the water in the hollow of my hand—carefully, lest the sand might be disturbed —and the sunlight gleamed on it as it slipped through my fingers. Alone in the green-roofed cave, alone with the sunlight and the pure water, there was a sense of something more than these. The water was more to me than water, and the sun than sun. The gleaming rays on the water in my palm held me for a moment, the touch of the water gave me something from itself. A moment, and the gleam was gone, the water flowing away, but I had had them. Beside the physical water and physical light I had received from them their beauty; they had communicated to me this silent mystery.

RICHARD JEFFERIES

We drank tea the night before I left Grasmere, on the Island in that lovely lake, our kettle swung over the fire hanging from the branch of a Fir-tree, and I lay and saw the woods, and mountains, and lake all trembling, and as it were *idealized* thro' the subtle smoke which rose up from the clear red embers of the fir-apples, which we had collected; afterwards, we made a glorious Bonfire on the margin, by some elder bushes, whose twigs heaved and sobbed in the uprushing column of smoke—and the Image of the Bonfire,

395

and of us that danced round it—ruddy laughing faces in the twilight
—the Image of this in a Lake smooth as that sea, to whose waves the
Son of God had said, *Peace!*

S. T. COLERIDGE

Felpham is a sweet place for Study, because it is more Spiritual
than London. Heaven opens here on all sides her golden Gates;
her windows are not obstructed by vapours; voices of Celestial
inhabitants are more distinctly heard, & their forms more distinctly
seen; & my Cottage is also a Shadow of their houses.

BLAKE

A roller & two harrows lie before my window. I met a plow on
my first going out at my gate the first morning after my arrival, &
the Plowboy said to the Plowman, "Father, The Gate is Open."

BLAKE

"What," it will be Question'd, "When the Sun rises, do you not
see a round disk of fire somewhat like a Guinea?" O no, no, I see an
Innumerable company of the Heavenly Host crying, "Holy, Holy,
Holy is the Lord God Almighty." I question not my Corporeal or
Vegetative Eye any more than I would Question a Window con-
cerning a Sight. I look thro' it & not with it.

BLAKE

THE INTRODUCTION TO 'EUROPE'

"Five windows light the cavern'd Man: thro' one he breathes the
    air;
Thro' one hears music of the spheres; thro' one the eternal vine
Flourishes, that he may receive the grapes; thro' one can look
And see small portions of the eternal world that ever groweth;
Thro' one himself pass out what time he please; but he will not,
For stolen joys are sweet & bread eaten in secret pleasant."

So sang a Fairy, mocking, as he sat on a streak'd Tulip,
Thinking none saw him: when he ceas'd I started from the trees
And caught him in my hat, as boys knock down a butterfly.
"How know you this," said I, "small Sir? where did you learn
    this song?"
Seeing himself in my possession, thus he answer'd me:
"My Master, I am yours! command me, for I must obey."

396

"Then tell me, what is the material world, and is it dead?"
He, laughing, answer'd: "I will write a book on leaves of flowers,
If you will feed me on love-thoughts & give me now and then
A cup of sparkling poetic fancies; so, when I am tipsie,
I'll sing to you to this soft lute, and show you all alive
This world, where every particle of dust breathes forth its joy."

I took him home in my warm bosom: as we went along
Wild flowers I gather'd, & he shew'd me each eternal flower:
He laugh'd aloud to see them whimper because they were pluck'd.
They hover'd round me like a cloud of incense: when I came
Into my parlour and sat down and took my pen to write,
My Fairy sat upon the table and dictated *Europe*.

BLAKE

THE TRANSFIGURATION

So from the ground we felt that virtue branch
Through all our veins till we were whole, our wrists
As fresh and pure as water from a well,
Our hands made new to handle holy things,
The source of all our seeing rinsed and cleansed
Till earth and light and water entering there
Gave back to us the clear unfallen world.
We would have thrown our clothes away for lightness,
But that even they, though sour and travel stained,
Seemed, like our flesh, made of immortal substance,
And the soiled flax and wool lay light upon us
Like friendly wonders, flower and flock entwined
As in a morning field. Was it a vision?
Or did we see that day the unseeable
One glory of the everlasting world
Perpetually at work, though never seen
Since Eden locked the gate that's everywhere
And nowhere? Was the change in us alone,
And the enormous earth still left forlorn,
An exile or a prisoner? Yet the world
We saw that day made this unreal, for all
Was in its place. The painted animals
Assembled there in gentle congregations,
Or sought apart their leafy oratories,
Or walked in peace, the wild and tame together,
As if, also for them, the day had come.

397

The shepherds' hovels shone, for underneath
The soot we saw the stone clean at the heart
As on the starting-day. The refuse heaps
Were grained with that fine dust that made the world;
For he had said, 'To the pure all things are pure.'
And when we went into the town, he with us,
The lurkers under doorways, murderers,
With rags tied round their feet for silence, came
Out of themselves to us and were with us,
And those who hide within the labyrinth
Of their own loneliness and greatness came,
And those entangled in their own devices,
The silent and the garrulous liars, all
Stepped out of their own dungeons and were free.
Reality or vision, this we have seen.
If it had lasted but another moment
It might have held for ever! But the world
Rolled back into its place, and we are here,
And all that radiant kingdom lies forlorn,
As if it had never stirred; no human voice
Is heard among its meadows, but it speaks
To itself alone, alone it flowers and shines
And blossoms for itself while time runs on.

But he will come again, it's said, though not
Unwanted and unsummoned; for all things,
Beasts of the field, and woods, and rocks, and seas,
And all mankind from end to end of the earth
Will call him with one voice. In our own time,
Some say, or at a time when time is ripe.
Then he will come, Christ the uncrucified,
Christ the discrucified, his death undone,
His agony unmade, his cross dismantled—
Glad to be so—and the tormented wood
Will cure its hurt and grow into a tree
In a green springing corner of young Eden,
And Judas damned take his long journey backward
From darkness into light and be a child
Beside his mother's knee, and the betrayal
Be quite undone and never more be done.

EDWIN MUIR

HORSES

Those lumbering horses in the steady plough,
On the bare field—I wonder why, just now,
They seemed terrible, so wild and strange,
Like magic power on the stony grange.

Perhaps some childish hour has come again,
When I watched fearful, through the blackening rain,
Their hooves like pistons in an ancient mill
Move up and down, yet seem as standing still.

Their conquering hooves which trod the stubble down
Were ritual that turned the field to brown,
And their great hulks were seraphim of gold,
Or mute ecstatic monsters on the mould.

And oh the rapture, when, one furrow done,
They marched broad-breasted to the sinking sun!
The light flowed off their bossy sides in flakes;
The furrows rolled behind like struggling snakes.

But when at dusk with steaming nostrils home
They came, they seemed gigantic in the gloam,
And warm and glowing with mysterious fire
That lit their smouldering bodies in the mire.

Their eyes as brilliant and as wide as night
Gleamed with a cruel apocalyptic light.
Their manes the leaping ire of the wind
Lifted with rage invisible and blind.

Ah, now it fades! it fades! and I must pine
Again for that dread country crystalline,
Where the blank field and the still-standing tree
Were bright and fearful presences to me.

EDWIN MUIR

THE GRAVEL-PIT FIELD
(Spring, 1941)

Beside the stolid opaque flow
Of rain-gorged Thames; beneath a thin
Layer of early evening light

Which seems to drift, a ragged veil,
Upon the chilly March air's tide:
Upwards in shallow shapeless tiers
A stretch of scurfy pock-marked waste
Sprawls laggardly its acres till
They touch a raw brick-villa'd rim.

Amidst this nondescript terrain
Haphazardly the gravel-pits'
Rough-hewn rust-coloured hollows yawn,
Their steep declivities away
From the field-surface dropping down
Towards the depths below where rain-
Water in turbid pools stagnates
Like scraps of sky decaying in
The sockets of a dead man's stare.

The shabby coat of coarse grass spread
Unevenly across the ruts
And humps of lumpy soil; the bits
Of stick and threads of straw; loose clumps
Of weeds with withered stalks and black
Tatters of leaf and scorched pods: all
These intertwined minutiae
Of Nature's humblest growths persist
In their endurance here like rock.

As with untold intensity
On the far edge of Being, where
Life's last faint forms begin to lose
Name and identity and fade
Away into the Void, endures
The final thin triumphant flame
Of all that's most despoiled and bare:
So these least stones, in the extreme
Of their abasement might appear

Like rare stones such as could have formed
A necklet worn by the dead queen
Of a great Pharaoh, in her tomb . . .
So each abandoned snail-shell strewn
Among these blotched dock-leaves might seem
In the pure ray shed by the loss

Of all man-measured value, like
Some priceless pearl-enamelled toy
Cushioned on green silk under glass.

And who in solitude like this
Can say the unclean mongrel's bones
Which stick out, splintered, through the loose
Side of a gravel-pit, are not
The precious relics of some saint,
Perhaps miraculous? Or that
The lettering on this Woodbine-
Packet's remains ought not to read:
Mene mene tekel upharsin?

Now a breeze gently breathes across
The wilderness's cryptic face;
The meagre grasses scarcely stir;
But when some stronger gust sweeps past,
Seeming as though an unseen swarm
Of sea-birds had disturbed the air
With their white wings' wide stroke, a gleam
Of freshness hovers everywhere
About the field: and tall weeds shake,

Leaves wave their tiny flags to show
That the wind blown about the brow
Of this poor plot is nothing less
Than the great constant draught the speed
Of Earth's gyrations makes in Space . . .
As I stand musing, overhead
The zenith's stark light thrusts a ray
Down through dusk's rolling vapours, casts
A last lucidity of day

Across the scene: and in a flash
Of insight I behold the field's
Apotheosis: No-man's-land
Between this world and the beyond,
Remote from men and yet more real
Than any human dwelling-place:
A tabernacle where one stands
As though within the empty space
Round which revolves Lao Tse's Wheel.

DAVID GASCOYNE

FROM "THE TRAVELLER"

Beneath him an immeasurable well
Of lustrous crystal motionlessly black
Deeped on. And as he gazed—marvel past words to tell—
It seemed to him a presence there gazed back:

Rapt, immaterial, remote; ev'n less
In substance than is image of the mind;
And yet, in all-embracing consciousness
Of its own inmost being; elsewise blind:

Past human understanding to conceive;
Of virgin innocence, yet source of all
That matter had the power to achieve
Ere Man created was, ere Adam's fall:

And in its midst a mote scarce visible—
Himself: the momentary looking-glass
Of Nature, which a moment may annul,
And with earth's hosts may into nothing pass:

The flux of change. Ay, this poor Traveller too—
Soon to be dust, though once erect, elate,
From whose clear gaze a flame divine burned through;
A son of God—no sport of Time or Fate:

It seemed his heart was broken; his whole life long
Concentred in this moment of desire;
Its woe, its rapture, transient as the song
The Phoenix sings upon her funeral pyre.

WALTER DE LA MARE

PLAGE

Sun on the rose-red tiles, the orange bricks,
Sun on the shifting sapphire of the sea,
Sun on the ancient sea-town where it lies
Beneath the green hills and the guardian tower,
Sun on the feast of youth, the opening flower,
Washed in the salt caresses of the sea.

The children sparkle in the sun and wind,
Their pale locks woven into threads of glass,
The golden ephebes race along the sand

402

Like colts at pasture, all athrill with life,
The virgins trail the beauty of their hair,
Dizzying in the azure-spiralled air.

Far out at sea the white sails spread like wings,
High in the air gulls' wings shine white like sails—
O Life, the beautiful moment, the swift kiss
On parted lips and upturned faces burning,
O Spirit, in the poet's heart, the yearning
Holy desire for far infinities! . . .

WILFRED ROWLAND CHILDE

THE LARCH WOOD

High up and dim the towering larches rise,
   The floor is green with bracken and the air
   Sweeter than incense breathes and Silence there
Broods with mute mouth and tense averted eyes.

But deeper in a darkling terror hides,
   The columns thicken and the shadowy floor
   Is heaped with muffling needles, the gradual store
Fallen to earth in endless winter-tides.

Old gnarlèd roots are gray with goblin moss;
   There red and white the mitred fungi grow;
   All is as still as death: above, below,
In glimmering deeps the ghostly branches cross.

O this immense cathedral of the wood,
   Strange in her soaring Gothic mystery!—
   In the high tree-tops rustles quietly
A sea-surge of soft sound, a multitude

Of murmuring wind-waves hushed and far away;
   High up the ring-dove moans, the hidden choir
   Of this enormous church, whose tapering spire
Ascends unseen into the vaults of day.

O sweet voice of the doves, the only sound
   Save the far rustling in the topmost-boughs
   Of this august and sanctuaried house,
O white dove-feathers fallen to the ground;

O pale-boled pillars in endless multitude,
Stretching away into the twilight aisles
Of absolute quiet where never the sun smiles,
Nor ever a flower blooms in all this solitude,

Where there sounds nothing, nothing, but the sigh
Of the wind soughing in the invisible crests
Of the steep soaring trees where the wild dove nests,
And the dove's sweet and melancholy cry!

A shudder of delight and piercing awe
Seizes me here, this temple is the place
Where I behold Thy Beauty face to face,
Whose Love is the fulfilling of the law!

WILFRED ROWLAND CHILDE

WINTER COMPANY

Blackbird silent in the snow;
Motionless crocus in the mould;
Naked tree; and, cold and low,
Sun's wintry gold . . .
Lost for the while in their strange beauty—self how far!—
Lulled were my senses into a timeless dream;
As if the inmost secret of what they are
Lay open in what they seem.

WALTER DE LA MARE

FROM "RELIGIOUS MUSINGS"

. . . Such delights
As float to earth, permitted visitants!
When in some hour of solemn jubilee
The massy gates of Paradise are thrown
Wide open, and forth come in fragments wild
Sweet echoes of unearthly melodies,
And odours snatched from beds of amaranth,
And they, that from the crystal river of life
Spring up on freshened wing, ambrosial gales!
The favoured good man in his lonely walk
Perceives them, and his silent spirit drinks
Strange bliss which he shall recognise in heaven.

S. T. COLERIDGE

A DAY DREAM

On a sunny brae alone I lay
One summer afternoon;
It was the marriage-time of May
With her young lover, June.

From her Mother's heart seemed loath to part
That queen of bridal charms,
But her Father smiled on the fairest child
He ever held in his arms.

The trees did wave their plumy crests,
The glad birds carolled clear;
And I, of all the wedding guests,
Was only sullen there.

There was not one but wished to shun
My aspect void of cheer;
The very grey rocks, looking on,
Asked, "What do you do here?"

And I could utter no reply:
In sooth I did not know
Why I had brought a clouded eye
To greet the general glow.

So, resting on a heathy bank,
I took my heart to me;
And we together sadly sank
Into a reverie.

We thought, "When winter comes again,
Where will these bright things be?
All vanished, like a vision vain,
An unreal mockery!

"The birds that now so blithely sing,
Through deserts frozen dry,
Poor spectres of the perished Spring
In famished troops will fly.

"And why should we be glad at all?
The leaf is hardly green,
Before a token of the fall
Is on its surface seen."

Now whether it were really so
I never could be sure;
But as, in fit of peevish woe,
I stretched me on the moor,

A thousand thousand glancing fires
Seemed kindling in the air;
A thousand thousand silvery lyres
Resounded far and near:

Methought the very breath I breathed
Was full of sparks divine,
And all my heather-couch was wreathed
By that celestial shine.

And while the wide Earth echoing rang
To their strange minstrelsy,
The little glittering spirits sang,
Or seemed to sing, to me:

"O mortal, mortal, let them die;
Let Time and Tears destroy,
That we may overflow the sky
With universal joy.

"Let Grief distract the sufferer's breast,
And Night obscure his way;
They hasten him to endless rest,
And everlasting day.

"To Thee the world is like a tomb,
A desert's naked shore;
To us, in unimagined bloom,
It brightens more and more.

"And could we lift the veil and give
One brief glimpse to thine eye
Thou would'st rejoice for those that live,
Because they live to die."

The music ceased—the noonday Dream
Like dream of night withdrew
But Fancy still will sometimes deem
Her fond creation true.

EMILY BRONTË

The day before he died Rabbi Shneur Salomon asked his grandson
"Is the ceiling still there?" When the boy said nothing, the Rabbi
continued, in a voice quivering with joy, "I can see no ceiling or walls:
I can only see the life of everything, and God creating everything
and making everything live."

HASIDIC TRADITION

The dying Boehme had asked his son to open the door as he
heard strains of distant music: William Blake welcomed death with
joyful songs, saying to his wife: "My beloved, they are not mine—
no—they are not mine."

MONA WILSON

§ 4

Poetry is the opening and closing of a door, leaving those who
look through to guess about what is seen during a moment.

CARL SANDBURG

It [poetry] is as it were the interpretation of a diviner nature
through our own . . . It strips the veil of familiarity from the
world, and lays bare the naked and sleeping beauty which is the
spirit of its forms.

SHELLEY

All the poems of the poet who has entered into his poethood are
poems of homecoming.

MARTIN HEIDEGGER

> . . . A hundred times when, roving high and low,
> I have been harassed with the toil of verse,
> Much pains and little progress, and at once
> Some lovely Image in the song rose up
> Full-formed, like Venus rising from the sea. . . .

WORDSWORTH

For all good poets, epic as well as lyric, compose their beautiful
poems not by art, but because they are inspired and possessed.
And as the Corybantian revellers when they dance are not in their
right mind, so the lyric poets are not in their right mind when they
are composing their beautiful strains: but when falling under the

407

power of music and metre they are inspired and possessed; like Bacchic maidens who draw milk and honey from the rivers when they are under the influence of Dionysus but not when they are in their right mind. And the soul of the lyric poet does the same, as they themselves say; for they tell us that they bring songs from honeyed fountains, culling them out of the gardens and dells of the Muses; they, like the bees, winging their way from flower to flower. And this is true. For the poet is a light and winged and holy thing, and there is no invention in him until he has been inspired and is out of his senses, and the mind is no longer in him: when he has not attained to this state, he is powerless and is unable to utter his oracles. Many are the noble words in which poets speak concerning the actions of men; but like yourself when speaking about Homer, they do not speak of them by any rules of art: they are simply inspired to utter that to which the Muse impels them, and that only; and when inspired, one of them will make dithyrambs, another hymns of praise, another choral strains, another epic or iambic verses—and he who is good at one is not good at any other kind of verse: for not by art does the poet sing, but by power divine. Had he learned by rules of art, he would have known how to speak not of one theme only, but of all; and therefore God takes away the minds of poets, and uses them as his ministers, as he also uses diviners and holy prophets, in order that we who hear them may know them to be speaking not of themselves who utter these price-less words in a state of unconsciousness, but that God himself is the speaker, and that through them he is conversing with us.

PLATO

Phidias did not make his Zeus from any model perceived by the senses; he understood what Zeus would look like if he wanted to make himself visible.

PLOTINUS

I really do not know how I paint. Armed with a white panel I take up a position in front of the spot that interests me, contemplate what lies before me, and say to myself "That white panel must be turned into something." Dissatisfied with my work I return home, put my panel out of sight, and after taking a little rest go back to my work, almost with qualms to see what it looks like. But even then I am not yet satisfied, for glorious Nature is still too vividly stamped upon my mind. Nevertheless I find in my work a certain reverberation of that which fascinated me. I know that Nature told me something, that she spoke to me, and that I took down her message in shorthand. Perhaps my stenographic transcript contains words that are undecipherable; belike there are faults and omissions in it too; still it may possess something that the wood, the beach, or the figures said. And this is never in a tame or conventional language that did not spring from Nature herself.

VINCENT VAN GOGH

In this theory [of early Chinese painting] every work of art is thought of as an incarnation of the genius of rhythm, manifesting the living spirit of things with a clearer beauty and intenser power than the gross impediments of complex matter allow to be transmitted to our senses in the visible world around us. A picture is conceived as a sort of apparition from a more real world of essential life.

LAURENCE BINYON

Harmonies unheard in sound create the harmonies we hear, and wake the soul to the consciousness of beauty.

PLOTINUS

Heard melodies are sweet, but those unheard
Are sweeter . . .

KEATS

We are the flute, our music is all Thine.

RUMI

Then lutes were played, and coiling away and away
The tune fell earthward, dropping from the grey clouds.

LI PO (tr. by Waley)

Now, what is music? This question occupied me for hours before I fell asleep last night. Music is a strange thing. I would almost say it is a miracle. For it stands halfway between thought and phenomenon, between spirit and matter, a sort of nebulous mediator, like and unlike each of the things it mediates—spirit that requires manifestation in time, and matter that can do without space.

We do not know what music is.

HEINRICH HEINE

Musical order, as recognized and evaluated by our mind, is not an end in itself. It is an image of a higher order which we are permitted to perceive if we proceed one step further to the sixth degree on our scale of musical assimilation: if we put our enjoyment of such knowledge ("enjoyment, the weight of the soul!") into the side of the balance that tends towards the order of the heavens and towards the unification of our soul with the divine principle.

PAUL HINDEMITH

The musician we may think of as being exceedingly quick to beauty, drawn in a very rapture to it: somewhat slow to stir of his own impulse, he answers at once to the outer stimulus: as the timid are sensitive to noise so he to tones and the beauty they convey; all that offends against unison or harmony in melodies and rhythms repels him; he longs for measure and shapely pattern.

This natural tendency must be made the starting-point to such a man; he must be drawn by the tone, rhythm and design in things of sense: he must learn to distinguish the material forms from the Real Being which is the source of all these correspondences and of the entire reasoned scheme in the work of art: he must be led to the Beauty that manifests itself through these forms; he must be shown that what ravished him was no other than the Harmony of the Spiritual world and the Beauty in that sphere, not some one shape of beauty but the All-Beauty, the Absolute Beauty; and the truths of the sanctified life must be implanted in him to lead him to faith in that which, unknowing it, he possesses within himself. What these truths are we will show later.

PLOTINUS

MUSIC AND THE BEATIFIC VISION

My introduction to music occurred on the first occasion that Mr. Pyatt invited me to dinner. . . . At the coffee stage we moved into another room, filled with very easy chairs and sofas, and containing a piano-player, a rather novel instrument at that time. Mr. Pyatt suggested trying a few rolls. . . . It so happened that the first one he put on was one of the mightiest and most immediately arresting of all compositions, Bach's great organ Toccata and Fugue in D minor. Even as arranged for the piano and played by a mechanical player it is, as I can testify, completely overwhelming. My first hearing of it was a cardinal experience in my life; perhaps, when all is summed up, it will prove to have been *the* cardinal experience of my life. For it was my first glimpse of those activities of the human spirit which are, I am convinced, the justification of life, and in which the meaning of life is to be found. Nothing that I had hitherto experienced belonged to that region. I experienced, quite literally, a revelation. All great art, I believe, is the record of a spiritual achievement, of a synthesis of experience, of a degree of understanding, that cannot be communicated in other terms. But, for myself, it is only in certain great music that the revelation is complete and unambiguous. Such music is my substitute for the mystic vision. It is, perhaps, an experience that can never be satisfactorily rationalised, nor ever communicated to others. It is also an experience that can never be denied. No account of life that denies its supreme importance can be even remotely true. In this position, however much it may seem to conflict with my liking for clear reasoning based on verifiable premises, I am quite unshakable. I have heard, and I know.

I passed the rest of the evening in a sort of bewildered happiness. Several more rolls were played—too many for my untrained attention. I cannot remember what they were. After that first shock I listened but vaguely. But it was not until very late that I suddenly became conscious of fatigue and rose to go. Mr. Pyatt shook hands with a pleased smile, obviously finding his experiment completely successful, but, with a tact that could not be missed, he refrained from questioning me about my sensations. The bus-ride home was through a transfigured London. How I loved it all—the bright lights, the traffic, the dark trees of the park, the great, impressive buildings! I was in a dreamy ecstasy at the wonder of life, at its range and complexity, its infinite possibilities. Life! The scale of it! The diversity of it! The greatness of this adventure to which the spirit of man is committed! What undreamed-of possibilities lie before him, what new ways of thinking, what new knowledge, what new heights of experience! And there, as it seemed to me, amongst the farthest reaches of the spirit, lonely and prophetic, was music such as I had heard that night, music informed with the new understanding, the new degree of realisation, that has been achieved by the pioneers of our race.

J. W. N. SULLIVAN

411

The seer of Lublin, having served a poor traveller with a meal, cleared away the dishes. He was asked why he troubled to do this. "Surely," he replied, "carrying the vessels out of the Holy of Holies was part of the duty of the High Priest."

HASIDIC TRADITION

IV. TIME AND ETERNITY

That which occurs in time and on earth occurs also in heaven and in eternity.

BERDYAEV

All transient things are permanent in God.

TRAHERNE

>   . . . but, in this life
> Of error, ignorance, and strife,
> Where nothing is but all things seem,
> And we the shadows of the dream,
>
> It is a modest creed, and yet
> Pleasant if one considers it,
> To own that death itself must be,
> Like all the rest, a mockery.
>
> That garden sweet, that lady fair,
> And all sweet shapes and odours there,
> In truth have never passed away:
> 'Tis we, 'tis ours, are changed; not they.
>
> For love, and beauty, and delight,
> There is no death nor change; their might
> Exceeds our organs, which endure
> No light, being themselves obscure.

SHELLEY

> The traces cannot, of mine earthly being,
> In aeons perish—they are there!

GOETHE

For every thing exists and not one sigh nor smile nor tear,
One hair nor particle of dust, not one can pass away.

BLAKE

In Eternity one Thing never Changes into another Thing. Identities or Things are Neither Cause nor Effect. Each Identity is Eternal. Eternity Exists, and All things in Eternity, Independent of Creation which was an act of Mercy.

BLAKE

Remembering our happy Christmas at lovely Felpham, our spirits seem still to hover round our sweet cottage and round the beautiful Turret. I have said *seem*, but am persuaded that distance is nothing but a phantasy. We are often sitting by our cottage fire, and often we think we hear your voice calling at the gate. Surely these things are real and eternal in our eternal mind and can never pass away.

BLAKE (*from a letter*)

The blunder is to estimate,—
"Eternity is *Then*,"
We say, as of a station.
Meanwhile he is so near,
He joins me in my ramble,
Divides abode with me,
No friend have I that so persists
As this Eternity.

EMILY DICKINSON

§ 2

Eternity both enfoldeth and unfoldeth succession.

NICOLAS OF CUSA

TIME THE IMAGE OF ETERNITY

Eternity, thus, is of the order of the supremely great; it proves on investigation to be identical with God: it may fitly be described as God made manifest, as God declaring what He is, as existence without jolt or change, and therefore as also the firmly living. It is a Life limitless in the full sense of being all the life there is and a Life which, knowing nothing of past or future to shatter its completeness, possesses itself intact for ever. To the notion of a Life all-comprehensive add that it never spends itself, and we have the statement of a Life instantaneously infinite.

What, then, is Time?

We start from Eternity, unwavering Life, undivided totality, limitless, knowing no divagation, at rest in unity and intent upon it. Time was not yet: or at least it did not exist for the Divine, though its being was implicit in the Idea and Principle of progressive derivation from the Divine.

416

But from the Divine thus at rest within itself, how did this Time first emerge?

We can scarcely call upon the Muses to recount its origin since they were not in existence then—perhaps not even if they had been. The engendered thing, Time, itself, can best tell us how it rose and became manifest; something thus its story would run:

Time at first—in reality before that "first" was produced by the divine desire for succession—Time lay, self-concentrated, at rest within the Divine: it was not yet Time; it was merged in the Divine and motionless with it. But there was an active principle in the Divine [namely, the All-Soul, God the Creator], one set on governing itself and realising itself, and it chose to aim at something more than its present: it stirred from its rest, and Time stirred with it. And we [namely, the individual human souls, included in the All-Soul] we, stirring to a ceaseless succession, to a next, to the discrimination of identity and the establishment of ever new difference, traversed a portion of the outgoing path and produced an image of Eternity, produced Time.

For the All-Soul was desirous of translating elsewhere what it saw in the Divine Realm, and it could not bear to retain within itself all the dense fullness of its possession.

A seed is at rest; the nature-principle within, uncoiling outwards, makes way towards what seems to it a large life; but by that partition it loses; it was a unity self-gathered, and now, in going forth from itself, it fritters its unity away; it advances into a weaker greatness. It is so with this faculty of the All-Soul, when it produces the Cosmos known to sense—the mimic of the Divine Sphere, moving not in the very movement of the Divine but in its similitude, in an effort to reproduce that of the Divine. To bring this Cosmos into being, the All-Soul first laid aside its eternity and clothed itself with Time; this world of its fashioning it then gave over to be a servant to Time, making it at every point a thing of Time, setting all its progressions within the bournes of Time. For the Cosmos moves only in the All-Soul—there is no other space within the range of the All open to it to move in—and therefore its movement has always been in the Time which inheres in Soul.

Putting forth its energy in act after act, in a constant progress of novelty, the All-Soul produces succession as well as act; taking up new purposes added to the old, it brings thus into being what had not existed in that former period when its purpose was still dormant and its life was not as it since became: the life is changed and that change carries with it a change of Time. Time, then, is contained in differentiation of Life; the ceaseless forward movement of Life brings with it unending Time; and Life as it achieves its stages constitutes past Time.

Would it, then, be sound to define Time as the Life of the Soul in movement as it passes from one stage of act or experience to another?

Yes; for Eternity, we have said, is Life in repose, unchanging, self-identical, always endlessly complete; and there is to be an image of Eternity—Time—such an image as this lower All presents of the Higher Sphere. Therefore over against that higher life there must be another life, known by the same name as the more veritable, life of the All-Soul; over against that identity, unchangeableness and stability there must be that which is not constant in the one hold but puts forth multitudinous acts; over against that oneness without extent or interval there must be an image of oneness, a unity of link and succession; over against the immediately infinite and all-comprehending, that which tends, yes, to infinity but by tending to a perpetual futurity; over against the Whole in concentration, there must be that which is to be a Whole by stages never final. The lesser must always be working towards the increase of its Being; this will be its imitation of what is immediately complete, self-realised, endless without stage: only thus can its Being reproduce that of the Higher.

PLOTINUS

THE HYACINTH

Time opens in a flower of bells
the mysteries of its hidden bed,
the altar of the ageless cells
whose generations never have been dead.

So flower angels from the holy head,
so on the wand of darkness bright worlds hang.
Love laid the elements at the vital root,
unhindered out of love these flowers spring.

The breath of life shapes darkness into leaves,
each new born cell
drinks from the star-filled well
the dark milk of the sky's peace.

The hyacinth springs on a dark star—
I see eternity give place to love.
It is the world unfolding into flower
the rose of life, the lily and the dove.

KATHLEEN RAINE

§ 3

THE DEAD WARRIOR

There were grass-grown tumuli on the hills to which of old I used to walk, sit down at the foot of one of them, and think. Some warrior had been interred there in the ante-historic times. The sun of the summer morning shone on the dome of sward, and the air came softly up from the wheat below, the tips of the grasses swayed as it passed sighing faintly, it ceased, and the bees hummed by to the thyme and heathbells. I became absorbed in the glory of the day, the sunshine, the sweet air, the yellowing corn turning from its sappy green to summer's noon of gold, the lark's song like a water-fall in the sky. I felt at that moment that I was like the spirit of the man whose body was interred in the tumulus; I could understand and feel his existence the same as my own. He was as real to me two thousand years after interment as those I had seen in the body. The abstract personality of the dead seemed as existent as thought. As my thought could slip back the twenty centuries in a moment to the forest-days when he hurled the spear, or shot with the bow, hunting the deer, and could return again as swiftly to this moment, so his spirit could endure from then till now, and the time was nothing . . .

It happened once that a man was drowned while bathing, and his body was placed in an outhouse near the garden. I passed the outhouse continually, sometimes on purpose to think about it, and it always seemed to me that the man was still living. Separation is not to be comprehended; the spirit of the man did not appear to have gone to an inconceivable distance. As my thought flashes itself back through the centuries to the luxury of Canopus, and can see the gilded couches of a city extinct, so it slips through the future, and immeasurable time in front is no boundary to it. Certainly the man was not dead to me.

Sweetly the summer air came up to the tumulus, the grass sighed softly, the butterflies went by, sometimes alighting on the green dome. Two thousand years! Summer after summer the blue

419

butterflies had visited the mound, the thyme had flowered, the wind sighed in the grass. The azure morning had spread its arms over the low tomb; and full glowing noon burned on it; the purple of sunset rosied the sward. Stars, ruddy in the vapour of the southern horizon, beamed at midnight through the mystic summer night, which is dusky and yet full of light. White mists swept up and hid it; dews rested on the turf; tender harebells drooped; the wings of the finches fanned the air—finches whose colours faded from the wings how many centuries ago! Brown autumn dwelt in the woods beneath; the rime of winter whitened the beech clump on the ridge; again the buds came on the windblown hawthorn bushes, and in the evening the broad constellation of Orion covered the east. Two thousand times! Two thousand times the woods grew green, and ring-doves built their nests. Day and night for two thousand years—light and shadow sweeping over the mound—two thousand years of labour by day and slumber by night. Mystery gleaming in the stars, pouring down in the sunshine, speaking in the night, the wonder of the sun and of far space, for twenty centuries round about this low and green-grown dome. Yet all that mystery and wonder is as nothing to the Thought that lies therein, to the spirit that I feel so close.

Realising that spirit, recognising my own inner consciousness, the psyche, so clearly, I cannot understand time. It is eternity now. I am in the midst of it. It is about me in the sunshine; I am in it, as the butterfly floats in the light-laden air. Nothing has to come; it is now. Now is eternity; now is the immortal life. Here this moment, by this tumulus, on earth, now; I exist in it. The years, the centuries, the cycles are absolutely nothing; it is only a moment since this tumulus was raised; in a thousand years more it will still be only a moment. To the soul there is no past and no future; all is and will be ever, in now.

RICHARD JEFFERIES

Before me and all around me was the soul of the Empress Mumtaz-i-Mahal.

The soul, so infinitely great, radiant and beautiful in comparison with the little body that had lived on earth and was now enclosed in the tomb.

In that moment I understood that the soul is not enclosed in the body, but that the body lives and moves in the soul. And then I remembered and understood a mystical expression which had arrested my attention in old books:

The soul and the future life are one and the same.

It even seemed strange to me that I had not been able to understand this before. Of course they were the same. Life, as a process, and that which lives, can be differentiated in our understanding only so long as there is the idea of disappearance, of death. Here, as in eternity, everything was united, dimensions merged, and our little earthly world disappeared in the infinite world.

OUSPENSKY

From the very beginning of the road from Gizeh I began to experience this strange sensation of past as present which for some reason was produced in me by the Egyptian landscape. But this time I felt a desire to understand this sensation better, and I looked with particular intentness at everything round me, trying to decipher the secret of this magic of Egypt. And I came to think that the secret might lie in the astonishing changelessness of the Egyptian landscape and its colours. In other countries nature changes its face several times a year. Even where for centuries the main features have been preserved, as in forests and steppes, the outer cover of nature, the grass, the leaves, is all new, just born. But here this sand and these stones are the same as those which had seen the people who built the pyramids, the Pharaohs and the Caliphs.

And it seemed to me that in these stones which had seen so much, something of what they had seen was preserved, and that because of this a certain link was established through them with the life which existed in these places before and seemed still to be invisibly present here . . .

And in everything I felt there was a not easily comprehensible but very subtle joy. I would describe it as the joy of liberation from oneself and the joy of feeling the incredible richness of life, which never dies but exists in an infinite variety of forms invisible and intangible for us.

OUSPENSKY

. . . there is a coherence in things, a stability; something, she meant, is immune from change, and shines out (she glanced at the window with its ripple of reflected lights) in the face of the flowing,

421

the fleeting, the spectral, like a ruby; so that again to-night she had
the feeling she had had once to-day already, of peace, of rest.

VIRGINIA WOOLF (from To The Lighthouse)

Our own insufficiency is that we live in a fraction of ourselves, in
a narrow *I*, in a narrow vision, *in time*, in a belief that the material
universe of the moment is *all*. The perfecting of oneself, the attainment of unity, is connected with . . . a full-filling which must mean,
to begin with, an overcoming of our narrow temporal vision—so
that now we can understand better why the Hermetist advises the
exercise of thinking of the life *as living at all points*, as a movement
towards 'eternal life'. But time—life—is only one track through the
fullness of things.

MAURICE NICOLL

Think that you are not yet begotten, think that you are in the
womb, that you are young, that you are old, that you are dead, that
you are in the world beyond the grave, grasp all that in your thought
at once, all times and places.

HERMETICA

A single minute released from the chronological order of time
has recreated in us the human being similarly released.

PROUST

O hours of childhood, when behind the figures
was more than the mere past, and when before us
no future loomed! We grew, of course, and sometimes
made haste to be grown-up, half for the sake
of those who'd nothing else but their grown-upness.
But when we were alone, we found our pleasure
in everlastingness; we would stand there,
in between world and plaything, on a spot
founded from the beginning of the world
for the enactment of a pure event.

RILKE

The apprehension of time is caused by the perception of the
changing instant, the apprehension of eternity by that of the
enduring instant.

ST. THOMAS AQUINAS

> Time past and time future
> Allow but a little consciousness.
> To be conscious is not to be in time.
> But only in time can the moment in the rose-garden,
> The moment in the arbour where the rain beat,
> The moment in the draughty church at smokefall
> Be remembered; involved with past and future.
> Only through time time is conquered.

T. S. ELIOT (from Four Quartets)

§ 4

'Child,' Lord Arglay said, 'I am an old man and I have known nothing all my life farther or greater than the work I have taken to do. I have never seen a base for any temple nor found an excuse to believe in the myths that are told there. I will not say *believe* or *do not believe*. But there is one thing only of which I have wondered at times, and yet it seemed foolish to think of it. It will happen sometimes when one has worked hard and done all that one can for the purpose before one—it has happened then that I have stood up and been content with the world of things and with what has been done there through me. And this may be pride, or it may be the full stress of the whole being and delight in labour—there are a hundred explanations. But I have wondered whether that profound repose was not communicated from some far source and whether the life that is in it was altogether governed by time. And I am sure that state never comes while I am concerned with myself. . . .'

CHARLES WILLIAMS (from Many Dimensions)

AN ARTIST IN KOUROO

There was an artist in the city of Kouroo who was disposed to strive after perfection. One day it came into his mind to make a staff. Having considered that in an imperfect work time is an ingredient, but into a perfect work time does not enter, he said to himself, It shall be perfect in all respects, though I should do nothing else in my life. He proceeded instantly to the forest for wood, being resolved that it should not be made of unsuitable material; and as he searched for and rejected stick after stick, his friends gradually deserted him, for they grew old in their works and died, but he grew not older by a moment. His singleness of purpose

423

and resolution, and his elevated piety, endowed him, without his knowledge, with perennial youth. As he made no compromise with Time, Time kept out of his way, and only sighed at a distance because he could not overcome him. Before he had found a stick in all respects suitable the city of Kouroo was a hoary ruin, and he sat on one of its mounds to peel the stick. Before he had given it the proper shape the dynasty of the Candahars was at an end, and with the point of the stick he wrote the name of the last of that race in the sand, and then resumed his work. By the time he had smoothed and polished the staff Kalpa was no longer the pole-star; and ere he had put on the ferule and the head adorned with precious stones, Brahma had awoke and slumbered many times. But why do I stay to mention these things? When the finishing stroke was put to his work, it suddenly expanded before the eyes of the astonished artist into the fairest of all the creations of Brahma. He had made a new system in making a staff, a world with full and fair proportions; in which, though the old cities and dynasties had passed away, fairer and more glorious ones had taken their places. And now he saw by the heap of shavings still fresh at his feet, that, for him and his work, the former lapse of time had been an illusion, and that no more time had elapsed than is required for a single scintillation from the brain of Brahma to fall on and inflame the tinder of a mortal brain. The material was pure, and his art was pure; how could the result be other than wonderful?

THOREAU

§ 5

The eternal life is not the future life; it is life in harmony with the true order of things—life in God. We must learn to look upon time as a movement of eternity, as an undulation in the ocean of being. To live, so as to keep this consciousness of ours in perpetual relation with the eternal, is to be wise; to live, so as to personify and embody the eternal, is to be religious.

AMIEL

I. RELIGION AND RELIGION

For John and Diana Collins

He who begins by loving Christianity better than truth, will proceed by loving his own sect or church better than Christianity, and end in loving himself better than all.

S. T. COLERIDGE

He who does reverence to his own sect, while disparaging the sects of others with intent to enhance the glory of his own sect, by such conduct inflicts the severest injury on his own sect.

ASOKA

I do not understand how people declare themselves to be believers in God, and at the same time think that God has handed over to a little body of men all truth, and that they are the guardians of the rest of humanity.

VIVEKANANDA

Seeing then that the body of Christ is mystically one, it follows that the fellowship of his members must also be mystical, and not confined to place and time, inasmuch as it is composed of individuals of widely separated countries, and of all ages from the foundation of the world.

MILTON

THE SHEPHERD'S PRAYER

Moses saw a shepherd on the way, crying, "O Lord Who choosest as Thou wilt,

Where art Thou, that I may serve Thee and sew Thy shoon and comb Thy hair?

That I may wash Thy clothes and kill Thy lice and bring milk to Thee, O worshipful One;

That I may kiss Thy little hand and rub Thy little feet and sweep Thy little room at bed-time."

On hearing these foolish words, Moses said, "Man, to whom are you speaking?

What babble! What blasphemy and raving! Stuff some cotton into your mouth!

Truly the friendship of a fool is enmity: the High God is not in want of suchlike service."

The shepherd rent his garment, heaved a sigh, and took his way to the wilderness.

427

Then came to Moses a Revelation: "Thou hast parted My servant
from Me.
Wert thou sent as a prophet to unite, or wert thou sent to sever?
I have bestowed on every one a particular mode of worship, I have
given every one a peculiar form of expression.
The idiom of Hindustan is excellent for Hindus; the idiom of Sind
is excellent for the people of Sind.
I look not at tongue and speech, I look at the spirit and the inward
feeling.
I look into the heart to see whether it be lowly, though the words
uttered be not lowly.
Enough of phrases and conceits and metaphors! I want burning,
burning: become familiar with that burning!
Light up a fire of love in thy soul, burn all thought and expression
away!
O Moses, they that know the conventions are of one sort, they
whose souls burn are of another" . . .

RUMI

Christ does not save all those who say to Him: 'Lord, Lord'. But
he saves all those who out of a pure heart give a piece of bread to a
starving man, without thinking about Him the least little bit. And
these, when He thanks them, reply: 'Lord, when did we feed
thee?' . . .

An atheist and an 'infidel', capable of pure compassion, are as
close to God as is a Christian, and consequently know Him equally
well, although their knowledge is expressed in other words, or
remains unspoken. For 'God is Love'.

SIMONE WEIL

§ 2

No religion is better than an unnatural one.

WILLIAM PENN

It were better to be of no church than to be bitter for any. To be
furious in religion is to be irreligiously religious.

WILLIAM PENN

Men never do evil so fully and so happily as when they do it for
conscience' sake.

PASCAL

The Outward Ceremony is Antichrist.

BLAKE

When Crucifixes upon Men's Hearts suppress not their bad commotions, and his Image who was murdered for us with-holds not from Blood and Murder; Phylacteries prove but formalities, and their despised hints sharpen our condemnations.

SIR THOMAS BROWNE

Religion is not a Hear-say, a Presumption, a Supposition; is not a customary Pretension and Profession; is not an Affectation of any Mode; is not a Piety of particular Fancy, consisting in some pathetic Devotions, vehement Expressions, bodily Severities, affected Anomalies and Aversions from the innocent Usages of others: but consisteth in a profound Humility, and an universal Charity.

BENJAMIN WHICHCOTE

And most certainly as men grow in grace and know the anointing of the word in themselves, the dispensation will be less in words (though in words) and more in life; and preaching will in great measure be turned into praising and the worship of God, more into walking with than talking of God. For that is worship indeed that bows to His will at all times and in all places, the truest, the highest worship man is capable of in this world. And it is that conformity that gives communion, and there is no fellowship with God, no light of His countenance to be enjoyed, no peace and assurance to be had farther than their obedience to His will, and a faithfulness to His word, according to the manifestation of the light thereof in the heart.

I say this is the truest and highest state of worship; for set days and places, with all the solemnity of them, were most in request in the weakest dispensation. Altars, ark, and temples, Sabbaths and festivals, etc., are not to be found in the writings of the New Testament. There every day is alike and every place is alike; but if there were a dedication let it be to the Lord. Thus the apostle, but he plainly shows a state beyond it, for to live (with him) was Christ, and to die was gain; for the life he lived was by the faith of the Son of God, and therefore it was not he that lived, but Christ that lived in him; that is, that ruled, conducted, and bore sway in him, which is the true Christian life, the supersensual life, the life of conversion and regeneration, to which all the dispensations of God and ministry of His servants have ever tended as the consummation of God's work for man's happiness. Here every man is a temple, and every family a church, and every place a meeting-place, and every visit a meeting. And yet a little while and it shall be so yet more and more; and a people the Lord is now preparing to enter into this Sabbath or degree of rest.

WILLIAM PENN

Religion to him had reference to an act of consciousness, by which he submerged his own will with the Will of Life, an act of creation, of abandonment to the stream of life.

STEPHEN POTTER (of S. T. Coleridge)

§ 4

The indifference of believers is something far more dreadful than the fact that unbelievers exist.

FATHER YELCHANINOV

If you wish to be commonly good, the easiest, indeed the only way, is to be heroically so.

COVENTRY PATMORE

In all ages, ardent and magnificent souls have thought that in order to do enough it was absolutely necessary to do too much, and that thus did one ravish the Kingdom of the Heavens. . . .

LÉON BLOY

With most people religion is a sort of intellectual assent and goes no further than a document. I would not call it religion. It is better to be an atheist than to have that sort of religion.

VIVEKANANDA

In every collective belief, religious or social, very rare are the men who believe, because very rare are the men who are men. Faith is an heroic force: its fire has kindled but a very few human torches, and even these have often flickered. . . . Not more than a few hundred Christians really believe in Christ. The rest believe that they believe, or else they only try to believe.

ROMAIN ROLLAND

It is not easy to realise how many waiting souls there are in this world. The greater number of men pass through life with souls asleep. They are like virgins of the sanctuary who sometimes feel a vague agitation; their hearts throb with an infinitely sweet and subtle thrill, but their eyelids droop; again they feel the damp cold of the cloister creeping over them; the delicious but baneful dream vanishes; and this is all they ever know of that love which is stronger than death.

It is thus with many men for all that belongs to the higher life. Sometimes, alone in the wide plain at the hour of twilight, they fix their eyes on the fading lights of the horizon, and on the evening breeze comes to them another breeze, more distant, fainter, and almost heavenly, awaking in them a nostalgia for the world beyond and for holiness. But the darkness falls, they must go back to their homes; they shake off their reverie; and it often happens that to the very end of life this is their only glimpse of the Divine; a few sighs, a few thrills, a few inarticulate murmurs—this sums up all our efforts to attain to the sovereign good.

Yet the instinct for love and the divine is only slumbering. At the sight of beauty love always awakes; at the appeal of holiness the divine witness within us at once responds; and so we see, streaming from all points of the horizon to gather around those who preach in the name of the inward voice, long processions of souls athirst for the ideal. The human heart so naturally yearns to offer itself up, that we have only to meet along our pathway some one who, doubting neither himself nor us, demands it without reserve, and we yield it to him at once. Reason may understand a partial gift, a transient devotion; the heart knows only the entire sacrifice, and, like the lover to his beloved, it says to its vanquisher, "Thine alone and forever".

That which has caused the miserable failure of all the efforts of natural religion is that its founders have not had the courage to lay hold upon the hearts of men, consenting to no partition. They have not understood the imperious desire for immolation which lies in the depth of every soul, and souls have taken their revenge in not heeding these too lukewarm lovers.

PAUL SABATIER

I LOOK AT THE WORLD AROUND ME

I look at the world around me, and at my own life. At the world of atom bombs; at the hatred between East and West; at the vileness

431

of the press; at the sadism of films; at the murder of children and old women; at murderers hung by the neck until they are dead; at millions and millions starving miserably, and no one caring anything about it; at my own wretched efforts to make profits for my firm and provide for my own present comfort and my future old age. And I know, I have long known, with every atom of my being, that there is only one answer: absolute pacifism, absolute communism (not in the Stalinist sense, but in the early religious sense of holding all things in common), an absolute living of the Christian ethic.

We were at *Fidelio* tonight, and when I unburdened myself to Ruth, at supper, of what I have just been saying, she asked me "But was Leonora wrong to threaten Pizarro with the pistol? She saved her husband's life." She couldn't have put the dilemma in a more agonising form, for Leonora's pistol and the simultaneous trumpet-call had long seemed to me the perfect expression of divine-human co-operation. But I had to answer "Yes, she was wrong." To interpose her own body, of course this was right: to threaten with the pistol was far better than just to have been indifferent, just to have done nothing about it: but to retaliate against violence with violence—this, absolutely, was wrong. And the absoluteness is everything. I do not believe that you can approximate to Christian ethics: that is why Christ told us, not merely to love our friends and do no injury to our enemies but positively to love our enemies, and not merely to be as good as we could manage to be but to be perfect as our Father is perfect. The question is not one of degree. You cannot be more or less of a Christian, just as you cannot be more or less of a lover. You either love or you do not. When absoluteness is reached, you are suddenly a Christian; before, however close you may have got, you have not been a Christian at all. And this absoluteness is the only possible road to the Kingdom of Heaven: it is the Kingdom of Heaven itself. Whether or not Christ actually said what he is quoted as saying in a Gospel fragment, he might very well have said it: "if ye keep not Sabbath for the whole week, ye shall not see the Father".

It follows that whether or not such absoluteness will "succeed" is utterly irrelevant. I don't mean only in the short run; I don't mean only, for instance, that it's utterly irrelevant whether total disarmament, and love in our life and in our hearts for Stalin and the Red Army and the G.P.U., would either hinder a communist conquest of the world or mitigate its horrors when it came. I mean in the long run too; I mean that whether or not, ages hence, the condition of the world might appear, in human judgment, to have been improved by such behaviour is utterly irrelevant too. The thing succeeds, in the real sense, by the fact of it happening: it is there, good, eternally, God realised and incarnate. Perhaps, as Samuel Alexander might say, it makes God. I am explaining this badly; perhaps I am trying to explain something one can only feel utterly convinced about but can never explain to others. Let me make another attempt. Elizabeth Pilenko, a Russian living in Paris, took the place of a Jewess who was going to the incinerators and was burnt in her stead. It happens that her action is known. But if it had never been known; if no one had witnessed it; if the Jewess had herself been killed immediately afterwards; if, therefore, what Elizabeth had done could never possibly have become known to anyone—nevertheless she was doing the only thing that can answer the world's evil, and her action lives and reigns eternally, whether or not, to mortal seeming, the world is a better place for it. And as irrelevant as this last consideration is the fact that, as I have little doubt, Elizabeth's life, in the ordinary sense, was a far more valuable one than the Jewess's, and that, if she had lived, she might have given spiritual strength and physical comfort to thousands.

I feel exactly the same about Christian communism as I do about pacifism. Meister Eckhart wrote, "He who withholds but a penny-worth of worldly goods from his neighbour, knowing him to be in need of it, is a robber in the sight of God. Further I declare, who spares a penny for himself to put it by against a rainy day, thinking, I may need that for tomorrow, is a murderer before God." I am utterly convinced that he is right. . . .

You will find an answer of sorts to all this, so far as public affairs are concerned, in Reinhold Niebuhr's *Moral Man and Immoral Society*. I admire Reinhold Niebuhr as much as I admire any man now living, but I reject his dualistic relativism utterly. His point of view is based, among other things, on a sharp differentiation between this world and the next: on a contrast, seen as basic and inevitable, between the individual man and the collective man (whereas, for me, the assumption of this inevitability is the cause of half our evils, and derives from a muddle-headed, bogus-mystical, unrealistic taking-it-for-granted that there is something in society, something ultimate, other than the men and women who make it up): and on a profoundly pessimistic estimate of human nature. "The demand of religious moralists" he writes in a typical passage

433

"that nations subject themselves to 'the law of Christ' is an unrealistic demand, and the hope that they will do so is a sentimental one. Even a nation composed of individuals who possessed the highest degree of religious goodwill would be less than loving in its relation to other nations. It would fail, if for no other reason, because the individuals could not possibly think themselves into the position of the individuals of another nation in a degree sufficient to ensure pure benevolence." But that is to beg the whole question. Side by side with this passage may be set a peculiarly horrible statement by Martin Luther: "It is indeed true that Christians, so far as they themselves are concerned, are subject to neither law nor sword, and need neither; but just take heed to fill the world with real Christians before ruling it in a Christian and evangelical manner. This you will never accomplish, for the world and the masses are and always will be unchristian." I don't want to be melodramatic, but really you can almost hear the nails on Calvary.

v. g. (from *My Dear Timothy*)

EITHER/OR

For what is either/or, if I am to say it, who surely must know? Either/or is the word before which the folding doors fly open and the ideals appear—O blissful sight! Either/or is the token which ensures entrance into the unconditional—God be praised! Yea, either/or is the key to heaven! On the other hand, what is, was, and continues to be man's misfortune? It is this 'to a certain degree', the invention of Satan or of paltriness or of cowardly shrewdness, which being applied to Christianity (by a preposterous miracle, or with miraculous preposterousness) transforms it into twaddle! No: Either/or! And as it is on the stage, that however tenderly the actor and actress embrace one another and caress one another, this remains nevertheless only a theatrical union, a theatre-marriage; so also in relation to the unconditional all this thing of 'to a certain degree' is theatrical, it grasps an illusion; only either/or is the embrace which grasps the unconditional . . .

The Biblical interpretation of mediocrity goes on interpreting and interpreting Christ's words until it gets out of them its own trivial meaning—and then, after having removed all difficulties, it is tranquillised, and appeals confidently to Christ's words!

It quite escapes the attention of mediocrity that hereby it generates a new difficulty, surely the most comical difficulty it is possible to imagine, that God should let himself be *born*, that the Truth

434

should have come into the world . . . in order to make trivial remarks. And likewise the new difficulty as to how one is to explain that Christ could be crucified. For it is not usual in this world of triviality to apply the penalty of death for making trivial remarks, so that the crucifixion of Christ becomes both inexplicable and comical, since it is comical to be crucified because one has made trivial remarks . . .

The Christianity of the New Testament simply does not exist. Here there is nothing to reform; what has to be done is to throw light upon a criminal offence against Christianity, prolonged through centuries, perpetrated by millions (more or less guiltily), whereby they have . . . succeeded in making Christianity exactly the opposite of what it is in the New Testament . . .

KIERKEGAARD

More! More! is the cry of a mistaken soul; less than All cannot satisfy Man.

BLAKE

§ 5

In his prayers he says, Thy Will be done: but means his own. At least acts so.

WILLIAM PENN

Some folk think they may scold, rail, hate, rob, and kill too, so it be but for God's sake.

But nothing in us unlike Him can please Him.

WILLIAM PENN

We have just enough Religion to make us hate, but not enough to make us love one another.

SWIFT

Christ rejects the law of Moses and gives his own. For a man believing in Christ there is no contradiction. Disregarding the law of Moses he believes in the law of Christ and fulfils it. For one believing in the law of Moses there is also no contradiction. The Jews consider the words of Christ vain, and believe in the law of Moses. There is a contradiction only for those who wish to live by the law of Moses but assure themselves and others that they believe the law of Christ—for those whom Christ calls hypocrites, the off-spring of vipers.

435

Instead of acknowledging one of the two, the law of Moses or of Christ, they acknowledge both to be divinely true.

But when the question touches life itself, the law of Christ is simply denied and the law of Moses acknowledged.

TOLSTOY

The Christian nations offer many illustrations of the law of irony. They profess the citizenship of heaven, the exclusive worship of eternal good; and never has the hungry pursuit of perishable joys, the love of this world, or the thirst for conquest, been stronger or more active than among these nations. Their official motto is exactly the reverse of their real aspiration. Under a false flag they play the smuggler with a droll ease of conscience. Is the fraud a conscious one? No—it is but an application of the law of irony. The deception is so common a one that the delinquent becomes unconscious of it. Every nation gives itself the lie in the course of its daily life, and not one feels the ridicule of its position.

AMIEL

Disbelief in Christianity is not so much to be dreaded as its acceptance with a complete denial of it in society and politics.

MARK RUTHERFORD

If Christianity refuses to realise social justice on the assumption that the sinfulness of human nature makes it impossible, the task will be undertaken by that sinful nature without its help, and the idea of justice will be distorted and spoiled.

BERDYAEV

First bread and then religion. We stuff them too much with religion, when the poor fellows have been starving. No dogmas will satisfy the cravings of hunger. There are two curses here, first our weakness, secondly our hatred, our dried-up hearts. You may talk doctrines by the millions, you may have sects by the hundreds of millions; aye, but it is nothing until you have the heart to feel; feel for them as your Veda teaches you, till you find they are parts of your bodies, till you realise that you and they, the poor and the rich, the saint and the sinner, are all parts of One Infinite Whole, which you call Brahman.

VIVEKANANDA

The dualism of Lutheran theology, which separated the realm of grace from the social order, and held each to be autonomous under God as Redeemer and as Creator, has made it possible for Christians . . . to acquiesce in policies which the Christian conscience would otherwise condemn.

A. E. GARVIE

When we love a person, we love all that belongs to him; we extend to the children the affection which we feel for the father. Now every Soul is a daughter of the Father in heaven. How can this world . . . be separated from the spiritual world? Those who despise what is so nearly akin to the spiritual world, prove that they know nothing of the spiritual world, except in name.

PLOTINUS

It is even possible to doubt, whether the anxiety for eternal safety, which bids a man neglect all social duty, and concentrate all the strength and every moment of existence upon the state of his own soul, be anything better than a most insidious and most dangerous form of selfishness.

CHARLES BEARD

CHRIST AND THIS WORLD

To those who are inclined to deny the immediate influence of theology upon society and to accept the necessity for a divorce between religion and life it is important to realize that if the fact of Christ constrained men to a radical change in their concept of God it also disclosed and made possible for them a radically new relationship to mankind in an unprecedented type of human community. It may indeed be argued that if St. Paul had not experienced in his dealings with his fellow Christians the love that he so fully and intimately describes to the Corinthians he could never have appreciated or proclaimed the sufficiency of this love as the supreme quality of God. Certainly it was out of the Pentecostal community, which was at once the end-product of the ministry of Jesus and the instrument for the perpetuation of his incarnate work, that the new interpretation of God and man was conceived. But it is plain that here as elsewhere the question of precedence is unimportant. In Christ all things had been made new, and the Christian concept of reality and the Christian way of living were alike due to the same

437

creative event. They have the same origin and, if either is to be healthy, must remain inseparably associated.

For Jesus himself the two are indivisible. In convincing men of the reality and character of God he is also and by the same means preparing them for fellowship with one another, and this fellowship is attained only when they have been released into a full experience of dependence and adoration. . . . A community of worship and service is the goal to which the Christian is committed, and to treat the contemplative and the practical as though they were alternatives, or to cultivate one while neglecting the other, is to imperil both. . . .

We Christians, and the Church, only too often have failed to harmonize devotion with action and, indeed, have deliberately separated the sacred from the secular by introducing a double standard of ethics and reserving the term religious for the life of the cloister. This alone is perhaps a sufficient reason for the weakness of our witness and the ineffectiveness of our lives. Surely it is not enough to urge that we should season our mundane activities with a little of the spice of contemplation, or pay some heed to the social, political and economic implications of our faith. More is required if our lives are to be "all of a piece and all in God", and it may well be that in this respect traditional practices and conventions need serious criticism. It can hardly be denied that fulness of life is not, as it should be, a general attribute of Christians, or that too few of them are successful in bringing their whole activities within the sphere of their religion.

It is at least clear from the example of Jesus that he not only regarded his two commandments as inseparable, but that both by his teaching and his practice he insisted that neither could be fulfilled in isolation. To say Lord, Lord and not to behave accordingly was as wrong as to suppose that human affairs would go well if God's Kingdom were not our first objective. Accordingly, in his training of his disciples he sent them out on a mission of service before they had more than begun to appreciate the meaning of his message. Faith and practice must go together; the doing of the works is a condition of the learning of the doctrine, and to see is inevitably to act; the two advance *pari passu*.

When we consider more closely the character of this new relationship, which Christians call the Fellowship of the Holy Spirit, and the means by which the earliest disciples were fitted to experience it, we shall discover how essential to its attainment was this combination. For no human society of which we have record has been so amazingly creative both in thought and deed, so passionately vital in its achievements, and so permanently influential in its effects. The energy that carried the religion of a crucified Jew in less than a century to the imperial palace; the courage that baffled Nero and won the admiration of his brutalized people; the spiritual quality of the writings that give the New Testament its unique and perennial value; the inspiration that fashioned out of the slaves and petty tradesmen of a pagan empire a society that revolutionized history; and the solidarity that enabled it to resist the disintegrating tensions of persecutions from without and of heresies from within—these testify to a fulness of life altogether unprecedented and to a fellowship in which the members could realize their full stature and the whole could function as a single organism.

CHARLES E. RAVEN

Religion is world loyalty.

A. N. WHITEHEAD

Beware of the man whose god is in the skies.

BERNARD SHAW

§ 6

God's mercy is over all his works, but divines of all sorts lessen that mercy too much.

SWIFT

THE EIGHTEENTH CENTURY

Sing, O ye Heavens, and shout, all ye lower parts of the earth, this is our God, that varies not, whose first creating love knows no change but into a redeeming pity towards all His fallen creatures.

Look now at warring Christendom. What smallest drop of pity towards sinners is to be found in it? Or how could a spirit all-hellish more fully contrive and hasten their destruction? It stirs up and kindles every passion of fallen nature that is contrary to the all-humble, all-meek, all-loving, all-forgiving, all-saving Spirit of Christ. . . .

Again, would you further see the fall of the universal Church from being led by the Spirit of Christ, to be guided by the inspiration of the great fiery dragon, look at all European Christendom

439

sailing round the globe with fire and sword and every murdering art of war to seize the possessions and kill the inhabitants of both the Indies. What natural right of man, what supernatural virtue, which Christ brought down from Heaven, was not here trodden underfoot? All that you ever read or heard of heathen barbarity was here outdone by Christian conquerors. And to this day, what wars of Christians against Christians, blended with scalping heathen, still keep staining the earth and the seas with human blood for a miserable share in the spoils of a plundered heathen world! A world which should have heard or seen or felt nothing from the followers of Christ but a divine love that had forced them from distant lands and through the perils of long seas to visit strangers with those glad tidings of peace and salvation to all the world, which angels from Heaven and shepherds on earth proclaimed at the birth of Christ. . . .

St. Paul speaks of a natural man that cannot know the things of God, but to whom they are mere foolishness. . . . This is the natural man who, having got into the Church and Church power, has turned the things of God into things of this world. Had this man been kept out of the Church, the Church had kept its first purity to this day, for its fallen state is nothing else but its fall into the hands of the natural man of this world. And when this is the state of the Church, the wisdom of this world (which always loves its own) will be in love with it, will spare no cost to maintain it, will make laws, fight battles in defence of it, and condemn every man as heretical who dares speak a word against this glorious image of a Church which the wisdom of this world has set up.

This is the great Antichrist, which is neither better nor worse nor anything else but the spirit of Satan working against Christ in the strength and subtlety of earthly wisdom.

If, therefore, you take anything to be Church-reformation but a full departure from the wisdom of this world, or anything to be your entrance into a salvation-Church but the nature, spirit, and works of Christ become living in you, then, whether Papist or Protestant, reformation or no reformation, all will be just as much good to you as when a Sadducee turns publican, or from a publican becomes a Pharisee. For the Church of Christ, as it is the door of salvation, is nothing else but Christ himself. Christ in us, or we in His Church, is the same thing. When that is alive, wills and works in you, which was alive in Christ, then you are in His Church; for that which He was, that must they be who are His.

WILLIAM LAW

THE TWENTIETH CENTURY

There was a silence, and then the aviator cried, "The padres were trying on both sides to hide their voices."

"What's that mean?" said the astonished zouave.

"Are you taking leave of 'em, old chap?" asked a chasseur wounded in the hand and with one arm bound to his body, as his eyes left the mummified limb for a moment to glance at the flying-man.

The latter's looks were distraught; he was trying to interpret a mysterious picture which everywhere he saw before his eyes—

"Up there, from the sky, you don't see much, you know. Among the squares of the fields and the little heaps of the villages the roads run like white cotton. You can make out, too, some hollow threads that look as if they'd been traced with a pin-point and scratched through fine sand. These nets that festoon the plain with regularly wavy marks, they're the trenches. Last Sunday morning I was flying over the firing-line. Between our first lines and their first lines, between their extreme edges, between the fringes of the two huge armies that are up against each other, looking at each other and not seeing, and waiting—it's not very far; sometimes forty yards, sometimes sixty. To me it looked about a stride, at the great height where I was planing. And behold I could make out two crowds, one among the Boches, and one of ours, in these parallel lines that seemed to touch each other; each was a solid, lively lump, and all around 'em were dots like grains of black sand scattered on grey sand, and these hardly budged—it didn't look like an alarm! So I went down several turns to investigate.

"Then I understood. It was Sunday, and there were two religious services being held under my eyes—the altar, the padre, and all the crowd of chaps. The more I went down the more I could see that the two things were alike—so exactly alike that it looked silly. One of the services—whichever you like—was a reflection of the other, and I wondered if I was seeing double. I went down lower; they didn't fire at me. Why? I don't know at all. Then I could hear. I heard one murmur, one only. I could only gather a single prayer that came up to me *en bloc*, the sound of a single chant that passed by me on its way to heaven. I went to and fro in space to listen to this faint mixture of hymns that blended together just the same although they were one against the other; and the more they tried to get on top of each other, the more they were blended together up in the heights of the sky where I was floating.

"I got some shrapnel just at the moment when, very low down, I made out the two voices from the earth that made up the one— '*Gott mit uns!*' and 'God is with us!'—and I flew away" . . .

HENRI BARBUSSE (from Under Fire)

§ 7

Love is the abridgement of all theology.

ST. FRANÇOIS DE SALES

II. CRIME AND PUNISHMENT

For Hugh Klare
and in memory of
Roy Calvert

The Spirit of the Lord God is upon me; because the Lord hath anointed me to preach good tidings unto the meek; he hath sent me to bind up the brokenhearted, to proclaim liberty to the captives, and the opening of the prison to them that are bound . . .

ISAIAH

A soul in trouble is near unto God.

APOCRYPHAL SAYING OF ST. PETER

At some time in the day or the night think upon and call to mind all who are sick and sorrowful, who suffer affliction and poverty, the pain which prisoners endure who lie heavily fettered with iron.

ANONYMOUS (from the Ancren Riwle)

§ 2

Therefore thou art inexcusable, O man, whosoever thou art that judgest: for wherein thou judgest another, thou condemnest thyself; for thou that judgest doest the same things.

ROMANS

Consider too that thou doest many a wrong thing thyself and art much as others are, and if thou dost refrain from certain wrong-doings, yet hast thou a disposition inclinable thereto even supposing that through cowardice or a regard for thy good name or some such base consideration thou dost not actually commit them.

MARCUS AURELIUS

The germs of all things are in every heart, and the greatest criminals as well as the greatest heroes are but different modes of ourselves.

AMIEL

'INCOMPREHENSIBLE'

Engrossed in the day's 'news', I read
Of all in man that's vile and base;
Horrors confounding heart and head—
Massacre, murder, filth, disgrace:
Then paused. And thought did inward tend—
On my own past, and self, to dwell.

445

Whereat some inmate muttered, 'Friend,
If you and I plain truth must tell,
Everything human we comprehend,
Only too well, too well!'

WALTER DE LA MARE

We dare not even look within ourselves. If we were to tell a hundredth part of the dreams that come to an ordinary honest man, or of the desires which come into being in the body of a chaste woman, there would be a scandal and an outcry. Silence such monsters! Bolt and bar their cage! But let us admit that they exist, and that in the souls of the young they are insecurely fettered.

ROMAIN ROLLAND

From lowest to highest the distance is not so great.

ROMAIN ROLLAND

We must relinquish the notion that humanity is divided into two hostile camps, two different breeds of men, the just and the sinners —the first predestined for beatitude, the second for perdition. Nothing of the sort is true. We are all sinful, all tainted, and our Lord suffered for all of us. All are equally dear to Him, and it is to Him that the final judgment belongs. That is why Christ's words about love are directly followed by the words about judgment: "Judge not, that ye be not judged".

FATHER YELCHANINOV

If we may not judge, how shall we help our erring brother? By turning our attention to the beam in our own eye; only then, after we have struggled to remove it, shall we understand how deep-seated are the causes of sin, how hard it is to fight, through what means it can be cured, how great the pity and sympathy deserved by the sinner; and these feelings of yours, and your experience of the struggle with sin, will help to remove the mote from your brother's eye—through sympathy, example, love. Judgment will fall away of itself.

FATHER YELCHANINOV

We should hate sin only for love.

JULIANA OF NORWICH

446

You felons on trial in courts,
You convicts in prison-cells, you sentenced assassins chain'd and
  handcuff'd with iron,
Who am I too that I am not on trial or in prison?
Me ruthless and devilish as any, that my wrists are not chain'd with
  iron, or my ankles with iron? . . .
Inside these breast-bones I lie smutch'd and choked,
Beneath this face that appears so impassive hell's tides continually
  run,
Lusts and wickedness are acceptable to me,
I walk with delinquents with passionate love,
I feel I am of them—I belong to those convicts and prostitutes
  myself,
And henceforth I will not deny them—for how can I deny myself?

WALT WHITMAN

Beware of the man of complete unquestionable virtue, the up-standing self-righteous citizen, who for all creatures of weakness has one general attitude: "Give them hell".

DAVID ABRAHAMSEN

The first prison I ever saw had inscribed on it *Cease to do evil: learn to do well*; but as the inscription was on the outside, the prisoners could not read it. It should have been addressed to the self-righteous free spectator in the street, and should have run *All have sinned, and fallen short of the glory of God*.

BERNARD SHAW

The evil for which we punish others is of the same substance as the evil in our own thinking and feeling.

DAVID ABRAHAMSEN

Even the struggle against evil can itself easily degenerate into evil. The victory of the good is always positive; it does not deny life, it affirms it. We must begin by struggling against the evil in ourselves and not against that which we see in others, for too often feelings of hatred towards evil-doers are merely a form of self-affirmation.

BERDYAEV

Go therefore, cast out devils in Christ's name,
Heal thou the sick of spiritual disease,
Pity the evil, for thou art not sent
To smite with terror & with punishments
Those that are sick, like to the Pharisees
Crucifying & encompassing sea & land
For proselytes to tyranny & wrath;
But to the Publicans & Harlots go,
Teach them True Happiness, but let no curse
Go forth out of thy mouth to blight their peace;
For Hell is open'd to Heaven; thine eyes beheld
The dungeons burst & the Prisoners set free.

BLAKE

May I be born again and again, and suffer thousands of miseries, so that I may worship the only God that exists, the only God I believe in, the sum total of all souls—and, above all, my God the wicked, my God the miserable, my God the poor of all races, of all species, is the special object of my worship.

VIVEKANANDA

If a man can successfully manage to pronounce no sentence of condemnation, to bind no man, to imprison no man, to torture no man—if all this can be managed, a Christian may be a magistrate.

TERTULLIAN

§ 3

Man's desires are limited by his perceptions, none can desire what he has not perciev'd.

BLAKE

The cases of no conscience are sometimes cases of unawakened conscience.

BERNARD SHAW

Every moment we are enjoying the absolute bliss, though covered up, misunderstood and caricatured. Wherever there is any blessing, blissfulness, or joy, even the joy of the thief in stealing, it is that Absolute Bliss coming out; only it has become obscured, muddled up, as it were, with all sorts of extraneous conditions, and misunderstood.

VIVEKANANDA

448

I am often struck by the word Jesus used for sin. It comes from archery practice; to sin (in the thought of Jesus) means to miss the mark: miss the target. To miss the target at least implies that you are aiming at something. However wide of the mark the shots are going, a sinner is aiming at something. Take the lecherous man, the sex addict. What's he aiming at? A real experience of love surely—mad though his efforts be ever so to find it. Take the gambler: what is *he* aiming at? Surely making a big thing out of life: taking real risks to get it; real risks and terrifying. Isn't he playing (however upside down) with that precious gift called faith? He risks all on an Act. And our drunkards ... what are they aiming at? Most solemnly I say it, they want to be filled: filled with life, filled with spirit. They want to recover hope. Faith, hope and love —that's their real target, all of them—Life! They want to be filled with it: they take appalling risks for it: they are determined to live; determined to love. I am not condoning it. Poor souls, they don't condone it themselves. They are missing their mark; and don't they know it? But at least they go on demanding Life. Dare we say this is why Jesus loved them? I am sure the sinners crowded round Him (in the market-place and pub) because they knew He understood. He didn't just love sinners; He liked them. He saw their possibility. He loved sinners—not as the Pharisees did, because it was their duty to save; He loved them for wanting something badly: for wanting Life at all costs.

G. F. MACLEOD

There is in man an upwelling spring of life, energy, love, whatever you like to call it. If a course is not cut for it, it turns the ground round it into a swamp.

MARK RUTHERFORD

Our sins are the misdirected steps of a seeking Power that aims, not at sin, but at perfection, at something that we might call a divine virtue. Often they are the veils of a quality that has to be transformed and delivered out of this ugly disguise: otherwise, in the perfect providence of things, they would not have been suffered to exist or to continue.

AUROBINDO

Even in the murderer the Pure Soul is there; It dies not. It was his mistake; he could not manifest It; he had covered It up.

VIVEKANANDA

The Jews would not willingly tread upon the smallest piece of paper in their way, but took it up; for possibly, said they, the name of God may be on it. Though there was a little superstition in this, yet truly there is nothing but good religion in it, if we apply it to men. Trample not on any; there may be some work of grace there, that thou knowest not of. The name of God may be written upon that soul thou treadest on; it may be a soul that Christ thought so much of, as to give His precious blood for it; therefore despise it not.

S. T. COLERIDGE

Do not be afraid of Brother Sin. He is a leper; but when thou hast washed his feet, then shalt thou see . . . in them . . . the wounds of Christ. Yea, when for us Christ died—with Him also died—Brother Sin.

ST. FRANCIS (in a Housman play)

'Tis Nature's law
That none, the meanest of created things,
Of forms created the most vile and brute,
The dullest or most noxious, should exist
Divorced from good—a spirit and pulse of good,
A life and soul, to every mode of being
Inseparably linked. Then be assured
That least of all can aught—that ever owned
The heaven-regarding eye and front sublime
Which man is born to—sink, howe'er depressed,
So low as to be scorned without a sin;
Without offence to God cast out of view. . . .

WORDSWORTH

There is no soul
But it's unlike all others in the world
Nor one but lifts a strangeness to God's love,
Till that's grown infinite, and therefore none
Whose loss were less than irremediable,
Although it were the wickedest in the world.

W. B. YEATS

Sometimes one would know a man for years in prison and despise him and think that he was not a human being but a brute. And suddenly a moment will come by chance when his soul will suddenly reveal itself in an involuntary outburst, and you see in it such wealth, such feeling, such heart, such a vivid understanding of its own suffering, and of the suffering of others, that your eyes are open and for the first moment you can't believe what you have seen and heard yourself.

DOSTOEVSKY (from *The House of the Dead*)

Year by year I had all these fellow creatures to look at and to talk to, for as long as I chose. It was a swift communion of souls, but in prison you come straight to the point. It is a temple of truth. No one else seemed to be interested, no one wanted to take them from me. Many people thought they did not get the truth from prisoners. These were the people who did not realize the colour of red tape. Prisoners themselves, not their classification, nor marks, nor industry, nor gruel, nor cell furniture, were the real objects of my scrutiny. These other things were my excuse for being there.

I soon became fairly expert at selecting from the long rows of cells, or from the associated working parties, the people who were worth my while. I had only to go to them in order to receive. They gave me so much that I was ashamed of my own poverty of response. They held up to me a mirror in which to see myself at new angles. They searched my soul, they showed me aspects of existence which I had ignored. They reflected their dumb pains upon me, and laid before me elemental secrets of character and inheritance. I could not begin to live until I had lived first with them. Whether hunted by or hunting life, they showed me an amount of glowing *élan vital* that was a denial of all theories of lost souls.

MARY GORDON, *at one time H.M. Inspector of Prisons*

In a pleasant spring morning all men's sins are forgiven. Such a day is a truce to vice. While such a sun holds out to burn, the vilest sinner may return. Through our own recovered innocence we discern the innocence of our neighbours. You may have known your neighbour yesterday for a thief, a drunkard, or a sensualist, and merely pitied or despised him, and despaired of the world; but the sun shines bright and warm this first spring morning, recreating the world, and you meet him at some serene work, and see how his exhausted and debauched veins expand with still joy and bless the new day, feel the spring influence with the innocence of infancy, and all his faults are forgotten. There is not only an atmosphere of good will about him, but even a savour of holiness groping for expression, blindly and ineffectually perhaps, like a new-born instinct, and for a short hour the south hill side echoes to no vulgar jest. You see some innocent fair shoots preparing to burst from his gnarled rind and try another year's life, tender and fresh as the youngest plant. Even he has entered into the joy of his Lord. Why the jailer does not leave open his prison doors—why the judge does not dismiss his case—why the preacher does not dismiss his congregation! It is because they do not obey the hint which God gives them, nor accept the pardon which he freely offers to all.

THOREAU

When, in 1925, I started my clinical clerkship at the Royal Norwegian University Clinic in Oslo, we were one day making the rounds with our professor. He was at that time in his sixties and we considered him old, although thinking today of my own age I believe he was young. The professor was comfortably seated in a chair while we were standing around listening to him, when we suddenly heard high screams in the corridor. We all rushed out and saw a young fellow running toward us with two men in close pursuit. The frightened young man took refuge behind us. At that point the professor asked what was the matter. The pursuers explained that the young man was a criminal whom they had been trailing for several days. They had seen him walking into the hospital and had orders to take him to the police station.

One of the detectives started to walk behind us to catch the man, but the professor shot out like lightning and placed himself between them. "This man is a criminal," said the detective in a determined voice and made a grab for him. The professor stood straight as a ramrod and retorted, "I have no criminals here, I have only sick people". And pointing, he added one word: "Go!" The detectives looked at each other, turned around and left slowly.

DAVID ABRAHAMSEN

Most people believe that criminals are solely responsible for their guilt. Crime and criminals have existed since man was born, and society, from the earliest primitive cultures until our own, has been more intent on punishing the wrongdoer than in understanding why he broke its laws.

My work has, for years, led me into the study of the maladjustments of individuals, especially delinquents, and through them to the riddle of crime itself. I found that I was faced not only with the problem of handling those unfortunates who were truant or who had stolen or raped or even killed. I was also faced with a necessity for complete reorientation of our basic understanding of criminal behaviour.

I reached the inescapable conclusion that society, with all its ramifications of family, school, community and government agencies, had to share the responsibility of guilt together with the particular individual involved. I had to believe that the offender becomes guilty because of the influence of his family, his education, and of society. This is not to say that there is no weakness in the person who commits the crime. But as we examined case after case we invariably asked ourselves: "Where were the parents, the school, the community, when this crime was committed?"

DAVID ABRAHAMSEN

For no man is voluntarily bad; but the bad become bad by reason of an ill disposition of the body and bad education, things which are hateful to every man and happen to him against his will.

PLATO

Every Criminal [was once] an Infant Love.

BLAKE

You know also that the beginning is the most important part of any work, especially in the case of a young and tender thing; for that is the time at which the character is being formed and the desired impression is more readily taken.

PLATO

From what has been stated, the nature of the education of little children in heaven should be evident, namely, that by the understanding of truth and the wisdom of love they are introduced into angelic life; this consists in love to the Lord and mutual love, in both of which there is innocence.

SWEDENBORG

A DIALOGUE ON YOUTH AND CRIME

But then, if I am right, certain professors of education must be wrong when they say that they can put a knowledge into the soul which was not there before, like sight into blind eyes.

453

They undoubtedly say this, he replied.

Whereas, our argument shows that the power and capacity of learning exists in the soul already; and that just as the eye was unable to turn from darkness to light without the whole body, so too the instrument of knowledge can only by the movement of the whole soul be turned from the world of becoming [i.e. this world of ever-changing phenomena] into that of being [i.e. the eternal world of unchangeable reality], and learn by degrees to endure the sight of being, and of the brightest and best of being, or, in other words, of the good.

Very true.

And must there not be some art which will effect conversion in the easiest and quickest manner?—convert, not implant the faculty of sight, for that exists already, but has been turned in the wrong direction, and is looking away from the truth.

Yes, he said, such an art may be presumed.

And whereas the other so-called virtues of the soul seem to be akin to bodily qualities, for even when they are not originally innate they can be implanted later by habit and exercise, the virtue of wisdom more than anything else contains a divine element which always remains, and by this conversion is rendered useful and profitable; or on the other hand, hurtful and useless. Did you never observe the narrow intelligence flashing from the keen eye of a clever rogue—how eager he is, how clearly his paltry soul sees the way to his end; he is the reverse of blind, but his keen eyesight is forced into the service of evil, and he is mischievous in proportion to his cleverness?

Very true, he said.

But if there had been a circumcision of such natures in the days of their youth; and had they been severed from those sensual pleasures, such as eating and drinking, which, like leaden weights, were attached to them at their birth, and which drag them down and turn the vision of their souls upon the things that are below—if, I say, they had been released from these impediments and turned in the opposite direction, the very same faculty in them would have seen the truth as keenly as they see what their eyes are turned to now.

PLATO

In the lost boyhood of Judas
Christ was betrayed.

A. E.

The man who has graduated from the flogging block at Eton to the bench from which he sentences the garotter to be flogged is the same social product as the garotter who has been kicked by his father and cuffed by his mother until he has grown strong enough to throttle and rob the rich citizen whose money he desires.

BERNARD SHAW

. . . That iron man was born like me,
    And he was once an ardent boy:
He must have felt, in infancy,
    The glory of a summer sky.

Though storms untold his mind have tossed,
    He cannot utterly have lost
Remembrance of his early home—
    So lost that not a gleam may come;

No vision of his mother's face
    When she so fondly would set free
Her darling child from her embrace
    To roam till eve at liberty:

Nor of his haunts, nor of the flowers
    His tiny hand would grateful bear
Returning from the darkening bowers,
    To weave into her glossy hair.

I saw the light breeze kiss his cheek,
    His fingers 'mid the roses twined;
I watched to mark one transient streak
    Of pensive softness shade his mind.

The open window showed around
    A glowing park and glorious sky,
And thick woods swelling with the sound
    Of Nature's mingled harmony.

Silent he sat. That stormy breast
 At length, I said, has deigned to rest;
At length above that spirit flows
    The waveless ocean of repose.

Let me draw near: 'twill soothe to view
    His dark eyes dimmed with holy dew;

Remorse even now may wake within,
And half unchain his soul from sin.

Perhaps this is the destined hour
When hell shall lose its fatal power
And heaven itself shall bend above
To hail the soul redeemed by love. . . .

EMILY BRONTË

§ 4

The conception of punishment as a moral duty to impose suffering in order to reform and regenerate the criminal is false and always has a touch of bigotry and hypocrisy about it.

BERDYAEV

"A good deal of punishment," she used to say, "is mere useless pain."

MARK RUTHERFORD

Crime cannot be hindered by punishment; it will always find some shape and outlet, unpunishable or unclosed. Crime can only be truly hindered by letting no man grow up a criminal—by taking away the will to commit sin; not by mere punishment of its commission. Crime, small and great, cannot truly be stayed by education of the intellect only, which is on some men wasted, and for others mischievous; but education of the heart, which is alike good and necessary for all.

JOHN RUSKIN

Once admit that if I do something wicked to you we are quits when you do something equally wicked to me, and you are bound to admit also that the two blacks make a white. Our criminal system is an organized attempt to produce white by two blacks. Common sense should doggedly refuse to believe that evil can be abolished by duplicating it. But common sense is not so logical; and thus we get the present grotesque spectacle of a judge committing thousands of horrible crimes in order that thousands of criminals may feel that they have balanced their moral accounts.

BERNARD SHAW

As part of the technique of definition and adjudication of the criminal act, we have blithely assumed that punishment for evil has a good outcome. Somewhere there is the assumption that by doing evil to evil-doers we shall achieve good ends in the person so treated. Every experience . . . proves the opposite. There is not a shred of evidence that punishment—severe or mild, with good intentions or bad ones—has beneficial effects on the future lives of the men punished. If experience proves anything, it proves the opposite. It proves that evil, even when done in a good cause, has evil consequences. All that we know about prisons indicates that punishment merely confirms the criminal in his career. There is implicit in our procedure, of course, the old Benthamite assumption that pain and pleasure can be balanced off at some equitable point. The assumption is false and derived from a false reading of human nature. Punishment does not reform. It does not alter the criminal who is already formed, nor does it act as a deterrent upon others who are thrown in the way of crime by the subtle incidence of companionship, habit, appetite, judgment, and opportunity. If we have learned nothing else from our experience, we have learned that to send a criminal to prison is almost to make certain that we shall have the task of sending him again, after his release . . .

The present method of punishment is an empty and expensive exercise in futility, ending only in chagrin and bitterness and further crime and further punishment. We need an alternative to punishment . . .

FRANK TANNENBAUM

Vengeance is mine, saith the Lord; and that means that it is not the Lord Chief Justice's.

BERNARD SHAW

That there is Justice in the world
Even the fool who hath said in his heart
There is no God
Would be unlikely wholly to deny:
But if he did, even he would not be such a fool
As the man who declares that there is Justice in the world
And that he can not only see it plainly but must proceed to
administer it with perfect justice.
There is no perfectly just man
Because the vision of Justice is the pleasure of God alone.

And that is why the divine part in all men
Longs to see justice and to live by it;
While the enemy of God that is in each of us
Is always trying to make us satisfied with what we can see of Justice
    without God,
As though He were bound to ratify automatically
Whatever a man-made judge with his own reason decides is just
Provided a sufficiently large number of other men be persuaded to
    agree with him.

DAVID GASCOYNE

Neither Jesus' teaching nor Paul's means that justice has been dethroned by love; it does mean that all human relationships must ultimately be based on the Gospel of love; that justice truly "fulfilled" is an outcome of love, rather than love a mere by-product of justice; that if we aim at love we shall establish justice by the way; that we can in fact secure justice only when we aim primarily not at it, but at the love out of which it springs.

G. H. C. MACGREGOR

The pearl of Justice is found in the heart of mercy.

ST. CATHERINE OF SIENA

First citizen: Is there to be no such thing as justice?
Francis: With God, Brother: but with men the only justice is—
    mercy.

IN A HOUSMAN PLAY

And now remember that in My Torah justice and mercy are commingled; for if it were all mercy, how would sin not destroy the world? and if it were all justice, how would justice not destroy the sinner? Wherefore, since it is permitted thee to behold Me face to face, when My face is justice let thine be mercy.

GOD TO MOSES (from a *Midrash*)

The actions of men send forth either direct or reflected rays. The first are mercy, the second justice. The reflected rays are many times weaker than the direct rays, even as justice is many times weaker than mercy.

RABBI PINHAS OF KORETZ

458

God Himself commanded Abraham to sacrifice Isaac, yet Abraham listened to an angel and saved Isaac's life. Why? Because to harm a man a command from a high tribunal is required, but to save a man only a word from the lowest authority is needed.

RABBI MOSHE LEIB OF SASOV

Man is not made for justice from his fellow, but for love, which is greater than justice, and by including supersedes justice. *Mere* justice is an impossibility, a fiction of analysis. . . . Justice to be justice must be much more than justice. Love is the law of our condition, without which we can no more render justice than a man can keep a straight line, walking in the dark.

GEORGE MACDONALD

What shall I do? what could I do if I could find these Criminals?
I could not dare to take vengeance, for all things are so constructed
And builded by the Divine hand that the sinner shall always escape,
And he who takes vengeance alone is the criminal of Providence.
If I should dare to lay my finger on a grain of sand
In way of vengeance, I punish the already punish'd. O whom
Should I pity if I pity not the sinner who is gone astray?
O Albion, if thou takest vengeance, if thou revengest thy wrongs,
Thou art for ever lost! What can I do to hinder the Sons
Of Albion from taking vengeance? or how shall I them perswade?

BLAKE

Whatever Book is for Vengeance for Sin and Whatever Book is Against the Forgiveness of Sins is not of the Father, but of Satan the Accuser and Father of Hell.

BLAKE

Every Christian must reject with detestation that covert propaganda for cruelty which tries to drive mercy out of the world by calling it names such as "Humanitarianism" and "Sentimentality".

C. S. LEWIS

Yea, truth and justice then
Will down return to men,
Orbed in a rainbow; and, like glories wearing,
Mercy will sit between,
Throned in celestial sheen,
With radiant feet the tissued clouds down steering;
And Heaven, as at some festival,
Will open wide the gates of her high palace hall.

MILTON (from *On the Morning of Christ's Nativity*)

THE LAW OF GOD AND THE LAW OF MAN

From childhood I was taught that Christ was God and that his teaching was divine, but at the same time I was taught to respect those institutions which secured by violence my safety from evil men. I was taught to respect these institutions by the priests. I was taught to resist the evil man, and it was inculcated that it is degrading and shameful to submit to the evil man and to endure him. They taught me to judge and to execute.

All my circumstances, my tranquillity, the safety of myself and my family and my property were all based on the law repudiated by Christ, on the law of a tooth for a tooth. The doctors of the Church taught that Christ's teaching was divine, but its performance impossible on account of human frailty, and only Christ's blessing can assist its performance. The worldly teachers and the whole construction of our life plainly admitted the impracticability and fantastic nature of Christ's teaching, and by words and deeds taught what was opposed to it. The admission of the impracticability of God's teaching had gradually to such a degree impregnated me and had become so familiar, and it coincided to such a degree with my desires, that I had never before noticed the contradiction with which I was faced.

Christ says: 'Resist not him that is evil'. The purpose of the courts is to resist the evil man. Christ tells us to return good for evil. The courts repay evil for evil. Christ tells us not to distinguish good people from bad. The courts are entirely concerned in making the distinction. Christ says, forgive all men. Forgive not once, not seven times, but endlessly. Love your enemies and do good to them that hate you. The courts do not forgive, but punish. They deal out not good but evil to those they call the enemies of society.

One need only understand the law of Christ in its full meaning, with all its consequences, in order to understand that Christ's teaching is not contrary to man's nature, but that it really consists in rejecting what is contrary to man's nature, namely, the visionary human doctrine of resistance to evil which now makes life unhappy.

Christ's doctrine of non-resistance to him that is evil is a dream! But that the life of men, in whose souls pity and love for one another is implanted, has been passed, and is now being passed, by some in organizing executions, lashes, handcuffs, penal servitude, gallows, shootings, solitary confinements, prisons for women and children— and the life of others in carrying out all these horrors, and the life of a third set in evading these sufferings and avenging themselves for them—is this not a dreadful dream?

One has but to understand Christ's teaching to understand that the world, not that which God gave for man's delight but the world men have devised for their own destruction, is a dream, and a very wild and terrible dream—the raving of a maniac from which one need but awake in order never to return to that terrible nightmare.

God descended to earth; the Son of God—one of the Persons of the Trinity—became flesh and redeemed Adam's sin; this God, we were taught to think, must have said something secret, mystical, difficult to understand, and only to be understood by the aid of faith and the sacraments; and suddenly it appears that the word of God is so simple, so clear, so reasonable. God says simply: Do not do evil to one another—and there will be no evil. Is it possible that God's revelation is so simple? Can it be that God only said that? It seems to us that we all knew that: it is so simple.

Elijah the prophet, fleeing from men, hid in a cave, and it was revealed to him that God would appear to him at the entrance to the cave. A storm arose that broke the trees. Elijah thought this was God, and looked; but God was not there. Then came thunder; the thunder and lightning were terrible. Elijah went out to look whether God was not there; but God was not there either. Then there came an earthquake; fire arose from the earth, the rocks were rent, and the mountains quaked. Elijah looked, but God was still not there. Then a light, quiet breeze arose, bringing the refreshing scent of the fields. Elijah looked—and God was there! Such, too, are these simple words of God: 'Resist not him that is evil'.

They are very simple, but in them is expressed the law of God and man, one and eternal. Only goodness, meeting evil and not infected by it, conquers evil. That this is so is in man's spiritual

461

world an immutable law comparable to the law of Galileo, but even *more immutable*, clearer and more complete. People may deviate from it and hide it from others, but nevertheless the progress of humanity towards what is good can only be accomplished by that path. Every step forward is made solely in the path of non-resistance to evil. And in the face of all possible temptations and threats the disciples of Christ may, with more assurance than Galileo, declare: 'And yet, not by violence, but by goodness alone can you destroy evil'. If that advance is slow, this is thanks solely to the fact that the clearness, simplicity, reasonableness, inevitability, and necessity of Christ's teaching is hidden from the majority of men in the most cunning and dangerous way, hidden under a different doctrine falsely called his.

TOLSTOY

For I desired mercy, and not sacrifice; and the knowledge of God more than burnt offerings.

HOSEA

§ 5

Brother, do not make prisoners; for he that puts others in prison is himself a prisoner.

ST. FRANCIS (*in a Housman play*)

Whilst we have prisons it matters little which of us occupy the cells.

BERNARD SHAW

Imprisonment cannot be fully understood by those who do not understand freedom.

BERNARD SHAW

Judges spend their lives consigning their fellow creatures to prison; and when some whisper reaches them that prisons are horribly cruel and destructive places, and that no creature fit to live should be sent there, they only remark calmly that prisons are not meant to be comfortable, which is no doubt the consideration that reconciled Pontius Pilate to the practice of crucifixion.

BERNARD SHAW

As long as the principle of punishment is admitted, and the Sermon on the Mount ridiculed as an unpractical outburst of anarchism and sentimentality, the public will always be reassured . . . by the romances of Prison Commissioners like Du Cane and Sir Evelyn Ruggles-Brise, who arrange prisons as children build houses with toy bricks, and finally become so pleased with their arrangements that they describe them in terms which make us wonder that they do not commit crimes themselves to qualify themselves for residence in their pet paradises.

BERNARD SHAW

> As he went through Cold-Bath Fields he saw
> A solitary cell;
> And the Devil was pleased, for it gave him a hint
> For improving his prisons in Hell.

S. T. COLERIDGE

GALSWORTHY'S "JUSTICE", ACT III, SCENE III

Falder's cell, a whitewashed space thirteen feet broad by seven deep, and nine feet high, with a rounded ceiling. The floor is of shiny blackened bricks. The barred window, with a ventilator, is high up in the middle of the end wall. In the middle of the opposite end wall is the narrow door. In a corner are the mattress and bedding rolled up (two blankets, two sheets, and a coverlet). Above them is a quarter-circular wooden shelf, on which is a Bible and several little devotional books, piled in a symmetrical pyramid; there are also a black hair-brush, tooth-brush, and a bit of soap. In another corner is the wooden frame of a bed, standing on end. There is a dark ventilator under the window, and another over the door. Falder's work (a shirt to which he is putting button-holes) is hung to a nail on the wall over a small wooden table, on which the novel "Lorna Doone" lies open. Low down in the corner by the door is a thick glass screen, about a foot square, covering the gas-jet let into the wall. There is also a wooden stool, and a pair of shoes beneath it. Three bright round tins are set under the window.

In fast-failing daylight, Falder, in his stockings, is seen standing motionless, with his head inclined towards the door, listening. He moves a little closer to the door, his stockinged feet making no noise. He stops at the door. He is trying harder and harder to hear something, any little thing that is going on outside. He springs suddenly upright—

463

as if at a sound—and remains perfectly motionless. Then, with a heavy sigh, he moves to his work, and stands looking at it, with his head down; he does a stitch or two, having the air of a man so lost in sadness that each stitch is, as it were, a coming to life. Then, turning abruptly, he begins pacing the cell, moving his head, like an animal pacing its cage. He stops again at the door, listens, and, placing the palms of his hands against it with his fingers spread out, leans his forehead against the iron. Turning from it presently, he moves slowly back towards the window, tracing his way with his finger along the top line of the distemper that runs round the walls. He stops under the window, and, picking up the lid of one of the tins, peers into it, as if trying to make a companion of his own face. It has grown very nearly dark. Suddenly the lid falls out of his hand with a clatter—the only sound that has broken the silence—and he stands staring intently at the wall where the stuff of the shirt is hanging rather white in the darkness—he seems to be seeing somebody or something there. There is a sharp tap and click; the cell light behind the glass screen has been turned up. The cell is brightly lighted. Falder is seen gasping for breath.

A sound from far away, as of distant, dull beating on thick metal, is suddenly audible. Falder shrinks back, not able to bear this sudden clamour. But the sound grows, as though some great tumbril were rolling towards the cell. And gradually it seems to hypnotize him. He begins creeping inch by inch nearer to the door. The banging sound, travelling from cell to cell, draws closer and closer; Falder's hands are seen moving as if his spirit had already joined in this beating, and the sound swells till it seems to have entered the very cell. He suddenly raises his clenched fists. Panting violently, he flings himself at his door, and beats on it. The curtain falls.

JOHN GALSWORTHY

AN AMERICAN PRISON

One Saturday afternoon at the prison * an inmate said, "The tension of these places is unbelievable." He had committed his first crime at the age of forty-five—turned thief to feed his family. He was an intelligent, educated man. "My weakness was a spiritual weakness. Not mental. And through the long hours of meditation in the silence of the night, I've learned. I got what I deserve. But the punishment never ends. This abnormal life, this regulated life, the dull, deadly, corroding monotony—you can't expect anything good to accrue from such a life. Of course we know this is no hotel,

464

it's a prison. There are many idiots here that must be disciplined. The knives—a man that would even think in terms of having a knife—" he gestured. "Some of them are like animals. This is a vicious place. It is devoid of love, built on hate and punishment. Hate begets more hate. Where does it end? Many good men go to prison, but very few come out. Prison brutalizes a man, brutalizes and humiliates him. You have a number and you are not allowed to forget it. You are looked on like the teeth in a gear wheel. They don't look for the best in you—they look for the worst. You go to the shower all naked like animals, it's coarse, never a kind word, there is no privacy. You cease to be looked upon as a human being. You are a pariah. It is intellectual and moral brutality. There is a wonderful field here for psychiatrists, men who ask, 'What's wrong with this human being?' You never hear that question here. Here there is no hope, nothing. Without hope you're a zombie, a living dead man. They come to life when there is a riot somewhere else. Then there is feverish excitement. I never saw such an outpouring of hatred as I saw in the riot. The hate in here would sicken a pig. Hate begets hate, violence begets violence. Here all you hear is lock up, lock up, lock up, day after day, year after year in this cold grey world, you lose touch with the decent men, no one ever says 'please' or 'thank you'—" He broke off, a red-faced Irishman, a devout Catholic, and looked upward, saying, "If God spares me I'll never come back." But they do.

    ★ Jackson, Michigan.   JOHN BARTLOW MARTIN

A BRITISH PRISON

During my service I found nothing in the prison system to interest me, except as a gigantic irrelevance—a social curiosity. If the system had a good effect on any prisoner, I failed to mark it. I have no shadow of a doubt of its power to demoralise, or of its cruelty. It appears to me not to belong to this time or civilisation at all.

My main argument here is that we not only do not deter, but that we do actually make over our criminal to crime. The fallacy of applying force to a being who is inherently insusceptible of being managed by force lies in the fact that the proceeding ends, not in the alteration of the prisoner's point of view, but in his spiritually triumphing over us, and bringing the strong arm of the law to naught. We merely ill-treat a man or woman who still ignores and escapes us. . . .

Upon the boy or girl, man or woman taken by force and confined under our penal discipline, *consequences descend in response to natural laws* which we are powerless to counteract. If we hold people captive under certain conditions, the results will certainly appear. All down the history of imprisonment they have confronted us if we would have looked at them. Yet our discipline, and restraint of prisoners under it, is about as humane or scientific as to render a caged animal irritable and savage by confinement, and then to treat its irritability, or nervous exasperation, by tying it up and beating it. . . . Man, the most untameable in spirit of all creatures, cannot be reduced to submission by any such means. He can be held so tightly in confinement that he explodes, as he occasionally does, in a paroxysm of nervous excitement, or until his mental condition calls aloud for enquiry, but the one thing that he will not do, under this treatment, is change his point of view, or abandon the crime upon which we have merely caused him to focus his unconscious desires. . . .

Do *we* never consciously or unconsciously wish for luxury, wish to escape from pain, desire oblivion, seek refuge from reality, wish for another's death, and could punishment change *our* fancies?

This is the question for us who make the laws that punish. For our answer let us not look to such means as the imposition of hours of solitude, hunger and deprivation, and repression, to severe rule and continual punishment, to making of our criminal a maimed, inert, or over-excited slave. Let us rather hand him over, not to the hangman, but to the doctor, to the man of science, to the student of the whole man, to the educator, to the man who knows himself in so far as human knowledge will allow of it, to the man who can bring the most of human knowledge, human resource, and human feeling to bear on the problem, which we—have utterly failed to solve.

MARY GORDON, *at one time H.M. Inspector of Prisons*

PENAL WORK

My first impression on entering the prison was most revolting, and yet strange to say it seemed to me that life in prison was much easier than on the journey I had fancied it would be. . . . The labour, for instance, seemed to me by no means so hard, so *penal*, and only long afterwards I realized that the hardness, the penal character of the work lay not so much in its being difficult and uninterrupted as in its being *compulsory*, obligatory, enforced. The peasant in freedom works, I dare say, incomparably harder, sometimes even all night, especially in the summer; but he is working for himself, he is working with a rational object, and it makes it much easier for him than for the convict working at forced labour which is completely useless to himself. The idea has occurred to me that if one wanted to crush, to annihilate a man utterly, to inflict on him the most terrible of punishments so that the most ferocious murderer would shudder at it and dread it beforehand, one need only give him work of an absolutely, completely useless and irrational character. Though the hard labour now enforced is uninteresting and wearisome for the prisoner, yet in itself as work it is rational; the convict makes bricks, digs, does plastering, building; there is sense and meaning in such work. The convict worker sometimes even grows keen over it, tries to work more skilfully, faster, better. But if he had to pour water from one vessel into another and back, over and over again, to pound sand, to move a heap of earth from one place to another and back again—I believe the convict would hang himself in a few days or would commit a thousand crimes, preferring rather to die than endure such humiliation, shame and torture. Of course such a punishment would become a torture, a form of vengeance, and would be senseless, as it would achieve no rational object. But as something of such torture, senselessness, humiliation and shame is an inevitable element in all forced labour, penal labour is incomparably more painful than any free labour—just because it is forced.

DOSTOEVSKY (from *The House of the Dead*)

THE EFFECT OF REPRESSION

The prison authorities are sometimes surprised that after leading a quiet, exemplary life for some years, and even being made a foreman for his model behaviour, a convict with no apparent reason suddenly breaks out, as though he were possessed by a devil, plays pranks, drinks, makes an uproar and sometimes positively ventures on serious crimes—such as open disrespect to a superior officer, or even commits murder or rape. They look at him and marvel. And all the while possibly the cause of this sudden outbreak, in the man from whom one would least have expected it, is simply the poignant hysterical craving for self-expression, the unconscious yearning for himself, the desire to assert himself, to assert his crushed personality, a desire which suddenly takes possession of him and reaches the pitch of fury, of spite, of mental aberration, of fits and nervous convulsions. So perhaps a man buried alive and awakening in his coffin might beat upon its lid and struggle to fling it off, though of course reason might convince him that all his efforts would be useless; but the trouble is that it is not a question of reason, it is a question of nerves. We must take into consideration also that almost every expression of personality on the part of a convict is looked upon as a crime, and so it makes no difference whether it is a small offence or a great one. If he is to drink he may as well do it thoroughly, if he is to venture on anything he may as well venture on everything, even on a murder.

DOSTOEVSKY (from *The House of the Dead*)

A PRISONER'S RIGHT TO LIVE

In all cases where detention and restraint are called for, the criminal's right to contact with all the spiritual influences of his day should be respected. Conversation, access to books and pictures and music, unfettered scientific, philosophic, and religious activity, change of scene and occupation, the free formation of friendships and acquaintances, marriage and parentage: in short, all the normal methods of creation and recreation must be available for criminals as for other persons, partly because deprivation of these things is severely punitive, and partly because it is destructive to the victim, and produces what we call the criminal type, making a cure impossible. Any specific liberty which the criminal's specific defects lead him to abuse will, no doubt, be taken from him; but his right to live must be accepted in the fullest sense, and not, as at present, as merely a right to breathe and circulate his blood. In short, a criminal must be treated, not as a man who has forfeited all normal rights and liberties by the breaking of a single law, but as one who, through some specific weakness or weaknesses, is incapable of exercising some specific liberty or liberties.

BERNARD SHAW

Nothing more unqualifies a Man to act with Prudence, than a Misfortune that is attended with Shame and Guilt.

SWIFT

Some people think that, if convicts are well fed and well kept and all the requirements of the law are satisfied, that is all that is necessary. This is an error, too. Everyone, whoever he may be and however down-trodden he may be, demands—though perhaps instinctively, perhaps unconsciously—respect for his dignity as a human being. The convict knows himself that he is a convict, an outcast, and knows his place before his commanding officer; but by no branding, by no fetters will you make him forget that he is a human being. And as he really is a human being he ought to be treated humanely. My God, yes! Humane treatment may humanize even one in whom the image of God has long been obscured. These "unfortunates" need even more humane treatment than others. It is their salvation and their joy. I have met some good-hearted, high-minded officers. I have seen the influence they exerted on these degraded creatures. A few kind words from them meant almost a moral resurrection for the convicts. They were as pleased as children and as children began to love them.

DOSTOEVSKY (from *The House of the Dead*)

Rabbi Baroka was walking one day through the crowded market-place of his town, and met Elijah. "Who of all this multitude has the best claim to Heaven?" asked the Rabbi. The prophet pointed to a disreputable, weird-looking creature, a turnkey. "That man yonder, because he is considerate to his prisoners."

THE TALMUD

Despite reforms here and there, despite a slow movement in public opinion, despite the efforts of a few devoted men and women, governors and warders and suchlike, to serve humanity, our prisons, by and large, still remain what they have continuously been since revengefulness and cruelty invented them—hideous landmarks of our paganism, very symbols of our unregenerate hostility to Christ. Their evil can be expressed in six short words: there is no love in them. They should be "vales of soul-making"—but what are they? Dead wastes of frozen matter, spiritless enclosures for an army of the damned. Everything about them is military: everything about them should be humane. How dreadful to think that a man in prison is no longer a man but a cipher: no longer Paul, no longer even Jones, but 10560! For it is in prison above all that a man should be Paul: there, above all, his quintessence, his uniqueness, what makes him Paul and no one else, must be released from the corruption that has spoiled it, and helped to come through in all its fruitfulness for himself and mankind. Coldness, impersonality, harsh commands, sullen obedience—these are the very last things required: living contact is required, the awakening of spirit by spirit. A prison is icy and static: it should be warm with a climate for growth.

And if there is no love in prisons, the cause is clear. Very few really believe in the ethics of Christ when the testing-point comes: when the sense of personal outrage is so great that hatred and revengefulness rise instinctively. But the testing-point is everything. Not to believe in Christian ethics, not to follow Christian ethics, at the testing-point is not to believe in them, not to follow them, at all. Well, little though I may follow them often, as I know very well, I do believe in them truly. I believe that every human soul is worth saving, infinitely worth saving; and that the human contribution towards saving it is to sympathise—which means suffer with—and love.

More and more, as I said earlier, I see our attitude to crime and punishment as the point on which everything turns: as more fundamental, even, than our attitude to wealth and poverty, to war and peace. For here at last is revealed, quite naked, the quality of our relation to our neighbour, and through him to God.

V. G.

Prisons have failed as deterrents to crime. They have failed as rehabilitative institutions. What then shall we do? Let us face it: Prisons should be abolished.

The prison cannot be reformed. It rests upon false premises. Nothing can improve it. It will never be anything but a graveyard of good intentions. Prison is not just the enemy of the prisoner. It is the enemy of society. This behemoth, this monster error, has nullified every good work. It must be done away with.

JOHN BARTLOW MARTIN

§ 6

THE "CAT" YESTERDAY

I do not know how it is now, but in the recent past there were gentlemen who derived from the power of flogging their victims something that suggests the Marquis de Sade and the Marquise de Brinvilliers. I imagine there is something in this sensation which

470

sends a thrill at once sweet and painful to the hearts of these gentlemen. There are people who are like tigers thirsting for blood. Anyone who has once experienced this power, this unlimited mastery of the body, blood and soul of a fellow man made of the same clay as himself, a brother in the law of Christ—anyone who has experienced the power and full licence to inflict the greatest humiliation upon another creature made in the image of God will unconsciously lose the mastery of his own sensations. Tyranny is a habit; it may develop, and it does develop at last, into a disease. I maintain that the very best of men may be coarsened and hardened into a brute by habit. Blood and power intoxicate; coarseness and depravity are developed; the mind and the heart are tolerant of the most abnormal things, till at last they come to relish them. The man and the citizen is lost for ever in the tyrant, and the return to human dignity, to repentance and regeneration becomes almost impossible. Moreover, the example, the possibility of such despotism, has a perverting influence on the whole of society: such power is a temptation. Society, which looks indifferently on such a phenomenon, is already contaminated to its very foundations. In short, the right of corporal punishment given to one man over another is one of the sores of social life, one of the strongest forces destructive of every germ, every effort in society towards civic feeling, and a sufficient cause for its inevitable dissolution.

DOSTOEVSKY (from *The House of the Dead*)

THE "CAT" TODAY

For flogging, as ordinarily understood, read a whipping with the cat o' nine tails. The effect of it is to tear the flesh off a man's back, whereupon a hurricane of strokes is rained down on the raw and bleeding surface. Some judges, however, prefer the birch—as making the recipient "look ridiculous". (The point is: you administer the whip to a man's back, but the birch to his bottom.) They believe, then, quite explicitly, in hurting and humiliating people; and these are high legal functionaries in an England nominally Christian.

*   *   *

There's more in the papers this morning to fill one with horror and shame. "Town demands the cat": "They say flog": "Bring back the lash"—these are some of the headlines I've read on my way to the office. At a Wimbledon meeting dissentients were howled down; and a single word, in enormous letters, caught my eye on the poster of a weekly with millions of readers—"FLOGGING". Why can't they be honest about it, and say "Bring back torture"? Because they dare not: because they must pay lip-service to Christianity. But I repeat and repeat again that the cat o' nine tails is torture, and I challenge anyone to deny it. In terms of the pain involved—the subject is so disgusting that one can hardly go on with it—there is little difference, for the time being, between lashing a man and flaying him: the two processes, indeed, are not dissimilar. And pain apart, what is the object, or if you like the result, of a lashing? Degradation: and to degrade still more thoroughly a man already steeped in degradation is the meanest, wickedest, stupidest thing I ever heard of. If you're going to make anything out of him, for the good of his own soul and of the society he menaces (and will continue to menace if he emerges from prison unchanged, not to say worsened), your object above all must be to give him, or give him back, self-respect.

A paragraph has just appeared in the papers about the flogging of a prisoner at Dartmoor. He was given twelve strokes of the cat, and "the doctor and Governor were present. *The man was medically examined after each stroke*". You understand why? His heart may give out, you may kill him: and while torture is permissible, murder isn't. So you flay and examine, you flay and examine, you flay and examine . . . up to ten, up to eleven, up to twelve. God in heaven, can we ever feel clean again?

V. G. (from More for Timothy)

§ 7

The condition of people's moral consciousness may be gauged in a sense by their attitude to capital punishment. It is an ominous moral sign that the peoples of Western Europe and America approve of capital punishment . . .

BERDYAEV

Criminals do not die by the hands of the law. They die by the hands of other men.

Assassination on the scaffold is the worst form of assassination, because there it is invested with the approval of society.

It is the deed that teaches, not the name we give it. Murder and

capital punishment are not opposites that cancel one another, but
similars that breed their kind.

BERNARD SHAW

And thou, man, who by these my labours dost look upon the
marvellous works of nature, if thou judgest it to be an atrocious act
to destroy the same, reflect that it is an infinitely atrocious act to
take away the life of man.

LEONARDO DA VINCI

A deep reverence for human life is worth more than a thousand
executions in the prevention of murder; and is, in fact, the great
security of human life. The law of capital punishment, whilst
pretending to support this reverence, does in fact tend to destroy it.

JOHN BRIGHT

Blood demands blood. Does it? The system of compensation
might be carried on ad infinitum—an eye for an eye and a tooth for a
tooth, as by the old Mosaic Law. Why, because you lose your eye,
is that of your opponent to be extracted? Where is the reason for
the practice? Knowing that revenge is not only evil but useless we
have given it up on minor points. Only to the last we stick firm. I
came away from Snow Hill that morning with a disgust for murder,
but it was for the murder I saw done. I pray to Almighty God to
cause this disgraceful sin to pass from among us, and to cleanse our
land of blood.

THACKERAY (from On Going to See a Man Hanged)

So, for instance, during my stay in Paris, the sight of an execution
revealed to me the instability of my superstitious belief in progress.
When I saw the head part from the body, and how they thumped
separately into the box, I understood, not with my mind but with
my whole being, that no theory of the reasonableness of our present
progress could justify this deed; and that though everybody from
the creation of the world, on whatever theory, had held it to be
necessary, I knew it to be unnecessary and bad; and therefore the
arbiter of what is good and evil is not what people say and do, nor is
it progress, but it is my heart and I.

TOLSTOY

473

When a certain proceeding or institution is shown to be very wrong indeed, there is a class of people who rush to the fountain-head at once, and will have no less an authority for it than the Bible, on any terms. So, we have the Bible appealed to in behalf of Capital Punishment.

It is enough for me to be satisfied, on calm inquiry and with reason, that an Institution or Custom is wrong and bad; and thence to feel assured that IT CANNOT BE a part of the law laid down by the Divinity who walked the earth. Though every other man who wields a pen should turn himself into a commentator on the Scriptures—not all their united efforts, pursued through our united lives, could ever persuade me that Executions are a Christian law. I could not, in my veneration for the life and lessons of Our Lord, believe it. If any text appeared to justify the claim, I would reject that limited appeal, and rest upon the character of the Redeemer, and the great scheme of His Religion, where, in its broad spirit, made so plain—and not this or that disputed letter—we all put our trust. But, happily, such doubts do not exist. The case is far too plain. We know that the law of Moses was delivered to certain wandering tribes, in a peculiar and perfectly different social condition from that which prevails among us at this time. We know that the Christian Dispensation did distinctly repeal and annul certain portions of that law. We know that the doctrine of retributive justice, or vengeance, was plainly disavowed by the Saviour. We know that on the only occasion of an offender, liable by the law to death, being brought before Him for His judgment, it was *not* death. We know that He said "Thou shalt not kill". And if we are still to inflict Capital Punishment because of the Mosaic law (under which it was not the consequence of a legal proceeding, but an act of vengeance from the next of kin, which would surely be discouraged by our later laws if it were revived among the Jews just now), it would be equally reasonable to establish the lawfulness of a plurality of wives on the same authority.

CHARLES DICKENS

Christ's Crucifix shall be made an excuse for Executing Criminals.

BLAKE

474

The Cross is the banner and standard of Him who has overcome and triumphed, not by fighting and slaying, but by His own bitter death. With the Cross do ye deprive of life your brother, whose life was rescued by the Cross?

ERASMUS

When God prohibits killing, He not only forbids us to commit brigandage, which is not allowed even by the public laws, but He warns us not to do even those things which are regarded as legal among men. And so it will not be lawful for a just man to accuse anyone of a capital offence, because it makes no difference whether you kill with a sword or with a word, since killing itself is forbidden. And so, in this commandment of God, no exception at all ought to be made to the rule that it is always wrong to kill a man, whom God has wished to be a sacrosanct creature.

LACTANTIUS

I can never help asking myself why, when one is called upon to superintend an execution, one should have been affected with such an acute sense of personal shame. . . . There must be something fundamentally wrong with a law which has the effect of lessening the self-respect of those whose duty it is to carry it out.

MAJOR BLAKE, *at one time Governor of Pentonville*

The final scene must always be a haunting and imperishable memory—the dreadful hooded figure on the scaffold, the thud of the falling drop, the awful plunge into the yawning pit, and the jerk as the rope tautens and sways. No one can leave the slaughter-shed without a deep sense of humiliation, horror and shame.

S. R. GLANVILLE MURRAY, *Prison Chaplain*

When we were all gathered together there, it seemed utterly impossible to believe what we were there to do.

PRISON CHAPLAIN (*of Mrs. Thompson*)

I think if she had been spared she could have become a very good woman.

HIGH PRISON OFFICER (*of Mrs. Thompson*)

475

FROM "YIELD TO THE NIGHT"

... The doctor bent over me.

"You've been asleep?"

I looked at him.

"I think it would be a good thing to give you something to make you sleep again . . . it is only ten o'clock."

"Please, Doctor. . . . I would rather not have anything tonight."

"As you wish."

He felt my pulse. Next time he felt it there would be no beat.

He let go of my wrist with a sudden movement. Perhaps he was thinking of the same thing.

Jim . . . Jim . . . there's something on at the local tonight . . . it's supposed to be good . . . you can't tonight . . . not tonight . . . something better, I suppose. Not good enough for you any more. . . . Don't come back . . . don't come back. . . .

I opened my eyes. McFarlane was sitting on the end of the bed.

"What time is it?"

She looked at her watch. "Twelve-thirty-five."

"I . . . I don't want it to be morning. . . . You won't be with me?"

"No . . . but you will be all right . . . won't you?"

"I don't know. . . . It doesn't take very long, does it?"

"No . . . only a few minutes."

She spoke quietly, but I was hardly conscious of the still seated figure of my other guard in the background.

"Do you believe in God, Miss McFarlane?"

"I'm a Catholic. . . . I believe in God."

"Your religion . . . and all that . . . it means a lot to you?"

"I couldn't live without it. . . ."

Jim couldn't live without Lucy . . . I couldn't live without Jim . . . now I'm going to die without anybody. . . .

She might have guessed my thoughts, for she said:

"God is with us all whether we believe in him or not . . . even when we cannot feel his presence."

"It's easy for you to talk . . . you are not going to die in the morning. . . ."

"Perhaps we all die some mornings . . . it can sometimes be harder to live, you know."

"I don't know. . . . I don't want to die. . . . I'm not ready to die. I know I have done wrong, but that doesn't make me want to die . . . not that way, anyway."

She did not say anything, only smoothed the blanket with her long pale fingers.

I knew that there was nothing she could do . . . yet I felt that she had failed me.

I turned over with my face to the wall. I touched the rough cotton sheet and my head pressed into the unyielding pillow. The jumbled nightmare of my thoughts could not stifle the fear that rose, like a scream, inside of me . . . and grew . . . and grew. . . .

The blankets were being moved up over me. . . . I opened my eyes. McFarlane had her hat on, and I knew that the watch was changing over.

She bent over me and her hand brushed mine.

"Good-bye, Mary."

I could not speak, but my eyes followed her until she passed through the door.

I remembered later that it was the only time that she had ever used my Christian name.

I fell into a kind of doze.

The officer touched my shoulder.

"Get up now, Hilton."

I stumbled out of bed. It seemed strange to be putting on my own clothes again. My brown skirt. . . . The open-necked white shirt had been washed; it was no longer crumpled as it had been when I'd worn it at my trial. I automatically straightened the collar. . . .

"No . . . no, I don't want anything to eat. . . ."

There is the window . . . it is morning, but it is all blurred now . . . it is the fade-out of the film . . . stand up for God save the Queen. . . . My clothes are real though . . . my own clothes. . . . I smooth the skirt with my hand . . . feel . . . feel . . . even my shoes . . . my own brown shoes. They seem a long way off when I look down at their polished toes. . . . Who polished them? . . . who polished them? Did I say that? . . .

"No . . . I don't want anything to eat. . . ."

They are coming for me . . . I know now. You told me I wouldn't know. . . . When the lift stops . . . when the bough breaks

477

. . . when the lift stops they will take me and then we will all go down together. . . . no . . . I will go down alone in my white shirt and my brown skirt and my polished shoes . . . down . . . down . . . and then they will come down after me to see. . . .

"Hilton . . . Hilton. . . ." What are they saying?

It is the chaplain . . . it is the chaplain. . . . Who is it? It is the chaplain saying his prayers. . . .

"Shall we kneel? . . ."

I could feel the hardness against my knees . . . feel . . . feel. . . .

"Let us pray. . . ."

"Our Father which art in heaven, Hallowed be thy name . . . and forgive us our trespasses, as we forgive them that trespass against us. . . . Amen. . . ."

". . . And he said unto me, it is done. I am Alpha and Omega, the beginning and the end. I will give unto him that is athirst of the fountain of the water of life freely. He that overcometh shall inherit all things; and I will be his God, and he shall be my son."

". . . your soul to everlasting life."

"Drink this. . . ."

I take the glass. Rum or brandy? . . . hot in my cold stomach . . . feel . . . feel . . .

I turn and hand her the glass. Her face is out of focus . . . at the same time I feel my arms being pinned behind my back. . . . Scream . . . no . . . no! . . . no use. . . . It's no use. . . .

We are walking . . . three blind mice . . . we are walking. . . . Something is over my face and round my neck . . . . alone in darkness. They are doing something to my legs . . . dark. . . . Loveliest of trees the cherry now. . . . Jim . . . Jim, where are you? . . . God . . . God help me . . . to see the cherry hung with . . .

JOAN HENRY

FROM "A BAD END"

. . . The last hope had gone, and the last full day of his remaining life was beginning to unfold itself. The warders, like old friends, played cards with him all day to take off his mind from the event. In the little intervals he wondered whether Hanbury who was to hang him on the morrow was not perchance the man who bit off the heads of live rats whom he and Weaver should have visited that fatal Sunday. Weaver had not disclosed his name. But there were few hangmen, he knew, and this might very well be the man in question. "Where does Hanbury, the hangman, come from?" he inquired from the warder.

"Up Manchester way."

It *was* the man!

What emotions, what a multitude of moods he experienced in those few brief hours. Till twelve he was sprightly and not very nervous. The hangman, peeping at him through the observation hole, to decide what "drop" to give him, saw him pacing up and down in the cell, puffing calmly at a cigarette. But as, at midnight, the prison clock boomed out the hours, he got agitated, threw away the cigarette and began counting the remaining hours on his fingers. He tried to think of the noble souls who went before him:—of Anton Chehov, gravely saying to the doctor who had been called to him during the night "I am dying," drinking the glass of champagne prescribed to him to the bottom and remarking, with a smile, to his wife "It's a long while since I have had champagne," turning over on one side, and presently being quiet for ever;—of Goethe asking that the window might be opened to admit of more air and more light, and the faithful Eckermann coming to look at him, lying dead. "And I turned aside," he records, "to give a free run to my tears." And with a shudder he recalled that *his* body would fall into lime to be instantly consumed like a foul thing. He must go not knowing why he lived, and nobody in those bleak immensities would know or care: no father, no mother, no love in the world would intervene on his behalf; not even memory would be left him to recall his single spell of life, as if he never had been, as if indeed he was never meant to matter. There was but to "curse God and die".

And suddenly his soul stirred within him, as if it had wings. "It's the end here," he thought. "But it's not the end there." Weaver believed in the world-soul—which meant that in a while he and Weaver would be one. It was night, but he could not sleep. Perhaps now, all over the world, there were people who could not sleep on his account and lay thinking of him. As by imponderable wireless waves he, alone in the dark cell with the gallows adjoining, felt himself linked to all compassionate souls; and to them he sent greetings—his desperate greetings. . . . At last he slept.

His sleep was troubled. He dreamt he had shrunk back from the pale gate of death, a bleak coldness in his chest and limbs, and was going past a park where there were children playing and people lounging wearily after their strenuous day's work. And he thought that the trivialities of living were manna compared with death. But by the faces of the people who came out of the park he knew that they, not realising it, could not enjoy the gift of life. He walked on, and suddenly found himself in a beautiful, totally unfamiliar part of the town, the existence of which he had not even suspected. And he told himself how he would come home and tell his father of it. He woke—and there was nothing to tell but that he had dreamt it. And at once an incredible coldness invaded his heart.

Besides, it was cold in the cell. Our courage is at its lowest ebb in the early morning: it is wicked to hang people at dawn, he reflected. The warder came in. "Get up. Here is your suit." His old suit that knew him in different circumstances. No collar today. "I'll go and fetch you yer breakfast now."

Perhaps at the last minute the Home Secretary might . . .? He remembered seeing a film where also at the last moment, also the Home Secretary. . . . How cold. They wouldn't tell his father. Or would they? The warder brought in a tray with some cocoa and porridge and an apple. He could not eat. He nibbled at the apple, and the savoury juice reminded him of some utopian land of fruit and flowers, like Italy, which he had never known. And he thought that when they had done their worst, and he was left in peace, perhaps in dreamland he would fly to such a land.

He looked strangely at the warder. "Is it very bad? Does it . . . hurt?" he asked uneasily.

"No. A second—and it's all over. Like having yer tooth out—no more. All over in a wink."

The chaplain, a young man, was more confused than he—and more miserable. "Perhaps some spiritual consolation?" he stammered.

"I don't understand," said Mr. Proudfoot. "The indivisible universe speaks and lives only through each separate creature, as if no other creature existed at all. But it is the same indivisible universe which so expresses itself. And they—absurd—they want to do away with me—that means with the universe."

"Perhaps a last communion . . ."

"Why?"

"Or a confession? After all, you've killed a human being."

He thought of Weaver, and would have felt sorry for him if he did not feel so overwhelmingly sorry for himself. If they'd let him off now he'd put back what he had taken, put back into the spiritual cosmos what he'd taken from it. If they would leave it to him, he'd see that humanity did not lose.

480

He was brave, resigned. But a quarter of an hour before time, suddenly he felt he wanted to live, love, breathe in through these nostrils the fresh air of, not this, but other, future mornings, when *he* would be no more. . . . He remembered a windy day when the big chestnuts swayed and lashed their branches like drunken things, and nuts and sticks fell off like missiles aimed at passers-by. A little boy had turned round to his mother, hiding his eyes from the dust and the wind in the folds of her skirt. This had moved him then somehow. And now an intolerable thought obsessed him—that when, in a few minutes from now, he would be buried in a pool of lime, he would feel the wind no more. And he thought that if this life he was leaving was the only life in a bleak universe, then he could not face the anguish of leaving it. But if there was another life, he wanted to hide his face in the lap of his Maker, hide from the missiles that fell all about him and hurt him, weep on His breast, and be quiet for ever. . . .

But perhaps—two minutes yet—perhaps the Home Secretary. . .? And before he could realise it the hangman stood in the cell. Was this it? Was it this? Was *this*, then, what he had to come to? Could mother but have known! But the warder, who up to this had been like a friend and confidant, suddenly began to shout at the executioner, "Come on, you there, get a move on and get about it quick!" (as though anxious to get the nasty job over). And Mr. Proudfoot felt almost as though his friend the warder had betrayed him to that other man. That other man had a soft, drooping, yellow moustache and glassy eyes, and seemed slow and good-natured. You wouldn't think by the mild look of him that he bit off the heads of live rats. Somehow Mr. Proudfoot wanted to claim acquaintance: to tell him about Weaver: that Weaver and himself were about to call on him that fatal Sunday: if they had called he would not now be here. But the man with his assistants and the warder were resolutely coming up to him as if they were intent on making a swift end of him, the governor, the chaplain and the doctor looking on. Yes, yes, he would die—if they would leave him alone, or do it—handsomely. He killed Weaver—however inadvertently, he killed him, and he would forfeit his life, on his word of honour he would. But not so—— The hangman and his assistant were trying to pinion him; and suddenly he put up a fight for his life. What right had they? All nonsense apart, what right? A glimpse of the jurymen all back in their homes, and at breakfast, flashed through his brain. What right? Where he got the strength

481

from he did not know, but the prison bell was already tolling for the soul departing, and its last stroke had boomed its melancholy message across the yard into the streets, but Mr. Proudfoot was still alive and struggling desperately with the executioner and three warders, who only knew that they had to despatch him: he should have been disposed of ten minutes ago: there was no document to account for his unwarranted existence after 8 a.m. They were shocked: it was improper in the extreme. "Don't! Oh!" He wanted to tell them—if they would only stop to listen—he wanted to tell them that—yes—he was a soul, a universe with things in it which had nothing to do with that devil in him they were intent on destroying. It was unjust. A whole universe. "Stop! Think: what are you doing? . . . *No!*" he cried, struggling in their grip and realising that nothing save his poor physical exertion now stood between him and their grim determination to do away with him. "No! You *mustn't!*" he pleaded, his soul filled with a sickening animal fear. But they dragged him on without respite, the chaplain leading the way, reading words from the Bible. And if—he thought —there was a God in heaven, why did He stand aside? What God was He to stand aside? "No! No! . . . *Oh!* . . ." But they were dragging him on none the less, dragging him on to his doom. Swiftly he looked at each of them, for a spark of compassion. But they were all men who valued their duty before everything else. He was in the open. And suddenly a wave of awe came over him, standing as he did on the brink of eternity or extinction: so that the hangman at his neck seemed like a friend who was assisting at a parting, and those others, too, seemed as if they'd come to see him off at the railway station as he was about to step into the train on his awful journey; and he clung to them with a fraternal, desperate farewell. But they only looked as though they had no time for that, but wanted to get the nasty business, long overdue, over at last. It seemed minutes before he toed the chalk line on the drop—when suddenly he fell, it seemed minutes, he expected it with drawn breath, the pulling up—when *snap!* it came!

And all was darkness.

The great harbour was awakening in the cold fog. From the terminus a tramcar set off half empty. The conductor strode inside and began collecting the fare. Then newspapers appeared on the street corners, and posters announced in red and black letters:

They were eagerly snapped up by busy hurrying people, who stopped and read:

"Proudfoot had a quiet night and is believed to have been greatly relieved at the end by confessing his crime to the chaplain. The condemned man breakfasted lightly and walked with a firm step to the scaffold. From the moment of prisoner leaving his cell to the execution of the sentence there barely elapsed twenty-five seconds."

WILLIAM GERHARDI

"I SAW AN EXECUTION IN FRANCE"

"Yes—I saw an execution in France—at Lyons. Schneider took me over with him to see it."

"What, did they hang the fellow?"

"No, they cut off people's heads in France."

"What did the fellow do?—yell?"

"Oh no—it's the work of an instant. They put a man inside a frame and a sort of broad knife falls by machinery—they call the thing a guillotine—it falls with fearful force and weight—the head springs off so quickly that you can't wink your eye in between. But all the preparations are so dreadful. When they announce the sentence, you know, and prepare the criminal and tie his hands, and cart him off to the scaffold—that's the fearful part of the business. The people all crowd round—even women—though they don't at all approve of women looking on."

"No, it's not a thing for women."

"Of course not—of course not!—bah! The criminal was a fine intelligent fearless man; Le Gros was his name; and I may tell you —believe it or not, as you like—that when that man stepped upon the scaffold he *cried*, he did indeed—he was as white as a bit of paper. Isn't it a dreadful idea that he should have cried—cried! Who ever heard of a grown man crying from fear—not a child, but a man who never had cried before—a grown man of forty-five years? Imagine what must have been going on in that man's mind at such a moment; what dreadful convulsions his whole spirit must have endured; it is an outrage on the soul, that's what it is. Because it is said 'thou shalt not kill', is he to be killed because he murdered some one else? No—it is not right—it's an impossible theory. I

483

assure you, I saw the sight a month ago and it's dancing before my eyes to this moment. I dream of it, often."

The prince had grown animated as he spoke, and a tinge of colour suffused his pale face, though his way of talking was as quiet as ever. The servant followed his words with sympathetic interest. Clearly he was not at all anxious to bring the conversation to an end. Who knows? perhaps he too was a man of imagination and with some capacity for thought.

"Well, at all events it is a good thing that there's no pain when the poor fellow's head flies off," he remarked.

"Do you know, though," cried the prince warmly, "you made that remark now, and everyone says the same thing, and the machine is designed with the purpose of avoiding pain, this guillotine I mean; but a thought came into my head then: what if it be a bad plan after all? You may laugh at my idea, perhaps—but I could not help its occurring to me all the same. Now with the rack and tortures and so on—you suffer terrible pain of course; but then your torture is bodily pain only (although no doubt you have plenty of that) until you die. But *here* I should imagine the most terrible part of the whole punishment is, not the bodily pain at all—but the certain knowledge that in an hour—then in ten minutes, then in half a minute, then now—this very *instant*—your soul must quit your body and that you will no longer be a man—and that this is certain, *certain!* That's the point—the certainty of it. Just that instant when you place your head on the block and hear the iron grate over your head—then—*that* quarter of a second is the most awful of all.

"This is not my own fantastical opinion—many people have thought the same; but I feel it so deeply that I'll tell you what I think. I believe that to execute a man for murder is to punish him immeasurably more dreadfully than is equivalent to his crime. A murder by sentence is far more dreadful than a murder committed by a criminal. The man who is attacked by robbers at night, in a dark wood, or anywhere, undoubtedly hopes and hopes that he may yet escape until the very moment of his death. There are plenty of instances of a man running away, or imploring for mercy—at all events hoping on in some degree—even after his throat was cut. But in the case of an execution, that last hope—having which it is so immeasurably less dreadful to die—is taken away from the wretch and *certainty* substituted in its place! There is his sentence, and with it that terrible certainty that he cannot possibly escape death—which, I consider, must be the most dreadful anguish in the world. You may place a soldier before a cannon's mouth in battle, and fire upon him—and he will still hope. But read to that same soldier his death-sentence, and he will either go mad or burst into tears. Who dares to say that any man can suffer this without going mad? No, no! it is an abuse, a shame—it is unnecessary—why should such a thing exist? Doubtless there may be men who have been sentenced, who have suffered this mental anguish for a while and then have been reprieved; perhaps such men may have been able to relate their feelings afterwards. Our Lord Christ spoke of this anguish and dread. No! no! no! No man should be treated so, no man, no man!"

DOSTOEVSKY (from The Idiot)

. . . And I am dumb to tell the hanging man
How of my clay is made the hangman's lime. . . .

DYLAN THOMAS

The doomed regard the sunrise
With different delight
Because when next it burns abroad
They doubt to witness it.

The man to die to-morrow
Detects the meadow bird,
Because its music stirs the axe
That clamors for his head.

Joyful to whom the sunrise
Precedes enamored day—
Joyful for whom the meadow bird
Has aught but elegy!

EMILY DICKINSON

Upon the gallows hung a wretch,
Too sullied for the hell
To which the law entitled him.
As nature's curtain fell
The one who bore him tottered in,
For this was woman's son.
" 'Twas all I had," she stricken gasped;
Oh, what a livid boon!

EMILY DICKINSON

Have you ever tried to visualise the feelings of a mother on the night before her boy is to be hanged? (and no crime is going to kill maternal love; rather it will make greater claims on the protective instinct). The agony and horror which you and I, representing the State, must inflict upon this perfectly innocent woman must be more terrible than any pain the murderer can inflict upon his victim. And as with the mother, so may it be with the wife, the lover, the sister, the father, the brother, the children and even the loyal friend. To all these people life must become numbed and meaningless at the time, and for ever after a haunted wilderness where the demons of revenge for ever lurk.

STACY AUMONIER

THE INSTITUTION OF HANGING

English hanging is an ancient institution, not in essence dissimilar from what social anthropologists call 'ritual sacrifice', which is as old as the hills. Our hanging represents and symbolizes many things. First of all, it is a fulfilment of established law. And with that it is a satisfaction, or catharsis, of public vengeance against the murderer. It is intended as an example, by way of deterrent, to other potential murderers (not a very effective one, it seems; for they keep on cropping up with the utmost regularity year in and year out). And then there is in it a scapegoat element. The person hanged can take the place of either of the goats which Old Testament Hebrews sacrificed on the Day of Atonement. There were two goats, the Bible reader will remember, one of which had the sins of Israel confessed on it by the high priest. This one was driven into the desert and somehow disposed of, often by being cast over a precipice (if there should happen to be one convenient). The other goat was ceremoniously killed as a sin-offering. Similarly a good hanging can be the cathartic sacrifice of a victim who, on being hanged in accordance with the traditional ritual, carries with him into eternity the murderous potentialities in all of us, and symbolizing a liberation from them. Hence its uplifting moral value to so many good people.

*　　　*　　　*

When we look at this question in the cold light of reason, is it not disgraceful that the directly civilizing and humanizing influence of hanging should be limited to the sheriffs of England, the prison officials and the clergy?—men who do not really require it. Public

486

imagination in England is so limited that it does not reap the full benefit of hangings. This defect, coupled with the official strangulation at birth of all information on the subject, has caused hanging to become an almost useless institution when it should be salutary. Every good judge will agree with the logic of an eminent Bishop, who, in reply to Mr. Josiah Oldfield's written question "Do you suggest any alternative for hanging a murderer in semi-secrecy?", wrote "*I should hang him publicly*".

With regard to the actual hanging process, this could be made extremely impressive if executions were held in public. To do full justice to the ceremony, it would be necessary to employ a good impresario, and then the State could reap considerable financial benefits from public executions (to the financial and economic aspects of the question I shall return later). There are around London many admirable open spaces suitable for the execution of criminals. Shambles could be appointed in convenient parts of the metropolis, say in Hyde Park, Regent's Park, Trafalgar Square, and on the Horse Guards Parade for the special convenience of Members of the Cabinet and their families, who from rooms in No. 10 Downing Street, the Foreign Office, the Treasury, etc., would be provided with a good view and be able to contemplate the hangman at work in reality and not in imagination. Binoculars would bring it all closer. Spectators would realize that the hangman's work is not all beer and skittles, and they would see their representative as a very worthy being, a great patriot, and a man of true virtue, acting in *their* name and fulfilling an unpleasant task in an estimable manner. They do not at present fully realize the virtue and quality of his act.

The massed bands of the Brigade of Guards could discourse sweet music, and a high Church dignitary, or his deputy on less important occasions, could preach a sermon based upon the text "*An eye for an eye; a tooth for a tooth*", or they could vary this with "*Whoso sheddeth man's blood, by man shall his blood be shed; for in the image of God made He man.*" Here I might interject that, although it is not generally publicized, both the hangman and the criminal are also made in the image of God. The pipers of the Scots Guards could no doubt add to the sermon a suitable lament, for the benefit of the assembled populace. There could not possibly be music more suitable for a hanging than that of the bagpipes. The Prime Minister would be able to watch the hangman put the finishing touches to his client, see him pause to make sure that all is ready;

the pull of the lever, the sudden fall, the crack of doom and the last paroxysms of the body. The jury who found the prisoner guilty could afterwards file up to shake hands with the executioner, and congratulate him upon his proficiency. A special gallery conveniently situated should be provided for the British Medical Association, and the Council should be present with stop-watches. As a final wind-up, the Archbishop of Canterbury or his deputy should say the Lord's Prayer, emphasizing the words "*Thy will be done on earth as it is in heaven.*" By way of further variety, an eminent theologian of modernist brand should make a speech showing that Christ was mistaken in His whole idea of redemption; that the Sermon on the Mount does not stand the test of higher criticism; or anything equally relevant that comes into his head.

*　　*　　*

If it were not that the prestige of the Church has so deplorably declined I would suggest a strong appeal to the bishops on behalf of the hangman's rapidly disappearing art. Most Christian Churches can be relied upon to support State killing: in 1810 there were six bishops and an archbishop in the majority of thirty-two votes to eleven which defeated the measure to abolish hanging for the theft of five-shillings' worth of anything. It must be a great comfort to all our hangmen to think that today they can be equally sure of Christian support for a continuance of their office. Indeed, when we come to look squarely at the present position in regard to the death penalty in England it will be found that its two greatest supporters are the Law and the Church, as they always have been in the past; for which, may the Lord make us truly thankful.

CHARLES DUFF

The Bishop of —— deplored present-day fear of the use of punishment and the opening of the door more widely to opinions of doctors and psychiatrists. On the question of reformative treatment he declared that "The more we have made provision by our prison treatment . . . for appealing to the better nature of criminals, the more frequently we find that there is less better nature to which to appeal." He thought that the death penalty helped to educate the conscience of the whole community and that it aroused among many people "a quasi-religious sense of awe".

The Bishop of —— said: "'Whoso sheddeth man's blood, by man shall his blood be shed' has appealed to man as . . . an approximation of justice . . ." He thought there was a good deal to be said for extending the death penalty for a period, e.g. for attempted murder or rape.

LORDS' DEBATE ON DEATH PENALTY, 1948

In the early ages, the social edifice rested on three columns—Superstition, Tyranny, Cruelty. A long time ago a voice exclaimed "Superstition has departed!" Lately another voice has cried "Tyrrany has departed!" It is now full time that a third voice shall be raised to say "The Executioner has departed!"

Thus the barbarous usages of the olden times fall one by one; thus Providence completes modern regeneration. . . .

Let it not be supposed that social order will depart with the scaffold; the social building will not fall from wanting this hideous keystone. Civilization is nothing but a series of transformations. For what then do I ask your aid? The civilization of penal laws. The gentle laws of Christ will penetrate at last into the Code, and shine through its enactments. We shall look on crime as a disease, and its physicians shall displace the judges, its hospitals displace the galleys. Liberty and health shall be alike. We shall pour balm and oil where we formerly applied iron and fire; evil will be treated in charity, instead of in anger. This change will be simple and sublime:

THE CROSS SHALL DISPLACE THE GIBBET

VICTOR HUGO

III. WAR AND PEACE

Then he answered and spake unto me, saying, This is the word of the Lord unto Zerubbabel, saying, Not by might, nor by power, but by my spirit, saith the Lord of hosts.

ZECHARIAH

> Nought can deform the Human Race
> Like to the Armour's iron brace.
> The Soldier, arm'd with Sword & Gun,
> Palsied strikes the Summer's Sun.

BLAKE

Children are nourish'd for the Slaughter; once the Child was fed With Milk, but wherefore now are Children fed with blood?

BLAKE

What! are we terrors to one another? Come, O brethren, wherefore Was this wide Earth spread all abroad? not for wild beasts to roam.

BLAKE

The whole world is wet with mutual blood; and murder, which in the case of an individual is admitted to be a crime, is called a virtue when it is committed wholesale.

ST. CYPRIAN

The slaying of multitudes is a matter for grief and tears; he that has conquered in battle is received with rites of mourning.

TAO TÊ CHING

We read in a Midrash that Cain and Abel quarrelled for the reason that each wished to establish the Holy Temple on his land. This excuse has ever since been brought forward for every shedding of blood and for every war. It is always maintained that the fight is on behalf of a holy purpose.

AUTHOR OF KOL OMER KERA

Satan mostly employs comparatively moral instruments and the language of ethics to give his aims an air of respectability. War is disciplined destruction, much more bloody than any yet committed by mobs. And yet war has been apostrophised, because we have been deceived by the temporary but brilliant results achieved by some wars.

GANDHI

493

In war the worst men have a free hand.

PLOTINUS

> I know that Justice holds in store
> Reprisals for those days of gore;
> Not for the blood but for the sin
> Of stifling mercy's voice within.

EMILY BRONTË

Modern civilisation as represented by the West of to-day, in my opinion, has given Matter a place which by right belongs to Spirit. It has therefore put Violence upon the throne of triumph and held under bondage Truth and Innocence.

GANDHI

It is political and commercial egoism which is the evil harbinger of war. By different combinations it changes its shape and dimensions, but not its nature. This egoism is still held sacred, and made a religion; and such a religion, by a mere change of temple, and by new committees of priests, will never save mankind. We must know that as, through science and commerce, the realisation of the unity of the material world gives us power, so the realisation of the great spiritual Unity of Man alone can give us peace.

TAGORE

SOCRATES ON THE ORIGIN OF WAR

In my opinion the true and healthy constitution of the State is the one which I have described. But if you wish also to see a State at fever-heat, I have no objection. For I suspect that many will not be satisfied with the simpler way of life. They will be for adding sofas, and tables, and other furniture; also dainties, and perfumes, and incense, and courtesans, and cakes, all these not of one sort only, but in every variety; we must go beyond the necessaries of which I was at first speaking, such as houses, and clothes, and shoes: the arts of the painter and the embroiderer will have to be set in motion, and gold and ivory and all sorts of materials must be procured.

True, he said.

Then we must enlarge our borders; for the original healthy State is no longer sufficient. Now will the city have to fill and swell with a

494

multitude of callings which are not required by any natural want; such as the whole tribe of hunters and actors, of whom one large class have to do with forms and colours; another will be the votaries of music—poets and their attendant train of rhapsodists, players, dancers, contractors; also makers of divers kinds of articles, including women's dresses. And we shall want more servants. Will not tutors be also in request, and nurses wet and dry, tirewomen and barbers, as well as confectioners and cooks; and swineherds, too, who were not needed and therefore had no place in the former edition of our State, but are needed now? They must not be forgotten: and there will be animals of many other kinds, if people eat them.

Certainly.

And living in this way we shall have much greater need of physicians than before?

Much greater.

And the country which was enough to support the original inhabitants will be too small now, and not enough?

Quite true.

Then a slice of our neighbours' land will be wanted by us for pasture and tillage, and they will want a slice of ours, if, like ourselves, they exceed the limit of necessity, and give themselves up to the unlimited accumulation of wealth?

That, Socrates, will be inevitable.

And so we shall go to war, Glaucon. Shall we not?

Most certainly, he replied.

PLATO

§ 2

SPRING MCMXL

London Bridge is falling down, Rome's burnt, and Babylon
The Great is now but dust; and still Spring must
Swing back through Time's continual arc to earth.
Though every land become as a black field
Dunged with the dead, drenched by the dying's blood,
Still must a punctual goddess waken and ascend
The rocky stairs, up into earth's chilled air,
And pass upon her mission through those carrion ranks,
Picking her way among a maze of broken brick
To quicken with her footsteps the short sooty grass between;

While now once more their futile matchwood empires flare and
  blaze
And through the smoke men gaze with bloodshot eyes
At the translucent apparition, clad in trembling nascent green,
Of one they can still recognise, though scarcely understand.

DAVID GASCOYNE

A WARTIME DAWN
(April, 1940)

Dulled by the slow glare of the yellow bulb;
As far from sleep still as at any hour
Since distant midnight; with a hollow skull
In which white vapours seem to reel
Among limp muddles of old thought; till eyes
Collapse into themselves like clams in mud . . .
Hand paws the wall to reach the chilly switch;
Then nerve-shot darkness gradually shakes
Throughout the room. *Lie still* . . . Limbs twitch;
Relapse to immobility's faint ache. And time
A while relaxes; space turns wholly black.

But deep in the velvet crater of the ear
A chip of sound abruptly irritates.
A second, a third chirp; and then another far
Emphatic trill and chirrup shrills in answer; notes
From all directions round pluck at the strings
Of hearing with frail finely-sharpened claws.
And in an instant, every wakened bird
Across surrounding miles of air
Outside, is sowing like a scintillating sand
Its throat's incessantly replenished store
Of tuneless singsong, timeless, aimless, blind.

Draw now with prickling hand the curtains back;
Unpin the blackout-cloth; let in
Grim crack-of-dawn's first glimmer through the glass.
All's yet half sunk in Yesterday's stale death,
Obscurely still beneath a moist-tinged blank
Sky like the inside of a deaf mute's mouth . . .
Nearest within the window's sight, ash-pale

Against a cinder coloured wall, the white
Pearblossom hovers like a stare; rain-wet
The further housetops weakly shine; and there,
Beyond, hangs flaccidly a lone barrage-balloon.

An incommunicable desolation weighs
Like depths of stagnant water on this break of day.—
Long meditation without thought.—Until a breeze
From some pure Nowhere straying, stirs
A pang of poignant odour from the earth, an unheard sigh
Pregnant with sap's sweet tang and raw soil's fine
Aroma, smell of stone, and acrid breath
Of gravel puddles. While the brooding green
Of nearby gardens' grass and trees, and quiet flat
Blue leaves, the distant lilac mirages, are made
Clear by increasing daylight, and intensified.

Now head sinks into pillows in retreat
Before this morning's hovering advance;
(Behind loose lids, in sleep's warm porch, half hears
White hollow clink of bottles,—dragging crunch
Of milk-cart wheels,—and presently a snatch
Of windy whistling as the newsboy's bike winds near,
Distributing to neighbour's peaceful steps
Reports of last-night's battles); at last sleeps.
While early guns on Norway's bitter coast
Where faceless troops are landing, renew fire:
And one more day of War starts everywhere.

DAVID GASCOYNE

WALKING AT WHITSUN
(May, 1940)

. . . Then let the cloth across my back grow warm
Beneath such comforting strong rays! new leaf
Flow everywhere, translucently profuse,
And flagrant weed be tall, the banks of lanes
Sprawl dazed with swarming lion-petalled suns,
As with largesse of pollen-coloured wealth
The meadows; and across these vibrant lands
Of Summer-afternoon through which I stroll

497

Let rapidly gold glazes slide and chase
Away such shades as chill the hillside trees
And make remindful mind turn cold . . .

                                    The eyes
Of thought stare elsewhere, as though skewer-fixed
To an imagined sky's immense collapse;
Nor can, borne undistracted through this scene
Of festive plant and basking pastorale,
The mind find any calm or light within
The bone walls of the skull; for at its ear
Resound recurrent thunderings of dark
Smoke towered waves rearing sheer tons to strike
Down through To-day's last dyke. Day-long
That far thick roar of fear thuds, on-and-on,
Beneath the floor of sense, and makes
All carefree quodlibet of leaves and larks
And fragile tympani of insects sound
Like Chinese music, mindlessly remote,
Drawing across both sight and thoughtlike gauze
Its unreality's taut haze.

                                    But light!
O cleanse with widespread flood of rays the brain's
Oppressively still sickroom, wherein brood
Hot festering obsessions, and absolve
My introspection's mirror of such stains
As blot its true reflection of the world!
Let streams of sweetest air dissolve the blight
And poison of the News, which every hour
Contaminates the aether.

                                    I will pass
On far beyond the village, out of sight
Of human habitation for a while.
Grass has an everlasting pristine smell.
On high, sublime in his bronze ark, the sun
Goes cruising across seas of silken sky.
In fields atop the hillside, chestnut trees
Display the splendour of their branches piled
With blazing candle burdens.—Such a May
As this might never come again . . .

                                    I tread
The white dust of a weed-bright lane; alone
Upon Time-Present's tranquil outmost rim,
Seeing the sunlight through a lens of dread,
While anguish makes the English landscape seem
Inhuman as the jungle, and unreal
Its peace. And meditating as I pace
The afternoon away, upon the smile
(Like that worn by the dead) which Nature wears
In ignorance of our unnatural tears,
From time to time I think: How such a sun
Must glitter on their helmets! How bright-red
Against this sky's clear screen will ruins burn . . .

How sharply their invading steel must shine!

                                    DAVID GASCOYNE

                          *

NINETEEN FIFTEEN

"Saturday night it was, at eleven o'clock. He had the top of his
back taken away by a shell," says Marchal, "cut off like a razor.
Besse got a bit of shell that went clean through his belly and
stomach. Barthélemy and Baubex got it in the head and neck. We
passed the night skedaddling up and down the trench at full speed,
to dodge the showers. And little Godefroy—did you know him?—
middle of his body blown away. He was emptied of blood on the
spot in an instant, like a bucket kicked over. Little as he was, it was
remarkable how much blood he had, it made a stream at least fifty
metres long. Gougnard got his legs cut up by one explosion. They
picked him up not quite dead. That was at the listening post. I was
there on duty with them. But when that shell fell I had gone into
the trench to ask the time. I found my rifle, that I'd left in my
place, bent double, as if some one had folded it in his hands, the
barrel like a corkscrew, and half of the stock in sawdust. The smell
of fresh blood was enough to bring your heart up."

"And Mondain—him, too?"

"Mondain—that was the day after, yesterday in fact, in a dug-out
that a shell smashed in. He was lying down, and his chest was
crushed. Have they told you about Franco, who was alongside

Mondain? The fall of earth broke his spine. He spoke again after they'd got him out and set him down. He said, with his head falling to one side, 'I'm dying', and he was gone. Vigile was with them, too; his body wasn't touched, but they found him with his head completely flattened out, flat as a pancake, and huge—as big as *that*. To see it spread out on the ground, black and distorted, it made you think of his shadow—the shadow one gets on the ground sometimes when one walks with a lantern at night."

*   *   *

Along the hazy, filthy, and unwholesome space, where withered grass is embedded in black mud, there are rows of dead. They are carried there when the trenches or the plain are cleared during the night. They are waiting—some of them have waited long—to be taken back to the cemeteries after dark.

We approach them slowly. They are close against each other, and each one indicates with arms or legs some different posture of stiffened agony. There are some with half-mouldy faces, the skin rusted, or yellow with dark spots. Of several the faces are black as tar, the lips hugely distended—the heads of negroes blown out in goldbeaters' skin. Between two bodies, protruding uncertainly from one or the other, is a severed wrist, ending with a cluster of strings.

Others are shapeless larvae of pollution, with dubious items of equipment pricking up, or bits of bone. Farther on, a corpse has been brought in in such a state that they have been obliged—so as not to lose it on the way—to pile it on a lattice of wire which was then fastened to the two ends of a stake. Thus was it carried in the hollow of its metal hammock, and laid there. You cannot make out either end of the body; alone, in the heap that it makes, one recognises the gape of a trouser-pocket. An insect goes in and out of it.

Around the dead flutter letters that have escaped from pockets or cartridge pouches while they were being placed on the ground. Over one of these bits of white paper, whose wings still beat though the mud ensnares them, I stoop slightly and read a sentence—"My dear Henry, what a fine day it is for your birthday!" The man is on his belly; his loins are rent from hip to hip by a deep furrow; his head is half turned round; we see a sunken eye; and on temples, cheek and neck a kind of green moss is growing.

*   *   *

A German sergeant-major is seated, here where we tread, supported by the riven timbers that once formed the shelter of a sentry.

There is a little hole under his eye; the thrust of a bayonet has nailed him to the planks through his face. In front of him, also sitting, with his elbows on his knees and his fists on his chin, there is a man who has all the top of his skull taken off like a boiled egg. Beside them—an awful watchman!—the half of a man is standing, a man sliced in two from scalp to pelvis, upright against the earthen wall. I do not know where the other half of this human post may be, whose eye hangs down above and whose bluish viscera curl spirally round his leg.

* * *

We arrive at last on the summit, which is marked as with a signal by a wounded and frightful man. He is upright in the wind, shaken but upright, enrooted there. In his uplifted and wind-tossed cape we see a yelling and convulsive face. We pass by him, and he is a sort of screaming tree.

* * *

The light of a candle shows us several men shaken with their efforts to hold a wounded soldier down on his stretcher. It is a man whose feet are gone. At the end of his legs are terrible bandages, with tourniquets to restrain the hæmorrhage. His stumps have bled into the linen wrappings, and he seems to wear red breeches. His face is devilish, shining and sullen, and he is raving. They are pressing down on his shoulders and knees, for this man without feet would fain jump from the stretcher and go away.

"Let me go!" he rattles in breathless, quavering rage. His voice is low, with sudden sonorities, like a trumpet that one tries to blow too softly. "By God, let me go, I tell you! Do you think I'm going to stop here? Let go, let me be, or I'll jump over you on my hands!"

So violently he contracts and extends himself that he pulls to and fro those who are trying to restrain him by their gripping weight, and I can see the zigzags of the candle held by a kneeling man whose other arm engirdles the mutilated maniac, who shouts so fiercely that he wakes up the sleepers and dispels the drowsiness of the rest. On all sides they turn towards him; half rising, they listen to the incoherent lamentations which end by dying in the dark.

* * *

"There were some chaps there that were blown to bits when the shells burst," said some one to me who was waiting there in the sickly ray of entombed light. "You talk about a mess! Look, there's the padre hooking down what was blown up."

The huge Red Cross sergeant, in a hunter's chestnut waistcoat which gives him the chest of a gorilla, is detaching the pendent entrails twisted among the beams of the shattered woodwork. For the purpose he is using a rifle with fixed bayonet, since he could not find a stick long enough; and the heavy giant, bald, bearded and asthmatic, wields the weapon awkwardly. He has a mild face, meek and unhappy, and while he tries to catch the remains of intestines in the corners, he mutters a string of "Oh's!" like sighs. His eyes are masked by blue glasses; his breathing is noisy. The top of his head is of puny dimensions, and the huge thickness of his neck has a conical shape. To see him thus pricking and unhanging from the air strips of viscera and rags of flesh, you could take him for a butcher at some fiendish task.

HENRI BARBUSSE (from Under Fire)

NINETEEN THIRTY-SIX

All night they marched, the infantrymen under pack,
But the hands gripping the rifles were naked bone
And the hollow pits of the eyes stared, vacant and black,
When the moonlight shone.

The gas mask lay like a blot on the empty chest,
The slanting helmets were spattered with rust and mold,
But they burrowed the hill for the machine-gun nest
As they had of old.

And the guns rolled, and the tanks, but there was no sound,
Never the gasp or rustle of living men
Where the skeletons strung their wire on disputed ground . . .
I knew them, then.

"It is eighteen years," I cried. "You must come no more.
We know your names. We know that you are the dead.
Must you march forever from France and the last, blind war?"
"Fool! From the next!" they said.

STEPHEN VINCENT BENÉT

NINETEEN FORTY-FIVE (THE ATOM BOMB)

As I watched, two things that looked like great big hideous lizards crawled in slowly, making croaking, groaning sounds. Others followed. I was paralysed with horror for minutes. Then the light got a little stronger and I could see they were human beings—skinned alive by fire or heat, their bodies all smashed where they had been thrown against something hard.

*   *   *

After a few minutes I saw something coming up the road along the river that looked like a parade of roast chickens. Some of them kept asking for 'Water! Water!'

They were all naked and they were skinned. The skin of their hands had been torn away at the wrists. It was hanging from their fingertips just behind the nails, turned inside-out like a glove. In the dim light I thought I saw many other children lying all about the yard.

TAKASHI NAGAI (from We of Nagasaki)

NINETEEN FIFTY-TWO (THE NAPALM BOMB)

In front of us a curious figure was standing, a little crouched, legs straddled, arms held out from his sides. He had no eyes, and the whole of his body, nearly all of which was visible through tatters of burnt rags, was covered with a hard black crust speckled with yellow pus. A Korean woman by his side began to speak, and the interpreter said: 'He has to stand, sir, cannot sit or lie'.

He had to stand because he was no longer covered with a skin, but with a crust like crackling which broke easily.

RENE CUTFORTH (from Korean Reporter)

THE ENEMY AND FRIEND

There was a lull just then in the place where Tamino was, and his men lay huddled together plunged in sleep. But he was awake and standing alone, looking out over the plain. And what he saw under the glimmering moon was a desolation—ruined houses, stumps of trees, black pits and hummocks, where once had been houses and orchards and waving corn. And all the scene was dotted with corpses, some fresh and bleeding, some blown into bladders, some with the flesh half rotted from their bones. Here was a head sticking out, with the dried skin black upon it; here a hand; there a foot. The still air reeked with putrefaction. And somewhere close at hand was the moaning of a wounded man. And Tamino said to himself:

"All this have I done. Why?"

503

And a voice beside him echoed—"Why?"

Tamino started and cried, "Who is there?" But he saw nothing, for Sarastro chose to remain unseen. But to the question "Who is there?" came the answer:

"You yourself."

"What do you want?" cried Tamino. And the voice said again: "Yourself."

"Well, I am here," Tamino said. And the voice asked:

"Why are you here?"

Now in the past Tamino would have answered, confidently enough, "To win Pamina." But that answer he could no longer make. Yet answer he must, so like a child he blurted out:

"I don't know why."

"If you do not know why you are fighting," said the voice, "tell me at least for whom."

And half-heartedly, and not believing himself, Tamino faltered: "For my friends."

But as he spoke he heard again the moaning of the wounded man. And the voice said:

"Go then and look at your friend." Tamino replied:

"That is an enemy."

But the voice repeated:

"Go and look," and Tamino had to go. And gazing at him out of a face that had lost all its features, he saw the eyes of an enemy, and they were the eyes of a friend. He gave a cry and fell senseless to the ground. And Sarastro watched beside him till the dawn.

G. LOWES DICKINSON (from *The Magic Flute*)

We shall never stop war, whatever machinery we may devise, until we have learned to think always, with a sort of desperate urgency and an utter self-identification, of single human beings.

V. G.

§ 3

There are things that a man must not do to save a nation.

JOHN O'LEARY THE FENIAN

To do evil that good may come of it is for bunglers in politics as well as morals.

WILLIAM PENN

504

"THEN WE MUST DO NO WRONG?"

Socrates Then we must do no wrong?

Crito Certainly not.

Socrates Nor when injured injure in return, as the many imagine; for we must injure no one at all?

Crito Clearly not.

Socrates Again, Crito, may we do evil?

Crito Surely not, Socrates.

Socrates And what of doing evil in return for evil, which is the morality of the many—is that just or not?

Crito Not just.

Socrates For doing evil to another is the same as injuring him?

Crito Very true.

Socrates Then we ought not to retaliate or render evil for evil to any one, whatever evil we may have suffered from him. But I would have you consider, Crito, whether you really mean what you are saying. For this opinion has never been held, and never will be held, by any considerable number of persons; and those who are agreed and those who are not agreed upon this point have no common ground, and can only despise one another when they see how widely they differ. Tell me, then, whether you agree with and assent to my first principle, that neither injury nor retaliation nor warding off evil by evil is ever right. And shall that be the premiss of our argument? Or do you decline and dissent from this? For so I have ever thought, and continue to think; but, if you are of another opinion, let me hear what you have to say. If, however, you remain of the same mind as formerly, I will proceed to the next step.

Crito You may proceed, for I have not changed my mind.

PLATO

One fire is not quenched by another fire, but fire by water.

CHRYSOSTOM

Ahimsa is not merely a negative state of harmlessness but it is a positive state of love, of doing good even to the evil-doer. But it does not mean meek submission to the will of the evil-doer: it means the putting of one's whole soul against his will. Working under this law of our being, it is possible for a single individual to defy the whole might of an unjust empire, to save his honour, his

505

religion, his soul, and lay the foundation for that empire's fall or its regeneration.

Non-violence in its dynamic condition means conscious suffering.

GANDHI

Where there is only a choice between cowardice and violence, I would advise violence. But I believe that non-violence is infinitely superior to violence, forgiveness is more manly than punishment.

GANDHI

One man abstains from resisting because he is weak, lazy, and cannot, not because he will not; the other man knows that he can strike an irresistible blow if he likes; yet he not only does not strike, but blesses his enemies. The one who from weakness resists not commits a sin, and as such cannot receive any benefit from the non-resistance; while the other would commit a sin by offering resistance.

VIVEKANANDA

*

And Christ is not divided, for in him there is peace.

GEORGE FOX

The Religion of Jesus, Forgiveness of Sin, can never be the cause of a War nor of a single Martyrdom.

BLAKE

We also believe that war ought to cease among the followers of the Lamb Christ Jesus, who taught His disciples to forgive and love their enemies, and not to war against them and kill them; and that therefore the weapons of His true followers are not carnal but spiritual; yea mighty, through God, to cut down sin and wickedness, and dethrone him that is the author thereof. And as this is the most Christian, so the most rational way; love and persuasion having more force than weapons of war. Nor would the worst of men easily be brought to hurt those that they really think love them. It is that love and patience must in the end have the victory.

WILLIAM PENN

THE BASIS OF PACIFISM

Christian pacifists derive their conviction not from the negative abhorrence of war nor from the utopian dream of a lotus-eater's world, but from the fact and significance of Jesus Christ. They concentrate attention on war because it is a typical symptom, and at this juncture the outstanding representative, of evil. They believe that here is the concrete issue upon which today evil can be challenged most effectively, and that to challenge it here would ultimately involve a conflict over the whole field. Their confidence is grounded in the faith that peace on earth is God's will for his children and that man is in fact capable of fellowship. They cannot regard this hope as utopian without abandoning the Lord's Prayer and repudiating faith in its author.

But prior to these considerations is the historic event of the life and death of Jesus, the belief in the uniqueness and the validity of that event, and consequently the conviction that a new, final and authentic means for the overcoming of evil has been revealed to us. Far from agreeing that the progress of theological studies, or the development of human society, or the experience of recent happenings have shaken their position, they would maintain that the sophistries and propaganda and despair of their critics have in fact simplified the issue and strengthened their case. Amid the confusion and tragedy of the times the way of Christ stands out plainly for what it is, the hope of the world; but it is the way of the Cross. Considering the unanimity with which Christendom accepts the one symbol of its faith and the devotion with which individual Christians take it up daily, it is amazing that in the most urgent problem of our time they generally reject it and explain it away.

Jesus "came into the world to save sinners". He fulfilled his mission by a deliberate acceptance of death, and his martyrdom has proved the most momentous victory in history. . . .

Such a brief statement is necessary if we are to appreciate the challenge and the novelty of the gospel. Adumbrated as we can see by the most profound of the prophets of Israel, vindicated to some degree at least by the experiences of that martyr-nation, it was yet a revelation running clean counter to the selfish instincts of men and nations, to the "common sense" of human wisdom, and to the traditional standards of human conduct and ambition. "To the Jews a scandal, to the Greeks a silliness": so the apostle Paul triumphantly admitted when he named it "the weakness and folly of God" . . .

Christ by his Cross presents to us his way of overcoming the sin of the world, and in this form at least the mass of mankind and even of Christians repudiate it. Twice in half a century the decision has been taken. . . .

The plain fact is that the Church since the First Century and with few exceptions has never, despite its protestations, taken Christ with complete seriousness. If it has not evaded the questions "Whom say ye that I am?" and "What think ye of Christ? Whose son is he?" it has given a credal answer but failed to endorse it or to act whole-heartedly upon it. "Let this mind be in you which was also in Christ Jesus"; "I live, yet not I; Christ lives in me"—a multitude of such sayings proves that in the New Testament the *Imitatio Christi* was not a devotional aspiration but an admitted obligation. "In Christ" is the characteristic phrase of St. Paul. Its significance implies that such real identification of the believer with his Lord was a basic feature of discipleship, and its constant repetition underlines its primacy as the true constituent condition of human wayfaring.

We have answered Christ's questions with Christologies of greater or less complexity: we have not realized that the occasion of the questions gives them an importance that demands for them much more than intellectual and conciliar discussions. It is not an accident that Jesus at the two crucial points in his ministry, at the close of his mission in Galilee, and at the end of the final day of questions in Jerusalem, turned away from his usual themes, the character of God's Kingdom, the quality of its members, the challenge it gives to every human aspiration or opinion, and confronted his followers with the supreme fact (be it parable or sacrament) of Himself. It is as if he were to say to us, "The macrocosm, God's revelation of himself in the Universe, is too large and vague and impersonal: you cannot find guidance and inspiration from it— come unto me. In the microcosm of the Son of Man you can perceive and act upon and be transformed by evidence of God's nature and purpose such as cannot be disclosed to you elsewhere or at a lesser cost."

Such a demand plainly involves not only a complete oblation of ourselves in faith and love, but therefore also the measure of self-identification with him which St. Paul and the writers of the New Testament and a succession of saints throughout the ages have in fact attained. . . . "That we may both perceive and know what things we ought to do, and also may have grace and power faithfully to fulfil the same"—the ancient collect sums up our obligation. And if this seems impossible, if on the human side it seems arrogant and even blasphemous to suggest its possibility, then let us remember that . . . our discipleship is not our own; we are not living in our own strength; we are vitalized and controlled by "the good gift of the Holy Ghost". Humanly speaking, our task is impossible; Christianly considered, our resources are infinite.

It is in this form—the contrast between task and resources—that the New Testament presents the paradox of our state . . . There is continuous and emphatic testimony to the character and cost of the Christian's adventure: it is the daily carrying of a cross; life must be lost if it is to be gained; if thine eye offend thee, pluck it out. Jesus never suggested that the way was easy or the gate wide. But neither did he ever lessen his demand, nor blur the distinction between acceptance and denial, nor indicate that those who count the cost will not be able to pay it. Plainly he had himself such complete trust in God, and was so sure that we could share his trust and follow under its constraint, that for him there was no other way. God's Kingdom would come, God's will would be done as in heaven so on earth, and if that will involved crucifixion, yet even so victory was assured. Confident of the resources available for us he could be recorded as saying "Be ye therefore perfect even as your father which is in heaven", and promising that we should be led into all the truth and should do even greater works than his . . .

It has long been common practice among Christians in defending themselves against charges of failure to quote G. K. Chesterton's saying: "Christianity has not been tried and found wanting: it has been tried, found too difficult and abandoned" . . . We have realized that Christianity has its symbol and centre in a crucifixion; we have had an uncomfortable knowledge that a resurrection without a crucifixion was a contradiction in terms; consequently in order to avoid the Cross we have denied the possibility of the crown. The cost of perfection has been too high for us. At such a price we cannot take Jesus seriously.

The plain fact is that the antithesis of task and resources was resolved by Christ, but only at the inevitable breaking-point. Jesus himself overcame the world and accomplished the impossible when he cried "My God, my God, why hast thou forsaken me?" By accepting the Cross, by suffering dereliction, by surrendering everything without reserve, he revealed and released the infinite energies of God. He had already prepared his disciples by precept, warning them that they must be broken; now by example he sacrificed them with himself that they might be crucified with him and so be raised and glorified. Defeat for them as for him was in fact victory. From it flowed the consequences that changed not only their lives but the course of history. Throughout the centuries where men have experienced the full manifestation of exaltation and self-emptying, of adoration and abasement, they have attained a similar victory. . . .

The heart of the Christian gospel is not safety but victory—the victory over evil that was won by the way of the Cross. Jesus when he undertook his mission of deliverance was constantly tempted to use other methods: the reformer's road of material satisfactions; the statesman's road of armed rebellion and imperial rule; the ecclesiastic's road of awe and wonder and the fulfilment of prophecy and the role of the Lord's anointed. Even at the Mission's crisis in the last days at Jerusalem, he could still have appealed to the Zealots and fought, or he could have fled and taken refuge in Galilee. He chose to meet evil unarmed and unafraid, to let it do its worst with him, and to bear its wounds in his own body on the tree. So by death came life, and the twin sayings—"I am come that they may have life and have it abundantly"·and "Whoso loveth his life shall lose it, whoso hateth his life in this world shall keep it unto life eternal"—are seen to be complementary.

Of course it is possible for us to say that we are incapable of following his example or else that the example is not one that ought to be followed. But if in this supreme lesson and achievement we are not to imitate him, either our discipleship becomes trivial or else his lordship is denied. To say "This is too high a price for me to pay" is natural enough, but we ought surely not to make such a confession without shame. To say "This was right for him, but it would be wrong for me" is to tear up those parts of his teaching in which he bade us follow and do his works and to assume that we can lightly disassociate ourselves from him whenever we think fit. In this matter of victory over evil—a matter fundamental to his whole ministry—what is not legitimate for us is to ignore his way or to replace it by some method of our own. But this is precisely what we do when we call pacifism a soft utopianism or decide that mass-killing is the lesser of two evils.

CHARLES E. RAVEN

510

PACIFISM AND REALISM

Christian pacifists have often been warned by self-styled "realists" that we shall never bring in the Kingdom of God by acting in an evil world as if it were already here. Yet this is, I suggest, exactly what Jesus *did* teach: if only men were prepared to take God at His word, and to order their lives here and now by the laws of a transcendent Kingdom, then the power of God would answer the cry of faith, and the Kingdom would break in upon them and take them unawares.

G. H. MACGREGOR

PACIFISM AND DISASTER

We must recognize frankly that the way of pacifism may bring worldly disaster. It may mean the subjugation of the world by an oppressive and murderous dictatorship. . . . If we deceive ourselves about this, our faith and our message will have no depth, and will wither.

All this is true. But at the last resort we cannot be brought to a nice judgment of consequences, to balancing death against tyranny and devastation against injustice; these are incommensurables. Furthermore, our estimate of results cannot go beyond a certain point. We picture the immediate but never the ultimate fruits of our action. The whole course of future history is changed because I act in one way rather than another, and the final outcome of that act is beyond our dreaming. Thinking of consequences forms a useful guide to action, and one that we habitually use, but it is not the ultimate criterion. When Jesus hung on the Cross on Good Friday, it was, to anyone who cared to weigh the consequences, the end of Christianity. The Master killed as a common criminal, His leading associates, a handful of rough peasants, skulking from the police, the populace turned against Him or indifferent. But Jesus was following the way of God, and Good Friday was succeeded by Easter Sunday. When the Early Church refused to sacrifice to the Emperor, it was, to anyone who cared to weigh the consequences, the end of Christianity. The whole might of Rome descended to exterminate this band of obstinate upstarts. But God was with them. The Church survived and expanded into every corner of the Empire, as Tertullian can boast. Those who ask thus ask the wrong question. The question which matters is "Is this God's way?" If so, however dark the future seems, the end will be God's. . . .

It is needful at this point to clarify one common confusion. Some three-quarters of philosophical argument is argument about words. It is important to realize that when we say "Sin is evil" and "Suffering is evil" we are using the word "evil" in two different senses; the one signifies moral evil, the other does not. Failure to understand this has led to enormous difficulties. Jesus suffered, but He did not sin. Hence, too, the paradox of Socrates, that it is better to suffer wrong than to commit it. . . . The norm by which the Christian acts should be not "Does this involve evil in the second sense?" but "Does it involve evil in the first sense?", because, if so, it is not God's way in God's world. To put it otherwise, he will ask "Is it loving?" or more simply "Is it the way of Christ?" The heart of Christ went out to the suffering of others, but He did not dissuade them from the cup He drank when that was the will of God. It is not an answer to the pacifist to show him that whatever way he chooses will involve others in suffering. It is an answer to the non-pacifist to show that the way of war is rejected by Jesus as not pleasing to God and therefore morally evil.

JOHN FERGUSON

PACIFISM AND FORCE

Reconciliation and redemption, which are the supreme ends of the Christian love which is itself the essence of Christian living, can never be achieved by force pure and simple; for force in itself is much more likely to thwart than to fulfil these ends. If then force is to find a place within the Christian ethic, it must only be in a form which is limited by such sympathetic discrimination that it may be expected to prepare the way for the final appeal of redemptive love. Any use of force, therefore, which by its very nature escapes from such control, and renders such an appeal abortive, can under no circumstances be countenanced. It is obvious that war utterly fails to pass this test, and for these reasons: Firstly, no sooner has war begun than there automatically follows the prostitution of every conceivable moral value, truth, honesty, decency, upon which all stable personal relationships, and the only possibility of recovering them when lost, depend. Secondly, war has, particularly in its modern form, become so entirely mechanical and impersonal that one can engage in it only by totally depersonalizing one's entire relationship to the object of one's action. And thirdly, its main aim is to kill, and therefore to remove the presumed object of redemption entirely from that sphere of personal relationship wherein alone love can make its appeal.

G. H. C. MACGREGOR

THE PACIFIST INITIATIVE

A nation, following the way of Christ, might feel called upon to adopt a policy of total disarmament. But it would do so, in the first instance, not with the deliberate purpose of courting martyrdom, but with the conviction that the best safety from the perils against which nations arm is to be found in a new national way of life, which would remove causes of provocation and lead progressively to reconciliation and peace. It would risk everything on the conviction that God's way would work. But such a nation must also be willing, if necessary, to incur the risk of national martyrdom by refusing to equip itself against the possibility of aggression. And it may be that the world must wait for its redemption from warfare until one nation is ready to risk crucifixion at the hands of its possible enemies. It might lose its own national life; but it would set free such a flood of spiritual life as would save the world.

G. H. C. MACGREGOR

PACIFISM AND THE HEAVENLY PATTERN

In heaven, I replied, there is laid up a pattern of the good city, methinks, which he who desires may behold, and beholding, may set his own house in order. But whether such a city exists or ever will exist on earth, is no matter; for the man of understanding will live after the manner of it, having nothing to do with any other.

I think so, he said.

PLATO

§ 4

PEACE

"But what are you doing, and where are you going?"

"I'm going to stop the war."

"So am I. Let us go together."

So together they went, Pamina leading them, till they came to the battlefield and the tent of Monostatos. And there Pamina vanished,

513

and Papageno danced away, but Tamino went into the tent, and took his seat unseen.

Now, as it happened, there was a council of war proceeding, and there were present, beside Monostatos and the other generals, the first minister and the Archbishop. For both of these were amateurs of war, and loved to discuss strategy and to watch the battle from a distance. Tamino listened for some time to their talk; and it was what he had heard so often before—new plans, new guesses, new hopes, and fears, and yet all so old, so old! He could not bear it. And suddenly, leaping to his feet, he shouted out: "There is only one good counsel—make peace." And as he shouted they saw him, with his flute in his hand, beautiful as he had never been before, with his flashing eyes and golden hair. They all stood up in a hubbub, and Monostatos made a grab at him, but he put his flute to his lips and began to play. And they stood like stone, while the flute sang:

> Lift, mist of blood!
>> Man-swallowing cataract of battle, cease!
> Flesh stamped in mud,
>> Emancipate the soul to her last peace.
>
> Love undismayed,
>> Comradeship shining far, and courage high,
> Fail not nor fade!
>> Burn on, bright fires, up to eternity!
>
> All else was vain,
>> Child of the brute unfathered by the soul.
> All sinks again
>> Back, whence it came, to Mother Night's control.
>
> Kind genders kind,
>> Murder from murder springs, and hate from hate.
> Who close the mind,
>> Precipitate run back to the beast's estate.
>
> Who will may learn;
>> Who will not in their children's children pay.
> Take now the turn
>> That sets your feet on the celestial way.

Thus sang the flute and finished; and for a while they kept silence, motionless as under a spell. Then softly the Archbishop began:

A pagan song I fear.
　It jars my lofty mood.
The meaning is not clear,
　And cannot well be good.

Yet creeping in and out
　Some magic in the song
Makes even a bishop doubt—
　What if I should be wrong?

So said the Archbishop.　Then the commander-in-chief spoke:

It's worse than printer's ink,
　This musical appeal.
It's bad enough to think,
　But even worse to feel.

The victory's secure.
　'Twill cost a million men.
We'll win it, kill or cure.
　But when it's won, what then?

So said the commander-in-chief.　And then the minister took
it up:

By clamour undeterred
　How prudently I wrought,
By censoring every word
　To stifle every thought.

For let one error free
　Such melodies as these,
And even old men like me
　Begin to dream of peace.

But when Monostatos saw what harm Tamino's flute had
wrought, fear and rage seized him. "What are you thinking of,
gentlemen?" he cried. "This man is a deserter and a traitor."
When he heard these words, the Archbishop shuddered, and
Monostatos called in the guard to arrest Tamino, who stood still in
the tumult, making no resistance.　But just as they laid hands on
him, there was heard the sound of a pipe and a great noise of feet
and voices. They threw open the door of the tent, and lo! there was
Papageno, dancing along and playing, and behind him both armies,
their own and the enemy's, fraternizing, embracing, laughing,
weeping, and dancing all the time, while high above all the pipe
sang:

What are you doing, silly boys,
Where are all your summer joys?
Have you forgotten mother earth,
And her sweet and friendly mirth?
Far away, far away,
Hear it call, the happy day!
Over the downs, a silver stream,
The sheep are drifting like a dream;
The mowers cut the lushy grass,
Their scythes go swishing as they pass;
The wild rose flutters on the briar;
The cows are quelching in the byre;
The milk along the happy vales
Is ringing in a thousand pails;
And every evening, in the shade,
The boy goes out to meet the maid.
Oh, 'tis the very month of June!
Listen, listen to her tune!
Far away, far away,
Hear it call, the happy day!

So he sang, and they all took it up, and went dancing away, friend with enemy and enemy with friend, over the scarred earth, past the ruined walls and towers, away, away, in a wavering farandole, to the sweet country and their homes long lost. Hour after hour they passed, and Tamino stood and watched, until, as evening fell, the last had vanished into the dusk, and shadow and silence fell upon the plain. Then began the deluge. It descended, not in drops, but in a sheer mass, as though a sluice had been suddenly drawn that held it up in the sky. But Tamino stood dry and unharmed on his hill. Quickly the plain became a lake, and the trenches torrents. The corpses and all the middens of sordid refuse, accumulated in the months of war, went sweeping away down to the cleansing sea; and dawn broke grey on a shining level of bare soil. But hardly had this become visible, when it flushed into tender colour. Garden and glebe, fallow and orchard and pasture, grew into green and golden life, and flourished fair and distinct, under the beams of the risen sun. From village and homestead, newly-built, the happy labourers streamed. Dogs barked, cocks crowed, and all the jocund life that had been on the earth from the beginning returned once more to run its ancient course. Then there came over Tamino that old doubt, what was real, this or that? Had there indeed ever been a war? Had all that horror

516

happened? And, for the very relief of it, he was inclined to think he had been dreaming. But as that thought came into his mind, the air round him seemed to turn into music; and a chorus of male voices, so sweet and solemn that his mortal sense could hardly bear it, chanted the words that here follow:

Be not deceived. What once hath been
Abides in that tremendous scene.
From pain that stung the cries were wrung.
The dead are dead, their flesh is dung.

Evil and Good their place assume
Irreparably on earth's great loom.
The moving pattern who would trace,
Sees the reflection of his face.

What hath been is. But human fate
Needs not to bow beneath the weight.
The moment's yours. O use it well!
There you will find your heaven or hell.

But though he heard the voices, Tamino could not see the singers. And revolving perplexedly in his mind all he had seen and done and felt, he made his way across the shining fields and back to the city.

G. LOWES DICKINSON (from *The Magic Flute*)

Coda to fourth part:
on Justice

JUSTICE

Why do I, and apparently so many others with me, find it so astonishingly difficult to think clearly about justice? Partly the difficulty is simply a revolt of man at his most human. When his manhood is at its best, and that is, most typically, when Christianity has awakened in him a true sense of human values, the impersonality of justice, even in the form of equity, stirs in him a deep unrest. True, this is justice, but what of the offender? True, as the moralists, with Bishop Butler at their head, assert, it is the business of the Moral Governor of the World to secure that virtue is rewarded and vice punished. But what becomes of that moralism in the face of Christ? What of the shepherd, going out to seek the sheep that is lost, *until he find it*: "there shall be joy in heaven over one sinner that repenteth, more than over ninety and nine righteous persons, which need no repentance"? What of the sayings which seem to deny us all claim upon the principles of equity: "love your enemies, and do them good, and lend, never despairing; and your reward shall be great, and ye shall be sons of the most High: for he is kind toward the unthankful and evil"; "it is my will to give unto this last, even as unto thee"—even if, as is probable enough, the result is a general strike in the vineyard? What of the Cross, and of the universal Christian conviction that it was and is for sinners that Jesus died? What of that interpretation of the Cross which lay at the heart of the first Christian preaching: "the wages of sin is death, but the free gift of God is eternal life in Christ Jesus our Lord"?

When I try to analyse my own share in this perplexity, I find that there are several sources of confusion in my mind.

One obstacle to clear thinking is the following. Almost everybody would admit at once that the administration of justice, human or divine, ought not to be influenced by personal considerations; and for the Christian this apparent truism is reinforced by the well-known text "There is no respect of persons with God". It is indeed obvious that if we have any worthy conception of God at all we cannot for an instant imagine Him to be swayed in His dealings with us by anything resembling a bribe or consideration. Still less can we suppose that His judgment of the sinner is in any way modified by regard for the sinner's status or social position. Neither God's justice, whatever that may mean, nor any human justice worthy of the name, can conceivably be reconciled with personal considerations of such a kind. This truth has only to be stated to be accepted, at any rate by the Christian, and we need not here concern ourselves with the widespread modern tendency to glorify any injustice which is done in the name of or for the sake of the State as such. What is not so easily seen is that the acceptance of this truth does not in fact or in logic lead to the very similar sounding truism from which we started this paragraph. It is simply untrue to say that justice should not be influenced by personal considerations. What is true is that justice should not be influenced by unworthy personal considerations, and that is a very different matter.

It is perfectly clear, so soon as we disabuse our minds of this confusion, that justice, in any proper meaning of the word, must be concerned entirely with persons. It is by persons that it is administered, in the name of some wider, organic community of persons, and it is upon persons that it takes effect. The whole question of its rightness and of its efficacy is inseparably bound up with what we must needs admit to be personal considerations. The one fundamental differential in the case of true justice, again in any proper meaning of the word, is that those considerations are worthy and not unworthy. In the case of human justice its application must be such that it does no violence to the highest meaning and worth of human nature, whether in those who administer it (a point worth remembering, as, for example, in the consideration of capital punishment, or of the possible justice of certain types of war), or in those upon whom it is administered. Even more must this be true of the Divine justice, supposing that such a phrase is permissible at all. Such justice must conform wholly to the full personality of God's dealings with man, and to that personality of His own being from which both man and God's way with man alike proceed.

Thus the conception of impersonal justice, a conception which has had such immense and, upon the whole, beneficent consequences, is seen to be a curious blending of a truth and a falsehood. At the secondary level of man's frailty and self-seeking it is a truth. At the primary level of God's way with man, which is ultimately the deepest level of our human dealings with one another, it is false. It is this that St. Paul saw and said when he pointed out that the Law was given because of transgressions. It was because of man's sin that he needed this impersonal, codified "tutor" to bring him to Christ. Apart from sin, there would have been no place for Law.

There is a real source of confusion in our thinking here. The vast and world-wide system of impersonal justice, in all its various codifications, is indeed impressive. But it is also cold, abstract, and negative. It is man's supreme endeavour to undo the consequences of his own inner weakness and failure. And it fails. The most that it can do is to secure a certain framework of social and civic order. It cannot deal with the inner corruption which makes that framework necessary. And, indeed, a generation which has twice seen a world-war may well ask whether it even secures the framework.

This is man's way. Justice is not a Christian virtue by birthright. Perhaps God has a better way.

But the most radical difficulty of all is one rather loosely linked with this impersonal conception of justice of which we have been speaking, though it comes into our thinking in another way and from a different part of our inheritance. It is due to the idea of justice as an absolute principle existent in its own right, having therefore a status and an authority of its own, and demanding for itself some satisfaction or vindication or reparation when it is violated. There is an inevitable tendency to transform abstractions into actual entities. Thus we find it desperately easy to slip into the use of such a phrase as "the obligation to truth", when our real obligation is to one another, binding us to a strict honesty and sense of responsibility in all our dealings with those facts which are the material of our common life. There is no meaning in saying that it is wrong to lie, unless we mean that it is wrong to lie to one another. We cannot in any case lie to God, though we may commit the sin of trying to do so.

In the case of justice the confusion produced by this transformation of abstractions into entities is especially marked, and its results have sometimes been disastrous, as in the cruder forms of the Penal Theory of the Atonement and in the terrible parallel developments of the penal laws in the seventeenth and eighteenth centuries, when a boy could be hanged for the theft of a few pence. Behind all this lay the belief that justice itself demanded a vindication of this kind, that without it some wrong would be done, not to man but to a principle. And it is surprisingly easy to slip into language which, whatever our intention, can only be interpreted on similar lines. We constantly use such phrases as "the demands of justice", and very often, almost without noticing it, set those demands in actual opposition to the real obligation that is laid upon us to seek the good of all men, whether they have wronged us or not, saint and sinner alike.

A common form of this quasi-personification of justice, one which even in careful writers often passes without challenge, is seen in the familiar argument that justice consists in rendering to every man his due, and that which is due to the sinner is retribution or punishment. This, though not always explicitly stated, is the real ground for the insistence, otherwise so astonishing, of some outstanding Christian leaders upon the necessity for retribution and reparation after a war.

What then is the matter with this argument? It is simply that it wholly mistakes the nature of a moral or personal obligation, and, in addition, transfers to the supposed offender that which has no meaning except as something due to justice itself. Justice is here truly an abstraction. That which is due to every human being, simply as personal, is, in Kant's phrase, that he should be treated "as an end and not as a means". And if we accept this view, we have at once excluded the treatment of human beings, however greatly they may have offended, as means towards the satisfaction of retributive justice, or indeed of any form of justice regarded as subsisting in its own right. To render to every man his due is one of the oldest, and still one of the best, definitions of justice. But its regard is wholly personal, and we must not attempt to determine the meaning of the phrase "what is due" by any process of thought which does not take into account the full meaning and worth of personality.

For the Christian, Kant's saying is an obvious truism. It is, indeed, rather a flat and unenterprising way of saying about human nature something which the Christian proclaims with all the warmth of news so good that it is capable of making sense of a sin-laden and war-worn world. That which is due to every man, however fallen, is the deep challenge and service of human love, and beyond and about and in that service, the masterful onset of the love of the God that made him and claims him for His own. It is due not as a legal right, but as the imperative demand of God's inmost Being, giving Himself in redemption as wholly as He gives Himself in Creation, a giving of which the only measure known to us is the Cross. We may, if we like, speak of this too as justice, but if we do so speak we must not forget how far we have transformed the meaning of the word.

One more source of confusion is worthy of mention, though it is perhaps of less importance than those which have been discussed. It is really an illusion, resulting from a logical fallacy, but it is not always easy to detect the illusion when it is presented in an indirect form. It might perhaps be termed the reverential fallacy, and its principle may be stated thus. Obviously we may not predicate of God anything unworthy. Therefore we must ascribe to Him the opposite of any such unworthiness. For example, we could not possibly bring ourselves to ascribe ugliness to God. Must we not therefore conceive Him as "in perfect beauty"? So again we cannot dare to say that God is unjust. Must we not therefore speak of Him as a just God? "Shall not the Judge of all the earth do right?"

This is sheer fallacy, for it rests upon the assumption that the pairs of alternatives "ugliness and beauty" "injustice and justice" may properly be applied to the being of God Himself. But there is no such propriety, evident or demonstrable. The argument falls entirely into the void. Logically it is as nonsensical as it would be to say that God must needs be red because we cannot possibly think of Him as green. But that would only make sense if we add the preliminary assumption that God is coloured, which is, of course, absurd.

Very often, when we find ourselves driven, in some unnecessary defence of our faith, to the assertion that God is just, with the corollary that the justice of God must needs be satisfied, not because justice is justice but because God is God, we are in fact slipping unawares into this fallacy. What we really want to assert is that God will under no circumstances become an accomplice in the human injustice which springs from our human sin. We can conceive no unworthy motive in Him, nor any expression of His purposes which either violates His own being or treats as less than human those beings which He made, and whose being has kinship, however small and remote, with His own. But to convert this assertion into the assertion that God is just, is to take an unwarrantable logical step, and it is only when we have realised that our logic is bad that we can go on to ask what is the truth which we are trying to state. For we do, all of us who believe in God, constantly use language of that kind. What do we mean by it? And what ought we to mean?

I am sure that this is one of the points at which confusion again and again slips into our thinking. But in clearing up the confusion, and the logical fallacy upon which it rests, we do get at least a clue as to the way in which our thinking ought to proceed. What we often mean, and what we must not mean, is that our human conceptions of justice are binding upon God. When we speak of God as just we must not conceive Him after the pattern of any human administrator or judge. The long history which lies behind our modern ideas of justice is the history of a quest, full of digressions and obscurities, and by no means ended. There is no such thing as an absolute and final conception of justice. And therefore to speak of God as just tells us very little about God. We learn about Him in another and a better way.

But it may be that it tells us something about justice. For if the phrase may be rightly used at all, it means that our conception of justice must in the end conform to what we know of God, must conform, that is to say, to God's revelation of Himself in Jesus Christ. And this gives us not a complete account of human justice, but a true starting point from which to think about it, and a real clue as to its ultimate purpose and meaning. The conflict between justice and love is a real conflict at our human level. But God is Love, and all justice that is true to God's purposes must in the end be conformed to that love. The justice of God is simply His love, operative and unveiled, and the key to that justice is not the Law, but the Cross. When we have realised that, and not before, we can rightly speak of God as just.

Often in the complexities of our life we shall find ourselves at one and the same time called to be ministers of our human justice and constrained by the claim of love that knows no limit to its range. Sometimes the two will not conflict. Sometimes they will. At that parting of the ways the Christian will make no mistake. For there, set up as a sign-post, he will find the Cross. He must needs choose love.

L. W. GRENSTED

FIFTH PART

I. THE JUST LIFE FOR MAN— THE ONE THING NEEDFUL

Love is the life of man.

SWEDENBORG

Compassion is the chief law of human existence.

DOSTOEVSKY

Essentially man is not a slave either of himself or of the world; but he is a lover. His freedom and fulfilment is in love, which is another name for perfect comprehension.

TAGORE

Have thy Heart in Heaven, and thy Hands on Earth: Ascend in Pietie, and Descend in Charity, for this is the Nature of Light, and the Way of the Children of it.

THOMAS VAUGHAN

All bodies together and all minds together and all their products are not equal to the least motion of love; that belongs to an order higher by infinity.

PASCAL

Every creative act of ours in relation to other people—an act of love, of pity, of help, of peacemaking—not merely has a future but is eternal.

BERDYAEV

The smallest atom of good realised and applied to life, a single vivid experience of love, will advance us much farther, will far more surely protect our souls from evil, than the most arduous struggle against sin, than the resistance to sin by the severest ascetic methods of chaining the dark passions within us.

FATHER YELCHANINOV

That man will love his greatest enemy, who knows that that very enemy is God Himself.

VIVEKANANDA

"Thou shalt love thy neighbour as thyself". Why? Because every human being has a root in the Unity, and to reject the minutest particle of the Unity is to reject it all.

THE BAAL-SHEM

Each natural compassion that a man hath on his fellow Christians with charity, it is Christ in him.

JULIANA OF NORWICH

Sympathy or no sympathy, a man's love should no more fail towards his fellows than that love which spent itself on disciples who altogether misunderstood it, like the rain which falls on just and unjust alike.

MARK RUTHERFORD

Charity is the great channel through which God passes all his mercy upon mankind. For we receive absolution of our sins in proportion to our forgiving our brother. This is the rule of our hopes, and the measure of our desire in this world; and in the day of death and judgement the great sentence upon mankind shall be transacted according to our alms, which is the other part of charity. Certain it is, that God cannot, will not, never did, reject a charitable man in his greatest needs and in his most passionate prayers; for God Himself is love, and every degree of charity that dwells in us is the participation of the Divine nature.

JEREMY TAYLOR

Our lack of compassion, our ruthlessness towards other men, is an impenetrable curtain between ourselves and God. It is as if we had covered a plant with a black hood, and then complained that it died from deprivation of sunlight.

FATHER YELCHANINOV

And still the uncombatable song rose to the light
From all the heights of Being, and from the depth of the last abyss:
'If every grain of my dust should be a Satan—
If every atom of my heart were Lucifer—
If every drop of my blood were an Abaddon,
—Yet should I love.'

EDITH SITWELL

With everything, whether it is above or below, remote or near, visible or invisible, thou shalt preserve a relation of unlimited love without any animosity or without a desire to kill. To live in such a consciousness while standing or walking, sitting or lying down till

you are asleep, is Brahma vihāra, or, in other words, is living and
moving and having your joy in the spirit of Brahma.

THE BUDDHA

*

In every act the good man seeks to save.

MENANDER

However innumerable sentient beings are I vow to save them.

BUDDHIST VOW

> If I can stop one heart from breaking,
> I shall not live in vain;
> If I can ease one life the aching,
> Or cool one pain,
> Or help one fainting robin
> Unto his nest again,
> I shall not live in vain.

EMILY DICKINSON

Let thy soul lend its ear to every cry of pain, as the lotus bares
its heart to drink the morning sun.

Let not the fierce sun dry one tear of pain before thyself has
wiped it from the sufferer's eye.

But let each burning human tear drop on thy heart and there
remain; nor ever brush it off until the pain that caused it is
removed.

THE VOICE OF THE SILENCE

How shall we comfort those who weep? By weeping with them.

FATHER YELCHANINOV

He loved and wept for all.

D'ANNUNZIO (OF VERDI)

Solitude and hunger and weariness of spirit—these sharpened my
perceptions so that I suffered not only my own sorrow but the
sorrow of those about me. I was no longer myself. I was man. I
was no longer a young girl. . . . I was the oppressed. I was that

531

drug addict, screaming and tossing in her cell, beating her head against the wall. I was that shoplifter who for rebellion was sentenced to solitary. I was that woman who had killed her children, murdered her lover.

DOROTHY DAY

When I see a hunchback, my back aches for him.

ROMAIN ROLLAND (from Jean-Christophe)

LUKE TEN

*And a certaine Priest comming that way, looked on him
and passed by.*
Why doest thou wound my wounds, o thou that passest by,
Handling & turning them with an unwounded eye?
The calme that cooles thine eye does shipwrack mine, for o,
Unmov'd to see one wretched is to make him so.

RICHARD CRASHAW

*

When your brother sins against you in any way—for instance, if he speaks ill of you, or transmits with an evil intention your words in a perverted form to another, or calumniates you—do not be angered against him, but seek to find in him those good qualities which undoubtedly exist in every man, and dwell lovingly on them, despising his evil calumnies concerning you as dross, not worth attention, as an illusion of the Devil. The gold-diggers do not pay attention to the quality of sand and dirt in the gold-dust, but only look for the grains of gold; and though they are but few, they value this small quantity, and wash it out of heaps of useless sand. God acts in a like manner with us, cleansing us with great and long forbearance.

Every person that does any evil, that gratifies any passion, is sufficiently punished by the evil he has committed, by the passions he serves, but chiefly by the fact that he withdraws himself from God, and God withdraws Himself from him: it would therefore be insane and most inhuman to nourish anger against such a man; it would be the same as to drown a sinking man, or push into the fire a person who is already being devoured by the flame. To such a man, as to one in danger of perishing, we must show double love,

532

and pray fervently to God for him; not judging him, not rejoicing at his misfortune.

JOHN OF CRONSTADT

If anyone abuses you be silent. Not in order to provoke your slanderer, but because of your love.

RABBI NAHMAN OF BRATZLAV

'When a man sees that his neighbour hates him', said Rabbi Rafael of Berschad, 'then he must love him more than he did before to fill up what is lacking . . .' Rabbi Rafael used always to warn against applying the measuring-rod in one's dealings with people: A surplus of love is necessary to fill up what is lacking of love in this world.

MARTIN BUBER

Our attitude to all men would be Christian if we regarded them as though they were dying, and determined our relation to them in the light of death, both of their death and of our own. A person who is dying calls forth a special kind of feeling. Our attitude to him is at once softened and lifted on to a higher plane. We then can feel compassion for people whom we did not love. But every man is dying, I too am dying and must never forget about death.

BERDYAEV

Tried friendship must go down perforce
Before the outward eating rage
And murderous heart of middle age,
Killing kind memory at its source,
If it were not for mortality,
The thought of that which levels all
And coldly pillows side by side
The tried friend and the too much tried.

Then think of that which will have made
Us and all else contemporary.
Look long enough and you must see
The dead fighting with the dead.
Now's the last hour for chivalry,
Now we can still escape the shame
Of striking the unanswering head,
Before we are changed put off the blame.

533

But should this seem a niggardly
And ominous reconciliation,
Look yet again until you see,
Fixed in the body's final station,
The features of immortality.
Try to pursue this quarrel then.
You cannot. This is less than man
And more. That more is our salvation.
Now let us seize it. Now we can.

EDWIN MUIR

THE WILL TO UNIVERSAL SALVATION

All must be saved and liberated from hell. This is the last and final demand of ethics. Direct all the power of your spirit to freeing everyone from hell. Do not build up hell by your will and actions, but do your utmost to destroy it. Do not create hell by thrusting the "wicked" into it. Do not imagine the Kingdom of God in too human a way as the victory of the "good" over the "wicked", and the isolation of the "good" in a place of light and of the "wicked" in a place of darkness. . . . The moral will must be directed in the first place towards universal salvation. This is an absolute moral truth and it does not depend upon this or that metaphysical conception of salvation and perdition. Do not create hell for anyone either in this world or in the next, get rid of the instincts of vengeance which assume lofty and idealistic forms and are projected into eternity. As immanent in experience and as a consequence of the dark freedom that has to be lived through, hell exists, anyway, but we must not create it as a place of retribution in which the "wicked" are to be segregated from "the good". The Kingdom of God, in any case, lies beyond our "good" and "evil", and we must not increase the nightmare of our sinful life on this side of the distinction. The "good" must take upon themselves the fate of the "wicked", share their destiny and thus further their liberation. I may create hell for myself and, alas, I do too much to create it. But I must not create hell for others, not for a single living being. Let the "good" cease being lofty, idealistic avengers . . .

There is very little good in goodness, and this is why hell is being prepared on all sides. The responsibility of good for evil, of "the good" for "the wicked", is a new problem for ethics. It is unjust to lay the whole responsibility upon "evil" and the "wicked".

534

They have come into being because "the good" were bad and had not enough good in them. Both the "wicked" and the "good" will have to give an answer to God, but His judgment will be different from the human. Our distinction between good and evil may prove to be a confusion. The "good" will have to answer for having created hell, for having been satisfied with their own righteousness, for having ascribed a lofty character to their vindictive instincts, for having prevented the "wicked" from rising up and for speeding them on the way to perdition by condemning them. . . .

Even if the knowledge that there shall be no hell is withheld from me, I do know, at any rate, that there ought to be no hell and that I must do my utmost to save and free everyone from it. I must not isolate myself in the work of salvation and forget my neighbours doomed to perdition. We must not abandon to the devil greater and greater stretches of existence but must win them back for God. Hell is not a triumph for God—it is the triumph of the devil and of non-being.

BERDYAEV

. . . and thence we know
That Man subsists by Brotherhood and Universal Love.
We fall on one another's necks, more closely we embrace.
Not for ourselves, but for the Eternal family we live.
Man liveth not by Self alone, but in his brother's face
Each shall behold the Eternal Father and love and joy abound.

BLAKE

In vain we supplicate the Powers above;
There is no resurrection for the Love
That, nurst in tenderest care, yet fades away
In the chilled heart by gradual self-decay.

S. T. COLERIDGE

§ 2

I want to paint humanity, humanity and again humanity.

I love nothing better than this series of bipeds, from the smallest baby in long clothes to Socrates. . . .

VINCENT VAN GOGH

THE VEGETABLE-SELLER

On one occasion, a certain excellent man who feared God in his life and works, and who was living in the world, went to Abbâ Poemen, and some of the brethren, who were also with the old man, were asking him questions. Then Abbâ Poeman said to the man who was in the world, "Speak a word to the brethren"; but he entreated him, saying, "Forgive me, father, but I came to learn." And the old man pressed him to [speak], and, as the force of his urging increased, he said, "I am a man living in the world, and I sell vegetables, and because I do not know how to speak from a book, listen ye to a parable. There was a certain man who had three friends, and he said to the first, 'Since I desire to see the Emperor, come with me'; and the friend said unto him, 'I will come with thee half the way'. And the man said to the second friend, 'Come, go with me to the Emperor's presence'; and the friend said unto him, 'I will come with thee as far as his palace, but I cannot go with thee inside'; and the man said the same unto his third friend, who answered and said, 'I will come with thee, and I will go inside the palace with thee, and I will even stand up before the Emperor and speak on thy behalf.'" Then the brethren questioned him, wishing to learn from him the strength of the riddle, and he answered and said unto them, "The first friend is abstinence, which leadeth as far as one half of the way; and the second friend is purity and holiness, which lead to heaven; and the third friend is loving-kindness, which stablisheth a man before God, and speaketh on his behalf with great boldness."

THE PARADISE OF THE FATHERS

Wouldst thou love God alone? God alone cannot be beloved. He cannot be loved with a finite love, because He is infinite. Were He beloved alone, His love would be limited. He must be loved in all with an illimited love, even in all His doings, in all His friends, in all His creatures. Everywhere in all things thou must meet His love. And this the Law of Nature commands. And it is thy glory that thou art fitted for it. His love unto thee is the law and measure of thine unto Him: His love unto all others the law and obligation of thine unto all.

His nature requireth that thou love all those whom He loveth, and receive Him in all those things wherein He giveth Himself unto thee. Their nature loveth to be beloved and being amiable require love, as well as delight in it. They require it both by desert and

desire. Thy nature urgeth it. For without loving thou art desolate,
and by loving thou enjoyest. Yea by loving thou expandest and
enlargest thyself, and the more thou lovest art the more glorious.
Thou lovest all thy friends' friends; and needest not to fear any
dearth of love or danger of insufficiency. For the more thou lovest
thy friend, thy Sovereign Friend, the more thou lovest all His
Friends. Which showeth the endless proneness of love to increase
and never to decay. O my Soul thou livest in all those whom thou
lovest: and in them enjoyest all their treasures.

TRAHERNE

ABOU BEN ADHEM

Abou Ben Adhem (may his tribe increase!)
Awoke one night from a deep dream of peace,
And saw, within the moonlight in his room,
Making it rich, and like a lily in bloom,
An angel writing in a book of gold:—
Exceeding peace had made Ben Adhem bold,
And to the presence in the room he said,
    'What writest thou?'—The vision rais'd its head,
And with a look made of all sweet accord,
Answer'd, 'The names of those who love the Lord.'
    'And is mine one?' said Abou. 'Nay, not so,'
Replied the angel. Abou spoke more low,
But cheerly still; and said, 'I pray thee, then,
Write me as one that loves his fellow men.'
    The angel wrote, and vanish'd. The next night
It came again with a great wakening light,
And show'd the names whom love of God had blest,
And lo! Ben Adhem's name led all the rest.

LEIGH HUNT

AMO ERGO SUM

Because I love
    The sun pours out its rays of living gold
    Pours out its gold and silver on the sea.

Because I love
    The earth upon her astral spindle winds
    Her ecstasy-producing dance.

537

Because I love
Clouds travel on the winds through wide skies,
Skies wide and beautiful, blue and deep.

Because I love
Wind blows white sails,
The wind blows over flowers, the sweet wind blows.

Because I love
The ferns grow green, and green the grass, and green
The transparent sunlit trees.

Because I love
Larks rise up from the grass
And all the leaves are full of singing birds.

Because I love
The summer air quivers with a thousand wings,
Myriads of jewelled eyes burn in the light.

Because I love
The iridescent shells upon the sand
Take forms as fine and intricate as thought.

Because I love
There is an invisible way across the sky,
Birds travel by that way, the sun and moon
And all the stars travel that path by night.

Because I love
There is a river flowing all night long.

Because I love
All night the river flows into my sleep,
Ten thousand living things are sleeping in my arms,
And sleeping wake, and flowing are at rest.

KATHLEEN RAINE

SYBIL CURES THE HURT ANKLE

Amabel smiled back, a thing she didn't much believe in doing as a rule, having been for some months with a lady who held that if you smiled at your servants they would do everything for you, and also held that you had a right to see that they did. The company proceeded slowly to the drawing-room, and Aaron was made as comfortable as possible on a divan. Sybil, kneeling by him, bared his ankle and looked at it.

'It doesn't,' she said, 'seem very bad.' She laid her hand over it; thinking how charming Aaron Lee's courtesy had been, very willing to be courteous in her turn. He looked up at her and met her eyes, and his anxious babblings stopped.

Her hand closed round the ankle; her mind went inwards into the consciousness of the Power which contained them both; she loved it and adored it: with her own thought of Aaron in his immediate need, his fear, his pain, she adored. Her own ankle ached and throbbed in sympathy, not the sympathy of an easy proffer of mild regret, but that of a life habituated to such intercession. She interceded; she in him and he in her, they grew acquainted; the republican element of all created things welled up in them both. Their eyes exchanged news. She throbbed for an instant not with pain but with fear as his own fear passed through her being. It did but pass through; it was dispelled within her, dying away in the unnourishing atmosphere of her soul, and with the fear went the pain. Her hand had fastened on him; she smiled at him, and then with the passing of that smile before her recovered serenity her hand was released. She sank back on to her heels, and said, her voice full of a deep delight: 'O, no, not very bad' . . .

Negligent of his supposed hurt, he put his feet to the floor and stood up. . . .

CHARLES WILLIAMS (from *The Greater Trumps*)

SYBIL SAVES HER BROTHER FROM THE STORM

Sybil Coningsby stepped out into the storm and tried to see before her. It was becoming very difficult, and the force of the wind for the moment staggered and even distressed her. She yielded to it a little both in body and mind; she knew well that to the oppositions of the world she could in herself offer no certain opposition. As her body swayed and let itself move aside under the blast, she surrendered herself to the only certain thing that her life had discovered: she adored in this movement also the extreme benevolence of Love. She sank before the wind, but not in impotence; rather as the devotee sinks before the outer manifestations of the God that he may be made more wholly one with that which manifests. Delaying as if both she and it might enjoy the exquisite promise of its arrival, it nevertheless promised, and, as always, came.

She recovered her balance, swaying easily to each moment's need, and the serene content which it bestowed filled again and satisfied her.

It satisfied, but for no more than the briefest second did she allow herself to remain aware of that. Time to be aware, and to be grateful for that awareness, she enjoyed; literally enjoyed, for both knowledge and thankfulness grew one, and joy was their union, but that union darted out towards a new subject and centre. Darted out and turned in; its occupation was Lothair Coningsby, and Lothair was already within it. It did not choose a new resting-place, but rather ordered its own content, by no greater a movement than the shifting of the accent from one syllable back to the other. So slight a variation as gives the word to any speaker a new meaning gave to this pure satisfaction a new concern. She was intensely aware of her brother; she drew up the knowledge of him from within her, and gave it back within her. In wave after wave the ocean of peace changed its 'multitudinous laughter' from one myriad grouping to another. And all, being so, was so.

Such a state, in which the objects of her concern no longer struck upon her thoughts from without, recalled by an accident, a likeness, or a dutiful attention, but existed rather as they did in their own world—a state in which they were brought into being as by the same energy which had produced their actual natures—had not easily been reached. That sovereign estate, the inalienable heritage of man, had been in her, as in all, falsely mortgaged to the intruding control of her own greedy desires. Even when the true law was discovered, when she knew that she had the right and the power to possess all things, on the one condition that she was herself possessed, even then her freedom to yield herself had been won by many conflicts. Days of pain and nights of prayer had passed while her lonely soul escaped; innocent joys as well as guilty hopes had been starved. There had been a time when the natural laughter that attended on her natural intelligence had been hushed, when her brother had remarked that 'Sybil seemed very mopy'. She had been shocked when she heard this by a sense of her disloyalty, since she believed enjoyment to be a debt which every man owes to his fellows, partly for its own sake, partly lest he at all diminish their own precarious hold on it. She attempted dutifully to enjoy and failed, but while she attempted it the true gift was delivered into her hands.

When the word Love had come to mean for her the supreme greatness of man she could hardly remember: one incident and another had forced it on her mind—the moment when her mother, not long before death, had said to her, 'Love, Sybil, if you dare; if you daren't, admit it'; the solemn use of the name in the great poets, especially her youthful reading of Dante; a fanatic in a train who had given her a tract: *Love God or go to Hell.* It was only after a number of years that she had come to the conclusion that the title was right, except perhaps for *go to*—since the truth would have been more accurately rendered by *be in Hell.* She was doubtful also about *God*; *Love* would have been sufficient by itself but it was necessary at first to concentrate on something which could be distinguished from all its mortal vessels, and the more one lived with that the more one found that it possessed in fact all the attributes of Deity. She had tried to enjoy, and she remembered vividly the moment when, walking down Kingsway, it had struck her that there was no need for her to try or to enjoy: she had only to be still, and let that recognized Deity itself enjoy, as its omnipotent nature was. She still forgot occasionally; her mortality still leapt rarely into action, and confused her and clouded the sublime operation of—of It. But rarely and more rarely those moments came; more and more securely the working of that Fate which was Love possessed her. For it was fatal in its nature; rich and austere at once, giving death and life in the same moment, restoring beyond belief all the things it took away—except the individual will.

Its power rose in her now and filled her with the thought of her brother. As she came from the drive into the road she looked as alertly as she could before her in case he staggered into sight. Whether she was going to find him or not she couldn't tell, but it was apparently her business to look for him, or she wouldn't have felt so strongly the conviction that, of all those in the house, she alone was to go out and search. That she should be walking so lightly through the storm didn't strike her as odd, because it wasn't really she who was walking, it was Love, and naturally Love would be safe in his own storm. It was, certainly, a magnificent storm; she adored the power that was displayed in it. Lothair, she thought, wouldn't be adoring it much at the moment: something in her longed passionately to open his eyes, so that the two of them could walk in it happily together. And Nancy, and Henry—O, and Aaron Lee, and Ralph, and everyone they all knew, until the vision of humanity rejoicing in this tumultuous beauty seemed to show itself to her, and the delight of creation answered the delight of the Creator, joy triumphing in joy.

CHARLES WILLIAMS (from *The Greater Trumps*)

§ 3

Mutual Forgiveness of each Vice,
Such are the Gates of Paradise.

BLAKE

Without Forgiveness of Sin, Love is Itself Eternal Death.

BLAKE

And Throughout all Eternity
I forgive you, you forgive me.
As our dear Redeemer said:
"This the Wine & this the Bread."

BLAKE

O point of mutual forgiveness between Enemies!
Birthplace of the Lamb of God incomprehensible!

BLAKE

In Heaven the only Art of living
Is Forgetting & Forgiving
Especially to the Female.

BLAKE

To Sin in the open face of day is cruel & pitiless! But
To record the Sin for a reproach, to let the Sun go down
In a remembrance of the Sin, is a Woe & a Horror,
A brooder of an Evil Day and a Sun rising in blood!
Come then, O Lamb of God, and take away the remembrance of
Sin.

BLAKE

There is not one Moral Virtue that Jesus Inculcated but Plato &
Cicero did Inculcate before him; what then did Christ Inculcate?
Forgiveness of Sins. This alone is the Gospel, & this is the Life &
Immortality brought to light by Jesus. . . .

BLAKE

The Spirit of Jesus is continual forgiveness of Sin: he who waits
to be righteous before he enters into the Saviour's kingdom, the
Divine Body, will never enter there. I am perhaps the most sinful

542

of men. I pretend not to holiness; yet I pretend to love, to see, to converse with daily as man with man, & the more to have an interest in the Friend of Sinners.

BLAKE

In Great Eternity every particular Form gives forth or Emanates
Its own peculiar Light, and the Form is the Divine Vision
And the Light is his Garment. This is Jerusalem in every Man,
A Tent and Tabernacle of Mutual Forgiveness.

BLAKE

If thou wouldst taste God's clemency and have him to forgive thy sins and dowse thee with his Holy Ghost in grace, then show the mercy due to all mankind made in Christ's image as they are, whether or not they shall have sinned against thee: needs must if thou art ever to find grace.

MEISTER ECKHART

Be Thou praised, O Lord, for those who forgive for love of thee, and bear sufferings and tribulations.

Blessed are they who are steadfast in peace, for by thee, Most High, shall they be crowned.

ST. FRANCIS

One of the old men said, "When a man saith unto his companion, 'Forgive me,' and at the same time humbleth himself, the devils are consumed."

THE PARADISE OF THE FATHERS

To what may this be likened, ask our Rabbis? To that king who had a son and a friend. Six times the son sinned against his father, and six times the friend obtained forgiveness for him. The seventh time the friend dared not intercede again. What, then, did the king? He gave his forgiveness without being asked for it.

EDMOND FLEG (*from a Midrash*)

One day God said to Moses: "Korah, sobbing, called you seventy times and you did not reply. If he had called me thus, once, I would have wrested his heart from the pit of polytheism and covered his breast with a vestment of faith. O Moses, you have caused him to perish in a hundred agonies, you have cast him into the earth with disgrace. If you had been his creator you would have been less stern with him."

FARID UD-DIN ATTAR

CYMBELINE

Cymbeline   See,
Posthumus anchors upon Imogen;
And she, like harmless lightning, throws her eye
On him, her brothers, me, her master, hitting
Each object with a joy: the counterchange
Is severally in all. Let's quit this ground,
And smoke the temple with our sacrifices.
(*To Belarius*) Thou art my brother; so we'll hold thee
     ever.

Imogen   You are my father too; and did relieve me,
To see this gracious season.

Cymbeline   All o'erjoyed,
Save these in bonds: let them be joyful too,
For they shall taste our comfort.

Imogen   My good master,
I will yet do you service.

Lucius   Happy be you!

Cymbeline The forlorn soldier that so nobly fought,
He would have well becomed this place and graced
The thankings of a king.

Posthumus   I am, sir,
The soldier that did company these three
In poor beseeming; 'twas a fitment for
The purpose I then follow'd. That I was he,
Speak, Iachimo: I had you down, and might
Have made you finish.

Iachimo   [*Kneeling*] I am down again:
But now my heavy conscience sinks my knee,
As then your force did. Take that life, beseech you,
Which I so often owe: but your ring first;
And here the bracelet of the truest princess
That ever swore her faith.

544

Posthumus	Kneel not to me:
	The power that I have on you is to spare you;
	The malice towards you to forgive you: live,
	And deal with others better.
Cymbeline	Nobly doom'd!
	We'll learn our freeness of a son-in-law;
	Pardon's the word to all.

SHAKESPEARE

THE PENITENT SINNER

Once upon a time a man lived in the world for seventy years, and lived all his life in sin. Then this man fell sick, but did not repent—except that, when death came to him in the last hour of all, he burst into tears and cried: "O Lord, pardon me as Thou didst the thief upon the cross." That was all he had time to say before his soul departed. Yet the soul of that sinner loved God, and trusted in His mercy, and thus it came to the doors of Paradise.

And the sinner began to knock thereat and beseech admittance to the Kingdom of Heaven. Then he heard a voice from within the doors saying: "What manner of man is this who is knocking at the doors of Paradise, and what deeds hath he performed during his lifetime?"

Then the voice of the Accuser answered, and recounted all the sinful deeds of the man, and named no good ones at all.

Thereupon the voice from within the doors spoke again. "Sinners," it said, "may not enter into the Kingdom of Heaven. Depart thou hence."

And the man cried: "O Judge, thy voice I hear, but thy face I cannot see, and thy name I do not know."

And the voice answered: "I am Peter the Apostle."

Then said the sinner: "Have compassion upon me, O Peter the Apostle, and remember the weakness of men and the mercy of God. Wert thou not a disciple of Christ, and didst thou not hear from His own lips His teaching, and didst thou not behold the example of His life? Dost thou not remember also the time when He was in agony of soul and did thrice ask of thee why thou didst sleep and not pray, and yet thou didst sleep, for thine eyes were heavy, and thrice He found thee sleeping?

"Dost thou not remember also how thou didst promise Him that thou wouldst not deny Him unto death, and yet how thou didst thrice deny Him when He was brought before Caiaphas? Thus hath it been with me.

"Dost thou not remember also how the cock did crow, and thou didst go out and weep bitterly? Thus hath it been with me. Thou canst not deny me admittance."

But the voice from within the doors of Paradise was silent.

Then, after waiting a little while, the sinner began once more to beseech admittance to the Kingdom of Heaven. Thereupon a second voice was heard from within the doors and said: "Who is this man, and in what manner hath he lived in the world?"

The voice of the Accuser answered, and once more recited all the evil deeds of the sinner, and named no good ones.

Thereupon the voice answered from within the doors: "Depart thou hence. Sinners such as thou may not live with us in Paradise."

But the sinner cried: "O Judge, thy voice I hear, but thy face I cannot see, and thy name I do not know."

Then the voice said to him: "I am King David the Prophet."

Yet the sinner would not desist nor leave the doors, but cried again:

"Have compassion on me, O King David, and remember the weakness of men and the mercy of God. God loved thee and exalted thee above thy fellows. Thou hadst all things—a kingdom, glory, riches, wives, and children—yet didst thou look from thy roof upon the wife of a poor man, and sin did enter into thee, and thou didst take the wife of Uriah, and didst slay Uriah himself with the sword of the Ammonites. Thou, the rich man, didst take from the poor man his one ewe lamb, and didst put the man himself to death. Thus also hath it been with me.

"But dost thou not remember also how thou didst repent and say—'I acknowledge my transgressions, and my sins are ever before me'? Thus is it with me now. Thou canst not deny me admittance."

But the voice from within the doors of Paradise was silent.

Then, after waiting a little while, the sinner began once more to knock and beseech admittance to the Kingdom of Heaven.

Thereupon a third voice was heard from within the doors and said: "Who is this man, and in what manner hath he lived in the world?"

And the voice of the Accuser answered, and for the third time recited the evil deeds of the man, and named no good ones.

Then the voice spoke again from within the doors. "Depart thou hence," it said. "Sinners may not enter into the Kingdom of Heaven."

546

But the sinner cried: "O Judge, thy voice I hear, but thy face I cannot see, and thy name I do not know."

And the voice answered: "I am John the Divine, the disciple whom Jesus loved."

Then the sinner rejoiced and said: "Now canst thou not deny me admittance. Peter and David might have let me in because they know the weakness of men and the mercy of God: but thou wilt let me in because in thee there is abounding love. Didst not thou, O John the Divine, write in thy book that God is Love, and that whoso loveth not, the same knoweth not God? Didst not thou in thy old age give to men this saying—'Brethren, love one another'? How therefore, canst thou hate me or drive me hence? Either must thou love me and yield me admittance to the Kingdom of Heaven, or thou must deny what thou thyself hast said."

Then the doors of Paradise were opened, and John received the penitent sinner, and admitted him to the Kingdom of Heaven.

TOLSTOY

UNCONDITIONAL FORGIVENESS

Forgiveness must be, both in its inner completeness and in its non-discrimination about objects, unconditional forgiveness: well-wishing must be, both in its inner completeness and in its non-discrimination about objects, unconditional well-wishing: and reconciliation must be unconditional reconciliation.

Let us examine for a moment only two of the limitations which it is commonly thought right or necessary to impose upon the practice of forgiveness and well-wishing; and please note that I say "thought right or necessary", for I have in mind, not the weakness of anyone who, like myself, is unable to rise to the full height of the argument, but conditions and limitations that are deliberately imposed. You sometimes hear it said, for instance—I have heard it said by a famous leader of religious thought in this country—that to wish a man well would be not only unreasonable but downright immoral, if he has wronged you or someone else or humanity in general *beyond a given point*, or if you judge him to have been guilty, *beyond a given point*, of cruelty or faithlessness or whatever wickedness it may be. One might retort with an adaptation of some famous words, and ask "If ye love only the obviously lovable, what reward have ye? Even the spiritually careless do the same". The moment you make this kind of distinction in your well-wishing, it is clear that you do not begin to understand what well-wishing really means. To wish a man well is to wish that as a personality, as a partaker in the universal personality, he may have life, spiritual life, in greater abundance. How can it be relevant whether he has harmed you or others, or transgressed the moral law, beyond a certain point? Or rather it *is* relevant: because his revolt from love and reality demands from you, and precisely in your meeting with him, a correspondingly greater loyalty to them: the more his lack, the more you have to give. It is *he*, he in his immortal essence, he as an everlasting personality, with which you are concerned: but the moment you begin judging, the moment you begin weighing and measuring, you are not with him but with yourself. It is surely by no means a paradox, but the simple truth, to say that it is far more important to wish a man well whom you judge to be very wicked than to wish a man well whom you judge to be rather wicked, and to wish a man well whom you judge to be rather wicked than to wish a man well whom you judge to be a saint. Or to put it another way, it is precisely the hater who has most need of our love: and if we can really love him unconditionally, if we can really love him in spirit and in truth, the hatred will go and love take its place.

I will give only one more example of the conditions and limitations which people impose on well-wishing. It is sometimes said—this also was said a year or two ago by one of our great religious leaders—that you cannot and ought not to forgive a wrongdoer until he has repented. There is here a quite radical misconception. What is in fact being said is that until the other has become good you ought not to be good yourself. How then can a start ever be made? I said before that to wish a man well whom we judge wicked is more important than to wish a man well whom we judge good: I will now go further and say that it is more important to wish a man well who has not repented than to wish a man well who has. It is precisely his repentance, his reunion with love and reality, that we desire to produce: and it is by loving him, we believe, that we produce it. To say that we will love him only if he repents is to propose a sort of bargain more relevant to the counting-house than to spiritual reality. I would add that while an expression of sorrow for having wronged, and perhaps restitution, are due to the wronged one, repentance is to God: only God can judge of it: and for a man to demand repentance, or to weigh up its quality, is Satanic presumption, and a breach of the commandment that forbids us to take the name of the Lord our God in vain.

What it all adds up to is this. We are called upon to love our neighbour: and our neighbour means not merely the good man, or the repentant man, or the man in the next street—indeed not chiefly these—but just man—man indifferently, man everywhere.

Humility also comes in. Unless it is in utter humility that we hold out our hands, the other will not grasp them: he cannot grasp them, because, in spirit and in truth, they are not there. Genuine charity is an act of complete self-surrender: if we are really to meet the other, we must cut and cast away our last moorings. If we judge the other, if we compare the other to ourselves, if, with whatever worthy motive, we play the schoolmaster or even the loving father and guide, there can be no spiritual meeting: for we have by no means cut our moorings: we have stayed on our own shore, and beckoned the other to us. He will not come.

V. G.

. . . Doth Jehovah Forgive a Debt only on condition that it shall
Be Payed? Doth he Forgive Pollution only on conditions of Purity?
That Debt is not Forgiven! That Pollution is not Forgiven!
Such is the Forgiveness of the Gods, the Moral Virtues of the
Heathen whose tender Mercies are Cruelty. But Jehovah's Salva-
tion
Is without Money & without Price, in the Continual Forgiveness of
Sins,
In the Perpetual Mutual Sacrifice in Great Eternity; for behold,
There is none that liveth & Sinneth not! And this is the Covenant
Of Jehovah: If you Forgive one-another, so shall Jehovah Forgive
You,
That He Himself may Dwell among You.

BLAKE

§ 4

One day a kid escaped from the flock. Moses hastened after it to a rocky place where he found it drinking at a spring. "Poor kid," he said to it, "thou didst flee in order to drink? Surely thou art now full weary." He took it on his shoulder and brought it back to the flock. Then God said: "Since he hath had pity upon a poor kid, bearing it upon his shoulder to take upon him its weariness, then will he have pity upon My poor people, bearing them in his heart to take upon him their sin."

549

For God, before entrusting the flocks of men to His kings and His prophets, entrusts to them, to try them, the flocks of His beasts.

EDMOND FLEG (*from a Midrash*)

ST. MALO AND THE WREN

And another miracle he wrought like to this, worthy of record for its compassion alone. He was a follower of Paul the Apostle, whose own hands supplied his wants, if aught were lacking: and when he had leisure from his task of preaching the Gospel, he kept himself by the work of his hands. One day he was busy with the brethren in the vineyard, pruning the vines, and for better speed in his work took off his cloak and laid it out of sight. When his work was done and he came to take his cloak, he found that the small bird whom common folk call a wren had laid an egg on it. And knowing that God's care is not far from the birds, since not one of them falls on the ground without the Father, he let his cloak lie there, till the eggs were hatched and the wren brought out her brood. And this was the marvel, that all the time that cloak lay there, there fell no rain upon it. And whoever came to hear of it, they glorified the power of God, and they praised God's own pity in man.

ACTA SANCTORUM (*tr. by Waddell*)

THE IMITATION OF ST. MALO

St. Malo would not move his cloak, because a wren had nested in it: and the other day a professional in a golf championship let go his chance of it, because he would not play his ball out of a thrush's nest.

HELEN WADDELL

ST. GODRIC AND THE HUNTED STAG

In the time of Rainulf, Bishop of Durham, certain of his household had come out for a day's hunting, with their hounds, and were following a stag which they had singled out for its beauty. The creature, hard pressed by the clamour and the baying, made for Godric's hermitage, and seemed by its plaintive cries to beseech his help. The old man came out, saw the stag shivering and exhausted at his gate, and moved with pity bade it hush its moans, and opening the door of his hut, let it go in. The creature dropped at the good father's feet, but he, feeling that the hunt was coming near, came out, shut the door behind him and sat down in the open: while the dogs, vexed at the loss of their quarry, turned back with a mighty baying upon their masters. They, none the less, following on the track of the stag, circled round about the place, plunging through the well-nigh impenetrable brushwood of thorns and briars; and hacking a path with their blades, came upon the man of God in his poor rags. They questioned him about the stag: but he would not be the betrayer of his guest, and he made prudent answer, "God knows where he may be." They looked at the angelic beauty of his countenance, and in reverence for his holiness they fell before him and asked his pardon for their bold intrusion. Many a time afterwards they would tell what had befallen them there, and marvel at it, and by their oft telling of it, the thing was kept in memory by those that came after. But the stag kept house with Godric until the evening: and then he let it go free. But for years thereafter it would turn from its way to visit him, and lie at his feet, to show what gratitude it could for its deliverance.

ACTA SANCTORUM (tr. by Waddell)

ST. GODRIC AND THE HARE

The gentleness of his heart did not betray itself only in kindness to men, but his wise solicitude watched over the very reptiles and the creatures of the earth. For in winter when all about was frozen stiff in the cold, he would go out barefoot, and if he lighted on any animal helpless with misery of the cold, he would set it under his armpit or in his bosom to warm it. Many a time would the kind soul go spying under the thick hedges or tangled patches of briars, and if haply he found a creature that had lost its way, or cowed with the harshness of the weather, or tired, or half dead, he would recover it with all the healing art he had. . . .

And if anyone in his service had caught a bird or little beast in a snare or a trap or a noose, as soon as he found it he would snatch it from their hands and let it gò free in the fields or the glades of the wood. So that many a time they would hide their captive spoils under a corn measure or a basket or some more secret hiding-place still: but even so they could never deceive him or keep it hidden. For often without any telling, and indeed with his serving-man disavowing and protesting, he would go straight to the place where the creatures had been hidden: and while the man would stand by crimson with fear and confusion, he would lift them out and set

them free. So, too, hares and other beasts fleeing from the hunts-
men he would take in, and house them in his hut: and when the
ravagers, their hope frustrated, would be gone, he would send them
away to their familiar haunts. Many a time the dumb creatures of
the wood would swerve aside from where the huntsmen lay in wait,
and take shelter in the safety of his hut: for it may be that by some
divine instinct they knew that a sure refuge abided their coming.

ACTA SANCTORUM (tr. by Waddell)

ST. FRANCIS AND THE TURTLE-DOVES

One day at Siena he asked for some turtle-doves, and, holding
them in the skirt of his tunic, he said: "Little sisters turtle-doves,
you are simple, innocent and chaste; why did you let yourselves be
caught? I shall save you from death, and have nests made for you,
so that you may bring forth young and multiply according to the
commandment of our Creator."

And he went and made nests for them all, and the turtle-doves
began to lay eggs and bring up their broods under the eyes of the
Brothers.

At Rieti a family of red-breasts were the guests of the monastery,
and the young birds made marauding expeditions on the very table
where the Brothers were eating. Not far from there, at Greccio,
they brought to Francis a leveret that had been taken alive in a
trap. "Come to me, brother leveret," he said to it. And as the poor
creature, being set free, ran to him for refuge, he took it up, caressed
it, and finally put it on the ground that it might run away; but it
returned to him again and again, so that he was obliged to send it
to the neighbouring forest before it would consent to return to
freedom.

One day he was crossing the Lake of Rieti. The boatman in whose
bark he was making the passage offered him a tench of uncommon
size. Francis accepted it with joy, but to the great amazement of
the fisherman put it back into the water, bidding it bless God.

We should never have done if we were to relate all the incidents
of this kind, for the sentiment of nature was innate with him; it was
a perpetual communion which made him love the whole creation. He
is ravished with the witchery of great forests; he has the terrors of a
child when he is alone at prayer in a deserted chapel, but he tastes
ineffable joy merely in inhaling the perfume of a flower, or gazing
into the limpid water of a brook.

This perfect lover of poverty permitted one luxury—he even commanded it at Portiuncula—that of flowers; the Brother was bidden not to sow vegetables and useful plants only; he must reserve one corner of good ground for our sisters, the flowers of the fields. Francis talked with them also, or rather he replied to them, for their mysteries and gentle language crept into the very depth of his heart.

*   *   *

He [the dying Francis] had lost the notion of time; believing that it was still Thursday he desired to take a last meal with his disciples. Some bread was brought, he broke it and gave it to them, and there in the poor cabin of Portiuncula, without altar and without a priest, was celebrated the Lord's Supper . . .

The sun was gilding the crests of the mountains with his last rays, there was silence around the dying one. All was ready. The angel of death might come.

Saturday, October 3, 1226, at nightfall, without pain, without struggle, he breathed the last sigh.

The Brothers were still gazing on his face, hoping yet to catch some sign of life, when innumerable larks alighted, singing, on the thatch of his cell, as if to salute the soul which had just taken flight and give the Little Poor Man the canonization of which he was most worthy.

PAUL SABATIER

AN INSECT

Writing, I crushed an insect with my nail
And thought nothing at all. A bit of wing
Caught my eye then, a gossamer so frail

And exquisite, I saw in it a thing
That scorned the grossness of the thing I wrote.
It hung upon my finger like a sting.

A leg I noticed next, fine as a mote,
"And on this frail eyelash he walked," I said,
"And climbed and walked like any mountain-goat."

And in this mood I sought the little head,
But it was lost; then in my heart a fear
Cried out, "A life—why beautiful, why dead!"

553

It was a mite that held itself most dear,
So small I could have drowned it with a tear.

KARL SHAPIRO

THE SNARE

I hear a sudden cry of pain!
There is a rabbit in a snare:
Now I hear the cry again,
But I cannnot tell from where.

But I cannot tell from where
He is calling out for aid!
Crying on the frightened air,
Making everything afraid!

Making everything afraid!
Wrinkling up his little face!
As he cries again for aid;
—And I cannot find the place!

And I cannot find the place
Where his paw is in the snare!
Little One! Oh, Little One!
I am searching everywhere!

JAMES STEPHENS

Leonardo was in the habit of paying the price demanded by the owners of captive birds, for the pleasure of setting them free.

VASARI

Buddha once said to a king, "If the sacrifice of a lamb helps you to go to heaven, sacrificing a man will help you better, so sacrifice me."

VIVEKANANDA

I fished for pike at Castle Dargan and shot at birds with a muzzle-loading pistol until somebody shot a rabbit and I heard it squeal. From that on I would kill nothing but the dumb fish.

W. B. YEATS

Even in the days when he had been happy he had always loved the beasts: he had never been able to bear cruelty towards them: he had always had a detestation of sport which he had never dared to express for fear of ridicule . . . We must kill to live, if, at the time, there is no other means of living. But the man who kills for the sake of killing is a miscreant. An unconscious miscreant, I know. But, all the same, a miscreant. The continual endeavour of man should be to lessen the sum of suffering and cruelty: that is the first duty of humanity.

ROMAIN ROLLAND (from *Jean-Christophe*)

Is it not a reproach that man is a carnivorous animal? True, he can and does live, in a great measure, by preying on other animals; but this is a miserable way—as any one who will go to snaring rabbits, or slaughtering lambs, may learn—and he will be regarded as a benefactor of his race who shall teach man to confine himself to a more innocent and wholesome diet. Whatever my own practice may be, I have no doubt that it is a part of the destiny of the human race, in its gradual improvement, to leave off eating animals, as surely as the savage tribes have left off eating each other when they came in contact with the more civilized.

THOREAU

§ 5

He who gives alms in secret is greater than Moses.

TALMUD

The saying is, that he who gives to the poor, lends to the Lord. But it may be said, not improperly, the Lord lends to us to give to the poor.

WILLIAM PENN

And Korah the rich asked Moses: "Moses, our master, it is written in thy Torah: 'Take not from the poor, for he is poor'. Who can take from the poor, since he hath nothing?" And Moses answered him: "That which thou shouldst give to the poor belongeth unto him; that which thou givest him not, that thou takest from him."

EDMOND FLEG (*from a Midrash*)

Be cheated millions of times and never ask a question, and never think of what you are doing. Never vaunt of your gifts to the poor or expect their gratitude, but rather be grateful to them.

VIVEKANANDA

555

I was walking along the street . . . I was stopped by a decrepit old beggar.

Bloodshot, tearful eyes, blue lips, coarse rags, festering wounds. . . . Oh, how hideously poverty had eaten into this miserable creature!

He held out to me a red, swollen, filthy hand. He groaned, he mumbled of help.

I began feeling in all my pockets. . . . No purse, no watch, not even a handkerchief. . . . I had taken nothing with me. And the beggar was still waiting . . . and his outstretched hand feebly shook and trembled.

Confused, abashed, I warmly clasped the filthy, shaking hand . . . 'Don't be angry, brother; I have nothing, brother.'

The beggar stared at me with his bloodshot eyes; his blue lips smiled; and he in his turn gripped my chilly fingers.

'What of it, brother?' he mumbled; 'thanks for this, too. That is a gift too, brother.'

I knew that I too had received a gift from my brother.

TURGENEV

"Go, give a penny to that blind beggar," said the Rabbi of Witkowo to his son when they were walking together. The boy did so. When he rejoined his father, "Why didst thou not raise thy hat?" asked the latter. "But he is blind," replied the boy. "He could not have seen me." "And how dost thou know," retorted the Rabbi, "that he is not an imposter? Go, raise thy hat."

RABBI MOSHE HAKOTUN

If a man astride upon a horse should stretch down his hand for alms, do not deny him, because he is then, without doubt, as needy as a beggar. And when you give, do so with magnanimity, with a friendly face, and provide more than was asked for. For by this you can attract even the unworthy to goodness: because through the body the soul is quickly drawn into the fear of God. So the Lord shared his dinner with publicans and harlots, and did not drive the unworthy away, thereby drawing all into the fear of God, so that through the flesh they should come to the spirit. Therefore through kind deeds and esteem make all men equal, be it Jew or pagan or murderer, all the more as he too is a brother to you, and has wandered from the truth unknowingly.

ST. ISAAK OF SYRIA

Charity is generous; it runs a risk willingly, and in spite of a hundred successive experiences it thinks no evil at the hundred-and-first. We cannot be at the same time kind and wary, nor can we serve two masters—love and selfishness. We must be knowingly rash, that we may not be like the clever ones of the world, who never forget their own interests. We must be able to submit to being deceived; it is the sacrifice which interest and self-love owe to conscience. The claims of the soul must be satisfied first if we are to be the children of God.

AMIEL

My master, the Rabbi of Witkowo, used to say: How shouldest thou give of thy possessions to a man in need? As a matter of duty? No: for if love be lacking the body is nourished but the soul is starved. Better thus, however, than not at all. With conscious pleasure? No: for thy thought is on thyself, and thou puffest thyself up and imaginest thyself God. How, then? Naturally, spontaneously, without thought, as the sun gives its light and the mother her milk.

RABBI MOSHE HAKOTUN

THE WIDOWS MITES

Two Mites, two drops, yet all her house and land
Falls from a steady heart though trembling hand:
The others wanton wealth foams high and brave;
The other cast away, she onely gave.

RICHARD CRASHAW

§ 6

THE OLD CITY

O Jerusalem, Jerusalem, I have forsaken thy Courts,
Thy Pillars of ivory & gold, thy Curtains of silk & fine
Linen, thy Pavements of precious stones, thy Walls of pearl
And gold, thy Gates of Thanksgiving, thy Windows of Praise,
Thy Clouds of Blessing, thy Cherubims of Tender-mercy
Stretching their Wings sublime over the Little-ones of Albion!
O Human Imagination, O Divine Body I have Crucified,
I have turned my back upon thee into the Wastes of Moral Law.
There Babylon is builded in the Waste, founded in Human desolation.

557

O Babylon, thy Watchman stands over thee in the night,
Thy severe Judge all the day long proves thee, O Babylon,
With provings of destruction, with giving thee thy heart's desire;
But Albion is cast forth to the Potter, his Children to the Builders
To build Babylon because they have forsaken Jerusalem.
The Walls of Babylon are Souls of Men, her Gates the Groans
Of Nations, her Towers are the Miseries of once happy Families,
Her Streets are paved with Destruction, her Houses built with
    Death,
Her Palaces with Hell & the Grave, her Synagogues with Torments
Of ever-hardening Despair, squar'd & polish'd with cruel skill.

BLAKE

THE NEW CITY

What are those golden builders doing? . . .
. . . is that
Mild Zion's hill's most ancient promontory, near mournful
Ever weeping Paddington? is that Calvary and Golgotha
Becoming a building of pity and compassion? Lo!
The stones are pity, and the bricks, well wrought affections
Enamel'd with love & kindness, & the tiles engraven gold,
Labour of merciful hands: the beams & rafters are forgiveness:
The mortar & cement of the work, tears of honesty: the nails
And the screws & iron braces are well wrought blandishments
And well contrived words, firm fixing, never forgotten,
Always comforting the remembrance: the floors, humility:
The cielings, devotion: the hearths, thanksgiving.
Prepare the furniture, O Lambeth, in thy pitying looms,
The curtains, woven tears & sighs wrought into lovely forms
For comfort; there the secret furniture of Jerusalem's chamber
Is wrought. Lambeth! the Bride, the Lamb's Wife, loveth thee.
Thou art one with her & knowest not of self in thy supreme joy.
Go on, builders in hope, tho' Jerusalem wanders far away
Without the gate of Los, among the dark Satanic wheels.

BLAKE

II. THE JUST LIFE FOR MAN— DESIRABLE THINGS

Who will justify him that sinneth against his own soul? and who will glorify him that dishonoureth his own life?

ECCLESIASTICUS

That action is ill, wherein we lose ourselves: and there is no Recompense for the loss.

BENJAMIN WHICHCOTE

Look within: within is the fountain of good, ready always to well forth, if thou wilt ever delve.

MARCUS AURELIUS

O Lady! we receive but what we give
And in our life alone does Nature live:
Ours is her wedding garment, ours her shroud!
  And would we aught behold, of higher worth,
Than that inanimate cold world allowed
To the poor loveless ever-anxious crowd,
  Ah! from the soul itself must issue forth
A light, a glory, a fair luminous cloud
    Enveloping the Earth—
And from the soul itself must there be sent
  A sweet and potent voice, of its own birth,
Of all sweet sounds the life and element!

O pure of heart! thou need'st not ask of me
What this strong music in the soul may be!
What, and wherein it doth exist,
This light, this glory, this fair luminous mist,
This beautiful and beauty-making power.
  Joy, virtuous Lady! Joy that ne'er was given,
Save to the pure, and in their purest hour,
Life, and Life's effluence, cloud at once and shower,
Joy, Lady! is the spirit and the power,
Which wedding Nature to us gives in dower
  A new Earth and new Heaven,
Undreamt of by the sensual and the proud—
Joy is the sweet voice, Joy the luminous cloud—
  We in ourselves rejoice!
And thence flows all that charms or ear or sight,
  All melodies the echoes of that voice,
All colours a suffusion from that light.

S. T. COLERIDGE

"Consult thy heart," the Prophet said to one of his followers, "and thou wilt hear the secret ordinance of God proclaimed by the heart's inward knowledge, which is real faith and divinity."

SUFI TRADITION

The moral good is not a goal but an inner force which lights up man's life from within.

BERDYAEV

God—we read—is outside of none, present unperceived to all; we break away from Him, or rather from ourselves; what we turn from we cannot reach; astray ourselves, we cannot go in search of another; a child distraught will not recognise its father; to find ourselves is to know our source.

PLOTINUS

It is not by running hither and thither outside of itself that the soul understands morality and right conduct: it learns them of its own nature, in its contact with itself, in its intellectual grasp of itself, seeing deeply impressed upon it the images of its primal state; what was one mass of rust from long neglect it has restored to purity.

Imagine living gold: it files away all that is earthy about it, all that kept it in self-ignorance, preventing it from knowing itself as gold; seen now unalloyed it is at once filled with admiration of its worth and knows that it has no need of any other glory than its own, triumphant if only it be allowed to remain purely to itself.

PLOTINUS

Become what thou art.

ORPHIC SAYING

We can live—and many do—our entire life as the pale reflection of someone else, as a copy of someone else. The first, original meaning of living is to be oneself, rising to the transformation of oneself into the image and likeness of God.

FATHER YELCHANINOV

He was like so many men: they have no opinions, except in so far as they disapprove of all enthusiastic opinion: but if a man is to be independent he must stand alone, and how many men are there who are capable of that? How many men are there, even amongst the most clear sighted, who will dare to break free of the bondage of certain prejudices, certain postulates which cramp and fetter all the men of the same generation? That would mean setting up a wall between themselves and others. On the one hand, freedom in the wilderness, on the other, mankind. They do not hesitate: they choose mankind, the herd. . . . Then those who have chosen pretend to think what they do not in fact think. It is not very difficult for them: they know so little what they think! . . . "Know thyself!" . . . How could they, these men who have hardly a Me to know?

ROMAIN ROLLAND (from *Jean-Christophe*)

When on the Sabbath day my room is full of people, I find it hard to interpret the Law. For each man needs his own law, and needs to be perfected therein; and what I interpret for all, I withdraw from each.

RABBI BUNAM OF PZHYSHA

The best way of serving God is the one to which your heart is drawn. Labour in it with your whole strength.

THE SEER OF LUBLIN

If we take the resolution of always obeying the voice of conscience —for this is God's voice in us—such a resolution will develop in us the lost organ of communion with God.

FATHER YELCHANINOV

The will to originality is not the will to be peculiar and unlike anybody else; it means the desire to derive one's consciousness from its primary source.

BERDYAEV

Cast conformity behind you, and acquaint men at first hand with Deity.

EMERSON

But if we fear to do the dictates of our Angels, & tremble at the Tasks set before us; if we refuse to do spiritual Acts because of Natural Fears or Natural Desires! who can describe the dismal torments of such a state! . . . Naked we came here, naked of Natural things, & naked we shall return; but while cloth'd with the Divine Mercy, we are richly cloth'd in Spiritual & suffer all the rest gladly. . . .

BLAKE

Every honest man is a Prophet; he utters his opinion both of private & public matters.

BLAKE

If I had ten thousand lives, I could freely and cheerfully lay down them all to witness in this matter. By God I have leaped over a wall; by God I have run through a troup, and by God I will get through this death, and He will make it easy to me. However men presume to call it by hard names, there was more of God in it than men are now aware of.

THOMAS HARRISON (*from the scaffold*)

The hackneyed and lavished title of Blasphemer—which, with Radical, Liberal, Jacobin, Reformer, &c., are the changes which the hirelings are daily ringing in the ears óf those who will listen— should be welcome to all who recollect on *whom* it was originally bestowed. Socrates and Jesus Christ were put to death publicly as *blasphemers*, and so have been and may be many who dare to oppose the most notorious abuses of the name of God and the mind of man. But persecution is not refutation, nor even triumph: the "wretched infidel", as he is called, is probably happier in his prison than the proudest of his assailants.

BYRON

Disobedience, the rarest and most courageous of the virtues, is seldom distinguished from neglect, the laziest and commonest of the vices.

BERNARD SHAW

Do always what you believe right, Brother; and if that is wrong, repent of it afterwards.

A FRANCISCAN (*in a Housman play*)

The greatest pride or dejection is the greatest ignorance of self.

SPINOZA

There are two states or conditions of pride. The first is one of self-approval, the second one of self-contempt. Pride is seen probably at its purest in the last.

AMIEL

There is a luxury in self-dispraise;
And inward self-disparagement affords
To meditative spleen a grateful feast.

WORDSWORTH

I should like to add one more beatitude to those of the gospels
and to say, Blessed are they who heal us of self-despisings. Of all
services which can be done to man, I know of none more precious.

MARK RUTHERFORD

We receive everything, both life and happiness; but the *manner*
in which we receive, this is what is still ours. Let us, then, receive
trustfully without shame or anxiety. Let us humbly accept from
God even our own nature, and treat it charitably, firmly, intelli-
gently. Not that we are called upon to accept the evil and the disease
in us, but let us accept *ourselves* in spite of the evil and the disease.

AMIEL

Our first duty is not to hate ourselves; because to advance we
must have faith in ourselves first and then in God. He who has no
faith in himself can never have faith in God.

VIVEKANANDA

Wretched is the soul that does not feel its own fruitfulness, and
know itself to be big with life and love, as a tree with blossom
in the spring!

ROMAIN ROLLAND

We see here the necessity for distinguishing between love of
one's-self regarded as non-disposable, and love of one's-self regarded as disposable, that is, love of what God may make of me.

GABRIEL MARCEL

One of the sources of human suffering is disgust with oneself
and inability to feel any self-love. There is a self-love which we
ought to have in accordance with God's will. We ought to love
ourselves as God's creation and love the Divine image and likeness
in us. We must love our neighbours as ourselves. This implies
that we must love ourselves too and respect the image of God in us.
Such a love is opposed to egoism and egocentricity, i.e. to the madness of putting oneself at the centre of the universe.

BERDYAEV

So long as a man seeks his self-will and his best as his, and for his own sake, he will never find it . . . For so long as he does this, he seeks himself, and imagines that he is himself the Best.

THEOLOGIA GERMANICA

Self-interest is but the survival of the animal in us. Humanity only begins for man with self-surrender.

AMIEL

In short, then, wherever man fairly and loyally throws the seat of his value outside his immediate self into something else which he worships, with which he identifies his will, and which he takes as an object solid and secure at least relatively to his private exist-ence—as an artist in his attitude to beauty or as a man of science to truth—there we have in its degree the experience of religion, and, also in its degree, the stability and security of the finite self.

BOSANQUET

Here is a problem: having renounced ourself, to remain ourself, to realise God's plan concerning us.

FATHER YELCHANINOV

THE TRUE SELF

The individual seeking for the law of his being can only find it safely if he regards clearly two great psychological truths and lives in that clear vision. First, the ego is not the self; there is one self of all and the soul is a portion of that universal Divinity. The fulfil-ment of the individual is not the utmost development of his egoistic intellect, vital force, physical well-being, and the utmost satisfaction of his mental, emotional, physical cravings, but the flowering of the divine in him to its utmost capacity of wisdom, power, love and universality, and through this flowering his utmost realisation of all the possible beauty and delight of existence.

The will to be, the will to power, the will to know are perfectly legitimate, their satisfaction the true law of our existence, and to discourage and repress them improperly is to mutilate our being and dry up or diminish the sources of life and growth. But their satis-faction must not be egoistic—not for any other reason moral or religious, but simply because they cannot so be satisfied. The attempt always leads to an eternal struggle with other egoisms, a mutual wounding and hampering, even a mutual destruction in which, if we are conquerors today, we are the conquered or the slain tomorrow; for we exhaust ourselves and corrupt ourselves in the dangerous attempt to live by the destruction and exploitation of others. Only that which lives in its own self-existence can endure. And generally, to devour others is to register oneself also as a subject and predestined victim of Death.

No doubt, so long as we live without self-knowledge, we can do no other; men and nations have to act and think egoistically, because in their self-ignorance that is the only life known to them, and to live is their God-given impulse; therefore they must live egoistically rather than not at all, with whatever curb of law, ethics and practical common sense of self-restraint nature and experience have taught them. But subjectivism is in its very nature an attempt at self-knowledge and at living by a true self-knowledge and by an inner strength, and there is no real gain in it if we only repeat the old error in new terms. Therefore we must find out that the true individual is not the ego, but the divine individuality which is through our evolution preparing to emerge in us; its emergence and satisfaction, and not the satisfaction of the mere egoistic will-to-live for the sake of one's lower members, is the true object at which a humanity subjectively seeking to know and fulfil its own deepest law and truth should increasingly aim.

The second psychic truth the individual has to grasp is this: that he is not only himself, but is in solidarity with all of his kind— let us leave aside for the moment that which seems to be not of his kind. That which we are has expressed itself through the individual, but also through the universality; and though each has to fulfil itself in its own way, neither can succeed independently of the other. The society has no right to crush or efface the individual for its own better development or self-satisfaction; the individual, so long at least as he chooses to live in the world, has no right to disregard for the sake of his own solitary satisfaction the development of his fellow-beings, and to live at war with them or seek a selfishly isolated good. And when we say "no right" it is from no social, moral or religious standpoint, but from the most positive, and simply with a view to the law of existence itself. For neither the society nor the individual can so develop to their fulfilment. Every time the society crushes or effaces the individual, it is inflicting a wound on itself and depriving its own life of priceless sources of stimulation and growth. The individual too cannot flourish by himself; for the

567

universal, the unity and collectivity of his fellow-beings, is his present source and stock; it is the thing whose possibilities he individually expresses, even when he transcends its immediate level, and of which in his phenomenal being he is one result. Its depression strikes eventually at his own sources of life; by its increasing he also increases. This is what a true subjectivism teaches us—first, that we are a higher self than our ego or our members, secondly, that we are in our life and being not only ourselves but all others; for there is a secret solidarity which our egoism may kick at and strive against, but from which we cannot escape. It is the old Indian discovery that our real "I" is a Supreme Being which is our true self and which it is our business to discover and consciously become; and, secondly, that that Being is one in all, expressed in the individual and in the collectivity—and only by admitting and realising our unity with others can we entirely fulfil our true self-being.

AUROBINDO

Let us not be in too furious a haste to acquire even peace, purity and perfection. Peace must be ours, but not the peace of an empty or devastated nature or of slain or mutilated capacities incapable of unrest because we have made them incapable of intensity and fire and force. Purity must be our aim, but not the purity of a void or of a bleak and rigid coldness. Perfection is demanded of us, but not the perfection that can exist only by confining its scope within narrow limits or putting an arbitrary full stop to the ever self-extending scroll of the Infinite.

AUROBINDO

Consider yourself a refractory pupil for whom you are responsible as mentor and tutor. To sanctify sinful nature, by bringing it gradually under the control of the angel within us, by the help of a holy God, is really the whole of Christian pedagogy and of religious morals. Our work—my work—consists in taming, subduing, evangelising, and *angelising* the evil self; and in restoring harmony with the good self. Salvation lies in abandoning the evil self in principle, and in taking refuge with the other, the divine self—in accepting with courage and prayer the task of living with one's own demon, and making it into a less and less rebellious instrument of good. The Abel in us must labour for the salvation of the Cain. To undertake it is to be converted, and this conversion must be re-

568

peated day by day. Abel only redeems and touches Cain by exercising him constantly in good works. To do right is in one sense an act of violence: it is suffering, expiation, a cross, for it means the conquest and enslavement of self. In another sense it is the apprenticeship to heavenly things, sweet and secret joy, contentment and peace.

AMIEL

Every hurtful passion draws us to it, as an abyss does, by a kind of vertigo. Feebleness of will brings about weakness of head, and the abyss, in spite of its horror, comes to fascinate us, as though it were a place of refuge. Terrible danger! For this abyss is within us; this gulf, open like the vast jaws of an infernal serpent bent on devouring us, is in the depth of our own being, and our liberty floats over this void, which is always seeking to swallow it up. Our only talisman lies in that concentration of moral force which we call conscience, that small inextinguishable flame of which the light is duty and the warmth love. This little flame should be the star of our life; it alone can guide our trembling ark across the tumult of the great waters; it alone can enable us to escape the temptations of the sea, the storms and the monsters which are the offspring of night and the deluge. Faith in God, in a holy, merciful, fatherly God, is the divine ray which kindles this flame.

How deeply I feel the profound and terrible poetry of all these primitive terrors from which have issued the various theogonies of the world, and how it all grows clear to me, and becomes a symbol of the one great unchanging thought—the thought of God about the universe! How present and sensible to my inner sense is the unity of everything! It seems to me that I am able to pierce to the sublime motive which, in all the infinite spheres of existence, and through all the modes of space and time, every created form reproduces and sings within the bond of an eternal harmony. From the infernal shades I feel myself mounting towards the regions of light; my flight across chaos finds its rest in paradise. Heaven, hell, the world are within us. Man is the great abyss.

AMIEL

Do no violence to yourself, respect in yourself the oscillations of feeling. They are your life and your nature; One wiser than you ordained them. Do not abandon yourself altogether either to instinct or to will. Instinct is a siren, will a despot. Be neither the slave of your impulses and sensations of the moment, nor of an abstract and general plan; be open to what life brings from within and without, and welcome the unforeseen; but give to your life unity, and bring the unforeseen within the lines of your plan. Let what is natural in you raise itself to the level of the spiritual, and let the spiritual become once more natural. Thus will your development be harmonious, and the peace of heaven will shine upon your brow—always on condition that your peace is made, and that you have climbed your Calvary.

AMIEL

> If with the great Divinity who dwells
> Within thy breast thou hast no controversy,
> Go not to Ganges' water to be cleansed,
> Nor make a pilgrimage to Kuru's fields.

THE CODE OF MANU

Anything which is at variance and enmity with itself is not likely to be in union or harmony with any other thing.

PLATO

We must not live superficially, but with the greatest possible tension of all our forces, both physical and spiritual. When we expend the maximum of our powers, we do not exhaust ourselves, but increase the sources of our strength.

FATHER YELCHANINOV

The majority of men have not vitality enough to give themselves wholly to any passion. They spare themselves and save their force with cowardly prudence. They are a little of everything and nothing absolutely. A man who gives himself without counting the cost, to everything that he does, everything that he suffers, everything that he loves, everything that he hates, is a prodigy, the greatest that is granted to us here on earth.

ROMAIN ROLLAND

A moderately honest man with a moderately faithful wife, moderate drinkers both, in a moderately healthy house: that is the true middle class unit.

BERNARD SHAW

Strange is the vigour in a brave man's soul. The strength of his spirit and his irresistible power, the greatness of his heart and the height of his condition, his mighty confidence and contempt of dangers, his true security and repose in himself, his liberty to dare and do what he pleaseth, his alacrity in the midst of fears, his invincible temper, are advantages which make him master of fortune. His courage fits him for all attempts, makes him serviceable to God and man. . . .

TRAHERNE

We never know how high we are
  Till we are called to rise;
And then, if we are true to plan,
  Our statures touch the skies.

The heroism we recite
  Would be a daily thing,
Did not ourselves the cubits warp
  For fear to be a king.

EMILY DICKINSON

TO THE RIVER DUDDON

I thought of Thee, my partner and my guide,
As being past away.—Vain sympathies!
For, backward, Duddon! as I cast my eyes,
I see what was, and is, and will abide;
Still glides the Stream, and shall for ever glide;
The Form remains, the Function never dies;
While we, the brave, the mighty, and the wise,
We Men, who in our morn of youth defied
The elements, must vanish;—be it so!
Enough, if something from our hands have power
To live, and act, and serve the future hour;
And if, as toward the silent tomb we go,
Through love, through hope, and faith's transcendent dower,
We feel that we are greater than we know.

WORDSWORTH

Every rank of creatures, as it ascends in the scale of creation, leaves death behind it or under it. The metal at its height of being seems a mute prophecy of the coming vegetation, into a mimic semblance of which it crystallizes. The blossom and flower, the acme of vegetable life, divides into correspondent organs with reciprocal functions, and by instinctive motions and approximations seems impatient of that fixure, by which it is differenced in kind from the flower-shaped Psyche, that flutters with free wing above it. And wonderfully in the insect realm doth the irritability, the proper seat of instinct, while yet the nascent sensibility is subordinated thereto—most wonderfully, I say, doth the muscular life in the insect, and the musculo-arterial in the bird, imitate and typically rehearse the adaptive understanding, yea, and the moral affections and charities, of man. Let us carry ourselves back, in spirit, to the mysterious week, the teeming work-days of the creator: as they rose in vision before the eye of the inspired historian of *the generations of the heaven and the earth, in the days that the Lord God made the earth and the heavens.* And who that hath watched their ways with an understanding heart, could, as the vision evolving still advanced towards him, contemplate the filial and loyal bee; the home-building, wedded, and divorceless swallow; and above all the mani-foldly intelligent ant tribes, with their commonwealths and confederacies, their warriors and miners, the husbandfolk, that fold in their tiny flocks on the honeyed leaf, and the virgin sisters with the holy instincts of maternal love, detached and in selfless purity—and not say to himself, Behold the shadow of approaching humanity, the sun rising from behind, in the kindling morn of creation! Thus all lower natures find their highest good in semblances and seekings of that which is higher and better. All things strive to ascend, and ascend in their striving. And shall man alone stoop? Shall his pursuits and desires, the reflections of his inward life, be like the reflected image of a tree on the edge of a pool, that grows downward, and seeks a mock heaven in the unstable element beneath it, in neighbourhood with the slim water-weeds and oozy bottom-grass that are yet better than itself and more noble, in as far as substances that appear as shadows are preferable to shadows mistaken for substance! No! it must be a higher good to make you happy. While you labour for any thing below your proper humanity, you seek a happy life in the region of death. Well saith the moral poet—

Unless above himself he can
Erect himself, how mean a thing is man!

S. T. COLERIDGE

The hope of mankind does not lie in the action of any corporate body, be it ever so powerful, but in the influence of individual men and women who for the sake of a greater have sacrificed a lesser aim.

KENNETH WALKER

Good is a product of the ethical and spiritual artistry of individuals; it cannot be mass-produced.

ALDOUS HUXLEY

Few are chosen, for the good reason that few choose themselves.

ALDOUS HUXLEY

I ought, therefore I can.

KANT

§ 2

Very few Men, properly speaking, live at present, but are providing to live another Time.

SWIFT

Our continual mistake is that we do not concentrate upon the present day, the actual hour, of our life; we live in the past or in the future; we are continually expecting the coming of some special hour when our life shall unfold itself in its full significance. And we do not observe that life is flowing like water through our fingers, sifting like precious grain from a loosely fastened bag.

FATHER YELCHANINOV

Be reverent before the dawning day. Do not think of what will be in a year, or in ten years. Think of to-day. Leave your theories. All theories, you see, even those of virtue, are bad, foolish, mischievous. Do not abuse life. Live in to-day. Be reverent towards each day. Love it, respect it, do not sully it, do not hinder it from coming to flower. Love it even when it is grey and sad like to-day. Do not be anxious. See. It is winter now. Everything is asleep. The good earth will awake again. You have only to be good and patient like the earth. Be reverent. Wait.

ROMAIN ROLLAND

573

The secret of good living is to live always both in the moment and in eternity: or, for this is the truer way of putting it, to live in the moment as eternity and in eternity as the moment: the two, for anyone who has mastered the secret, being one.

V. G.

To the question of what had been the essential point in the life of his late teacher, a disciple answered: "Just that which he dealt with at the moment."

MARTIN BUBER (*of a Hasid*)

If in obedience to right reason thou doest the thing that thy hand findeth to do earnestly, manfully, graciously, and in no sense as a by-work, and keepest that divine 'genius' of thine in its virgin state, just as if even now thou wert called upon to restore it to the Giver—if thou grapple this to thee, looking for nothing, shrinking from nothing, but content with a present sphere of activity such as Nature allows, and with chivalrous truth in every word and utterance of thy tongue, thou shalt be happy in thy life. And there is no one that is able to prevent this.

MARCUS AURELIUS

The problem set before us is to bring our daily task into the temple of contemplation and ply it there, to act as in the presence of God, to interfuse one's little part with religion. So only can we inform the detail of life, all that is passing, temporary, and insignificant, with beauty and nobility. So may we dignify and consecrate the meanest of occupations. So may we feel that we are paying our tribute to the universal work and the eternal will. So are we reconciled with life and delivered from the fear of death. So are we in order and at peace.

AMIEL

§ 3

To enjoy—to love a thing for its own sake and for no other reason.

LEONARDO DA VINCI

How much Easier is it quietly to enjoy, than eagerly to contest! How vastly wiser!

BENJAMIN WHICHCOTE

To bring forth and preserve, to produce without possessing, to act without hope of reward, and to expand without waste, this is the supreme virtue.

TAO TÊ CHING

Purification is the separation of good from covetousness.

SIMONE WEIL

Happiness and Beauty are by-products. Folly is the direct pursuit of Happiness and Beauty.

BERNARD SHAW

It is storied of that prince [Pyrrhus], that having conceived a purpose to invade Italy, he sent for Cineas, a philosopher and the King's friend: to whom he communicated his design, and desired his counsel. Cineas asked him to what purpose he invaded Italy? He said, to conquer it. And what will you do when you have conquered it? Go into France, said the King, and conquer that. And what will you do when you have conquered France? Conquer Germany. And what then? said the philosopher. Conquer Spain. I perceive, said Cineas, you mean to conquer all the World. What will you do when you have conquered all? Why then said the King we will return, and enjoy ourselves at quiet in our own land. So you may now, said the philosopher, without all this ado. Yet could he not divert him till he was ruined by the Romans. Thus men get one hundred pound a year that they may get another; and having two covet eight, and there is no end of all their labour.

TRAHERNE

THE DERVISH WITH A BEAUTIFUL BEARD

In the time of Moses there was a dervish who spent days and nights in a state of adoration, yet experienced no feeling for spiritual things. He had a beautiful long beard, and often while praying would stop to comb it. One day, seeing Moses, he went to him and said: 'O Pasha of Mount Sinai, ask God, I pray you, to tell me why I experience neither spiritual satisfaction nor ecstasy'.

The next time Moses went up on Sinai he spoke to God about the dervish, and God said, in a tone of displeasure: 'Although this dervish has sought union with me, nevertheless he is constantly thinking about his long beard'. When Moses came down he told the

575

Sufi what God had said. The Sufi thereupon began tearing out his beard, weeping bitterly. Gabriel then came along to Moses and said: 'Even now your Sufi is thinking about his beard. He thought of nothing else while praying, and is even more attached to it while he is tearing it out!'

O you who think you have ceased to be pre-occupied with your beard, you are plunged in an ocean of affliction. When you can regard it with detachment you will have a right to sail across this ocean. But if you plunge in with your beard you will have difficulty in getting out.

FARID UD-DIN ATTAR

THE LAND WHERE TÊ RULES

'I would have you strip away not your fine fur only, but every impediment of the body, scour your heart till it is free from all desire, and travel through the desolate wilds. For to the south there is a place called the Land where Tê Rules. Its people are ignorant and unspoiled, negligent of their own interests, and of few desires. They know how to make, but do not know how to hoard. They give, but seek no return. The suitabilities of decorum, the solemnities of ritual are alike unknown to them. They live and move thoughtlessly and at random, yet every step they take tallies with the Great Plan. They know how to enjoy life while it lasts, are ready to be put away when death comes.

'I would have you leave your kingdom and its ways, take Tao as your guide and travel to this land.'

'It is a long way to go,' said the prince of Lu, 'and dangerous. There are rivers too swift for any boat, mountains that no chariot can cross. What am I to do?' 'Humility,' said Shih-nan I-liao, 'shall be your boat. Pliancy shall be your chariot.' 'It is a long way to go,' said the prince, 'and the lands through which it passes are not inhabited. There would be no villages where I could buy provisions or take a meal. I should die long before I reached my journey's end.' 'Lessen your wants, husband your powers,' said Shih-nan I-liao, 'and you will have no need to buy provisions on your way. You will cross many rivers and come at last to a lake so wide that, gaze as you will, you cannot see the further shore. Yet you will go on, without knowing whether it will ever end. At the shores of this lake all that came with you will turn back. But you will still have far to go. What matter? "He who needs others is for

576

ever shackled; he who is needed by others is for ever sad." . . . I would have you drop these shackles, put away your sadness, and wander alone with Tao in the kingdom of the Great Void.'

CHUANG TZU (*tr. by Waley*)

The healthy man should be able to live on a piece of bread and keep at work all day. He should also be able to bear a pipe of tobacco and a good drink; for without these things nothing can be done. And withal he ought to have some feeling for the stars and the infinite heavens. Then it is a joy to live!

VINCENT VAN GOGH

My father had brought me up never when at school to think of the future or of any practical result. I have even known him to say, "When I was young, the definition of a gentleman was a man not wholly occupied in getting on."

W. B. YEATS

Let us work for what we consider useful and good, but not up-buoyed by the hope of a speedy and marvellous success, nor lured by the imagination of a social apocalypse: every apocalypse dazzles and deceives. Let us not expect any miracles. Let us resign ourselves, each doing his imperceptible part, to bequeath a better future which we shall not live to see.

ANATOLE FRANCE

Ecoutons l'ensemble du concert! The present moment is but a transitional chord—bitter, rich and cruel maybe, but it will resolve in the next phase in the chord that succeeds. Let each of us care only for playing the part allotted to him with conscientiousness, sincerity and unselfishness. And if it so happens that those whose parts belong to the noblest and deepest are misunderstood, they do not stand in need of commiseration. They are amply repaid by the joy they experience of the beautiful music which falls to their lot. What matters if "others" misjudge them? The "others" are not the judges. The judge is the Invisible Master of the Symphony.

ROMAIN ROLLAND

You stress the word progress again and again: but whatever do you really mean by the term? Can anybody really tell us whither we are being led? Let us suppose, hypothetically, that we have satisfac-

577

torily solved all the problems that confront us today. What next? Do you mean to say that our day's work will then have been done for good and all? Is life like the story of a fairy king and queen who after the initial vicissitudes just go on living happily ever afterwards? Is that conceivable? No, my friend, creation could never have a well-defined end, any more than it had a precise beginning. We have therefore no choice but to try to know more, still more, fighting injustice and oppression sleeplessly. 'Progress'? If by that word you mean our complete deliverance from the global evils, then I confess I believe that to be a Utopia, especially when we see that the human life has been built on the sepulchres of millions of creatures big and small. So I am for each of us doing his bit, that is, the utmost bit of good that he can achieve, and let the consequences take care of themselves. I know at least that this is good and this is bad. My native sense of right and wrong tells me this in unmistakable accents. You may contend that this sense of right and wrong isn't a sure guide for all, since human conscience is so variable. I admit it *is* difficult for the majority of men to distinguish the eternal values in life from the temporal, so that conscience as a guide to objective morality is no less bound up with our evolution than is our intelligence or artistic gift. All the same, you have only this light within you wherewith to pick your way and shift for yourself as best you can. I would therefore say: 'Let us act up to our highest lights available and let our aims be the highest we can focus our gaze on. Never mind if they are temporal glimmers or shining orbs for all time. The essential thing is that these convictions should be sincere and that there should be no falsehood nor compromise with ourselves'. Why worry about the finality of it all? There is an old French proverb which says: *'Fais ce que dois! Advienne que pourra'!*

ROMAIN ROLLAND

§ 4

Let not, therefore, the frailty of man go on thus inventing needless troubles to itself, to groan under the false imagination of a strictness never imposed from above; enjoining that for duty which is an impossible and vain supererogating. 'Be not righteous overmuch,' is the counsel of Ecclesiastes; 'why shouldst thou destroy thyself?' Let us not be thus over-curious to strain at atoms, and yet to stop every vent and cranny of permissive liberty, lest nature, wanting those needful pores and breathing-places, which God hath not debarred our weakness, either suddenly break out into some wide rupture of open vice and frantic heresy, or else inwardly fester with repining and blasphemous thoughts, under an unreasonable and fruitless rigour of unwarranted law.

MILTON

The Visions of Eternity, by reason of narrowed perceptions,
Are become weak Visions of Time & Space, fix'd into furrows of
   death,
Till deep dissimulation is the only defence an honest man has left.
O Polypus of Death! O Spectre over Europe and Asia,
Withering the Human Form by Laws of Sacrifice for Sin!
By Laws of Chastity & Abhorrence I am wither'd up:
Striving to create a Heaven in which all shall be pure & holy
in their Own Selfhoods; in Natural Selfish Chastity . . .

BLAKE

And many of the Eternal Ones laughed after their Manner:
"Have you known the Judgment that is arisen among the
Zoas of Albion, where a Man dare hardly to embrace
His own Wife for the terrors of Chastity that they call
By the name of Morality?"

BLAKE

      What is it men in women do require?
      The lineaments of Gratified Desire.
      What is it women do in men require?
      The lineaments of Gratified Desire.

BLAKE

    All is not Sin that Satan calls so: all the Loves & Graces of Eternity.

BLAKE

    O how I abhor this abominable heart-haunting impurity in the envelope of modesty!

S. T. COLERIDGE

He who does harm to his body does harm to his soul.

HASIDIC SAYING

579

It is very difficult, almost impossible, to conquer evil passions negatively, through negative asceticism and prohibitions. They can only be conquered positively, through awakening the positive and creative spiritual force opposed to them. Creative fire, divine Eros, overcomes lust and evil passions. It burns up evil, boredom and the false strivings engendered by it. The will to evil is at bottom objectless and can only be overcome by a will directed towards an object, towards the valuable and divine contents of life. Purely negative asceticism, preoccupied with evil and sinful desires and strivings, so far from enlightening the soul, intensifies its darkness. We must preach, therefore, not the morality based upon the annihilation of will but upon its enlightenment, not upon the humiliation of man and his external submission to God but upon the creative realisation by man of the divine in life—of the values of truth, goodness and beauty. The ethics of creativeness can alone save the human soul from being warped by arid abstract virtue and abstract ideals transformed into rules and norms. The ideas of truth, goodness and beauty must cease to be norms and rules and become vital forces, an inner creative fire.

BERDYAEV

Cold snows drifted around him: ice cover'd his loins around.
He sat by Tyburn's brook, and underneath his heel shot up
A deadly Tree: he nam'd it Moral Virtue, and the Law
Of God who dwells in Chaos hidden from the human sight.

BLAKE

The Moral Virtues are continual Accusers of Sin and promote Eternal Wars and Dominency over others.

BLAKE

Men are admitted into Heaven not because they have curbed and govern'd their Passions or have No Passions, but because they have Cultivated their Understandings. The Treasures of Heaven are not Negations of Passion, but Realities of Intellect, from which all the Passions Emanate Uncurbed in their Eternal Glory.

BLAKE

§ 5

THE STANDARD OF LIVING

There is a new fetish, the Standard of Living, a material measure hardly related to the enjoyment of life. Its worshippers believe that the 'dirt, stink and noise' so long ago recognized by Young, with the additional massive ugliness of the nineteenth century and the shoddiness of the twentieth, are of no importance when set beside this artificial measure. So far have we in Britain been enslaved to this fetish that when we go to another country and see people with light in their faces and beauty all round them we dare not think them fortunate if at the same time we see they have not very much money. Yet here in this once most lovely island people will spend all that they have been able to save and their few most precious days of holiday in flying from the dirt, stink, noise and ugliness in which they must spend the other fifty weeks of the year. Surely it is time to recognize not a standard of living but a standard of values, in which beauty, comeliness and the possibility of solitude have a high place among human needs? It must be established that it is not sentimental to value a fine stretch of farming land more highly than the five thousand tons of iron ore which can be snatched from it, or to believe that life and amenity should not be sacrificed to production, to the rapacity of the machine. In America vast stretches of countryside have the lack of form and sanctity which shows it only to have been tilled since the age of exploitation; the American people, the most successful materialists in the history of the world, are now often to be found speaking with loathing of their own life and with nostalgic envy of the happiness of primitive peoples.

JACQUETTA HAWKES

ECONOMICS AND THE SPIRIT

... The whole purpose of society lies in enabling its members to pursue their transcendent obligations; particularly to truth, justice and charity. Society is of course also an economic organization. But the social achievements of ancient Athens compared with those of, say, Stockport—which is of about the same size as Athens was— cannot be measured by the differences in the standard of living in the two places. The advancement of well-being therefore seems not to be the real purpose of society but rather a secondary task given to it as an opportunity to fulfil its true aims in the spiritual field.

Such an interpretation of society would seem to call for an extension in the direction towards God.

MICHAEL POLANYI

MONEY AND POWER

In recent centuries a devastating change has come over our mentality with regard to the acquisition of money. Whereas in former ages men treated it with condescension, even with disrespect, now they bend their knees to it. That it should be allowed a sufficiently large place in society, there can be no question; but it becomes an outrage when it occupies those seats which are specially reserved for the immortals, by bribing us, tampering with our moral pride, recruiting the best strength of society in a traitor's campaign against human ideals, thus disguising, with the help of pomp and pageantry, its true insignificance. Such a state of things has come to pass because, with the help of science, the possibilities of profit have suddenly become immoderate. The whole of the human world, throughout its length and breadth, has felt the gravitational pull of a giant planet of greed, with concentric rings of innumerable satellites, causing in our society a marked deviation from the moral orbit. In former times the intellectual and spiritual powers of this earth upheld their dignity of independence and were not giddily rocked on the tides of the money market. But, as in the last fatal stages of disease, this fatal influence of money has got into our brain and affected our heart. Like a usurper, it has occupied the throne of high social ideals, using every means, by menace and threat, to seize upon the right, and, tempted by opportunity, presuming to judge it. It has not only science for its ally, but other forces also that have some semblance of religion, such as nation-worship and the idealising of organised selfishness. Its methods are far-reaching and sure. Like the claws of a tiger's paw, they are softly sheathed. Its massacres are invisible, because they are fundamental, attacking the very roots of life. Its plunder is ruthless behind a scientific system of screens, which have the formal appearance of being open and responsible to inquiries. By whitewashing its stains it keeps its respectability unblemished. It makes a liberal use of falsehood in diplomacy, only feeling embarrassed when its evidence is disclosed by others of the trade. An unscrupulous system of propaganda

582

paves the way for widespread misrepresentation. It works up the crowd psychology through regulated hypnotic doses at repeated intervals, administered in bottles with moral labels upon them of soothing colours. In fact, man has been able to make his pursuit of power easier today by his art of mitigating the obstructive forces that come from the higher region of his humanity. With his cult of power and his idolatry of money he has, in a great measure, reverted to his primitive barbarism, a barbarism whose path is lit up by the lurid light of intellect. For barbarism is the simplicity of a super-ficial life. It may be bewildering in its surface adornments and complexities, but it lacks the ideal to impart to it the depth of moral responsibility.

TAGORE

OUTER AND INNER

We have built a monumental world round about us, and have slaved for it with unequalled energy. But it is so imposing only because we have spent upon the outside all that is imposing in our natures—and what we find when we look within must necessarily be as it is, shabby and insufficient.

C. G. JUNG

THE RICHES OF DARKNESS

The riches of darkness are those which men have made, during their ignorance of God Almighty's treasures: That lead us from the love of all, to labour and contention, discontentment and vanity. The works of Darkness are Repining, Envy, Malice, Covetousness, Fraud, Oppression, Discontent and Violence. All which proceed from the corruption of Men and their mistake in the choice of riches: for having refused those which God made, and taken to themselves treasures of their own, they invented scarce and rare, insufficient, hard to be gotten, little, movable and useless treasures. Yet as violently pursued them as if they were the most necessary and excellent things in the whole world. And though they are all mad, yet having made a combination they seem wise; and it is a hard matter to persuade them either to Truth or Reason. There seemeth to be no way, but theirs: whereas God knoweth they are as far out of the way of Happiness, as the East is from the West. For, by this means, they have let in broils and dissatisfactions into the world, and are ready to eat and devour one another: particular and feeble interests, false proprieties, insatiable longings, fraud, emulation, murmuring and dissension being everywhere seen; theft and pride and danger, and cousenage, envy and contention drowning the peace and beauty of nature, as waters cover the sea. Oh how they are ready to sink always under the burden and cumber of devised wants! Verily, the prospect of their ugly errors is able to turn one's stomach: they are so hideous and deformed.

Would one think it possible for a man to delight in gauderies like a butterfly, and neglect the Heavens? Did we not daily see it, it would be incredible. They rejoice in a piece of gold more than in the Sun; and get a few little glittering stones and call them jewels. And admire them because they be resplendent like the stars, and transparent like the air, and pellucid like the sea. But the stars themselves which are ten thousand times more useful, great, and glorious they disregard. Nor shall the air itself be counted anything, though it be worth all the pearls and diamonds in ten thousand worlds. A work of God so Divine by reason of its precious and pure transparency, that all worlds would be worth nothing without such a treasure.

TRAHERNE

ECONOMIC BARBARISM

But if Science has thus prepared us for an age of wider and deeper culture, and if in spite of and even partly by its materialism it has rendered impossible the return of the true materialism, that of the barbarian mentality, it has encouraged more or less indirectly both by its attitude to life and its discoveries another kind of barbarism—for it can be called by no other name—that of the industrial, the commercial, the economic age which is now progressing to its culmination and its close. This economic barbarism is essentially that of the vital man who mistakes the vital being for the self and accepts its satisfaction as the first aim of life. The characteristic of Life is desire and the instinct of possession. Just as the physical barbarian makes the excellence of the body and the development of physical force, health and prowess his standard and aim, so the vitalistic or economic barbarian makes the satisfaction of wants and desires and the accumulation of possessions his standard and aim. His ideal man is not the cultured or noble or thoughtful or moral or religious, but the successful man. To arrive, to succeed, to produce, to accumulate, to possess is his existence.

The accumulation of wealth and more wealth, the adding of possessions to possessions, opulence, show, pleasure, a cumbrous inartistic luxury, a plethora of conveniences, life devoid of beauty and nobility, religion vulgarised or coldly formalised, politics and government turned into a trade and profession, enjoyment itself made a business, this is commercialism. To the natural unredeemed economic man beauty is a thing otiose or a nuisance, art and poetry a frivolity or an ostentation and a means of advertisement. His idea of civilisation is comfort, his idea of morals social respectability, his idea of politics the encouragement of industry, the opening of markets, exploitation and trade following the flag; his idea of religion at best a pietistic formalism or the satisfaction of certain vitalistic emotions. He values education for its utility in fitting a man for success in a competitive or, it may be, a socialised industrial existence, science for the useful inventions and knowledge, the comforts, conveniences, machinery of production with which it arms him, its power for organisation, regulation, stimulus to production. The opulent plutocrat and the successful mammoth capitalist and organiser of industry are the supermen of the commercial age and the true, if often occult, rulers of its society.

The essential barbarism of all this is its pursuit of vital success, satisfaction, productiveness, accumulation, possession, enjoyment, comfort, convenience for their own sake. The vital part of the being is an element in the integral human existence as much as the physical part; it has its place but must not exceed its place. A full and well-appointed life is desirable for man living in society, but on condition that it is also a true and beautiful life. Neither the life nor the body exist for their own sake, but as vehicle and instrument of a good higher than their own. They must be subordinated to the superior needs of the mental being, chastened and purified by a greater law of truth, good and beauty before they can take their proper place in the integrality of human perfection. Therefore in a commercial age—with its ideal, vulgar and barbarous, of success, vitalistic satisfaction, productiveness and possession—the soul of man may linger a while for certain gains and experiences, but cannot permanently rest. If it persisted too long, Life would become clogged and perish of its own plethora or burst in its straining to a gross expansion. Like the too massive Titan it will collapse by its own mass, *mole ruet sua.*

AUROBINDO

585

RESPECT FOR PERSONALITY

Our central value—or, to put it in another way, the value that includes all our other values—is respect for personality.

It is important to understand precisely what is meant, in this phrase, by the word "respect" and the word "personality". Respect does not mean (as it means when used with a narrower significance) admiring, or fearing, or looking up to, or dutifully obeying, or regarding as good, or recognising as superior in character or intellect or station; nor does it mean some of or all these attitudes, or similar attitudes, combined in various proportions. And "personality" does not mean "certain selected personalities".

Negatively, respect for personality can be understood by reflecting on a statement which uses the word "respect" in one of the narrower senses. Consider, for instance, the phrase "I respect my father". If anyone who said that were asked "Why?" he would probably answer "Because he's my father". Further pressed, he might insist that the reason was sufficient, or might be prepared to amend his reply to "Because he's a good father". Similarly, a man might say "I respect the King: because he's the King: because he has carried out with courage and devotion the duties of a constitutional monarch." Or, rather differently, "I respect Mr. Churchill, not because he was Prime Minister nor yet because I agree with his politics, but because during the most critical years of our history, and with a burden of responsibility such as no other Englishman has ever borne, he had the faith of a child and the heart of a lion."

Now the very fact that in these sentences my father, the King, and Mr. Churchill are *selected* as objects of respect shows that the word "respect" is being used in a sense other and narrower than that which we intend when we speak of "respect for personality": and this at once becomes apparent when such reasons as "because he's my father" or "because he's a good father" are adduced in explanation. The very reason for which we respect them in the broader sense would itself preclude us from *particularizing* them for respect in that sense. I personally do in fact respect, in the narrower sense also, all three of them; but if I were asked "Why do you respect your father, and the King, and Mr. Churchill?", and if I understood that respect in the broader sense were intended, my reply in all three cases would be the same, namely "because he's a personality".

When we say that we respect personality, we mean that we recognize in every human being, and to a certain extent (or even completely, perhaps) in every living thing, something special, particular, concrete, individual, unique: something, as the Greeks would have said, αὐτὸ καθ' αὑτό: something—and this is perhaps the nearest that can be got to expressing what from its very nature must elude definition—something in its own right. There is in every human being, we say, something as much in *its* own right as my self-consciousness tells me I am in *mine*.

As much as I am in mine, but no more; for I also am a personality that I must respect. Fénelon, anticipating Freud (as so often theology, from its different approach, anticipated modern psychology), said somewhere that we should be in charity with ourselves as well as with our neighbours. There is indeed nothing self-abasing in respect for personality. In spite of *accidental* differences, and very wide ones, in spiritual development—the difference, for instance, between St. Francis at one end of the scale and Herr Streicher at the other; in spite, too, of greatly varying levels of capacity and intellect: respect for personality recognises the *essential* spiritual equality of all human beings, including ourselves, and perhaps of every living thing.

If I have made myself clear, it must at once be apparent that the real test of respect for personality is our attitude towards people we "don't like", towards those whom, in the narrower sense, we "don't respect", and to all whom we think of as enemies or criminals or sinners. To be concrete, the test was our attitude, during the war, to Germans and Italians and Japanese; was our attitude, a few months ago, to John Amery and William Joyce; is our attitude, as I write this, to Goering and Ribbentrop and Streicher and the rest. To talk of Huns and Wops: to rejoice when Joyce and Amery are sentenced to a shameful end: to think with pleasurable triumph of those wretched men in the dock at Nuremberg—all this is to blaspheme against respect for personality.

Only one person on earth, so far as the records go, has shown a respect for personality utter and without reservation. Christ consorted with harlots and sinners neither in condescension nor without recognition of their sins: he thought of them quite naturally, quite as a matter of course one might say, as fellow human beings, and therefore, to him as a man, essentially and beyond their sins his equals. "Why callest thou me good?" he asked: "there is none good but one, that is, God." And he preached respect for personality in

587

words of a beauty and conviction which never have been and never can be surpassed. There is some great music—Beethoven's Fifth Symphony, for instance—which overfamiliarity has spoiled: only when a Toscanini conducts it, or when there is a magic fitting of the music to our need, does it mean for us what it meant when we were young and freshly receptive to its message. So only when they are spoken by a voice of great spiritual power, or when at some climax of disgrace, such as Belsen or Hiroshima, we fly to what may save us from terror and despair—only at moments such as these do we experience once again the full revelation of verses which teach respect for personality in its ultimate form—the verses which begin with the words "But I say unto you, love your enemies."

But *why*, it may be asked, should we respect personality—not this or that personality, but personality as such? What is the sanction? There are many answers: one, and an obvious one, would be given by pantheism, and others by various systems of eastern wisdom and western philosophy. But there are two answers, I think, which come naturally to people trained in the European tradition; and they are not, as will be seen, mutually exclusive. They may be loosely called the religious and the non-religious.

In western religious thought, respect for personality is demanded by three interrelated religious doctrines: that God created all men in His own image, that God is the Father of all men, and that all men are therefore brothers. Both before and after the birth of Christianity, Judaism—prophetic, talmudic and cabbalistic—insisted on this Fatherhood of God and brotherhood of men. "Are ye not" cries the prophet Amos—"Are ye not as children of the Ethiopians unto me, O children of Israel? saith the Lord. Have not I brought up Israel out of the land of Egypt? and the Philistines from Caphtor, and the Syrians from Kir?" Which is as if a modern Jew or Russian, or some refugee from Lidice, were to ask, in spite of all the wrong that had been done to him, "Is not my God also the God of the Nazis?" There is a legend in the Talmud which is remarkable not so much for what it says as for the light it throws on the religious consciousness of men who, regarding Egypt as the national enemy, could nevertheless invent it. The story runs like this: that when the Egyptians were drowning in the Red Sea, and Miriam was singing her song of triumph and thanksgiving, the angels in heaven began to take up the refrain; but God stopped them, saying "What? My children are drowning, and ye would rejoice?" To this day orthodox Jews preserve the memory of that

588

legend. It is customary on all joyful occasions to sing the Hallel, or Song of Praise. But during Passover, which commemorates the deliverance from Egypt, it is sung in full only on the first three days; on the four remaining days it is sung in a shortened form, because some thirty-three centuries ago the Egyptians, who were also God's children, were destroyed. In the same spirit, but even more directly, the Cabbala insists that every man, however sinful, is in some degree divine. With that mixture of nonsense and profound wisdom which is characteristic of it, it relates that God has divided Himself and placed a particle of Himself in the soul of every human being: and that there it will remain, pure and undefiled no matter how wicked the individual may be, until men, reuniting with one another in perfect brotherhood, recreate at last the Unity of God.

But it was Christ who was to experience the universality of God's Fatherhood with a directness and immediacy never approached before or since. Or if that is too bold a claim, for no one can know what is in other men's hearts, it is at least true to say that he alone has had the power to communicate some measure of this experience to countless others. "Are not two sparrows" he asked, "sold for a farthing? and one of them shall not fall on the ground without your Father." I have already suggested that in the injunction to love our enemies respect for personality finds its ultimate expression. And we are immediately told *why* we should love our enemies: "That ye may be the children of your Father which is in heaven: for he maketh his sun to rise on the evil and on the good, and sendeth rain on the just and on the unjust." These few words, so rebuking to the self-righteous, are the greatest of all Christ's gifts—the greatest of all the gifts, I would dare to say, of Hebrew prophecy—to the religion of the western world.

The non-religious man of our tradition, if asked why we should respect personality, would give a different answer, though many may think that it is in the last analysis the same. I recognize (he would say), with a sense of necessity or inevitability independent of logical processes, my own uniqueness, my own "being in my own right". I recognize that there is in me an inner citadel that must be for ever inviolate. And because I recognize this I understand, by imaginative sympathy, that what is true of me is true of others: that every human being is unique, and has a citadel which is sacred: and that I must imperatively respect in others what I know, from the very nature of my being, must be respected in me.

V. G. (1946)

Mutual respect implies discretion and reserve even in love itself; it means preserving as much liberty as possible to those whose life we share. We must distrust our instinct of intervention, for the desire to make one's own will prevail is often disguised under the mask of solicitude.

AMIEL

§ 7

Respect, for others and for oneself, is at the root of every virtue: disrespect, at the root of every vice. The respect and disrespect take many forms.

RABBI MOSHE HAKOTUN

Some examples follow

No work noble or lastingly good can come of emulation any more than of greed: I think the motives are spiritually the same.

GEORGE MACDONALD

Bear well thy heart against the assaults of envy, which kills even sooner than death itself; and know no envy at all, save such envy of the merits of virtuous men as shall lead thee to emulate the beauty of their lives.

ELEAZAR ROKËACH

The jealous are troublesome to others, but a torment to themselves.

Jealousy is a kind of civil war in the soul, where judgment and imagination are at perpetual jars.

This civil dissension in the mind, like that of the body politic, commits great disorders and lays all waste.

Nothing stands safe in its way: nature, interest, religion must yield to its fury.

It violates contracts, dissolves society, breaks wedlock, betrays friends and neighbours. Nobody is good, and every one is either doing or designing them a mischief.

It has a venom that more or less rankles wherever it bites. And as it reports fancies for facts so it disturbs its own house as often as other folks.

Its rise is guilt or ill-nature, and by reflection it thinks its own

590

faults to be other men's; as he that is overrun with the jaundice takes others to be yellow.

A jealous man only sees his own spectrum when he looks upon other men and gives his character in theirs.

WILLIAM PENN

I cry: Love! Love! Love! happy happy Love! Free as the mountain
    wind!
Can that be Love that drinks another as a sponge drinks water,
That clouds with jealousy his nights, with weepings all the day,
To spin a web of age around him, grey and hoary, dark,
Till his eyes sicken at the fruit that hangs before his sight?
Such is self-love that envies all, a creeping skeleton
With lamplike eyes watching around the frozen marriage bed!

BLAKE

The sin of self-righteousness is not only the final sin in the subjective sense but also in the objective sense. It involves us in the greatest guilt. It is responsible for our most serious cruelties, injustices and defamations against our fellowmen. The whole history of racial, national, religious and other social struggles is a commentary on the objective wickedness and social miseries which result from self-righteousness.

REINHOLD NIEBUHR

An ambitious man is like a common bit of glass, glistening and gay in rays of light; and the stronger the light, the more the glass sparkles; but in the absence of light it is dull and colourless.

FATHER YELCHANINOV

We cannot be too circumspect how we receive praise. For if we contemplate ourselves in a false glass we are sure to be mistaken about our dues; and because we are too apt to believe what is pleasing, rather than what is true, we may be too easily swelled beyond our just proportion by the windy compliments of men.

Make ever therefore allowances for what is said on such occasions, or thou exposest as well as deceivest thyself.

For an over-value of ourselves gives us but a dangerous security in many respects.

We expect more than belongs to us; take all that is given us

591

though never meant us; and fall out with those that are not as full of us as we are of ourselves.

In short it is a passion that abuses our judgment and makes us both unsafe and ridiculous.

Be not fond therefore of praise, but seek virtue that leads to it.

And yet no more lessen or dissemble thy merit than overrate it. For though humility be a virtue, an affected one is none.

WILLIAM PENN

Be humble, if thou would'st attain to Wisdom. Be humbler still, when thou hast mastered Wisdom.

THE VOICE OF THE SILENCE

Humility is the chasuble of God. The Word made man clad itself with it, and through it talked to us within our bodies. And every one who wears it truly resembles the One who descended from his heights and hid the valour of His greatness and covered His glory with humility, so that his creatures should not be scorched by the sight of Him. For they would not have been able to look at Him had He not taken part of them into Himself and thus begun to talk to them.

ST. ISAAK OF SYRIA

Without freedom there can be no humility. . . . Humility is the victory achieved through freedom over all the pride which arises from self-assertion and over all those hatreds which spring from the lower aspects of our nature. Humility is the way to rebirth and to the centring of life, not on that which is without, but on that which lies in the innermost depths. . . . It means freedom from the influence of everything arbitrary, external, and alien to humanity. . . . An act of humility is not the act of a will alien to my own, but that of my own will enlightened and transfigured by a higher spiritual nature.

BERDYAEV

It is not impossible that there may be in some an affected pride in the meanness of apparel, and in others, under either neat or rich attire, a very humble unaffected mind . . . Great is he who enjoys his earthenware as if it were plate, and not less great is the man to whom all his plate is no more than earthenware.

S. T. COLERIDGE

The grateful soul of the wise man is the true altar of God.

PHILO

Gratitude or thankfulness is another virtue of great lustre, and so esteemed with God and all good men. It is an owning of benefits received, to their honour and service that confer them. It is indeed a noble sort of justice, and might in a sense be referred as a branch to that head; with this difference though, that since benefits exceed justice, the tie is greater to be grateful than to be just; and consequently there is something baser and more reproachful in ingratitude than injustice. So that though you are not obliged by legal bonds or judgments to restitution with due interest, your virtue, honour, and humanity are naturally pledges for your thankfulness; and by how much the less you are under external ties, esteem your inward ties so much the stronger.

WILLIAM PENN

When thou hast done well to another and another has fared well at thy hands, why go on like the foolish to look for a third thing besides, that is, the credit also of having done well or a return for the same?

MARCUS AURELIUS

Be grateful to the man you help, think of him as God. Is it not a great privilege to be allowed to worship God by helping your fellow-man?

VIVEKANANDA

It is more blessed to give than to receive; yet a noble nature can accept and be thankful.

STRINDBERG

One day a good-natured king gave a rare and beautiful fruit to a slave, who tasted it and thereupon said that never in his life had he eaten anything so delicious. This made the king wish to try it himself, and he asked the slave for a piece. But when he put it into his mouth he found it very bitter and he raised his eyebrows in astonishment. The slave said: 'Sire, since I have received so many gifts at your hand how can I complain of one bitter fruit? Seeing that you shower benefits on me why should one bitterness estrange me from you?'

FARID UD-DIN ATTAR

While thou so hotly disclaimest the Devil, be not guilty of Diabolism. Fall not into one name with that unclean Spirit, nor act his nature whom thou so much abhorrest; that is to Accuse, Calumniate, Backbite, Whisper, Detract, or sinistrously interpret others; degenerous depravities, and narrow minded vices, not only below St. Paul's noble Christian, but Aristotle's true Gentleman. Trust not with some that the Epistle of St. James is Apocryphal, and so read with less fear that Stabbing Truth, that in company with this vice thy Religion is in vain.

SIR THOMAS BROWNE

It is a moral imperative that we should rise above suspicion and morbid imagination, and never suspect anybody of anything. To suspect evil in others always means being blind to evil in oneself. Not to succumb to suspiciousness and evil imaginings is the first rule of moral and mental hygiene.

BERDYAEV

Believe nothing against another but upon good authority. Nor report what may hurt another, unless it be a greater hurt to others to conceal it.

WILLIAM PENN

When you speak evil of another man, Satan will compel you to be his witness against the object of your words. Would you become Satan's assistant? Blame the fault, not the man.

RABBI PINHAS OF KORETZ

Darts, barbëd arrows, iron-headed spears,
However deep they penetrate the flesh,
May be extracted; but a cutting speech,
That pierces, like a javelin, to the heart,
None can remove; it lies and rankles there.

THE MAHA-BHARATA

Do not despise others because, as it seems to you, they do not possess the virtues you thought they had: they may be pleasing to God for other reasons which you cannot discover.

ST. JOHN OF THE CROSS

594

It is absurd not to eschew our own wickedness, which is possible, but to eschew that of others, which is not possible.

MARCUS AURELIUS

When the actions of a neighbour are upon the stage, we can have all our wits about us, are so quick and critical we can split a hair and find out every failure and infirmity. But are without feeling or have but very little sense of our own.

Much of this comes from ill nature, as well as from an inordinate value of ourselves. For we love rambling better than home, and blaming the unhappy rather than covering and relieving them.

In such occasions some show their malice and are witty upon misfortunes; others their justice, they can reflect apace; but few or none their charity; especially if it be about money matters.

You shall see an old miser come forth with a set gravity, and so much severity against the distressed to excuse his purse, that he will, ere he has done, put it out of all question that riches is righteousness with him. This, says he, is the fruit of your prodigality (as if, poor man, covetousness were no fault) or of your projects or grasping after a great trade. While he himself would have done the same thing but that he had not the courage to venture so much ready money out of his own trusty hands, though it had been to have brought him back the Indies in return.

WILLIAM PENN

He that willingly drinks in tales and calumnies, will, from the delight he hath in evil hearing, slide insensibly into the humour of evil speaking. It is strange how most persons dispense with themselves in this point, and that in scarcely any societies shall we find a hatred of this ill, but rather some tokens of taking pleasure in it; and until a Christian sets himself to an inward watchfulness over his heart, not suffering in it any thought that is uncharitable, or vain self-esteem, upon the sight of others' frailties, he will still be subject to somewhat of this, in the tongue or ear at least.

S. T. COLERIDGE

Our souls may lose their peace and even disturb other people's if we are always criticising trivial actions which often are not real defects at all, but we construe them wrongly through ignorance of their motives.

ST. TERESA

595

It is easy to acknowledge a man to be great & good while we Derogate from him in the trifles & small articles of that goodness. Those alone are his friends who admire his minutest powers.

BLAKE

The more perfect the man, the more compliant he is, even towards his fellows; we must temper our importance, not thrusting insolently beyond what our nature warrants; we must allow other beings, also, their place in the presence of the Godhead; we may not set ourselves alone next after the Godhead in a dream-flight which deprives us of our power of attaining identity with the Godhead in the measure possible to the human soul.

PLOTINUS

It is the part of wisdom—and this is true of the Christian life as well as in general—not to be over-exacting of human nature.

FATHER YELCHANINOV

It is not because Angels are Holier than Men or Devils that makes them Angels, but because they do not Expect Holiness from one another, but from God alone.

BLAKE

And now I say unto you, Refrain from these men, and let them alone: for if this counsel or this work be of men, it will come to nought: But if it be of God, ye cannot overthrow it; lest haply ye be found even to fight against God.

THE ACTS

Toleration is a herb of spontaneous growth in the soil of indifference; but the weed has none of the virtues of the medicinal plant, reared by humility in the garden of zeal.

S. T. COLERIDGE

He that never changed any of his opinions, never corrected any of his Mistakes: and He, who was never wise enough, to find out any mistakes in Himself, will not be charitable enough, to excuse what he reckons mistakes in Others.

BENJAMIN WHICHCOTE

596

After all, it is rating one's conjectures at a very high price to roast a man alive on the strength of them.

MONTAIGNE

Holy indignation is a proof that we should do the same thing ourselves.

COVENTRY PATMORE

We learn to recognise a mere blunting of the conscience in that incapacity for indignation which is not to be confounded with the gentleness of charity, or the reserve of humility.

AMIEL

By letting gentleness have sway it is possible to continue as a child.

TAO TÊ CHING

You cannot believe in honour until you have achieved it. Better keep yourself clean and bright: you are the window through which you must see the world.

BERNARD SHAW

Magnanimity and contentment are very near allied; like brothers and sisters they spring from the same parents, but are of several features. Fortitude and Patience are kindred to this incomparable virtue. Moralists distinguish Magnanimity and Modesty by making the one the desire of greater, the other of less and inferior honours. But in my apprehension there is more in Magnanimity. It includes all that belongs to a Great Soul: a high and mighty courage, an invincible Patience, an immoveable Grandeur which is above the reach of injuries, a contempt of all little and feeble enjoyments, and a certain kind of majesty that is conversant with great things; a high and lofty frame of spirit, allied with the sweetness of Courtesy and Respect; a deep and stable resolution founded on humility without any baseness; an infinite hope and a vast desire; a Divine, profound, uncontrollable sense of one's own capacity; a generous confidence, and a great inclination to heroical deeds; all these conspire to complete it, with a severe and mighty expectation of Bliss incomprehensible. It soars up to Heaven, and looks down upon all dominion of fortune with pity and disdain. Its aims and designs are transcendent to all concerns of this little world. Its objects and its

597

ends are worthy of a soul that is like God in Nature; and nothing less than the Kingdom of God, his Life and Image; nothing beneath the friendship and communion with Him can be its satisfaction. The terrors, allurements, and censures of men are the dust of its feet: their avarice and ambition are but feebleness before it. Their riches and contentions, and interests and honours, but insignificant and empty trifles. All the world is but a little bubble; Infinity and Eternity the only great and sovereign things wherewith it conserveth. A Magnanimous Soul is always awake. The whole globe of the earth is but a nutshell in comparison of its enjoyments. The sun is its lamp, the sea its fishpond, the stars its jewels, men, angels, its attendants, and God alone its sovereign delight and supreme complacency. The earth is its garden, all palaces its summer houses, cities are its cottages, empires its more spacious Courts, all ages and kingdoms its demeans, monarchs its ministers and public agents, the whole Catholick Church its family, the Eternal Son of God its pattern and example. Nothing is great if compared to a Magnanimous Soul but the sovereign Lord of all Worlds.

TRAHERNE

Young man, or rather, comparatively young man! You began life by accepting everything, then went on to denying everything on principle. Now end your life by comprehending everything. Be exclusive no longer. Do not say 'either—or': say rather 'not only—but also!' In a word, or two words, Humanity and Resignation!

STRINDBERG

§ 8

Give up the awful disease that is creeping into our national blood, that idea of ridiculing everything.

VIVEKANANDA

How malign, infectious, and unwholesome is the eternal smile of that indifferent criticism, that attitude of ironical contemplation, which corrodes and demolishes everything, that mocking pitiless temper, which holds itself aloof from every personal duty and every vulnerable affection, and cares only to understand without committing itself to action! Criticism become a habit, a fashion, and a system, means the destruction of moral energy, of faith, and of all spiritual force. . . . This kind of temper is very dangerous among us, for it flatters all the worst instincts of men—indiscipline, irreverence, selfish individualism—and it ends in social atomism.

AMIEL

§ 9

When I say a Christian, I mean one with whom to see is to act.

JOHN OMAN

And Jesus went into the temple of God, and cast out all them that sold and bought in the temple, and overthrew the tables of the moneychangers, and the seats of them that sold doves. . . .

ST. MATTHEW

Give me a knowledge that's fertile in performances, for Theories without their effects are but Nothings in the dress of things.

THOMAS VAUGHAN

Activity is the only road to knowledge.

BERNARD SHAW

Not in being acted upon but in activity lies the evil and the good of the rational and civic creature, just as his virtue too and his vice lie in activity and not in being acted upon.

MARCUS AURELIUS

Accident is the omission of act in self & the hindering of act in another; This is Vice, but all Act is Virtue.

BLAKE

Unless at one time perspiration has streamed down your back, you cannot see the boat sailing before the wind.

ZEN BUDDHIST SAYING

And Tamino persevered, and entered the seventh stage [of the Buddhist road]. And there he was aware of nothing, and his soul was like nothing. And this state was beyond even peace, and he would have been glad to remain in it for ever. But as it so happened, on that day, he had gone out to meditate in the little wood that surrounded the monastery. And as he sat there by the way, lost in meditation, there passed a traveller. And thieves leapt out upon

him and wounded and robbed him and left him for dead. He cried
for aid to Tamino, but Tamino sat there unconscious, seeing and
hearing nothing. And so the man lay bleeding on the ground, and
there he was when Tamino returned to earth. Tamino was dazed
and for a long time did not understand what he saw nor know what
he had to do. But presently, as the current of his life in the flesh set
in again, he went up to the man and bound up his wounds as best
he could. But the man's blood had flowed too long. He looked at
Tamino and died. And in his eyes, before he died, Tamino saw the
look he had seen once on the battle field. And all his peace, so
painfully won, fled from him. And he went back to the monastery,
and passed over on to the island, and mounted to the topmost
terrace, and there sat down beside one of the images of Gautama. It
was evening, and the setting sun shone on the stone face, till it
seemed to flush into life. And Tamino, looking into the eyes of the
face, said:

'Lord Buddha, was your gospel true?'

And the image answered back:

'True and false.'

'What was true in it?'

'Selflessness and Love.'

'What false?'

'Flight from Life.'

'Must I go back to Life?'

But the light had faded from the face and it turned to stone again.

G. LOWES DICKINSON (from *The Magic Flute*)

The seduction of a life purely contemplative assailed St. Francis,
and he asked himself if instead of preaching to the multitudes he
would not do better to live in retreat, solely mindful of the inward
dialogue between the soul and God.

This aspiration for the selfish repose of the cloister came back to
him several times in his life; but love always won the victory. He
was too much the child of his age not to be at times tempted by
that happiness which the Middle Ages regarded as the supreme bliss
of the elect in paradise—peace. Beati mortui quia quiescunt! His
distinguishing peculiarity is that he never gave way to it.

PAUL SABATIER

I have understood that one who aimeth at his individual peace
and happiness adopteth the Lower Path. But he who, from the very

start, devoteth the merit of his love and compassion to the cause of others, I understand belongeth to the Higher Path.

MILAREPA

Christ was the greatest contemplative that ever lived, yet He was ever at the service of men, and never did His ineffable and perpetual contemplation diminish His activity, or His exterior activity.

RUYSBROEK

[In reply to an old man who expressed anguish at not having yet atoned.] O my friend, you are thinking only of yourself. How about forgetting yourself and thinking of the world?

RABBI ELIEZER OF DZIKOV

§ 10

Nothing is more unchristian than the "idealization" of reality; it is precisely the Christian more than anybody else who must put aside fear whenever the exposure and condemnation of a horrible and wicked reality is called for.

BERDYAEV

From every human being whose body has been racked by pain; from every human being who has suffered from accident or disease; from every human being drowned, burned, or slain by negligence, there goes up a continually increasing cry louder than the thunder. An awe-inspiring cry dread to listen to, which no one dares listen to, against which ears are stopped by the wax of superstition and the wax of criminal selfishness. . . . These miseries are your doing, because you have mind and thought, and could have prevented them. You can prevent them in the future. You do not even try.

RICHARD JEFFERIES

It is an easy thing to talk of patience to the afflicted,
To speak the laws of prudence to the houseless wanderer,
To listen to the hungry raven's cry in the wintry season
When the red blood is fill'd with wine & with the marrow of lambs.
It is an easy thing to laugh at wrathful elements,
To hear the dog howl at the wintry door, the ox in the slaughter
   house moan;
To see a god on every wind & a blessing on every blast;

601

To hear sounds of love in the thunder storm that destroys our
    enemies' house;
To rejoice in the blight that covers his field, & the sickness that cuts
    off his children,
While our olive & vine sing & laugh round our door, & our children
    bring fruits and flowers.
Then the groan & the dolor are quite forgotten, & the slave grinding
    at the mill,
And the captive in chains, & the poor in the prison, & the soldier in
    the field
When the shatter'd bone hath laid him groaning among the happier
    dead.
It is an easy thing to rejoice in the tents of prosperity. . . .

BLAKE

I dreamt (no "dream" awake—a dream indeed)
    A wrathful man was talking in the Park:
"Where are the Higher Powers, who know our need
    And leave us in the dark?

"There are no Higher Powers; there is no heart
    In God, no love"—his oratory here,
Taking the paupers' and the cripples' part,
    Was broken by a tear.

And then it seemed that One who did create
    Compassion, who alone invented pity,
Walked, as though called, in at that north-east gate,
    Out from the muttering city;

Threaded the little crowd, trod the brown grass,
    Bent o'er the speaker close, saw the tear rise,
And saw Himself, as one looks in a glass,
    In those impassioned eyes.

ALICE MEYNELL

This thing must be put bluntly: every man who has more than is
necessary for his livelihood and that of his family, and for the normal
development of his intelligence, is a thief and a robber. If he has too
much, it means that others have too little. How often have we smiled
sadly to hear tell of the inexhaustible wealth of France, and the
number of great fortunes, we workers, and toilers, and intellectuals,

602

and men and women who from our very birth have been given up to
the wearying task of keeping ourselves from dying of hunger, often
struggling in vain, often seeing the very best of us succumbing to
the pain of it all—we who are the moral and intellectual treasure
of the nation! You who have more than your share of the wealth of
the world are rich at the cost of our suffering and our poverty.
That troubles you not at all: you have sophistries and to spare to
reassure you: the sacred rights of property, the fair struggle for life,
the supreme interests of that Moloch, the State and Progress, that
fabulous monster, that problematical Better to which men sacrifice
the Good—the Good of other men. But for all that, the fact remains,
and all your sophistries will never manage to deny it: "You have
too much to live on. We have not enough."

ROMAIN ROLLAND (from Jean-Christophe)

It is vain to assert the dignity and vocation of human personality
if we do not strive to transform the conditions that oppress these;
strive to deal so that men can live worthily and gain their bread in
honour.

JACQUES MARITAIN

But first a word or two about "practicality". If you are going to
grow up the sort of person who is always saying "we must be practical", "that's all very well, but it can't be done", "what about
human nature?", and so on, you had better skip everything that
follows. There is nothing more mean-minded than this cult of a
bogus "practicality", and I shall be horrified if you turn out to be
addicted to it.

People misuse words so vilely. They call a nation peace-loving
if it happens to be backing them in a war. They call a man sentimental if he doesn't talk and behave like a cynic, cynicism being the
seediest expression of that emotional shallowness in which sentimentality consists. They talk about toughness when what they
mean is brutality. And to be unpractical, according to this type of
terminology, is to take anything but the lowest possible view, which
is a false view, of human potentialities, and to go a millimetre
outside the radius of what the humdrum take for granted because
they've never made the effort to think for themselves.

For God's sake let's get straight about it all, Timothy. To be
practical, genuinely practical, is more important than anything
else in the world; and what it means is this: to do away with that

breach between the so-called ideal and the so-called practical, to abandon that lie at the heart of our living, which has brought us to such a pass that we are busily preparing, at this very moment as I write, for the final practicality of ending human existence by atomic inventions: by inventions which have issued—and here is the heart of the matter, this is the breach to be healed—from that purest, most "ideal" characteristic of human nature, the search after truth. To be practical is to be revolutionary, as the gospels are revolutionary: to turn everything upside down—all the values of this world—as Christ recommended: to rate the first as last, and the last as first: to bring heaven down to earth and take earth up to heaven: to stop fighting against God: to establish the Kingdom. There is no other practicality: everything else is self-contradiction and self-destruction.

v. g. (from My Dear Timothy)

The part which he [St. Francis] had taken at Assisi in the controversies of his fellow-citizens he would willingly have taken in all the rest of Italy, for no man has ever dreamed of a more complete renovation; but if the end he sought was the same as that of many revolutionaries who came after him, their methods were completely different; his only weapon was love.

PAUL SABATIER

§ II

All that can be expected from the most perfect institutions is that they should make it possible for individual excellence to develop itself, not that they should produce the excellent individual. . . . The political life is but the means of the true life.

AMIEL

Every single person, says St. Thomas, is in regard to the community as a part is in regard to the whole and is thereby subordinate to the whole. . . . But the point of this is only and indispensably completed by St. Thomas's other saying: that man has in him a life and good which surpass the ordering of the social polity. Why? Because he is a person. The human person is a member of society as a *part* of a greater whole—but *not to the whole extent* of his being or of all that belongs to him! The core of his life as a person takes him beyond the temporal city, of which, nevertheless, it has need.

JACQUES MARITAIN

A SPIRITUALISED SOCIETY

A spiritualised society would treat in its sociology the individual, from the saint to the criminal, not as units of a social problem to be passed through some skilfully devised machinery and either flattened into the social mould or crushed out of it, but as souls suffering and entangled in a net and to be rescued, souls growing and to be encouraged to grow, souls grown and from whom help and power can be drawn by the lesser spirits who are not yet adult. The aim of its economics would be, not to create a huge engine of production whether of the competitive or the cooperative kind, but to give to men—not only to some but to all men, each in his highest possible measure—the joy of work according to their own nature, and free leisure to grow inwardly; as well as a simply rich and beautiful life for all. In its politics it would not regard the nations within the scope of their own internal life as enormous State machines, regulated and armoured, with man living for the sake of the machine and worshipping it as his God and his larger self, content at the first call to kill others upon its altar and to bleed there himself so that the machine may remain intact and powerful and be made ever larger, more complex, more cumbrous, more mechanically efficient and entire. Neither would it be content to maintain these nations or States in their mutual relations as noxious engines, meant to discharge poisonous gas upon each other in peace and to rush in times of clash upon each other's armed hosts and unarmed millions, full of belching shot and men missioned to murder like hostile tanks in a modern battle-field. It would regard the peoples as group souls, the Divinity concealed and to be self-discovered in its human collectivities, group souls meant like the individual to grow according to their own nature, and by that growth to help each other, to help the whole race in the one common work of humanity. And that work would be to find the divine Self in the individual and collectivity, and to realise spiritually, mentally, vitally, materially its greatest, largest, richest and deepest possibilities in the inner life of all and their outer action and nature.

For it is into the Divine within each man and each people that the man and nation have to grow; it is not an external idea or rule that has to be imposed on them from without. Therefore the law of a growing inner freedom is that which will be most honoured in the spiritual age of mankind. True it is that so long as man has not come within measurable distance of self-knowledge and has not set his face towards it, he cannot escape from the law of external compulsion, and all his efforts to do so must be vain. He is and always must be, so long as that lasts, the slave of others, the slave of his family, his caste, his clan, his church, his society, his nation; and he cannot but be that, and they too cannot help throwing their crude and mechanical compulsion on him, because he and they are the slaves of their own ego, of their own lower nature. We must feel and obey the compulsion of the Spirit if we would establish our inner right to escape other compulsion: we must make our lower nature the willing slave, the conscious and illumined instrument or the ennobled but still self-subjected portion, consort or partner of the divine Being within us; for it is that subjection which is the condition of our freedom, since spiritual freedom is not the egoistic assertion of our separate mind and life, but obedience to the Divine Truth in ourself and our members and in all around us. But we have, even so, to remark that God respects the freedom of the natural members of our being, and that he gives them room to grow in their own nature so that by natural growth and not by self-extinction they may find the Divine in themselves. The subjection which they finally accept, complete and absolute, must be a willing subjection of recognition and aspiration—to their own source of light and power and their highest being. Therefore even in the unregenerated State we find that the healthiest, the truest, the most living growth and action is that which arises in the largest possible freedom, and that all excess of compulsion is either the law of a gradual atrophy or a tyranny varied or cured by outbreaks of rabid disorder. And as soon as man comes to know his spiritual self, he does by that discovery, often even by the very seeking for it—as ancient thought and religion saw—escape from the outer law and enter into the law of freedom.

A spiritual age of mankind will perceive this truth. . . . Its aim will be to diminish as soon and as far as possible the element of external compulsion in human life, by awakening the inner divine compulsion of the spirit within; and all the preliminary means it will use will have that for its aim. In the end it will employ chiefly, if not solely, the spiritual compulsion which even the spiritual individual can exercise on those around him—and how much more should a spiritual society be able to do it—that which awakens within us, in spite of all inner resistance and outer denial, the compulsions of the Light, the desire and the power to grow through one's own nature into the Divine. For the perfectly spiritualised society will be one in which, as is dreamed by the spiritual anarchist, all men will be deeply free, and it will be so because the preliminary condition will have been satisfied. In that State each man will be not a law to himself, but *the* law, the divine Law, because he will be a soul living in the Divine, and not an ego living mainly if not entirely for its own interest and purpose. His life will be led by the law of his own divine nature liberated from the ego.

Nor will that mean a breaking up of all human society into the isolated action of individuals; for the third word of the Spirit is unity. The spiritual life is the flower not of a featureless but of a conscious and diversified oneness. Each man has to grow into the Divine within himself through his own individual being; therefore is a certain growing measure of freedom a necessity of the being as it develops, and perfect freedom the sign and the condition of the perfect life. But also, the Divine whom he thus sees in himself he sees equally in all others, and as the same Spirit in all. Therefore, too, is a growing inner unity with others a necessity of his being, and perfect unity the sign and condition of the perfect life. Not only to see and find the Divine in oneself, but to see and find the Divine in all, not only to seek one's own individual liberation or perfection, but to seek the liberation and perfection of others, is the complete law of the spiritual being. If the divinity sought were a separate godhead within oneself and not the one Divine, or if one sought God for oneself alone, then indeed the result might be a grandiose egoism, the Olympian egoism of a Goethe or the Titanic egoism imagined by Nietzsche; or it might be the isolated self-knowledge or asceticism of the ivory tower or the Stylites pillar. But he who sees God in all will freely serve God in all with the service of love. He will, that is to say, seek not only his own freedom, but the freedom of all, not only his own perfection, but the perfection of all. He will not feel his individuality perfect except in the largest universality, nor his own life to be full life except as it is one with the universal life. He will not live either for himself or for the State and society, for the individual ego or the collective ego, but for something much greater, for God in himself and for the Divine in the universe.

AUROBINDO

AFTER THE BOOK
PRAYER · AND PRAYERS

Prayer is
The world in tune.

HENRY VAUGHAN

Prayer is the effort to live in the spirit of the whole.

S. T. COLERIDGE

The prayer of the heart is the source of all good, which refreshes
the soul as if it were a garden.

ST. GREGORY OF SINAI

The prayer of one pure heart, I think, hath might
To atone for many.

SOPHOCLES

Our prayers are always answered.
Oh, to be wise in prayer!

A. E.

God only comes to those who ask him to come; and he cannot
refuse to come to those who implore him long, often and ardently.

SIMONE WEIL

One night a certain man cried "Allah!" till his lips grew sweet with
  praising Him.
The Devil said, "O man of many words, where is the response
  'Here am I' to all this 'Allah'?
Not a single response is coming from the Throne: how long will you
  say 'Allah' with grim face?"
He was broken-hearted and lay down to sleep: in a dream he saw
  Khadir amidst the verdure,
Who said, "Hark, you have held back from praising God: why do
  you repent of calling unto Him?"
He answered. "No 'Here am I' is coming to me in response: I fear
  that I am turned away from the Door."
Said Khadir, "Nay; God saith: That 'Allah' of thine is My 'Here
  am I', and that supplication and grief
And ardour of thine is My messenger to thee. Thy fear and love
  are the noose to catch My Favour:
Beneath every 'O Lord' of thine is many a 'Here am I' from Me."

RUMI

611

Do never pray,
But only say
—O Thou!

JAMES STEPHENS

Do not speak before God from knowledge, but approach Him
with childish thoughts and so walk before Him, that you may be
blessed with the fatherly care which fathers bestow upon their
children. For it is written: "The Lord preserveth the simple".

ST. ISAAK OF SYRIA

Prayer unites the soul to God. For though the soul be ever like
to God in nature and substance, restored by grace, it is often unlike
in condition by sin on man's part. Then is prayer a witness that the
soul wills as God wills, and it comforts the conscience and enables
man to grace. And so He teaches us to pray and mightily trust that
we shall have it. For He beholdeth us in love and would *make us
partners of His good deed.* And therefore He moves us to pray for
that which it pleases Him to do.

JULIANA OF NORWICH

For St. Francis, as for his Master, the end of prayer is communion with the heavenly Father, the accord of the divine with the
human; or rather it is man who puts forth his strength to do the
work of God, not saying to him a mere passive, resigned, powerless
Fiat, but courageously raising his head: "Behold me, Lord, I
delight to do thy will." . . .

But it is not without difficulty that the soul unites itself to God,
or, if one prefers, that it finds itself. A prayer ends at last in divine
communion only when it began by a struggle. The patriarch of
Israel, asleep near Bethel, had already divined this: the God who
passes by tells his name only to those who stop him and do him
violence to learn it. He blesses only after long hours of conflict.

PAUL SABATIER

That man is perfect in faith who can come to God in the utter
dearth of his feelings and desires, without a glow or an aspiration,
with the weight of low thoughts, failures, neglects, and wandering
forgetfulness, and say to Him, 'Thou art my refuge'.

GEORGE MACDONALD

She found help in prayer, except when her heart could not pray, as sometimes happens—when it was, as it were, withered and dry. Then she could only wait in silence . . . for the return of grace.

ROMAIN ROLLAND (from Jean-Christophe)

Perfect purity alone cannot be defiled. If at the moment when the soul is invaded by evil the attention can be turned towards a thing of perfect purity, so that a part of the evil is transferred to it, this thing will be in no way tarnished by it, nor will it send it back. Thus each minute of such attention really destroys a part of the evil.

SIMONE WEIL

Pray only for the suppression of evil, and never for one's material well-being, for a separating veil arises if one admit the material into the spiritual.

THE BAAL-SHEM

One prays: *How may I lie with that woman!* Thou: *How may I not lust to lie with her!* Another: *How may I be quit of that man!* Thou: *How may I not wish to be quit of him!* Another: *How may I not lose my little child!* Thou: *How may I not dread to lose him.* In a word, give thy prayers this turn, and see what comes of it.

MARCUS AURELIUS

Meanwhile I was also reading my Bible and became aware of a clearer understanding of it than before, when I had failed to grasp a multitude of things and had many perplexities. The Holy Fathers were right in their assertion that the *Philocalia* represents a key to the mysteries of the Scripture. It helped me to understand, to a certain degree, the Word of God in its hidden meaning. I began to perceive the significance of the following sayings: 'The inner secret man of the heart', 'true prayer', 'worships in the spirit', 'the kingdom of God within us', 'the intercession of the Holy Spirit with unspeakable groanings', 'abide in Me', 'give Me thy heart', 'to put on Christ', 'the betrothal of the Spirit to our hearts', the cry from the depths of the heart 'Abba, Father', and so forth. And when I prayed in my heart bearing all this in mind, everything about me appeared to be pleasing and lovely. It was as though the trees, the grass, the birds, the earth, the air and the light were saying that they existed for the sake of man, in testimony and proof of the love

613

of God for mankind. It was as if they were saying that everything prayed and praised God.

In this manner I began to get the meaning of what the *Philocalia* describes as 'the understanding of the language of the creation' and I saw that there were ways of conversing with all the creatures of God.

'THE PILGRIM'

I pray for a gift which perhaps would be miraculous: simply to be able to see that field of waving grass as I should see it if association and the 'film of custom' did not obscure it.

MARK RUTHERFORD

I am trying to recall, as I write this, what I meant by praying. I think I meant a process in which getting outside oneself, getting inside oneself, communing with God (very vaguely felt as something all-pervading and good), communing with the leaves and the sky and London and the dahlias in the market gardens, flinging up one's arms and expressing gratitude for the joy of living as one sniffed the air, and making up one's mind to be a better boy so that one shouldn't feel shut out from all these cleannesses and beauties—I think I meant a process in which things of this kind and others like them were somehow all mixed up.

V. G.

I was utterly alone with the sun and the earth. Lying down on the grass, I spoke in my soul to the earth, the sun, the air, and the distant sea far beyond sight. I thought of the earth's firmness—I felt it bear me up; through the grassy couch there came an influence as if I could feel the great earth speaking to me. I thought of the wandering air—its pureness, which is its beauty; the air touched me and gave me something of itself. I spoke to the sea: though so far, in my mind I saw it, green at the rim of the earth and blue in deeper ocean. . . . I turned to the blue heaven over, gazing into its depth, inhaling its exquisite colour and sweetness. The rich blue of the unattainable flower of the sky drew my soul towards it, and there it rested, for pure colour is rest of heart. By all these I prayed. . . . Then, returning, I prayed by the sweet thyme, whose little flowers I touched with my hand; by the slender grass; by the crumble of dry chalky earth I took up and let fall through my fingers. Touching the crumble of earth, the blade of grass, the thyme flower, breathing

614

the earth-encircling air, thinking of the sea and the sky, holding out my hand for the sunbeams to touch it, prone on the sward in token of deep reverence, thus I prayed . . .

RICHARD JEFFERIES

I seemed alone with immensity, and there came at last that melting of the divine darkness into the life within me for which I prayed.

A. E.

When you pray, endeavour to pray more for others than for yourself alone, and during prayer represent to yourself vividly all men as forming one body with yourself, and each separately as a member of the Body of Christ and your own member, "for we are members one of another". Pray for all as you would pray for yourself, with the same sincerity and fervour; look upon their infirmities and sicknesses as your own; their spiritual ignorance, their sins and passions as your own; their temptations, misfortunes, and manifold afflictions as your own. Such prayer will be accepted with great favour by the Heavenly Father, that most gracious, common Father of all, with Whom "there is no respect of persons", "no shadow of alteration", that boundless Love that embraces and preserves all creatures.

When you are saying a prayer for all men, and not praying from your heart for all men, then your soul is oppressed, for God does not favour such prayer; but as soon as you begin to pray for all men from your heart, then you will immediately feel relieved, for the Lord listens mercifully to such prayers.

When you are struck by other people's suffering, and the contraction of their souls, so that you are induced to pray for them with a pitying and contrite heart, pray to God to have mercy upon them and to forgive them their sins, as you would pray for the forgiveness of your own sins—that is, implore God with tears to pardon them; likewise pray for the salvation of others as you would pray for your own salvation. If you attain to this and make it a habit, you will receive from God an abundance of spiritual gifts, the gifts of the Holy Ghost, Who loves the soul that cares for the salvation of others, because He Himself, the most Holy Spirit, wishes to save us all in every possible way, if only we do not oppose Him and do not harden our hearts.

JOHN OF CRONSTADT

615

If he might have had but one request of God Almighty, it should have been, above all other, that he might be a blessing to mankind. That was his daily prayer above all his petitions. He wisely knew that it included all petitions; for he that is a blessing to mankind must be blessed, that he may be so, and must inherit all their affections, and in that their treasures.

TRAHERNE

Why has our sincere prayer for each other such great power over others? Because of the fact that by cleaving to God during prayer I become one spirit with Him, and unite with myself, by faith and love, those for whom I pray; for the Holy Ghost acting in me also acts at the same time in them, for He accomplishes all things. "We, being many, are one bread, one body". "There is one body and one Spirit".

JOHN OF CRONSTADT

Of prayer in the morning:

I will begin here also with the beginning of time, the morning; so soon as you wake, retire your mind into a pure silence from all thoughts and ideas of worldly things, and in that frame wait upon God to feel His good presence, to lift up your hearts to Him, and commit your whole self into His blessed care and protection.

WILLIAM PENN

Of prayer at night:

Stand in awe, and sin not: commune with your own heart upon your bed, and be still.

THE HEBREW PRAYER BOOK

§ 2

Let us adore now, you and I.

A. E.

§ 3

O Sacred Providence, who from end to end
Strongly and sweetly movest! shall I write,
And not of thee, through whom my fingers bend
To hold my quill? shall they not do thee right?

616

Of all the creatures both in sea and land
Onely to Man thou hast made known thy wayes,
And put the penne alone into his hand,
And made him Secretarie of thy praise. . . .

All things that are, though they have sev'rall wayes,
Yet in their being joyn with one advise
To honour thee: and so I give thee praise
In all my other hymnes, but in this twice.

*

And still, O Lord, to me impart
An innocent and grateful heart.

*

Let the remembrance of all the glory wherein I was created make
me more serious and humble, more deep and penitent, more pure
and holy before Thee.

*

O God if I worship Thee from hope of Paradise, exclude me
thence. But if I worship Thee for Thyself alone, then withhold
not Thyself from me.

*

O thou immortall light and heat!
Whose hand so shines through all this frame,
That by the beauty of the seat,
We plainly see, who made the same.
        Seeing thy seed abides in me,
        Dwell thou in it, and I in thee.

*

Lord, who has form'd me out of mud,
    And hast redeem'd me through thy bloud,
    And sanctifi'd me to do good;

Purge all my sinnes done heretofore:
    For I confesse my heavie score,
    And I will strive to sinne no more.

Enrich my heart, mouth, hands in me,
With faith, with hope, with charitie;
That I may runne, rise, rest with thee.

*

I confess I can see, but I cannot moderate, nor love as I ought. I pray Thee for Thy loving kindness sake supply my want in this particular. And so make me to love all, that I may be a blessing to all: and well pleasing to Thee in all. Teach me wisdom, how to expend my blood, estate, life, and time in Thy service for the good of all, and make all them that are round about me wise and holy as Thou art. That we might all be knit together in Godly Love, and united in Thy service to Thy Honor and Glory.

*

O Adorable and Eternal God! Hast Thou made me a free agent? And enabled me if I please to offend Thee infinitely? What other end couldst Thou intend by this, but that I might please Thee infinitely? That having the power of pleasing or displeasing, I might be the friend of God! Of all exaltations in all worlds this is the greatest. To make a world for me was much, to command Angels and men to love me was much, to prepare eternal joys for me was more. But to give me a power to displease Thee, or to set a sin before Thy face, which Thou infinitely hatest, to profane Eternity, or to defile Thy works, is more stupendous than all these. What other couldst Thou intend by it but that I might infinitely please Thee? And having the power of pleasing or displeasing, might please Thee and myself infinitely, in being pleasing! Hereby Thou hast prepared a new fountain and torrent of joys greater than all that went before, seated us in the Throne of God, made us Thy companions, endued us with a power most dreadful to ourselves, that we might live in sublime and incomprehensible blessedness for evermore. For the satisfaction of our goodness is the most sovereign delight of which we are capable. And that by our own actions we should be well pleasing to Thee, is the greatest Felicity Nature can contain. O Thou who art infinitely delightful to the sons of men, make me, and the sons of men, infinitely delightful unto Thee. Replenish our actions with amiableness and beauty, that they may be answerable to Thine, and like unto Thine in sweetness and value. That as Thou in all Thy works art pleasing to us, we in all our works may be so to Thee; our own actions as they are pleasing to Thee being an offspring of pleasures sweeter than all.

618

Lord, not for light in darkness do we pray,
Not that the veil be lifted from our eyes,
Nor that the slow ascension of our day
    Be otherwise.

Not for a clearer vision of the things
Whereof the fashioning shall make us great,
Not for the remission of the peril and stings
    Of time and fate.

Not for a fuller knowledge of the end
Whereto we travel, bruised yet unafraid,
Nor that the little healing that we lend
    Shall be repaid.

Not these, O Lord. We would not break the bars
Thy wisdom sets about us; we shall climb
Unfetter'd to the secrets of the stars
    In Thy good time.

We do not crave the high perception swift
When to refrain were well, and when fulfil,
Nor yet the understanding strong to sift
    The good from ill.

Not these, O Lord. For these Thou hast reveal'd,
We know the golden season when to reap
The heavy-fruited treasure of the field,
    The hour to sleep.

Not these. We know the hemlock from the rose,
The pure from stain'd, the noble from the base,
The tranquil holy light of truth that glows
    On Pity's face.

We know the paths wherein our feet should press,
Across our hearts are written Thy decrees:
Yet now, O Lord, be merciful to bless
    With more than these.

Grant us the will to fashion as we feel,
Grant us the strength to labour as we know,
Grant us the purpose, ribb'd and edged with steel,
    To strike the blow.

Knowledge we ask not—knowledge Thou hast lent,
But, Lord, the will—there lies our bitter need,
Give us to build above the deep intent
    The deed, the deed.

*

O my God, guard my tongue from evil and my lips from speaking guile; and to such as curse me let my soul be dumb, yea, let my soul be to all as the dust.

*

O Lord God our heavenly Father, regard, we beseech thee, with thy divine pity the pains of all thy children, and grant that the passion of our Lord and his infinite merits may make fruitful for good the miseries of the innocent, the sufferings of the sick, and the sorrows of the bereaved; through him who suffered in our flesh and died for our sake, thy Son our Saviour Jesus Christ.

*

O Lord God our heavenly Father, put love into our hearts, we beseech thee, for all who lie in prison, and especially for those who are under sentence of death; and grant that our love may bring them some measure of assuagement. Through the infinite merits of Him who bade us not to judge and Himself condemned not, and in whose Passion all men are brothers.

*

When,
—At the mid of moon,
At end of day—
My lamp is lit,
Grant me a boon,
I pray,
And do
So order it

—That the small creatures,
Terrified and blind:
The gold and silvern moths
Of lovely kind,

620

Do not whirl to my taper,
Nor, therein,
Die, painfully,
And bring my light
To sin.

My light
Is innocent!
Grant
—That it may be
Harmless,
And helpful,
And remarked
Of Thee.

★

There follow six prayers for a time of dereliction

★

Here am I now cast down
Beneath the black glare of a netherworld's
Dead suns, dust in my mouth, among
Dun tiers no tears refresh: am cast
Down by a lofty hand,

Hand that I love! Lord Light,
How dark is thy arm's will and ironlike
Thy ruler's finger that has sent me here!
Far from Thy face I nothing understand,
But kiss the Hand that has consigned

Me to these latter years where I must learn
The revelation of despair, and find
Among the debris of all certainties
The hardest stone on which to found
Altar and shelter for Eternity.

★

Ah my deare angrie Lord,
Since thou dost love, yet strike;
Cast down, yet help afford;
Sure I will do the like.

I will complain, yet praise;
I will bewail, approve:
And all my sowre-sweet dayes
I will lament, and love.

★

Lord, since Thou hast taken from me all that I had of Thee, yet
of Thy grace leave me the gift which every dog has by nature: that
of being true to Thee in my distress, when I am deprived of all
consolation. This I desire more fervently than Thy Heavenly
Kingdom.

★

Lord! thou didst put a soul here; If I must
Be broke again, for flints will give no fire
Without a steel, O let thy power cleer
Thy gift once more, and grind this flint to dust!

★

How should I praise thee, Lord! how should my rymes
Gladly engrave thy love in steel,
If what my soul doth feel sometimes,
My soul might ever feel!

Although there were some fourtie heav'ns, or more,
Sometimes I peere above them all;
Sometimes I hardly reach a score,
Sometimes to hell I fall.

O rack me not to such a vast extent;
Those distances belong to thee:
The world's too little for thy tent,
A grave too big for me.

Wilt thou meet arms with man, that thou dost stretch
A crumme of dust from heav'n to hell?
Will great God measure with a wretch?
Shall he thy stature spell?

622

O let me, when thy roof my soul hath hid,
O let me roost and nestle there:
Then of a sinner thou art rid,
And I of hope and fear.

Yet take thy way; for sure thy way is best:
Stretch or contract me thy poore debter:
This is but tuning of my breast,
To make the musick better.

Whether I flie with angels, fall with dust,
Thy hands made both, and I am there:
Thy power and love, my love and trust
Make one place ev'ry where.

*

Thou, Lord, art with me, and I will not fear.

*

There follow two prayers for the deathbed

*

Before the beginning Thou has foreknown the end,
Before the birthday the death-bed was seen of Thee:
Cleanse what I cannot cleanse, mend what I cannot mend,
O Lord All-Merciful, be merciful to me.

While the end is drawing near I know not mine end;
Birth I recall not, my death I cannot foresee:
O God, arise to defend, arise to befriend,
O Lord All-Merciful, be merciful to me.

*

I acknowledge unto thee, O Lord, that both my cure and my
death are in thy hands. If my death be determined by thee, I will
in love accept it at thy hand. Make known to me the path of life:
in thy presence is fulness of joy. Into thy hand I commend my
spirit. Amen, and Amen.

There follows a prayer for the nation and the world

Yet O for his sake who sits now by thee
    All crown'd with victory,
So guide us through this Darknes, that we may
    Be more and more in love with day;

Settle, and fix our hearts, that we may move
    In order, peace, and love,
And taught obedience by thy whole Creation,
    Become an humble, holy nation.

Give to thy spouse her perfect, and pure dress,
    Beauty and holiness,
And so repair these Rents, that men may see
    And say, *Where God is, all agree.*

★

Let the words of my mouth, and the meditation of my heart, be
acceptable in thy sight, O Lord, my strength, and my redeemer.

Courtesy of the Metropolitan Museum of Art

L'ENVOI I

'What then is Love?' I asked. 'Is he mortal?' 'No.' 'What then?' 'As in the former instance he is neither mortal nor immortal, but in a mean between the two.' 'What is he, Diotima?' 'He is a great spirit, and like all spirits he is intermediate between the divine and the mortal.' 'And what,' I said, 'is his power?' 'He interprets,' she replied, 'between gods and men, conveying and taking across to the gods the prayers and sacrifices of men, and to men the commands and replies of the gods; he is the mediator who spans the chasm which divides them, and therefore in him all is bound together, and through him the arts of the prophet and the priest, their sacrifices and mysteries and charms, and all prophecy and incantation, find their way. For God mingles not with man; but through Love all the intercourse and converse of God with man, whether awake or asleep, is carried on. The wisdom which understands this is spiritual; all other wisdom, such as that of arts and handicrafts, is mean and vulgar.'

PLATO

L'ENVOI II

A cry from the green-grained sticks of the fire
   Made me gaze where it seemed to be:
'Twas my own voice talking therefrom to me
On how I had walked when my sun was higher—
   My heart in its arrogancy.

"*You held not to whatsoever was true,*"
   Said my own voice talking to me:
"*Whatsoever was just you were slack to see;*
Kept not things lovely and pure in view,"
   Said my own voice talking to me.

"*You slighted her that endureth all,*"
   Said my own voice talking to me;
"*Vaunteth not, trusteth hopefully;*
That suffereth long and is kind withal,"
   Said my own voice talking to me.

"*You taught not that which you set about,*"
   Said my own voice talking to me;
"*That the greatest of things is Charity . . .*"
—And the sticks burnt low, and the fire went out,
   And my voice ceased talking to me.

THOMAS HARDY

NOTES ON WRITERS AND BOOKS, SOURCES AND ACKNOWLEDGMENTS, AND INDEX

NOTES ON WRITERS AND BOOKS

[I have written a note in the case of all writers who are dead—and of such books as the *Acta Sanctorum*—except when it would clearly have been absurd to do so: and have preferred to err on the side of absurdity. I have written a note in the case of every living writer.]

Abrahamsen, David. Contemporary American psychologist and psychiatrist.

Acta Sanctorum. A collection of biographies and legends of the saints, publication of which began, under the auspices of the Belgian Jesuits, in 1643.

Acts of John, The. An early Christian uncanonical writing.

Acts of Pilate, The. An early Christian uncanonical writing.

Addison, Joseph. British essayist, poet and man of letters, 1672–1719.

A. E. Pseudonym of George Russell, Irish poet, writer and painter, 1867–1935.

Allen, Warner H. Contemporary British writer on mysticism.

al-Hallaj. Mystic of Islam, executed for blasphemy in 922.

al-Junaid. Mystic of Islam, *d.* 910.

Amiel, Henri Frédéric. Swiss philosopher and critic, 1821–81.

Andrews, C. F. British clergyman, 1871–1940; lifelong and beloved friend of India.

Angela of Foligno, St. Franciscan mystic, 1248–1309.

Annunzio, Gabriele d'. Italian poet and novelist, 1864–1934.

Aratus. Greek poet, *c.* 315–*c.* 245 B.C.

Asoka. Buddhist Emperor of India, reigned 3rd century B.C.

Aumonier, Stacy. British novelist, 1887–1928.

Aurobindo, Sri. Indian philosopher and teacher, 1872–1950.

Ausonius. Roman poet, *c.* 310–95.

Baal-shem, The. Rabbi Israel ben Eliezer Baal Shem Tov ("Rabbi Israel, son of Eliezer, Master of the Good Name"), the leader of Hasidism (*q.v.*) and one of the world's greatest religious geniuses. 1700–60.

Bacon, Roger. British philosopher and scientist, *c.* 1214–92.

Barbusse, Henri. French novelist and man of letters, 1874–1935.

Barnes, William. British poet, 1800–86.

Basho. Japanese poet, 1643–94.

Baudelaire, Charles Pierre. French poet, 1821–67.

Beard, Charles. British writer and divine, 1827–88.

Beerbohm, Max. Contemporary British writer, cartoonist and wit.

Bellay, Joachim du. French poet, 1525–60.

Benet of Canfield, Father. Capuchin friar, 1563–1611.

Benêt, Stephen Vincent. American poet and critic, 1898–1943.

Bentley, E. C. Contemporary British writer, author of the famous detective story "Trent's Last Case".

Berdyaev, Nicolas. Russian philosopher and theologian, 1874–1948.

Bhagavad-Gita, The. Perhaps the most famous book in Hindu religious literature, probably of some date between the 5th and 2nd centuries B.C.

Binyon, Laurence. British poet and writer on art, 1869–1943.

Blackwood, Algernon. British novelist, 1869–1951.

Bloy, Léon Marie. French writer and mystic, 1846–1917.

Boehme, Jakob. German mystic, 1575–1624.

Boethius. Roman and Christian philosopher and statesman, *c.* 480–524.

Bosanquet, Bernard. British philosopher, 1848–1923.

Brown, T. E. Manx poet and divine, 1830–97.

Browne, William. British poet, 1591–1643.

Browne, Sir Thomas. British physician and writer, 1605–82.

Bunam of Pzhysha. Hasidic Rabbi, *d.* 1827.

Bussierre, Renouard de. French author of a 19th-century Life of St. Rose of Lima.

Campanella, Tommaso. Italian philosopher, 1568–1639.

Carpenter, Edward. British man of letters and social reformer, 1844–1929.

Carmina Burana. A collection of mediæval Latin lyrics, mainly of French origin.

Carpenter, Joseph Estlin. British divine, 1844–1927.

Castiglione, Baldassare. Italian writer and diplomatist, 1478–1529.

Catherine of Siena, St. Dominican, 1347–80.

Childe, Wilfred Rowland. British poet, 1890–1952.

Chrysostom, St. John. Greek Father, 345–407.

Chuang Tzu. Chinese thinker of the 4th and 3rd centuries B.C.

Clark, Leonard. Contemporary British poet.

Clare, John. British poet, 1793–1864.

Clement of Alexandria. Christian philosopher and theologian, probably born *c.* 150.

Cowlyd, Gwilym. Welsh poet, 1827–1905.

Crashaw, Richard. British poet, 1613?–49.

Cutforth, René. Contemporary British journalist.

Cyprian, St. Christian writer and sometime Bishop of Carthage; *c.* 200–58.

D'Arcy, M. C. Contemporary British philosopher and theologian.

Day, Dorothy. Contemporary American lover of humanity: founder of the Catholic Worker Movement.

Dickinson, Emily. American poet, 1830–86.

Dickinson, G. Lowes. British man of letters, 1862–1932.

Dionysius the Areopagite. The "Pseudo-Dionysius", a Christian philosopher writing probably in the 5th century A.D. under the name of the Dionysius mentioned in Acts xvii, 34.

Dixon, Richard Watson. British poet and divine, 1833–1900.

Donne, John. British poet and divine, 1573–1631.

Drinkwater, John. British poet and playwright, 1882–1937.

Drummond, William. British poet, 1585–1649.

Duff, Charles. Contemporary Irish writer and satirist.

Eckhart, Meister. German mystic, 1260?–1327.

Eliezer of Dzikov. Hasidic Rabbi, 18th–19th centuries.

Eliot, T. S. Contemporary Anglo-American poet.

Emerson, Ralph Waldo. American poet and man of letters, 1803–82.

Erigena, Johannes Scotus. ("*John the Scot*".) Philosopher and theologian, *c.* 815–*c.* 877.

Evans, Thomas Telynog. Welsh poet, 1840–65.

Evelyn, John. British diarist, 1620–1706.

Eyth, Max. German mechanical engineer and writer, 1836–1906.

Farid ud-din Attar. Persian poet and mystic, 1119–1229.

Fechner, Gustav Theodor. German psychologist, 1801–87.

Ferguson, John. Contemporary British classicist and theologian.

Fleg, Edmond. Contemporary French writer on Jewish themes.

Fox, George. British lover of humanity, whose ministry was the origin of Quakerism.

France, Anatole. French novelist and man of letters, 1844–1924.

François de Sales, St. Sometime Bishop of Geneva; 1567–1622.

Galsworthy, John. British playwright and novelist, 1867–1933.
Gardner, Alice. British historian and philosopher, 1854–1927.
Garvie, A. E. British theologian, 1861–1945.
Gascoyne, David. Contemporary British poet.
Gerhardi, William. Contemporary British man of letters.
Gould, Gerald. British poet and critic, 1884–1936.
Green, Peter. Contemporary British divine.
Gregory of Nyssa, St. A Father of the Eastern Church, *c.* 331–*c.* 396.
Gregory of Sinai, St. A Father of the Eastern Church, *d.* 1360.
Grensted, L. W.. Contemporary British philosopher, psychologist and theologian.
Guérin, Maurice de. French poet, 1810–39.

Hanokh of Alexander. Hasidic Rabbi, *d.* 1870.
Harrison, Thomas. British parliamentarian, 1606–60. Martyred at Charing Cross.
Hasid, Hasidic, Hasidism. Hasid is a Hebrew word meaning "pious" or "devout". The word and its derivatives are used in this book with exclusive reference to the remarkable Jewish movement which originated in Podolia just before the middle of the 18th century under the inspiration of the Baal-shem (*q.v.*), and which soon had millions of adherents, particularly in Eastern Europe. Martin Buber is its greatest contemporary interpreter. Louis I. Newman has well described the movement as follows: "Its chief emphasis has been upon a sense of mystical ecstasy in the communion of God and man; upon the joyful affirmation of life; upon compassion, charity and love; upon democracy and brotherhood between rich and poor; and upon the moral values of the religious system."
Hawkes, Jacquetta. Contemporary British writer.
Hayyim of Mogielnica. Hasidic Rabbi, *d.* 1849.
Hegel, Georg Wilhelm Friedrich. German philosopher, 1770–1831.
Heidegger, Martin. Contemporary German philosopher.
Heine, Heinrich. German poet, 1797–1856.
Henry, Joan. Contemporary British writer and novelist.
Herbert, George. British poet, 1593–1633.
Hermes Trismegistos. A designation of the Egyptian Hermes, god of wisdom.
Hermetica. A collection of writings associated with Hermes Trismegistos (*q.v.*), partly Egyptian and partly Greek in origin.

Herrick, Robert. British poet, 1591–1674.
Hindemith, Paul. Contemporary German composer.
Housman, Laurence. Contemporary British man of letters.
Hügel, Baron von. Catholic theologian, 1852–1925.
Hughes, John A. Quaker, *d.* 1942.
Humphreys, Christmas. British barrister and Buddhist.
Hunt, Leigh. British poet and essayist, 1784–1859.
Huxley, Aldous. Contemporary British novelist and man of letters.

Iamblichus. Syrian Neoplatonist, died *c.* 330.
Ibn 'Arabi. Muslim mystic, 1165–1240.
Ibsen, Henrik. Norwegian dramatist, 1828–1906.
Ignoto. Signature to a 17th-century poem.
Inge, W. R. British philosopher and divine, 1860–1954.
Irenaeus. Christian theologian, born *c.* 130.
Isaak of Syria, St. 6th-century Desert Father.

Jacopone da Todi. Italian Franciscan poet, *c.* 1230–1306.
James, Henry. Anglo-American novelist, 1843–1916.
James, William. American psychologist, 1842–1910.
Jaspers, Karl. Contemporary German philosopher.
Jefferies, Richard. British novelist and writer on the countryside, 1848–87.
John of Cronstadt. Father John Sergieff, 1829–1908. Russian parish priest.
John of the Cross, St. Spanish mystic, 1542–91.
Johnson, James Weldon. American (Negro) poet, 1871–1938.
Johnson, Lionel. British poet, 1867–1902.
Jones, David. Contemporary Welsh poet, painter and man of letters.
Juliana of Norwich. British mystic, 14th and 15th centuries.
Jung, C. G. Contemporary Swiss psychologist.

Keller, Helen. Contemporary American worker for the blind. Deaf and blind almost from birth.
Kierkegaard, Sören. Danish philosopher and theologian, 1813–55.
Kinge, H. Signature to 17th-century poem. Perhaps Henry King, British poet, 1591–1669, and sometime Bishop of Winchester.
Kingsley, Charles. British poet, novelist and Christian Socialist, 1819–75.
Kol Omer Kera, The author of. A Hasid.

Lactantius. Christian writer, *c.* 260–*c.* 340.

Lammennais, H. F. R. de. French priest and writer on philosophy and politics, 1782–1854.

Larbaud, Valery. Contemporary French poet.

Law, William. British divine and mystic, 1686–1761.

Leon, Luis de. Spanish poet and mystic, 1527–91.

Leon, Moses de. Spanish-Jewish scholar, *d.* 1305.

Lewis, C. S. Contemporary British philosopher and writer.

Li Po. Chinese poet, 701–62.

Linus. A saint of the Gregorian canon.

Little Flowers of St. Francis, The. The "Fioretti"—an Italian translation of a Latin MS. (composed some time after 1322) which records memories of St. Francis of Assisi.

Macdonald, George. British novelist and poet, 1824–1905.

Macgregor, G. H. C. Contemporary British theologian.

Mackenna, Stephen. Irish scholar and journalist, *d.* 1934.

MacLeod, George F. Contemporary Presbyterian divine, and leader of the Iona Community.

Macmurray, John. Contemporary British philosopher.

Malaval, François. French mystic, 1627–1719.

Maha-Bharata, The. One of the two great Hindu epics. Probably completed by about A.D. 200

Manu, The Code of. An ancient compilation of Hindu rules, moral teaching, etc.

Marcel, Gabriel. Contemporary French philosopher.

Marcus Aurelius Antoninus. Roman Emperor and Stoic philosopher, A.D. 121–80.

Mare, Walter de la. Contemporary British poet.

Maritain, Jacques. Contemporary French philosopher, theologian and sociologist.

Martin, John Bartlow. Contemporary American writer and journalist.

Martyrdom of Peter, The. An early Christian uncanonical writing.

Masefield, John. Contemporary British poet.

Maximus St., "the Confessor". Christian theologian, *c.* 580–662.

Mechthild of Magdeburg. German poet and mystic, 13th century.

Mekilta, The. A pre-Talmudic commentary on the Book of Exodus.

Melville, Herman. American author, 1819–91.

Menander. Greek comic poet, *fl.* 4th century B.C.

Mencius. Chinese moral philosopher, *fl.* 3rd century B.C.

Meredith, George. British novelist and poet, 1828–1909.

Merejkowski, Dmitri. Russian novelist, 1865–1941.

Meynell, Alice. British poet, 1849–1922.

Midrash, The. Rabbinic homilies on the Bible, 3rd–10th centuries. A single homily is called a Midrash.

Milarepa. Tibetan Yogi, *c.* 1052–1135.

Millay, Edna St. Vincent. American poet, 1892–1950.

Mirror of Perfection, The. A record of St. Francis, said to be based on memories of him, and completed *c.* 1318.

Monnin, A. French biographer of the Curé of Ars.

Montaigne, Michel de. French essayist, 1533–92.

Moore, George. Irish novelist, 1852–1933.

More, Henry. British philosopher, 1614–87. Cambridge Platonist.

Morris, William. British poet, writer and artist, 1834–96.

Moshe Hakotun, Rabbi ("Rabbi Moses the small"). A legendary figure among the Hasidim. Many sayings, in various languages, are attributed to him. His dates are uncertain: some think he is still alive.

Moshe Leib of Sasov. Hasidic Rabbi, *d.* 1807.

Muir, Edwin. Contemporary British poet and critic.

Murray, Gilbert. Contemporary British classical scholar and humanist.

Nagai, Takashi. A Japanese Christian, who survived the Nagasaki catastrophe. He spent the last six years of his life studying the effect of the atom bomb, and of treatment, on himself and others: and died of radiation sickness just before his book was published in England.

Nahman of Bratzlav. Hasidic Rabbi, *d.* 1810.

Nedoncelle, Maurice. Contemporary French Abbé.

Nicolas of Cusa. Philosopher and mystic, born at Cues on the Moselle in 1401. Became Cardinal.

Nicoll, Maurice. British psychiatrist, philosopher and teacher, 1884–1953.

Niebuhr, Reinhold. Contemporary American philosopher and divine.

Norris, John. British philosopher and divine, 1657–1711.

O'Connor, Flannery. Contemporary American novelist.

O'Leary the Fenian, John. Irish journalist, 1830–1907. (The

Fenian Brotherhood was an Irish–American secret society, founded in America in 1858.)

Oman, John. British theologian and divine, 1860–1939.

Orphism. A Greek cult, of which Orpheus was the legendary founder.

Osuna, Francisco de. Spanish mystic, *c.* 1497–*c.* 1541.

Otto, Rudolf. German theologian, 1869–1937.

Ouspensky, P. D. Russian philosopher and teacher, 1878–1947.

Paradise of the Fathers, The. "The Paradise or Garden of the Holy Fathers, being Histories of the Anchorites, Recluses, Monks, Coenobites and Ascetic Fathers of the Desert of Egypt between A.D. 250 and A.D. 400 *circiter,* compiled by Athanasius, Archbishop of Alexandria: Palladius, Bishop of Helenopolis: St. Jerome, and others."

Pascal, Blaise. French philosopher and mathematician, 1623–62.

Pater, Walter. British man of letters, 1839–94.

Patmore, Coventry. British poet and man of letters, 1823–96.

Péguy, Charles. French author, poet, Catholic, republican, socialist, patriot and Dreyfusard. 1873–1914.

Penn, William. British Quaker, 1644–1718.

Peter of Alcántara, St. Spanish mystic, 1499–1562.

Philo Judaeus. Jewish philosopher, probably born *c.* 20–10 B.C.

"Pilgrim, The". The unknown author of "The Candid Narrations of a Pilgrim to His Spiritual Father", first printed in Kazan in 1884.

Pinhas of Koretz. Hasidic Rabbi, *d.* 1791.

Plotinus. Neoplatonic philosopher and mystic, born in Egypt A.D. 204 or 205, died 270.

Poincaré, Jules Henri. French mathematician, 1854–1912.

Polanyi, Michael. Contemporary British sociologist.

Porphyry. Neoplatonic scholar and historian, 233–*c.* 304.

Potter, Stephen. Contemporary British critic and wit.

Prezzolini, Guiseppe. Contemporary Italian-American critic and historian.

Proclus. Neoplatonic philosopher and mystic, 410–85.

Proust, Marcel. French novelist, 1871–1922.

Rabi'a. A woman mystic of Islam, *d.* 801.

Raine, Kathleen. Contemporary British poet.

Randolph, Thomas. British poet and dramatist, 1605–35.

Raven, Charles E. Contemporary British divine.

Rechung. Disciple of the Yogi Milarepa (*q.v.*) and author of his biography.

Rilke, Rainer Maria. German poet, 1875–1926.

Rokëach, Eleazar. Jewish mystic and hymn-writer, 13th century.

Rolland, Romain. French man of letters, 1866–1944.

Rolle, Richard. British mystic, *d.* 1349.

Roscoe, William Caldwell. British poet, dramatist and critic, 1823–59.

Rossetti, Christina. British poet, 1830–94.

Ruddock, Margot. British poet, artist and actress, *b.* 1907.

Rumi, Jalalu D-Din. Persian poet and mystic, 1207–73.

Rutherford, Mark. Pseudonym of William Hale White, British author, 1829–1913.

Ruysbroeck, Jan van. Dutch mystic, 1293–1381.

Sabatier, Paul. French theologian and historian, 1858–1928.

Saint-Cyran. Jean Du Vergier de Hauvanne, French theologian, 1581–1643.

Saint-Exupéry, Antoine de. French airman and writer, 1900–45.

Saint-Martin, Louis Claude de. French philosopher, 1743–1803.

Sales, St. François de. 1567–1622. Bishop of Geneva.

Sandburg, Carl. Contemporary American poet.

Schleiermacher, F. D. E. German theologian and philosopher, 1768–1834.

Scholem, Gershom. Contemporary Jewish scholar. Professor of Jewish Mysticism in the Hebrew University of Jerusalem.

Seer of Lublin, The. Hasidic Rabbi, *d.* 1815.

Shapiro, Karl. Contemporary American poet.

Siepmann, Eric. Contemporary British writer.

Sitwell, Edith. Contemporary British poet.

Smith, John. Cambridge Platonist, 1618–52.

Spinoza, Baruch. Dutch philosopher, 1632–77.

Stanley, Arthur. Pseudonym of Arthur Megaw, contemporary anthologist: a native of County Down.

Stephens, James. Irish novelist and poet, 1882–1950.

Strindberg, August. Swedish dramatist and man of letters, 1849–1912.

Stuart, Francis. Contemporary Irish novelist.

Sufism. The doctrine, or way of life, of certain Muslim mystics, quietists and ascetics.

Sullivan, J. W. N. Irish man of letters, 1886–1937.

Suso, Heinrich. German mystic, *c.* 1300–66.
Suzuki, D. T. Contemporary Japanese writer on Buddhism.
Swift, Jonathan. British satirist, 1667–1745.
Symeon the New Theologian, St. Abbot of Saint-Mamas of Constantinople. ?949–1022.

Tadhg Óg Ó hUiginn. Irish poet, 16th century.
Tagore, Rabindranath. Indian poet and writer, 1861–1941.
Talmud, The. A great collection of Rabbinical treatises, etc., reduced to writing in the early centuries of our era.
Tannenbaum, Frank. Contemporary American sociologist, economist and criminologist.
Taoism, Tao. Taoism is a system of Chinese philosophy, said to date from the 6th century B.C. Tao is the eternal energy behind all phenomena.
Tao Tê Ching. The classic of Taoism.
Taylor, Jeremy. British writer and divine, 1613–67.
Teasdale, Sara. American poet, 1884–1933.
Teresa, St. Spanish mystic, 1515–82.
Tertullian. Christian theologian, *c.* 155–*c.* 222.
Theocritus. Greek pastoral poet, 3rd century B.C.
Theologia Germanica. One of the most beautiful works of German mysticism, written perhaps in the second half of the 14th century.
Thomas of Celano. A follower of St. Francis of Assisi (whom he joined probably about 1214) and his biographer.
Thomas, Dylan. Welsh poet and writer, 1914–53.
Thoreau, Henry David. American writer and naturalist, 1817–62.
Traherne, Thomas. British poet, 1637?–74.
Turgenev, Ivan, Russian novelist, 1818–83.

Underhill, Evelyn. British writer on mysticism, 1874–1941.
Upanishads, The. Indian scriptures.

Van Gogh, Vincent. Dutch painter, 1853–90.
Vasari, Giorgio. Italian painter, architect and historian of art, 1511–71.
Vaughan, Henry. British poet, 1622–95.
Vaughan, Thomas. British mystic, 1622–66.
Vedanta, The. A philosophical system, developing and systematizing the Upanishads (*q.v.*).

Vedas, The. Indian scriptures.·

Verlaine, Paul. French poet, 1844–96.

Vivekananda, Swami. Indian philosopher and teacher, 1863–1902.

Voice of the Silence, The. A book of extracts, chosen by Madame Blavatsky, from a body of precepts current among mystic students in the East.

Waddell, Helen. Contemporary British novelist, poet and woman of letters.

Waley, Arthur. Contemporary British poet, writer and translator from the Chinese and Japanese.

Walker, Kenneth. Contemporary British physician and writer.

Ward, James. British philosopher and logician, 1843–1925.

Weil, Simone. French writer and servant of humanity, 1909–43.

Whichcote, Benjamin. British philosopher, 1609–83. Cambridge Platonist.

Whitehead, A. N. British mathematician and philosopher, 1861–1947.

Whitman, Walt. American poet, 1819–92.

Williams, Charles. British poet, novelist and critic, 1886–1945.

Wilson, Mona. British administrator and woman of letters, 1872–1954.

Woolf, Virginia. British novelist, 1882–1941.

Wordsworth, Dorothy. British writer and diarist, sister of the poet. 1771–1855.

Yelchaninov, Father. A leader of the Russian Christian Student Movement in exile. 1881–1934.

Zen. A way of life followed by certain Buddhists.

Zohar, The. A great work of Jewish mysticism; perhaps 1290.

SOURCES AND ACKNOWLEDGMENTS

My debt to my wife is sufficiently conveyed by the extract from *Fidelio* which accompanies the dedication. My most loving thanks are due to Tessa (Elinor) Murphy, whose devotion and efficiency are alike incomparable: I thank her, also, for her translation of some French passages. I am most grateful to Mr. Nicolas Zernoff for translating some sentences of St. Isaak of Syria, and to Mr. Robin Skelton for introducing me to the work of Margot Ruddock, as well as for other benefits. I wish to thank Dame Edith Sitwell, Professor D. Mac-Kinnon, the Rev. George MacLeod, Mr. Warner Allen and Mr. H. F. Rubinstein for very special courtesies: my daughter Livia for preparing the musical illustrations: and Mr. John Rosenberg, not only for careful proof-reading, but also for his skill in tracking down a number of references that I had lost. Miss Barbara Dicks and Mrs. Queenie Matthews have helped me greatly by the speed and efficiency of their transcriptions: and Miss Dorothy Horsman has supervised the details of the production with her usual care.

Miss Kathleen Raine has generously given me a great deal of her time, and has made a number of very valuable suggestions. In particular, I am most grateful to her for pointing out to me the parallelism between Thomas Taylor's paraphrase of Proclus on the sunflower, and Blake's poem on the same subject (see page 376).

Miss Sheila Hodges' last-minute reading has meant a great deal to me.

Finally, I wish to thank Messrs. Richard Clay and Co. of Bungay: their skill in typography, and the efficiency of their admirable readers, have been of great assistance to me.

*　　*　　*　　*　　*　　*

In the pages that follow I have, in the great majority of cases, cited the author's work from which the particular passage is taken. When I have not done so, this is because I have failed (or not thought it worth the time that would be involved) to trace the exact source of a passage copied out and checked some years ago.

*　　*　　*　　*　　*　　*

THE BIBLE. For the Old and New Testaments the Authorised Version has been used, except in one instance, and except that chapter and verse numbers are not given, italics have been romanised, and the word "Lord" is not printed in capitals. The Authorised Version is Crown Copyright, and is used by permission. For the Apocrypha the Revised Version has been used, by permission of the University Presses of Oxford and Cambridge.

★   ★   ★   ★   ★   ★

THE HEBREW PRAYER BOOK. The extracts are from the Authorised Daily Prayer Book of the United Hebrew Congregations of the British Empire (which was translated by the late Rev. S. Singer) and are printed by permission of the Singer Prayer Book Publication Committee.

★   ★   ★   ★   ★   ★

The citing of the names of authors, publishers and translators below will please be understood as acknowledging kind permission to reprint the relevant passages in the Anthology. It should be assumed that all items are fully protected by copyright, unless this is obviously not the case. The letter following a page number refers to the position of the passage on the page: thus 7a means the first passage (by the author in question) that *begins* on page 7.

★   ★   ★   ★   ★   ★

ABRAHAMSEN, DAVID. From *Who are the Guilty?* (Rinehart).

ACTA SANCTORUM. From *Beasts and Saints* tr. by Helen Waddell (Constable).

ACTS OF JOHN. From *The Apocryphal New Testament* tr. by Montague James (Clarendon Press).

ACTS OF PILATE. From *The Apocryphal New Testament* tr. by Montague James (Clarendon Press).

ADDISON. From *The Spectator*.

A.E. The poems are from *The Selected Poems of A.E.* (Macmillan) and are reproduced by permission also of Mr. Diarmuid Russell. The passage on p. 207 is an extract from *Ancestry*; p. 380 from *The Unknown God*; p. 454 from *Germinal*; p. 611 from *Companions*; p. 616 from *Prayer*. The prose extracts are from *The Candle of Vision*. I thank Mr. Diarmuid Russell.

AL-HALLAJ. From *Sufism* by A. J. Arberry (Allen and Unwin).

AL-JUNAID. From *Sufism* by A. J. Arberry (Allen and Unwin).

ALLEN, WARNER. From *The Happy Issue* (Faber).

AMIEL. From his *Journal* tr. by Mrs. Humphry Ward (Macmillan).

ANDREWS, C. F. From *The Sermon on the Mount* (Macmillan).

ANGELA OF FOLIGNO, ST. From *The Book of Divine Consolation*, tr. by Mary G. Steegman (Chatto).

643

ANONYMOUS. The passage on p. 393 is quoted by William James in *Varieties of Religious Experience* (Holt). The extract on p. 445 from the *Ancren Riwle* is tr. by James Morton.

APOCRYPHAL SAYING OF ST. PETER. Quoted in the *Apocryphal New Testament* tr. by Montague James (Clarendon Press).

AQUINAS, ST. THOMAS. The passage p. 208*b* is quoted by Warner Allen in *The Happy Issue* (Faber), and tr. by him. Pp. 163, 422 from *Summa Theologica*; p. 208*a* from *III Contra Gentes*; p. 327 from *Commentary, I. Ethics*; p. 334 from *Disputations, I. de Veritate*; p. 355 from *Commentary, I. de Anima*. The last six are tr. by Thomas Gilby in *Philosophical Texts of St. Thomas Aquinas* (Oxford University Press).

ARATUS. Tr. by G. R. Mair (Loeb Classical Library, Harvard).

ASOKA. Quoted in *Zen Buddhism* by Christmas Humphreys (Heinemann).

AUGUSTINE, ST. P. 208 from the *Encheiridion*. P. 209 from *The Confessions*, quoted in *The Happy Issue* by Warner Allen (Faber), and tr. by him.

AUROBINDO. Pp. 302, 332, 333, 340, 566, 584, 605 from *The Human Cycle* (Dutton). Pp. 177, 287, 311, 314, 449, 568 from *Synthesis of Yoga* (Dutton). P. 215 from *The Life Divine* (Dutton). These passages are reproduced by kind permission of the Sri Aurobindo Ashram, Pondicherry. The extract on p. 73 is from a letter to D. K. Roy, published in *Among the Great*. I thank Mr. Roy for permission.

AUSONIUS. From *Mediaeval Latin Lyrics* tr. by Helen Waddell (Constable).

BACON, ROGER. From *The Mirror of Alchemy*.

BARBUSSE. From *Le Feu*, tr. as *Under Fire* by Fitzwater Wray (Everyman, Dutton).

BASHO. Quoted in *Zen Buddhism* by Christmas Humphreys (Heinemann).

BEARD, CHARLES. From *Port Royal* (Longmans).

BEERBOHM, MAX. From *Seven Men* (Heinemann).

BENÉT, STEPHEN VINCENT. From *The Selected Works of Stephen Vincent Benét* (Rinehart, New York). I thank Mrs. Benét for permission.

BENTLEY, E. C. From *Trent's Last Case*, reprinted by permission of Alfred A. Knopf, Inc.

BERDYAEV, NICHOLAS. Pp. 63, 159, 242, 244, 245*a*, *b*, 256, 257, 301*a*, *b*, 415, 447, 592 are from *Freedom and the Spirit* tr. by Oliver Fielding Clarke (Bles). P. 214: the first and last paragraphs are from *Freedom and the Spirit*, the second paragraph is from *The Destiny of Man*. Pp. 311, 436, 456, 472, 529, 533, 534, 562, 563, 565, 580, 594 are from *The Destiny of Man* tr. by Natalie Duddington (Bles). P. 601 is from *Christianity and the Class War*, tr. by Donald Attwater (Sheed and Ward).

BHAGAVAD-GITA. From the translation by Swami Prabhavananda and Christopher Isherwood, entitled *The Song of God* (Harper), except p. 171.

BINYON, LAURENCE. From *Painting in the Far East* (St. Martin's Press).

BLACKWOOD, ALGERNON. The publishers are St. Martin's Press, and the passage is reproduced by permission of the Owner of the Copyright.

BLAKE, MAJOR. From *Quod* (Hodder).

BLAKE, WILLIAM. I have followed the text in *Poetry and Prose of William Blake*, ed. by Geoffrey Keynes (Nonesuch Press). Pp. 39*a*, *b*, 109, 353, 380, 396*a*, *b*, 563 are from letters. Pp. 69, 591, from *Visions of the Daughters of Albion*. Pp. 112, 113, 158, 241*a*, 493*b*, *c*, 535, 601 from *The Four Zoas*. P. 474, a note written on a page of *The Four Zoas*. P. 132 from *Songs of Innocence*. P. 379*b* from *Europe*. P. 396*d*: in the Nonesuch text the final word *Europe* is printed in capitals. I have printed it in upper and lower-case italic for typographical reasons. Pp. 147, 183, 186, 207, 241*b*, 243*a*, *b*, 245, 339*a*, 340*a*, 375*c*, 415*a*, 429, 448*a*, 453, 459*a*, 506, 542*b*, *d*, *e*,*f*, *h*, 543, 549, 557, 558, 579*a*, *b*, 580*a*, 596*a* from *Jerusalem*. (P. 243*a*: I have inserted a comma between "Fear not" and "Albion" in order to make the meaning clear.) Pp. 200, 368, 375*b* from *Milton*. P. 304 is cited in Crabb Robinson's *Diary* for December 10th, 1825: he had met Blake at dinner with the Adens. Pp. 208, 599 from notes on Lavater's *Aphorisms*. P. 240 from notes on Swedenborg's *Divine Love and Divine Wisdom*. Pp. 329, 493*a* from *The Auguries of Innocence*. P. 334 from *The Marriage of Heaven and Hell*. Pp. 339*b*, 579*d* from *The Laocoon Group*. Pp. 340*b*, *c*, 580*b* from notes on Berkeley's *Siris*. Pp. 340*d*, *e*, 355, 379*a* from notes on Reynolds's *Discourses*. P. 375*a* from *The First Book of Urizen*. Pp. 396*c*, 580*c*, 596*b* from *A Vision of the Last Judgment*. P. 415*b* is a composite passage from *A Vision of the Last Judgment* and a note on Reynolds's *Discourses*. Pp. 435, 448*b* from *There is no Natural Religion*. P. 459*b* from *Notes on the Illustrations to Dante*. P. 542*a* from *The Gates of Paradise*. P. 542*c* is a stanza from a longer (untitled) poem. (The initial "And" appears in the Nonesuch edition as an ampersand.) P. 542*g* from the Preface to *The Everlasting Gospel*. P. 564 is from *Annotations to Watson's "Apology"*.

BLOY, LÉON. P. 245 is quoted by Berdyaev in *Freedom and the Spirit* (Scribner). P. 430 is from *Dans les Tenèbres*, included in *Pilgrim of the Absolute* by Léon Bloy tr. by John Coleman and Harry Lorin Binsse (Pantheon).

BOEHME. P. 361 from the *Aurora* tr. by Law. P. 369 from the *Signatura Rerum* tr. by Law. P. 302 from *The Threefold Life of Man* tr. by J. Sparrow, the translation having been corrected and amended (Watkins). P. 174*b* is also from *The Threefold Life of Man*: it is quoted in Evelyn Underhill's *Mysticism* (Dutton) and may have been translated by her.

BOETHIUS. From *Mediaeval Latin Lyrics* tr. by Helen Waddell (Constable).

BOSANQUET, BERNARD. From *The Value and Destiny of the Individual*. I thank Mrs. Ellen Bosanquet for permission.

BRIHADARANYAKA UPANISHAD. P. 171 from Max Müller's translation of *The Sacred Books of the East* (Clarendon Press).

BRONTË, EMILY. I have mainly relied on *The Complete Poems of Emily Jane Brontë*, edited from the manuscripts by C. W. Hatfield (Columbia University Press). P. 81 is an extract from *Julian M. and A. G. Rochelle*. P. 455 is an extract from *Lines* (April 28, 1839).

BROWNE, SIR THOMAS. From *Christian Morals*.

BROWNE, WILLIAM. From *Britannia's Pastorals*.

BROWNING, ELIZABETH BARRETT. From *Mystery*.

BROWNING, ROBERT. Pp. 243, 363 are from *Saul*.

BUBER, MARTIN. Pp. 533, 574 are from *Mamre* (Cambridge University Press).

BUDDHA, THE. Quoted in Tagore's *Sadhana*, and presumably translated by him.

BUNAM OF PZHYSHA, RABBI. From the *Hasidic Anthology*, q.v.

BUSSIERRE, RENUARD DE. Quoted in Evelyn Underhill's *Mysticism* (Dutton) and probably translated by her.

BYRON. Pp. 157, 301 from *Don Juan*. P. 564 from the Preface to Cantos 6, 7 and 8 of *Don Juan*.

CARPENTER, EDWARD. From *Towards Democracy* (Mitchell and Kennerley). P. 162 is an extract from *Disentanglement*.

CARPENTER, JOSEPH ESTLIN. From *Joseph Estlin Carpenter* by C. H. Herford (Clarendon Press).

CASTIGLIONE. From *The Courtier*.

CHILDE, WILFRED ROWLAND. I thank Mr. Godfrey Childe. Some of the poems are from *Blessed Pastures* (Lotus Press): others from manuscript. P. 183 is an extract from *The Expostulation of St. John*.

CHRYSOSTOM. P. 245 from *Homil. de Prodit. Judae*. P. 505 from the *Eighteenth Homily*.

CHUANG TZU. Pp. 83, 173, 207, 307, 576 are from *Three Ways of Thought in Ancient China*, tr. by Arthur Waley (Macmillan) and reprinted by permission of Allen and Unwin.

CLARE, JOHN. From *The Poems of John Clare*, edited by J. W. Tibble (Dent).

CLARK, LEONARD. From *English Morning and Other Poems* (Hutchinson).

CLEMENT OF ALEXANDRIA. Pp. 67, 77 are from *Stromateis*, quoted by Inge in *Faith and Its Psychology* (Duckworth). P. 245 from *To the Newly Baptised* in the Loeb Classical Library edition of *Clement of Alexandria*, tr. G. W. Butterworth (Harvard).

COLERIDGE, S. T. Pp. 27, 561 are from *Dejection: an Ode*. Pp. 28, 395 from letters. P. 123 from *The Nightingale*. Pp. 197, 329, 353 from the *Notebooks*. Pp. 306a, b, 328, 336, 427, 450, 571, 592, 595, 596 from *Aids to Reflection*. P. 368 from *Frost at Midnight*. P. 463 from *The Devil's Thoughts*. P. 579 from *Literary Remains*, ed. H. N. Coleridge.

COWLYD, GWILYM. From *A Celtic Miscellany* tr. by Kenneth Hurlstone Jackson (Harvard).

CRASHAW. P. 241 is from *Hymn of the Nativity*.

CUTFORTH, RENÉ. *Korean Reporter* is published by Wingate.

CYPRIAN, ST. From his *Letters*.

D'ARCY, M. C. From *The Mind and Heart of Love* (Holt).

DAY, DOROTHY. From *The Long Loneliness, Autobiography of Dorothy Day* (Harper).

DICKENS. From a letter to the *Daily News*, March 16th, 1846. The passage is abridged.

DICKINSON, EMILY. Pp. 143 and 416 are from *The Single Hound* (Little, Brown). Pp. 263 and 485 are from *Further Poems* (Little, Brown). I also thank the Library and the President and Fellows of Harvard College.

DICKINSON, G. LOWES. *The Magic Flute* (Macmillan) is reprinted by permission of Allen and Unwin.

DIONYSIUS THE AREOPAGITE. P. 171 is from *The Divine Names*, tr. by C. E. Rolt (Macmillan). The passage is shortened. P. 363 is from *De Mystica Theologia* and is quoted in Evelyn Underhill's *Mysticism* (Dutton) and may have been translated by her, or may be from Rolt's translation.

DOSTOEVSKY. Extracts from *The Idiot* are taken from the edition tr. by Eva M. Martin (Everyman, Dutton). Those from *Crime and Punishment*, *The House of the Dead* and *The Brothers Karamazov* are from Constance Garnett's translations (Macmillan). P. 183 is from *The Brothers Karamazov*. Pp. 304, 328 are from *Crime and Punishment*. P. 529 is from *The Idiot*.

DUFF, CHARLES. From *A New Handbook of Hanging* (Melrose).

ECKHART, MEISTER. Pp. 197, 246a, b, 543 are from the two-volume edition tr. by C. de B. Evans (Watkins). P. 242 is quoted in Niebuhr's *The Nature and Destiny of Man* (Scribner). Pp. 245, 363 are quoted in Evelyn Underhill's *Mysticism* (Dutton) and are translated by Margaret Robinson.

ELIEZER, RABBI. From Martin Buber's *Tales of the Hasidim* (Schocken).

ELIOT, T. S. P. 311 is from *Four Quartets* (Faber).

ERIGENA. Pp. 174, 337 are quoted in *The Happy Issue* by Warner Allen (Faber), and tr. by him.

EURIPIDES. From *The Bacchae*, tr. by Gilbert Murray (Allen and Unwin).

EVANS, THOMAS TELYNOG. From *A Celtic Miscellany*, tr. by Kenneth Hurlstone Jackson (Harvard).

EVELYN, JOHN. From a letter to Thomas Henshaw.

FARID UD-DIN ATTAR. From *The Conference of Birds*, tr. by S. C. Nott (Janus Press).

FECHNER, GUSTAV THEODOR. Quoted in *The Centaur* by Algernon Blackwood (Macmillan) and presumably translated by him. I thank the Owner of the Copyright.

FERGUSON, JOHN. From *The Enthronement of Love* (Fellowship of Reconciliation).

FLEG, EDMOND. Pp. 173, 188, 458 ("God to Moses"), 543, 549, 555 from *The Life of Moses*, tr. by Stephen Haden Guest (Dutton).

FOX, GEORGE. From the *Journal*.

FRANCE, ANATOLE. From *Among the Great* by D. K. Roy. I thank Mr. Roy for permission.

FRANÇOIS DE SALES, ST. P. 185, 442 from *Treatise on the Love of God*; p. 258 from *Letters to Persons in Religion*. All quoted in *The Spirit of Love* by C. F. Kelley (Harper).

FRANCIS, ST. P. 543 is from *The Canticle of the Sun*.

GALSWORTHY, JOHN. *Justice* is reprinted by permission of Charles Scribner's Sons.

GARDNER, ALICE. From *Studies in John the Scot* (Oxford University Press).

GARVIE, A. E. From an article *Features and Factors of the World Crisis* in the *Hibbert Journal* of October 1940.

GASCOYNE, DAVID. Pp. 72, 399, 495, 496, 497 are from *Poems, 1937–1942* (Mandeville Publications). P. 72 is entitled *Dichters Leben*. From the poem on p. 497 I have omitted the quotation from Apollinaire. Pp. 77, 305, 457 are from *A Vagrant* (Lehmann). The poem on p. 305 is entitled *Rex Mundi*. P. 457 is from *Fragments towards a Religio Poetae*.

GERHARDI, WILLIAM. *A Bad End.* I thank Mr. William Gerhardi for permission.

GOETHE. P. 415 from *Faust*.

GOLLANCZ, VICTOR. *Our Threatened Values* (Regnery). *My Dear Timothy* (Simon & Schuster).

GORDON, MARY. From *Penal Discipline* (Routledge and Kegan Paul).

GREEN, PETER. From *Our Lord and Saviour* (Longmans).

GREGORY OF NYSSA, ST. Pp. 208, 241, 242 from *The Great Catechism*. Pp. 231, 234, 236, 238 from *On the Making of Man*. P. 257 from *On the Soul and the Resurrection*.

GREGORY OF SINAI. Quoted by St. Nilus Sorsky in *A Treasury of Russian Spirituality*, ed. G. P. Fedotov (Sheed and Ward).

GRENSTED, L. W. P. 77 is from *The Philosophical Implications of Christianity* (Clarendon Press). The essay on *Justice* is an abridgment of a longer essay published by the Fellowship of Reconciliation.

GUÉRIN, MAURICE DE. From *The Journal of Maurice de Guérin* tr. by Jessie P. Frothingham (Chatto). The passage on p. 29 is shortened and slightly modified.

HANOKH OF ALEXANDER, RABBI. From *The Hasidic Anthology*, q.v.

HARDY, THOMAS. From *Collected Poems*, by permission of the Trustees of the Hardy Estate and Macmillan.

649

HASIDIC ANTHOLOGY is translated, selected, compiled and arranged by Louis I. Newman, in collaboration with Samuel Spitz.

HASIDIC LEGEND. P. 289 is from the *Hasidic Anthology*, q.v. I owe the beautiful saying on p. 412 to Martin Buber, who quotes it in one of his essays.

HAWKES, JACQUETTA. From *A Land* (Cresset Press).

HAYYIM OF MOGIELNICA, RABBI. P. 176 is from Martin Buber's *Tales of the Hasidim* tr. by Olga Marx (Schocken).

HEBREW DOCTRINE. From *Major Trends in Jewish Mysticism* by Gershom Scholem (Schocken, Jerusalem).

HEGEL. From *The Philosophy of Religion*.

HEIDEGGER, MARTIN. From *Existence and Being* tr. Douglas Scott (Vision Press).

HEINE. Included in *Pleasures of Music*, ed. Jacques Barzun. Reprinted by permission of The Viking Press, Inc.

HENRY, JOAN. *Yield to the Night* is reprinted by permission of Doubleday & Company, Inc. I also thank Miss Henry.

HERBERT, GEORGE. P. 362 is from *The Elixir*. P. 363 is from *Love*.

HERMETICA. From the edition edited and translated by Walter Scott (Clarendon Press).

HIGH PRISON OFFICER. Reported by Margery Fry in a statement sent to Sir Ernest Gowers' Royal Commission on the Death Penalty.

HINDEMITH, PAUL. From *A Composer's World* (Harvard).

HOUSMAN, LAURENCE. From *The Little Plays of St. Francis* (Sidgwick and Jackson).

HUGHES, JOHN A. From *What the Cross Means to Me: A Theological Symposium* (James Clarke and Co.).

HUGO, VICTOR. From the Preface to *Le Dernier Jour d'un Condamné*.

HUMPHREYS, CHRISTMAS. From *Zen Buddhism* (Heinemann).

HUXLEY, ALDOUS. All published by Chatto. Pp. 573*a*, *b* are from *Grey Eminence*.

IBN 'ARABI. From *Sufism* by A. J. Arberry (Allen and Unwin).

IBSEN. From *Brand*.

IGNOTO. From Grierson's *Metaphysical Lyrics and Poems of the 17th Century* (Clarendon Press).

INGE, W. R. P. 22 is from *Religion* in *The Legacy of Greece* (Clarendon Press). P. 74 is from *Faith and Its Psychology* (Duckworth). Pp. 180, 184, 197, 207 are from *The Philosophy of Plotinus* (Longmans).

IRENAEUS. From *Contr. Haer.*

650

IRISH. From *A Celtic Miscellany* tr. by Kenneth Hurlstone Jackson (Harvard).

JACOPONE DA TODI. Quoted in Evelyn Underhill's *Mysticism* (Dutton). The translation is either her own, or may be taken from *Jacopone da Todi: with a selection from the Spiritual Songs translated by Mrs. T. Beck, London, 1919* (Dent).

JAMES, HENRY. I thank Messrs. Paul R. Reynolds and Son of New York. P. 119 is from *The Golden Bowl*.

JAMES, WILLIAM. From *The Will to Believe*. I thank Messrs. Paul R. Reynolds and Son of New York.

JASPERS, KARL. From *Tragedy is not Enough*, tr. by Harald Reiche, Harry Moore, Karl Deutsch (Beacon). I thank the Beacon Press, Boston, for Canadian permission.

JEFFERIES, RICHARD. Pp. 36, 234, 381, 419, 601, 614 from *The Story of my Heart*. Pp. 87, 117, 395 from *The Life of the Fields*.

JOHN OF CRONSTADT. From *My Life in Christ*, tr. by Goulaeff (Cassell).

JOHN OF THE CROSS, ST. Pp. 28, 38 are from *The Dark Night of the Soul* tr. Gabriela Cunninghame Graham (Watkins). The passage on p. 28 is abbreviated. P. 594 is from *The Living Flame of Love* tr. by David Lewis (Thomas Baker).

JOHNSON, JAMES WELDON. From *God's Trombones*. Reprinted by permission of The Viking Press, Inc.

JONES, DAVID. From *Anathemata* (Faber).

JULIANA OF NORWICH. Most of the extracts are from *Juliana of Norwich: an Appreciation and an Anthology* by P. Franklin Chambers (Harper). I thank Mr. Chambers. Pp. 255, 258b, are from Grace Warrack's translation entitled *Revelations of Divine Love* by Julian of Norwich (Methuen).

JUNG. From *Modern Man in Search of a Soul*, tr. by W. S. Dell and Cary F. Baynes (Harcourt, Brace).

KEATS. P. 380 from *Ode to a Nightingale*. P. 409 from *Ode to a Grecian Urn*.

KELLER, HELEN. From *The Story of My Life* reproduced by permission of Doubleday, New York.

KIERKEGAARD. Pp. 269, 270, 334 are from *Christian Discourses* tr. by Walter Lowrie (Oxford University Press). P. 434 is from *Attack upon "Christendom"* tr. by Walter Lowrie (Princeton University Press).

KINGE, H. From Grierson's *Metaphysical Lyrics and Poems of the 17th Century* (Clarendon Press).

KINGSLEY, CHARLES. From his call to the workmen of England in 1848 in rejoinder to the Communist Manifesto.

KOL OMER KERA, AUTHOR OF. From the *Hasidic Anthology* (q.v.).

LACTANTIUS. From *Divine Institutions*.

LAMENNAIS. Quoted by Saint-Beuve in his Memoir on *Maurice de Guérin*.

LARBAUD, VALERY (Doubleday). I thank Messrs. Gallimard of Paris.

LAW, WILLIAM. From *Selected Mystical Writings of William Law* ed. Stephen Hobhouse, 2nd edition, Harper, 1948.

LEON, LUIS DE. P. 90 is from the *Book of Job* and is quoted in *The Names of Christ* tr. by a Benedictine of Stanbrook. Pp. 242, 250, 362 are from *The Names of Christ*. P. 351 from *The Lyrics of Luis de Leon* tr. Aubrey Bell. Both books published by Burns, Oates.

LEONARDO DA VINCI. From *The Notebooks of Leonardo da Vinci* tr. Edward MacCurdy (Macmillan).

LEWIS, C. S. From *The Problem of Pain* (Bles).

LINUS. From *The Apocryphal New Testament* tr. by Montague James (Clarendon Press).

LI PO. From *The Poetry and Career of Li Po* by Arthur Waley (Macmillan).

LITTLE FLOWERS OF ST. FRANCIS. Tr. by T. Okey (Everyman, Dutton).

MACDONALD, GEORGE. From *George Macdonald: An Anthology* by C. S. Lewis (Macmillan).

MACGREGOR, G. H. C. From *The New Testament Basis of Pacifism* (Fellowship of Reconciliation).

MACKENNA, STEPHEN. From the Introduction to his translation of Plotinus (Faber, and Pantheon Books).

MACMURRAY, JOHN. From *Reason and Emotion* (Faber).

MAHA-BHARATA. From *Indian Wisdom* by Sir Monier Monier-Williams (Luzac).

MALAVAL. Quoted by Evelyn Underhill in *Mysticism* (Dutton). The translation may be her own, or may be from *A Simple Method of Raising the Soul to Contemplation* tr. by Lucy Menzies (Dent).

MANU, CODE OF. From *Indian Wisdom* by Sir Monier Monier-Williams (Luzac).

MARE, WALTER DE LA. All the following Walter de la Mare items are reprinted by permission of The Viking Press, Inc. Pp. 29, 68, 112*a*, *b*, 366, 445 are from *The Inward Companion*. P. 29 is entitled *See, Here's the Warrant*. Pp. 349, 404 are from *The Burning Glass*. P. 366 is from *The Traveller*. P. 115 is from *O Lovely England* and is entitled "Why then comes in . . ." P. 142 is an extract from *Fare Well* from *Collected Poems* and is reprinted by permission of Henry Holt & Company, Inc. I also thank Mr. de la Mare for permission to reproduce these poems.

MARCEL, GABRIEL. From *Being and Having* tr. by Katharine Farrar (Beacon).

MARCUS AURELIUS. From the Loeb Classical Library edition tr. C. R. Haines (Harvard). I have slightly modified the passage on p. 327.

MARITAIN, JACQUES. From *True Humanism* tr. by M. R. Adamson (Bles).

MARTIN, JOHN BARTLOW. From *Break Down the Walls* (Ballantine).

MASEFIELD, JOHN. By permission of The Society of Authors and Dr. John Masefield, O.M. I thank Macmillan of New York. P. 143 is an extract from a sonnet. All selections are copyrighted.

MEKILTA, THE. Quoted in *The Rabbinic Anthology* ed. C. G. Montefiore and H. Loewe (Macmillan & Company Ltd. and St. Martin's Press).

MENANDER. Quoted in the Loeb edition of *Clement of Alexandria* (Heinemann).

MENCIUS. Tr. by H. A. Giles in his *History of Chinese Literature* (Heinemann).

MEREDITH, GEORGE. From *Richard Feverel*.

MEREJKOWSKI. From *The Death of the Gods* tr. B. G. Guerney (Random House, New York).

MEYNELL, ALICE. I thank Sir Francis Meynell. The poem on p. 19 is entitled *Christ in the Universe*; that on p. 602 is entitled *In Sleep*.

MIDRASH. P. 246 is from *The Rabbinic Anthology* ed. C. G. Montefiore and H. Loewe (Macmillan).

MILAREPA. See Rechung.

MILLAY, EDNA ST. VINCENT. From *Renascence and Other Poems* (Harper, New York).

MILTON. Pp. 90, 241, 270, 375 from *Paradise Lost*. Pp. 161, 163 from *Tetrachordon*. P. 329 from *Areopagitica*. P. 427 from *A Posthumous Treatise on the Christian Doctrine*. P. 578 from *The Doctrine and Discipline of Divorce*.

MIRROR OF PERFECTION. From *"The Little Flowers" and the Life of St. Francis with the "Mirror of Perfection"* tr. by Robert Steele (Everyman, Dutton).

MONNIN. From *The Life of the Curé D'Ars*.

MOORE, GEORGE. From *Memoirs of My Dead Life* (Heinemann). I thank Messrs. Field Roscoe & Co.

MORRIS, WILLIAM. From a letter to Miss Kate Faulkner, August 8th (1890 given by MacKail in MS notes for his *Life*). I thank the Librarian, William Morris Gallery, Walthamstow.

MOSHE LEIB OF SASOV, RABBI. From Martin Buber's *Tales of the Hasidim* tr. by Olga Marx (Schocken).

MOZART. From *The Letters of Mozart and his Family* ed. by Emily Anderson (Macmillan & Company Ltd.).

MUIR, EDWIN. The poems are from his *Collected Poems, 1921–1951* (Faber, and Grove Press). P. 159 is an extract from *Song*. P. 186 is entitled *The Debtor*. P. 533 is entitled *The Letter*. The prose is from *An Autobiography* (Hogarth).

MURRAY, GILBERT. P. 22 is from *The Value of Greece to the Future of the World* in *The Legacy of Greece* (Clarendon Press).

NAGAI, TAKASHI. *We of Nagasaki* is published by Duell, Sloan and Pearce, New York.

NÉDONCELLE, MAURICE. From *Suffering: The Christian View* tr. by M. Vernon (Burns, Oates).

NEWMAN, LOUIS I. See *Hasidic Anthology*.

NICOLAS OF CUSA. From *The Vision of God* tr. by Emma Gurney Salter (Dutton).

NICOLL, MAURICE. Pp. 188, 422 from *Living Time* (Vincent Stuart). P. 238 from *The New Man* (Vincent Stuart).

NIEBUHR. From *The Nature and Destiny of Man* (Scribner).

NIETZSCHE. From *Thus Spake Zarathustra* ed. by Dr. Oscar Levy, and tr. by Thomas Common. I thank Mrs. Maud Rosenthal.

NORRIS, JOHN. From *Beauty*.

O'CONNOR, FLANNERY. From *The Artificial Nigger* in *A Good Man is Hard to Find* (Harcourt, Brace, New York).

OSUNA, FRANCISCO DE. From *Mystics of Spain* tr. by Allison Peers (Macmillan).

OTTO, RUDOLF. From *The Idea of the Holy* tr. by John W. Harvey (Oxford University Press).

OUSPENSKY. From *A New Model of the Universe* and reprinted by permission of Alfred A. Knopf, Inc.

PARADISE OF THE FATHERS. Tr. by Sir E. A. Wallis Budge (Chatto).

PASCAL. From *Pensées*.

PATMORE, COVENTRY. From *The Rod, the Root and the Flower*.

PÉGUY. From *Basic Verities* tr. by Anne and Julian Green. I thank Pantheon Books, Inc., New York.

PETER OF ALCÁNTARA, ST. From *Mystics of Spain* by Allison Peers (Allen and Unwin).

PHILO. P. 339 is from *Quis rer. div. haeres sit*, quoted by Warner Allen in *The Happy Issue* (Faber). P. 593 is included in *A Book of Jewish Thoughts* by Dr. J. H. Hertz. I thank Mr. Samuel Hertz.

"PILGRIM, THE". From *The Way of a Pilgrim* tr. Nina Toumanova in *A Treasury of Russian Spirituality* ed. G. P. Fedotov (Sheed and Ward).

PINHAS OF KORETZ, RABBI. Pp. 458, 594 are from the *Hasidic Anthology*, q.v.

PLATO. The translation of all passages is by Benjamin Jowett. Pp. 70, 86 from the *Phaedo*. Pp. 279, 626 from the *Symposium*. P. 327, 328 from the *Gorgias*. P. 334 from *The Laws*. P. 345 from the *Phaedrus*. P. 354 from the *Meno*. P. 408 from the *Ion*. Pp. 255, 453a from the *Timaeus*. Pp. 453b, c, 494, 513 from *The Republic*. P. 505 from the *Crito*. P. 570 from the *Lysis*.

PLOTINUS. With some exceptions, all the passages are from Stephen Mackenna's translation, sometimes as it stands, sometimes slightly or considerably modified. My thanks are due to Messrs. Faber and Faber, who have in preparation a revised edition of the Mackenna translation. Pp. 210b, 234b, 283, 346, 416 are abbreviated. The exceptions are as follows: pp. 207, 437 are quoted in Inge's *The Philosophy of Plotinus* (Longmans) and are probably translated by him. Pp. 377, 408 are from *Plotinus* tr. Armstrong (Macmillan). In the passage on p. 377 Professor Armstrong has retained the word "Nous": for the convenience of the English reader, I have substituted the word "Spirit".

POINCARE, HENRI. From *Science and Method* tr. by F. Maitland (Nelson).

POLANYI, MICHAEL. From *Science, Faith and Society* (Oxford University Press). I thank Professor Polanyi.

PORPHYRY. From Stephen Mackenna's translation of Plotinus, q.v.

POTTER, STEPHEN. From *Coleridge and S.T.C.* (Cape).

PREZZOLINI. From an article in *La Voce* of April 13th, 1911.

PRISON CHAPLAIN. Reported by Margery Fry in a statement sent to Sir Ernest Gowers' Royal Commission on the Death Penalty.

PROCLUS. P. 179 is from *The Elements of Theology* ed. by Professor E. R. Dodds (Clarendon Press). This is a composite passage. P. 376 is from Thomas Taylor's preface to *The Mystical Initiations: or Hymns of Orpheus*.

PROUST, MARCEL. From *A la Recherche* . . . tr. by Frederick Blossom (Random House, New York).

RAINE, KATHLEEN. From *Collected Poems* (Hamish Hamilton). P. 178 is entitled *Word Made Flesh*. P. 183 is an extract from the second *Invocation of Death*. P. 368 is entitled *Tu non se' in terra, si come tu credi* . . .

RANDOLPH, THOMAS. From *A Platonic Elegy*.

RAVEN, CHARLES. From *The Theological Basis of Christian Pacifism* (Fellowship of Reconciliation).

RECHUNG. From *Tibet's Great Yogi Milarepa* by his disciple Rechung, tr. by Lama Kazi Dawa-Samdup, ed. by W. Y. Evans-Wentz (Oxford University Press).

RENAN, ERNEST. From *The Life of Jesus* tr. by C. E. Wilbour (Everyman, Dutton).

RILKE, RAINER MARIA. P. 202 from *Requiem and other Poems* tr. by J. B. Leishman (Hogarth). Pp. 203, 422 from *Later Poems* tr. by J. B. Leishman (Hogarth).

ROKËACH. Included in *A Book of Jewish Thoughts* by Dr. J. H. Hertz. I thank Mr. Samuel Hertz.

ROLLAND, ROMAIN. From the translation of *Jean-Christophe* by Gilbert Cannan (Holt) except pp. 270, 577a, which are from letters to D. K. Roy, quoted in *Among the Great* by D. K. Roy, and p. 577b, which is from a conversation quoted in the same volume. I thank Mr. Roy.

ROLLE, RICHARD. From *The Fire of Love*.

RUDDOCK, MARGOT. The poems are from *The Lemon Tree* (Dent).

The prose passage is quoted in Yeats's Introduction to that volume.

RUMI. From *Rumi: Poet and Mystic* tr. by Reynold A. Nicholson (Macmillan), except p. 39, which is quoted from *Sufism* by A. J. Arberry (Macmillan), and reprinted by permission of Allen and Unwin.

RUTHERFORD, MARK. Pp. 37, 456, 530, 565 from *The Autobiography of Mark Rutherford* (Oxford University Press). Pp. 213, 234, 366, 391, 436, 449, 614 from *More Pages from a Journal* (Oxford University Press). I thank Mrs. D. V. White.

RUYSBROEK. P. 28 from *De Orn. Spir. Nupt.* quoted in Evelyn Underhill's *Mysticism* (Dutton) and presumably tr. by her. P. 601 is from *Flowers of a Mystic Garden*.

SABATIER, PAUL. From *The Life of St. Francis of Assisi* tr. Louise Seymour Houghton (Scribner).

SAINT-EXUPÉRY, ANTOINE DE. From *Le Petit Prince* (Harcourt, Brace).

SANDBURG, CARL. From *Ten Definitions of Poetry* in *Good Morning, America* (Harcourt, Brace, New York).

SCHLEIERMACHER. From *The Monologen* tr. by Horace L. Fliess (Open Court Publishing Co.).

SCHOLEM, GERSHOM. From *Major Trends in Jewish Mysticism* (Schocken, Jerusalem).

SEER OF LUBLIN. From the *Hasidic Anthology*, q.v.

SHAPIRO, KARL. From *Poems, 1940–1953* (Random House, New York).

SHAW, BERNARD. I thank The Public Trustee and The Society of Authors. P. 83 from *Music in London* (Dodd, Mead). Pp. 302, 439, 455, 462*a*, 472, 564, 570, 575, 597, 599 from *Man and Superman* (Dodd, Mead). Pp. 447, 448, 456, 457, 462*b*, *c*, 463, 468 from his Preface to *English Prisons under Local Government* by Sidney and Beatrice Webb.

SHELLEY. P. 393 is an extract from *To Jane: The Recollection*. P. 407 is from *A Defence of Poetry*. P. 415 is an extract from *The Sensitive Plant*.

SIEPMANN, ERIC. From *Confessions of a Nihilist* (Gollancz).

SITWELL, EDITH. P. 27 is from *A Love Song* in *Gardeners and Astronomers* (Vanguard). P. 530 is an extract from *A Song of the Dust* in the same volume (it is founded on a passage in one of Donne's sermons). P. 119 is from *The Canticle of the Rose* (Vanguard).

SOPHOCLES. P. 234 from the *Antigone*. Pp. 274, 611 from the translation of the *Oedipus Coloneus* by Gilbert Murray (Clarendon Press).

SPENSER, EDMUND. Pp. 157, 208 from *An Hymne in Honour of Beautie*.

SPINOZA. From the *Ethics*.

STANLEY, ARTHUR. From *The Testament of Man* (Gollancz). I thank Mr. Stanley.

STEPHENS, JAMES. From *Collected Poems:* Copyrighted (Macmillan). P. 612 is an extract from *Paternoster;* Copyrighted. I also thank Mrs. Stephens.

STUART, FRANCIS. *Redemption* is published by Gollancz.

STRINDBERG. From *The Road to Damascus* tr. by Graham Rawson (Cape). The translation of the passage on p. 598 has been slightly modified.

SUFI TRADITION. From *Sufism* by A. J. Arberry (Allen and Unwin).

SULLIVAN, J. W. N. Pp. 381, 410 from *But for the Grace of God* (Cape). I have used the passage from *Beethoven* by permission of Mr. Navin Sullivan, and Alfred A. Knopf, Inc. The passage is a composite one, put together from various parts of the book.

SUSO. P. 365a is from the *Leben*, quoted in Evelyn Underhill's *Mysticism* (Dutton). This is either her own translation or that of T. F. Knox in *The Life of Blessed Henry Suso, by Himself* (Methuen). I cannot trace the source of 365b.

SUZUKI, D. T. P. 109 from *Buddhism in the Life and Thought of Japan* (Buddhist Society, London). Pp. 185, 338 from *The Essence of Buddhism* (Buddhist Society).

SWEDENBORG. Pp. 162, 190, 256, 377, 453 from *Heaven and Hell*. The passage on p. 377 is a composite one. Pp. 179, 529 from *The Divine Love and Wisdom*. In the case of both books I have used the revised translation by F. Bayley, on the basis of the F'cap 8vo edition issued by the Swedenborg Society (Everyman, Dutton).

SWIFT. Pp. 336, 439 from *Thoughts on Religion*. Pp. 435, 468, 573 from *Thoughts on Various Subjects*.

SYMEON THE NEW THEOLOGIAN, ST. Quoted by St. Nilus Sorsky in *A Treasury of Russian Spirituality* ed. G. P. Fedotov (Sheed and Ward).

TADHG ÓG Ó HUIGINN. From *A Celtic Miscellany* tr. by Kenneth Hurlstone Jackson (Harvard).

TAGORE. Pp. 107, 338, 529 from *Sadhana*. P. 349 from *The Gardener*. Pp. 215, 301, 304, 494, 582 from *Creative Unity*. P. 315 from *Gitanjali*, all copyrighted, and published by Macmillan; I thank also the author's Trustees.

TALMUD, THE. P. 469 is quoted in *A Book of Jewish Thoughts* by Dr. J. H. Hertz. I thank Mr. Samuel Hertz. P. 555 is quoted in the *Rabbinic Anthology* ed. Montefiore and Loewe (Macmillan & Company Ltd. and St. Martin's Press).

TALMUDIC LEGEND. This is quoted by Ouspensky in *A New Model of the Universe* (Routledge and Kegan Paul) from *Agada* by Ravnitsky and Bialik.

TANNENBAUM. From *Crime and the Community* (Columbia University Press).

TAO-TÊ-CHING. Pp. 211, 575, 597 from the translation by W. G. Old entitled *Lao Tze: The Tao-Teh-King* (Rider). P. 493, tr. by Arthur Waley in *The Way and Its Power* (Allen and Unwin).

TEASDALE, SARA. From *Collected Poems*, Copyrighted. I thank the Macmillan Co. of New York. The original title is *August Night*.

TERESA, ST. From *The Interior Castle*. I thank the Right Rev. the Lady Abbess of Stanbrook Abbey for permission to use this version.

TERTULLIAN. P. 208 from the *De Anima*. P. 448 is shortened.

THEOLOGIA GERMANICA. From the edition with Susanna Winkworth's translation revised by Willard Trask to accord with Bernhart's version (Pantheon). I have slightly modified the passage on p. 184. I thank Pantheon Books, New York, for Canadian permission.

THOMAS OF CELANO. From *Legenda Prima*, quoted in Evelyn Underhill's *Mysticism* (Dutton) and possibly translated by her.

THOMAS, DYLAN. Published by New Directions. Pp. 140, 141, 150 from *Quite Early One Morning*. P. 485 is an extract from *The Force that through the Green Fuse . . .* from *Collected Poems, 1934–1952*.

THOREAU. From *Walden*.

TOLSTOY. Pp. 69, 115, 382 from *Anna Karenina* tr. by Rochelle S. Townsend (Everyman, Dutton). P. 545 from *Master and Man, etc.* (Everyman, Dutton). Pp. 435, 460 from *What I Believe* tr. by Aylmer Maude (Oxford). (P. 460 is abbreviated.) P. 315

from *The Death of Ivan Ilych and Hadji Murad* tr. by Louise and Aylmer Maude (Oxford). P. 473 from *A Confession* tr. by Aylmer Maude (Oxford). All the Oxford items are in the World's Classics edition.

TRAHERNE. Pp. 5, 107a, b, 108, 125, 234, 245, 259, 361, 362, 536, 575, 583, 616 from *Centuries of Meditation*. P. 133 from *Poetical Works*. (In the fourth verse, line 5, I have changed "then" to "they", as this seems to be required by the sense.) Pp. 571, 597 from *Christian Ethicks*. I thank the Clarendon Press for permission to reproduce these extracts.

TURGENEV. From *Dream Tales and Prose Poems* tr. Constance Garnett (Macmillan).

UNDERHILL, EVELYN. From *Mysticism* (Dutton).

VAN GOGH, VINCENT. From *Letters of a Post-Impressionist* tr. by Anthony Ludovici (Constable). I thank Mr. Ir. V. W. van Gogh.

VAUGHAN, HENRY. P. 363 is an extract from *The Incarnation*, & *Passion*. P. 364 is an extract from *The Proffer*. P. 611 is an extract from *The Morning-watch*.

VAUGHAN, THOMAS. Pp. 116, 375, 529 from *Anima Magica Abscondita*. Pp. 207, 231 from *Anthroposophia Theomagica*. P. 599 from *Aula Lucis*.

V.G. All passages are from *My dear Timothy* or *More for Timothy* with three exceptions. P. 586 from *Our Threatened Values*. P. 35b from the Introduction to *A Year of Grace* (expanded). P. 547 from *On Reconciliation*. All published by Gollancz.

VIVEKANANDA. The works of Vivekananda from which the extracts are taken are published by the Advaita Ashrama, India.

WADDELL, HELEN. All published by Barnes & Noble, and reprinted by permission of Constable & Co., Ltd. P. 115 is an extract from a poem from the *Carmina Burana* tr. by Helen Waddell in *Mediaeval Latin Lyrics*. P. 550 from *Beasts and Saints*.

WALEY, ARTHUR. P. 309 from *Three Ways of Thought in Ancient China* (Macmillan) and reprinted by permission of Allen and Unwin.

WALKER, KENNETH. From *Diagnosis of Man* (Cape).

WARD, JAMES. From *The Realm of Ends* (Cambridge University Press).

WEIL, SIMONE. Pp. 67, 255a, b, 329c, 428 from *Letter to a Priest* tr. by

A. F. Wills. Pp. 225, 269, 329*a*, *b*, 611, 613 from *Waiting for God* tr. by Emma Craufurd. P. 575 from *Gravity and Grace* tr. by Emma Craufurd. All published by Putnam.

WELSH (TRADITIONAL). From *A Celtic Miscellany* tr. by Kenneth Hurlstone Jackson (Routledge and Kegan Paul).

WILLIAMS, CHARLES. All published by Farrar, Straus and Cudahy. I thank also Mrs. Williams. P. 174 is from *The Place of the Lion.*

WILSON, MONA. From *A Life of William Blake* (Hart-Davis).

WOOLF, VIRGINIA. *To the Lighthouse* (Harcourt, Brace).

WORDSWORTH, DOROTHY. From *The Journals of Dorothy Wordsworth* ed. de Selincourt (Macmillan).

WORDSWORTH, WILLIAM. Pp. 108, 110, 112, 116, 135*a*, *b*, 137, 201, 235, 238, 362, 365, 407 from *The Prelude.* P. 307 from the *Ode to Duty.* P. 450 from *The Old Cumberland Beggar.* P. 565 from *The Excursion.* P. 571 is entitled *Afterthought*, with the subtitle *To the River Duddon.*

YEATS. Prose passages from *Autobiographies* (Macmillan). P. 450 from *The Countess Kathleen* in *Collected Plays* (Macmillan). I thank Mrs. Yeats.

YELCHANINOV, FATHER. From his *Diary* tr. by Helen Iswolsky and included in *A Treasury of Russian Spirituality* ed. G. P. Fedotov (Sheed and Ward).

ZEN BUDDHISM, A MASTER OF. Quoted in *The Buddhist Sects of Japan* by Steinilber-Oberlin (Allen and Unwin).

THE PRAYERS

P. 616   From George Herbert's *Providence.*

P. 617*a*.   From Coleridge's *A Child's Evening Prayer.*

P. 617*b*.   From Traherne's *Centuries of Meditation.* (See Traherne.)

P. 617*c*.   By Rabi'a, quoted in *The Spirit of Love* by C. F. Kelley. (See St. François de Sales.)

P. 617*d*.   From Henry Vaughan's *Cock-crowing.*

P. 617*e*.   From George Herbert's *Trinitie Sunday.*

P. 618*a*.   From Traherne's *Centuries of Meditation.* (See Traherne.)

P. 618*b*.   From Traherne's *Centuries of Meditation.* (See Traherne.)

P. 619.   From John Drinkwater's *Poems, 1908–1914* (Sidgwick and Jackson).

P. 620*a*.   From the Hebrew Prayer Book (q.v.).

P. 620*b*.   From the Scottish Book of Common Prayer, 1929.

P. 620*c*.   Anonymous.

P. 620d. James Stephens' *Student Taper*. (See James Stephens.)

P. 621a. *Ex Nihilo* from David Gascoyne's *Poems, 1937–1942*. (See David Gascoyne.)

P. 621b. George Herbert's *Bitter-sweet*.

P. 622a. By Mechthild of Magdeburg from *Das fliessende Licht der Gottheit*, quoted in Evelyn Underhill's (q.v.) *Mysticism*, where Margaret Robinson is acknowledged as the translator.

P. 622b. From Henry Vaughan's *The Tempest*.

P. 622c. George Herbert's *The Temper*.

P. 623a. From the Hebrew Prayer Book (q.v.).

P. 623b. Christina Rossetti's *Last Prayer*.

P. 623c. This is an abbreviated version of a prayer in the Hebrew Prayer Book.

P. 624a. From Henry Vaughan's *The Constellation*.

P. 624b. From Psalm XIX.

THE MUSIC

The sources are as follows: The quotation on the title-page, the phrase *mein Engel Leonore* from Beethoven's *Fidelio*; p. 35, the opening of the (consolatory) middle section from Chopin's *Funeral March;* p. 80, from Beethoven's Fourth Symphony; p. 97, the opening of the last movement of Bach's Violin Concerto in E major; p. 156, Florestan's opening phrase in the duet *O namenlose Freude* from the prison scene in Beethoven's *Fidelio*; p. 276, the opening phrase of Beethoven's Quartet in C sharp minor, opus 131; p. 610, the *Heiliger Dankgesang* from Beethoven's Quartet in A minor, opus 132. For this last I thank C. F. Peters Corporation, New York, sole agents for Eulenburg Miniature Scores.

THE ENGRAVINGS

I am most grateful to Mr. Reynolds Stone for the illustration on the title-page. The other two illustrations are reproduced from Blake's engravings for the *Book of Job*.

THE HEBREW

When an orthodox Jew has recovered from a grave physical or spiritual sickness, or has been saved from a disaster, it is customary for him to attend a synagogue service on the Sabbath and to make a public affirmation, over a scroll of the *Torah*, in the form of words printed on page 63. They mean: "Blessed art Thou, O Lord our God, King of the Universe, who doest good to the undeserving, and hast done all good to me."

INDEX OF AUTHORS

Abrahamsen, David, 447, 452
Acta Sanctorum, 128, 550, 551
Acts, The, 596
Acts of John, The, 176, 270
Acts of Pilate, The, 328
Addison, 379
A. E., 138, 174, 207, 355, 370, 380, 387, 390, 454, 611, 615, 616
Allen, Warner H., 211
al-Hallaj, 362
al-Junaid, 366
Amiel, 34, 84, 87, 107, 118, 137, 269, 270, 279, 327, 337, 352, 424, 436, 445, 557, 564, 565, 566, 568, 569, 574, 590, 597, 598, 604
Andrews, C. F., 213
Angela of Foligno, St., 233
Anonymous, 393, 445. See also under "The Prayers", p. 660
Aquinas, St. Thomas, 163, 208, 327, 334, 355, 422
Aratus, 173
Aristotle, 22
Asoka, 427
Augustine, St., 208, 209, 302
Aumonier, Stacy, 486
Aurobindo, 20, 73, 177, 215, 287, 302, 311, 314, 332, 333, 340, 449, 566, 568, 584, 605
Ausonius, 166

Baal-Shem, The, 212, 246, 529, 613
Bacon, Roger, 7
Barbusse, 441, 499
Barnes, William, 116
Basho, 111
Baudelaire, 378
Beard, Charles, 437
Beerbohm, Max, 154
Beethoven, 49, 51, 55, 124
Bellay, Joachim du, 7

Benet of Canfield, Father, 82
Benét, Stephen Vincent, 502
Bentley, E. C., 127
Berdyaev, 63, 159, 214, 242, 244, 245, 256, 257, 301, 311, 415, 436, 447, 456, 472, 529, 533, 534, 562, 563, 565, 580, 592, 594, 601
Bhagavad-Gita, The, 171, 240, 310
Binyon, Laurence, 409
Blackwood, Algernon, 384
Blake, Major, 475
Blake, William, 18, 39, 69, 109, 112, 113, 132, 147, 158, 183, 186, 200, 207, 208, 240, 241, 243, 245, 304, 329, 334, 339, 340, 353, 355, 368, 375, 376, 379, 380, 396, 415, 416, 429, 435, 448, 453, 459, 474, 493, 506, 535, 542, 543, 549, 557, 558, 563, 564, 579, 580, 591, 596, 599, 601
Bloy, Léon, 245, 430
Boehme, 174, 302, 361, 369
Boethius, 357
Book of Common Prayer, The, 107
Bosanquet, Bernard, 207, 566
Bright, John, 473
Brontë, Emily, 39, 62, 71, 81, 89, 117, 175, 256, 405, 455, 494
Brown, T. E., 264
Browne, Sir Thomas, 429, 594
Browne, William, 90
Browning, Robert, 102, 243, 257, 363
Browning, Elizabeth Barrett, 362
Buber, Martin, 533, 574
Buddha, The, 530
Buddhist Vow, 531
Bunam of Pzhysha, Rabbi, 563

Bunyan, 225, 261
Bussierre, Renouard de, 129
Byron, 114, 157, 301, 564

Campanella, 197
Carmina Burana, 115
Carpenter, Edward, 162, 279
Carpenter, Joseph Estlin, 390
Castiglione, Baldassare, 171
Catherine of Siena, St., 458
Childe, Wilfred Rowland, 89, 183, 350, 402, 403
Chrysostom, St. John, 245, 505
Chuang Tzu, 83, 173, 207, 307, 310, 576
Clark, Leonard, 88, 91, 124, 128, 138
Clare, John, 31, 367
Clement of Alexandria, 67, 77, 245
Coleridge, S. T., 27, 28, 92, 121, 123, 197, 306, 328, 329, 336, 340, 353, 368, 395, 404, 427, 450, 463, 535, 561, 571, 579, 592, 595, 596, 611. See also under "The Prayers", p. 660
II Corinthians, 301
Cowlyd, Gwilm, 111
Cowper, 30
Crashaw, Richard, 241, 532, 557
Cutforth, René, 503
Cyprian, St., 493

D'Annunzio, 531
D'Arcy, M. C., 158
Day, Dorothy, 531
Deuteronomy, 28
Dickens, 474
Dickinson, Emily, 108, 109, 110, 143, 263, 306, 356, 379, 416, 485, 531, 571
Dickinson, G. Lowes, 164, 503, 513, 599
Dionysius the Areopagite, 171, 363
Dixon, Richard Watson, 188
Donne, 363
Dostoevsky, 29, 34, 86, 108, 183, 304, 328, 388, 392, 450, 466, 467, 469, 470, 483, 529

Drinkwater, John. See under "The Prayers", p. 660
Drummond, William, 367
Duff, Charles, 486

Ecclesiasticus, 157, 561
Eckhart, Meister, 197, 242, 245, 246, 363, 543
Eliezer of Dzikov, Rabbi, 601
Eliot, T. S., 311, 423
Emerson, 363, 563
Erasmus, 475
Erigena, 174, 178, 337
Euripides, 22, 67
Evans, Thomas Telynog, 116
Evelyn, John, 154
Eyth, Max, 273
Exodus, 362

Farid Ud-Din Attar, 543, 575, 593
Fechner, Gustav Theodor, 393
Ferguson, John, 511
Fleg, Edmond, 15, 173, 188, 543, 549, 555
Fox, George, 506
France, Anatole, 577
Francis of Assisi, St., 81, 153, 450, 462, 543
Franciscan, A, 564

Galsworthy, 463
Gandhi, 493, 494, 505, 506
Gardner, Alice, 178
Garvie, A. E., 437
Gascoyne, David, 72, 77, 305, 399, 457, 495, 496, 497. See also under "The Prayers", p. 660
Genesis, 361
Gerhardi, William, 478
Goethe, 364, 415
Gordon, Mary, 451, 465
Gould, Gerald, 73
Green, Ann and Julian, 95
Green, Peter, 389
Gregory of Nyssa, St., 208, 231, 234, 236, 238, 241, 242, 257
Gregory of Sinai, 611
Grensted, L. W., 77, 521

Guérin, Maurice de, 29, 111, 198

Hanokh of Alexander, Rabbi, 246
Hardy, Thomas, 67, 627
Harrison, Thomas, 564
Hasidic legends, traditions and sayings, 289, 407, 412, 579
Hawkes, Jacquetta, 108, 581
Hayyim of Mogielnica, Rabbi, 176
Hebrew doctrine, 363
Hebrew Prayer Book, The, 616. See also under "The Prayers", p. 660
Hegel, 364
Heidegger, Martin, 407
Heine, 409
Henry, Joan, 476
Herbert, George, 238, 262, 362, 363. See also under "The Prayers", p. 660
Hermetica, 422
Herrick, 242
High Prison Officer, 475
Hindemith, 353, 410
Homer, 173
Hosea, 462
Housman, Laurence, 81, 137, 153, 291, 450, 458, 462, 564
Hügel, Baron von, 209
Hughes, John A., 270
Hugo, Victor, 200, 489
Humphreys, Christmas, 288, 305, 308, 339
Hunt, Leigh, 537
Huxley, Aldous, 44, 184, 209, 214, 225, 573

Iamblichus, 247
Ibn 'Arabi, 233
Ibsen, 328
Ignoto, 261
Inge, W. R., 22, 74, 180, 184, 197, 207
Irenaeus, 240
Irish, 110, 113
Isaak of Syria, St., 81, 556, 592, 612
Isaiah, 445

Jacopone da Todi, 304
James, Epistle of, 310
James, Henry, 119, 157, 163
James, William, 217
Jaspers, Karl, 270, 334
Jefferies, Richard, 36, 87, 117, 234, 381, 395, 419, 601, 614
Job, 362
John, St., 240
John of Cronstadt, 532, 615, 616
John of the Cross, St., 28, 38, 594
Johnson, James Weldon, 229
Johnson, Lionel, 148
Jones, David, 132
Juliana of Norwich, 174, 255, 258, 446, 530, 612
Jung, C. G., 187, 209, 301, 583

Kant, 573
Keats, 380, 409
Keller, Helen, 134
Kierkegaard, 269, 270, 334, 434
Kinge, H., 70
Kingsley, Charles, 244
Kol Omer Kera, Author of, 493

Lactantius, 475
Lamennais, 198
Larbaud, Valery, 141
Law, William, 182, 364, 439
Leonardo da Vinci, 86, 179, 202, 473, 574
Leon, Luis de, 90, 242, 250, 351, 362
Leon, Moses de, 181
Lewis, C. S., 459
Li Po, 409
Linus, 176
Little Flowers of St. Francis, The, 129
Lords' Debate on Death Penalty, 488
Luke, St., 259

Macdonald, George, 305, 362, 380, 459, 590, 612
Macgregor, G. H. C., 212, 458, 511, 512, 513
Mackenna, Stephen, 215
MacLeod, G. F., 272, 449

Macmurray, John, 162
Malaval, 361
Maha-Bharata, The, 594
Manu, The Code of, 570
Marcel, Gabriel, 565
Marcus Aurelius, 86, 327, 337, 445, 561, 574, 593, 595, 599, 613
Mare, Walter de la, 29, 68, 112, 115, 139, 142, 349, 366, 402, 404, 445
Maritain, Jacques, 603, 604
Martin, John Bartlow, 464, 470
Martyrdom of Peter, The, 176
Masefield, 143, 147, 167
Matthew, St., 599
Maximus, St., "the Confessor", 247
Mechthild of Magdeburg. See under "The Prayers", p. 660
Mekilta, The, 234
Melville, Herman, 132
Menander, 531
Mencius, 211
Meredith, George, 113
Merejkowski, 247
Meynell, Alice, 19, 152, 602
Midrash, 246, 458
Milarepa, 184, 256, 303, 600
Millay, Edna St. Vincent, 120
Milton, 71, 90, 101, 159, 161, 163, 226, 241, 270, 301, 329, 375, 427, 460, 578
Mirror of Perfection, The, 199
Monnin, A., 288
Montaigne, 597
Moore, George, 150
More, Henry, 335
Morris, William, 149
Moshe Hakotun, Rabbi, 137, 556, 557, 590
Moshe Leib of Sasov, Rabbi, 459
Mozart, 140
Muir, Edwin, 68, 131, 152, 159, 186, 397, 399, 533
Murray, Gilbert, 22, 274
Murray, S. R. Glanville, 475

Nagai, Takashi, 502
Nahman of Bratzlav, Rabbi, 533

Nédoncelle, Maurice, 271
Nicolas of Cusa, 176, 179, 362, 416
Nicoll, Maurice, 188, 239, 422
Niebuhr, Reinhold, 591
Nietzsche, 93, 234
Norris, John, 364

O'Connor, Flannery, 266
O'Leary the Fenian, John, 504
Oman, John, 599
Orphic Hymn, 171
Orphic Saying, 562
Osuna, Francisco de, 82
Otto, Rudolf, 273
Ouspensky, 212, 420, 421

Paradise of the Fathers, The, 536, 543
Pascal, 428, 529
Pater, Walter, 118
Patmore, Coventry, 7, 210, 214, 234, 239, 355, 430, 597
Péguy, 95
Penn, William, 167, 235, 249, 256, 303, 327, 328, 428, 429, 435, 504, 506, 555, 590, 591, 593, 594, 595, 616
Peter, St., 445
Peter of Alcántara, St., 248
Philo, 339, 593
"Pilgrim, The", 613
Pinhas of Koretz, Rabbi, 458, 594
Plato, 70, 86, 255, 279, 327, 328, 334, 345, 354, 407, 453, 494, 505, 513, 570, 626
Plotinus, 172, 177, 179, 188, 207, 210, 215, 234, 250, 255, 280, 283, 311, 346, 363, 364, 365, 377, 379, 380, 408, 409, 410, 416, 437, 494, 562, 596
Poincaré, Henri, 355
Polanyi, Michael, 581
Porphyry, 180, 375
Potter, Stephen, 430
Prezzolini, Guiseppe, 327
Prison Chaplain, 475
Proclus, 179, 376
Proust, 422
Proverbs, 163

Psalms, 62, 63, 92, 107, 127, 279. See also under "The Prayers", p. 660

Rabi'a. See under "The Prayers", p. 660
Raine, Kathleen, 31, 32, 178, 183, 185, 198, 347, 368, 418, 537
Raleigh, Sir Walter, 73
Randolph, Thomas, 158
Raven, Charles E., 437, 507
Rechung, 184
Renan, 301
Revelation, 379
R. G., 108
Rilke, 202, 203, 422
Rokëach, Eleazar, 590
Rolland, Romain, 72, 134, 158, 246, 269, 270, 327, 333, 334, 430, 446, 532, 554, 562, 565, 570, 573, 577, 602, 613
Rolle, Richard, 107
Romans, 301, 445
Roscoe, William Caldwell, 167
Rossetti, Christina. See under "The Prayers", p. 660
Ruddock, Margot, 81, 92, 306
Rumi, 39, 182, 210, 233, 248, 263, 350, 364, 409, 427, 611
Ruskin, 456
Rutherford, Mark, 37, 213, 234, 366, 391, 436, 449, 456, 530, 565, 614
Ruysbroek, 28, 601

Sabatier, Paul, 431, 552, 600, 604, 612
Saint-Cyran, 258
Saint-Exupéry, 366
Saint-Martin, 378
Sales, St. François de, 185, 258, 442
Sandburg, Carl, 407
Schleiermacher, 239
Scholem, Gershom, 181
Scottish Book of Common Prayer. See under "The Prayers", p. 660
Seer of Lublin, The, 563

Shakespeare, 23, 92, 207, 335, 544
Shapiro, Karl, 199, 553
Shaw, Bernard, 83, 302, 439, 447, 448, 455, 456, 457, 462, 463, 468, 472, 564, 570, 575, 597, 599
Shelley, 393, 407, 415
Siepmann, Eric, 329
Sitwell, Edith, 27, 119, 530
Smith, John, 247, 285, 328, 336
Sophocles, 234, 274, 611
Spenser, Edmund, 157, 208, 371
Spinoza, 564
Stanley, Arthur, 289
Stephens, James, 186, 264, 307, 554, 612. See also under "The Prayers", p. 660
Strindberg, 185, 593, 598
Stuart, Francis, 272
Sufi Tradition, 305, 562
Sullivan, J. W. N., 48, 381, 410
Suso, 365
Suzuki, D. T., 109, 185, 197, 338
Swedenborg, 162, 179, 190, 256, 377, 453, 529
Swift, Jonathan, 336, 435, 439, 468, 573
Symeon the New Theologian, 233

Tadhg óg ó Huiginn, 111
Tagore, Rabindranath, 107, 215, 301, 304, 315, 338, 349, 494, 529, 582
Talmud, The, 469, 555
Talmudic Legend, 220
Tannenbaum, Frank, 457
Tao Tê Ching, 211, 493, 575, 597
Taylor, Jeremy, 530
Taylor, Thomas, 376
Teasdale, Sara, 200
Teresa, St., 595
Tertullian, 208, 448
Thackeray, 473
Theocritus, 118
Theologia Germanica, 184, 244, 361, 566

667

Thomas of Celano, 366
Thomas, Dylan, 108, 140, 141, 150, 485
Thoreau, 423, 451, 555
Tolstoy, 69, 115, 315, 382, 435, 460, 473, 545
Traherne, 5, 107, 108, 125, 133, 234, 245, 259, 361, 362, 415, 536, 571, 575, 583, 597, 616. See also under "The Prayers", p. 660
Turgenev, 556

Underhill, Evelyn, 380
Upanishad, Brihadaranyaka, 171, 333
Upanishad, Swetaswatara, 176
Upanishad, Taittiriya, 107

Van Gogh, 108, 408, 535, 577
Vasari, 554
Vaughan, Henry, 7, 90, 110, 127, 197, 347, 363, 364, 611. See also under "The Prayers", p. 660
Vaughan, Thomas, 116, 207, 231, 365, 375, 529, 599
Vedanta, The, 174, 207
Vedas, The, 107
Verlaine, 91
V. G., 16, 34, 35, 126, 134, 136, 151, 153, 154, 183, 187, 188, 216, 245, 248, 273, 279, 303, 330, 382, 431, 469, 471, 504, 547, 574, 586, 603, 614
Vivekananda, 174, 176, 178, 186, 211, 234, 269, 304, 308, 427, 430, 436, 448, 449, 506, 529, 554, 555, 565, 593, 598

Voice of the Silence, The, 531, 592

Waddell, Helen, 39, 115, 128, 166, 357, 550, 551
Waley, Arthur, 83, 173, 207, 307, 309, 409, 493, 576
Walker, Kenneth, 573
Ward, James, 209
Weil, Simone, 67, 225, 255, 269, 329, 428, 575, 611, 613
Welsh (Traditional), 27
Whichcote, Benjamin, 336, 429, 561, 574, 596
Whitehead, A. N., 439
Whitman, Walt, 379, 447
Williams, Charles, 125, 140, 174, 335, 386, 423, 538, 539
Wilson, Mona, 407
Woolf, Virginia, 421
Wordsworth, Dorothy, 87, 120, 198, 201, 394
Wordsworth, William, 23, 38, 107, 108, 110, 112, 116, 135, 137, 201, 235, 238, 307, 346, 356, 362, 365, 407, 450, 565, 571

Yeats, W. B., 249, 389, 450, 554, 577
Yelchaninov, Father, 82, 240, 244, 305, 430, 446, 529, 530, 531, 562, 563, 566, 570, 573, 591, 596

Zechariah, 493
Zen Buddhism, A Master of, 109
Zen Buddhist Saying, 599
Zohar, The, 189, 258

INDEX OF SUBJECTS

Absolute, the, 288, 340, 363, 410, 432, 448, 523
Abstinence, 536
Action, 85, 310–15, 599–601, 620; conviction and, 164; devotion and, 438; of mercy or justice, 458. *See also* Creativeness *and* Labour
Adolescence, 327
Adoration, 21, 131–32, 616. *See also* Worship
Affliction, 30, 48–53, 269, 270, 445. *See also* Suffering
Age, 86, 166, 167–68
Ahimsa, 505
Air, 377, 419, 538, 584, 614
Almsgiving, 555, 556. *See also* Charity
Ambition, 286, 591
Angels, 190–94, 263, 347, 418, 459, 596
Anguish, 34, 485–86. *See also* Suffering
Animals. *See* Beasts
Antichrist, 429, 440
Art, 52, 339, 370, 408–9, 410, 411, 423–24, 585
Asceticism, 529, 580, 607
Atheism, 234, 329, 333
Atom bomb, 502–3, 604
Atonement, 21, 523
Attention, 329–30, 613
Authority, 249, 337
Autumn, 89, 119–20, 136, 420

Barbarism, 583; economic, 584–85
Beasts, 127, 128, 200–202, 399; adoration of, 131–32; bliss of, 305; compassion for, 549–55;

Beast (*continued*)
recognition between man and, 349
Beauty, 7, 22, 74–76, 107, 142–43, 171–72, 174, 235, 237, 281, 283, 327, 333, 341, 345–46, 363, 575, 580, 581, 585; divine, 237, 238, 404; heavenly, 371–75; ideal, 355; love and, 431; perception of, 126, 364–84, 392, 393–96, 402–4, 409, 410–11; sadness and, 279
Bees, 110, 117, 123, 201, 572
Belief, 271, 329, 336, 391, 430. *See also* Faith
Bigotry, 456. *See also* Prejudice
Birds, 67–68, 110, 111, 113, 118, 127, 129–30, 201, 349–50, 496, 538, 552, 553, 572
Bitterness, 40–41, 428, 457
Blasphemy, 212, 286, 564
Blessedness, 237, 303, 616, 618
Blindness, 134, 138, 258, 306, 366
Bliss, 17, 46, 102, 134, 237, 305, 597; absolute, 448
Bondage. *See* Slavery
Brahma, 338, 531
Brahman, 174, 178, 287, 311, 436
Brotherhood, 22, 243, 535, 588, 589. *See also* Fellowship *and* Love
Brutality, 465, 471, 603. *See also* Cruelty
Buddha, Buddhism, 288, 308, 554, 600

Calm. *See* Peace
Capital punishment, 472–89, 522
Cat o' nine tails, 470–72
Cause and effect, 335
Ceremony, 429, 486

Changelessness, 240, 415, 421, 569
Chaos, 23, 215, 272, 309–10
Character formation, 453
Charity, 191, 194, 255, 271, 429, 489, 530, 549, 557, 595, 596, 597, 627. *See also* Love
Chastity, 579
Children, childhood, 305–6, 318, 320, 347-48, 382, 402, 422, 454, 455
Christ: attitude of, towards humans, 212, 213; as blasphemer, 564; contemplation and activity of, 601; crucifixion of, 242–43, 244, 273, 274, 435, 474–75, 511, 620; doctrine of non-resistance of, 460–62; and fatherhood of God, 589; and forgiveness, 542 (*see also* Forgiveness); God in, 240, 241, 332, 339; and Greece, 22–23; hostility to, 469; incarnation of, 16–21; law of, 434, 435–36; love of and for, 243–44; meaning of life and death of, 332, 507, 521; and the moneychangers, 599; not taken seriously, 508, 509; passion of, 295, 296, 397; peace of, 506, 507–10; retributive justice repudiated by, 474; second coming of, 398; on sin, 258, 449; and sinners, 213, 259–61, 449, 542–43, 587; and suffering, 273, 512, 620; 'supposed impracticability of teaching of, 460, 463; and this world, 437–39; and truth, 328, 329; war rejected by, 512; and the way of the Cross, 507, 508, 509, 510, 511
Christianity, 214, 256, 270, 427, 432, 434–35, 437–42, 521; disbelief in, 436; heart of, 510; lip-service to, 472; task and resources of, 509
Church: death penalty supported by, 488; dereliction of, 439–40; failure of, to take Christ seriously, 508. *See also* Pentecostal community

Civilization, 489, 494, 555, 585
Comfort, 35–63, 84, 258, 558, 585
Commercialism, 216, 585. *See also* Economics *and* Materialism
Commonplace, the wonderful in, 380, 381
Common sense, 456, 507
Communism, Christian, 432, 433
Compassion, 264–65, 269, 428, 529–32, 545–47, 558, 602; divine, 255–66, 439; towards beasts, 549–55. *See also* Mercy
Compensation, 288, 473
Complacency, 272, 353
Compromise, 328, 570, 578
Conflict, inner, 188–90, 216–17, 218–19, 221. *See also* War
Conformity, 83, 429, 563
Conquest: Self-, 288, 312, 568–69 (*see also* Self-knowledge); thirst for, 436, 440, 567, 575
Conscience, 448, 557, 563, 569, 578; blunting of, 597; evil done in the name of, 428
Consciousness, 209, 306; Self-, 85, 587. *See also* Perception
Contemplation, 85, 250, 599–600, 601
Contentment, 569, 597. *See also* Happiness *and* Joy
Contraries. *See* Opposites
Conversion, 454, 568–69
Convicts. *See* Prisons, prisoners
Co-operation with God, 246
Corporal punishment, 455, 456–57, 461, 470–72
Correspondences, 225, 377, 378, 410
Corruption, 125, 208, 345. *See also* Evil
Cosmos, 417. *See also* Universe *and* World
Courage, 54, 56, 271, 281, 439, 571, 595, 612
Courtesy, 597
Covetousness, 575, 583, 595
Cowardice, 445, 506, 570
Creation, 101, 108, 229–32, 255,

Creation (*continued*)
296, 572, 578; God in, 362, 363,
369–70, 393; of man, 107, 231,
232, 565, 572
Creativeness, 50–51, 53–62, 108,
245, 302, 311, 439, 529, 580
Credulity, 336. *See also* Belief
Creeds, 332, 341, 391, 415, 508
Crime, criminals, 225, 445–89, 532,
587
Criticism, 18, 19, 438, 595, 598
Cross of Christ, 474, 475, 489, 507,
508, 509, 510, 511, 521, 524, 526.
See also Crucifixion
Crucifixion, 242–43, 273, 274, 435,
462, 474–75, 509, 511
Cruelty, 459, 462, 465, 469, 489,
554, 591. *See also* Punishment
and Torture
Cynicism, 603

Damnation, 30–31, 45, 210, 469
Darkness, 208, 214, 272, 583–84
Dawn, 72, 496
Day, 112. *See also* Dawn, Eve-
ning, Morning, Night, Noon
Day dream, 405
Death, 31–32, 48, 69, 70–71, 83,
242–43, 244, 274–76, 315–24,
385–86, 391, 407, 415, 533, 553,
567, 571; life in, 86, 510; person-
ality and, 419; prayers at, 623;
as punishment, 472–89; science
and, 339; in war, 499–504. *See
also* Immortality *and* Life
Defiance, 49–50, 53
Degradation, 341, 472
Democracy of suffering, 274
Demoralization, 465
Depravity, 266, 471. *See also* Sin
Dereliction, 27–35, 273, 509; of the
Church, 439–40; prayers in, 621–
23; recovery from, 35–63
Desire, 256, 311, 312, 313, 446,
448, 449, 584, 597; divine, 369;
for God, 279–98; gratified, 579;
to sin, 225. *See also* Need

Desolation, 27–35, 339, 497, 503,
557
Despair, 35, 40, 45, 54, 81, 340,
484–85
Despotism. *See* Tyranny
Destiny. *See* Fate
Destruction, 215, 271, 272, 439,
462, 468, 471, 493, 558, 567, 598.
See also Execution *and* War
Detachment, 84, 219, 308, 311,
313
Devil, 212, 214, 328, 463, 535, 594;
kingdom of, 287. *See also* Satan
Dew, 89, 91, 110, 350
Dharma, 289, 308, 333
Diabolism, 214, 594
Dictatorship, 511. *See also* Tyran-
ny
Dignity: human, 469, 471, 603; of
work, 574
Disarmament, 513. *See also* Paci-
fism
Disaster, 338; pacifism and, 511–12
Disbelief, 226, 329, 330, 430, 436
Disciples, discipleship, 438, 508,
509, 510, 530
Disobedience, 564
Disrespect, 590. *See also* Respect
Distance, 416, 419, 446
Distrust, 304
Divinity, 215, 234, 250, 281, 288,
336, 361, 416–17, 562, 566, 570,
605; realisation of, 580. *See also*
God
Doctrine: and feeling, 436; of
the liberty of the soul, 301; of
non-resistance, 460–62; of resist-
ance, 460–61; and works, 438.
See also Action
Doubt, 28, 68, 69, 261, 329, 330,
332, 337, 366
Dreams, 131–32, 352, 366, 405,
446, 461, 602
Drunkenness, 210, 449, 451
Duality, 184, 207–21, 225–26, 284,
433, 437. *See also* Oneness
Dullness, 74–75, 450
Duty, 108, 307, 308, 312, 456, 482,
540, 555, 569, 598

671

Earth, 107, 246, 372, 537, 614. *See also* Nature *and* World

Economics, 581–82, 584–85, 605

Ecstasy, 118, 297, 352, 368, 370, 378, 388–89

Eden, 72, 183, 244, 348, 350

Education, 327, 453, 585; of the heart, 456

Egoism, 217, 311–15, 494, 566–67, 568, 607. *See also* Personality

Either/or, 434

Emotions: and love, 281; music and, 353. *See also* Hate, Joy, Sorrow, *etc.*

Emulation, 584, 590

Enemies: love for, 264, 432, 460, 521, 529, 588, 589; of society, prisons as, 470

Energy, 181, 240, 287, 302, 306, 439, 449

Enjoyment, 125–26, 134–35, 232, 233, 410, 537, 540, 541, 574, 576. *See also* Joy

Enlightenment, 37–39, 42–44, 46, 340–41, 580

Envy, 581, 583, 590, 591. *See also* Jealousy

Equality, 280, 312–13, 314, 587

Error, 210, 332, 333, 334, 449, 470, 567, 583, 584, 596; emancipation from, 338

Eternity, 367, 382; forecourt of, 361; life and, 416, 418; as the moment, 574; visions of, 579; voice of, 270. *See also* Time and eternity

Ethics, Christian: disbelief in, 470; double standard of, 438; force and, 512; salvation and, 534; and war, 493

Evening, 90, 114–15

Everlastingness, 347, 422

Evil, 86, 331, 431–32; committed in God's name, 435; concentration on, 214; for conscience' sake, 428; good and, 86, 207–21, 305, 339, 450, 461–62, 473, 505, 532–33, 534–35; hearing and speaking of,

Evil (*continued*)
594, 595; means for overcoming, 215, 433, 461–62, 489, 507, 508, 510, 532–33, 580; meeting of, with evil, 456, 457, 460, 505; moral, 512; purity and, 613; represented by war, 507; resistance and non-resistance to, 460–62; sin as, 512; suffering as, 271, 512. *See also* Sin

Evolution, 239, 257

Exclusion, 304

Execution, 432, 473–89

Exile, 32–33, 45, 51, 348, 381

Existence, world of, 74, 76. *See also* Life

Experience, 184, 211, 285, 332, 366, 410–11, 438, 457; and faith, 75–76; inner and outer aspects of, 381

Exploitation, 567, 581

Failure, 282, 431, 523. *See also* Error

Faith, 62–63, 73–78, 95, 271, 329, 429, 430, 449, 461, 507, 511, 562, 571; absence of, 226, 329, 330, 430, 436; of Christ, in human goodness, 213; in God, 62–63, 509, 569, 612; in ourselves, 565; perfect, 612; personal qualifications for, 74–75; and practice, 438; scepticism and, 333; truth and, 330–32. *See also* Hope

Falsehood, 333, 334, 522, 578, 582. *See also* Lying

Fame, 261, 353, 354

Fate, 271, 273, 314, 541

Fatherhood of God, 240, 242, 332, 437, 569, 588, 589, 615

Fear, 28, 261, 272, 275, 477, 483, 498, 554; of looking upon God, 362. *See also* Terror

Fellowship, 22, 507; Christian, 437–39; mystical, 427. *See also* Brotherhood

Fire, 202, 257, 263, 365, 505, 580; of love, 428; of separation, 248

First Cause, 179, 338, 377
Flogging, 455, 470–72
Flowers, 32–33, 69, 70, 108, 109, 113, 124, 198, 199–200, 279, 348, 366, 376, 418, 553, 614
Force: and crime, 465–66; moral, 569, 580 (*see also* Conscience); pacifism and, 512–13. *See also* Power
Forced labour, 466–67
Forgiveness, 258–61, 263–65, 266, 331, 389, 451, 452, 460, 506, 530, 542–49, 558
Fortitude, 312, 597. *See also* Courage *and* Heroism
Freedom, 22, 23, 38, 39, 246, 301–11, 333, 398, 462, 563; from egoism, 311–15; and error, 332; and health, 489; from hell, 534; humility and, 592; of imagination, 339; from inner turmoil, 216–17; joy of, 421; and the Kingdom of God, 245; paradox of, 301; and philosophy, 338; spiritual, 269, 301, 304, 337, 605–6, 607; struggle for, 211, 301, 302; work in, 467
Freudianism, 209
Friendship, 192–93, 243, 244, 248, 275–76, 381, 416, 533
Futility, 73, 457, 470

Gaiety, 353. *See also* Happiness *and* Joy
Generosity, 217, 556–57. *See also* Charity
Genius, 50, 53, 54, 306, 409, 574
Gentleness, 137, 217, 597
Giving, 451, 555–57, 561; of self, 570
Glory: of God, 181, 247, 370, 393; of people, 381; of the soul, 133, 173, 234
God: action directed towards, 314–15; in Christ, 240, 241, 332, 339; concepts of, 172, 255, 365, 437; co-operation with, 246; the Creator, 101, 172, 229–33, 246, 255,

God (*continued*)
258, 407, 572; eternity identified with, 416; in everything, 207, 233, 241, 363; and evil, 208, 209; as father, 240, 242, 332, 437, 569, 588, 589, 615; forgiveness by, 258, 266 (*see also* Forgiveness); freedom to deny, 333; goodness of, 255; grace of, 67, 217, 249, 256, 261, 263; heart of, 174; help of, 245, 564; humility of, 233, 592; justice of, 255, 521, 522, 525–26; killing forbidden by, 475; kingdom of, *see* Kingdom of God; knowledge of, 248–49, 305, 462; law of, and law of man, 460–62; life in, 424; longing for, 47, 279–97; as love, 237, 243, 428, 526, 530; love for, 248, 269, 453, 536; love of, 240, 245, 246, 257, 389, 439, 524, 536, 613–14, 615; loving-kindness of, 263; meeting with, 331, 332; mercy of, 45, 439, 530, 543, 545, 563, 569; naturalist attitude towards, 256; nature of, 181, 246; new interpretation of man and, 437; oneness with, 84, 171–90, 283–85, 338, 589, 596, 612; peace of, 47–48; praise to, 63, 82, 101, 107–12, 118, 124, 125–26, 127, 128–34, 137, 138–39, 173, 212, 246, 247, 249, 427–28, 429, 614, 617 (*see also* Worship); prayers to, 248–49, 611–24 (*see also* Prayer); relation of, to man, 233, 235–36, 470; seeing of, 75, 362–63, 390, 404; sensations of, 379; service to, 563; and the soul, 261–62; spirit of, 445, 493; strength of, 39; trust in, 62, 63, 509, 612 (*see also* Faith); undifferentiated and particularized, 189; in us, 241–42, 448, 562; will of, 44, 258, 314, 370, 507, 509; withdrawal from, 532
Golden Age, 391
Good, 179, 184, 257, 281, 282, 288,

Good (*continued*)
329, 331, 333, 529, 561, 562, 573; divine, 190; and evil, 86, 207–21, 305, 339, 450, 461–62, 473, 505, 532–33, 534–35; victory of, 447. *See also* Evil
Goodness, 74–76, 183, 187, 194, 208, 580; evil conquered by, 461–62; of God, 255; heroic, 430
Grace, 48, 250–51, 261, 281, 429, 437, 450, 543, 613; of God, 67, 217, 249, 256, 263
Gratitude, 109, 551, 555, 556, 593, 614, 617
Greatness, 261, 288, 315, 382, 571, 592
Greed, 85, 308, 335, 582–83, 584–85, 590
Grief, 27, 40, 73, 86, 270, 275, 353, 406, 493
Guilt, 262, 452–53, 468, 590, 591

Hanging, 432, 478–83, 486–88
Happiness, 85, 89, 93–94, 102, 117, 279, 430, 574, 575; envy of, 581; heavenly, 190–94; of love, 239; search for, 286; and suffering, 269, 271. *See also* Joy
Harmony, 85, 171–94, 309, 392, 569; of development, 570; of evil and good self, 568; of the spiritual world, 410. *See also* Oneness
Hate, 30, 317, 331, 431, 435, 436, 446, 447, 465, 470, 533, 548, 592
Health, 489, 577, 584
Heart: education of, 456; feeling with, 436; inward knowledge of, 562
Heaven, 125, 176, 190–94, 246, 257, 263, 352, 364, 371–75, 377, 460, 513, 580; earth and, 375, 377; entrance into, 545–47; key to, 434; world as gate of, 361
Hell, 207, 257; good man in, 68–69; liberation from, 534–35; man on way to, 263
Hellenism, 22
Heresy, 329

Heroism, 430, 445, 571, 597
Holiness, 236, 240, 293, 354, 431, 451, 536, 551, 596
Holy Ghost, Holy Spirit, 83, 212–13, 509, 543, 615, 616; fellowship of, 437–39
Home, 114, 347–49
Honesty, 446, 558, 564; intellectual, 329
Honour, 597, 603
Hope, 44, 67–78, 95, 96, 334, 449, 484, 571, 597
Hopelessness, 29, 35, 465
Human nature, 23, 81, 211, 213, 236–37, 238, 271, 433, 436, 445–47, 457, 460, 522, 596, 603; Christ's sharing of, 241, 242–43, 273. *See also* Man
Humane treatment of prisoners, 468–69
Humanitarianism, 459
Humiliation, 465, 467, 471, 475, 580
Humility, 43, 217, 233, 328, 429, 543, 549, 558, 576, 592, 596, 597
Hunger, 432; for the good, 282; for love, 557; for nature, 122; for pleasure, 436. *See also* Desire
Husbands and wives, 157–68, 579
Hypochondria, 37
Hypocrisy, 248, 435, 456

Ideal: of beauty, 355; of nature, 87; and the practical, 604; thirst for, 431
Idolatry, 214, 256, 583
Ignorance, Self-, 564, 567
Ill nature, 590, 595
Illness, 37, 269, 274, 315–24, 392, 452, 453; crime as, 489
Illumination, 216, 235, 250, 340–41, 380. *See also* Enlightenment
Illusion, 337–38, 391, 424, 524–25
Imagination, 76, 247, 339, 380; false, 578; morbid, 594
Imitation, 562. *See also* Emulation
Immolation, desire for, 431

Immortality, 137, 174, 175–76, 179–80, 182, 183, 236, 237, 261, 354, 355, 415, 419–20, 424, 534. *See also* Soul

Impartiality, 337

Imperfection, 19, 312, 313

Imprisonment. *See* Prisons, prisoners

Impulse, 312, 570

Incarnation, 16–21

Independence, 562–63, 582

Indifference, 75, 255, 313, 430, 596, 598; of thought, 329

Indignation, 597

Individuality, 189, 239, 566–68, 607; good and, 573. *See also* Society, individual and

Indivisibility, 171–94, 437–38. *See also* Oneness

Infinite, 234, 279, 340, 370, 418, 421

Innocence, 271, 451, 452, 453, 494, 617

Inquiry, 328, 330, 337, 354

Insects, 116–17, 118, 124, 200, 201, 368, 498, 553–54, 572

Insight, 233, 338, 355, 379, 388–93, 401

Inspiration, 345, 354, 407–8, 439

Instinct, 569, 572, 590

Instrument: creation as, 370; egoism of, 314–15; knowledge as, 454

Integrity, 83–84, 335

Intellect, 333, 335, 338, 339, 340, 341, 391; adherence through, 330; honesty of, 329; pain and, 270; realities of, 580; religion and, 430. *See also* Reason

Intelligence, 329, 330, 340, 341, 454

Intention, 303

Intuition, 239, 305, 338, 339, 355

Irony, 436

Isolation, 51, 55–56, 60, 87, 88, 93, 186, 534

Israel, 15–16, 507, 588

Jealousy, 255, 590–91

Jesus. *See* Christ

Joy, 82, 86, 87, 102, 269, 307, 338, 339, 341, 370, 383, 406, 407, 469, 541, 561, 577; in Christ, 245; heavenly, 190–94; in nature, 107–43; pain and, 270, 271; perishable, 436; of work, 605. *See also* Happiness

Judaism, 588

Judas, 244, 398, 454

Judgement, 445, 460, 462; of consequences, 511; divine, 45, 446, 530, 535, 577

Jungian psychology, 210

Justice, 22, 42, 236, 247, 255, 257, 457–58, 463–64, 595; concern of, with persons, 522, 524; of God, 255, 521, 522, 525–26; gratitude as, 593; impersonal, 521–25; and love, 458, 459, 526; and mercy, 458, 460, 494, retributive, 474, 524 (*see also* Vengeance); social, 436. *See also* Mercy

Karma-Yoga, 304, 314

Kavvanah, 187, 248

Killing: legal, 432, 472–89; as sport, 555. *See also* Murder

Kingdom of God, 47, 176, 184, 244, 245, 287, 361, 438, 509, 511, 534, 598, 604. *See also* Heaven

Knowledge, 330–31, 335, 337, 338, 340, 379, 390, 454; action and, 599; of beauty, 355; faith and, 75, 76, 77; of God, 248–49, 305, 462; intellectual, 338; intuitive, 355; inward, of the heart, 562; joy as, 338; of mercy, 265–66; self, 269, 284, 563, 566–68, 605, 607

Krishna, 174–75

Labour: delight in, 423, 605; dignity in, 574; forced, 466–67; God-directed, 314. *See also* Action

Language: confusion in, 512, 523, 525; limitation of, 85; misuse of, 85; symbolical, 353, 363

Laughter, 135, 339. *See also* Joy

Law: of God and law of man, 460–62; and the institution of hanging, 486, 488; interpretation of, 563; Mosaic, 435–36, 473, 474; self-respect lessened by, 475; sin and, 522; spiritual, 215

Learning, power and capacity for, 454. *See also* Education *and* Knowledge

Lechery, 449

Liberty. *See* Freedom

Life: acceptance of, 288, 570; affirmation of, 447; art and, 339; blindness of, 306; community of, 190; conflict of, 328; as divine manifestation, 288; eagerness for, 134–35, 136, 137, 449, 451; and eternity, 416, 418; immortal, *see* Immortality; loss of, to find, 509, 510, 513; meaning and justification of, 411; miracle of, 143, 182; natural, 309; oneness of, *see* Oneness; in the present, 305, 573, 574, 577; psychic, 187, 209–10; reverence for, 473, 474; source of, 348, 378; synthesis of, 392; tragedy and joy of, 218 (*see also* Joy). *See also* Death

Living standard, 581

Loneliness, 51, 55–56, 284, 319–20

Love, 32, 33, 36, 39, 67, 69, 77, 107, 115, 117, 187, 243, 247, 258, 262, 279, 281, 282, 296, 331, 338, 361, 418, 437, 442, 449, 453, 505, 512, 529–41, 548, 557, 569, 571, 591, 600, 604, 607, 620, 626; absence of, in prisons, 465, 469, 470; blindness of, 306; for Christ, 244; Divine, 190, 240, 245, 246, 257, 389, 439, 524, 536, 613–14, 615; for enemies, 264, 432, 460, 521, 529, 588, 589; as every man's due, 524; expression of, 198; force of, 506; of friends, 243, 244, 275–76; God as, 237, 243, 428, 526, 530; for God, 248, 269, 453, 536; happiness of, 239;

Love (*continued*)
heavenly, 190, 192, 193; instinct for, 431; justice and, 458, 459, 526; married, 157–68, 192; maternal, 485, 486, 572; of neighbour, 529, 535, 537, 549, 565; parental, 192; perfect, 280; redemption by, 456; self, 219, 427, 557, 565, 591, 595; source of, 346; of this world, 436

Loving-kindness, 536; of God, 263

Loyalty, 439, 566

Lying, 327, 523, 594, 595

Madness, 271, 339, 345, 408

Magnanimity, 556, 597–98

Maladjustment, 452–53

Malice, 595

Man, 187, 188, 234–35, 238; as co-heir with Christ, 242; creation of, 107, 231, 232, 565, 572; duality in, 208; the God-like in, 212, 213, 234, 237, 238–39, 241–42; Gospel conception of, 239; ideal, 87, 584; in image of God, 237, 239; individual and collective, 433; love of man for, 239, 529, 535, 537, 549; natural, 270, 309, 440; nature of, 208, 236–37, 327; oneness of, with God, 84, 174, 175, 177, 178–79, 180, 280–85, 338, 589, 596, 612; perfect, 233; as projected design, 63; recognition between beasts and, 349; relation of, with God, 235–36, 470; struggle within, 188–90, 216–17, 218–19, 221; subconscious in, 209–10; successful, 284–85; things valued by, 85, 304, 308, 494, 581, 582–84; true treasure of, 309; and woman, 87, 157–68, 579. *See also* Human nature

Manichaeanism, 214

Manifestation, divine, 288, 369–70, 416

Marriage, 157–68

Martyrdom, 506; of Christ, *see* Christ, crucifixion of; national, 513. *See also* Suffering
Materialism, 85, 581, 582–83, 584–85
Matter, 215–16, 280, 409, 494
Maya, 287
Meaninglessness, 273, 467, 486
Mediocrity, 434
Meditation, 85, 248, 285. *See also* Contemplation
Meekness, 247, 258
Melancholy, 35, 37, 340
Memory, 86, 87, 137, 416, 455; of feelings, 353; of the other world, 345–57; of sin, 542; of suffering, 269
Mental freedom, 304, 337
Mental hygiene, 594
Mental needs, 313, 585
Mercy 45, 236, 247, 258, 265–66, 415, 439, 462, 530, 543, 545, 563; justice and, 458, 460, 494. *See also* Compassion
Mind: freedom of, 304, 337; health of, 594; needs of, 313, 585; pain and, 270, 271. *See also* Intellect *and* Reason
Miracles, 7, 108, 111, 143, 215, 220, 290, 298, 381, 550, 553
Misery, 29, 35, 304, 432, 601. *See also* Affliction
Misunderstanding, 190
Moderation, 570
Modesty, 281, 579, 597
Money, 304, 308, 582–83, 595
Monotheism, 256
Months, 120–21, 279, 516
Moon, 90, 91, 92
Moral consciousness, 472
Moral drought, 36, 585
Moralism, 433–34, 521, 597
Morality, 216, 309, 562, 578, 579, 580
Morning, 112, 279, 367, 381, 393, 419, 420, 451; prayer in, 616
Moses, 220–21, 239, 362, 427–28, 543–44, 549, 575; law of, 435–36, 473, 474, 555

Motives, 216, 306, 313, 590, 595
Murder, 432, 449; by sentence, 432, 472–89; in war, 493
Music, 34, 53–62, 92, 101, 138, 140, 350–53, 370, 407, 409–11, 495, 588; Bach, 410–11; Beethoven, 20, 48–62, 588; Mozart, 140; reactions to, 353
Mutilation, 499–501, 502–3, 504, 566
Mystery, 176, 182, 271, 273, 286, 330, 345, 357, 362, 369, 370, 381, 395, 420, 613

Napalm bomb, 503
Nation: prayer for, 624; risk of martyrdom of, 513
Nationalism, 214, 582
Naturalism, 256, 257, 270
Nature, 22–23, 107–43, 159–60, 229–32, 348, 364–65, 368–69, 378, 614; corruption of, 208; gifts of, 238; ideal of, 87, 395; law of, 536; pensiveness in, 279–80; reason and, 337; rhythm of, 308; unities of, 249
Necessity, 23, 263, 301, 607
Need, 164, 313, 530, 576–77, 581, 585, 620
Neglect, 564
New Testament, 429, 435, 439, 509
Night, 90–91, 368, 406, 420; prayer in, 616
Nirvana, 85. *See also* Paradise
Non-discrimination, 547
Non-resistance, 460–62, 506; to Christ, 244
Non-violence, 505–6
Nonsense, 328, 339
Noon, 93–95, 420

Obedience, 245, 328, 470, 574
Omnipotence, 273, 369
Oneness, 279–85, 339, 390, 436, 529, 568, 569, 607; of God and Christ, 332; with God, 84, 171–90, 280–85, 338, 589, 596, 612; of good and evil, 207–21; of life

677

Oneness (*continued*)
and eternity, 418; peace and, 494; of the spirit, 312, 313; of Truth, Good, Beauty, God, 333
Opposites, 140, 173, 174–75, 176, 179, 207–21, 225–26, 241, 287, 301, 339, 363
Original Sin, Original Virtue, 209–10, 274
Originality, 563

Pacifism, 432–33; basis of; 507–10; disaster and, 511–12; force and, 512–13; and the heavenly pattern, 513; initiative by, 513; realism and, 511. *See also* Peace
Paganism, 469
Pain, 270, 271, 272, 315–24, 445, 456, 471, 472, 484, 486, 531, 539, 554; and pleasure, 457. *See also* Suffering
Painting, 220–21, 237, 408–9
Parables, 213, 259–60, 536
Paradise, 71–72, 83, 85, 127, 352, 361, 387–88, 393, 404, 600
Pardon, 452. *See also* Forgiveness
Passion of Christ, 295, 296, 297
Patience, 52, 236, 269, 573, 597
Patriotism, 22, 214, 582
Peace, 38, 47–48, 61–62, 81, 82–96, 114, 115, 118, 124, 219, 220, 307, 377, 394, 396, 422, 494, 506, 507, 513–17, 568, 570, 600. *See also* Pacifism
Penal laws, 523
Penal system. *See* Prisons, prisoners
Penal work, 466–67
Penitence, 31–32, 258, 259–62, 263–64, 545–47, 548, 564
Pentecostal community, 437–39. *See also* Christianity
Perception: desire limited by, 448; of God, 75, 362–63, 379, 390, 404; heightened, 126, 364–84, 392, 393–96, 402–4, 409, 410–11; knowledge as, 340
Perfection, 83, 233, 255, 256, 257,

Perfection (*continued*)
265, 280, 288, 335, 338, 363, 369, 423, 432, 449, 568, 585, 607, 612; cost of, 509
Persecution, 439, 564. *See also* Punishment *and* Torture
Personality: of the dead, 419, 420; development of, 76; everlasting, 548; expression of, 468; justice and, 522; meaning and worth of, 524; quickening of, 392; repressed, 215; respect for, 586–89, 603
Perversity, 225–26, 287
Pessimism, 75, 433–34
Philosophy, 22, 313, 333, 334, 337–38, 345, 588; the problem of, 74
Pity. *See* Compassion
Places: Assisi, 153, 604; Babylon, 557–58; Bibury, 149–50; Egypt, 421; England, 23, 147–50, 279; Florence, 153; Greece, 22–23; Jerusalem, 147, 244, 340, 375, 543, 557, 558, destruction of, 269; London, 136, 150, 411; Lucca, 154; Meran, 153–54; Naples, 257; New York, 151; Oxford, 147–49; Paris, 150–51; Rome, 152, 495, 511; The Thames, 125, 381, 399; Torcello, 154; Venice, 154
Plants, 197, 198, 199–200, 376, 538. *See also* Flowers *and* Trees
Pleasure, 346, 436, 454, 618; pain and, 457. *See also* Enjoyment
Poetry, 339, 354, 407–8, 585
Poise, 82
Politics, 504, 585, 604, 605; denial of Christianity in, 436
Possession, 304, 584, 585
Poverty, 286, 304, 445, 553, 555, 556, 603
Power: derived from suffering, 271–72; expression of, 311 (*see also* Action); of God, 233; heavenly, 83, 84; in material unity, 494; money and, 582–83; of money and propaganda, 304;

Power (*continued*)
temptation of, 471; using the maximum of, 570, 571
Practicality, 603–4
Praise, 327, 591–92; to God, 63, 82, 101, 107–12, 118, 124, 125–26, 127, 128–34, 137, 138–39, 173, 212, 246, 247, 249, 427–28, 429, 614, 617. *See also* Worship
Prayer, 137, 139, 248, 249, 289, 427, 441, 611–24
Preaching, 130, 429
Prejudice, 337
Preoccupation, 248–49, 575–76, 580
Present, living in, 305, 573, 574, 577
Pride, 43, 217, 313, 315, 564, 592
Prisons, prisoners, 445, 447, 450–51, 457, 461, 462, 463–70, 488, 489, 523
Prodigality, 570, 595
Profit, 582
Progress, 462, 473, 577–78
Propaganda, 304, 459, 507, 582
Prophecy, 70, 71
Prudence, 570
Psychic life, 187, 209–10. *See also* Egoism
Psycho-analysis, 216, 217
Psychology, 217, 587; crowd, 583
Punishment, 257, 264, 455, 456–57, 460, 461, 462, 463–89, 506, 532, 587; alternative to, 457, 466; capital, 472–89, 522; corporal, 455, 456–57, 461, 470–72
Purification, 269, 271, 575
Purity, 75, 84, 137, 237, 256, 281, 398, 424, 428, 449, 536, 561, 562, 568, 613

Quietness, 82, 83, 84–85, 87, 89, 90. *See also* Peace

Rain, 68, 109, 111, 125, 136
Rapture. *See* Ecstasy
Realism and pacifism, 511
Reality, 580; "idealization" of, 601

Reason, 22, 286, 335–41, 431; errors of, 333
Recompense, 311–12
Reconciliation, 86, 259, 265, 274, 512, 513, 547, 574
Redemption, 181, 218, 269, 456, 512, 513, 524
Reflection, 22, 246, 335
Reformation, 440
Relativism, dualistic, 433
Religion: birth of, 271; conventional, 341, 391; credulity in, 336; dogmatic, 333; to the economic man, 585; egoism and, 494; embodiment of the eternal in, 424; experience of, 566; and hate, 435; humility in, 429; intellectual, 430; natural, 431; reason and, 336; unnatural, 428; western, and respect for personality, 588–89. *See also* Christianity *and* Judaism
Reminiscence, 345–57. *See also* Memory
Remorse, 456
Renunciation, 282, 285, 287, 310, 314
Reparation, 524
Repentance. *See* Penitence
Repression, 215, 466, 467–68, 529
Resignation, 49, 219, 312, 313, 598; of self to God, 336
Resistance to evil, 460–61, 506, 529
Respect, 590, 597; self, 472, 475, 565
Rest, 83, 84, 246, 285, 422. *See also* Peace
Resurrection, 272, 509, 511, 535
Retaliation, 505
Retribution, 474, 524, 534
Revelation, 241, 340, 355, 388–93, 411, 428, 461, 507
Revenge. *See* Vengeance
Reverence, 282, 473, 474, 573
Ridicule, 197, 436, 463, 598
Right and wrong, sense of, 578
Righteousness, 237, 281, 542, 578, 595; Self-, 447, 589, 591

Rights, prisoner's, 468
Ritual, 309, 399, 486
Rocks, 197, 202, 306, 394, 395
Ruthlessness, 217, 530

Sacraments, 381, 383, 461
Sacrifice, 314, 327, 431, 510, 549, 557, 573; ritual, 486, 554
Sadism, 432, 470–71. *See also* Cruelty *and* Torture
Sadness. *See* Sorrow
Saints, 72, 128–29, 210, 508, 550–53; Francis of Assisi, 129–30, 137, 199, 293–97, 366, 552–53, 600, 604, 612; Paul, 75, 219, 303, 437, 440, 507, 508, 522, 550
Salvation, 440, 531, 549, 568, 615, 620; of prisoners, 469; universal, 470, 534–35
Sanctions, posthumous, 257
Sanctity, 210, 247, 568, 581
Satan, 264, 440, 459, 493, 579, 594. *See also* Devil
Scapegoat, 486
Scepticism, 21, 75, 331, 332, 333, 338
Scholasticism, 337
Science, 22, 333, 339, 582, 585
Sea, 36, 377, 614
Seasons, 136, 369, 419–20. *See also* Autumn, Spring, Summer, Winter
Sects, 427
Security, 306, 307, 473, 571, 591
Self-acceptance, 219, 565
Self-approval, 564
Self-consciousness, 85, 587
Self-consecration, 287
Self-contempt, 564–65
Self-denial, 336
Self-discipline, 312
Self-expression, 468
Self-government, 236, 417
Self-identification, 504, 508
Self-knowledge, 269, 284, 563, 566–68, 605, 607
Self-love, 219, 427, 557, 565, 591, 595

Self-respect, 472, 475, 565, 569
Self-righteousness, 447, 589, 591
Self-sufficiency, 286
Self-surrender, 250, 314, 549, 566
Selfhood, 18, 126, 183, 185, 579
Selfishness, 75, 304, 437, 557, 582, 601
Senses, 309, 341, 365, 379, 454. *See also* Perception
Sensitivity, 410
Sentimentality, 459, 463, 603
Separation, 248, 419
Serenity. *See* Peace
Sermon on the Mount, 463, 488
Service, mission of, 438, 601. *See also* Charity
Shame, 34, 35, 262, 266, 467, 468, 475, 510
Sharing, 157, 160, 190, 257, 290
Silence, 82, 116, 137, 173, 289, 394, 395, 613
Simplicity, 84, 305, 306, 461, 583
Sin, 207–26; against self, 561; causes of, 446; Christ and, 259, 449, 450; confession of, 261; as evil, 512; forgiveness of, 258–61, 263, 265, 266, 451, 506, 530; 542–49; Jesus on, 258–59; and law, 303, 522; liberty and, 302; as missing one's goal, 449; original, 209–10; repentance of, *see* Penitence; struggle against, 446, 447, 529; universal tendency towards, 225, 445–47. *See also* Evil
Sincerity, 305, 337
Singleness of purpose, 423–24
Sky, 38, 90, 91, 362, 372, 538, 614
Slander, 212–13
Slavery, 301–2, 304, 308, 466, 606
Sleep, 92–96, 349, 368, 538
Social justice, 436
Society: contamination of, by power to punish, 471; denial of Christianity in, 436; individual and, 567–68, 604, 605; materialist, *see* Materialism; prisons as enemy of, 470, 471; products of, 455; purpose of, 581–82; respon-

Society (*continued*)
sibility of, for crime, 453; spirit-
ualized, 302, 605–7; unhappiness
of, 215
Socrates, 70–71, 86, 494, 505, 512,
564
Solicitude, 590
Solidarity: of the Christian fellowship, 439; with God, 269, 568;
of humanity, 567
Solitariness. *See* Isolation
Sorrow, 27–39, 60, 271, 279, 383,
405, 531
Soul, 28, 46–47, 84, 85, 181, 182,
184, 188, 234–35, 236, 257, 284,
285–86, 287, 562; and future life,
420–21; God and, 246, 259, 612;
goodness of, 207, 208; group,
605; manifestation of, 174; memories of, 345–57; purification of,
269, 271; resignation of, to God,
336 (*see also* Self-surrender);
revelation of, 450–51; training of,
284; uniqueness of, 239, 389,
450, 469, 589; universal, 378;
upward journey of, 280–83
Source of all things, 172, 182, 283,
348, 377, 562
Spirit: compulsion of, 606; desolation of, 27–35; economics and,
581–82; matter and, 409, 494;
nature and life of, 301; oneness
of, 312, 313; rediscovery of life
of, 301; strength of, 571; universal, 378. *See also* Holy Ghost
and Soul
Spiritual development, 53–62,
301–3
Spiritual universe, 172, 214
Spiritual wealth, 74
Spirituality, 214, 332–33, 341
Spiritualization, 302, 605–7
Spontaneity, 303, 305
Spring, 27, 102–3, 115, 140, 198,
377, 391, 393, 451, 495–97
Standard of living, 581
Stars, 90, 91, 101, 110, 368, 377,
420, 584

Stoics, stoicism, 22, 255, 286, 312,
313
Stupidity, 75
Subconscious, 209–10; community, 215
Subjectivism, 567, 568
Submission, 55, 61, 312, 466, 580
Subsistence, 377
Succession, 416, 417, 418
Suffering, 34, 38, 58, 63, 242–43,
245, 269–76, 315–24, 486, 487,
531; as evil, 271, 512; as a means
to good, 274; non-violence as,
506; as punishment, 456, 470,
471–72, 476–85; sympathy as,
470; understanding of, 451; undeserved, 271, 272–73, 274
Summer, 116–18, 368, 369, 381,
419, 497
Sun, 34–35, 112–13, 119, 135–36,
362, 381, 382, 383, 395, 396, 402,
419, 451, 497, 498, 537, 614;
sunrise, 112, 151, 153, 367; sunset, 151, 420
Superficiality, 85, 271, 570, 583
Supernatural, 256, 382
Superstition, 335, 450, 489, 601
Supreme, 380; aspiration towards,
210–11; mingling with, 283–85,
568; and subordinate, 376
Surrender, Self-, 250, 314, 549,
566
Suspicion, 594
Symbolism, 84, 279, 309, 353, 363,
486, 507, 509, 569
Sympathy, 376, 446, 470, 530, 539

Tao, 173, 207, 308, 309, 577
Temptation: against faith, 330; of
Jesus, 510; to sin, 225–26
Terror, 28, 39, 51, 69, 282, 380,
554, 569
Thankfulness. *See* Gratitude
Theology, 239, 274, 437, 587
Theophany, 174
Thought, 420; indifference of, 329;
law of, 333; of sin, 225
Thoughtfulness, 336

Time and eternity, 264, 415–24.
  See also Eternity
Tiredness, 114, 197
Toleration, 339, 596
Torture, 257, 264, 265, 467, 472,
  476–86. *See also* Suffering
Tradition, 327, 507
Tragedy, 218, 270, 273
Trains, 141–42
Tranquillity, 38, 220, 250, 286,
  307. *See also* Peace
Transfiguration, 63, 393, 397–98,
  411
Trees, 38, 111, 119, 123–24, 198,
  203, 369, 393–94, 395, 403, 498
Triviality, 434–35, 510
Trust in God, 62–63, 509, 612.
  See also Faith
Truth, 16, 20, 22, 74–76, 257, 281,
  287, 327–34, 335, 337, 340, 341,
  357, 427, 451, 460, 494, 580, 585;
  obligation to, 523; search after,
  604
Twilight. *See* Evening
Tyranny, 471, 489

Unconditional, the, 172, 434, 547
Understanding, 82, 233, 237, 248,
  286, 451, 513, 580, 613–14
Unhappiness, 215. *See also* Sorrow
Union: material and spiritual, 494,
  570; yearning for, 171–94, 279–
  85. *See also* Oneness
Uniqueness, 239, 389, 450, 469,
  589
Universe, 180–81, 184, 377–78; as
  product of the struggle for freedom, 211; rhythm of, 308;
  spiritual, 172, 214
Unmanifest, God the, 240

Values: moral, prostitution of, 512;
  standard of, 75, 580; world of,
  74, 76
Vengeance, 30, 331, 431, 457, 459,
  461, 467, 469, 470, 473, 474, 486,
  534

Vice and virtue, 207–21, 302, 447,
  449, 564, 575, 580, 590, 593, 599
Violence, 432, 465, 494, 506, 583
Vision, 235, 250, 280–83, 284, 285,
  291–97, 309, 361, 368–69, 370–
  71, 380, 386–93, 397–98, 402,
  410–11, 541, 543, 572, 579

War, 215, 440, 441, 493–504, 506,
  512, 522, 605; origin of, 494.
  See also Pacifism *and* Peace
Weakness, 306, 436, 438, 447, 453,
  464, 468, 506, 507, 523, 579
Wealth, 585; of nature, 232; and
  poverty, 602–3; spiritual, 74
Weapons, spiritual, 506, 604
Weariness. *See* Tiredness
Well-wishing, 217, 547–48
Western nations, 85, 304, 581
Wholeness. *See* Oneness
Wickedness. *See* Sin
Wilfulness, 246
Will, 76, 248, 286, 314, 315, 330,
  430, 435, 456, 534, 566, 569, 574,
  590, 592, 612; of God, 44, 258,
  314, 370, 507, 509
Winter, 116, 128, 404, 420
Wisdom, 67, 83–84, 219, 247, 424,
  454, 592, 626; earthly, 440
Witnesses, 246
Wives and husbands, 157–68,
  579
Wonder, 126, 133–34, 276, 281
Woods, 123–24, 393–94, 395, 403–
  4. *See also* Trees
Work. *See* Labour
Works. *See* Action
World, 184; Christ and, 437–39;
  differentiation between this and
  the next, 433, 437; of existence
  and of values, 74; as gate of
  heaven and house of God, 361,
  363, 375; natural and spiritual,
  287, 364, 377, 437, 583; other,
  memories of, 345–57; outer and
  inner, 365, 583; prayer for, 624.
  See also Heaven, Nature, *and*
  Universe

Worship, 17–18, 42, 249, 427–28, 429, 593. *See also* Praise

Wrong-doing. *See* Sin

Yoga, 240, 287, 288, 304, 312, 314, 315

Youth, 86, 136, 424; and crime, 453–54

Zarathustra, 92–95

Zen, 305, 309